LIBRARY OF THE HISTORY OF IDEAS

VOLUME VIII

Race, Gender, and Rank:
Early Modern Ideas of Humanity

LIBRARY OF THE HISTORY OF IDEAS

ISSN 1050–1053

Series Editor: JOHN W. YOLTON

RACE, GENDER, AND RANK

EARLY MODERN IDEAS OF HUMANITY

Edited by

MARYANNE CLINE HOROWITZ

UNIVERSITY OF ROCHESTER PRESS

This collection first published 1992

University of Rochester Press
200 Administration Building, University of Rochester
Rochester, New York 14627, USA
and at PO Box 9, Woodbridge, Suffolk IP12 3DF, UK

ISBN 1 878822 15 2

Library of Congress Cataloging-in-Publication Data
Race, gender, and rank : early modern ideas of humanity / edited by
Maryanne Cline Horowitz.
    p. cm. – (Library of the history of ideas, ISSN 1050–1053 ;
v. 8)
    Includes bibliographical references.
    ISBN 1–878822–15–2 (alk. paper)
    1. Social history – Modern, 1500– 2. Race relations – History.
3. Ethnic relations – History. 4. Sex role – History. 5. Social
classes – History. I. Horowitz, Maryanne Cline, 1945– .
II. Series.
HN13.R33   1992
306'.09–dc20   92–23111

       British Library Cataloguing-in-Publication Data
       Race, Gender and Rank : Early Modern Ideas
       of Humanity. – (Library of the History of
       Ideas Series, ISSN 1050–1053 ; Vol.8)
          I. Horowitz, Maryanne Cline II. Series
       128
       ISBN 1–878822–15–2

This publication is printed on acid-free paper

Printed in the United States of America

TABLE OF CONTENTS

ACKNOWLEDGEMENTS

The articles in this volume first appeared in the *Journal of the History of Ideas* as indicated below, by volume, year and pages.

Barker-Benfield, G. J., "Mary Wollstonecraft: Eighteenth-Century Commonwealthwoman", 50 (1989) 95–115.

Clouatre, Dallas L., "The Concept of Class in French Culture Prior to the Revolution", 45 (1984) 219–44.

Colish, Marcia L., "The Mime of God: Vives on the Nature of Man", 23 (1962) 3–20.

Constantin, Charles, "The Puritan Ethic and the Dignity of Labor: Hierarchy vs. Equality", 50 (1979) 543–61.

Fiering, Norman S., "Irresistible Compassion: An Aspect of Eighteenth-Century Sympathy and Humanitarianism", 37 (1976) 197–218.

Gabriel, Astrik L., "The Educational Ideas of Christine de Pisan", 16 (1955) 3–21.

Glausser, Wayne, "Three Approaches to Locke and the Slave Trade", 51 (June 1990) 199–216.

Greene, John C., "The American Debate on the Negro's Place in Nature, 1780–1815", 15 (1954) 384–96.

Horsman, Reginald, "Origins of Racial Anglo-Saxonism in Great Britain before 1850", 37 (1976) 387–410.

Hunting, Claudine, "The *Philosophes* and Black Slavery: 1748–1765," 39 (1978) 405–18.

Klaiber, Jeffrey L., "The Posthumous Christianization of the Inca Empire in Colonial Peru", 37 (1976) 507–20.

Lebovics, Herman, "The Uses of America in Locke's *Second Treatise of Government*", 47 (1986) 567–81.

Margolis, Nadia, "Christine de Pizan: The Poetess as Historian", 47 (1986) 361–75.

Nadelhaft, Jerome, "The Englishwoman's Sexual Civil War: Feminist Attitudes Towards Men, Women, and Marriage 1650–1740", 43 (1982) 555–79.

Nicholson, Mervyn, "The Eleventh Commandment: Sex and Spirit in Wollstonecraft and Malthus", 51 (1990) 401–21.

Richards, Judith, Lotte Mulligan, and John K. Graham, " 'Property' and 'People': Political Usages of Locke and Some Contemporaries", 42 (1981) 29–51.

Thomas, Keith, "The Double Standard", 20 (1959) 195–216.

Wallech, Steven R., " 'Class versus Rank:' The Transformation of Eighteenth-Century English Social Terms and Theories of Production", 57 (1986) 409–31.

Winfrey, John C., "Charity versus Justice in Locke's Theory of Property", 42 (1981) 423–438.

Zeeveld, W. Gordon, "Social Equalitarianism in a Tudor Crisis", 7 (1946) 35–55.

I

INTRODUCTION: RACE, GENDER, AND RANK

By Maryanne Cline Horowitz

Race, Gender, and Rank: Early Modern Ideas of Humanity, together with *Race, Class, and Gender in 19th-Century Culture* (Volume III in the *Library of the History of Ideas*) contribute to the exposure of particularity, difference, and hierarchy in Western ideas of human nature. In both volumes, a section focusing on human unity and compassion provides balance, counteracting the current trend of pointing at sexism, racism, and elitism (found throughout world cultures) to debunk in particular Western "civilization." Tracing developments in thought from the fifteenth through the twentieth centuries, these two volumes provide historical and philosophical contexts for understanding and transforming Western constructs of human nature: stratification and unity, prejudice and compassion.

The chronological span of this volume is the fifteenth through nineteenth centuries, focusing particularly on the seventeenth and eighteenth centuries. Through the title's substitution of "rank" for "class" in our contemporary theoretical triad "race, class and gender," *Race, Gender, and Rank* emphasizes that national variations in systems of legal rank are fundamental to the historical sociology of pre-industrial European society. The historical shift from rank to class is presented in Steven Wallech's " 'Class versus Rank': The Transformation of Eighteenth Century English Social Terms and Theories of Production" and Dallas L. Clouatre's "The Concept of Class in French Culture Prior to the Revolution." The development of "rank-consciousness" into "class-consciousness," which questions the medieval belief in a divinely ordained static social order, is only one of several important transformations. Intellectuals from Christine de Pizan to Mary Wollstonecraft explain how men and women are socially constructed through the institutions of childcare, education, church, government, and press; today we recognize that form of consciousness-raising as an awareness of gender distinctions. This book likewise shows the increasing presence of "race-consciousness" among intellectuals and within their categories of thought: both a growing focus on the particulars of the "Anglo-Saxons," the "Celts," and the "Franks" (what we would now call "ethnicity" rather than "race") as well as the discovery of the "European" or the "Whiteman" through encounters with and enslavement of Blacks of Africa and Indians of the Americas. The controversy on the biases in English and American liberalism has focused on John

Locke, who declares the natural right of life, liberty, and property. We shall examine case studies of Locke on the slave trade in Part One, "Race and Ethnicity," and case studies on Locke on property rights and citizenship in Part Four, "Human Nature and Compassion."

In Part I, "Race and Ethnicity," Jeffrey Klaiber studies Indian and Mestizo chroniclers of ancient Peru and shows their rewriting of ancient Peruvian history and culture in the context of the Old and New Testament. While Spanish chroniclers, such as Acosta, claim the devil was at work fooling the Indians into "idolatry," the local chroniclers take a more positive view of the ancient Inca religion; they creatively apply theories of the ancient arrival of descendants of Noah, of a previous evangelization by followers of Jesus, and of parallels in world religions. Juan de Santa Cruz Pachacuti relates an Inca theory of the creation of Adam and an early evangelization by T. Thomas; Felipe Huamán Poma de Ayala relates the arrival in Peru of descendants of Noah and later of St. Bartholomew. The anonymous Mestizo Jesuit makes parallels between the Inca religion and the Christian: he finds among the Incas both an ancient celibate church hierarchy and the customs of communion and confession. Garcilaso de la Vega suggests that the Incas were a model to all the Andean peoples for adopting Christianity. Klaiber approves the Indian and Mestizo chroniclers' syncretist techniques, concluding that they succeed in creating a bridge between the Incan and the Christian heritage that has precedent in the ecumenical approach of some of the church fathers.

In "The *Philosophes* and Black Slavery: 1748–1765," Claudine Hunting discusses Voltaire and several authors of articles in the *Encyclopédie*. In defending them against modern scholars who have accused them of "racism," Hunting presents Enlightenment writing as constrained by censorship and by the French official policy on slavery in the West Indies. Inspired by Montesquieu's *L'Esprit des lois*, Enlightenment thinkers point out the absurdity of royal decrees authorizing slavery in order to convert the slaves to Christianity and draw attention to the underlying real motive of national greed. The *philosophes'* argument that liberty and equality are natural to humankind juxtaposes effectively with their descriptions of the horrors of slavery. A particularly troublesome matter of interpretation is the appearance in Montesquieu and Voltaire of extremist defenses of slavery: Hunting views those as wit effectively challenging official censorship.

The evidence that Locke invested in slave trading companies and was a policy advisor concerning the provision and regulation of slaves in American colonies is the topic of Wayne Glausser's "Three Approaches to Locke and the Slave Trade." Glausser categorizes the main schools of thought for reconciling Locke's theoretical discussions of slavery in

Two Treatises of Government and *Essay Concerning Human Understanding* with his personal involvement: practice opposite to theory, practice conforming to some of the details of his theory, and practice as a fulfillment of his theory. Analyzing examples of each type, Glausser concludes "that Locke has written himself into the institutions of both slavery and abolition." On the other hand, Herman Lebovics, in "The Use of America in Locke's *Second Treatise on Government*," argues that the availability of usable land in the Americas was essential to Locke's philosophy of "the emergent world system". While Locke's notion that one might mix one's labor with land to acquire property was no longer feasible to the propertyless in England, it was a working formula overseas: by arguing how increase in productivity yields societal benefits, Locke justifies both the enclosure of English commons and the dispossession of Indian land. In distinction from Lenin's analysis of imperialism as the highest stage of capitalism, imperialism (Locke's version) thus appears to be an early stage of liberalism.

John C. Greene, in "The American Debate on the Negro's Place in Nature, 1780–1815," explores the spectrum of treatises on physical anthropology contemporary with Thomas Jefferson. The issue of the formation of races challenges the defenders of one human species, such as William Wells, to speculate on theories of random variation and natural selection. Samuel Smith's environmentalist argument of the impact of climate and civilization on race characteristics contrasts with Jefferson's focus on inheritance. One one hand, Edward Long, comparing the Negro to the orang-outang, argues that there are several species of human beings; on the other hand, Benjamin Rush argues that there is only one human species but explains differences by comparing Blackness to leprosy. Charles White, also defending the unity of one species, contributes to the nineteenth-century pseudo-science of studying skull differences for proclaiming the gradation of races (and of sexes). That characteristics of European peoples are the standard by which other peoples are judged underlies many such absurd statements of these influential nineteenth-century works.

Another important topic is how differences among European peoples come to be viewed as racial in nature. Reginald Horseman's "Origins of Racial Anglo-Saxonism in Great Britain before 1850" traces the transformations in the myths of Anglo-Saxon history. In the sixteenth- and seventeenth-century accounts, Anglo-Saxons are characterized as descendants of Germanic tribes who are well-suited to representative government; in the Romantic period, attention shifts to racial characteristics on the assumption that linguistic affinity indicates commonality of race. Notions of superiority and inferiority permeate ethnological studies in England even before the influx of American ideas in the

1830s and 40s. In thinkers such as Carlyle, the argument for racial superiority as a civilizing mission becomes a path to justify Anglo-Saxon imperialism around the globe.

While the emergence of the fields of ethnology and anthropology in early modern Europe gives "scholarly credence" to divisions of humans into racial groupings along lines of easily observed physical characteristics, and freezes popular social stereotypes into a pseudo-science of "natural" differences, the emergence of the woman question pamphlets and treatises raises questions about the heretofore assumed "natural" characteristics and societal roles of women. Part II, "Gender Distinctions," begins with an analysis of the medieval/renaissance author who initiated the pamphlet war on the woman question – Christine de Pizan – and concludes with an analysis of the English enlightenment thinker Mary Wollstonecraft. Asrik L. Gabriel's "The Educational Ideas of Christine de Pizan" documents the educational background of the woman who takes up the pen against the misogyny of the *Romance of the Rose* and who explores in a multitude of scholarly books the paths to women's moral wisdom. In "Christine de Pizan: The Poetess as Historian," Nadia Margolis examines Christine's historical writings from the *Mutation on Fortune* (1403) to her poem on Joan of Arc (1423); Margolis draws attention to Christine's innovative introduction of a female narrative voice within the genre of history and her creative adoption of classical examples such as the sex-transforming Tiresias. Both articles highlight Christine de Pizan's emphasis on the writer's moral responsibility to society, a major theme of the humanist discourse of the Renaissance.

"The Double Standard" by Keith Thomas raises the question of why there persisted in law and social mores the notion that pre- and extra-marital sex is pardonnable in a man but inexcusable and punishable in a woman. His case study documents the sexist situation of sexuality in England from the seventeenth through the nineteenth centuries. Poking holes in the Freudian explanation that males are not satisfied with marital sex, the Marxist claim that capitalism turns women into men's property, and the naturalist argument that men need to be assured that their inheritance will not go to bastards, Thomas argues that the root cause for the double-standard lies in "the desire of men for absolute property in women." Critics of the double-standard include advocates of either Puritan or middle-class morality who suggest a single standard – that men conform to the standard expected of women. Thomas' article reminds us that defenders of a single standard based on traditional male libertine behavior – "sexual liberation" – do not gain a significant audience until the twentieth century.

The accomplishment of early modern feminists is to arouse controversy on the ontological nature of womankind – inferior, equal or superior? – and to move on from a premise of equality or moral superiority to proposing the opening up of educational institutions and professions to women. However, early modern authors in general do not appear to be very knowledgeable concerning working-class women of their own and previous generations. Only becoming apparent now under the scrutiny of quantitative historians and women's historians, during the early modern epoch working women's opportunities in many trades (not only midwifery) decline as professionalization yields new formal requirements – legal, educational, economic, and political restrictions.

Jerome Nadelhaft's "The Englishwoman's Sexual Civil War: Feminist Attitudes Towards Men, Women and Marriage 1650–1740" assembles the views of Margaret Cavendish, Mary Astell and the anonymous Sophia to suggest that their analyses of family roles – especially the servitude of wives – echo the Civil War debates on "power, allegiance, liberty and slavery." To reject claims of women's natural inferiority, these intellectuals give evidence of female achievement in both the private and public realm; they attribute women's inferior societal position to the usurpation of men, the inequality of marital law, and the process of victimization by which women live a life of masquerade. They suggest that women not be educated merely for marriage, that women gather in groups to discuss their condition, and that women of talent take on other societal roles.

Like Nadelhaft, G. J. Barker-Benfield emphasizes the echoes in English feminism of English political life. Writing on "Mary Wollstonecraft: Eighteenth-Century Commonwealthwoman," Barker-Benfield amasses evidence of the influence on Wollstonecraft of James and Hannah Burgh, who imparted to her the English tradition of the Rational Dissenters. Already when taking on Edmund Burke in her *A Vindication of the Rights of Men*, Wollstonecraft extends to women the Commonwealthian republican virtue through reason and civic participation, and categorizes together the luxurious idleness of "effeminate" upper-class men and of "effeminate" upper and middle class women. She and other women who exhibit republican virtue represent "the rights of man" and the "manly spirit of independence." Trying to utilize the Commonwealthian masculinist terms for virtue as gender-inclusive terms for human virtue, she expands her domain in *Vindications of the Rights of Women* to criticize the cult of sensibility – whose main spokesman is Rousseau – which turns women into emotional private creatures. Wollstonecraft proclaims the goal that women have employments to engage their minds and earn them income, as well as civic and political rights to establish their duty beyond the household. Contributing to a trans-

Atlantic tradition, Abigail Adams and Catherine Macaulay share in the same feminist application of the Commonwealthian tradition. Despite these feminist efforts, the liberal movement for "universal male suffrage" is to turn the lower orders of men into full participating citizens well before women vote.

In "Sex and Spirit in Wollstonecraft and Malthus," Mervyn Nicholson exposes the underpinnings of both Wollstonecraft's radical and Malthus' conservative philosophies of sex relations. From different perspectives, each elaborates the negative moral, social, and political effects of sexuality, and each assumes that God's aim is that body convert to spirit. To Nicholson, Malthus' "population" is a "codeword" for "sex": the overpopulating effects of unbridled sexuality of the lower classes are only contained by famine and disease. While Malthus starts from an assumption of different prerogatives for the propertied and the unpropertied, Wollstonecraft starts from an assumption of the equality of man (including the equality of women); by that standard, sexuality is condemned for allowing the political tyranny of man over woman. Malthus disguises the image of a God who created a world where population outstrips production by claiming God wants those who cannot afford children to become spiritual and apply not birth control but moral restraint; Wollstonecraft, anticipating liberation theology (but also recalling the tradition of nuns), recommends education for the development of reason and virtue to encourage a feminine life not directed to marriage but to spirituality.

Part III, "Politics and Economics of Rank," seeks to trace the emergence of the modern concepts of class analysis in the shift from the political hierarchy of rank to the socio-economic hierarchy of class. W. Gordon Zeeveld gives evidence of "Social Equalitarianism in a Tudor Crisis." Rather than finding the early democratic spirit in the German Peasants' War or in the English Lollard movement, Zeeveld locates it in Henry VIII's raising of commoners such as Thomas Cromwell to professional service for the crown and the subsequent official tracts defending this policy against the aristocratic protest in the Pilgrimage of Grace of 1536. Utilizing the hardy idea that all humans are created equal, Christian belief in spiritual equality before God, and Aristotelian and humanist notions that virtue is the source of nobility, Henry's "new men" argue that rank and degree is a violation of the natural order of society. While in 1536, those fearing "equality" interpret it to mean the opportunity for some commoners to rise to be become gentlemen, by 1549 those fearing "equality" interpret it to mean the threat of the leveling of all ranks so that no one can be rich, a fear that is realized in the Leveller movement of the English Revolution.

Max Weber's argument for the powerful influence of a "Protestant

Work Ethic" continues to evoke controversy and refinement. Charles Constantin in "Puritan Ethic and Dignity of Labor: Hierarchy vs. Equality" exposes several strands of the idea of "calling" in colonial New England, some supporting the hierarchical ranking of society and some supporting the equality of opportunity. Cotton Mather and his grandson, like Luther and Calvin, recognize the equal dignity before God of commoners' labor, viewing each station of work in the hierarchy of society as a path to expressing one's faith and subsequent service to God. On the other hand, Jonathan Edwards incorporates the notions of hierarchy and plenitude of the great chain of being into his version of the Puritan ethic: subjecting one's will to God aids the work of God's redemption in history. Within Samuel Hopkins' theology, virtue becomes a spontaneous expression of the heart, rather than the intellect, common to people of all stations; in contrast, to conservatives Charles Chauncy and Jonathan Mayhew, virtue comes from recognizing one's place of subordination in the chain of being within human society. Constantin's examination of these theologians provides evidence of a continuation to the early nineteenth century of a religious-aesthetic, traditional and hierarchical Puritan ethic, despite the emergence of the secular-utilitarian, egalitarian and modern Puritan ethic of Benjamin Franklin, John Adams, and Alexander Hamilton, by which one justifies attaining riches and gaining upward mobility as proof of one's faith and service through work.

"Rank," "degree," "estate," and "station" characterize the vocabulary of societal hierarchy before the severe social strife of the French Revolution and the emergence of the field of political economy in France and England. This view of Asa Briggs is the starting point of Steven Wallech's "'Class versus Rank': the Transformation of Eighteenth Century English Social Terms and Theories of Production." In 1755, Cantillon contributes a theory of intrinsic value based on land productivity and labor in which there are two classes, the entrepreneurs and the hired laborers. Quesnay applies Cantillon's system to found the physiocrats; defending "laissez-faire," Quesnay disregards the feudal ranks and proposes that society is functionally divided into three: landlords, laborers working the soil, and laborers or artisans working in industry. The latter two working groups he views as classes, while Turgot proposes that all three are classes. All three French theorists contribute to a new conception of "status in terms of production." Working from these French theories, Joseph Harris, Adam Smith, and David Richardo create a British theory of production. At first the language of rank persists even in Adam Smith, for whom rank becomes dependent on one's relationship to production, and the "labouring classes" takes on sociological significance in the distinctions of productive versus unproductive laborers. By the time of David Ricardo's work of 1817, the language of class, based on a changing mobile society, wins out. Ricardo, influenced by Malthus, breaks with the Commonwealthian tradition based on a common community, and asserts class conflicts between upper-class landlords, middle-class capitalists, and lower-class workers which explains contemporary positions on the Poor Laws and the Corn Laws. The Industrial Revolution and the popularization of the field of economics ensure the success of the new conceptualization.

Seeking in dictionaries for earlier linguistic evidence of the shift from political to economic terminology, Dallas L. Clouatre's "The Concept of Class in French Culture Prior to the French Revolution" distinguishes the early modern new vocabulary of *classe*, "class," from the medieval and early modern old vocabulary of *rang*, "rank." While the Latin root *classis* refers to a group, even sometimes the highest or most preeminent class, the root of "classical," by the sixteenth century, the French *classe* takes on the meaning of a general "category," sometimes applying to a school-class. In Cotgraves' dictionary of 1606, the new vocabulary gets defined by the old vocabulary: claşse is "a rank, order, or distribution of people according to their several degrees." By the end of the reign of Louix XIV, classe becomes the term in vogue in the inductive sense as the "Grade or rank *attributed* to persons or things according to their importance or qualities."

Among the physiocrats, class analysis becomes the way to describe social groups of the economic system. The transformation indicates the overthrow of an essentialist system of a fixed social hierarchy of rank and order focused on political status by an inductive and quantitative system focused on economic productivity. Precedents to physiocratic class analysis include the Head Tax of 1695, wherein a class might contain a rich peasant as well as a poor nobleman whose incomes are assessed the same, and Boisguilbert's writings which point to societal corruption in the division of society into two classes, those who do not work and enjoy "privilege" and those who work and possess little. The juxtaposition of the vocabulary of *ordre* and *rang* and the vocabulary of classe allows by the 1760s such theorists as Rousseau to suggest that the order of the nobility not only does not represent the common good of the nation, but prevents the common good by its service to its class interests. By the time of that transformation, "class," especially "productive classes," begins to take on some of the essentialist characteristics of the discarded terms "rank" and "ordre". Clouatre concludes: "The history of the emergence of 'class' in the early modern period, more than anything else, is the history of the development of this concept of social stratification."

We have seen that the development of the economic concept of "class" serves as a radical tool to break the elitist political privileges of the nobility. Likewise, we have seen the development of feminist writing question the fixed essentialist characterization of women's nature and societal role. The European exploration of other continents and the enterprise of the slave trade are very conspicuous aspects of the early modern era, which influence the development of the fields of anthropology and especially ethnology. Among some scholars, distinctions among peoples shift to essentialist racial categorization; yet at the same time critics emerge questioning the equity, the justice, and the humanity of the slavery business. Nevertheless, the overwhelming impression is that multiple layers of ideologies bulwark the walls of societal hierarchies: ideologies of gender behavior appropriate to one's sex, and ideologies of political and economic behavior appropriate to one's rank and race. The most potent paradigms for change are theories of resistance to government and examples of revolution which creative thinkers apply to the micropolitical realm of wife/husband, laborer/nobleman, and slave/owner, as well as to the macropolitical realm of the state. Part IV, "Human Nature and Compassion," considers whether there are some other redeeming social and moral ideas that ease the strain of the racist, sexist, and elitist social mores of early modern Europe.

Renaissance humanist viewpoints are considered in Marcia L. Colish's "The Mime of God: Vives on the Nature of Man." Colish reminds us, as do Constantin and Clouatre, that hierarchy in Western thought is fundamentally tied to a notion of a great chain of being linking the lowest form of life to the highest. Pico della Mirandola's suggestion in his famous oration on human dignity that humans have no fixed place in the chain takes literary form in Vives' *Famula de homine* of 1518, which describes a human actor before the court of Jupiter and the ancient gods: the actor successively poses as each stage of life – plant, animal, human, and then Jupiter himself. Colish argues that Vives differs in significant ways from Pico, and writes consistently within the movement of Christian humanism. While Vives thus plays with Pico's notion of the indeterminacy and changeability of human nature, he also reveals that in a divinely-ordained universe human potential is limited and constrained and that the mimicry of Jupiter is only a pretense. Nevertheless, to us, Vives' fable does reveal that the growth of theatrical productions and theatrical modes of thinking in the sixteenth century expands awareness that specific societal roles are acts possible to numerous other players.

Analysis of key concepts and of significant silences in a text is a combined contribution of Judith Richards, Lotie Mulligan, and John K. Graham in " 'Property' and 'People': Political Usages of Locke and Some Contemporaries." This article views Locke as a moralist and a radical political theorist, whose Two Treatises of Government disturbs Whigs in the aftermath of the 1688 English Revolution. Locke defines "property" expansively – "Property, that is, his Life, Liberty and Estate" – and does not make ownership of land a prerequisite for consent to government. Unlike contemporary Whigs Sidney, Tyrrell, and Neville, Locke proclaims the rationality of people of all ranks in society, and refrains from limiting those eligible for the franchise and those who share in the right of resistance to government. While Richards, Mulligan, and Graham praise Locke for rejecting the family as a model for political society because a family has a natural head (i.e., the father), they do not mention Locke's obvious acceptance of woman's subordination in the micropolitics of the family with implications for the macropolitics of the state. Likewise, they confirm the concerns of Glausser and Lebovics by pointing out that Locke attributes dignity to servants by distinguishing them from slaves. Locke appears here as a supporter for widening the political electorate among the working men of England.

John C. Winfrey in "Charity versus Justice in Locke's Theory of Property" clarifies that to Locke "charity" is Christian responsibility to provide for those "in need," and "justice" is honoring the property claims established by one's own or ancestors' "desert." Winfrey argues that three meanings of Locke's state of nature mutually reinforce one another: humanity after Adam's fall, existing conditions in the Americas, and everyman's position before consenting to society. Winfrey shows that by a sleight of hand Locke claims that the distribution of property in England is just: "Locke used the labor theory of value to justify initial accumulation; and secondly he assumes that subsequent transactions are voluntary." In addition, the natural state in the Americas allows for a continuation of economic opportunity and a proof that day workers in England are better off than those in a state of nature; for Locke, one may claim charity only when one lacks subsistence and exhibits honest industry. Winfrey argues for the consistency of Locke's Whig position which justifies the power of the landed gentry and merchants following the Glorious Revolution; the Locke of Winfrey is much less sympathetic to the workingmen of England than is the Locke of Richards, Mulligan, and Graham.

Norman S. Fiering gives evidence of eighteenth-century "irresistable compassion," the belief that humans have a moral instinct to feel compassion and come to the aid of other humans in need. While tracing ideas of compassion back to Juvenal, Cicero, and St. Paul, Fiering views faith in human compassion as blossoming in the seventeenth-century among Cambridge Platonists, English Latitudinarians, and Malebranche, who object to Calvinists' and Hobbes' depreciation of human nature. In "Irresistable Compassion: An Aspect of Eighteenth Century Sympathy and Humanitarianism," Fiering argues that Englishman William Wollaston extends compassion into the realm of punishments for criminals and that Scottish thinker Frances Hucheson applies compassion to overriding arguments for slavery. While pleased at the development of the "man of feeling" as a new social type, Fiering points out that much of the compassion, rather than expressing itself in acts of kindness, dissipates into emotional reading or theatre-going; furthermore, the excesses of the French Revolution and the philosophical sadism of Marquis de Sade follow on the heels of this age of humanitarianism. Nevertheless, a very important theological dilemma emerges, especially among American theologians. William Ellery Charring tries to modify the doctrine of the eternal punishment of sinners, finding it incompatible with a notion that humans, and consequently their creator, are naturally compassionate, while Edward Wigglesworth defends the doctrine of Hell, apparently unaware of how unconvincing his arguments are to those whose sensibilities have been altered by belief in irresistable compassion. From this theological perspective, we see that Mervyn Nicholson's discomfort with Malthus' God ordaining overpopulation reflects modern compassionate sensibilities against suffering and a modern sense of injustice in a universe in which suffering is part of a divine plan. Overall, the articles in this volume show that compassion and humane concerns are very evident in historical and philosophical circles today, and continue to inspire scholars to investigate topics relatively neglected before. Especially in response to exposure of the collective horrors of World War II, totalitarianism, and colonialism, and in sympathy with the liberation movements (anti-colonial, feminist, theological, and democratic) of our post-colonial period, some scholars have been seeking out the intellectual culprits who might be held responsible for some of the negative attitudes toward and negative treatment of specific groups of human beings. Likewise, some are seeking to discover and give renewed attention to the foremothers and forefathers of our contemporary outrage at institutional racism, sexism, and elitism: in this way, historical work contributes to the philosophical work of building upon and refining the intellectual traditions of those who suggest paths to creating a more egalitarian, just, and compassionate world order.

What *Race, Gender and Rank: Early Modern Ideas of Humanity* reveals most explicitly is the difficulty of placing our predecessors, as well as ourselves, in clear-cut categories of villains and heros. In-depth readings expose controversies everywhere: as we have seen, Christine de Pizan protests on women's behalf without questioning the double-standard on sexuality; John Locke proclaims natural human rights in a political economy which compromises his views of the political rights of working men, of Amerindians, and of Black slaves; the eighteenth-century *philosophes* question the privileges of legal rank and seek for a more compassionate and expansive system of justice, yet they, too, have left a mixed record containing slurs of racial, ethnic, and gender bias.

The prize-winning, anti-Stalinist *glasnost* film *Repentance* reminds us that we, too, will be held accountable to future generations, who will dig up bodies (as well as texts) to find out what we tried to hide. As the scholars herein have examined early modern European theorists for their consideration of "slavery," "wifedom," and "commoners' servitude," as well as "human unity," "natural rights," and "natural affections," so will future generations examine our deeds and thoughts by categories that they deem important. Hopefully, a future human generation – one effectively striving for compassionate human unity with recognition of human diversity – will appreciate the accomplishment of our generation in clarifying the conceptual distinctions of "race/ethnicity," "gender roles/sex differences/sexuality" and "rank/class."

PART ONE

RACE AND ETHNICITY

II

THE POSTHUMOUS CHRISTIANIZATION OF THE INCA EMPIRE IN COLONIAL PERU

By Jeffrey L. Klaiber

A problem which has increasingly concerned Christian missiologists and missionaries in the twentieth century is the continuing existence of a Christian-pagan syncretism in the Andean regions. In the decade of the twenties the Peruvian Marxist, José Carlos Mariátegui antedated this anthropological concern among churchmen when he observed in his *Siete Ensayos* that the aboriginal paganism of the highland Indians continued to subsist under the guise of Catholicism long after the presumed evangelization of Peru had taken place.[1] Yet, the lack of a real evangelization and the tenacious survival of prehispanic rites and myths is not a modern theme at all: government and church officials lamented this phenomenon all through the colonial period. The movement to extirpate idolatry in Peru in the late sixteenth and early seventeenth centuries, so associated with the name of the Jesuit, Pablo de Arriaga, stemmed from the realization that Christianity had made little headway among the Indians for decades after most of the Indians had been baptized.[2] A manual for priests working among the Indians, which appeared in 1771, deplored the continual recurrence of idolatry among the Indians as well as their widespread ignorance of Christianity.[3]

In the light of the persistence of these hybrid forms of Christianity and older native ways it may be of value to refocus some of the usual perspectives in which the problem is studied and look for other avenues of approach. On the one hand, much attention is paid to the more articulate and erudite religious writers of the evangelization process such as the Jesuits, José de Acosta, Pablo de Arriaga or Bernabé Cobo. On the other hand, the tendency exists to place lesser importance on the testimonies of certain mestizo and Indian chroniclers of the same period whose sense of critical objectivity is doubtful, especially as regards interpretations of the history of their own people. Thus, the Peruvian man of letters, José de la Riva-Agüero dismissed the relation of the so-called "Anonymous Jesuit" as "deceitful,"[4] while the historian, Raúl Porras Barrenechea belittled the chronicle of Felipe Huamán Poma de Ayala as the result of "mental confusion."[5] Readers of Garcilaso de la Vega, author of the *Royal Commentaries of the Incas,* are almost always cautioned against his "romanticizing" of the Inca empire.

---

[1] José Carlos Mariátegui, *Siete Ensayos de interpretación de la Realidad Peruana* (11th ed.; Lima, 1967), 150.

[2] José Pablo de Arriaga, *Extirpación de la Idolatría en el Perú,* in *Crónicas Peruanas de interés indígena,* ed. F. E. Barba (Madrid, 1968), 191–277.

[3] Alonso de la Peña Montenegro, *Itinerario para Párrocos de Indios* (Madrid, 1771), 177.

[4] José de la Riva-Agüero, *La Historia en el Perú* (2nd. ed.; Madrid, 1952), 23.

[5] Raúl Porras Barrenechea, *El Cronista Indio Felipe Huamán Poma de Ayala* (Lima, 1948), 7.

3

However, from another point of view, while the less objective historical narration of these chroniclers may pale before the works of the greater luminaries of that period, their more pronounced and positive attempt to reconcile their Inca past with Christianity was more in accord with the ecumenical missiology of the early Church, and in many respects more of an anticipation of modern mission theory. As a matter of fact, in one important area, the missionary outlook of the early Church did serve as a model for the sixteenth-century Church in Peru. Both Acosta and the Italian Jesuit, Anello Oliva, cite the early Church's fight against the idolatry of Greece and Rome as an early parallel to their own efforts in Peru.[6] While it is true that the early apologists and Fathers of the Church fulminated against idolatry, which most saw as the main obstacle to evangelization, they also shared, in one degree or another, a positive apologetical outlook by which they sought to incorporate the best of the surrounding pagan culture into a Christian synthesis. One example of this was the attempt to reinterpret certain "noble pagan" philosophers, especially Plato and Socrates, as precursors of Christianity. One of the first Gentile apologists, Justin, claimed that Plato derived much of his wisdom from his having come into contact with the writings of Moses.[7] In the fifth century St. Augustine theorized that Plato must have come into contact with the Septuagint during a visit to Egypt.[8]

However, some of the early Fathers went beyond this more extrinsic approach to the pagan philosophers and also touched upon means of bridging the gap between Christianity and the non-Christian world which were more intrinsic to the nature of man himself. Justin, for example, held that Christ, as the Word of God, preexisted His own coming in time and was known, albeit obscurely, by all men who lived according to reason. According to his doctrine of the all-present Word of God, Justin believed that Christ "was partially known even by Socrates, for He was and is the Word Who is in every man. . . ."[9] The African Father, Tertullian, referred to the "Testimony of the soul which is naturally Christian" (*Testimonium animae naturaliter Christianae*) in speaking of the capacity of all men to find God.[10] Augustine, asking why it is that even ungodly men reach a knowledge of God, answered by pointing to the testimony of the natural world and the stars which speak of their maker.[11] Finally, in spite of his Manichaean background which led him to distrust natural inclinations, Augustine summed up this universalizing viewpoint of the early Church in his statement that God is loved, "wittingly or unwittingly by everything that is capable of love."[12]

[6] José de Acosta, *Historia Natural y Moral de las Indias*, in *Obras de José de Acosta, S.J.*, ed. Francisco Mateos (Madrid, 1954), LXXIV, 139. Anello Oliva, *Historia del Reino y Provincias del Perú* (Lima, 1895), 125.

[7] Justin Martyr, *First Apology*, XIII, 8, *The Ante-Nicene Fathers*, ed. A. Roberts and J. Donaldson (New York, 1926), I, 183.

[8] St. Augustine, *City of God*, Book VIII, Ch. 11, *The Nicene and Post-Nicene Fathers*, trans. R. G. MacMullen (New York, 1903), 151.

[9] Justin Martyr, *Second Apology*, X, *The Ante-Nicene Fathers*, 191–92.

[10] Tertullian, *Apologia*, XVII, 5, 6., trans. T. R. Glover (London, 1931), 89.

[11] St. Augustine, *Sermons on New Testament Lessons*, XCI, 1. *The Nicene and Post-Nicene Fathers*, VI, 531.

[12] St. Augustine, *Soliloquies*, Book I, Ch. I, 2, *The Nicene and Post-Nicene Fathers*, trans. C. C. Starbuck, VII, 537.

One searches in vain for such an ecumenical view toward the Inca religion and philosophy among the leading religious writers of sixteenth-century Peru. Certainly, the reason cannot be that they looked upon the Inca culture as so inferior that it did not merit much attention or consideration. On the contrary, Acosta, Oliva, Cobo, and others stood in great admiration of Inca culture, and went to great lengths to portray the humanity and intelligence of the Peruvian Indians to their contemporary Europeans. Almost all of them compared the Inca civilization with the glories of Greece and Rome, and Cobo had no hesitation in declaring that the Inca's religion was by far the highest in the New World.[13] The most famous apologist for the Indians, José de Acosta, stood apart from many other Spaniards of his time with his courageous humanism which led him to refute views of the Indians which belittled their capacity. Acosta chose to place the blame for the slow progress in evangelization not on the low capacity of the Indians, but on the faulty catechizing techniques of previous missionaries among the Indians: "The difficulty of the natives in understanding the Gospel does not arise from their nature as much as from their lack of education."[14] Acosta found the Indians quite amenable to hearing the Christian message, if it were correctly presented. The Indians, said Acosta, were "simple, docile, humble, friends of good priests, and obedient."[15] On the other hand, Acosta warned, it is also the Indian's nature to be "inconstant and disloyal."[16]

Acosta's humanism and sense of balance in portraying the Indian's character also carried over into some of his missionary advice. On the question of idolatry Acosta warned that though idols should be destroyed, it is far more important to destroy the "idols of the heart."[17] Before any catechizing should take place, Acosta urged his fellow Jesuits and other missionaries to engage in a thorough study of Inca history and customs in order to distinguish between correct practices and erroneous ones among the Indians. With respect to the Inca empire, Acosta admired the "order and reason" which prevailed among the Incas.[18]

However, in assessing the Inca religion, Acosta was less sympathetic and more a man of his age. He was skeptical of the claims of some that the Incas had been pre-evangelized by an apostle.[19] Although he admired the Incas for coming to a knowledge of a supreme being and creator, he compared this belief to the *Ignoto Deo* which had confounded St. Paul in Athens. The Incas' one God was a dark and tenuous being which existed alongside myriad other gods.[20] The apparent similarities between certain Inca rites and practices and those of Christianity were discounted by Acosta as the work of the Devil. For Acosta, as for most Spaniards of his day, the great enemy of both faith and civilization

[13] Bernabé Cobo, *Historia del Nuevo Mundo*, ed. F. Mateos (Madrid,1956), 146–47.

[14] José de Acosta, *De Procuranda Indorum Salute*, in *Obras*, 413.

[15] *Ibid.*, 428.

[16] *Ibid.*, 452; cf. an article which treats of the Jesuit's view of the Peruvian Indian by Antonio de Egaña, "La Visión Humanística del Indio Americano en los Primeros Jesuitas Peruanos," *Analecta Gregoriana*, **70** (Oct. 1953), 291–306.

[17] Acosta, *De Procuranda*, 564.

[18] Acosta, *Historia Natural y Moral*, 181–83; also, León Lopetegui, *El Padre José de Acosta y las Misiones* (Madrid, 1942).

[19] Acosta, *De Procuranda*, 397. [20] Acosta, *Historia Natural y Moral*, 141–42.

was the Devil. From the very beginning, both the Spanish soldiers and missionaries looked upon the destruction of idols and temples not as a mere clearing away of past relics in order to preach the Gospel, but as an assault on the resting place of the Evil One himself.[21] In this titanic struggle of God and man against the Prince of Darkness, one of the most insidious tactics of the Devil was to parody Christian practices in prehispanic times among the Incas. Thus, Acosta and others were aware of the existence of such Inca practices as a type of confession and communion, the institution of consecrated virgins, symbols of the trinity, etc. But they felt that these rites and symbols, instead of serving as bridges between the Inca past and the Christian present, actually made the Christianization process more difficult. For example, Acosta cites the custom of eating a morsel of bread dipped in ram's blood during the feast of *Inti Raymi* as a sign of allegiance to the Inca. He termed this Inca rite as "diabolical communion," and offered it as another example of the malicious work of the Devil in corrupting the good religious instincts of the people.[22]

Acosta saw the Devil paralleling the work of God everywhere. Somewhat in the same way in which St. Augustine conceived of the natural order as a hierarchy ascending from the material to the spiritual, Acosta perceived a hierarchy of idolatry descending from the invisible lord creator to the natural world and finally to man. At the apex of the hierarchy is the idolatry of natural things, such as the sun, moon, and stars. Next comes the idolatry of particular things, such as hilltops, rivers, and rocks. A third type of idolatry was the cult of the dead. Finally, there was the idolatry of man-made objects, such as sacred images and statues.[23] Thus, both the natural world and the world of man were thoroughly infiltrated by the Devil on every level of being.

Given his belief in the all-maleficent influence of the Devil over the religious customs and aspirations of the Incas, Acosta was very skeptical of attempts to find salvific elements in the Inca past. Rather, he held that a radical break with the past was a necessary condition for evangelization. Citing St. Augustine as his source, he held that explicit belief in Christ is necessary for salvation, and that a mere belief in one God who rewards and punishes is not sufficient.[24] While Acosta urged that many elements of the Inca civil and political order be imitated as guidelines for Spanish colonial administration, he felt that in matters of religion, the Inca past offered little of value for the missionary needs of the Catholic Church.

Other Spaniards displayed differing degrees of skepticism in recording the religious legends and myths of the Incas, especially those which suggested some type of pre-evangelization. Many were impressed by the belief in a supreme creator, by the abundance of rites and symbols externally similar to Christian

[21] E.g., cf. Hernando Pizarro's account of the idol of the temple of Pachacamac in the "Carta de Hernando Pizarro a la Audiencia Real de Santo Domingo," in Gonzalo Fernández Oviedo y Valdés, *Historia General y Natural de las Indias* (Asunción, 1945), XII, 88.

[22] Acosta, *Historia Natural y Moral*, 166; also the remarks of Pierre Duviols on demonic parodies in colonial Peru, *La Lutte Contre les Religions Autochtones dans le Pérou Colonial* (Lima, n.d.), 67–78.

[23] *Ibid.*, 140–52ff.

[24] Acosta, *De Procuranda*, 546–51.

ones and by the high moral standards of the Incas. The Mercedarian, Martín de Morúa, who worked for many years among the Indians in the highlands around Cuzco, made much of the Inca's quest for the one, true God whom, he believed, they had indeed discovered, and to whom they gave the name, "Tipsi Viracocha."[25] He also reported a cross which the Indians revered and which served as a "sort of prophecy of the coming of the Christians."[26] However, Morúa, who was otherwise sympathetic towards the Indians, found the Inca religion infested with gods and idols through which the Devil worked to mislead the people.[27] The Augustinians in Huamachuco reported a belief in a triune god worshipped by the Indians in that region. Unimpressed, the friars dismissed this as a "false trinity" invented by the Devil.[28]

The same Morúa also offered an explanation for some of the advanced, that is, quasi-Christian, religious notions of the Incas. He told of a "poor Spaniard" who had come through the Tiahuanaco region preaching the Gospel in the time of the Inca Túpac Yupanqui, father of Huayna Capac.[29] The soldier-chronicler, Cieza de Léon, hearing of a statue near Chucuito which some Spaniards claimed to be that of an "apostle," examined the statue and concluded skeptically that he doubted if the Word of God had been heard in Peru before the coming of the Spanish.[30] Another explanation commonly put forth to link the American Indians with the primitive Judaic-Christian revelation was that they were descended in one way or another from Noah after the Flood. The cleric, Fernando de Montesinos, was even able to fix with exactitude the progenitor of the Peruvian Indians as Ophir, son of Shem, son of Noah.[31] The Dominican bishop, Reginaldo Lizárraga, however, was less certain of "what sons or grandsons or descendants of Noah the Indians might be."[32]

However, whether or not they believed in some type of pre-evangelization, most missionaries found that the Devil had so vitiated the good intentions and practices of the people so as to outweigh the original positive influence of any possible earlier pre-Christianization. One anonymous religious writer, who believed that the practice of confession among the Indians had been inspired by a Christian "holy man," observed that this prehispanic custom had

[25] Martín de Morúa, *Historia del origen y genealogía de los Reyes Incas del gran reino del Perú,* in *Colección de libros y documentos referentes a la historia del Perú,* ed. H. Urteaga and C. Romero (Lima, 1922), IV, 2nd series, 14, 217. On the confusion of names given to this supreme being: Acosta, *Historia Natural y Moral,* 142.

[26] Morúa, 30. [27] *Ibid.,* 113, 143.

[28] *Relación de la Religión y Ritos del Perú hecha por los primeros religiosos Agustinos que allí pasaron para la conversión de los naturales,* in Urteaga-Romero (Lima, 1919), XI, 11.

[29] Morúa, 77–78.

[30] Cieza de León, *Del Señorío de los Incas* (Buenos Aires, 1943), 42–47. For a fuller account of the widespread belief in the prehispanic appearance of a Christian evangelizer in Peru: Rubén Vargas, "La Venida del Apóstol," *Historia de la Iglesia en el Perú* (Lima, 1953), 62–79.

[31] Fernando de Montesinos, *Memorias Antiguas y Políticas del Perú,* in Urteaga (Lima, 1930), VI, 4–5.

[32] Reginaldo Lizárraga, *Descripción Breve de toda la Tierra del Perú, Tucumán, Río de la Plata y Chile,* in *Historiadores de Indias,* ed. Serrano y Sanz (Madrid, 1909), II, 486.

degenerated into a "bad and superstitious" rite by the time of the Spanish.[33] The Italian Jesuit, Anello Oliva, who believed that the Incas had once reached a high moral plateau under the Inca Pachacuti, described Inca history from that time on as a continual moral backsliding under the influence of the Devil, a phenomenon arrested only by the advent of the Jesuits in Peru in 1568.[34] Cieza de León grudgingly admitted that the Incas had, indeed, fashioned a concept of a single creator god, but he was quick to interject his opinion that the people were too much in the power of the Devil for this higher concept to have much meaning for them.[35]

Finally, from Spain, Bartholomew de las Casas lamented the duplicity of the Devil in the temple of Pachacamac, who fooled the newly converted Indians of that region into believing that they could worship both him as well as their new Christian God.[36] The great spokesmen and conductors of the movement to extirpate idols in Peru found that the old Inca Devil, far from being defeated, never ceased to muddle and confuse the Indians in their halting attempts to practice their new religion. Arriaga deplored the custom of the Indians of secretly carrying huacas with them in the very procession of Corpus Christi.[37] The parish priest Francisco de Avila, who set off one of the major waves of idol hunting, claimed that the Indians were so bold as to stoop to the "diabolical artifice" of actually using images of Christ and the Virgin as disguised idols.[38]

In the light of the rather dim view which many churchmen, government officials, and chroniclers, both illustrious and humble, took of the Inca religion, the task of devising an apology for it as the basis for a more positive missiology was fraught with great difficulties from the very beginning. The mestizo and Indian writers who did attempt to "baptize" the Inca religion lacked the theological sophistication and prestige of the great Spanish theologians of the day, and some of them still conceived of historical events in terms of the mythical world view inherited from their fathers. Nevertheless, a few of the mythical intuitions of these writers came closer to some of the insights of the early Fathers of the Church than did the narrower, Devil-filled missiology of sixteenth-century Spaniards.

An example of such an attempt to rewrite Inca history from a Christian perspective was the chronicle of Juan de Santa Cruz Pachacuti. Writing around 1600, Pachacuti was an Indian *curaca* (chieftain) whose ancestors from the Cajamarca region probably sided with Atahualpa. This Indian chronicler seemed moved to write his history of the Incas in order to counteract the opinion of many Spaniards that the Incas had been idolatrous barbarians and

---

[33] *Parecer Acerca de la perpetuidad y buen gobierno de los Indios del Perú, y Aviso de lo que deben hacer los encomenderos para salvarse,* in Urteaga (Lima, 1920), III, 150–51.

[34] Oliva, 130–31.

[35] Cieza de León, *La Crónica del Perú* (Buenos Aires, 1945), 85, 136.

[36] Bartholomew de las Casas, *Apologética Historia de las Indias,* cited in Raúl Porras Barrenechea, *Cronistas del Perú* (Lima, 1962), 164.

[37] Arriaga, 223.

[38] Francisco de Avila, *Prefación al libro de los sermones o homilías del Dr. Francisco Dávila en la lengua Castellana y en la índica general Quechua,* in Urteaga-Romero (Lima, 1918), XI, 77.

that their descendants did not make good Christians. It was this concern which led him to preface his chronicle with a long profession of faith to establish his credentials as a believing Christian. While his declaration was basically a restatement of the Nicene Creed, he also inserted a few personal additions. For one thing, he expanded upon the stark statement of God's creation of Heaven and Earth to include: "And all the things in them, such as the Sun and Moon, stars, comets, lightning and thunder. . . ."[39] While such a detailed litany added a poetic note to the creed, it probably also served the apologetic purpose of emphasizing the chronicler's Christianized vision of the natural world in which all the heavenly things formerly held to be gods were now pointedly placed under the power of the Christian God.

Another addition to the creed was the insertion of the Incas into the biblical scheme of creation:

Then He created the first man, Adam, Eve his woman, in his image, progenitors of the human race, and from whom we inhabitants of Tahuantinsuyo are descended, as are the other nations which inhabit the whole world. . . . (*Ibid.*)

Santa Cruz Pachacuti went even further by developing the story of the Incas within a New Testament frame of reference. He tells of pre-Inca times in Peru when the land was overrun by demons (*hapiñuños*) who fomented wars and sowed discord everywhere. One night, amidst shouting and cries, the demons were forceably ejected from the land. The author piously explains that this was the very night of Christ's death on the cross.[40] To further insure that his point is not lost, namely, that Inca history is not extraneous to but contiguous with Christian history, Pachacuti narrates the coming of the Apostle St. Thomas to Peru a few years after the rout of the demons. St. Thomas, or "Tonapa," after leading a campaign against the idols and huacas and leaving a deep imprint on all those who heard him, was eventually driven out of the land by other, less comprehending Indians.[41] Nevertheless, shortly thereafter, the founders of the Inca empire, Manco Capac and his wife-sister, Mama Ocllu, appear on the scene and proceed to implement many reforms associated with the higher religions. Besides putting into effect many "good moral laws," Manco Capac also waged a vigorous war against the worship of idols and inaugurated the cult of the supreme creator of Heaven and Earth.

However, the element of drama reenters the story when the exiled demons surreptitiously return to challenge the good works set in motion under Inca leadership. Working upon an innocent and unlearned people, the demons seduce many of the Indians by leading them to make secret pacts with them in "caves" and other out of the way places. Mysteriously, idols begin to appear again in the hills and caves around the new capital, Cuzco—a sure sign that the "old enemy," as the author terms him, is back. From that time forward till the last Inca an epic struggle between the Evil One and the Incas marks the climactic high and low points of all of Inca history. The fourth Inca, Mayta Capac, who was inspired enough to foresee the coming of the Christian Gospel, won fame as the most rigorous enemy of the huacas. It was this enlightened

---

[39] Juan de Santa Cruz Pachacuti Yamqui Salcamayhua, *Relación de Antiguedades deste reyno del Perú,* in Urteaga-Romero (Lima, 1917), IX, 129-31.

[40] *Ibid.,* 131. [41] *Ibid.,* 132-34; 165-67.

Inca who made it definitively clear to the simple folk that the sun and moon are but creatures of the One God, Ticci Capac, who placed them in the heavens in order to serve man.[42]

Another high point in the narration is reached when the son of Mayta Capac, Capac Yupanqui, decides deliberately to confront the Evil One. Knowing of the Devil's habit of speaking through the huacas, the young Inca shuts himself up in a house full of idols and huacas, and soon finds himself in a spirited debate with the Devil. When Capac Yupanqui invokes the name of the creator (*Hacedor*), the Devil flees. "From that time on," Pachacuti adds, "the huacas feared the Incas."[43]

In spite of the good efforts of some of the wiser Incas, such as Pachacuti and Topa Inca, others allowed the people to backslide into huaca-worship again. By the time of the civil war between Huascar and Atahualpa, the land was thoroughly overrun by the minions of the Devil. As a preparation for the upcoming conflict, Huascar publicly renounced the cult of the huacas and swore to become in his time another Mayta Capac. As the verdict of history seems to indicate, his resolution apparently came much too late. At the very moment that the vanquished Huascar cries out to the Lord Creator, he is reminded of his many past sins of idolatry.[44] However, Pachacuti's story of the Incas has an ending which is both happy and fitting. After a victorious march through Peru, the Spanish conqueror, Pizarro, his chaplain, Valverde, and the newly chosen Inca, Manco, enter Cuzco together. In the words of the chronicler:

And the Marquis and the Inca, in the company of the Holy Gospel of Jesus Christ our Lord, entered with great pomp and majesty. . . . At last, the law of God and His Holy Gospel, so eagerly awaited, had come to take possession of the New Vine. . . .[45]

The triumphant entrance of the Gospel into the heart of the Inca empire marked the successful climax of the long struggle of the Incas against the enemies of God. In reality, Pachacuti's chronicle is a morality play in which the main protagonists, the Inca leaders and the demons battle it out over the ages under the watchful eyes of a Christian heavenly court. The fact that his chronology of the Incas failed to accord with other, more history minded chroniclers mattered little to this Indian son of Christian converts. For him, the real and great drama dominating all of Inca history was the struggle of his people to fulfill their appointed task within the confines of Christian sacred history. Given this perspective, Pachacuti's recasting of Inca history as an essentially religious drama places him within a Christian providentialist tradition, epitomized earlier by St. Augustine's *City of God,* a classic example of theologized history, and later popularized in the twentieth century under the term, "Salvation History" (*Heilsgeschichte*).

More well known is the graphic chronicle of Felipe Huamán Poma de Ayala, Indian chief and descendant of Inca nobility. Poma de Ayala's many travels throughout Peru as well as his keen pride in his own history led him to

---

[42] *Ibid.,* 158–59.   [43] *Ibid.,* 164.
[44] *Ibid.,* 231.   [45] *Ibid.,* 234–35.

level a sweeping indictment against the many abuses of Spanish officials and clergymen. Although he admitted the existence of human sacrifices and idolatry in the time of the Incas, Poma also emphasized the greater justice and charity which reigned under the "Gentile" Incas than under the Christian Spanish.[46] He also introduced his own prehispanic apostle in Peru, St. Bartholomew, who worked many miracles among the first Incas. Poma's Christian vision of the past, however, is especially evident in his "Ages of the World." Like his fellow Christian, Pachacuti, Poma weaves Inca history into the general fabric of Old and New Testament history. During the period of the Second Age, for example, one of Noah's descendants is brought to the Indies by God, presumably to populate that part of the world.[47] Finally, after a long period, Christ initiates the Fifth Age with his birth, and Inca history begins as well:

At this time the Savior, Our Lord Jesus Christ was born, and in this kingdom of the Incas, the first Inca, Manco Capac, began to reign in the city of Cuzco. . . .[48]

If Poma's chronology is somewhat overextended to fit his Christian notions, his portrayal of the Spanish doctrinero as autocratic and mean was poignant and clear. As Poma saw it, the priest who worked among the Indians and the King's officials were the "mortal enemies" of the Indians.[49]

Among the more controversial chronicles, both as regards authorship as well as content, is that of the so-called "Anonymous Jesuit." Most authors agree that this Jesuit chronicler, who wrote roughly around the same time as Pachacuti and Poma, was a mestizo, and possibly even the same Blas Valera cited by Garcilaso. In any case, his view of Inca religion and customs is so highly positive that Riva-Agüero considered him as simply "deceitful," while Raúl Porras Barrenechea accused him of "finding in Inca ritual an anticipation of Catholic worship." At the same time, however, Porras defended the Jesuit as a valuable source for Inca customs and ritual.[50]

The author begins his *relación* in the style of the *Genesis* narration: in the beginning, according to Inca mythology, Illa Tecce, the "Eternal Light," created the heavens and the earth. All things, stars, moon, and sun, were but servants of the one God, who assigned different tasks to each one. In those days there were no idols in Peru, as the inhabitants adored only Illa Tecce and the celestial bodies.[51] Later, however, the people manufactured idols in order to honor particular celestial divinities. The anonymous author also introduces an angelology of both good and bad angels, a phenomenon absent in most other

---

[46]Felipe Huamán Poma de Ayala, *Primer Nueva Corónica* [sic] *y Buen Gobierno*, ed. A. Ponansky (La Paz, 1944), 912. A short biography of Poma de Ayala is in Raúl Porras Barrenechea, *El Cronista Indio Felipe Huamán Poma de Ayala* (Lima, 1948).

[47]Poma de Ayala, Folio 93.

[48] *Ibid.,* Folio 31.   [49] *Ibid.,* 933.

[50] Porras coined the phrase, "The Posthumous Christianization of the Inca empire," to express his general skepticism toward the anonymous Jesuit and other religious writers. *Cronistas del Perú,* 45–46; see also the discussion by Francisco Esteve Barba on the lineage of the Anonymous Jesuit, XLIV–LI.

[51] *Relación de las Costumbres Antiguas de los naturales del Perú,* in Esteve Barba, 153.

chronicles. Furthermore, the author stands nearly alone in holding that the Incas had no human sacrifices.[52]

The writer introduces another interesting distinction between "natural" and "artificial" temples. The former are all the things of nature, such as the heavens, the seas, mountains and rocks. The Incas, claimed the author, did not worship these "natural temples" as though they were divine things in themselves. Rather, they merely held them in greater reverence as dwelling places of the one God. It was only later, the author explains, that the Devil perverted this reverence for created things by turning it into idolatry. Similarly, the author denies that the Incas adored the mummies of their ancestors; they only rendered them simple filial homage.[53]

With respect to the hierarchical structure of the Inca religion, the anonymous chronicler asserts that at the apex was the great Vilahoma, "a type of supreme Pontiff," who was held in high esteem by all, even by the Inca himself. One of the principal duties of this chief priest was to choose qualified confessors for the people. Next in line in the hierarchy was a select group of general visitors and overseers who, the author explains, were "like bishops." Finally, at the base of the hierarchy were the ordinary priests. All of these Inca religious officials were bound by a vow of chastity. Moreover, within this religious structure there were two types of religious orders: the ordinary religious who served Illa Tecce, and the special virgins of the Sun. Both groups made vows of poverty, chastity, and obedience, and both underwent a novitiate training and lived a monastic-type life. However, as the Anonymous Jesuit points out, even those special elite groups had their peccadillos, which consisted of occasional lapses into idolatry.[54]

The author also mentions two rites which had much external semblance of Christian sacraments: confession and "communion." In Inca confession, some of the sins which the people were obliged to confess were the adoration of "foreign" gods, cursing one of the acceptable gods, failing to participate in the feasts, killing a fellow human being, or committing sodomy. The better instructed among them also confessed their bad interior thoughts as well. A penance appropriate to the offense was assigned to each one.[55] At the yearly feast of the Harvest the great pageants and spectacles ended with the distributing of a morsel of bread, "like a host," which all reverently received. However, the author cautions, this was an "act of religion and idolatry."[56]

In discussing the customs of the ordinary people, the author singles out drinking as the great vice which was the root of "all evils and even of idolatry." The ensuing detailed description of the process of making the native brew, *chicha,* is one of the telling signs mentioned by Porras to establish the author's Indian background.[57] The final analysis which the author makes of the Incas in their religion and government is that though

---

[52] *Ibid.,* 154–57. The main opponent against whom the author directs his remarks is Juan de Polo de Ondegardo, the Corregidor of Cuzco, whose studies of the "superstitious" and idolatrous practices of the Indians served as confessional manuals for priests. The works of Ondegardo are in the collection of Urteaga-Romero, Vol. IV.

[53] *Ibid.,* 157–61.   [54] *Ibid.,* 161–66; 168–74.

[55] *Ibid.,* 64–65.   [56] *Ibid.,* 173.   [57] *Ibid.,* 174.

The Inca, as a Gentile, erred in many things and carried the people along with him, he was also a man of reason who hit the mark correctly in many other things, especially in government affairs, because in this he knew how to govern the Peruvians according to their nature.[58]

This rather balanced judgment seems far distant from the anti-Inca diatribes in the chronicles of Polo de Ondegardo or Pedro Sarmiento de Gamboa, both of whom wrote under the Viceroy Toledo to justify the reductions and other "reforms" of that period. Nor does the Anonymous Jesuit completely merit Porras' charge of over-anticipating Christianity in the Inca religion. The author is quite clear in stating that the Inca religion was invented by the Devil and that the Incas were the most superstitious people in the world.[59] He contrasts their blindness in religious affairs with their great wisdom in civil and political administration. What causes skepticism in the author's views of the Incas is rather his attempt to balance apparently irreconcilable extremes in his description of their character. On the one hand, he notes that the Indians are "meek, bland, loving, compassionate and docile"; on the other hand, he also finds them to be "cruel, arrogant, merciless and recalcitrant."[60]

Furthermore, the author's attempt to describe Inca realities by the occasional indiscriminate use of certain Christian terms may have confused rather than clarified some issues. However, he consistently qualifies his description of the Inca realities as "like a Pontiff," "like a Bishop," or "like a host," and so forth. He expressly states that the communion received at the feast of the Harvest was an idolatrous act. His description of Inca confession is essentially that of most other chronicles, with the exception of his emphasis on the admission of interior sins.[61] His weakest point, in which he is supported by few others, is his denial of human sacrifices among the Incas. Other points are, at best, controversial. His distinction between the one supreme God and the lesser divinities of nature was probably not one so clearly made in the animistic religious world view of the ordinary highland dweller in Inca times. Nevertheless, he seems to be essentially accurate in portraying a hierarchical religion in which some gods have more importance than others, and certain places and things were more sacred than others. In short, the Incas were discriminating in their idolatry: they subordinated many particular objects to other objects which seemed of more universal significance as sources of life and energy, such as the sun or the Mother-Earth.[62]

The great value of the Anonymous Jesuit is his attempt to describe the Inca religion systematically in Christian terms and concepts, an essential of any positive missiology. In fact, the author deplored the Spaniard's ignorance of the Indian's religion, which he felt to be one of the prime reasons for the failure to effect a profound evangelization of the Indians. On the subject of idols, the author was no enlightened prophet before his time. He, too, wanted to see the

---

[58] *Ibid.*, 176.   [59] *Ibid.*, 177.   [60] *Ibid.*, 180.

[61] See, e.g., the accounts of prehispanic confession by Cristóbal de Molina, *Relación de las Fábulas de los Incas*, in Urteaga-Romero, I, 23–24; and that of Fernando de Avendaño, in José Toribio Medina, *La Imprenta en Lima* (Santiago de Chile, 1904), I, 381.

[62] See John Alden Mason's chapter on religion in *The Ancient Civilizations of Peru* (Baltimore, 1957), 202–23.

idols destroyed as a precondition for evangelization. Yet, he also claimed that whenever the Indians experienced a true conversion, they destroyed their own idols, because they had come to understand why it was necessary for them to do so. On the other hand, the author observes, it was typical of the superficial tactics of evangelization, before the arrival of the Jesuits, for the Christian preacher to destroy the idols in a town but leave the people unchanged.[63] Although his chronicle was probably composed primarily to encourage other missionaries to adopt Jesuit methods of evangelizing, the Anonymous Jesuit's account also served, given the limitations of possibilities and knowledge of his time, as an excellent model of a sympathetic and positive introduction to the Inca religion for Christians.

The most renowned of the mestizo chroniclers is, of course, the Inca, Garcilaso de la Vega. Although Garcilaso gathered together many pro-Inca apologetical lines of thought already proposed by other chroniclers, it was his masterful storytelling ability and superior command of Spanish in recreating the glories of the Inca empire and civilization which made the greatest impact on the Spaniards of his day and subsequent generations of Europeans. The fact that Garcilaso relied heavily upon the mestizo Jesuit, Blas Valera, is of little importance here: insofar as Garcilaso cited and used Valera for his own literary ends, he was still presenting a "mestizo" point of view on the Inca religion and civilization.

The key notion in Garcilaso's view of the religion of his forefathers is that the Incas prepared the way for the Christian Gospel by serving providentially as a "Natural Light" (*Lex Natura*) by which all the Andean peoples came to see, albeit obscurely, the face of the true God. For the non-Inca peoples Garcilaso, of Inca nobility, had nothing but contempt. From his Inca and Christianized point of view, they were nothing but crass idolaters of the lowest sort, worshipping anything and everything, animal, plant, or mineral. God sent the Incas to rule over these peoples, declared Garcilaso somewhat haughtily, so that when He "should deign to send the light of his divine rays over those idolaters, he would find them less savage and more amenable to receive the Catholic faith. . . ." By reason of this high mission, Garcilaso believed that the Incas were the "Natural Kings" of Peru. In Garcilaso's narrative, the founding fathers, Manco Capac and Mama Ocllu fulfill roles as prototypes of all ensuing Inca history. These divine children of the Sun left the region of Lake Titicaca and began announcing the good news of how their Father the Sun had chosen them to civilize and enlighten all the other inhabitants of the Cuzco area. The Indians, according to this official fable, responded to this hopeful message by placing themselves under the tutelage of the illustrious pair. Manco Capac introduced the neophytes to the ways of civilization as well as the ways of higher morality by outlawing homicide, adultery, robbery, polygamy, and sodomy.[64]

Furthermore, the first Incas set a high religious standard by inveighing against the idols of their new followers and by directing their gaze upward to the visible god, the Sun, and even beyond to Pachacamac, the invisible lord

---

[63] *Relación de las Costumbres Antiguas,* 184.

[64] Garcilaso de la Vega, *Los Comentarios Reales de los Incas,* ed. P. Carmelo Saenz de Santa María (Madrid, 1960), CXXXIII, 19–28ff.

creator. Naturally, the first Incas ruled out all human sacrifices and cannibalism. Thus, the pattern for the Inca's great historic mission was established in the Cuzco valley. As related by Garcilaso, the Inca's conquest of Peru seemed hardly a conquest at all, but rather a peaceful expansion carried out over a long period of time, perhaps best described as an ingathering of the eager but unenlightened masses. Although Garcilaso does mention a few battles (glorious victories for the Incas), as well as a few glossed over setbacks, it would be closer to his view of Inca expansion not to conceive of it as a military operation, but as a mission in civilizing and moral uplifting. Everywhere that the Incas spread they implemented Manco Capac's original designs and set the conquered peoples on the high road of the Natural Law.

Given this Garcilasen perspective, the meeting between Pizarro and Atahualpa at Cajamarca acquires even more dramatic significance. Garcilaso casts both Pizarro and Atahualpa into roles as symbolic representatives of their respective cultures. His portrayal of the encounter between the Inca and Valverde, the Dominican chaplain, is by far the longest and most imaginative of all the chronicles. What is a mere perfunctory reading of the *requerimiento* in the other accounts becomes a lengthy theological exchange between Valverde, the Christian apologist, and Atahualpa, the pagan philosopher-king. Atahualpa is so moved by the Dominican's explanations that he expresses a desire to come to know Jesus Christ.[65] Within the context of Garcilaso's moralized drama, the Inca's interest in hearing the Christian Gospel was undoubtedly the symbolic culmination of all of Inca history.

Garcilaso's treatment of idolatry is similar to that of the Anonymous Jesuit. He limits the idolatry of the Incas to sun worship, explaining that the moon and stars were but members of the family and heavenly court of the sun. Furthermore, Garcilaso claimed that the huacas were considered as sacred things only because they had been offered to the sun. By way of contrast, Garcilaso makes much of the Inca's quest for the one, true God. If they did not build temples to this invisible creator and animator of the universe, Garcilaso explains, at least the Incas "adored him in their hearts."[66] For Garcilaso, Pachacamac was truly the *Deus Ignotus* of the noble pagans.

In other areas, however, Garcilaso is more restrained in his judgment of the Inca's religion. Influenced by the demonology of the day, Garcilaso, too, believed that the Devil spoke through the huacas and perverted the original good instincts of the people. Furthermore, Garcilaso cites Blas Valera to refute the thesis of pre-evangelization either in Mexico or in Peru, and he discounts prehispanic confession as a prototype of the Christian sacrament. Although he claims that the Incas did believe in the immortality of the soul and in a type of general resurrection, the afterlife of the Incas was strictly a non-spiritual continuation of the present life.[67] Yet, for Garcilaso, these were but minor flaws compared to the Inca's successful carrying out of their divine mission of preparing the way in the natural order for God's fuller supernatural revelation in the Gospel brought by the Spanish.

This overview of a few of the mestizo and Indian chroniclers clearly shows

[65] *Ibid.,* CXXXIV, 51.
[66] *Ibid.,* CXXXIII, 41–43ff.   [67] *Ibid.,* 50–52.

that the elements of a positive mission theory did exist in early colonial Peru. It was not the more learned Spanish missionaries, but rather the native sons of Peru who first established a Christian dialogue with the Inca culture and history. The reasons why some of the Spanish could not conceive of these approaches were rooted, in part, in the ardent crusading nationalism of medieval Spain which had been relatively unaffected by renaissance humanism. In part, also, a belief in the all-pervasive power of the Devil, from which not even Luther or Calvin were liberated, colored the Spaniard's view of Inca religion. However, the Spanish missionaries in Peru cannot be exculpated completely with the excuse that they were only acting as men of their time in failing to conceive of ways by which to incorporate the best of the Inca past into a Christian synthesis. For example, in their reading of the early Fathers of the Church, with whom they were all familiar, they selectively ignored some of the more ecumenical passages, again, perhaps because of their conditioning.

In this regard it is interesting to compare the views of some of the missionaries in Mexico, especially the Franciscan Gerónimo de Mendieta and the Dominican Diego Durán, who in "discovering" Aztec parallels to Christian rites and beliefs,[68] were far advanced over their contemporaries in Peru. Even more innovative than these were the experiments with "going native" of the Italian Jesuits, Matteo Ricci in China (after 1583) and Robert de Nobili in India (after 1603), both contemporaries of Acosta and Garcilaso. The ecumenical perspective of the early Church was certainly alive in this creative minority. In light of this, the achievement of the Christian Indian and mestizo chroniclers of colonial Peru is even more remarkable. For these writers, acting on artistic intuitions largely their own, and in contradiction on many points to the opinions of most of the learned Spanish missionaries in Peru, fashioned an intellectual bridge linking the best of their Inca past with the more universal thrust of the early Church, as well as the more humanistic Christianity of renaissance Europe.

Carroll House, Washington, D.C.

[68] Cf. Robert Ricard's discussion of the theories of providential pre-evangelization in Mexico in *La Conquista Espiritual de México,* trans. Angel María Garibay (Mexico City, 1947), 475–88.

III

THE *PHILOSOPHES* AND BLACK SLAVERY: 1748-1765

By Claudine Hunting

Recent studies tend to minimize and even discredit the struggle of the French *philosophes* against black slavery in the eighteenth century. In an otherwise interesting article, Delesalle and Valensi, for example, draw erroneous conclusions about the attitude of the Encyclopedists toward Blacks because the authors consider only one article in Diderot's and D'Alembert's *Encyclopédie,* entitled "Nègres," which states some of the conservative views then held on Negroes.[1] However, the *Encyclopédie,* a communal endeavor, expresses a great diversity of opinions from its many different collaborators on any given subject. As will be seen, sentiments regarding black servitude are no exception, a fact seemingly ignored by the two critics.

In another article, published by *Les Temps Modernes,* Leila Sebbar-Pignon deliberately takes the anachronistic standpoint of a twentieth-century Marxist in judging eighteenth-century French writers, who according to her were "unknowingly the proponents of slavery and slave trade, which they thought they were condemning."[2] She blames "the enlightened 'philosopher' " for being "trapped by his bourgeois morality"; like his contemporaries, he belongs to a social system based on a colonial ideology which she sees as a dominant feature of eighteenth-century French culture (p. 2351).

Sebbar-Pignon may have been influenced by the analysis of Michèle Duchet's *Anthropologie et histoire au siècle des lumières* (Paris, 1971). Duchet admits in the introduction to her book that one of its main objectives is:

to denounce the myth of the *philosophes'* anticolonialism and to reduce their campaign in favor of Negroes and Indians to more modest proportions. When comparing, under close scrutiny, their attitude with the position of those responsible for colonial policies, one cannot but conclude that essentially the *philosophes* were in agreement with them to prevent excessive abuse and, thereby, helped maintain the status quo. The liberation of slaves, the protec-

---

[1] Simone Delesalle and Lucette Valensi, "Le mot 'Nègre' dans les dictionnaires français de l'Ancien Régime; histoire et lexicographie," *Langue Française* (Sept. 1972), 85-104.—*Encyclopédie, ou dictionnaire raisonné des sciences, des arts et des métiers par une Société de Gens de Lettres* (Paris/Neufchastel, 1751-65). The volumes of the *Encyclopédie* mostly mentioned in this study concerning Blacks and slavery are: V (1755); IX, XI, and XVI (1765).

[2] "Le mythe du bon nègre ou l'idéologie coloniale dans la production romanesque du XVIIIe siècle," I, *Les Temps Modernes* (juillet 1974), 2350. The translation of the quotation is mine, as are all other translations from the French in this paper.

tion of Indians, and civilization of "savages" are, despite appearances, mere elements of the same basic structure: that of a colonial ideology, which was to have in the nineteenth century the full development we all know (18).

The present study disregards these habits of thought, value judgments, and prejudices of our society today in appraising the *philosophes'* fight against black slavery and in analyzing the methods they used in their combat. This is done by returning to a more authentic historical context, that of the "ancien régime" in eighteenth-century French society with its own political background, power structures, and collective consciousness. It is imperative to consider the *philosophes'* combat from their standpoint and not from ours, if we are to evaluate their intentions and conduct more equitably and accurately.

We must first point out a major political fact which prevented the *philosophes* from being outspoken initially on the subject of slavery, a fact completely neglected by the critics mentioned above: slavery—a distant reality accepted then by general opinion with indifference as a normal institution—was a long-standing official policy of the French government and of its absolute monarch, who derived substantial benefits from slave trade and slavery in the colonies. The sinister *lettres de cachet,* the shadows of the Bastille or Vincennes prisons and vigilant censorship threatened any opponent of governmental authority. The *Encyclopédistes* and *philosophes* were perforce wary and tried to avoid the pitfalls which had already trapped some of them, e.g., Voltaire and Diderot who had both spent time in prison because of their "subversive" ideas and publications. It is not surprising in that historical context to see Jean-Jacques Rousseau driven to madness by what he felt to be a universal plot against him and his writings.

The *philosophes,* however, were not fundamentally intimidated. Cautiously, but courageously, they managed to criticize official policy effectively without incurring drastic governmental retaliation. This paper will explore the methods the *philosophes* used in the initial stage of their combat, between 1748 and 1765, the period of their first concerted efforts against slavery.[3] In those two crucial decades a gradually bolder

---

[3] Earlier protests in France against black slavery were sparse and uncoordinated. Among the predecessors of Montesquieu and the Encyclopedists, who expressed noteworthy anti-slavery opinions, we can cite French economist and political writer Jean Bodin in the sixteenth century, and Du Tertre, a seventeenth-century Dominican missionary in the French West Indies. Germain Fromageau, a theologian and casuist of the same period, after ministering to prisoners condemned to death focused on "cas de conscience" (or moral and religious dilemmas) among Christian slave-owners in the colonies and had his humanitarian decisions published in the eighteenth century. For further data, cf. R. P. Jameson's *Montesquieu et l'esclavage* (Paris, 1911) and E. D. Seeber's *Anti-Slavery Opinion in France during the Second Half of the Eighteenth Century* (New York, 1969; 1st ed. London, 1937). The considerable English and American influence on the

approach to the problem can be observed as the *philosophes'* writings, propagating a new ideal, by degrees changed general opinion on black servitude.

The dates 1748 and 1765 correspond to the publication of two very influential works, from our viewpoint, in ethics, politics, and economics. Montesquieu's *L'Esprit des lois* appeared in 1748, and the volumes of the *Encyclopédie* most important for our study came out between 1751 and 1765.[4] The first works of major *philosophes,* mentioning slavery incidentally, such as those of Voltaire and Rousseau, were also published during that period. Unlike earlier years, when only a few solitary, barely audible voices protested in France against black slavery, the middle of the eighteenth century saw a gradual awakening of the French collective consciousness under the prodding of the *philosophes.*

We may wonder what incited *philosophes* and Encyclopedists to take risks in defending black slaves whose plight was known to them only through travel books and *relations* about distant lands, the French colonies, where they had never set foot, while daily abuses of power at home solicited their full attention and fighting spirit—such an abuse, for example, as the pervasive religious intolerance against which Voltaire fought relentlessly all his life.[5] But the question of the Blacks was of significant importance to the *philosophes* because it concerned issues fundamental to their major preoccupations. It was part of their basic fight to obtain more justice and freedom for *all* men, and to defend their dignity wherever they lived, as Jaucourt pointedly says: "Everything concurs to let man enjoy dignity, which is natural to him. Everything tells us that we cannot take away from him that natural dignity which is liberty" (*Encyclopédie*, V, 937).[6] It was in the name of these principles that enlightened writers were assailing contemporary political and re-

---

philosophes, regarding black slavery, is not referred to here, as it has already been studied amply by Seeber.

    [4] *L'Esprit des lois* was the first book on international law, by a major *philosophe,* that dealt vigorously with the black question. Its renown and influence made it an ideal vehicle for the propagation of philosophical ideas to a vast public. The *Encyclopédie,* particularly the articles by Jaucourt concerning black slavery in 1755 and 1765, borrowed heavily from *L'Esprit des lois,* often transcribing verbatim whole paragraphs from Montesquieu, as Jaucourt himself acknowledges in his article "Esclavage."

    [5] Voltaire personally helped and defended, in both his writings and his actions, Protestants persecuted in France such as Sirven and Calas. He rehabilitated the latter's memory in his *Traité sur la tolérance, à l'occasion de la mort de Jean Calas,* 1763.

    [6] This obsession with liberty, among the *philosophes,* is pointed out by Peter Gay in his *The Enlightenment: An Interpretation* (New York, 1966), I, 3: "The men of the Enlightenment united on a vastly ambitious program of secularism, humanity, cosmopolitanism, and freedom, above all, freedom in its many forms."

ligious institutions, as well as the ethics those institutions generated. In the case of slavery, moral values unquestionably hinged on double-talk and pious hypocrisy, boldly exposed by the *philosophes*. For the old inequitable system, they wished to substitute a new humanism based on trust in man, in his discoveries, and in his achievements. Each man, with a novel awareness of himself, of his fellow men, and of his environment, would find his rightful place in the universe. Stripped of the age-old veneers that social differentiations had established between him and his fellow men, and which had masked his real self, each individual would appear as he was fundamentally: a "natural" man, brother to all men, whatever their creed, culture, or race.

Thus, black slavery was totally incompatible with the *philosophes'* basic tenets, and the question of human servitude gradually became fundamental in their fight against the abuses of their time, as appears in both their discursive and imaginative writings. The latter reveal the *philosophes'* system of thought in their combat, the dialectics, techniques, and devices they used to reach their goal. Fighting slave trade and slavery, predominant in the French West Indies and colonies on the American continent, the *philosophes'* primary objective was to enlighten the public and convince governmental authorities of the inequity of such practices. To that end, they made use in their writings of every argument at their disposal, whether religious, rationalistic, or satirical.

The servitude of man had theoretically been abolished in France by the end of medieval times and with the advent of Renaissance humanism. However, the *Encyclopédie*—on which this study relies extensively, as it represents an important body of eighteenth-century French thought —states that there still were in France, in the middle of the eighteenth century, cases of peasant bondage: "There still exist in a few of our regions mainmorte serfs who could pass for slaves" (V, 940; "Esclave"). But those are relatively isolated cases, peculiar to certain French provinces which had retained from the past a special legal understanding of land ownership. Personal slavery as such had ceased to exist in France long before it was legally restored in the French colonies in the seventeeth century, a fact mentioned in the *Encyclopédie:* "There are no longer any slaves as such in the countries under the jurisdiction of France except in the French isles of America" (*ibid., 941*).

The main argument for the reinstatement of slavery in French territories would itself become, for the Encyclopedists, a powerful argument against it, a reason for advocating its abolition, because of its inhumanity and, essentially, its absurdity. King Louis XIII of France had agreed, however reluctantly, to authorize slave trade in the French colonies, on the express urging of the Catholic Church and its missionaries, for the alleged purpose of saving their souls, more than a century after Portugal and Spain had adopted that policy in their own colonies.

The *Encylopédie* summarily stated the fact with underlying sarcasm: "Masters who acquire new slaves are obligated by law to have them instructed in the Catholic faith. This was the motive that determined Louis XIIII to authorize the commerce of human flesh" (XI, 81; "Nègres").

It was a most absurd decision, since in order to save his soul a Black was in fact "losing" it. By becoming a slave he was deprived of his essential human prerogative, *liberty*—the loss of which, according to Rousseau, was equivalent to "renouncing the quality of being human."[7] He was sold like an animal, which in Catholic doctrine has no soul. The deprivation of human nature in black slaves was pointed out by Voltaire in his *Essai sur les moeurs et l'esprit des nations:*

. . . to those slaves were added Negroes bought in Africa and transported to Peru like animals destined to serve man.

Neither the Negroes nor the inhabitants of the New World were, in fact, ever treated like creatures of the human species (Paris, 1963; II 360).[8]

And Voltaire added: "We tell them that they are men like us, that a God died to redeem them, and then we make them work like beasts of burden" (*ibid.,* 380). An *Encyclopédie* contributor observed bluntly:

They are trying to justify the odious character of slave trade and its violation of natural rights by arguing that with the loss of liberty slaves ordinarily find religious salvation; that the Catholic instruction they are given . . . tempers what may appear to be inhuman in a commerce whereby men buy and sell other men as they would do cattle, for tilling the land (XI, 79).[9]

The justification of black slavery for professedly religious purposes was legally recognized by an edict under Louis XIV, in March 1685, called *Code noir.* One of its first regulations concerned the enforcement of religious instruction: "The second article of the Black Code orders masters to have their slaves instructed in the Catholic religion, etc., with heavy penalties should they not comply" (*ibid.,* XI, 82).

[7] *Contrat social,* 1762; "De l'esclavage," I, iv, 239 (Paris, 1962). My emphasis in all cases unless indicated otherwise.

[8] From its first chapters published without the author's consent in 1753, Voltaire's *L'Essai sur les moeurs* grew steadily through its many successive editions until his death in 1778. Notable editions are that of 1761, which contains new chapters on the European possessions in America, and the Kehl ed. of 1785 with Voltaire's last additions and corrections.

[9] The bulk of this particular entry bears a close resemblance to the article "Negres" from Savary Desbruslons's *Dictionnaire universel de commerce* (Paris, 1723), precisely quoted as a source at the end of this passage in the Encyclopedia. But the first sentence in the *Encyclopédie* article shows an interesting modification of the original, already indicative of a notable change in attitude toward black slavery from 1723 to 1765. This is how Savary begins the paragraph in his own dictionary: "It is difficult to justify completely the commerce of Negroes; but it is true that . . . those miserable slaves ordinarily find their Salvation in the loss of their freedom."

The *Encyclopédie,* which had gradually become the official mouth-piece of the *philosophes* and a powerful medium for the propagation of their doctrine, repeatedly made veiled attacks on the intolerance and misguided policies of the Church. Encyclopedists often castigated it for neglecting basic Christian maxims in favor of an over-zealous propaganda of the Catholic faith and, most importantly, for its ultimate mundane concerns:

It is a direct violation of human rights and against nature to believe that the Christian religion gives those who profess it the right to reduce to servitude those who do not, in order to propagate their faith with greater ease. This was, however, the manner of thinking which encouraged in their crimes the men who destroyed America. It is not the first time that religion has been used in a fashion contrary to its basic principles, which teach us that man qualifies as *our brother* wherever he lives in the vast expanse of the universe (V, 938; "Esclavage").

The Chevalier de Jaucourt, directly quoting Montesquieu's *L'Esprit des lois* here, as he would often do on the question of slavery, also revealed the actual political and economic considerations which, under the guise of religious fervor, prompted the Christian countries of Europe to condone and even encourage black slavery: "After conquering countries where they deemed it *advantageous* to have slaves, Christian nations have authorized their buying and selling, and forgotten the basic principles of Nature and Christianity, which made *all men equal"* (V, 936).

Voltaire denounced slavery, noting that the Quakers were the only Christians opposed to it: "Those who call themselves 'whites' are buying Negroes cheaply to sell them at high prices in America. Only Pennsylvanians have solemnly renounced recently a trade which they deem dishonest" (*Dictionnaire philosophique* [Paris, 1878], XVIII, 602).

Another article, emphasizing the commercial value of Blacks, would direct the reader's attention to the real motive of slavery in the colonies: "the indispensable necessity and need for black slaves to cultivate sugar cane, tobacco, and indigo plants etc." (*Enc.,* XI, 79). So would Diderot, wryly remarking: "How in the world did Christian powers not consider that their religion, independently from natural law, was fundamentally opposed to black slavery? The reason is that they need them for their colonies, their plantations, and mines. *Auri sacra fames!"* (IX, 471-72; Liberté naturelle). Human greed, particularly the search for gold, was also Voltaire's lucid evaluation of the reason for slavery in the Spanish colonies; Voltaire was thus obliquely referring to the same practice in the New World territories belonging to France: "It is the object of all those voyages; patriarchs, missions, conversions were but pretexts. Europeans only propagated their religion from Chile to Japan to have men, like beasts of burden, serve their insatiable greed" (*Essai sur les moeurs,* II, 328).

Jaucourt's "all men are equal" suggests clearly that, from the *philosophe*'s standpoint, black slavery could not be confined to the domain of religious or economic necessity, but had to be viewed as a philosophical and moral issue. Jaucourt did not hesitate to say in another article, on "Slave trade": "If a commerce of this kind can be justified by a moral principle, then there is no crime, however atrocious, that cannot become legitimate" (XVI, 532). This is certainly one of the strongest moral condemnations ever directed against slavery. Encyclopedists insist that "nothing in the world can make of slavery a legitimate enterprise" (V, 938), and that "buying Negroes, to reduce them to slavery, is a trade that violates religion, morality, the natural law, and all the rights of human nature" (XVI, 532). The *philosophes* thus asserted unequivocally that no accepted principle of human conduct would ever sanction the practice of slavery.

Since Christian nations pursued with flagrant sophistry a fundamentally unchristian policy, the *philosophes,* profoundly distrusting established religions, would not invoke a divine principle to support human morality. With the progress of science, a new kind of "deity" or absolute principle, rediscovered by French thinkers after the Ancients and Renaissance humanists, became the foundation of eighteenth-century philosophical and ethical thought: NATURE.[10]

By his very nature, man is born free. *Liberty,* as defined by the *Encyclopédie,* is an inalienable right granted him by nature: "a right that nature gives all men to have control over their own person and possessions, in the manner that they consider the most appropriate to their happiness, with the restriction that they do so within the limits of natural law, and not misuse it to the prejudice of other men" (IX, 471).

Alluding to the condition of men who had lost that precious gift through slavery, Diderot emphatically added: "The first state granted man by nature, and considered the most valuable of all his possessions, is that of liberty; it can neither be exchanged for another, nor sold or lost, for every man is born naturally free; this means he cannot be submitted to the tyranny of a master, and nobody has the right to own him" (*ibid.*).

[10] The author of the *Encyclopédie* article on "Nature" points out the ambiguity of the word 'nature,' discussing its different meanings through time (XI, 40-44, 1765), as A. O. Lovejoy and G. Boas do in *Primitivism and Related Ideas in Antiquity,* where they give sixty-six different definitions of the word (Baltimore, 1935), 447-56. In our particular context, however, the term "nature" is very clear and precise; and the eighteenth-century *philosophes* were using it widely with this meaning, i.e., the "principle which acts on the whole universe . . . the cause of all the changes affecting matter," whether this cause be God or a substitute for God (XI, 40-41). Thus Nature, in this sense, is for the eighteenth-century *philosophe* the force that moves the Universe within a system, an order characterized by universal, external, and immutable laws. Also see Boas' and Lovejoy's definitions 13, 14, and particularly 15 (*Primitivism . . .* 448).

A corollary of the previous proposition, *equality* is a state natural to all men. If all enjoy liberty, all are fundamentally equal. No one, therefore, can be the slave of his fellowman:

Natural or *moral equality* is based on the constitution of human nature that is common to *all men* who are born, grow, live, and die alike.

Since human nature is the same in every man, it is clear that, according to natural law, every one must regard others as creatures who are naturally equal to him, that is to say, who are men like him (V, 415).

The postulate can be inverted, so interdependent are the two concepts. If we are all equal because of our intrinsic liberty, we are free too because of our basic equality, as Jaucourt noted in the *Encyclopédie:* "Natural equality is that which exists between all men by the very nature of their constitution. Such equality is the principle and foundation of liberty" (*ibid.*).

Liberty, equality, *fraternity*—an analysis of this ternary axiom, which was to become the motto of the French Revolution in 1789, is essential to understanding eighteenth-century French political and moral thought. The *philosophes* were not only motivated by arguments of reason; they also had to be moved. Emotions played an important part in the elaboration and propagation of their "philosophy." To convince, and be convinced themselves, they had to use reasons of the heart; their special eristics stood firm on the harmonious functioning of apparently antagonistic concepts: *le coeur et l'esprit,* heart and mind.

To the arguments of reason against human bondage—liberty and equality, considered as essential human prerogatives—a third important, emotional one was thus added: fraternity. Black slavery was morally wrong not just because every man is free and equal by nature to all others, but because a deep sense of solidarity and love links him to his *alter ego.* As we saw earlier, in the *Encyclopédie,* "man qualifies as *our brother* wherever he lives in the vast expanse of the universe" (V, 938). Acquiescing in the slavery of one's brother was immoral, heart-rending and against all the basic principles of humanitarianism. It demeaned one's own humanity, as noted by the same Encyclopedist: "slavery is not only a humiliating state for the person subjected to it, but for all mankind who is thus degraded" (*ibid.*).

Saint-Preux, in Jean-Jacques Rousseau's novel *La Nouvelle Héloise* (1761), admirably expresses that pity and horror, that sense of human debasement and shame, felt by all humanitarians of the period confronted with black slavery:

I have seen those vast unfortunate lands that seem only destined to be covered with herds of slaves. I have averted my eyes from that sordid sight with loathing, horror and pity; and seeing one fourth of my fellow men changed into beasts for the service of others, I have grieved to be a man (Part IV, Letter 3).

Though Voltaire himself has been, by a few modern critics, occasionally accused of racism, the great *philosophe* could stir his contemporaries' compassion and revulsion by describing the plight of escaped slaves and their maimed bodies with merciless precision in Chapter 19 of *Candide* (1759):[11]

As they drew near to the city they met a Negro lying on the ground, half naked, with only short underpants of blue cloth on; the poor man's left leg and right hand were missing. "Dear God!" said Candide in Dutch, "What are you doing here, friend, in this horrible condition?" "I am waiting for my master, Mr. Vanderdenhard, a famous merchant," the Negro answered.[12] "Did Mr. Vanderdenhard treat you in this fashion?" "Yes, sir," said the Negro. "It is the custom here. Our only clothing is blue cloth undershorts, given us twice a year. When we work in the sugar mill, and get one finger caught under the stone, they cut off our hand; when we attempt to run away, they cut off one leg. I found myself in both predicaments. *It is at that price you eat sugar in Europe.* Yet when my mother sold me for ten Patagonian crowns on the coast of Guinea, she told me: "My dear child, render thanks to our idols, always adore them, they will make your life happy; you have the great honor of becoming a slave to our lords, the Whites, and by so doing you are making your father and mother rich." Alas! I don't know whether I really made them rich, but they certainly did not make me so. Dogs, monkeys, and parrots are infinitely less unfortunate than we are; the

---

[11] Primarily a historian rather than a "philosopher" in the strictest sense of the word, Voltaire viewed man in a historical perspective. He had observed that the different civilizations achieved by social man around the globe did not correspond equally in time. For example, Voltaire considered the European civilization of his age as more advanced than that of the inhabitants of central Africa. In this respect, Voltaire thought that black "savages" were inferior to "civilized" man in Europe, and were nearer to the level of animals, just as Occidental man himself had been centuries before while the Chinese had long been enjoying a high level of refinement and culture. It was all a question of time. The forces of "progress" would eventually extend to "savages" too. This was basically Voltaire's view of man and of his evolution, though such a summary appraisal of the *philosophe's* thought on the subject should be tempered by his skepticism and even pessimism as to the ability of the common man to ever reach such a high level of culture. Voltaire's sarcastic comments on the French peasants of his time as compared to American Indians are a good example of this: "They were content to call Northern Americans *Savages,* though the latter were less 'savage' in most respects than the peasants living near our European coasts" (*Essai sur les moeurs,* II, 371). To consider Voltaire a "racist" in this perspective would be to misunderstand him seriously, as Michèle Duchet seems to do, for example, in her book mentioned earlier; see particularly 281-321.

[12] In the French text, the Dutch merchant is called "Vanderdendur." I have transposed his name in English to "Vanderdenhard" so as to express the cruelty of the slave driver implied by the French syllable "dur."

Dutch sorcerers who converted me declare every Sunday that we are all Adam's children, Blacks and Whites. I am not a genealogist, but if these preachers tell the truth, we are all second cousins. Now you won't deny that one cannot use one's relatives in a worse manner.

After hearing the slave's horrible story, sensitive Candide, calling that barbarity an "abomination," began to "shed tears looking at his Negro, and entered Surinam crying."

No religious, moral, or economic consideration therefore could justify black slavery in the eyes of the *philosophes*. In fact, Encyclopedists were advocating the destruction of an economic system that allowed such inequity. For what was slavery but a method by which a few profited and enriched themselves by the unremunerated forced labor of multitudes? Quoting the *Dictionnaire universel de commerce*—a commercial dictionary of the time by Savary Desbruslons Encylopedists noted: "Blacks constitute the main riches of residents in the isles. Whoever owns a dozen of them is considered rich. They multiply greatly in tropical countries; when treated with any degree of kindness by their masters, the initial family will gradually grow, slavery being hereditary" (XI, 80; "Nègres").

Jaucourt gives a more incisive and striking utilitarian definition of slaves: "those animate, organic units of economy" (V, 935; "Esclavage").[13] As a matter of fact, that was all black slaves were. From the French colonist's point of view, it was the basic reason for their existence. The three overlapping groups of *philosophes,* Encyclopedists, and economists of eighteenth-century France courageously revealed, in detail, to an often unsuspecting and gradually shocked public the shameful and barbarian treatment of other human beings, the religious fallacies permitting it, and the fundamental economic motives that actually instigated it.

Economy and morality appeared to be inescapably interrelated. Changing one meant drastically modifying the other. An economic system based on the immoral exploitation of man had to disappear, giving way to one more equitable. Many *philosophes* were aware of this. Voltaire, for instance, voiced a general conviction when he said: "One cannot too earnestly do battle against the notion, humiliating to mankind, that there are countries where millions of people ceaselessly labor for one man who devours everything" (*Essai sur les moeurs*, II, 322).

The principle under consideration had, in fact, greatly preoccupied eighteenth-century French *philosophes* and economists on a much wider scale than that of mere governmental policies regarding colonial slavery.

---

[13] Referring to Roman slaves, Jaucourt gives a definition that applies perfectly to black slaves in the French colonies at the time. Here is the exact quotation in French from the *Encyclopédie:* "ces organes vivans et animés de l'économique" [sic].

It belonged to the more general question of labor, its inadequacies and inequities in France. And, very near to the concerns of modern man, it dealt with the basic problem of an economy geared towards the superfluous and luxurious instead of simple basic human needs. A new Spartan morality was called for by many *philosophes* like Montesquieu and most Encyclopedists, who advocated a frugal way of life to permit an equitable repartition of wealth. Voltaire himself, who in his youth had considered luxury an essential factor in economic growth and progress (see his poem *Le Mondain* of 1736, for example), altered his position in later years in view of the impact such a policy had on slavery. In his *Essai sur les moeurs,* Voltaire deplored the fact that in the French part of Santo Domingo there were "one hundred thousand slaves, blacks or mulattoes, who worked in sugar mills, indigo and cocoa plantations, sacrificing their lives to gratify our newly acquired appetites, unknown to our forefathers" (II, 379). These new luxuries—sugar, cocoa, coffee, tobacco, etc.— became for the Europeans a "necessity" that "caused men to perish" (*ibid.,* 380).

Jaucourt's article, "Traite des nègres" (Slave Trade), published in the *Encyclopédie* in 1765, ten years after his first article on "Esclavage," showed a growing virulence of tone in his denunciation, on economic grounds, of the slave trade. This illustrates the increasing combativeness of the *philosophes* concerning black slavery, on both moral and economic planes, between 1755 and 1765. Jaucourt did not hesitate to compare colonial settlers to highway robbers and to recommend the destruction of colonies, since the luxuries they provided, like sugar cane and tobacco, were not of vital necessity to the French:

You might say that these colonies would be quickly ruined, if negro slavery were to be abolished. Well, should this be so, must we conclude from it that mankind has to be horribly wronged in order to make us rich or provide us with luxuries? It is true that the purses of highway robbers would be empty if thefts were absolutely suppressed; but do men have the right to grow richer in a cruel and criminal way? What right has a bandit to rob passers-by? Who is permitted to become affluent by making his fellow men miserable? Can it be considered lawful to deprive mankind of its most sacred rights for the sole purpose of gratifying one's greed, vanity or idiosyncrasies? No . . . Let European colonies perish rather than have so many suffer! (XVI, 533).

Like most *philosophes,* Jaucourt was not satisfied with mere destruction. He opposed a policy, not the proper development of new lands. While recommending the abolition of slavery, he urged the implementation of a new economic system based on freedom and private enterprise, in order to maintain prosperity and expand it:

I do not believe that the abolition of slavery could cause the ruin of the colonies. Trade would suffer for a time, I grant it; this is the usual effect of all new arrangements and, in this case, we could not find immediately an alternative system to implement. But many other advantages could result from *abolition.*

It is the slave trade and practice of servitude that have prevented America from becoming populous as promptly as it should have. *Set Negroes free,* and in a few generations this vast, fertile land will have numerous inhabitants. Arts and talents will flourish; and instead of being almost solely peopled by savages and wild beasts, it will soon be crowded with industrious settlers. *Liberty* and *industry* are the real sources of abundance. As long as a people maintain industry and liberty, they will have nothing to fear. Industry, like necessity, is ingenious and inventive; it discovers a thousand different ways to acquire wealth. If one of the canals of opulence gets clogged, a hundred others open up at once (*ibid.*).

If European nations remained unconvinced and unwilling to free their colonial slaves, Encyclopedists did not hesitate to encourage Blacks to rebel and take their destiny into their own hands:

There is not one of those unfortunates, whom we claim to be but slaves, who is not entitled to be declared a free man immediately, since he never lost his liberty. He could not lose it. . . . A Negro does not and cannot deprive himself of his natural right; he bears it in him wherever he goes, and can demand that we let him enjoy it wherever he lives (XVI, 532; Traite des Nègres).

In an earlier article on slavery, Jaucourt's position was even more vigorous, though he was speaking in more general terms: "Whoever attempts to usurp an absolute power over another places himself in a *state of war* with him" (V, 937). The implications of possible violence were inescapable. The prospect of serious open revolts by black slaves in the French colonies—they had already occasionally happened—became another argument in the *philosophes'* arsenal of opposition to slavery. Even Voltaire, indomitable pacifist, viewed a slaves' war against their masters as a legitimate act of violence: "We must admit that, of all wars, that of Spartacus is the most just and perhaps the only just one" (*Dictionnaire philosophique,* Moland ed., XVIII, 600).

Finally, one of the most striking and often least understood methods of the *philosophes* in fighting slavery was their use of irony and satire. They would seem to take the opposite stance and outrageously favor slavery, defending it as passionately as they had opposed it. They would feign to support slavery's proponents—to such extremes that their reasonings would be reduced to absurdity. A classic example of this appears in Montesquieu's *L'Esprit des lois* (Book XV, Ch. 5; [Paris, 1973], I, 265-66). Here are eight of his arguments "supporting" slavery (mostly consisting of the traditional reasons and motives invoked by partisans of slavery, but unabashedly carried to untenable excess, particularly when they are considered in the serious context of a treatise on international laws):

Of the Slavery of Negroes

If I were to defend the right we have to make Negroes our slaves, here is what I would say:

After exterminating the natives of America, the people of Europe had to enslave those from Africa to use them for clearing such vast areas of land.

Sugar would be far too expensive if the plant producing it were not cultivated by slaves.

The creatures in question are black from head to toe, and their nose is so flat that it is almost impossible to feel compassion for them.

One cannot imagine God, who is most wise, placing a soul, especially a good one, in a thoroughly black body.

It is so natural to think that color constitutes the essence of human nature that the people of Asia, who castrate Blacks in their employ, always deprive them of the distinctive attribute which they would otherwise have in common with us. . . .[14]

Here is a very good proof that Negroes lack common sense: they find glass beads more desirable than gold, which civilized nations so greatly value.[15]

It is impossible for us to assume that these creatures are men for, if we should, who would believe that we are Christians ourselves?

Petty minds exaggerate far too much the injustices dealt the Africans. If such were really the case, wouldn't it have occurred to the princes of Europe, who draw up so many useless conventions among themselves, to make a valuable one in favor of humanity and compassion?

Though the underlying irony can be easily detected, some readers outside France were sometimes unaware of it. Surprisingly as late as 1914, for instance, the editor of an English edition of *The Spirit of Laws* wrote the following footnote to the chapter just quoted: "The above arguments form a striking instance of the prejudice under which even a liberal mind can labour" (London, 1914; I, 257).

Even some of Voltaire's readers have been baffled and misled by the *philosophe*'s irony and irrepressible wit. Often treating with apparent levity problems that were uppermost in his philosophical reflections, Voltaire would also deal with the question of Blacks in this ambiguous fashion.[16] Nonetheless, in the eighteenth century Montesquieu's and

---

[14] This refers to black eunuchs employed then in Middle East harems.

[15] This is a sarcastic reference to the Europeans' "stupidity" in confusing a sign with reality. Gold for Montesquieu (as well as for Voltaire in *Candide*) was just a "sign" of riches; it had no intrinsic value, since it was useless. Its accumulation just "represented" wealth. Consequently, Blacks here were more correct in their evaluation of gold than Europeans. Theoretically gold had no greater value than the shiny colored beads preferred by the "savages."

[16] A point in question is, for example, Voltaire's controversial 7th letter from Amabed to Shastasid in *Lettres d'Amabed* (1769), which expresses some of his contemporaries' feelings and ideas about Blacks, carried to unreasonable extremes and therefore, by implication, seeming improbable and satirical (*Oeuvres complètes,* Moland ed., XXI, 462). If the letter appears to be so ambiguous, however, it may be due to the fact that Voltaire also also refers in it to Amabed's belief in the African's "progress" with *time* (see Voltaire's own position, note 11 above).

Voltaire's satire became a brilliantly effective weapon against slavery, perfectly understood by most of their contemporaries, and a device by which they could challenge official policies with impunity. At a time when the spoken or written *word* was omnipotent, particularly if clever or witty, and in a nation where vanity and susceptibility were high, derision and ridicule could "kill." It would deal one of the most effective blows to the yet undecided or to the last of those resisting the abolition of slavery.

But before the abolition of slavery could take place—as it temporarily did for the first time in 1792 during the French Revolution—a major change had to occur in the image of Blacks in the French collective consciousness. For over a century, many of the French had viewed the Black as an ignorant African primitive or a dejected slave in the colonies who, according to Jean-Jacques Rousseau's words, had let go of "his person, . . . his reason, his very identity, . . . in a word, had *ceased to exist* before even dying."[17] It would take time before "existence" would be restored to the Black in French literature, along with his identity, dignity, and self-respect. From the status of a brute to that of an exotic hero in French plays, novels, and short stories during the last decades of the eighteenth century, the road to regeneration would be arduous and long.

Thus, the preliminary work of the French *philosophes* in criticizing official economic policies and in proposing and propagating a new moral and social ideal in the middle of the eighteenth century was of paramount importance; it stirred and began changing public opinion in France on the question of black slavery. Their ideas and militancy concerning justice and equality for all played an essential part in the subsequent regeneration of Blacks in French ideology. The *philosophes* had cleared the ground for new esteem and interest in a vilified people, and paved the way for their liberation.

Texas A. and M. University.

[17] *Emile* (1762), [Paris, 1964], 587.

IV

Three Approaches to Locke and the Slave Trade

Wayne Glausser

Every modern scholar who takes him seriously has had to confront an embarrassing fact: John Locke, preeminent theorist of natural liberties, and an influential resource for abolitionist thinkers of the eighteenth and nineteenth centuries, actually participated in the slave trade.

Interpreters of Locke have responded to this embarrassment in three different ways. A first group treats it as an unfortunate but minor lapse in the public conduct of a man deservedly known for adherence to liberal principles. Locke's conduct here, according to this first mode of explanation, constitutes a deviation from his theory. A second group would agree that his participation in slave trading seems to contradict his basic principles; but instead of merely dismissing his conduct as a deviation from theory, these interpreters draw out of Locke's writings an elaborate, unworthy justification of the kind of slavery in which he participated. For this second group, then, Locke did manage to accommodate theory to practice, but only by an embarrassingly tortured logic. A third group concludes that Locke's accommodation of slavery does not proceed from the violation or torture of his basic theories. Instead, these interpreters argue, his treatment of slavery should be seen as part of the fabric of Lockean philosophy, however embarrassing that might be for modern admirers of one of the founding liberals.[1]

Two difficulties hinder any final judgment about the relative validity of the three approaches. First, as we shall see, the evidence by which

---

[1] James Farr also finds three versions of accounting for Locke's involvement in slavery, in "So Vile and Miserable an Estate: The Problem of Slavery in Locke's Political Thought," *Political Theory*, 14 (1986), 263-89. Farr's three versions are similar to mine, although his third group is defined much more narrowly and includes only the argument about Lockean theory as a foundation for racism. Farr argues that all of the existing accounts are inadequate, and he offers a new approach. I would classify his arguments as a combination of my third or integral approach (like David Brion Davis, he finds that Locke's theory of natural rights permits a justification of slavery) and my first or deviation approach (there can be no Lockean grounds for justifying Afro-American chattel slavery).

they may be evaluated has flaws and ambiguities. It would be unproductive, however, simply to declare the material undecidable, and aban-
don the project to a premature indeterminacy. Second, the conclusions
reached by various interpreters appear to depend as much on critical
predisposition as on evidence. The deviation approach emanates from a
kind of tempered idealism: theory will govern practice, except in certain
obvious cases of temptation and lapse. The torture approach recognizes
a specific area in which practice governs theory, rather than vice-versa;
but a seam remains visible, where something different intruded on the
theory and was joined to it. The third approach recognizes no such seam.
Theory and practice are inseparable, a seamless text of power relations.
The three approaches can thus be situated—and at least to some extent
ask to be validated—as different (but complementary) responses to familiar questions of idea and act.

To examine these three approaches, we first need to look at the
available facts about Locke's involvement in slavery. Scholars have
reached a fairly settled consensus about the facts, if not about how to
evaluate them; and the consensus comes despite lingering uncertainties
surrounding some of these facts. Locke participated in the institutions
of slavery in two basic ways. First, he invested in slave trading companies.
Second, he acted as secretary and to some degree policy advisor to three
different groups involved in the affairs of the American colonies, including
the provision and regulation of slaves.

Facts about the investments are solid enough, if not complete. (Investment records in the seventeenth century were often discarded after
a transaction was finished.) Among his various investments two stand
out for this discussion. Locke put money in two companies whose commercial activities depended on slavery: the Royal African Company, and
a company of adventurers formed to develop the Bahama Islands. The
first of these was explicitly a slave trading enterprise. Locke invested six
hundred pounds in the Royal African Company, shortly after its formation in 1672.[2] Lord Ashley (Locke's friend and patron, soon to become
the First Earl of Shaftesbury) had invested two thousand pounds, which
made him the third largest investor.[3] Locke's investment, then, was no
inconsequential matter either to the company or to Locke, who was
always so careful with his money. The Royal African Company was
formed in 1672 to trade along the West Coast of Africa and primarily

[2] The figure of six hundred pounds I take from Maurice Cranston, *John Locke: A
Biography* (New York, 1957), 115.
[3] See K. H. D. Haley, *The First Earl of Shaftesbury* (Oxford, 1968), 233. Only the
Duke of York and Sir Robert Viner made larger investments, and Haley assumes that
Shaftesbury advised Locke to put money in the company. This seems reasonable, although
Locke would never have risked money without careful consideration or under any sort
of coercion.

to provide the slaves considered indispensable by planters in America. It was chartered to replace the Company of Royal Adventurers into Africa, which had proved unsuccessful in its ten years of operation. The new company included more businessmen and fewer nobles, and was determined to attend more to profits than to subtle affairs of state. Certainly Locke was the sort of investor they sought, and Ashley, despite being a nobleman, had a great interest in the mercantile practicalities of American plantations. Ashley as a young man had owned acreage and slaves in Barbados as well as a fourth share in the *Rose*, a slave trading ship.[4] The new Royal African Company named him Sub-Governor, a post which he held through 1673, and until 1677 he served in its Court of Assistants. No doubt Locke and Ashley looked carefully both at the company's charter—which granted a monopoly for the trade of "Gold, Silver, Negroes, Slaves," and any other minor Guinea goods—and at a report of its first year's activities, which mentions gold, elephants' teeth, and a few other items, but places by far the greatest emphasis on slave shipping and slave factories. The slaves, this report assures, "are sent to all his Majesty's American Plantations, which cannot subsist without them."[5] The Royal African Company fared better than its predecessor, although it was never successful enough to justify its monopoly, and it had trouble meeting the considerable demand for slaves.[6] Ashley sold his stock in 1677 for a reasonable profit, and no doubt Locke did likewise, although not necessarily at the same time.

Locke also invested in a company of Bahamas Adventurers. Here again he was collaborating with Ashley. Ashley and five other Carolina proprietors had been granted the Bahama Islands, and in 1672 they formed a company with eleven "Adventurers to Bahamas" to pursue development. Locke was one of the eleven adventurers. He initially invested one hundred pounds; before long he doubled his share by taking over the one hundred-pound investment of his friend John Mapletoft. Fox Bourne calculates that Locke thus "became altogether responsible for a ninth" of the project, and he speculates that Locke must have spent much more than two hundred pounds:

The calls afterwards made upon him were doubtless far in excess of the original 200 pounds. He was present on the 8th of November [1672] at a meeting on board the ship *Bahamas Merchant*, moored in the Thames, and ready for sailing. A good deal of money must have been spent in so promptly fitting out this

[4] *Ibid.*, 230. Haley notes cautiously that the *Rose* was said to be in the "Guinea Trade," which "might refer to the trade in gums, wood, ivory . . . but it is more likely to refer to the usual triangular trade."

[5] Both documents (the Charter of the Royal African Company, and the report of the first year) can be found in Elizabeth Donnan, *Documents Illustrative of the History of the Slave Trade to America* (2 vols.; New York, 1965), I, 177-92, 192-93.

[6] For this overview of the company's performance, I am relying primarily on Michael Craton, *Sinews of Empire: A Short History of British Slavery* (London, 1974), 58-66.

vessel. But, as only the first minute-book of the Bahamas company is extant, there is not much to be said about the sequel to Locke's enterprise in colonial trade.[7]

We may not know a great deal more about Locke's Bahamas adventure, but some further details and background can help. In *A History of the Bahamas* Michael Craton explains the terms of the proprietors' grant: they were to stimulate planting and trading of profitable crops, in a colony that had been struggling under Spanish and now English rule. The plantations supported by Locke and the other adventurers were using slaves, of course. Craton cites a 1671 census of the islands, recording 443 slaves out of a total population of 1,097.[8] Another document has been found from about the time of the adventurers, computing the "expense of settling and improving the Bahama Islands for the first three years." According to this estimate, three hundred families would need to bring along six hundred slaves (costing thirty pounds each), and to "trade for 4,000 negroes per annum, being 8,000 for the first two years . . . at 25 pounds per head."[9] The adventurers were evidently not up to these stakes, and planters in the Bahamas complained that the proprietors and their company provided insufficient support. Locke and his patron, however, remained interested in the Bahamas. Shaftesbury tried to bolster planters' confidence with plans for new crops and a hereditary nobility. Locke attended to Bahamian matters for some years, and apparently at one point he was considering a more active involvement in planting. This can be inferred from a letter to Locke from his friend Sir Peter Colleton, a West Indies planter:

I find I am your partner in the Bahama trade which will turn to accompt if you meddle not with planting, but if you plant otherwise then for provizion for your factor you will have your whole stock drowned in a plantation and bee never the better for it. . . . If other men will plant there, I mean the Bahamas, hinder them not, they improve our province, but I would neither have you nor my lord ingadge in it . . . (28 May 1673).[10]

Fox Bourne interprets this as Colleton discouraging Locke from managing a full plantation at a great distance; Craton reads it differently and infers that Locke had inquired about moving to the Bahamas as a planter.[11] Either way, Locke apparently entertained notions of increasing his moderate but serious participation in American planting and trade.

---

[7] H. R. Fox Bourne, *The Life of John Locke* (2 vols.; New York, 1876), I, 291-92.

[8] *A History of the Bahamas* (London, 1962), 69-70.

[9] This document (from the Colonial State Papers, West Indies) is cited by both Fox Bourne and Craton. Fox Bourne prints an extract (I, 290).

[10] E. S. DeBeer (ed.), *The Correspondence of John Locke* (8 vols.; Oxford, 1976), I, 380.

[11] Fox Bourne, I, 292; Craton, *A History of the Bahamas*, 69.

His second kind of participation in the institutions of slavery called for investments of time rather than money. Locke held three relevant administrative positions: (unofficial) secretary to the Lords Proprietors of Carolina, Secretary to the Council of Trade and Plantations, and Commissioner of the Board of Trade.

In the first of these positions he helped Ashley and seven other noblemen who had been granted proprietorship of Carolina in 1663. Locke acted as a secretary for them, and probably as an advisor—but to what extent, remains uncertain. The most significant document in the Carolina papers is the *Fundamental Constitutions of Carolina*, which sets out an interesting mixture of liberal policies and restrictive social hierarchies. A scheme of nobility was invented; Locke was granted the second highest rank, of "Landgrave" (probably Locke's coinage), and forty-eight thousand acres that came with the title. Most relevant to our discussion is a provision that "every freeman of Carolina shall have absolute power and authority over his negro slave of what opinion or religion soever."[12] The proprietors thus clarified that the religious freedom granted Carolina slaves did not imply another sort of freedom. Scholars have variously proposed that Locke (a) authored the entire Carolina constitution (there is a manuscript in Locke's hand; and many editions of his work include it); (b) had no part in it, except as amanuensis; and (c) effectively co-authored it with Ashley. Most recent scholars have argued for this third conclusion, which seems the most plausible, given the two men's respect for each other. But did Locke endorse the slavery clause? There is evidence that he disagreed with at least one other clause, that establishing the Church of England;[13] so some would like to assume a similar objection to the slavery clause. Such an objection seems unlikely, however. Not only did Locke go on to make the slave investments already described but, in the much later commentaries to St. Paul, he carefully restated the distinction between religious and civil freedom articulated in the Carolina constitution. According to the constitution, slaves are free to attend the church of their choice, "but yet no slave shall hereby by exempted from that civil dominion his master hath over him, but be in all other things in the same state and condition he was in before."[14] Here is part of Locke's paraphrase of St. Paul, 1 Corinthians 7:20-24: "Christianity gives not anyone any new privilege to change the state . . . which he was in before. Wert thou called, being a slave? . . . In whatsoever state a man is called, in the same he is to remain, notwith-

---

[12] *The Works of John Locke* (10 vols.; London, 1801), X, 196.

[13] See Haley, 245: "Some of Locke's friends later maintained that Locke had told them that this clause providing for the establishment of the Church of England as the state church was inserted contrary to his wishes by 'some of the chief of the proprietors.' " Haley cites for this claim Des Maizeaux, *A Collection of Several Pieces of Mr. John Locke* (1720).

[14] *Works* (1801), X, 197.

standing any privileges of the gospel, which gives him no dispensation, or exemption, from any obligation he was in before . . "; to which he adds this commentary: "The thinking themselves freed by Christianity, from the ties of civil society and government, was a fault, it seems, that those Christians were very apt to run into."[15] Apparently Locke could endorse the Carolina slavery clause without qualms even if he did not himself compose it.

Locke's other two offices were government appointments. In 1673 he became Secretary to the Council of Trade and Plantations, a position he held for over a year. As Secretary he had to correspond with proprietors, governors, planters, merchants, and anyone else connected with the colonies who brought a complaint, made a proposal, or held useful information. Much of the Council's work went toward expediting the triangular trade of slaves, sugar, and manufactured goods. One of the Council's directives was to oversee the provision of slaves, and to investigate disputes between the chartered slaving company and the American plantations. (As we have seen, Locke held investments on both sides of such disputes; putting him in an interested but neutral position.) For over a year, then, Locke spent much of his time immersed in these matters. But it is difficult to say how actively he contributed to the Council's decisions: "In all the voluminous correspondence . . . [there is nothing] to show how far he acted merely as a secretary, and how far he initiated the proceedings that he had to direct."[16] There is no such uncertainty about Locke's second stint as colonial administrator. In 1696 he took office as a Commissioner of the new Board of Trade created to solve problems such as poor colonial government, piracy, and abused or ineffective trade regulations. In this position he was unquestionably an active policy-maker. Cranston concludes that "documents of the Board of Trade make abundantly clear that Locke was the leading Commissioner in nearly everything which was undertaken."[17] This opinion has been reinforced by Peter Laslett, who emphasizes Locke's contribution to the Board's formation and early policies.[18] He served until 1700, when he became too ill to continue.

Given all this evidence, scholars must account for the incongruity between Locke's actions in these matters and his place in the ordinary history of ideas. There are three main approaches, as set out above: practice as deviating from theory, as torturing theory, and as fulfilling theory. In the deviation approach, no one, to my knowledge, has accused

[15] *Ibid.*, VIII, 116-17.
[16] Fox Bourne, I, 287.
[17] *A Biography*, 406.
[18] "John Locke: The Great Recoinage and the Board of Trade, 1695-1698," *William and Mary Quarterly*, 14 (1957), 370-402.

Locke of blatant hypocrisy. Influenced primarily by idealist histories, most deviation theorists have privileged theory over practice (even for a man known as "the practical philosopher") and have taken Locke's participation in slavery as an embarrassing but insignificant lapse—an effect of local negotiations of personal interest. The importance and influence of the grand theory overwhelms such lapses. Historians of slavery such as Craton, for example, will pause to note the lapse, but as a parenthesis to the main fact of Locke as anti-slavery theorist. A more extreme version of deviation idealism is to discount the actions so drastically as to consider them unworthy of mention. Kathy Squadrito's 1975 essay does mention them but only to judge them irrelevant: defending Lockean empiricism against a charge of racism, she will "consider irrelevant any references to Locke's supposed involvement in, or support of, the slave trade."[19] Ruth W. Grant, in a more recent book, is not squeamish about admitting his involvement, but she argues for practice as deviation from theory, "which can in no way support that institution [slavery]."[20]

It would be useful here to highlight some anti-slavery passages from the *Two Treatises of Government*. Source books of abolitionist thinking like to quote the beginning of the *First Treatise*: "Slavery is so vile and miserable an Estate of Man, and so directly opposed to the generous Temper and Courage of our Nation; that 'tis hardly to be conceived, that an *Englishman*, much less a *Gentleman*, should plead for't" (1).[21] Snobbishness aside, this sounds like a clear, spirited denunciation; yet context alters the message. This is Locke's exordium to his attack on Filmer's theory of patriarchal monarchy. The slavery he refers to in this first sentence is the condition to which Filmer would reduce all English subjects. Locke is thus using slavery in a general rather than a specific sense, more figurative than literal. This does not simply disqualify the sentence as an abolitionist text, but it does suggest that Locke's anti-slavery theories need careful reading. Near the end of the *Second Treatise* he returns to his opening theme and attacks Filmer-like tyrannists who would resolve "all Government into absolute Tyranny, and would have all Men born to, what their mean Souls fitted them for, Slavery" (239). Here the rhetorical flourish again complicates an apparent repudiation of slavery. By suggesting that a "mean soul" makes a person fit for

---

[19] "Locke's View of Essence and Its Relation to Racism: A Reply to Professor Bracken," *The Locke Newsletter*, 6 (1975), 53n.

[20] *John Locke's Liberalism* (Chicago, 1987), 68n. Grant questions what I am calling the tortured approach of Seliger and Laslett. She charges that Laslett "misuses" his two sources (the *Fundamental Constitutions*, and a letter to Governor Nicholson of Virginia), but she does not explain further. The most likely objections would focus on questions of authorship.

[21] *Two Treatises of Government*, ed. Peter Laslett (Cambridge, 1960), 159. Parenthetical citations refer to numbered sections of the treatises.

slavery, Locke slips toward two ancient traditions justifying slavery: the classical model of natural inferiority (accepted easily enough by Plato and Aristotle) and the Judaeo-Christian model of slavery as divine punishment.[22] But, one might argue, this is only a rhetorical flourish. And even if it reveals traces of antique paradigms, Locke in his *Second Treatise* fought to counteract whatever influence the old paradigms might have on his thinking. Men are not born into or fitted for slavery, according to the real Locke. "No body can give more Power than he has himself; and he that cannot take away his own Life, cannot give another power over it" (23). Everyone is naturally free "from any Superior Power on Earth" (22), and anyone who attempts to enslave a person "puts himself into a State of War" with that person (17).

There is one technical exception within this anti-slavery doctrine, but deviation theorists can discount its importance. Locke allows that captives taken in a just war may be kept as slaves: "This is the Perfect condition of *Slavery*, which is nothing else, but *the State of War continued between a lawful Conqueror, and a Captive*" (24). He uses here the primary justification of slavery from the Justinianian Code—and a principle written into, among other things, the 1641 Laws and Liberties of Massachusetts. But deviationists can observe that Locke adds a liberal condition to the old justification. Once victor and vanquished have made a formal "agreement for a limited Power on the one side and Obedience on the other, the State of War and *Slavery* ceases, as long as the Compact endures..." (24). Clearly, they would argue, Locke did not expect the old slavery to impinge on modern government, with its sophisticated diplomatic machinery. Furthermore, Locke denies to conquerors any claims on the children of captives (189). In no way can Locke's theory be said to support chattel slavery as practiced on the American plantations.

Interpreters of a second kind agree that Locke deserves his reputation as an opponent of slavery, but they regretfully explain how he tortured his basic theories in order to accommodate American slavery. Advocates of the distortion approach are not as confident about the integrity of Lockean theory. The theory is vulnerable to contamination by misjudged practical interests. Still, this second approach recognizes a clear distinction between normal and intruding elements.

Locke's tortured justification of American slavery has been set out

[22] A useful discussion of these models can be found in David Brion Davis, *The Problem of Slavery in Western Culture* (Ithaca, 1966), 65-92. Thomas Wiedemann has collected a number of texts relevant to classical theories and institutions of slavery: see *Greek and Roman Slavery* (Baltimore, 1981).

most thoroughly by M. Seliger.[23] Seliger finds in the *Second Treatise* a special defense of colonization and slavery, two pillars of the first British empire. The justification represents an "inane" and localized (but still systematic) affirmation of territorial annexation and enslavement, elsewhere so forcefully repudiated in the *Second Treatise*. Seliger begins with the admission of slavery for captives in a just war (as noted above). A just war, for Locke, was a war fought in defense of one's possessions against an aggressor. One society cannot legitimately use war to subjugate another society, by attacking the lives, liberties, and possessions of its citizens. Locke's principles of just and unjust war are not among his more complex and sophisticated ideas. Even if his simple distinction between offensive and defensive war will admit some complications (e.g., the matter of justifiable preventive war), the *Second Treatise* insists on defensive motivations. Locke appears confident that he can distinguish between an aggressor and a defender in a given set of circumstances. His confident principles of just and unjust war serve to disqualify one possible defense of the African slave trade. The defense would be a simple one. As Craton observes, "most English writers believed that the majority of slaves were captives in the wars that were endemic to West Africa."[24] It was commonly thought (if not scrupulously verified) that Africans taken as slaves would be worse off as war captives in Africa than as slaves in America. But even if Locke held this view of the origin of enslavement, he could not on these grounds alone justify the Royal African Company slaving. Only captives taken in a just war deserve to be enslaved. All the English buyers could be sure of in an African war— if they gave it any thought at all—was who had superior force. The *Second Treatise* grants no privilege to conquerors with only this claim to superiority.

But Seliger identifies another line of thinking by which Locke appears to justify colonial slavery. Again it begins with the legitimate enslavement of war captives. The real torture comes in the next link of the logical chain: native Africans and Americans can be considered aggressors in a war against the Europeans who would colonize and develop their lands. Hence, Peter Laslett says, "Locke seems satisfied that the slave raiding forays of the Royal African Company were just wars."[25] Laslett says "seems" because Locke never actually drew such a conclusion. Seliger has to put together premises culled from the *Second Treatise* and find the "unavoidable implication" about colonizers as just conquerors. De-

---

[23] Seliger's discussion can be found in *The Liberal Politics of John Locke* (New York, 1969), 114-24. For a more condensed version of the same argument, see Seliger's "Locke, Liberalism, and Nationalism," John W. Yolton (ed.), *John Locke: Problems and Perspectives* (Cambridge, 1969), 27-29.

[24] *Sinews of Empire*, 72.

[25] *Two Treatises of Government*, 303n.

viation theorists object that he is putting words into Locke's mouth, but
Seliger's case should not be dismissed lightly.

The difficult link, the one about natives being aggressors, needs more
inspection. This idea seems an absurd violation of *Second Treatise* principles. In the chapter on war, Locke asserts that "he who makes an
attempt to enslave me thereby puts himself into a State of War with me"
(17), and the aggressor-enslaver deserves to be punished or killed. How
can the African and American victims of such aggression be turned into
the aggressors themselves? The answer, according to Seliger, is Locke's
theory of waste land, in which he may have been influenced by More's
Utopia.[26] According to this principle, people occupying (or claiming as
property) land that they either cannot or will not develop may become
aggressors against those who can and would develop that land. In Utopia,
when the population rises above fixed quotas, Utopians colonize a nearby
mainland area where "the natives have much unoccupied and uncultivated land." Ideally, the natives will agree to live under Utopian laws;
but those who

refuse to live according to their laws, they drive from the territory which they
carve out for themselves. If they resist, they wage war against them. They
consider it a most just cause for war when a people which does not use its soil
but keeps it idle and waste nevertheless forbids the use and possession of it to
others who by the rule of nature ought to be maintained by it.[27]

Locke's version of this thinking resides in two *Second Treatise* passages.
As part of his analysis of property, he mentions that "there are still *great
Tracts of Ground* to be found, which . . . *lie waste*, and are more than
the People, who dwell on it, do, or can make use of . . ." (45). Later,
in a discussion of war reparations, Locke explains that no victor may
justly seize possession of a defeated enemy's land—except that, "where
there being more *Land*, than the Inhabitants possess, and make use of,
any one has liberty to make use of the waste" (184). Thus, if a native
population should "resist conquest of their waste land, they become
aggressors in war,"[28] and the developers may justly kill them and enslave
captives.

Squadrito, following Seliger, has had to supply this last piece of
reasoning: Locke nowhere says that those who would develop a waste
land may justly kill or enslave those who resist. Indeed, the principle is

---

[26] Seliger mentions the similarity between Locke's argument and the passage from
More (*Liberal Politics*, 114), but he makes no definite claim of influence. We know that
Locke owned a copy of *Utopia*; but he does not discuss it anywhere in his writings,
except for an occasional reference to something "Utopian." Of course, Locke was influenced by many books to which he never acknowledged a debt. Most notoriously he
denied the influence of Hobbes, against both internal and external evidence to the contrary.

[27] Tr. by Edward Surtz, S. J. (New Haven, 1964), 76.

[28] Kathleen Squadrito, *John Locke* (Boston, 1979), 128.

clearer in *Utopia* than in the *Second Treatise*. Ashley preferred, where possible, to purchase land from Indians (although Haley cynically points out that this method was cheaper as well as more humane than combat).[29] It seems a reasonable surmise that Ashley and Locke wanted to think of plantations in the benign way of Bacon: "I like a Plantation in a Pure Soile; that is, where People are not Displanted, to the end, to Plant in Others." Bacon is nevertheless alert to problems of planting "where Savages are." These natives should be treated "justly and gratiously"; but even before the Virginia massacre of 1622, he advises colonists to keep "sufficient Guard."[30] Locke, coming after this massacre and consequent changes in English policy, can adjust his liberal principles to suit colonial realities. Here is a minor but revealing passage from the *First Treatise*: "A Planter in the *West Indies* . . . might, if he pleased (who doubts) Muster [a personal army] . . . against the *Indians*, to seek Reparation upon any Injury received from them . . ." (130). Locke is engaged in an entirely different argument (against Filmer), but this casual illustration shows that he assumes native resistance in the waste land, and that he takes for granted the justice of a developer's "resistance" to such "aggression." The wastes of Africa were less promising to the developer's eye than those of America, but the justification would have applied well enough to Africa, and hence to Africans, who were of course so useful to American development.[31] However tortured and incomplete this chain of logic, it is not simply an illusion conjured up by imaginative interpreters. Locke the opponent of slavery cannot entirely suppress Locke the Landgrave, eager to make his mark on the *tabula rasa* of American waste land.

Locke must have entertained complications to any *vacuus locus* model of a new world, as he did for his *tabula rasa* model of a new mind. In 1671 he was asked to write a description of Carolina to accompany publication of a map; although he never wrote it, he did sketch a bibliography and a list of topics, which included "Inhabitants—Number, Bodies, Abilities of Mind, Temper and Inclinations, Morality and Cus-

---

[29] *Shaftesbury*, 250.

[30] "Of Plantations," *The Essays or Counsels, Civill and Morall*, ed. Michael Kiernan (Oxford, 1985), 106-8.

[31] Farr's strongest objection to what I call the tortured approach is that Locke "could not have extended this view to cover black Africans, for the simple reason that there was at that time no intention by Englishmen to settle in Africa. Africa proved to be a vast uncharted graveyard for so many of the early traders that it was not conceived of as the next colonial outpost of the burgeoning English empire" (275). Although Locke and the English apparently did not envision grand settlements, they nevertheless saw Africa as a waste land that could be turned to more productive use. The land could be developed to produce gold, silver, ivory, and various other goods, as specified in the charter and reports of the Royal African Company. Since slaves were clearly the most important product, one can sympathize with Farr's objection to this justification; but his objection does not rule out the tortured justification on its own grounds.

toms, Religion, Economy." [32] His works elsewhere reveal a curiosity about what would now be called anthropological topics, especially matters of cultural difference. He was clearly not oblivious to developments within native culture. Still, he seems content with his own definition of development, embedded in reasonings about labor and property, as set forth most clearly in the "Property" sections of the *Second Treatise*. Virtue resides in productive labor toward the replenishment of the earth, and only through this labor do people earn title to lands and goods. Such thinking, as well as his actions in support of colonial slavery, would suggest that he sympathized with the Utopians on matters of waste and development. And at least one American Puritan, a Connecticut minister, used Locke's arguments about waste land to justify the dispossession of native inhabitants. [33]

Seliger considers this line of thinking a torture rather than a fulfillment of basic liberal theories, because elsewhere Locke shows such respect for self-determination and such sympathy for the dispossessed. Theorists of the final group instead see the justification of slavery as an integral part of Lockean theory. Three very different versions of this approach can be isolated. One sees Locke as an advocate of capitalism above all other considerations; another finds in Locke's empiricism a foundation for racism; and another concludes that his justification of slavery depends upon the same assumptions as his defense of natural liberties.

The first version comes from C. B. Macpherson, Leo Strauss, and their followers. They have proposed a bourgeois Locke, whose political philosophy rationalizes capitalist appropriation. For Macpherson, the primary confusion in Locke derives from his holding two contradictory conceptions of human nature and society, both of which originate in bourgeois ideology: "A market society generates class differentiation in effective rights and rationality, yet requires for its justification a postulate of equal natural rights and rationality. . . . Most of Locke's theoretical conceptions, and most of his practical appeal, can be traced to this ambiguous position." [34] Strauss's Locke is more devious than Macpherson's—Strauss accuses Locke of being a crypto-Hobbesian, whose efforts to conceal unpleasant premises left a trail of inconsistencies—but his purposes are similar:

To say that public happiness requires the emancipation and the protection of the acquisitive faculties amounts to saying that to accumulate as much money

[32] Fox Bourne, I, 245.

[33] The minister was John Bulkley, who made his argument in an introduction to Roger Wolcott's *Poetical Meditations* (New London, 1725). For excerpts and a brief analysis, see John Dunn, "The Politics of Locke in England and America," Yolton (ed.), *Problems and Perspectives*, 72-73.

[34] *The Political Theory of Possessive Individualism* (Oxford, 1962), 269.

and other wealth as one pleases is right or just. . . . Locke's followers in later generations no longer believed that they needed "the phraseology of the law of nature" because they took for granted what Locke did not take for granted: Locke still thought that he had to prove that the unlimited acquisition of wealth is not unjust or morally wrong.[35]

Macpherson's and Strauss's conclusions have been challenged over the years by a number of scholars, who have charged them with neglecting evidence, misreading intention, and oversimplifying historical context. One recent challenge proposes an extreme counter-version: James Tully's Locke is egalitarian and anti-capitalist. But the bourgeois theory has remained respectable. Richard Ashcraft's recent work, which criticizes the bourgeois Locke, nevertheless upholds Macpherson's approach as substantially useful.[36] To those who believe wholly or partially in this version of Locke, his participation in slavery comes as no particular surprise. Protections against enslavement are less fundamental to his theory than provisions for capitalist growth. Historians continue to argue about the actual economic advantages or disadvantages of slavery in the British colonies; but since Locke must have assumed that slave labor enabled planters to make greater profits, these scholarly debates make no difference to the bourgeois explanation of Locke's participation in slavery.

According to a second explanation, Locke's empiricism opens the door to racism and hence to an acceptance of slavery. Evidence for this charge comes from the *Essay Concerning Human Understanding*, instead of the *Two Treatises of Government*.[37] Leon Poliakov claims that the *Essay* promoted, beneath its explicit arguments, an Enlightenment myth of white superiority.[38] H. M. Bracken is more attentive to Locke's acceptance of slavery, and he argues that Locke's theory of substance and nominal essence "has been crucial as an ideological bulwark behind which racially biased pseudo-science continues to flourish."[39] Although some scholars

[35] *Natural Right and History* (Chicago, 1953), 246.

[36] James Tully, *A Discourse on Property: John Locke and his Adversaries* (Cambridge, 1980); Richard Ashcraft, *Revolutionary Politics and Locke's "Two Treatises of Government"* (Princeton, 1986). Another recent discussion of the bourgeois Locke and its challengers can be found in Neal Wood, *John Locke and Agrarian Capitalism* (Berkeley, 1984).

[37] It has been argued that the *Essay* and the *Treatises* differ so radically in purpose and style, that they can effectively be considered the work of different authors; see, for example, Peter Laslett's introduction to *Two Treatises of Government* (New York, 1965). But most recent interpreters, while acknowledging the dangers of simply combining the two books into one grand theory, would allow cross-fertilization.

[38] *The Aryan Myth: A History of Racist and Nationalist Ideas in Europe*, tr. Edmund Howard (1974; rpt. New York, 1977), 145-50.

[39] "Essence, Accident, and Race," *Hermathena*, 116 (1973), 93. Another presentation of the argument can be found in Richard H. Popkin, "The Philosophical Bases of Modern

have defended Locke by pointing out mitigating passages from the *Essay* or contrary tendencies in the *Second Treatise*, the charge is far from being dismissed. Eugene Miller says that he "can find no basis in Locke's account of substances for criticizing someone who chooses to define the essence of man in such a way as to exclude Negroes or any other racial group."[40]

In brief, Locke's argument about nominal essence goes as follows. He admits into his empiricism the terms "substance" and "essence," to convey what might be called the inner constitution of a thing. But he wishes to revise radically the Aristotelian discourse of substance. Although real substances may be assumed to exist, we cannot know them. We presume to speak of substances, but we can produce in our knowledge only conventional representations. What we call substances are in fact abstract and variable inferences collected from particular sensory ideas. Thus we categorize things not by real substance, but by nominal essence. Applied to ideas of human essence, this theory disrupts scholastic and rationalist assumptions about what constitutes a human being. We delude ourselves into believing that nature has established strict boundaries between humans and other species, but this is not so: "Wherein then, would I gladly know, consists the precise and *unmovable Boundaries of that Species*? 'Tis plain, if we examine, there is *no* such thing *made by Nature*, and established by her amongst Men. . . . *The boundaries of the Species, whereby Men sort them, are made by Men*" (3.6.27, 37).[41] One person's or one society's idea of human essence, therefore, may differ significantly from another's. And there is no convenient distinction between essential and accidental human properties.

Interpreters like Poliakov and Bracken see this as a foundation for racism. Bracken suggests that Locke's involvement in slavery fits easily inside such a theory. Critics of this approach have argued that in the *Second Treatise* Locke does establish—but within moral rather than epistemological discourse—identifying characteristics of a human being.[42] Some have looked to the *Essay* for counterevidence. One reply to Bracken cites a passage in which Locke warns against taking "the measure of a Man only by his out-side" (4.4.16).[43] Neal Wood observes that Locke's "view of natives and tribesmen was not marked by the negative attitude and anti-primitivism to be found in much contemporary and later lit-

---

Racism," *Philosophy and the Civilizing Arts*, ed. Craig Walton and John P. Anton (Athens, Ohio, 1974), 126-65.

[40] "Locke on the Meaning of Political Language," *The Political Science Reviewer*, 9 (1979), 178n.

[41] *An Essay Concerning Human Understanding*, ed. P. H. Nidditch (Oxford, 1975), 454, 462.

[42] See discussions by Eugene Miller and by Ruth Grant in previously cited works.

[43] Squadrito, "A Reply," 54n.

erature on the subject."[44] These defenses certainly have merit. But they cannot remove all suspicions. Even apparently innocuous material like Locke's illustrations can raise doubts. For instance, in a passage about nominal essence, he composes the following example to clarify his argument:

> First, a Child haveing framed the *Idea* of a *Man*, it is probable, that his *Idea* is just like that Picture, which the Painter makes of the visible Appearances joyned together; and such a Complication of *Ideas* together in his Understanding, makes up the single complex *Idea* which he calls *Man*, whereof White or Flesh-colour in *England* being one, the Child can demonstrate to you, that *a Negro is not a Man.* . . . (4.7.16)

Obviously, Locke is not arguing in favor of the child's construction, which is supposed to violate the common sense of readers. But his point is to show the constructed quality of all definitions of a man, and hence to entertain the validity of this one. Locke's convenient child also appears earlier in the *Essay*—"The Child certainly knows, that the *Nurse* that feeds it, is neither the *Cat* it plays with, nor the *Blackmoor* it is afraid of" (1.2.25)—as well as in Draft A: "A child unused to that sight & haveing had some such descriptions of the devil would call a Negro a devil rather then a Man & at the same time call a dryl a man."[45] Locke's choice of examples can make modern readers uneasy, especially those aware of his slavery connections. To Poliakov they "suggest a prejudice already well rooted in English society," and compatible with Locke's empiricist theories.[46]

Because these two references decorate rather than found Locke's argument, strict readers will dismiss them as accidents of convention. With David Brion Davis's version of the integral approach, no casual dismissal is possible. Davis reasons from the very foundation of Locke's argument:

> How can it be that so great a defender of the inalienable rights of man was not at heart a determined enemy of slavery? . . . It was precisely the same opening

---

[44] Neal Wood, *The Politics of Locke's Philosophy* (Berkeley, 1983), 81-82.

[45] *Draft A of Locke's Essay Concerning Human Understanding: The Earliest Extant Autograph Edition*, ed. Peter H. Nidditch (Sheffield, 1980), 33.

[46] *Aryan Myth*, 145. Poliakov cites two of the three passages mentioned in this essay, as well as an additional one (2.25.1), in which Locke's deep-rooted prejudice, according to Poliakov, accompanies defective logic. His argument against Locke's logic is persuasive (and bolstered by Leibniz), but the evidence of prejudice seems less telling here than in other passages. Farr recognizes that Locke may have been a "bigot," but he argues that "weak racism or bigotry of this kind need not and does not undermine the Lockean premise that all humans—even 'savages'—are born free and equal, with a full complement of natural rights" (278). Calling this a "weak" racism, however, does not rule it out as a contributing element within a body of theory flexible enough to abhor slavery and to allow it.

in Locke's theory of social contract that allowed both a justification of slavery and the preservation of natural rights. For in Locke's view, the origin of slavery, like the origin of liberty and property, was entirely outside the social contract. When any man, by fault or act, forfeited his life to another, he could not complain of injustice if his punishment was postponed by his being enslaved. . . . [Locke] had turned the traditional Stoic and Christian conception of slavery upside down, for instead of picturing bondage as a product of sinful society, he found its origins and justification outside the limits of a free and rational society. It followed, though Locke did not press the point, that slavery was in conformity with natural law and was as universally valid as private property.[47]

In contrast with general arguments about capitalism and racism, Davis attends to the specifics of Locke's slavery for war captives. Unlike torture or deviation theorists, Davis sees this provision as a coherent part of his system. Locke wants to authorize natural, pre-social individuals, whose rights and property precede social contract. With complementary reasoning he asserts that some individuals, by a willful turn against natural rights, can forever lose those natural rights. He creates a zone outside of social agreements which acts both as the repository of natural rights and as a kind of detention area for unnatural criminals.

I would like to extend Davis's argument by looking at how Locke uses the word "common" in the *Second Treatise* to define these criminals who deserve slavery. A man may kill an aggressor or a thief "for the same Reason, that he may kill a *Wolf* or a *Lyon*; because such Men are not under the ties of the Common Law of Reason . . ." (16). This "Common Law of Reason" defines a community of those who respect natural rights of self-preservation and property. Locke calls these rights "natural," but he also calls them "common"; and with this word he drifts away from the absolute law of nature and toward contingent laws of specific human communities. One of the main reasons men form societies is to put themselves under a "common Judge" (19). When Locke builds his justification of slavery by turning enemies into beasts of prey, he reduces a conflict of social interests into a simple difference of natural type. Humans become beasts become slaves by means of community judgments held up as natural.

"Common" again plays a crucial role in the waste land extension of justified slavery. As Seliger has noticed, Locke defines waste landers as people who have not "joyned with the rest of Mankind, in the consent of the Use of their common Money" (45). These are not beasts outside of common reason, then, but a new version of the outsider, undeveloped in their failure to use common money. Here the common values are more obviously conventional rather than natural. Money and other symbols of wealth, Locke explains elsewhere, "are none of Natures Goods, they have but a Phantastical imaginary value: Nature has put no such upon

---

[47] *The Problem of Slavery*, 119-20.

them" (184). The waste landers may have their "Wampompeke," but they have not joined the communal imaginings of "European silver money," with its specific codes of property, exchange value, and development.[48] Hence "*great Tracts of Ground . . . lie waste*, and are more than the People, who dwell on it, do, or can make use of, and so still lie in common" (45).

Waste land is common land, according to this logic; and it awaits the virtuous energy of European developers, who may find themselves killing, enslaving, and philosophizing in the interests of development. But earlier in his discussion of property Locke uses "common" with a different inflection: " 'Tis very clear, that God, as King *David* says, *Psal.* cxv.16 *has given the Earth to the Children of Men*, given it to Mankind in common" (25). Here "common" implies a community of all humans, with no exclusions. Tully looks at this passage and this version of community to articulate his anti-capitalist Locke. In such a community, people live as small-holders, tenants in common under God, in an egalitarian golden age.

But Tully's Locke is just one of many available to the shapers of intellectual history. The interesting trail left by "common" shows how his justification of slavery can lead back to his abhorrence of it. Perhaps one useful message to draw from all of this would be a caution against totalizing interpretations. Interpreters who wish to choose one of the three approaches—or finally to uphold or subvert a body of liberal theory—are apt to find what they look for. The same might be said of an analysis such as this one, which expects indeterminacy and ends up producing a variety of competing claims to truth. Such an analysis, whatever its inherent limitations, can help to show how Locke has written himself into the institutions of both slavery and abolition. His treatises, essays, secretarial records, and constitutions are sufficient to place him but insufficient to confine him in either camp. Locke has built in too many confusions of theory and practice, too many defenses against either being caught in the act or missing the boat. It may also be helpful to remember, at this point, that Locke wrote some letters in code and

---

[48] Herman Lebovics has observed that Locke's "ethnographic reading proved a great aid" to his theory here, as it taught him "that Wampompeke was used in ceremonial situations not primarily as a means of commercial exchange ('common Money') in the sense that coins of precious metals were in Europe." See "The Uses of America in Locke's *Second Treatise of Government*," *JHI*, 47 (1986), 578. Selinger, on the other hand, is inclined to belittle Locke's discussion of common money as a convenience. Locke's knowledge of Wampompeke, however accurate, would not strengthen what Seliger considers an "inane" defense of colonization. Seliger also points to a hint of contradiction in the argument. Locke justifies annexation on the grounds that American natives do not recognize common money; but he also implies, in *Second Treatise* 184, that they have now begun to do so: they "formerly" knew nothing of European silver money (*Liberal Politics*, 117).

invisible ink, and that he anxiously refused, until on his death bed, to identify himself as the author of the *Two Treatises*. If one were tempted to improve on this valuable but frustrating message and to distinguish one approach as most useful, it would probably be a modified version of the third or integral group. The first two approaches cannot be refuted conclusively, but they tend to imply too simple a distinction between "disinterested" theory and the personal interests of John Locke. Locke's investments, friendships, and quirks of personality (such as his secretiveness, or his tenacious care with money), to the extent we can determine them, should neither be dismissed as irrelevant nor elevated above theory to a domain of privileged causes. Locke's work with slavery consists of theory interwoven with practice. It would be misleading, however, to assume that the resulting "integrated" texts should cohere under the authority of one resolute purpose or value. The integral approach will be helpful only to the extent that it recognizes within Locke's work a destabilizing competition of values. Underlying Locke's involvement in slavery is a difficult marriage of development and natural rights.

DePauw University.

V

THE USES OF AMERICA IN LOCKE'S
SECOND TREATISE OF GOVERNMENT

By Herman Lebovics

John Locke was the first modern philosopher to discover the New World and to make its existence the major component of a political philosophy.* "In the beginning all the World was America," he wrote in the *Second Treatise of Government*,[1] thereby making that vast undeveloped continent an integral part of Western political philosophy. The pages of that essay are filled with references to the world across the Atlantic, which was in Locke's day just coming under systematic colonialization and settlement.[2]

Locke's interest in the New World extended beyond the philosophical discussion of the *Second Treatise*. He avidly collected and devoured books of great voyages and of explorations. Through his patron Anthony Ashley Cooper, the First Earl of Shaftesbury, he became proprietor of thousands of acres of undeveloped land in the province of Carolina as well as a member of a number of companies created to profit from the overseas possessions. He served on governmental bodies instituted to oversee the colonial empire. A significant portion of his income came to him from his work as a colonial civil servant and from his investments in the colonies. Locke's life was intimately tied up with America, the West Indies, and India. And so was his thought.

It is the thesis of this essay that as a thinker, Locke employed the vast unexploited resources of the New World to supply the key premise which lay at the foundation of the argument of his political philosophy. In his *Second Treatise* he summoned up the New World to validate the

* Knowledgeable individuals in various fields helped me pursue the ideas in this paper across dangerous disciplinary frontiers. I wish to thank especially Michael Zweig, Karl Bottigheimer, Bernard Semmel, Sidney Gelber, Hal Benenson, and Dick Howard for their ideas and criticism.

[1] Peter Laslett, *Locke's Two Treatises of Government: A Critical Edition with Introduction and Notes* (2nd ed.; Cambridge, 1970), 319. Hereafter cited as *Two Treatises*. Peter Laslett and John Harrison, *The Library of John Locke* (Oxford, 1965), hereafter cited as *Locke's Library*. The standard biography remains Maurice Cranston, *John Locke: A Biography* (New York, 1957); cf. 153-54.

[2] See the first volumes in Immanuel Wallerstein's series on the world system, *The Modern World-System*, I, *Capitalist Agriculture and the Origins of the World-Economy in the Sixteenth Century* (New York, 1974), esp. 346-57, and II, *Mercantilism and the Consolidation of the European World-Economy, 1600-1750* (New York, 1980). In general the World-System school has not pursued the intellectual aspects of the questions it raises. Resting on a world-system analysis but attempting to take the perspective of the "discovered" peoples is Eric R. Wolf, *Europe and the People without History* (Berkeley, 1982), esp. 3-23, 158-94.

society emerging in the old. He was the first philosopher of the emergent world system.

Taking up Quentin Skinner's welcome challenge, if not the Skinnerian method, this essay will pursue "the possibility of a dialogue between philosophical discussion and historical evidence."[3] It will first outline Locke's justifications for the existence of private property as he put them forth in his *Second Treatise of Government.* It will then demonstrate the logical inadequacy of these arguments as well as their irrelevance to English society both at the moment of the composition of the *Treatise* and that of its publication. Finally, it will extract the subtle argument Locke wove into the discussion of the *Second Treatise,* an argument depending upon the existence of land for the taking in the New World. By uncovering his unstated assumption of the availability of infinite resources, we may transcend both the factual and logical weaknesses which a historically naive reading of his text reveals and rightly adjudge Locke to be the wise organic intellectual both of the seventeenth-century British elite and of future generations of the British ruling classes.

Locke's explanation of the origins of the commonwealth and of private property in his *Second Treatise of Government* is so full of sweet reasonableness that finding fault with it borders on churlishness. And yet Locke's argument is vulnerable. Like his predecessors Grotius, Pufendorf, and Hobbes, he started his analysis of human society from the notion that mankind once lived in a state of nature: "'Tis often asked as a mighty Objection, where are, or ever were, there any Men in such a State of Nature?"[4] Unlike other thinkers who began their discussions of the origins of society by positing a state of nature, Locke granted historical, and indeed current, reality to that state. He offered as evidence of his claim two examples from contemporary life. To this day, he argued, nations and therefore their rulers dwell in a state of nature one with another. Moreover, "The Promises and Bargains for Truck, etc. between the two Men in the Desert island mentioned by Garcilasso De la Vega, in his

---

[3] See Quentin Skinner's "Meaning and Understanding in the History of Ideas," *History and Theory,* 8 (1969), 3-53. The methodological premise of Neal Wood's essay, *The Politics of Locke's Philosophy: A Social Study of "An Essay Concerning Human Understanding"* (Berkeley, 1983), offers good guidance: "Dehistoricizing a philosophic classic depoliticizes and dehumanizes it, separating it from any genuine role in the life and conflict of the age and artificially and mechanically divorcing thought from action" (7). Of equal importance is Wood, *John Locke and Agrarian Capitalism* (Berkeley, 1984), which takes us part of the way by seeing Locke as a theorist of early agrarian capitalism (14).

[4] *Two Treatises,* 294. With the important exceptions of Neal Wood and Richard Ashcraft, most recent reinterpretations of Locke's political philosophy have concentrated on refuting the reading in C. B. Macpherson, *The Political Theory of Possessive Individualism: Hobbes to Locke* (Oxford, 1962), of Locke's Chapter V, "Of Property," of the *Second Treatise,* and have rather seen Locke as a less modern (i.e. non-capitalist) thinker than does Macpherson (cf. below, notes 8-10).

History of Peru, or between a Swiss and an Indian, in the Woods of America are binding to them, though they are perfectly in a State of Nature, in reference to one another."[5]

According to Locke both "natural Reason which tells us that Men, being once born, have a right to their Preservation," and revelation, which gives us an account of God's giving "the Earth to the Children of Men, giv[ing] it to Mankind in common," substantiate an original state of common ownership of the things of this earth.[6] But the same God who "hath given the World to Men in common, hath also given them reason to make use of it to the best advantage of Life, and convenience." And yet to give the earth to all mankind and not provide for its appropriation and undisputed use by any particular man would be unreasonable on God's part, and Locke's God was an especially reasonable—one might say—an accommodating, Enlightenment personage. Here too at a key point in his argument Locke took his evidence from the New World: "The Fruit or Venison, which nourishes the wild Indian, who knows no Inclosure, and is still a Tenant in common, must be his, and so his, i.e. a part of him, that another can no longer have any right to it, before it can do him any good for the support of his Life."[7]

Thence, Locke could offer his famous formulation that, if "the Earth, and all inferior Creatures be common to all Men, [and] yet every Man has a Property in his own Person . . . ," it followed that "whatsoever that he removes out of the state that Nature hath provided, and left it in, he hath mixed his Labour with, and joyned to it something that is his own, and thereby makes it his property."[8]

Two important observations are in order here. First, this act did not require the common consent of the rest of mankind, for we would have starved long ago had we been obliged to await this sanction upon our survival.[9] Second, Locke did not differentiate between our own labor and

---

[5] *Two Treatises*, 295.

[6] *Ibid.*, 303-04. See further Laslett's Introduction, in *Two Treatises*, 100.

[7] *Ibid.*, 305.

[8] *Ibid.*, 306. Johannes Rohbeck, "Property and Labour in the Social Philosophy of John Locke," *History of European Ideas*, 5 (1984), 65-77. Karl Olivecrona's attempts to place Locke in a Roman law tradition is, I think, incorrect for a man writing in a land of common law and common law definitions of property. See his "Das Meinige nach der Naturrechtslehre," *Archiv für Rechts- und Sozialphilosophie*, 59 (1973), 197ff; "Locke's Theory of Appropriation," *Philosophical Quarterly*, 24 (1974), 220, 226; "Appropriation in the State of Nature: Locke on the Origin of Property," *Journal of the History of Ideas*, 35 (1974), 211, 218, 227; "The Term 'Property' in Locke's Two Treatises of Government," *Archiv für Rechts- und Sozialphilosophie*, 61 (1975), 110-14.

[9] *Ibid.*, 306-08. Both Grotius and Pufendorf grounded the transition from common ownership to private property on common consent because they desired to justify government by consent. See Martin Seliger, *The Liberal Politics of John Locke* (New York, 1969) 181 and 187ff. Locke carefully avoided using this argument from common consent, however, as Robert Filmer, the target of the attack on the *First Treatise*, had hit home

that of our living chattels and employees: "Thus the Grass my Horse has bit; the Turfs my Servant has cut; and the Ore I have digg'd in any place where I have a right to them in common with others, becomes my Property, without the assignation or consent of any body."[10] Despite his location of its origins in the state of nature, Locke wrote about property in what was for the seventeenth century the most modern of contexts, namely, property as capital: "my Horse," as embodied in hired labor: "my Servant," and as resources: "the Ore I have digg'd."

At this juncture of the argument, Locke again turned to the New World with evidence of the practice of people still in the state of nature. "This Law of reason," he explained, "makes the Deer, that Indian's who hath killed it; 'tis allowed to be his goods who hath bestowed his labour upon it, though before, it was the common right of every one." And then to connect the life of the primitive Indian with that of the contemporary Englishman, and thus the old world with the new, he added that "amongst those who are counted the Civiliz'd part of Mankind . . . this original Law of Nature for the beginning of Property, in what was before common, still takes place" in respect to the fruits of the efforts of fishermen and hunters.[11]

Why does Locke draw his examples almost indifferently at one moment from the most modern capitalist society and at the next moment from the life of the first inhabitants of America? Was he employing what would become the not uncommon Enlightenment strategy of framing arguments to speak of all of humankind, to articulate a natural law of society as true in the time of Adam and Eve as now; as valid for English

---

in his critique of Grotius with the observation that if private property were secured by the consent of mankind, then the withdrawal of that consent by individuals or groups would dissolve all government and throw mankind back to a state of nature. On this point see further James Daly, *Sir Robert Filmer and English Political Thought* (Toronto, 1979), 24, 90, 158-59. Daly finds the argument from appropriation used contemporaneously in the anti-Filmer polemic, *Patriarchia non Monarcha* (1681), by Locke's good friend James Tyrrell.

[10] *Two Treatises*, 307. Both James Tully, *A Discourse on Property: John Locke and his Adversaries* (Cambridge, 1980), 139, and Keith Tribe, *Land, Labour, and Economic Discourse* (London, 1978), 49-50, reject a reading of this passage (Macpherson's, e.g.), which understands the servant to have "sold" his labor to the master. Tully argues "The turf-cutter, who is Locke's servant, does not and cannot alienate his labor activity"; Tribe seeks to distinguish the servant's labor from that of Locke's horse as evidence that Locke meant to analyze the two efforts differently (50-51). Historically the Tully-Tribe reading leaves the servant with no reason to agree either to cut or not to cut the turf; he appears merely to make a decision to enter a contract to perform a service or not. It is not clear how he decides. It is however true that Locke's writing on labor gains ideological force by straddling the ambiguity of labor seen as a commodity and labor as activity. On this point—but situating the argument in a dense historical context—see the excellent article by E. J. Hundert, "The Making of *Homo Faber*: John Locke Between Ideology and History," *Journal of the History of Ideas*, 33 (1972), 3-22.

[11] *Two Treatises*, 307.

landowners, merchants, and their employees as for the natives of Jamaica, and the Carolinas? Certainly this must have been one of his motives, but only one. However, we must see where his doctrine of the origins and rights of property led him before we are in a position to assess the full import of Locke's pervasive exoticism. To this end, we must now turn to the limits which Locke set—and then overcame—to the appropriation of the possessions of God's earth.

Locke argued that the same divinely-given law of nature which allows us to own things necessary for our survival by mixing our labor with them "does also bound [the use of] that Property too." We are given the things of this earth to enjoy "as much as anyone can make use of to any advantage of life before it spoils." But, he wrote empathetically, "Nothing was made by God for Man to spoil or destroy." Moreover, the new owner of land, for example, cannot claim all for himself; there must remain "enough, and as good," with which others may mix their labor.[12] Voicing moral qualms of this sort seems scarcely the work of a great apologist for the economically most rapacious part of the population of the seventeenth century. Peter Laslett has correctly questioned whether such moral scruples would have deterred a man who was simply "the spokesman of a rising class, the middle class, the capitalists, the bourgeoisie."[13] As we shall see, Locke was both much more and much less than what those simple recipe-words describe.

He did need to provide a means for relaxing these stern Calvinist injunctions not to waste or misuse in order to preserve the principle of equal access to resources, but the realities of seventeenth-century English commercial society were not so easily overcome. The commercial society of the day was a reality which no sensible man could gainsay. But the moral law governing property was also still alive in the popular spirit; a political thinker of the age took a grave risk to ignore it.

The means Locke hit upon was, in his quaint phrase, "a little piece of yellow metal." He argued:

it is plain that Men have agreed to disproportionate and unequal Possession of the Earth, they have *by a tacit and voluntary consent* found out a way, how a man may fairly possess more land than he himself can use the product of, by receiving in exchange for the overplus, Gold and Silver, which may be hoarded

---

[12] *Ibid.*, 308-09. "But if they [property acquired in an early primitive sometimes he called "in the beginning"] perished, in his Possession, without their due use; if the Fruits rotted, or if the Venison putrified before he could spend it, he offended against the common Law of Nature. . . ."

[13] Laslett, Introduction to the *Two Treatises*, 43, and E. J. Hundert, "Market Society and Meaning in Locke's Political Philosophy," *Journal of the History of Philosophy*, 15 (1977), 33-44.

up without injury to any one, these metalls not spoileing or decaying in the hands of the possessor.[14]

Although it may strike some that the suspension of injunctions grounded in natural law by the provision of a few gold and silver coins is an unseemly, not to say inelegant, solution to a philosophical problem—on the order of Descartes's use of the pineal gland to solve the mind-body problem he had created for himself—this infelicity is not the chief problem with Locke's argument. Rather, his greatest difficulties grew from his uses of *consent*, that most delicate and most explosive issue of seventeenth-century political life and political philosophy.

Locke was intent on basing his doctrine of the right to property on a notion of property-for-survival, a version of a labor theory of value. He eschewed the positions taken by both Grotius and Pufendorf—whose analyses of the origins of property he knew well—for they based the right of property on the concurrence of the rest of mankind. And throughout the *Second Treatise* he held fast to his refusal to rest the right of exclusive ownership on the consent of one's fellows.[15] How then could he argue that the great act of suspending the limits on the acquisition of possessions set by a God-given natural law might be accomplished by "a tacit and voluntary consent" of men in society?[16] How could a law of nature be suspended by human agreement? If this were so, men could compact—if they could fashion a majority—to make of the commonwealth a democracy of the rabble and then vote to remove property from the propertied. Such was neither an idle nor an unheard-of fear. The issue of who might properly and safely participate in the political leadership of the nation had not been laid to rest in the course of the Revolution, and Locke's intent on resolving just this issue in no small

---

[14] Locke, *Two Treatises*, 311-12, 319-20, italics mine. See also Richard Ashcraft's valuable essay, "The *Two Treatises* and the Exclusion Crisis: The Problem of Lockean Political Theory as Bourgeois Ideology," in *John Locke, Papers read at a Clark Library Seminar, 10 December, 1977* (Los Angeles, 1980), 62-63.

[15] There is but one compact for the creation of property; Locke has no need for a two-stage theory of property, one for the first ages of the world and one for life in a commonwealth, as Tully suggests he does. All the important agreements—including that of using money—are made in the state of nature. In this essay I employ the concept of "consent" to mean the agreement of mankind to use money. For its use in his theory of government see John Dunn, "Consent in the Political Theory of John Locke, *The Historical Journal*, 10 (1967), 153-182 and his *The Political Thought of John Locke* (Cambridge, 1969), 128ff.

[16] In one passage he wrote that "Gold, Silver, and Diamonds [were] things which Fancy or Agreement hath put the Value on, more then real Use, and the necessary Support of Life" (*Second Treatise*, 318), thereby giving evidence of his awareness of the dimension of human arbitrariness and even of caprice in the selection of the medium which is to absolve us of our obligations under Natural Law. On this illogicality see Karen Iversen Vaughan, *John Locke: Economist and Social Scientist* (Chicago, 1980), 92-93.

degree determined the strategies of argument he employed in the *Two Treatises*.[17]

We are used to encountering these sorts of blatant inconsistencies in Locke. That all our ideas originate in experience, as he asserted in the *Essay Concerning Human Understanding*—except the idea of God, whose existence we can deduce—is perhaps the most famous.[18] We have been accustomed to forgiving Locke his philosophical errors because his sense of reality, his metaphysical and political savvy, was so keen. We honor him in the history of philosophy as the outstanding English representative of Cartesian *bon sens*, unlike his empiricist predecessor Hobbes, whose rigor led him to frame a logic of tyranny, or his heir Bishop Berkeley, whose unrelenting empiricism required him to commend our experienced ideas to God's mind when they were not being thought by us.

However, even if we allowed Locke his coin trick as the way individuals might own more than they could cultivate, store, or consume, we would have to forgive him further lapses of logic. If Locke's main concern had been purely the divine and human abhorrence of spoilage and waste, he did not have to provide a money economy—at least not from the point of view of philosophical argumentation—to avoid this violation of natural law. Barter was practiced by many of the peoples about whom Locke read in his books of voyages and travel. Moreover, one can store valuable things available in excess of needs in many forms other than gold and silver coins. Ingots of iron, carved stones, elegant

[17] Whether we locate the center of gravity of the *Two Treatises* in the succession crisis and the years 1679-1680 as Laslett persuasively argues (Laslett, *Two Treatises*, Introduction, 65), or connect them to the Glorious Revolution and 1690, the date of their anonymous publication, the question of who was to rule the commonwealth, and by what right, pervades Locke's essays. In this regard I must mark my distance from the work of Keith Tribe, *Land, Labour, and Economic Discourse*. His study, which touches on Locke (46-51), attempts a structuralist reading of the economic theorizing and theorists of the epoch. Thus neither history nor authorship matter: "[W]hile this book deals with archaic discursive forms, it cannot be said that it is historical. . . . The use of authors and texts in this book is no more than a bibliographical device, enabling the reader to locate the terms and form of discussion as it proceeds" (159-60). This method leads Tribe to conclude that Hobbes and Locke were involved in a discourse which "turn[ed] obstinately on a patriarchal form of organization that had been the currency of 'civil society' since the time of Plato" (51), and thereby to flatten history to an unchanging and predictable set of problems. A similarly overly abstract and ahistorical approach to the history of ideas, also structuralist in basis, is that of the more nuanced, James Tully, *A Discourse on Property*, e.g. 153. See the elaborate critique in Wood, *Locke and Agrarian Capitalism*, 72-92.

[18] Cf. his *Essay Concerning Human Understanding*, ed. Peter H. Nidditch (Oxford, 1979), 618-30. In Book II, Chapter I (104), Locke wrote: "Whence has [the mind] all the materials of Reason and Knowledge? To this I answer, in one word, From Experience: In that, all our Knowledge is founded; and from that it ultimately derives it self." In Book IV, Chapter XI (630), he wrote, "The Knowledge of our own Being, we have by intuition. The Existence of GOD, Reason clearly makes known to us. . . ."

clothing, and utensils have all been employed by various peoples to store unneeded wealth; nor did these repositories of social surplus serve as means of exchange in any modern sense. To display their opulence and thus gain great status, individuals, or more usually families, in certain New World cultures, e.g., the sophisticated native inhabitants of the Northwest Coast of North America, held great ceremonies, which amazed European visitors because of the splendor and volume of treasure given away or consumed. Naturally, competing families had to reciprocate, and thereby exchange of goods and services was facilitated among a scattered and warlike people. More than most contemporaries, Locke knew the many ways other cultures solved their version of the spoilage and exchange problem.

A more important point is that, even if we were to take Locke's point that accumulated coins liberate us from our moral qualms about keeping barnsful of wheat and root cellars overflowing with rotting crops, we would not thereby be freed from the other limit imposed upon us by natural law. The storage of wealth in the form of money does not leave "enough, and as good" so that others might live. Locke's theory of property violates this second limit set by a natural law the validity of which Locke never questioned or claimed suspended.

Was Locke then simply a hopelessly muddled ideologue of the new breed of men of wealth like his patron and investment advisor Shaftesbury? The answer, I believe, is no. In his justification for private property, and for differences in wealth, Locke made a philosophical move which in its seeming illogicality puts in relief the substance of his lasting contribution to Western political thought.

The problem lies with Locke's paradox of property. After the experience of civil war followed by continuing conflict over authority in the state, Locke's proposal of property as the basis of public order in the commonwealth was at once an astute insight into the deeper meaning of the troubles of his century and prescient advice for future rulers and statesmen charged with rendering societies immune to periodic outbreaks of revolutionary fevers. Writing of the limits upon the Supreme Power in the commonwealth, the doctor turned policy advisor prescribed the cure for popular revolution:

For the preservation of Property being the end of Government, and that for which Men enter into Society, *it necessarily supposes and requires, that the People should have Property*, without which they must be suppos'd to lose that by entring into Society, which was the end for which they entered into it. . . .[19]

The social and economic setting in which Locke wrote the *Second Treatise*—a conjunction of intensified development of the nation's land, now overwhelmingly in the hands of private owners, with a large landless

[19] *Two Treatises*, 378, italics mine.

population of poorly-paid laborers and masterless men—renders paradoxical a theory of property whereby one simply mixed labor with unused land and became the owner of the land and a person presumably devoted to the continuing good order of the realm. For in late seventeenth century England what meaning could be attached to the injunction (which, we must recall, Locke neither lifted nor found means of satisfying) that we are obliged to leave "enough, and as good" for others? In the sense in which he understood the word not many people possessed "property," i.e., land in freehold, in Locke's day.[20] Locke was not a naive thinker. Moreover, neither his public service nor his business connections could have left him unmindful of the absolute shortage of land in England in his own day.

But there was land, quite enough and very good, and in the New World. Locke, better than most men in public life of late seventeenth-century England, knew this too. It must be emphasized that in his own day he was credited with being one of the most knowledgeable of Englishmen about the colonial world. He came by this knowledge in several ways.

Locke was tied to this New World by the three most powerfully binding forces of his life. First, his imagination was excited by the poorly-mapped and little known places across the seas. He loved to read books of travel, geography, and explorations. By their perusal he gained an extensive knowledge of what was known of the new overseas lands coming into the European consciousness.[21]

[20] Gregory King, *Natural and Political Observations and Conclusions upon the State and Condition of England, 1696* (London, 1896), sections reproduced in C. B. Macpherson, *Political Theory of Possessive Individualism*, Appendix, 279. D. C. Coleman, "Labour in the English Economy of the Seventeenth Century," *Economic History Review*, 2nd series, 8 (1955), 280-95, esp. 283. H. J. Habbakkuk, "English Landownership, 1680-1740," *Economic History Review*, 10 (1940), 4. Robert Brenner, "Agrarian Class Structure and Economic Development in Pre-Industrial Europe," *Past and Present*, no. 70 (1976), 63. Professor Brenner's article ignited a great scholarly debate (seven comments/attacks and Brenner's long Rejoinder) which raged in the pages of *Past and Present*, nos. 78 (Feb., 1978), 79 (May, 1978), 80 (Aug., 1978), 85 (Nov., 1979), and 97 (Nov., 1982). E. S. De Beer "Introduction to the *Correspondence of John Locke*" (8 vols.; London, 1976-), I, xxxii, and n. 1; Wood, *The Politics of Locke's Philosophy*, 19, 26; as well as his *Locke and Agrarian Capitalism*, 30. J. P. Cooper, "The Social Distribution of Land and Men in England, 1436-1700," *Economic History* Review, 2nd series, 20 (1967), 419-37. F. M. L. Thompson, "The Social Distribution of Landed Property in England since the Sixteenth Century, *Economic History Review*, 2nd series, 19 (1966), 505-17. See also E. L. Jones, "Agriculture and Economic Growth in England, 1660-1750: Agricultural Change," in E. L. Jones (ed.), *Agriculture and Economic Growth in England, 1650-1815* (London, 1967), 152ff. Joyce Oldham Appleby, *Economic Thought and Ideology in Seventeenth Century England* (Princeton, 1978), 153.

[21] Peter Laslett, "John Locke and his Books," introductory essay in Harrison and Laslett, *Locke's Library*, 4, 15-18, 22-25, 28-29. See further Cranston, 463; Wood, *The Politics of Locke's Philosophy*, 31-32. In the part of his library on which we have infor-

Second, his economic well-being depended in part on his investments in various colonial ventures. The patronage of Shaftesbury secured him the office of Secretary to the Lords Proprietors of Carolina.[22] His friend put him onto investments with the Bahamas Adventurers (another undertaking of the Lords Proprietors), Richard Thompson's Company, The Royal Africa Company, and the East India Company.[23] On the eve of his retirement perhaps half of his living was drawn from these investments.[24]

Third, his career in public service brought him his practical knowledge of colonial matters and much of the rest of his income. Locke spent his two terms in state service helping to fashion and direct imperial colonial policy. From 1673 to 1675, while he served the Lords Proprietors of Carolina, he obtained, through Shaftesbury, a similar post with the Council of Trade and Plantations.[25] In the latter year the Earl of Danby, the new minister of Charles II and an enemy of Shaftesbury, dissolved the Council. Only some years after the Glorious Revolution and Locke's return from the continent was it recreated. From 1696 to his retirement in 1700 he served on its successor which William III had had reconstituted as the Board of Trade.[26]

---

mation—perhaps half his books—he had more titles on medicine, his first profession (some 11.1%), on law and politics (10.7%), and Greek and Latin classics (10.1%). But books of religion and theology, comprising 23.8% of the Oxford collection, were the largest single category. Cf. Appleby, 220ff.; Cranston, 396; Peter Laslett, "John Locke, The Great Recoinage, and the Origins of the Board of Trade, 1695-1698," in John W. Yolton (ed.), *John Locke: Problems and Perspectives, A Collection of Essays* (Cambridge, 1969), 137ff. The editors of *The Works of Locke* include a Preface written by Locke for the four-volume anthology of his friend Awnsham Churchill's *Collection of Voyages* (London, 1704). The Preface, is a long and careful catalogue-style narrative of important voyages and discoveries. In this text Locke supplied elaborately detailed information about useful natural products and trade items, as well as geographical and navigational information. He offered future explorers advice about precautions to take as they undertook new ventures and proposed as yet unexplored regions for future efforts. *The Works of John Locke* (10 vols.; London, 1923), X, 358-511. See further in the *Works*, X, 511-64, his essay "A Catalogue and Character of Most Books of Voyages and Travels," which lists books on voyages and explorations in Latin, Italian, French, Spanish, and English, with detailed critiques of the quality, credibility, and utility of each.

[22] E. S. De Beer (ed.), *The Correspondence of John Locke*, I, xxxii and n. 1.

[23] Wood, *The Politics of Locke's Philosophy*, 26. At Shaftesbury's suggestion, for example, Locke put up £200 the Bahamas Adventurers just before he took up his post as Secretary to the Council of Trade and Plantations. He sold out at a profit. Cranston, 155-56.

[24] Cranston, 153-54.

[25] *Ibid.*, 404ff.

[26] Laslett, *John Locke: Problems and Perspectives*, 137ff. A bureaucratic struggle about minor administrative questions touching on the Virginia plantation put Locke on the side of greater self-rule for the colony. One of Locke's concerns at his new post was the proper relation of the Irish to the English economy. The role of Ireland in Locke's thought is discussed in Cranston, 408-09, Laslett, *ibid.*, 159-60, Hugh Kearney, "The Political

Thus both theoretical need and practical experience converged to point Locke towards the solution of his problem. If in the beginning the whole world was America, Locke understood that in the late seventeenth century a great part of it still remained in the circumstances he defined as the state of nature. In the *Second Treatise* he wrote of "the first Ages of the World, when Men were more in danger to be lost, by wandering from their Company, in the then vast Wilderness of the Earth, than to be straitned from want of room to plant in."[27] But such vastness still existed, for he continued:

And the same measure may be allowed still, without prejudice to any body, as full as the World seems. For supposing a Man, or Family, in the state they were, at first peopling of the World by the Children of Adam, or Noah; let him plant in some in-land, vacant places of America, we shall find that the Possessions he could make himself upon the measures we have given, would not be very large, nor, *even to this day*, prejudice the rest of Mankind, or give them reason to complain, or think themselves injured by this Man's Incroachment, though the race of Men have now spread themselves to all corners of the World, and do infinitely exceed the small number (which) was at the beginning.[28]

Locke here was offering the New World, specifically the colonial settlements of America, as validation of his sociopolitical philosophy. For "even to this day" one could go there, and taking neither too much nor denying another his share, mix one's labor with the meadows and forests to join the ranks of England's proprietors. If one possessed neither adequate land nor gold and silver money in England—as were the circumstances of the vast majority of the nation—Locke offered America as the key which would give access to participation in the life of the commonwealth. But what of the aboriginal inhabitants of these lands, the Indians, for example; were they not the owners of the land even before the first vessel had embarked from Europe?

Locke offered two arguments for why European settlers had the right to take possession of these "new" lands. First, although he granted that indeed God had given the world to men in common, he reminded the reader that "he gave it them for their benefit, and the greatest Conveniences of Life they were capable to draw from it." Therefore, "it cannot be supposed he meant it should remain common and uncultivated. He gave it to the use of the Industrious and Rational, (and Labour was his title to it)."[29] Accordingly, to obtain the right to a part of nature a person must not simply mix his labor with it, he is obliged to maximize the

---

Background to English Mercantilism, 1695-1700," *Economic History Review*, 12 (1959). See in the *Correspondence* the letters between Locke and his Irish admirer William Molyneux.

[27] *Two Treatises*, 310-11.
[28] *Ibid.*, italics mine.
[29] *Ibid.*, 309.

productivity of the effort. As he wrote, "If either the Grass of his Inclosure rotted on the Ground, or the Fruit of his planting perished without gathering, and laying up, this part of the Earth, notwithstanding his Inclosure, was still to be looked on as Waste, and might be the Possession of any other."[30] With this philosophical *tour de force* Locke managed with the same argument both to justify the dispossession of the ancestral lands of the Indians in distant America and the ongoing enclosure of the commons once set aside by custom for the use of the peasants of the English countryside.

Locke's double-duty argument gives us further encouragement to accept the correctness of reading him as a great philosopher of the developing world system which linked the old world with the new with ties of domination and subordination. Clearly, by both the prime measure—that of human energy expended to modify nature—and, for Locke, the necessary correlative—that of the maximization of production—most Native Americans failed to meet the principal qualifications for owning a part of America.

Second, Europeans were warranted to displace the original inhabitants of Europe's overseas colonies because the natives of these regions did not use money as a means of exchange. Locke reasoned,

There are still great Tracts of Ground to be found, which (the Inhabitants thereof not having joyned with the rest of Mankind, in the consent of the Use of their common Money) lie waste, and are more than the people, who dwell on it, do, or can make use of, and so still lie in common.[31]

Locke granted that certain Indians used artifacts known as Wampompeke (wampum), which he understood to perform some of the functions of money. But here his ethnographic reading proved a great aid to the philosophy of the world system. He understood that Wampompeke was used in ceremonial situations not primarily as a means of commercial exchange ("common Money") in the sense that coins of precious metals were in Europe. Accordingly, the aboriginal inhabitants of America on this count, too, continued in the state of nature. The lands that the Amerindians hunted and even farmed were not theirs as the rents from Locke's estate in Somerset were his even while he lived in Oxford, or London, or in continental exile.[32]

[30] *Ibid.*, 310, 313.

[31] *Ibid.*, 317.

[32] *Ibid.*, 409. See further Martin Seliger, *The Liberal Politics of John Locke* (New York, Washington, 1969), 114-18. The European image of the native Americans is ably dissected in Robert F. Berkhofer, Jr., *The White Man's Indian: Images of the American Indian from Columbus to the Present* (New York, 1978), esp. Part One and 75. On the sacred significance the Algonkian attributed to wampum and its transformation into a money-like trade item, see Ruth M. Underhill, *Red Man's America* (rev. ed.; Chicago, London, 1975), 67-69. In 1725 the Rev. John Bulkley published a preface to Roger

Locke, even more than we have hitherto realized, captured the essence of his age in his treatment of the relation of property, colonial expansion, and good government. Property as the criterion for participation in the political life of the country, property as a guarantee of conservative demeanor, the *promise* of property as an inducement for social tranquility—these were the key functions Locke assigned to the ownership of resources in the *Second Treatise.* One had but to mix one's labor with the bounty of God's nature to create this property. Locke's political writings—however much aimed at contemporary issues—sought to lay a sound foundation for a theory of government which would both satisfy the elite and placate the governed of the day, and beyond this hold the loyalties of future generations.[33]

Commentators have noted the curious ambiguity of Locke's political writings which permitted him to justify the actions of rapacious and rebellious men of wealth of his and later ages and at the same time hold forth a promise of unprecedented political participation for the many.[34] This ambiguity works in a number of ways. Readers of the *Second Treatise* quickly note the slippage between "property" and "life, liberty, and Property," as if they were the same concept. But by so tying life and liberty to property, he excluded the vast bulk of the people from government. Again, in his *Letters Concerning Toleration* Locke described the government which terminated the state of nature as one which should see to "the peace, riches, and public commodities of the whole people,"[35]

Wolcott's *Poetical Meditations* at New London, Connecticut. In this piece (see esp. xiiff.) he invoked the authority of Mr. Locke to justify the claim that New England colonists might hold land without possessing a title granted by the appropriate Indians. In the Rev. Mr. Bulkley's view the Indian claims on land admittedly justified by virtue of first occupancy had to yield to the superior claims to the same land conferred by the settlers' labor. See further on Locke and the Indians of America, John Dunn, "The Politics of Locke in England and America in the Eighteenth Century," in Yolton, *John Locke: Problems and Perspectives,* 71-72 and *passim,* and for the implications of equating America with an earlier primitive stage of Old World life, Ronald Meek, " 'In the Beginning all the World was *American,*' " *Social Science and the Ignoble Savage* (Cambridge, 1978), ch. 2.

[33] On the slight immediate impact of the *Two Treatises,* see Martyn P. Thompson, "The Reception of Locke's *Two Treatise of Government,* 1690-1705," in *Political Studies,* 24 (1976), 184-91. On Locke's standing among contemporaries see also the nuanced discussion in John Dunn's essay in Yolton, *John Locke: Problems and Perspectives,* 45ff. However, by the eighteenth century Locke had taken his familiar, and altogether appropriate, place as England's greatest political philosopher. J. G. A. Pocock in his *Machiavellian Moment: Florentine Political Thought and the Atlantic Republican Tradition* (Princeton, 1975), 423-24, dismisses Locke's political writings as of little importance to the great movement of civic humanism he argues is the key to the Augustan age.

[34] E.g., Dunn, *ibid.,* 53.

[35] *Letters Concerning Toleration* (London, 1905), 178. See this more democratic reading, or one at least sympathetic to Irish nationalist claims, in Paschal Larkin, *Property*

and not one, as we might expect from knowing the argument of the *Second Treatise*, which catered only to the needs of the property owners. Moreover, no age which had seen both great bands of ideologically-aroused and armed men call to account their king and numbers of newly-monied men find their way to the top could easily accept a political theory which envisioned rule by an absolute monarch or a closed political elite. We may understand Locke's own attack on Sir Robert Filmer's defense of absolute rule in the *First Treatise* as evidence on this point. And yet that coalition of aristocrats and new men with whom Locke moved was not yet prepared to open the door to power so that the strata below them in wealth and eminence might enter.

C. B. Macpherson has proposed a way he believes Locke resolved this ambiguity. In Macpherson's view Locke's doctrine of the right of exclusive possession created by adding one's labor to resources pointed the way both to the modern capitalist notion of private property and, by implication, to a contemporary theory of political participation.[36] However, as we have seen, in terms both of the unresolved tensions of seventeenth-century life and more importantly, of Locke's estimate of future developments, this is no solution at all. There simply did not exist in Locke's England enough unclaimed land, mines, or forests with which a rapidly growing landless majority of the population might mix its labor. As we have seen also, his doctrine of money involved Locke in hopeless muddles and blatant violations of natural law.

In the late nineties when his experiences on the Board of Trade had brought him once more into direct connection with the workings of empire, and perhaps when he had meditated some on the implications of the arguments he had advanced in the *Second Treatise*, he added to his text of the *Second Treatise* the judgment "that the increase of lands and the right imploying of them is the great art of government."[37] Locke's own insight that the solution to his philosophical problem of how to ground a theory of a dynamically stable social order lay just across the Atlantic now stands out in its full, if ominous, clarity. Going well beyond the simplistic social theories of the mercantilism of his day, his political philosophy integrated the reality of colonialism and the beckoning riches of colonial resources into modern political philosophy in a new way. He made the colonial empire a vital bond between Britain's new elite and those they governed. He thereby strengthened the nascent liberalism of British society by building into it the promise of growth, of more for all,

---

in the Eighteenth Century with Special Reference to England and Locke (London, 1930), 64ff.

[36] C. B. Macpherson, "Capitalism and the Changing Concept of Property," in Eugene Kamenka and R. S. Neale (eds.), *Feudalism, Capitalism, and Beyond* (Canberra, 1975), 112-13.

[37] *Two Treatises*, 314-15 and notes to par. 42.

of social peace through empire. Moreover, understanding his idea of empire in this way suggests the direction for a reassessment of those theories of modern imperialism—Lenin's included—which see such expansion as a "last stage," rather than as a constitutive element of the liberal tradition.

In the history of philosophy Locke's use of a whole continent, indeed, several continents, as a *deus ex machina* for his philosophical system, is unprecedented. But then again the violent expansion of the domination of European societies over the rest of the world—a process in its infancy in Locke's day—is also unprecedented. Nearly three hundred years later we can still learn from Locke. For his comprehension of the relation between the old and the new worlds, however imperfect it may have been, has deepened our own understanding of important currents of thought and of their correlative praxis which, from their early modern beginnings, put the most powerful western societies on the road to enhancing their power and buttressing their internal stability by appropriating the labor of the people and resources of distant ancient cultures baptized by the minions of European civilization as a "New World."

SUNY, Stony Brook.

VI

THE AMERICAN DEBATE ON THE NEGRO'S PLACE IN NATURE, 1780–1815

By John C. Greene

Are all human beings of one biological species? This was a momentous question in Jefferson's day. Theologically it bore upon the Christian doctrine of the spiritual unity of mankind in their common descent from Adam. Politically it colored conceptions of the white man's rights and duties with respect to the inhabitants of those regions of the earth which were being subjected to his control. Scientifically it involved the distinction, enormous in the eyes of eighteenth-century naturalists, between a species and a variety. If the various types of human beings were separate species, the task of the natural historian was to classify them according to their specific characters, accepting these as permanent and divinely ordained. But if human races were but varieties of a single species, science must account for their peculiarities by natural causes.

In the United States there were special incentives to the study of these questions. The Americans were themselves a mixture of European peoples undergoing transformation by intermarriage and by exposure to a new physical and social environment. On the frontier they came into conflict with the Indian tribes. In the settled areas, particularly in the South, were the Negroes, an alien race transplanted from Africa and held in bondage to the white man despite the resounding affirmations of the Declaration of Independence. It is not surprising, then, that the current of anthropological speculation ran strong in the United States and that it swirled around the question of the Negro's place in nature.

The most ambitious and best known American treatise on physical anthropology in the period before 1815 was the Reverend Samuel Stanhope Smith's *Essay on the Causes of the Variety of Complexion and Figure in the Human Species,*[1] first published in 1787. Smith was Professor of Moral Philosophy at the College of New Jersey and later became its President. His main concern in this work was to vindicate the Scriptural doctrine of the unity of the human race against objections drawn from the apparent diversity of mankind, in particular those set forth by the Scotch jurist Lord Kames in his *Sketches of the History of Man,* first published in 1774.[2] With respect

[1] Samuel Stanhope Smith, *An Essay on the Causes of the Variety of Complexion and Figure in the Human Species. To Which Are Added, Strictures on Lord Kames's Discourse on the Original Diversity of Mankind* (Philadelphia, 1787). A second, enlarged edition was published at New Brunswick, N. J., in 1810.

[2] Henry Home (Lord Kames), *Sketches of the History of Man* (Edinburgh, 1774). A second enlarged and revised edition was issued in four volumes in 1788.

to the Negro, therefore, he confines himself to showing that the physical peculiarities of this, as of every, human race are the product of two great kinds of natural causes: climate and the state of society. On the subject of climate he echoes the arguments of Buffon, Montesquieu, and others, maintaining the slow and imperceptible modification of the human constitution by heat and cold, the transmissibility of the characteristics thus acquired, and the general correlation of latitude and skin color. He speculates that the complexion in any climate will be changed towards black, in proportion to the degree of heat in the atmosphere, and the quantity of bile in the skin."[3] The hair, he declares, follows the law of the complexion, hence it is not surprising that Negroes born in the United States have longer, straighter, denser hair than those brought directly from Africa, or that their body odor is less powerful. The change wrought in the Negro constitution by the American environment appears most strik-

---

Smith's "Strictures" on this work were appended to both editions of the *Essay*. Kames was a common sense polygenist, theologically heterodox but decidedly conservative in his general view of nature. He had no use for fine-spun distinctions between species and varieties. To him it seemed axiomatic that every kind of creature had been perfectly adapted by the Creator to its peculiar environment and function in nature. He conceded that environment might produce random variations from the original models of nature but denied that it could ever create a new type. Applying these principles to the case of man, he concluded that the various human types found on the earth had been created separately and adapted by their Maker to the regions which they were to inhabit. No other hypothesis, he felt, could account for the racial peculiarities of the Negro and the Indian or explain the tendency of varieties to degenerate when exposed to climates different from their native ones. None other could illustrate so clearly the wisdom of the Creator. As for the Scriptural account of man's descent from a single pair, it could be saved by supposing that the confusion of tongues at the tower of Babel had plunged mankind into barbarism and scattered them far and wide, so that it became necessary for God to alter their makeup so as to adapt them to the variety of conditions in which they found themselves. "Without immediate change of bodily constitution, the builders of Babel could not possibly have subsisted in the burning region of Guinea, or in the frozen region of Lapland." Smith was equally solicitous to uphold the wisdom of the Creator, of course, but found it to consist in man's being given a constitution sufficiently plastic to adapt itself to the whole range of climates on the globe. Lord Kames' reconciliation of sacred and profane history Smith rejected as both disingenuous and unnecessary.

[3] Smith, *op. cit.*, 16. Smith did not discover until later that Blumenbach had advanced a similar theory in 1775 in his *De Generis Varietate Humani Nativa*. He cites Buffon and Montesquieu, however. P. M. Spurlin, *Montesquieu in America 1760–1810* (Louisiana State University Press, 1940), shows that Montesquieu's works were widely read in the United States at this time. In general, however, the writers discussed in the present paper drew more heavily on European naturalists, such as Buffon, Camper, Cuvier, and Charles White, than on Montesquieu.

ingly in domestic slaves, because in their case the influences of civilized society are added to those of the climate. How much more rapidly, then, would the Negro take on the physical characteristics of the white man if he were admitted to the society of his masters.

In Jefferson's *Notes on Virginia* a quite different view of the matter was set forth. There the Negro is represented as inferior to the white man in both body and mind. Negro men, Jefferson asserts, confess the superior beauty of white women by preferring them to black as uniformly as the orang-outang prefers the Negro woman to the female of his own species. If superior beauty is thought worthy of preservation in breeding animals, why should it not be regarded in controlling the intercourse of human beings? In mental endowment, he continues, Negroes lack foresight and imagination; they are equal to the whites in memory but vastly inferior in the powers of reason, more ardent in sexual passion but less delicate. " In general, their existence appears to participate more of sensation than of reflection." [4] Jefferson admits that the Negro slaves' condition of life has not been favorable to the development of their faculties, but he adduces the artistic and intellectual achievements of the Roman slaves and the art and oratory of the Indians as proof that adverse conditions cannot completely suppress natural genius. He thinks that interbreeding with the whites produces a marked physical and mental improvement in the Negro and regards this supposed fact as proof that the Negro's inferiority is grounded in nature as well as in social condition.

The question whether the Negro is a separate species of man, distinct from all others since the day of creation, or merely a variety, "made distinct by time and circumstances," Jefferson leaves open. He is not concerned to corroborate Scripture, nor does he feel that any moral issue hangs on the answer to this problem in natural history. His denunciation of slavery in another passage of the *Notes on Virginia* and his reply in 1809 to the remonstrances of the Abbé Grégoire show that he viewed the question of the Negro's rights as one quite distinct from that of his rank in the scale of being. The real problem from Jefferson's point of view was: how to give the Negro the liberty which is his due without deteriorating the dignity and beauty of human nature by removing obstacles to the intermixture of white and Negro blood. " Among the Romans emancipation required but one effort. The slave, when made free, might mix with, without staining the blood of his master. But with us a second is necessary, unknown

---

[4] Thomas Jefferson, *Notes on the State of Virginia* . . . , in Saul K. Padover, *The Complete Jefferson Containing his Major Writings, Published and Unpublished, except his Letters* (New York, 1943), 662.

to history. When freed, he is to be removed beyond the reach of mixture." [5]

The American public was exposed to a much less cautious and temperate view of the Negro's endowments and rights when, in 1788, the *Columbian Magazine* reprinted two extracts from Edward Long's *History of Jamaica.*[6] The work had been published anonymously in 1774, five years after Long's return to England from a residence in Jamaica. In the chapter on " Negroes," extracted in the *Columbian Magazine,* Long attempts to prove that the African Negroes constitute a separate species of human beings. He finds them peculiar not only in their black skin but also in their woolly hair, their features, their odor, and even in their lice. Mentally, says Long, they are void of genius, destitute of moral sense, and incapable of making progress in civilization or science. As plantation slaves they do their work " perhaps not better than an *orang-outang* might, with a little pains, be brought to do." [7]

These differences, Long claims, prove a difference of species. They cannot be explained as effects of climate and living conditions. In one hundred and fifty years of residence in North America the Negro has remained as black and woolly-headed as ever, except where he has mixed with the whites. Moreover, the whole analogy of nature leads one to expect a multiplicity of human species analogous to the variety of animal species and an arrangement of these human species in a graded series bridging the gap between the apes and the most perfect type of man. The facts known about the orang-outang indicate, says Long, that the creature may be a savage man. An animal which walks erect, lives in society, builds huts, learns easily to perform menial services, and shows a passion for Negro women cannot be summarily excluded from the human family. Indeed, there is not much to choose as between Hottentot and an orang-outang, nor would an orang-outang husband dishonor a Hottentot female. Too little is known of the orang-outang to render it certain that he is incapable of speech and education. No one has tried seriously to train one from infancy.

[5] *Ibid.,* 665. In his letter to the Abbé Henri Grégoire, dated Washington, 25 February, 1809, Jefferson says: " . . . whatever be their degree of talent it is no measure of their rights. Because Sir Isaac Newton was superior to others in understanding, he was not therefore lord of the person or property of others." See A. A. Lipscomb, ed., *The Writings of Thomas Jefferson* (Washington, 1903–1904), XII, 255.

[6] [Edward Long], *The History of Jamaica, or, General Survey of the Antient and Modern State of That Island: with Reflections on Its Situation, Settlements, Inhabitants, Climate, Products, Commerce, Laws, and Government* (London, 1774).

[7] [Edward Long], " Observations on the Gradation in the Scale of Being between the Human and the Brute Creation. Including Some Curious Particulars respecting Negroes," *The Columbian Magazine or Monthly Miscellany,* 2 (1788), 15.

" For my own part," concludes Long, " I conceive that probability favors the opinion, that human organs were not given him for nothing: that this race have some language by which their meaning is communicated; whether it resembles the gabbling of turkies like that of the Hottentots, or the hissing of serpents, is of very little consequence, so long as it is intelligible among themselves: nor, for what hitherto appears, do they seem at all inferior in the intellectual faculties to many of the Negroe race; with some of whom, it is credible that they have the most intimate connexion and consanguinity." [8]

But even supposing with Buffon that intellect proceeds from a principle superior to matter and that the orang-outang's brain, for all its similarity to man's is but a parody of the human, the probability is still strong that there is a natural diversity of intellectual endowment among the various types of human beings. Since the Negro resembles the orang-outang in general form and structure, is it not probable that his brain too, though similar in appearance to the white man's, does not give rise to the same effects?

The Negroe race (consisting of varieties) will then appear rising progressively in the scale of intellect, the further they mount above the orangoutang and brute creation. The system of man will seem more consistent, and the measure of it more compleat, and analagous [sic] to the harmony and order that are visible in every other line of the world's stupendous fabric . . . . The series and progression from a lump of dirt to a perfect human being is amazingly extensive; nor less so, perhaps, the interval between the latter and the most perfect angelic being, and between this being and the Deity himself. Let us shake off those clouds with which prejudice endeavours to invelope the understanding; and, exerting that freedom of thought which the Best of Beings has granted to us, let us take a noon-tide view of the human genus; and shall we say, that it is totally different from, and less perfect than, every other system of animal beings? [9]

The extracts from Long's *History of Jamaica* were followed in the next issue of the *Columbian Magazine* by a reprint of Jefferson's views on the intellectual faculties of the Negro. In May, 1788, appeared " An Answer to a Circumstance on Which Some Writers, in Defense of the Slave-Trade Have Founded Much of Its Legality." The circumstance indicated was the supposition that many of the Negroes transported from Africa as slaves were the offspring of intercourse between orang-outangs and Negroes. From this it had been argued that the institution of slavery in the West Indies had contributed indirectly toward humanizing these hybrid creatures by promoting their intercourse with the white colonists, " ' to the honour of the

[8] *Ibid.,* 74.
[9] *Ibid.,* 74–75.

human species, and to the glory of the Divine Being.' " [10]   The author of the article, who signs himself " R," is not disposed to deny that intercourse between orang-outangs and Negroes may sometimes occur, but he objects vehemently to the idea that these unions could produce fertile offspring. If fertile crosses between species were possible, the distinctions in nature would soon become effaced and the whole animal economy would be thrown into confusion. Fortunately, says " R," the Creator has guarded against this eventuality by rendering crosses between species sterile. Conversely, the fact that all human beings can interbreed freely proves that they belong to a single species. If further proof is required, it can be found in the anatomical differences between man and the apes observed by Tyson, Buffon, Camper, and others. The absence of calf muscles and the inability of the orang-outang to speak mark him off from man as a separate species, a species which connects the rational to the brute creation.

In July, 1792, Benjamin Rush, a leading figure in American medical circles, entered the lists on the side of the unity of mankind by communicating to the American Philosophical Society his " Observations Intended to Favor a Supposition That the Black Color (as it is called) of the Negroes Is Derived from the LEPROSY." The phenomenon of albinism shows, says Rush, that skin color is often affected by disease. If albinos are white because of a diseased condition, may not the black skin of the Negro be produced by a similar cause? In Africa the climate and the diet and mode of life of the Negroes make them very susceptible to leprosy. There is a striking correspondence, moreover, between the typical Negro features and the characteristic effects of leprosy on the human being: black skin, insensibility in the nerves, strong venereal desires, big lips, flat noses, and woolly heads. Since leprosy is hereditary, its effects continue from generation to generation. Perhaps, then, congenital leprosy which has lost its virulent and infectious quality is the cause of the Negro's physical peculiarities.

If this be true, Rush goes on, " all the claims of superiority of the whites over the blacks, on account of their color, are founded in ignorance and inhumanity." [11]   There is, indeed, a sound medical reason for discouraging interbreeding between whites and Negroes until such time as the disease will have been cured. But there is no basis for denying the specific unity or the natural equality of all human beings.

[10] " R.," " An Answer to a Circumstance on Which Some Writers, in Defence of the Slave-Trade, Have Founded Much of Its Legality," *Columbian Magazine*, 2 (1788), 266.

[11] Benjamin Rush, " Observations Intended to Favor a Supposition That the Black Color (As It Is Called) of the Negroes is Derived from the LEPROSY," *Trans. Amer. Philos. Soc.*, 4 (1799), 295.

The racial issue becomes a medical problem of discovering a cure for leprosy. Thus, the leprosy hypothesis not only confirms revealed anthropology but also removes a barrier to the exercise of Christian benevolence.

Rush's " Observations " were published in the *Transactions* of the American Philosophical Society in 1799. In the same year appeared an English work which soon played an important part in the American controversy concerning the Negro, providing an arsenal of arguments for those who would assign him an inferior rank in the scale of being. This was Charles White's *Account of the Regular Gradation in Man, and in Different Animals and Vegetables.* In it the author, a Manchester physician, disclaims any purpose to justify Negro slavery. His only interest, he declares, is to investigate nature and discover her laws. " Nature exhibits to our view an immense chain of beings, endued with various degrees of intelligence and active powers suited to their stations in the general system." [12] The gradation of natural forms is not simply an observed fact; it is a law of nature. Hence, says White, Lord Monboddo's notion that some human beings have tails is patently absurd, for such a condition would break nature's law of gradation.

The idea that the principle of gradation applies to human as well as to animal types came to White upon hearing the British anatomist John Hunter discuss the gradation of skulls in some lectures on midwifery. Hunter illustrated his remarks with the skulls of a European, an Asiatic, an American, an African, a monkey, and a dog. It occurred to White that " nature would not employ gradation in one instance only, but would adopt it as a general principle." He undertook, therefore, to compare several characters of Europeans and Negroes to see whether in every case the Negro character was intermediate between that of an ape and that of a European. Upon comparing a Negro skeleton with several European skeletons, he discovered that the Negro skeleton had longer arm bones and a flatter arch in the foot. Extending his comparisons to living persons, he became convinced of the existence of constant constitutional differences between the Negro and the European in cartilages, muscles, tendons, skin, hair, sweat, odor, size of brain, reason, speech, and language, as well as in the skeleton. Even the body lice proved different. He concluded that in mankind, as in all nature, there is a steady gradation of forms, leading in the case of man from the ape-like Negro to the European.

Ascending the line of gradation, we come at last to the white European;

[12] Charles White, *An Account of the Regular Gradation in Man, and in Different Animals and Vegetables; and from the Former to the Latter* (London, 1799), 1.

who being most removed from the brute creation, may, on that account, be considered as the most beautiful of the human race. No one will doubt his superiority in intellectual powers; and I believe it will be found that his capacity is naturally superior also to that of every other man. Where shall we find, unless in the European, that nobly arched head, containing such a quantity of brain, and supported by a hollow conical pillar, entering its centre? Where the perpendicular face, the prominent nose, and round projecting chin? Where that variety of features, and fulness of expression; those long, flowing, graceful ringlets; that majestic beard, those rosy cheeks and coral lips? In what other quarter of the globe shall we find the blush that overspreads the soft features of the beautiful women of Europe, that emblem of modesty, of delicate feelings, and of sense. Where that nice expression of amiable and softer passions in the countenance; and that general elegance of features and complexion? Where, except on the bosom of the European woman, two such plump and snowy white hemispheres, tipt with vermillion? [13]

Having described the characteristic differences between Negro and European, White turns to the problem of accounting for them. He is certain that they cannot be explained by climate and mode of life, since skeletal formations are largely removed from these influences. Even color is not permanently affected by climate. One hundred and fifty years of residence in North America have not blanched the Negro's skin. If, says White, the Reverend Samuel Stanhope Smith, " one of the latest and ablest writers who attribute the color of the human race to climate," would look into the cases he reports of modification of Negro characters in America, he would discover that they result from miscegenation. If he would then consider the distribution of quadrupeds and human beings between the Old and the New Worlds, he would realize that the types of men and animals found in America must have been placed there in the beginning by the hand of the Creator.

In November, 1808, the medical students of the College of Physicians and Surgeons in New York were introduced to the controversy concerning the unity of mankind and the Negro's place in nature by their professor of anatomy, John Augustine Smith, a young man recently returned from his studies in London. Smith's lecture appeared in the *New York Medical and Philosophical Journal and Review* in the following year.[14] The lecturer begins by disclaiming any intention to settle the question whether the observable differences

[13] *Ibid.*, 134–135.

[14] John Augustine Smith, " A Lecture Introductory to the Second Course of Anatomical Instruction in the College of Physicians and Surgeons for the State of New York," *The New York Medical and Philosophical Journal and Review*, 1 (1809), 32–48.

among men are native and original or produced by climate and mode of life. He proposes instead to show that the European is superior in anatomical structure to the Asiatic, the American Indian, and the African in the sense of being farther removed from the brute creation. To this end, he undertakes to prove that the European and the Negro constitute the two extreme types in the scale of human anatomy.

As if to create a presumption in favor of his thesis, Smith turns for a moment to the subject of man's place in nature. He adopts Buffon's idea of a gradation of forms descending from man to the polyp and illustrates it with reference to Camper's facial angle and Cuvier's statistics on the relative proportions of face and cranium in man, orang-outang, and monkey. He states that he has tested a collection of human skulls in his own possession by these criteria and found them to form a series rising from the Negro to the European. He laments with Jefferson the black man's inability to blush and recapitulates White's table of anatomical differences between European and Negro.

He then turns to the problem of accounting for these differences. Scripture, he declares, states incontrovertibly that all mankind are offshoots of one stock, but those writers who have attempted to corroborate revelation by attributing the differences among men to the agency of climate and the state of society have injured both science and religion. Their works are distinguished more for piety than for sound philosophy. The Reverend Samuel Stanhope Smith displays a vast ignorance of anatomy in his discussion of pigmentation and grossly exaggerates the correlation between complexion and climate. Moreover, even supposing that climate can permanently alter complexion, how can it affect the structure of the bones? The reverend doctor's supposition that cold enlarges the heads of the Laplanders by contracting their faces and limbs is ludicrous. The causes of most variations in the human form being unknown, it is better to confess one's ignorance than to invent preposterous explanations. On this note of humility Smith closes the lecture, leaving his audience to form their own conclusions. " Different minds are satisfied with different degrees of evidence; and far be it from me to fix the bounds of your faith."

In 1810 Samuel Stanhope Smith returned to the fray with a second, considerably enlarged edition of his *Essay,* to which he appended some remarks on the arguments advanced by White, J. A. Smith, and Jefferson concerning the Negro. In these addenda he concedes that White's description of the African Negro is fairly accurate. He argues, however, that climate and mode of life have made the Negro what he is and hence are capable of making him a quite different creature. In proof of this contention he offers his own observations and measurements on the Negroes of Princeton, many of whom he finds as well-formed as the laboring classes of Europe. The anatomical differences *within* the white and the black races are more striking than those *between* them, says Smith. As for the Negro's black color, it must be expected to change very slowly. In one case, however, a Maryland Negro named Henry Moss turned from black to white in the course of a lifetime.

The change commenced about the abdomen, and gradually extended over different parts of the body, till, at the end of seven years, the period at which I saw him, the white had already overspread the greater portion of his skin. It had nothing of the appearance of a sickly or albino hue, as if it had been the effect of a disease. He was a vigorous and active man; and had never suffered any disease either at the commencement or during the progress of the change.[15]

This case, argues Smith, disposes of the notion that the Negro is a species immutably different from the European.

He then turns his attention to his countryman of the same name, Dr. J. A. Smith. He repays the young doctor's insults in kind, quoting at length from Blumenbach's treatise to show that his critic cannot be so well acquainted with that work as he pretends to be. " Can it be because Blumenbach's work is written in Latin! " Why, if the young professor of anatomy has really read Blumenbach, does he not inform his students that Blumenbach is highly skeptical concerning Camper's theory of gradation in the facial angle, instead of leaving them to infer that this hypothesis is generally accepted in the scientific world. The Negroes of Princeton, Smith declares, exhibit a range of variation from seventy to seventy-eight degrees in their facial angles. Many of them have high and prominent foreheads. Who, then, is the smatterer in philosophy, the Princeton Smith or the New York Smith? The young doctor's ignorance can be forgiven but not so the disingenuous manner in which he appeals to the authority of Scripture to settle the question of the unity or diversity of mankind. It is a favorite trick of infidels to assert the infallibility of Scripture at the same time that they labor to show that the facts cannot be reconciled with it. " These puny and half-learned scientists, who affect to treat with sarcastic leer the oracles of God, would do well

[15] Samuel Stanhope Smith, *An Essay on the Causes of the Variety of Complexion and Figure in the Human Species. To Which Are Added, Animadversions on Certain Remarks Made on the First Edition of This Essay, by M . Charles White . . . Also, Strictures on Lord Kaims' Discourse on the Original Diversity of Mankind. And an Appendix* (2nd ed., New Brunswick, 1810), 92-93.

to remember, if they are susceptible to advice, or of shame, with what modesty and humility of heart those sublime and genuine sons of nature, from Newton, down to Sir William Jones have thought it their glory to submit their superior minds to that wisdom which came down from heaven."[16]

Toward Jefferson, Smith is more lenient. He observes that the arguments by which Jefferson defends the Indian and the Anglo-American from the charge of mental and physical debility apply with equal force to the Negro. Indeed, they apply with greater force, since the Negro has the added disadvantage of being a slave. No wonder he has not produced noble flights of oratory. The Indians themselves degenerate into lazy, wretched, demoralized creatures when subjected to the influences of civilization. "They afford a proof of the deterioration of the mental faculties which may be produced by certain states of society, which ought to make a philosopher cautious of proscribing any race of men from the class of human beings, merely because their unfortunate condition has presented to them no incentives to awaken genius, or afforded no opportunities to display its powers."[17]

Not long after Smith's second edition appeared, it was reviewed in the *Medical Repository*, published in New York City by Dr. Samuel Latham Mitchill and colleagues. The review, though ostensibly laudatory, has an undertone of antagonism. It begins with a long summary of the Biblical account of man's origin and goes on to state that Smith is a firm believer in the veracity of Scripture, bent on corroborating Genesis by showing that all mankind can be derived from a single stock. The reviewers agree that this hypothesis is more defensible philosophically than the gratuitous assumption of several species of mankind, but they object to limiting the causes of human diversity to the agency of climate and mode of life. The most important single source of variety in successive generations is the mechanism of heredity, say the reviewers. "Enough for our present purposes is the statement of the fact, established on broad induction, 'that a man and woman may beget a child of a different complexion from either of the parents, and the complexion of the offspring may be perpetuated in his or her descendants.'"[18] Secondly, there may

[16] *Ibid.*, 305.

[17] *Ibid.*, 270.

[18] *Medical Repository*, 15 (1812), 159. See also *ib.*, 9 (1806), 64–70, in which the editors of the *Repository* review with approval Felix d'Azara's *Essays on the Natural History of the Quadrupeds of the Province of Paraguay*, M. Moreau-Saint-Méry, tr. 2 vols. (Paris, 1801). Say the reviewers: "... he traces the variegated forms of the hair, skin, and exterior parts of man and other animals, to a generative agency, or operation coeval with the production of the creature."

have been differences in "the primitive family" which were propagated to their posterity. Thirdly, the power of imitation operates powerfully to recreate in each generation family, national, and other group resemblances. The agency of climate is thus but one, and by no means the most important, source of variation in man.

This argument suggests that there were those in the United States who questioned the careless environmentalism of the day, who doubted the transmissibility of acquired characters and sought the secret of race formation in the unpredictable functioning of the mechanism of heredity. The problem from this point of view was to find some selective agency by which random heredity variation could eventuate in the production of stable types. When the Englishman Prichard attempted a solution of this problem in 1813, he found Samuel Stanhope Smith's notion of the selective influence of cultural standards a considerable help. By assuming the operation of a " natural standard of human beauty " in the choice of marriage partners Prichard thought to account for " the transmutation of the characters of the Negro into those of the European, or the evolution of white varieties in black races of men." [19] He thus opened the way to conceiving the process of race formation as a progress from rude and savage beginnings rather than as a decline from a perfect model of the species, to regarding Negroid traits as the traits of the human species at an early stage in its development. It was an Anglo-American, William Wells, however, who hit upon the idea of struggle for existence and survival of the fittest as the means whereby stable varieties might result from the sporting of the generative mechanism. His investigations into a case of a white woman with patches of black skin confirmed him in the opinion that difference of skin color was no sure proof of a difference of species and that the dark hue of the Negro was not produced by long exposure to the tropical sun. He was impressed with the susceptibility of both Negroes and whites to disease when they were transplanted to unaccustomed climates. Perhaps, he suggested, the prevalence of dark-skinned people in Africa could be explained by assuming an unknown cause correlating darkness of skin color with resistance to African diseases. If such were the case, those tribes with an hereditary tendency to dark skin would eventually drive out those tending toward a fair complexion. Thus, different human types might come to predominate in different regions of the earth by a process of natural selection. As to Prichard's

[19] James Cowles Prichard, *Researches into the Physical History of Man* (London, 1813), 233. Prichard makes specific acknowledgment of Smith's suggestions along this line (p. 41, note a).

idea that men become light-skinned in proportion as they become civilized, Wells was in doubt. He agreed that the features and woolly hair of Negroes were "somehow connected with their low state of civilization." But whether they were connected as *effects* of that low state or rather, in some obscure way, as *causes* of its continuance he was not prepared to say.[20]

Several conclusions may be drawn from the foregoing review of opinions concerning the Negro's place in nature. In the first place, the tendency to look to anthropology for a "scientific" defense of the institution of slavery, though clearly present in the years before 1815, had not yet become a major theme in American anthropology. Instead, the chief extra-scientific source of interest in the question of the Negro's origin and characteristics was its bearing on the credibility of revealed religion. The issue forced the defenders of Scripture to argue the mutability of the human constitution, while their theologically heterodox opponents were appealing to the old notion of the great chain of being—a highly conservative notion, scientifically speaking. Actually, the monogenists were as convinced of the stability and wise design of nature as their polygenist opponents, but the necessity which they felt to discover mechanisms whereby the variety of human types might have evolved in a few thousand years was bound, in the long run, to influence speculations concerning the nature and stability of species. Long before the origin of species had become a scientific problem in biology the related problem of race formation was challenging the best efforts of monogenist anthropologists. These efforts produced, among other ideas, the related concepts of random variation and natural selection with which Darwin was later to revive the languishing "development hypothesis." [21]

University of Wisconsin.

[20] William Wells, " An Account of a Female of the White Race of Mankind, Part of Whose Skin Resembles That of a Negro; with Some Observations on the Causes of the Differences in Color and Form between the White and Negro Races of Men," appended to *Two Essays: One upon Single Vision with Two Eyes; the Other on Dew* . . . (London, 1818), 425–439. Wells' " Account " was submitted to the Royal Society in 1813 but not published until 1818.

[21] This is not to say that Wells was the first to advance ideas of this kind. On the history of speculation along this line, see Conway Zirkle, " Natural Selection before the ' Origin of Species,' " *Proceedings Amer. Philos. Soc.*, 84 (1941), 71–123. Also Arthur O. Lovejoy, " Some Eighteenth Century Evolutionists," *Popular Science Monthly*, 65 (1904), 238–251, 323–340. The present article is not the place for an extended discussion of the relation of theories of race formation to the development of the idea of organic evolution. The author intends, however, to develop the subject more fully in a work now in progress, to be entitled *The Genesis of the Evolutionary Idea.*

ORIGINS OF RACIAL ANGLO-SAXONISM
IN GREAT BRITAIN BEFORE 1850

BY REGINALD HORSMAN

Although a belief in Anglo-Saxon racial superiority was a vital ingredient in English and American thought of the nineteenth century, the study of this belief has been largely neglected by historians. The best work is that of L. P. Curtis who in studying anti-Irish prejudice in the second half of the nineteenth century has analyzed far broader aspects of Anglo-Saxonism. Curtis points out that this Anglo-Saxonism of the middle and late nineteenth century was far different from the earlier sixteenth- and seventeenth-century adulation of the Anglo-Saxon period as a golden age of free institutions. A belief in Anglo-Saxon freedom, once used to defend popular liberties, had by the middle of the nineteenth century been transformed into a rationale for the domination of peoples throughout the world. The heyday of Anglo-Saxonism came in the late nineteenth century, but the essential transformation had occurred earlier. Although Curtis has effectively analyzed aspects of Anglo-Saxonism in the last half of the nineteenth century, little detailed attention has been devoted to the process by which an earlier stress on Anglo-Saxon liberties was by 1850 transformed into a racist doctrine.[1]

The myth of Anglo-Saxon England had its origins in the sixteenth century. The break with Rome and the creation of an English Church stimulated an interest in a primitive Anglo-Saxon church. Reformers wished to demonstrate that England was merely returning to older, purer, religious practices dating from before the Norman Conquest; practices which had been lost in subsequent centuries. Although the motives for this interest in Anglo-Saxon England were originally propa-

[1] Cf. L. P. Curtis, Jr., *Anglo-Saxons and Celts: A Study of Anti-Irish Prejudice in Victorian England* (Bridgeport, Conn., 1968). Christine Bolt, *Victorian Attitudes to Race* (London, 1971) also concentrates on the years after 1850, but does not concern herself specifically with problems of Anglo-Saxonism. The most important essay dealing with the earlier Anglo-Saxonism, from its origins to the early nineteenth century, is Christopher Hill, "The Norman Yoke," *Puritanism and Revolution: Studies in the Interpretation of the English Revolution of the 17th Century* (London, 1958). There is also information in Léon Poliakov, *The Aryan Myth: A History of Racist and Nationalist Ideas in Europe*, trans. Edmund Howard (New York, 1974), and in two lectures: Asa Briggs, *Saxons, Normans, and Victorians* (The Hastings and Bexhill Branch of the Historical Association, 1966), and Stuart Piggott, *Celts, Saxons, and the Early Antiquaries* (Edinburgh, 1967). Sir Herbert Butterfield, *The Englishman and His History* (Cambridge, 1944; rept., Archon Books, 1970) is a useful survey. Donald A. White, "Changing Views of the *Adventus Saxonum* in Nineteenth and Twentieth Century English Scholarship," *JHI*, **32** (Oct. 1971), 585–94, discusses a continuation of Germanist bias.

gandistic, the efforts of Archbishop Matthew Parker and his co-re-
ligionists brought to light a variety of sources which could be used in the
creation of a distinctly English history. These served to justify the break
with Rome, and also eventually overturned the Arthurian legends which
had dominated medieval accounts of England's origins.[2]

In the late sixteenth and early seventeenth century the interest in
the purity of Anglo-Saxon religious practices was subordinated to a vital
concern with their political and legal institutions. Parliamentarians
found in the Anglo-Saxons a historical base for their arguments; the
supposed antiquity of Parliament and of English common law provided a
rationale for opposition to royal pretensions. Throughout the Stuart period Anglo-Saxon institutions formed a constant theme in the arguments of the contending parties. Moreover, by the Restoration era the
seeds of Anglo-Saxon scholarship which had been planted in the Tudor
period flowered into a sustained interest in the language and sources of
the pre-Conquest period. At Oxford two generations of scholars delved
into the Anglo-Saxon language, sources, and history.[3]

The intensive efforts of the sixteenth and seventeenth centuries
meant that a well-defined myth of Anglo-Saxon history was available to
subsequent generations. The Anglo-Saxons were viewed as a freedom-
loving people, enjoying representative institutions and a flourishing
primitive democracy. This early freedom was crushed by the Norman
Conquest, and only gradually through Magna Carta and the subsequent
struggles were the English people able to regain their long lost
freedoms.

The Anglo-Saxonism of these early centuries was in large part
nonracial. Although Anglo-Saxon institutions were praised, there was
generally little interest in specific racial characteristics, in innate
physical or intellectual attributes separating the Anglo-Saxons from
other peoples. There was, however, a definite emphasis on the links

---

[2]The sixteenth-century developments can best be examined in Fred J. Levy, *Tudor
Historical Thought* (San Marino, Cal., 1967); T. D. Kendrick, *British Antiquity*
(London, 1950); May McKisack, *Medieval History in the Tudor Age* (Oxford, 1971);
and Eleanor N. Adams, *Old English Scholarship in England from 1566 to 1800* (New
Haven, 1917). Richard T. Vann, "The Free Anglo-Saxons: A Historical Myth," *JHI*, 19
(April 1958), 259–72, examines the origin of Leveller ideas.

[3]There is a discussion of seventeenth-century aspects of interest in the Anglo-Saxons
in Hill, Butterfield, Adams, and Vann. Indispensable, however, are J. G. A. Pocock, *The
Ancient Constitution and the Feudal Law: A Study of English Historical Thought in the
Seventeenth Century* (New York, 1967), and David C. Douglas, *English Scholars,
1660–1730* (2nd ed., rev., London, 1951). There is also considerable information on this
subject in Samuel Kliger, *The Goths in England: A Study in Seventeenth and Eighteenth
Century Thought* (Cambridge, Mass., 1952); Richard Foster Jones, *The Triumph of the
English Language: A Survey of Opinions Concerning the Vernacular from the Introduction of Printing to the Restoration* (Stanford, 1953); and Roberta Brinkley, *Arthurian
Legend in the Seventeenth Century* (Baltimore, 1932). There is considerable
disagreement on the exact nature of seventeenth-century interest in the Anglo-Saxons.

between the Anglo-Saxons and their Germanic ancestors. It was well understood that freedom was brought by Germanic tribes from the forests of Germany to the shores of England, and it was in defining links with their Germanic forbears that the English came nearest to describing racial characteristics rather than institutional excellence. As Tacitus was the most important source for the history of the Germanic tribes, his point of view inevitably colored this early interest in the history of their Anglo-Saxon descendants. "In the peoples of Germany," wrote Tacitus, "there has been given to the world a race untainted by intermarriage with other races, a peculiar people and pure, like no one but themselves."[4] The views of Tacitus on the Germanic tribes were common in seventeenth-century discussions of the origin of the English.

Laudation of the peculiar qualities of the Germanic people had been revived on the Continent as early as the Reformation; German reformers drew an analogy between the earlier destruction of the universal Roman Empire and the new destruction of the universal Roman Church. Interest in Germanic qualities continued in one form or another on the Continent from that time forward.[5] In England the emphasis on Germanic peoples rather than merely Saxon institutional origins was given a major impetus by Richard Verstegan and William Camden in the early seventeenth century. Verstegan emphasized the glories of England's Anglo-Saxon and German past, the Germanic roots of the English language, and the common racial origin of the Anglo-Saxons, Danes, and Normans. Camden also stressed the honor of descent from a great German people. As yet there were no specific racial definitions, but the emphasis on the Anglo-Saxons as the most distinguished branch of the sturdy, free-growing Germanic tree became a well-known facet of writings on the Anglo-Saxons in the seventeenth century. The love of liberty, a trait of the Germanic peoples had, according to these arguments, been transposed by the Anglo-Saxons in England into a system of free institutions.[6]

The theme of independent Germans and free Anglo-Saxons was given wide dissemination in the eighteenth century. The popular histories of Rapid de Thoyras and Catherine Macaulay embodied this myth, and across the Atlantic many of the makers of the American Revolution saw themselves as regaining the freedom of their Anglo-Saxon ancestors. Thomas Jefferson had an intense interest in Saxon

[4]Tacitus, *Germania* (London, 1914; rept., 1963), 269; Jones, *Triumph of the English Language,* 214–18, 269–70; Kliger, *Goths in England,* 112.

[5]Kliger, *Goths in England,* 33–66. There is a good discussion of the developments in France, in relation to general Continental developments, in Jacques Barzun, *The French Race: Theories of Its Origin and Their Social and Political Implications Prior to the Revolution* (Port Washington, N.Y., 1966).

[6]Levy, *Tudor Historical Thought,* 143; Jones, *Triumph of English,* 220–23, 232; Brinkley, *Arthurian Legend,* 55–61; Kliger, *Goths in England,* 115–19; Kendrick, *British Antiquity,* 116–20.

origins, and proposed putting the fifth-century Hengist and Horsa on one side of the Great Seal of the United States.[7] Particularly influential in the eighteenth century was Montesquieu's *De l'Esprit des lois*. While he believed in the innate capacity for improvement of the whole human race, Montesquieu stressed the peculiar excellence of the Germanic peoples. He carried the British political system back into the woods of Germany, and used Tacitus to support his view of liberty among the ancient Germans.[8] Eighteenth-century English Whigs and radicals accepted as axiomatic the view that English political institutions had enjoyed a continuous history from Saxon times, and that subsequent changes had destroyed earlier freedoms.

Yet, for all the interest in the Anglo-Saxons and the German tribes, racial factors continued to be subordinated to institutional discussions. Not until the 1760's and 1770's did a variety of new tendencies foreshadow a shift in emphasis from the continuity of free institutions to the inherent racial traits which supposedly explained them. Although England in the following decades shared in a general European movement, the interest in Anglo-Saxons was to take a distinct form, both because of the long established belief in the "free Anglo-Saxons," and because of the unparalleled success of Great Britain and the United States in the first half of the nineteenth century. As the English language, and English power, girdled the earth, Anglo-Saxons were given empirical "proofs" of their innate racial superiority.

The surge of interest in primitive European peoples, an interest which encompassed their history, their language, and their myths, and which eventually became a main thread of the Romantic movement, ultimately helped to give a whole new emphasis to the Anglo-Saxons as a "race." On the one hand, those studying the history and mythology of "the northern nations" firmly linked the Saxons to an heroic age of German-Scandinavian peoples; on the other, comparative philologists linked language to race and nation, and traced Anglo-Saxon roots deep into a prehistoric Indo-European or Aryan past. And while historians

---

[7] Barzun, *French Race*, 151–52; Alice Chandler, *A Dream of Order: The Medieval Ideal in Nineteenth Century English Literature* (Lincoln, Neb., 1970), 24–25; Thomas Preston Peardon, *The Transition in English Historical Writing, 1776–1830* (New York, 1933). There is an excellent account of the impact of these ideas in the American colonies in H. Trevor Colbourn, *The Lamp of Experience: Whig History and the Intellectual Origins of the American Revolution* (Chapel Hill, 1965).

[8] Baron de Montesquieu (Charles de Secondat), *The Spirit of the Laws*, trans. Thomas Nugent (rev., 2 vols., New York, 1899), I, 161, 163; Barzun, *French Race*, 200–04; M. Seliger, "Race Thinking During the Restoration," *JHI*, **19** (April 1958), 275, emphasizes that Montesquieu's views should not be confused with a later racism, but Théophile Simar, *Étude Critique sur La Formation de la Doctrine des Races au XVIII Siècle et son Expansion au XIXe Siècle* (Bruxelles, 1922), points out how Montesquieu furnished arguments for later racists; also Thor J. Beck, *Northern Antiquities in French Learning and Literature (1755–1855); A Study in Preromantic Ideas* (New York, 1934), 20–23.

and philologists gave the "free Anglo-Saxons" a far more complex, vigorous, and noble historical heritage than had ever been possible before, a shift in scientific interest from the universal human species to the classification of different varieties and, ultimately, different races made possible a contemporary comparison of superior and inferior breeds.

The most influential work in expanding Saxon-Germanic interests into the whole Norse tradition was Paul-Henri Mallet's *L'Introduction à l'histoire de Dannemarc* which idealized the ancient Scandinavians in the manner of Tacitus's idealization of the Germanic tribes. Mallet incorporated the still frequent confusion on race by failing to separate Scandinavians and Celts, but this was corrected by Thomas Percy when he published his English translation of Mallet's work in 1770 under the title *Northern Antiquities*. He pointed out that the Gothic or Teutonic peoples were distinct from the Celtic, and descended from the former were the Germans, the Saxons, and the Scandinavians. Moreover, argued Percy, the Celts did not have that peculiar love of liberty which distinguished the Gothic peoples.[9] Percy's influence was particularly strong because of his earlier publication of the *Reliques of Ancient English Poetry,* which stirred pride and interest in English national origins and greatly influenced the English Romantics, including Sir Walter Scott. In the brief essays accompanying the poems Percy emphasized the Germanic origins of the Anglo-Saxons, and also stressed that the Danish invasions of England merely reunited the Germanic peoples.[10]

The clear separation of Celt and Teuton, and the emphasis on the importance of race, took a marked step forward in 1787 with the publication of John Pinkerton's *Dissertation on the Origin of the Scythians or Goths.* Pinkerton, who possessed a striking polemic style, argued that the Celts were an inferior people who had been driven out of much of Europe by the Goths; a term which included Greeks and Romans as well as Germans and Scandinavians. Pinkerton had firm views on race, which differed from most of his contemporaries, and accurately foreshadowed nineteenth-century developments in scientific writing: "A Tartar, a Negro, an American &c. &c. differ as much from a German, as a bull-dog, or lap-dog, or shepherd's cur, from a pointer," wrote Pinkerton. "The differences are radical; and such as no climate or chance could produce: and it may be expected that as science advances,

[9] Paul Henri Mallet, *Northern Antiquities* (2 vols., London, 1770); Hans Aarsleff, *The Study of Language in England, 1780-1860* (Princeton, 1967), 166–67; Peardon, *Transition in English Historical Writing,* 106; Beck, *Northern Antiquities in French Learning,* 9–13, 23–26, 73; Frank E. Farley, *Scandinavian Influences in the English Romantic Movement* (Boston, 1903).

[10] *Reliques of Ancient English Poetry* (3 vols., London, 1812); Hoxie Neale Fairchild, *The Romantic Quest* (5th ed., Philadelphia, 1931), 259, 278; Chandler, *Dream of Order,* 26–27.

able writers will give us a complete system of the many different races of men."[11] Pinkerton was unusual in that rather than merely praising Germanic characteristics, he was prepared to make comparative racial judgments. He wrote of Celts who "have been savages since the world began, and will be for ever savages while a separate people; that is, while themselves, and of unmixt blood."[12] By violently attacking contemporary Scots and Welsh, Pinkerton assured wide publicity for his work as well as inspiring bitter rebuttals. Many disagreed with Pinkerton, but an interest in the northern nations, their history, and mythology flourished in England and on the Continent in the last decades of the eighteenth century. This interest gave the Anglo-Saxons a fuller historical past; it also ultimately made possible a new sense of national racial unity. For the Viking invasions, and even the Norman Conquest, could be viewed as making possible reunification of the ancient Germanic-Norse peoples. In England it meant that in the first half of the nineteenth century old interpretations of the Saxons under a Norman yoke existed side by side with newer ideas of an overriding Norse mystique.

The emphasis on language as a basis of nationality and of the common past of a people, although not originally intended by Herder to promote racial divisiveness, was rapidly used in this manner by many of those who took up the theme of the historic greatness of the German tongue. The idealization of the German language and of the German past was of direct use to English Anglo-Saxonists. The German *Volk* were the ancestors of the English, and they shared a common heritage. Indeed, it could be argued that England in her institutions and spreading empire had best realized the potential in the spirit of the Germanic tribes. Even German historians turned to England for proof of the capabilities of their race. Of particular use to the Anglo-Saxonists were the philological researches into the Indo-European language family from which the German and English languages were descended. The effort to determine the origin of the Indo-European language group assumed strong racial overtones. The fundamental error was the assumption that affinity of language proved affinity of race. This led to a search for an original homeland of the Indo-European or Aryan peoples. In the first half of the nineteenth century philologists not only described the ancient links between languages but also wrote historical descriptions of a tightly knit racial group that had spread out from its original homeland to encompass much of Europe and India. As it spread it brought new vigor to Europe, and the Germanic tribes regenerated a decaying Roman Empire.[13]

[11] John Pinkerton, *A Dissertation on the Origin and Progress of the Scythians or Goths Being an Introduction to the Ancient and Modern History of Europe* (London, 1787), 33–34; also 24–31, 51, 69.   [12] *Ibid.,* 91.

[13] Several older studies are useful for examining the Aryan controversy: Isaac Taylor, *The Origin of the Aryans: An Account of the Prehistoric Ethnology and Civilisation of Europe* (2nd ed., London, 1892); F. H. Raskin, *Racial Basis of Civilization* (New

Although there was a continuing controversy regarding the exact location of the original Indo-European homeland, from 1820 to 1850 there
was an increasing elaboration of J. G. Rhode's suggestion of an origin in
the plateau of central Asia. This hypothesis reached full flowering in the
work of F. Augustus Pott who with false certainty placed the Indo-
European cradle in the valleys of the Oxus and Jaxartes, and on the
slopes of the Hindu Kush. Pott painted imaginary scenes of tribesmen
pulled west by a pervading impulse as they followed the course of the
sun; their route became the route of civilization, and "*ex oriente lux*"
achieved reality. Jacob Grimm in the late 1840's essentially accepted
Pott's ideas, and provided a wider dissemination for them.[14]

By the 1830's German philology entered England to the extent of
forming its own school, led by the work of Benjamin Thorpe and John
M. Kemble. Thorpe had worked in Copenhagen under Rasmus Kristian
Rask, and Kemble had intimate ties with Germany. He studied there,
and became a friend of the Grimms. Thorpe and Kemble delved anew
into the Anglo-Saxon manuscripts, and were able to integrate their
work into the mainstream of Indo-European scholarship.[15] As the
English had already formed a firm link between their "free Anglo-
Saxons" and the Germanic tribes of the declining years of the Roman
Empire, they were now able to take over this new extension of their history, and make their past even more glorious. It was possible to trace a
continuous chain from a homeland in central Asia, through the forests
of Germany, to the shores of England. Moreover, as Anglo-Saxons
dominated the United States and extended toward the Pacific, the irresistible march following the sun took on a new meaning.

German philology, with all its extensions into race, history, and
mythology had comparatively little impact on English writing on the
Anglo-Saxons in the first three decades of the nineteenth century. The
quickening of interest in the Saxon past depended more on the new me-
dievalism which had arisen in the late eighteenth century, and it still had
its roots deep in the "free Anglo-Saxon" arguments of the seventeenth
century. Although the basic arguments were along traditional lines, a
new Romanticism was present; an emphasis on personal, individual
traits rather than on abstract institutional excellence. This approach
was exemplified in the works of Sharon Turner, Sir Walter Scott, and
Augustin Thierry, who helped bridge the gap between the older idealiza-

---

York, 1926); Salamon Reinach, *L'Origine des Aryens: Histoire d'une Controverse*
(Paris, 1892); Harold Peake, *The Bronze Age and the Celtic World* (London, 1922);
George L. Mosse, *The Crisis of German Ideology: Intellectual Origins of the Third
Reich* (New York, 1964); Rohan D'O. Butler, *The Roots of National Socialism* (New
York, 1942); Aarsleff, *Study of Language,* 143–53.

[14] Peake, *Bronze Age,* 132–43; Aarsleff, *Study of Language,* 154–60; Reinach,
L'Origine des Aryens, 8–15; Taylor, *Origin of the Aryans,* 3–10; Victor Rydberg, *Teutonic Mythology: Gods and Goddesses of the Northland* (3 vols., London, 1907), I, 5–17.

[15] Aarsleff, *Study of Language,* 161, 166, 182–203.

tion of Anglo-Saxon institutions and the new mid-nineteenth-century racialism.

Turner's classic *History of the Anglo-Saxons*, published between 1799 and 1805, was for the most part traditional in its ideas although it was more advanced in its scholarship than earlier studies. Turner believed that the English "language, our government, and our laws, display our Gothic ancestors in every part."[16] He stressed the love of liberty among the Anglo-Saxons, and the early origin of parliamentary institutions, but he was realistic in his depiction of the ferocity of his English ancestors in their uncivilized state. He also specifically defended the idea of a single human species, and though he praised Thomas Percy for his clear analysis of the distinction between the Celts and the Goths, he attacked Pinkerton's abuse of the Celts. Turner did, however, stress a constant nineteenth-century argument by contending that the conquest of the Roman Empire by the Germanic nations was a healthy recasting of human society rather than a barbarization.[17] Turner was extremely popular in the first decades of the nineteenth century, and greatly helped in stimulating an interest in Saxon studies.

The impact of new Romantic tendencies on the view of the Anglo-Saxons is muted in Turner's history, but reaches a fuller realization in the novels and poems of Sir Walter Scott, who acknowledged his indebtedness both to Turner and to Percy. Scott in turn was to influence historians, particularly Thierry, to present a more vivid and personalized depiction of the medieval past. In *Ivanhoe* (1817) he inspired a whole generation with a view of Saxon freedom and honesty. As a novelist he was able to depict these attributes more effectively as individual and racial traits than as an abstract institutional excellence. He wrote in the first chapter of *Ivanhoe* that four generations had not been enough to blend the hostile blood of the Normans and the Anglo-Saxons, and throughout the novel he constantly praises the homely, blunt, simple, honest qualities of his Saxon heroes. Even the Anglo-Saxon language was "far more manly and expressive" than French. *Ivanhoe* captured the imagination as no history could; the image of free, honest, chivalrous Anglo-Saxons had never before been so bright and clear in the eyes of the English.[18]

The most immediate historical impact of Scott was in France, not England. The long lasting French argument over racial origins, and the Celtic and Germanic elements in their own country, had influenced British Saxonists since the sixteenth century, but art now entwined with

[16] Sharon Turner, *The History of the Anglo-Saxons from the Earliest Period to the Norman Conquest* (3 vols., London, 5th ed., 1828), I, 88.

[17] *Ibid.*, I, 2–5, 251; III, 1-2.

[18] *Ivanhoe* (Boston, 1913), ch. 1, and 450; also Chandler, *Dream of Order*, 25–51; H. G. Schenk, *The Mind of the European Romantics: An Essay in Cultural History* (New York, 1967), 34–36.

reality as Augustin Thierry, profoundly influenced by Sir Walter Scott, in 1825 published his *Conquest of England*. For Thierry the history of England for centuries after the Norman Conquest could be explained as a racial struggle between Saxon and Norman. Thierry was no thoroughgoing racialist, and did not concern himself with innate differences in capacity, but he did subordinate political and religious considerations to those of race; even Becket and Henry II contended as Saxon and Norman.[19]

The Romantic pride in the Saxon past, which was already beginning to shift the emphasis from institutions to individuals and to race, received two additional streams of influence in the 1820's and 1830's. One, the Germanic pride in language and race, gave the Anglo-Saxonists a more deep-rooted and broader historical heritage; the other, the flowering of the new science of man, gave a firm physical, "scientific" base to the long entrenched ideas of Anglo-Saxon excellence. The work of the early nineteenth-century ethnologists was decisive in giving a definite racial cast to Anglo-Saxonism. Rather than merely praising Anglo-Saxons or Germanic tribes, the ethnologists were able by comparative methods to establish reasons for superiority and inferiority; an essential shift in emphasis occurred when the arguments about the inferiority of other "races" assumed an importance as great or even greater than arguments about the excellence of Anglo-Saxons. In studying the races of mankind these ethnologists ranged over a variety of materials, both cultural and physical. Some of them leaned heavily on the work of historians and philologists while others attempted to measure physical differences between races. Whatever the specific method used, and works on race ranged from impressionistic studies to those of supposed exact scientific measurement, there was in the first half of the nineteenth century a sharp increase in the number of those who were prepared to defend inherent, unchangeable differences between races. Also, it is clear that many of these "ethnologists" were responding to that interest in national identity, uniqueness, and separateness that had come to dominate European thought since the last decades of the eighteenth century. The Anglo-Saxons had already been firmly linked to their Germanic ancestors, they were in process of being linked to the linguistic racial group from which they were descended, now ethnologists were to place them firmly within a superior Caucasian race. The Anglo-Saxons were to become the final product of a long line of superior beings who stretched back through an Indo-Germanic cradle to the very creation of a superior race. Finally, this broadening of the base of Anglo-Saxonism was to produce a reaction, as some Englishmen dis-

---

[19]Augustin Thierry, *History of the Conquest of England by the Normans* (3 vols., London, 1825); Seliger, "Race Thinking," *JHI,* **19** (1958), 275–81; Simar, *Étude Critique,* 74–75; G. P. Gooch, *History and Historians in the Nineteenth Century* (1913; New York, 1949), 169–72.

covered they were being given close relatives, both linguistically and racially, whom they did not choose to recognize.

The most influential ethnologists in the first half of the nineteenth century still maintained the religiously orthodox position that there was one human species descended from Adam through Noah, although an increasing number of writers were prepared to flout religious opinion by maintaining the polygenesist position that there was more than one human species, and that there had been multiple creations. Significantly, however, writers on both sides of the monogenesis-polygenesis argument devoted attention to the differences between races rather than their common features, and concepts of inherent inferiority and superiority became increasingly common as the century progressed.[20]

Even in the eighteenth century some writers—though usually not those regarded as specialists—had shown a definite interest in inherent differences, and even in polygenesis. The standard viewpoint inherited from that century, however, was that of Johann Friedrich Blumenbach, who had argued for one human species which contained five varieties—Caucasian, Mongolian, American, Ethiopian, and Malay. Although Blumenbach denied the inherent inferiority of any race, he coined the name "Caucasian" because he thought a skull from the region of the Caucasus the most beautiful in his collection. He also emphasized the ways—shape of skull, face, hair, color—in which the different varieties could be physically classified. Although George Cuvier suggested a threefold division of the human species—Caucasian, Mongolian, and Negro—which became of great importance, Blumenbach's five-fold division continued to be popular until the middle of the century.[21]

By far the most influential ethnologist in England in the first half of the nineteenth century was James Cowles Prichard who was a firm believer in monogenesis, and who was intent on not offending the religiously orthodox. Although Prichard laid stress on physical comparison, he was also a distinguished philologist, and in 1831 clearly established

---

[20] John S. Haller, Jr., *Outcasts from Evolution: Scientific Attitudes of Racial Inferiority, 1859-1900* (Urbana, Ill., 1971), 70-78; J. C. Greene, *The Death of Adam: Evolution and its Impact on Western Thought* (Ames, Iowa, 1959), 221; George W. Stocking, *Race, Culture, and Evolution: Essays in the History of Anthropology* (New York, 1968), 39; Earl Count, "The Evolution of the Race Idea in Modern Western Culture during the Period of the Pre-Darwinian Nineteenth Century," *Transactions of the New York Academy of Sciences*, 2d ser., 8 (Feb. 1946), 139-65; Herbert H. Odom, "Generalizations on Race in Nineteenth Century Physical Anthropology," *Isis*, 58 (Spring 1967), 5-18.

[21] Haller, *Outcasts from Evolution*, 4-5; Count, "Evolution of the Race Idea," 147; L. Perry Curtis, *Apes and Angels: The Irishman in Victorian Caricature* (Washington, D.C., 1971), 8-9; Philip D. Curtin, *The Image of Africa: British Ideas and Action, 1780-1850* (Madison, 1964), 230-36. In the eighteenth century the Scottish jurist and natural philosopher Lord Kames, Voltaire, and British physician Charles White all argued at different times for polygenesis.

that the Celtic languages were of the Indo-European stock.[22] Prichard's major ethnological work was his *Researches into the Physical History of Man,* first published in one volume in 1813, and reaching its final state in the five volume fifth edition published between 1836 and 1847. Throughout his writings Prichard defended the concept of one human species, and refused to believe in the inherent inferiority of any race. Yet, by the 1840's Prichard had so defined "permanent variety" as to make it in practical terms little different from the "race" of the believers in polygenesis. Prichard wrote that permanent varieties were very like species in that they displayed characteristic peculiarities that were permanently transmitted. The difference from a species was that such deviations had not been present from the creation of the group.[23] If traits were now permanently transmitted it made little difference, except of course to the religiously orthodox, that they had not always been there. Prichard also had a high opinion of the Germanic tribes. "In moral energy," he wrote, "the German race was superior to the rest of mankind." He added that "the Goths were a people susceptible of civilisation, remarkable for the soundness of their understanding, and for intellectual qualities of the highest kind."[24]

The establishing of racial hierarchies proceeded rapidly in the first half of the nineteenth century. Even those views which were sharply attacked by the orthodox were given a wide dissemination. William Lawrence's *Lectures on . . . the Natural History of Man,* first published in 1819, went through numerous editions by the 1840's. Lawrence accepted the five-fold classification of Blumenbach, and argued that the Caucasians were clearly a superior race; he also wrote of the inferiority common to the "dark-coloured people of the globe." Even in the least advanced stages of civilization the superiority of the white races could be distinguished—one had only to compare the ancient Germans to the Hottentots or to a tribe of American Indians. Lawrence was able to argue for all this while still maintaining that these races were but varieties of one human species.[25]

The development of a belief in the different innate capacities of the various races or varieties, and of the superiority of the Caucasian race, was considerably helped in the 1830's and 1840's by an influx of ideas from the United States. A country in which a great many were intent on justifying the enslavement of the blacks and the extermination of the American Indians proved a fertile ground for the growth of racism. Eu-

[22] James Cowles Prichard, *The Eastern Origin of the Celtic Nations* (London, 1831).

[23] *Researches into the Physical History of Man* (3rd ed., 5 vols., London, 1836–47), I (1836), 105–09, V (1847), 548, 550; also Prichard, *The Natural History of Man,* ed. Edwin Norris (2 vols., London, 1855), I, 10, 68–69.

[24] Prichard, *Researches,* III (1841), 342, 377–78.

[25] *Lectures on Comparative Anatomy, Zoology, and the Natural History of Man* (1819; 9th ed., London, 1848), 328–30; William F. Edwards, *Des Caractères Physiologiques des Races Humaines* (Paris, 1829).

ropean defenses of innate differences were eagerly seized upon by American theorists, and by the 1830's public defenses of the inherent inferiority of the blacks were common in the South, and the first prominent school of American ethnologists—led by Samuel G. Morton of Philadelphia—advanced theories that threatened the belief in monogenesis. These American ethnologists showed no hesitation at all in ascribing different innate capacities to different races. Morton had a distinguished international reputation, and the work of his less distinguished followers was well known in England. Josiah C. Nott, whose frenetic defenses of white ability and black inferiority reached absurd lengths, was regarded with the greatest respect by the British ethnological community of the middle years of the nineteenth century.[26]

Distinctions between science and pseudoscience continued to be blurred in the first half of the nineteenth century, and the popularization of racial ideas was helped by the phrenologists who enjoyed a great vogue from the 1820's through the middle of the century. By the 1840's phrenology was deserted by the serious scientists, yet for many years it influenced popular opinion. The phrenologists preached an optimistic doctrine of improvability for the Caucasians, but questioned whether the other races of the world could ever equal them.[27] The most famous of the phrenologists after the death of Spurzheim in 1832 was the Scotsman George Combe. Combe praised the Caucasians above all other races, the Teutonic branch over all Caucasians, and the Anglo-Saxons over all Teutons. "The inhabitants of Europe, belonging to the Caucasian variety of mankind," wrote Combe, "have manifested, in all ages, a strong tendency towards moral and intellectual improvement." Among the Caucasians the Celtic race remained far behind the Teutonic, and "the Anglo-Saxon race," wrote Combe, "has been richly endowed by nature with mental qualities."[28] The phrenologists consistently maintained that Anglo-Saxon supremacy stemmed from the physical conformation of the brain, and that the improvability of non-Caucasian races was limited by the deficiencies of their original organization.

By the 1840's the importance of race, of "blood," was assumed in a

[26]The "American School" of Ethnology is discussed in William Stanton, *The Leopard's Spots: Scientific Attitudes Toward Race in America, 1815-1859* (Chicago, 1960).

[27]There is a convenient summary of the principles of phrenology in John D. Davies, *Phrenology: Fad and Science: A 19th-Century American Crusade* (New Haven, 1955), although he concentrates on the impact on reform rather than racial theory. There is considerable information on British aspects of phrenology in Charles Gibbon, *The Life of Combe* (2 vols., London, 1878).

[28]Combe, "Phrenological Remarks on the relation between the natural Talents and Dispositions of Nations, and the Development of their Brains," in Samuel G. Morton, *Crania Americana* (Philadelphia, 1839), 271; Combe, *Notes on the United States of America during a Phrenological Visit in 1838-9-40* (2 vols., Philadelphia, 1841), II, 242.

manner quite unlike that of one hundred years before. In reviewing Michelet's *History of France* in 1844 the *Edinburgh Review* commented that "of the great influence of Race in the production of National Character no reasonable inquirer can now doubt." There was a similarity in national character between the French and the Irish, the reviewer asserted, and this had to be ascribed to "their Gaelic blood."[29] Race was becoming a topic of popular discussion. Even Robert Chambers's *Vestiges of the Natural History of Creation,* which was bitterly attacked on its appearance in 1845, served to stimulate discussion of what once had been indisputable. "He believes that the human family may be (or ought to be) of many species," wrote the *Edinburgh Review* critic, "and all sprung from apes."[30] No longer was the idea of multiplicity of species, or of inherent differences, rare, and even those who insisted on the religiously orthodox position of one human species descended from Adam and Eve increasingly stressed distinct varieties.

The 1840's were a watershed in the surging growth of Anglo-Saxonism. Those ideas of Anglo-Saxon freedom that had persisted in English thought since the sixteenth century were now melded, on the one hand, with the ideas of Teutonic greatness and destiny developed by the comparative philologists and German nationalists, and on the other, with the ideas of inherent Caucasian superiority developed by those interested in the science of man. Many of course resisted the surge of racist doctrines, but an increasing number were swept away in an emotional tide of racial theory. The Anglo-Saxon doctrines that were being shaped were fed by the increasing power of Great Britain and the United States. This was an age in which the English language, English law, and English institutions seemed ready to dominate the entire world. The new racial ideas rapidly began to permeate English publications, and found articulate and able spokesmen. Through the views of Carlyle, Thomas Arnold, Disraeli, and Charles Kingsley one can readily perceive how a variety of threads had been woven into a new Anglo-Saxon racial tapestry.

Carlyle was the first great British writer to view Saxon triumphs as clearly a product of racial superiority. This Lowland Scot had little sympathy for the Celts, stressed the Norse origins of Scotland's population, and wrote of Robert Burns as "one of the most considerable Saxon men of the eighteenth century."[31] His inspiration was Germany, and among his mentors were Herder, Fichte, Goethe, Kant, Friedrich von Schlegel, and Novalis, but the passion of his arguments was peculiarly his own. He was imbued with a sense not only of the power of the individual hero, but also of the power of an individual race—the Teutonic. He saw in the

[29] *Edinburgh Review,* **79** (Jan. 1844), 9.

[30] *Ibid.,* **82** (July 1845), 6. For the *Vestiges:* Milton Millhauser, *Just Before Darwin: Robert Chambers and Vestiges* (Middletown, Conn., 1959).

[31] Carlyle, *On Heroes and Hero Worship* (London, 1897), 189; also 19, 144.

vigor of that race a transforming force in the world. Individual men and individual races were created unequal.[32]

To Carlyle the Teutonic people were the whole amalgam of Germans, Norsemen, and Anglo-Saxons; including those English who had colonized throughout the world. Race was more important to him than any religious division: "at bottom, Danish and Norse and Saxon have no destinction, except a superficial one,—as of Heathen and Christian, or the like." The old Norse sea kings were the "progenitors of our own Blakes and Nelsons."[33] Teutonism had revivified a Europe dominated by Rome, and now "once more, as at the end of the Roman Empire, a most confused epoch and yet one of the greatest, the Teutonic countries find themselves too full. . . . And yet, if this small western rim of Europe is overpeopled, does not everywhere else a whole vacant Earth as it were, call to us, Come and till me, come and reap me!"[34]

England had been assigned two special tasks in world history: the industrial task of conquering "half or more" of the planet, "for the use of man," and the constitutional task of sharing the fruits of conquest, and showing other peoples how this might be done. The tribe of Saxons, fashioned "on the shores of the Black Sea" or elsewhere, "out of Hartzgebirge rock" still had this great work of conquest to accomplish: "No property is eternal but God the Maker's: whom Heaven permits to take possession, his is the right; Heaven's sanction *is* such permission." Carlyle would not accept the idea of a post-Conquest racial split between Saxons and Normans: the "Normans were Saxons who had learned to speak French."[35]

For Carlyle the supreme destiny belonged to the race not simply to the nation. He wrote to Emerson that he believed the great "Wen" of London might for some centuries be the meeting place for "All the Saxons," but after centuries "if Boston, if New York, have become the most convenient '*All-Saxondom*,' we will right cheerfully go thither to hold such festival, and leave the Wen."[36] While the Saxons were a race destined for greatness and accomplishment, other races could be viewed as obstacles to progress. In his famous "Occasional Discourse on the Nigger Question" Carlyle wrote of the whole black population of the West Indies equalling "in *worth* (in quantity of intellect, faculty, docility, energy, and available human valour and value) perhaps one of the streets of Seven Dials." The West Indies now grew tropical fruits

[32]Charles F. Harrold, *Carlyle and German Thought: 1819–1834* (1934; Hamden, 1963) surveys the main influences on Carlyle; also Frederick E. Faverty, *Matthew Arnold: The Ethnologist* (Evanston, 1951), 14–15.

[33]Carlyle, *On Heroes and Hero Worship,* 19, 28, 32.

[34]Carlyle, "Chartism," *Critical and Miscellaneous Essays,* IV (London, 1899), 200.

[35]*Ibid.,* 171–75.

[36]Carlyle to Emerson, June 24, 1839, in Charles Eliot Norton, ed., *The Correspondence of Thomas Carlyle and Ralph Waldo Emerson, 1834–1872* (2 vols., Boston, 1883), I, 247.

and spices; Carlyle hoped that they would one day grow "beautiful Heroic human lives too . . . beautiful souls and brave; sages, poets, what not; making the Earth nobler round them, as their kindred from of old have been doing; true 'splinters of the old Harz Rock'; heroic white men, worthy to be called old Saxons."[37] Carlyle's popularity, both in England and the United States, did much to disseminate the idea of a superior Anglo-Saxon race with a world mission to fulfill.

Those who saw race as a key to historical explanation, and the basis of England's nineteenth-century power, did not all agree on the details of their racial explanations. They selected those parts of the various hypotheses that were attractive to them, and they discarded the rest. Both Carlyle and Thomas Arnold in large part paid little heed to ethnological theories on the Caucasian race, and placed their strongest emphasis on the Teutonic heritage. Thomas Arnold, who in his inaugural lecture at Oxford in 1841 lauded the Germanic roots of the English nation, expressed uncertainty on the question of the inherent superiority of some races of men over others, but leaned in the direction of an imbalance of inherent qualities.[38]

Arnold warned of the dangers of arrogance, but in describing the English race he had no doubts about its heritage, its power, and its destiny. He emphasized that while the English owed a great deal morally to Rome and Greece, they owed nothing to them in race: "Our English race is the German race; for though our Norman forefathers had learnt to speak a stranger's language, yet in blood, as we know, they were the Saxons' brethren: both alike belong to the Teutonic or German stock." The key to medieval and modern history was the impact of the German races on the Roman Empire. The Roman Empire of the fourth century, argued Arnold, possessed Christianity, and the intellectual and political legacies of Greece and Rome: "What was not there, was simply the German race, and the peculiar qualities which characterize it." The English race and language were now overrunning the earth, and together with the Germanic peoples had dominated the world, "half of Europe, and all America and Australia, are German more or less completely, in race, in language, or in institutions, or in all."[39] Arnold's views became best known in the 1840's, when they greatly influenced the next generation of Saxonists including E. A. Freeman, but they were clearly emerging when he was young. In the late 1820's when he first saw the valley of the Rhine he rhapsodized "before us lay the land of our Saxon and Teutonic forefathers—the land uncorrupted by Roman or any other mixture; the birthplace of the most moral races of men the

---

[37] Carlyle, "Occasional Discourse on the Nigger Question," *Critical and Miscellaneous Essays,* IV, 350, 376–77.

[38] Thomas Arnold, *Introductory Lectures on Modern History Delivered in the Lent Term MDCCCXLII, with the Inaugural Lecture Delivered in December 1841* (5th ed., London, 1860), 158.　　　[39] *Ibid.,* 26–28.

world has yet seen—of the soundest laws—the least violent passions, and the fairest domestic and civil virtues." The Teutonic nation was "the regenerating element" in modern Europe.[40]

By the early 1840's the position of England and the Anglo-Saxons within a general Teutonic racial framework was well established. When in 1845 Samuel Laing wrote a passionate defense of the Scandinavians as the supreme Teutons, the *Edinburgh Review* redressed the balance with a discussion of the whole Teutonic position. The reviewer pointed out that the researches of living antiquaries had finally shown that "the different tribes of Teutonic blood"—Germans, Anglo-Saxons, Scandinavians—were similar in the main elements of their national life. This unity began with language: some centuries before the Christian era "a single Teutonic language must have existed, from which, as from a common centre, all the existing dialects of that name have radiated and diverged." Also, throughout the Teutonic nations "the same political and judicial system prevailed"—all of them embodied the principles "of popular freedom and popular influence." Finally, before the Christian era, all the Teutonic nations had the same system of religious worship. Present differences between the Teutonic nations could largely be accounted for by the different times at which Christianity had been introduced.[41] Rather than wanting to disparage the Scandinavians in opposition to Laing's views, the *Edinburgh Review* argued for a common cause: "We would wish indeed that all the tribes of Teutonic kindred, embracing we believe, a hundred millions of mankind, should look upon each other with a kindly partiality . . . glorying with a national pride in the common honours of their Teutonic ancestry."[42]

When in 1847 a new edition of Percy's translation of Mallet's *Northern Antiquities* was issued, I. A. Blackwell developed in his introduction the same themes of Teutonic supremacy, while making passing reference to the divisions of the ethnologists. After commenting that "the Caucasian Variety is unquestionably the highest" in the human scale,[43] Blackwell went on to discuss the Teutonic regeneration of mankind; a mankind which had stagnated under Roman imperial despotism: "But the hardy tribes of the Teutonic race then issued from the forests of Germania," Blackwell wrote, "and after a long period of desolation and slaughter, regenerated the Romanized nations of Europe, by infusing into them, along with their Teutonic blood, a portion of that spirit of personal independence which appears to be the peculiar characteristic of the Teutonic race." This heritage went back even beyond the German forests. "The civilization that germinated on the plains of the Ganges

[40] Arthur Penryhn Stanley, *The Life and Correspondence of Thomas Arnold, D.D.* (12th ed., London, 1881), II, 324.

[41] *Edinburgh Review*, 82 (Oct. 1845), 142–43.   [42] *Ibid.*, 164.

[43] Paul Henri Mallet, *Northern Antiquities*, trans. Bishop Percy, ed. I. A. Blackwell (rev., London, 1847), 28.

some forty centuries ago," wrote Blackwell, "has been transmitted from race to race, until we now find it in the north-west of Europe, with the Germans in the possession of the more intellectual, and the English of the more practical, elements that constitute its essence."[44] The *Edinburgh Review* in 1851 placed the original homeland a little differently, but reached essentially the same conclusion: "the Arian nations . . . carried the germs of civilisation from a common centre on one side into India, and, on the other side, into Asia Minor, Greece, Italy, and the rest of Europe."[45]

John M. Kemble was cautious in his racial judgments compared to many of his contemporaries, but his *Saxons in England*, published in 1849, placed English-German kinship on a firm scholarly base. His main discussion was institutional, and he stressed land division and the mark, but he emphasized the common blood of the Anglo-Saxons and Teutons, and the destiny of the Germanic tribes: "dimly through the twilight in which the sun of Rome was to set for ever, loomed the Colossus of the German race, gigantic, terrible, inexplicable."[46] The *Edinburgh Review* in praising Kemble's work pointed out the great advances in Anglo-Saxon studies and philology that had thrown new light on the whole earlier period, and drew conclusions that were based on more than Kemble: "the true mission of the Germanic people was to renovate and re-organize the western world. In the heart of the forest, amid the silence of unbroken plains, the Teuton recognized a law and fulfilled duties, of which the sanctity if not the memory, was nearly extinct among races who deemed and called him *barbarian*. He felt and reverenced the ties of family life, chastity in woman, fealty in man to his neighbour and his chief, the obligations of oaths, and the impartial supremacy of the laws. And it is the portraiture of the Teuton doing his appointed work, in re-infusing life and vigour and the sanctions of a lofty morality into the effete and marrowless institutions of the Roman world, which is drawn in the volumes before us."[47]

While links with Aryan and Germanic tribesmen carrying the seeds of civilization and freedom gave a noble heritage to most Englishmen, this could not satisfy the young Disraeli. Carlyle and Arnold above all else had wanted the Anglo-Saxons to be Teutons, the young Disraeli above all else wanted them to be Caucasians. He needed a link between the tribes of the German forests and the tribes of the eastern Mediterranean; he found it in the Caucasian race of the ethnologists. Disraeli's novels of the 1840's popularized the word Caucasian while exalting the

[44]*Ibid.*, 44–45.

[45]*Edinburgh Review*, **94** (Oct. 1851), 167.

[46]John Mitchell Kemble, *The Saxons in England: A History of the English Commonwealth Till the Period of the Norman Conquest* (2 vols., London, 1849), I, 5.

[47]*Edinburgh Review*, **89** (Jan. 1849), 82.

Jews.[48] Most of the British were to reject what he had to say about Jewish supremacy, but many were to accept his contention that the influence of race on human action was "the key to history." "Progress and reaction," wrote Disraeli in 1852, "are but words to mystify the millions. They mean nothing, they are nothing, they are phrases and not facts. All is race. In the structure, the decay, and the development of the various families of man, the vicissitudes of history will find their main solution."[49] Although Disraeli was given to extravagant statements which he had no intention of living by, he was consistent in his espousal of the idea that race lay at the heart of human affairs.

Disraeli accepted Blumenbach's division of the human species into five varieties. The Caucasian, he believed, was "the superior class," and among the Caucasians the Jews "could claim a distinction which the Saxon and the Greek, and the rest of the Caucasian nations, have forfeited. The Hebrew is an unmixed race." The Caucasians in general were granted an original "first-rate organisation," and the Jews had retained their original structure in an "unpolluted" form. The Jews had survived their centuries of persecution because "you cannot destroy a pure race of the Caucasian organisation."[50] This adulation of the Jews as the purest of the pure was the dominant racial theme in Disraeli's works, but throughout his novels he also paid homage to his own country as well as his ancestors. Most of what the Romantics had to offer was of supreme appeal to Disraeli the novelist; he lauded passion over reason, medieval over modern, imagination over intellect, and race as an enduring, unconquerable thread.

When Coningsby as a "Saxon" protests that he also comes from Caucasus, the Jew Sidonia's answer is that "your race is sufficiently pure. You come from the shores of the Northern sea, land of the blue eye, and the golden hair, and the frank brow: 'tis a famous breed, with whom we Arabs have contended long; from whom we have suffered much: but these Goths, and Saxons and Normans were doubtless great men."[51] Even in *Tancred* (1847), which is a long hymn in praise of the Jewish race, Disraeli explained the greatness of England: "It is her inhabitants that have done this; it is an affair of race. A Saxon race, protected by an insular position, has stamped its diligent and methodic character on the century. And when a superior race with a superior idea to work and order, advances, its state will be progressive. . . . All is race; there is no other truth."[52]

[48] Racial writer Robert Knox claimed that the word "Caucasian" had risen to such popularity because of its use by Disraeli in his novels; Henry Lonsdale, *A Sketch of the Life and Writings of Robert Knox The Anatomist* (London, 1870), 380.

[49] Quoted in William F. Monypenny and George E. Buckle, *The Life of Benjamin Disraeli Earl of Beaconsfield* (rev., 2 vols., New York, 1929), I, 871.

[50] *Coningsby* (1844; New York, 1904), ch. XXXII, 292–93; ch. XXXVII, 331–32.

[51] *Ibid.,* ch. XXXVII, 334.

[52] *Tancred* (1847; New York, 1904), ch. XX, 191.

Disraeli's espousal of theories of Caucasian superiority reveals a dilemma for the Anglo-Saxonists. Although many were happy to accept scientific theories maintaining that a nation's power and prosperity stemmed from inherent physical and mental differences between races, they were less enthusiastic to accept particular racial categories which lumped Anglo-Saxons together with Jews and other supposedly distinct groups. In a similar manner even the philological theories regarding the original Indo-European people, theories which gave the Anglo-Saxons a long and distinguished history, also meant accepting a kinship with a variety of peoples, including Indians. Throughout the 1840's praise of the Teutons was a stronger theme than praise of the Caucasians, and by 1850 two well-known efforts were made to place the Anglo-Saxon-Teutonic strain into a more exclusive category; one, that of R. G. Latham, was in the main stream of scholarly research, although controversial, the other, that of Robert Knox, was more emotional racism.

Latham, a philologist, in his *Natural Varieties of Man,* suggested a tripartite division of the human species—the Mongolidae of Asia, Polynesia, and America, the Atlantidae of Africa, and the Iapetidae of Europe. The original "Caucasians" (that is, the Circassians and the Georgians) were placed not with the Europeans but with the Mongolidae. He objected to the classification, which had been used "in more than one celebrated work of fiction," which lumped together under the Caucasian name "Jews, Greeks, Circassians, Scotchmen, ancient Romans, and other heterogeneous elements." Of the three divisions, the influence of the Atlantidae on the history of the world had been "Inconsiderable," that of the Mongolidae "Material rather than moral," but that of the Iapetidae "Moral as well as material."[53] A logical extension of Latham's views came in the following year when he argued against the Asiatic origin of the Aryans, and instead proposed a European homeland. This idea was taken up with more enthusiasm later in the century.[54]

A more sensational attack on the broad depiction of Caucasians, and a passionate espousal of racial doctrines, came in Robert Knox's *Races of Men,* published in 1850. The anatomist who had been responsible for buying the hardly cold, murdered bodies provided by the notorious Burke and Hare in the Edinburgh of the 1820's could hardly be expected to be squeamish in racial matters, and Knox preached a frenetic racial doctrine. From 1846 Knox had spread his ideas in lectures throughout England.[55] Knox contemptuously dismissed earlier writers, even the greatest. Blumenbach and Prichard, according to Knox, had failed to understand basic racial division and antagonism, and Thomas Arnold

[53] Robert G. Latham, *The Natural History of the Varieties of Man* (London, 1850), 13–14, 107–08.
[54] Latham, *The Germania of Tacitus* (London, 1851), Epilegomena, cxxxix–cxlii.
[55] For his life see Lonsdale, *Life of Knox,* op. cit.

had confused a variety of races under the name Teutonic. "Race is everything," wrote Knox, "literature, science, art—in a word, civilization, depends on it."[56] In this he agreed with Disraeli, but he agreed with little else. The five-fold division of Blumenbach made no sense to Knox. There was no such thing as a Caucasian race; instead there were numerous unmixeable races even within Europe itself. Since the earliest historic times mankind had been divided into distinct races, races which had remained unchanged and were unchangeable. Races could not successfully intermingle; when they intermarried they gradually died out, overwhelmed by pure races. Strangely, along with this absolute racism, came a revival of old environmentalism, in a new guise. Races could not live successfully in all climates—without the influx of new blood, Europeans could not survive in tropical countries.[57]

Knox's preference was to use "Scandinavian" where others had used "Germanic" or "Teutonic." The Scandinavian was about to become the dominant race of the earth; a section of that race, the Anglo-Saxon, "had for nearly a century been all-powerful on the ocean." The race had always enjoyed noble qualities. The Romans at no period conquered "the Saxon or true German, that is, Scandinavian race." This "Scandinavian" race provided the only democrats on earth, "the only race which truly comprehends the meaning of the word liberty." Free government was the peculiar talent of the Anglo-Saxons: "their laws, manners, institutions, they brought with them from the woods of Germany, and they have transferred them to the woods of America."[58]

Except for the overriding theme of the supreme importance of race, Knox had little coherence of thought, and there was hardly any logical progression in his arguments. In spite of the talent of the Saxons for freedom, Knox argued that Great Britain still suffered from a Norman yoke in its government, and he failed to explain why the Normans failed to have his "Scandinavian" genius for government. He also had a harsh, at times realistic, view of the Anglo-Saxons. He painted them as a vigorous, acquisitive, aggressive race, natural democrats, but lacking men of artistic genius or abstract thought. They were a race "of all others the most outrageously boasting, arrogant, self-sufficient beyond endurance, holding in utter contempt all other races and all other men." What is more, although no race perhaps exceeded them in a sense of justice and fair play, this was "*only to Saxons.*" They did not extend their love of justice to other races.[59]

For the non-Scandinavian-Saxon races of men Knox had little respect or hope. He thought the Caucasian theory could not be right, because Jews and Gypsies were included in that grouping. Disraeli's

[56] Robert Knox, M.D., *The Races of Men: A Philosophical Enquiry into the Influence of Race over the Destinies of Nations* (2nd. ed., London, 1862), v, 15, 23–24, 341.
[57] *Ibid.*, 36, 44, 89, 107, 156, 380–81, 488.   [58] *Ibid.*, 9–10, 46, 59.
[59] *Ibid.*, 57, 131, 135, 370–71, 374.

ideas on the supremacy of the Jewish race he dismissed as idle romance, and the Celts also felt Knox's lash. The Celtic character was an amalgam of "Furious fanaticism; a love of war and disorder; a hatred for order and patient industry; no accumulative habits; restless, treacherous, uncertain: look at Ireland." Although Ireland had suffered from "Norman" rule, "the source of all evil lies in *the race,* the Celtic race of Ireland." Wales and Scotland gave similar examples, and the Celtic race should be forced from the soil, "by fair means, if possible; still they must leave. England's safety requires it. I speak not of the justice of the cause; nations must ever act as Machiavelli advised: look to yourself."[60]

The "dark races" of the earth, according to Knox, could never be taught true civilization: "Destined by the nature of their race to run, like all other animals, a certain limited course of existence, it matters little how their extinction is brought about." The inferiority of the dark races (and here Knox included a great variety of peoples, including Chinese) stemmed from "specific characters in the quality of the brain itself." If they were to survive it would be in the tropical regions, unsuitable for the Anglo-Saxons, where the blacks might hold out.[61] Although Robert Knox had a wild, irrational streak, and formed theories peculiarly his own, much of what he wrote, however illogically put together, was a selection from a variety of theories put forward in the previous half century or more. He was a peculiar example of what a confused, and perhaps dangerous, mind could make of what had often been put forward as precise scholarship in linguistic origins, history, race, and mythology.

The harsh philosophy of Knox was at one extreme of the Anglo-Saxonism that was flourishing by the middle of the century. At the other were the pious, vague platitudes filling the justly short-lived magazine *The Anglo-Saxon,* published in London in 1849 and 1850. Its tone was set by the emblem on the front cover—Gregory looking at a group of cherubic children, with the motto "Non Angli sed Angeli." The magazine quoted Knox, but also referred to his "erratic and frequently . . . unsteady pen."[62] Whereas Knox dealt with crude realities of power, the *Anglo-Saxon* stressed the Christian mission of the Anglo-Saxon race.

At the basis of the magazine's philosophy was a familiar Saxonism—the race had an innate love of liberty, equal laws, and free institutions. Although the "arts and sciences of Greece and Rome" were grafted "on the native stock of Saxon genius," not foreign enlightenment but "the inborn spirit of the race produced the germs which have unfolded into a civilization more noble and grand than ever flourished in

---

[60] *Ibid.,* 26, 194–95, 208, 379.   [61] *Ibid.,* 224–26, 450, 456, 598–99.
[62] *The Anglo-Saxon* (London, 1849–50). "Non Angli Sed Angeli" were also the first words of the lead article in the first issue. Comment on Knox: 1 (April 1849), 163.

the capitals of Athens or of Rome." The Saxons were also firmly tied
into their Teutonic ancestry. Anglo-Saxon readers (and it is difficult to
imagine many others) were asked to "be proud that we belong to the
great Teutonic stock," which "appears destined to people and rule the
East as well as the West." This Teutonic race had peculiar abilities
which were permanent, and had existed from the beginning of the race.
The Anglo-Saxon branch was now rapidly taking over the world.[63]

Although criticisms were levelled at the Celts, the *Anglo-Saxon* was
prepared to include them in its vague concept of family, for a mystical
faith was placed in the English language. The spreading of the English
language would somehow enable the Anglo-Saxons to absorb and
transform those Celts who spoke English. Moreover, as the Anglo-
Saxons spread they would afford "shelter, and protection, and support
to other families and less favoured races of mankind." A great stress
was laid on "the *Destiny*, the *Mission*" of the Anglo-Saxon race, and
above all else this was a Christian mission: "The whole Earth may be
called the *Father-land* of the Anglo-Saxon. He is a native of every
clime—a messenger of heaven to every corner of this Planet."[64] It was
even maintained that when a community began to speak the English language it was "half Saxonised," even if there were no Anglo-Saxons
there. The magazine emphasized that pride of race was not pride of nation or conquest, but in effect it was more confident than Knox that the
Anglo-Saxon race would rule the world: "Feebling dwindling day by
day/All other races are fading away." In practical terms the magazine
praised Rajah Brooke's expeditions into Sarawak, omitting the bloody
aspects of these endeavors, and depicted him as an agent of Saxon
destiny.[65]

By the time the young E. A. Freeman was taking his degree at Oxford in the 1840's the ingredients for the new racial interpretation of
Anglo-Saxon destiny were all present. By the end of the 1840's Freeman
was already writing of "Teutonic greatness," and was able to compare
those seeds planted in the "German forest or on . . . Scandinavian rock"
with all the legacy of Greece and Rome, and to decide clearly in favor of
the former.[66] Freeman's main work, however, lay in the future, and it is
Charles Kingsley who best typifies the impact of the new ideas in the
middle years of the century. Although one does not have to accept the
suggestion of one biographer that Kingsley typifies the Victorian man as
Queen Victoria typifies the Victorian woman,[67] Kingsley did reach a
whole middle class audience that shunned more esoteric explanations of

[63] *Ibid.*, 1 (April 1849), 144, 205.
[64] *Ibid.*, 1 (Jan. 1849), 3–4; 1 (July 1849), 5–16.
[65] *Ibid.*, 2 (1850), 6–14, 39, 453, 467.
[66] W. R. W. Stephens, *The Life and Letters of Edward A. Freeman* (2 vols., London, 1895), I, 108, 120, 126.
[67] Margaret Farrand Thorp, *Charles Kingsley, 1819–1875* (Princeton, 1937), 1.

England's past. In racial matters he absorbed, and transmitted, in simplistic form a whole host of themes that had permeated the first half of the nineteenth century. That Kingsley was able to blend a marked Anglo-Saxon racism into his defense of Christianity, home, family, womanhood, monarchy, and empire is an indication of the pervasiveness of the new Anglo-Saxonism.

From the late 1840's until his death in 1875 Kingsley expounded the virtues of the English branch of the great Teutonic race, and their role in world history. His religion had a curious, pagan tinge: "I say that the Church of England is wonderfully and mysteriously fitted for the souls of a free Norse-Saxon race," he wrote to his wife in 1851, "for men whose ancestors fought by the side of Odin, over whom a descendant of Odin now rules."[68] Kingsley was particularly influenced by the concept of a strong Norse element in Teutonism and Anglo-Saxonism. When in 1849 he gave up lecturing at Queen's College he described to his successor what his next lecture would have been. The essence of it was that in the late Anglo-Saxon period the system was rotting for lack of original thinking—the "Anglo-Saxon, (a female race) required impregnation by the great male race,—the Norse introduction of Northmen by Edward paving the way for the Conquest, &c." He asked his successor to give the students a lecture "on the rise of our Norse forefathers—give them something from the Voluspa and Edda."[69]

Yet, for all his Norse emphasis, Kingsley gave what had become a common interpretation of the overrunning of the Roman Empire: regeneration of the degenerate peoples of Europe by vigorous Teutons. According to Kingsley, not only the future Europe but also the Church needed this infusion. Kingsley fully developed these ideas in his strange, impressionistic Cambridge lectures of 1860–61, but he had suggested them much earlier. In his preface to *Hypatia* in the early 1850's he had pointed out that "the *mens sana* must have a *corpus sanum* to inhabit." This was provided by the Teutonic or Gothic nations. Into a world drained by the influence of Rome came "the infusion of new and healthier blood." The Teutonic nations brought with them "comparative purity of morals; sacred respect for women, family life, law, equal justice, individual freedom, and, above all, . . . honesty in word and deed."[70] Later, in his Cambridge lectures, Kingsley argued that God had fitted the Teutonic race to become the ruling race of the world, indeed "the welfare of the Teutonic race is the welfare of the world." Although

[68] Kingsley to his wife, Jan. 26, 1851, in *Charles Kingsley. His Letters and Memories and His Life*, ed. by his wife (5th ed., 2 vols., London, 1877), I, 253.
[69] Kingsley to Rev. Alfred Strettell, April 17, 1849, *ibid.*, I, 201. The idea of active (male) races, and passive (female) races was most fully developed by Gustav Klemm in his *Allgemeine Cultur-Geschichte der Menschheit* (10 vols., Leipzig, 1843–52); Michael D. Biddiss, *Father of Racist Ideology: The Social and Political Thought of Count Gobineau* (New York, 1970), 110.
[70] Kingsley, *Hypatia* (2 vols., 1853; New York, 1899), Preface, xviii.

those tribes that swept over the Roman Empire had no supreme general on earth, they may have had "a general in Heaven."[71] For all his sense of Christian destiny, Kingsley could on occasion be as ruthless as Robert Knox in describing the fate of other races. He believed that degenerate races, including the North American Indian, were better off dead. Like the writers of the the *Anglo-Saxon* magazine, Kingsley admired Rajah Brooke (he dedicated *Westward Ho* to him), and he was Brooke's ardent defender when many criticized his attacks on the Sarawak "pirates." "The truest benevolence," wrote Kingsley in 1849, "is occasional severity. It *is* expedient that one man die for the people. One tribe exterminated, if need be, to save a whole continent. 'Sacrifice of human life?' Prove that it is *human* life." Kingsley was confident that the Anglo-Saxons were spreading the virtues of the Teutonic race throughout the world, and in doing so extending God's kingdom: "Because Christ's kingdom is a kingdom of peace; because the meek alone shall inherit the earth, therefore, you Malays and Dyaks of Sarawak, you are also enemies to peace . . . you are beasts, all the more dangerous, because you have a semi-human cunning."[72] The reign of world peace, order, and morality was to be established by the Anglo-Saxon-Teutonic Christians, and if necessary it was to be founded on the bodies of inferior races.

By the middle years of the nineteenth century the simple praise of Anglo-Saxon institutions and love of freedom, which had assumed such importance in the sixteenth and seventeenth centuries, had undergone a profound change. Racial emphases which influenced the whole of Europe in the first half of the nineteenth century fell on peculiarly fertile ground in England and in the countries colonized from Great Britain, particularly the United States. An interest in national origins, in the intimate relationship of race, language, and nation was of course not peculiar to Great Britain, but the Anglo-Saxons combined a long idealization of their early institutions with overt signs of nineteenth-century success; of the apparently inevitable drive of Great Britain and the United States to world domination. "Anglo-Saxons" were pouring across the North American continent while British power reached to the Antipodes. Many national groups have believed they were the chosen people, but few have had such apparent evidence to feed their delusions. By the middle years of the nineteenth century the idea of a superior Anglo-Saxon race regenerating a world of lesser races was firmly ingrained in English thinking.

University of Wisconsin, Milwaukee.

[71] Kingsley, *The Roman and the Teuton. A Series of Lectures Delivered Before the University of Cambridge* (1864; London, 1891), 305–06.
[72] Kingsley to J. M. Ludlow, Dec. 1849, Kingsley, *Letters and Memories*, I, 222–23.

PART TWO

GENDER DISTINCTIONS

VIII

THE EDUCATIONAL IDEAS OF CHRISTINE DE PISAN *

By Astrik L. Gabriel

The life problem of Christine de Pisan was to refute the false conception of Aristotelian anti-feminism, that woman is nothing else than defective man, a *mutilated male* (*vir occasionatus*) and to show that the compliment given to her by Gerson, *femina ista virilis*, is applicable to her sex.[1] Christine, one of the greatest moralists of Christian literature, approached with courageous frankness the problem of woman's place in society.

Christine's father, Thomas, was a native of Bologna and became a master in medicine in 1343. His daughter, Christine, was born in 1364.[2] His fame as a physician was growing; and Louis, King of Hungary and Charles V of France both tried to get him to their court.[3] Thomas accepted the offer of Charles V. His wife and daughter joined him at the court in 1368. Christine never regretted her father's decision, for she had loved France from her childhood:

No nation of the world has such benign and humane princes as France. I say it without flattery, because it is the truth.[4]

At the court of Charles V, her father's main preoccupation was making astrological predictions. He invented a "natural experiment" a kind of "secret weapon" of the Hundred Years War [5]—for

---

* Lecture given at Marygrove College, Detroit, Mich., on March 8, 1953.

[1] Aristotle, *De generatione animalium*, IV, 6: "We must look upon the female character as being a sort of natural deficiency"; II, 3: "The female is, as it were a mutilated male": *The works of Aristotle, translated into English* under the editorship of J. A. Smith and W. D. Ross, V, 775a, 16–17 and 737a, 28; St. Thomas quoting Aristotle: "Sicut enim Philosophus dicit in XVI. *De animalibus*, mulier est vir occasionatus": *Script. Super Sent.* II, Dist. 20, q. 2,a. 1, obj. 1. On Gerson: C. Ward: *The epistles on the Romance of the Rose and other documents in the debate* (Chicago, 1911), 79.

[2] E. Wickersheimer, *Dictionnaire biographique des médecins en France au moyen âge* (Paris, 1926), 764b.

[3] *Mutacion de Fortune*, Bk. 7, ch. 55, f. 312: Marie J. Pinet, *Christine de Pisan (1364-1430)* (Paris, 1927), 4, note 3: "The good king of Hungary helped by fortune during his life ruled for a long time. He governed his country well and conducted his wars wisely. He had two kind and beautiful daughters. The oldest was engaged to the virtuous Louis of France, but the bitterness of war destroyed this union."

[4] Paris, B. N. Ms. Fr. 12493, f. 210v; S. Solente, "Un traité inédit de Christine de Pisan, 'L'epistre de la prison de vie humaine,'" *Bibl. École des Chartes*, 85 (1924), 264.

[5] L. Thorndike, *A History of Magic and Experimental Science* (New York, 1923), II, 802.

expelling the English companies and mercenaries from French soil. He was well liked in the King's entourage. The marriage contract of Louis of France with the daughter of Louis, King of Hungary, was witnessed by him.[6] The learned physician gave Christine a thorough education in Latin, in philosophy, and in the various branches of science. She proved herself a good student and showed an extraordinary predilection for learning.

When Christine was fifteen, she married the King's secretary, Etienne de Castel, a gentleman from Picardy. Union of heart and mind characterized this marriage:

> Our love and our two hearts were far more than that of brother and sister. We were joined in a unity of joy and pain.[7]

Two years after her marriage her father's royal protector died. The year 1380 marked the beginning of the turning of the Wheel of Fortune. The cruel fate of her childhood justified a later poem: *La Mutacion de Fortune*,[8] wherein she wrote:

> " Fortune " is more inconstant than the moon.

After the death of the King, her father lost his position at the court. He could not share the enthusiasm of Jean des Mares: *Novus rex, nova lex, novum gaudium* (New king, new law, new joy).[9] He died shortly afterwards in 1385.

Sorrows never come singly. A still heavier misfortune, the epidemic of Beauvais, took Christine's husband, in 1389. With three small children to provide for, at the age of twenty-five she was left alone.

> Seulete suy et seulete vueil estre
> Seulete m'a mon doulz ami laissiée
>
> Alone am I, alone I wish to be,
> Alone my sweetest friend hath left me here,
> Alone am I, in my sole company,
> Alone in sorrow bent, and without cheer.
> Alone am I in langourous disgrace,
> Alone far more than wanderer from God's grace,
> Alone, without a friend, the world I face.[10]

---

[6] E. Wickersheimer, *op. cit.*, note 8.

[7] *Le chemin de long estude*, vv. 87–90; *Le livre du Chemin de Long Estude par Christine de Pizan*, ed. R. Puschel (Berlin, Paris, n.d.).

[8] The *Mutacion de Fortune* is unpublished: Paris, B. N. Ms. Fr. 604; Pinet, *op. cit.*, 306, note 1; Alice Kemp-Welch, *Of six mediaeval women*, (London, 1913), 142.   [9] Pinet, *op. cit.*, 15, n. 2.

[10] French text: M. Roy, *Oeuvres poétiques de Christine de Pisan*, Paris, 1886 (Soc. Anc. Textes, 33), I, 12; English translation: W. A. Nitze and E. Preston Dargan, *A History of French Literature* (New York, 1938), 93.

Her happy life was ended. She entered into the hermitage of her heart, surrounding herself with a wall of learning. In the inconstancy of the world, knowledge became her only consolation, that learning which can change the mortal to immortal. Her only pastime was that of Charles d'Orléans, playing with her own thoughts:

There is no better pastime than to play at thinking.[11]

Harrassed by her husband's creditors and unable to collect what had been bequeathed to her children, she was involved in endless lawsuits throughout the following years.

Her one consolation was her visit to the famous convent of Poissy, where her daughter had become a nun. This monastery of Dominican nuns was founded by Philippe Auguste in 1304. Placed under the patronage of St. Louis, it enjoyed the most generous privileges of the royal house. Marie de France, daughter of Charles VI and of Isabel of Bavaria, lived there. A special authorization of the King was required for admission of girls or nuns.[12]

II

The solicitous mother was a frequent visitor at the convent that housed her beloved daughter. In an enchanting poem, Christine tells with charming simplicity of her pleasure-pilgrimage from Paris to the convent of Poissy. She describes all the beauties of the country. We feel the air of spring, we hear the warbling of the birds, we assist at the cheerful outing of a noble society. The soft flowing of the river, the calm trees of St. Germain give a picturesque background for the tableau painted by Christine.[13] The poem reveals the loving mother who is happy to see her daughter:

My daughter, so they say, is beautiful and kind, young, learned and gracious, and also a nun in a fine rich abbey.[14]

Joyous and happy they arrive at the convent. Then she gives a charming description of the convent and a vivid picture of the nuns, who are always ready to serve, wisely and with simplicity:

Simples, sages et a Dieu servir prestes.[15]

She meets her daughter, so dear to her heart:

Then she whom I love much and hold so dear, approached me humbly

[11] J. Bédier, P. Hasard and P. Martino, *Littérature Française* (Paris, 1948, I), 122b.
[12] M. Roy, *op. cit.*, II, notes 312.
[13] A beautiful analysis of the poem by Alice Kemp-Welch, *op. cit.*, 140.
[14] *Le livre du dit de Poissy*, vv. 42–46; M. Roy, *op. cit.*, II, 160.
[15] *Ibid.*, v. 230; II, 166.

and knelt down before me, and I kissed her soft, sweet face.[16]

In that earthly paradise, where even visitors from the world were compelled to talk about devotion and of how to serve God with right intention, she could hardly restrain her tears, when bidding her farewell. When she left the sacred walls she became again a reticent soul, hiding a broken heart.

> I know not how my life I bear!
> For sad regrets my hours employ,
> Yet may I not betray a tear,
> Nor tell what woes my heart destroy.[17]
> Je ne sçay comment je dure;
> Car mon dolent cuer font d'yre.

Compelled to earn her daily bread, she set to work with extraordinary diligence. "Men must work, and women must weep." [18] She did both. The Christian paideia became her consolation.

III

Qui bien aime, tout endure. She was most fitted to understand the sorrows of the widows who lost their husbands in the battle of Agincourt (Oct. 25, 1415). Friend and sympathizer of many of the great families decimated by the calamities of the time, she composed a consolatory treatise.[19]

The sorrows of the invaded land are reflected in her *l'Epistre de Prison de la vie humaine.* Moved by the sight of so many killed and taken prisoner, she decided to follow in the footprints of Vincent of Beauvais, who composed one of the earliest Consolatory Letters.[20]

Christine begins by showing from texts of St. Bernard and St. Albert the Great that life is a poor thing, and that this mortal life can be best portrayed as a prison from which we await deliverance at the hour of death. Hence the title, *The Prison of Human Life.* If perchance anyone should trust in worldly grandeur, there are enough historical examples to prove that only the dead are truly happy and

---

[16] *Ibid.*, vv. 233–236.

[17] Translation by Louisa S. Costella in Ch. W. Jones, *Mediaeval Literature in Translation* (New York, London, Toronto, 1950) p. 688; no source given by the translator. This is the seventh rondeau: M. Roy, *op. cit.*, I, 151:

[18] A. Kemp-Welch, *op. cit.*, 121.

[19] Treatise written between the 15th of June 1416 and the 20th of January 1418. It was dedicated to Marie de Berry, her learned and charitable benefactress: S. Solente, *op. cit., Bibl. École des Chartes*, 85 (1924), 282–301.

[20] Vincentius Bellovacensis, *Opuscula* (Basel, Johann Amerbach, 13 Dec. 1481). Consolacio pro morte amici; Cf. M. B. Stillwell, *Incunabula in American Libraries* (New York, 1940), 516, V. 248.

assured of escaping the fantasies of rude Fortune. *Virtue* is no shield against such blows, and *vice* only serves to precipitate the final disaster, since the wicked often begin their hell even in this world. With such thoughts in mind why should we not exclaim with Christine:

Oh, world, is it then such a great joy and victory to rule over Thee! [21]

What are the remedies counselled by Scripture and the holy doctors for any adversity of life? The best is " hope in God and do well " and the other " suffer patiently for the love of Our Lord." The necessary patience is usually troubled by our pride when we are reluctant to accept even the smallest insults or injuries. We must strive also to conquer human sorrow, impatience, or anger for fear of sinning against Providence.

No matter what misfortune strikes us, we still have some reasons for rejoicing. God has bestowed on us gifts of *Grace, Nature,* and *Fortune.* In the midst of adversities we must recall that with *Grace* we have received the gift of understanding and discerning; with *Nature* we have obtained strength, beauty, health, the gift of speech, pleasant manners and graciousness. (Christine de Pisan has definitely in mind Marie de Berry, daughter of Jean de France, niece of Charles V, and charming Duchess of Bourbonnais, to whom she has dedicated the present treatise.) *Fortune* gives us power, riches and good adventure. Discretion, the mother of all virtues, should direct us in the use of the goods of Fortune.

Towards the end of this meditation, Christine de Pisan shows that the Duchess Marie de Berry is sufficiently endowed with the gifts of Grace, Nature, and Fortune, not that she should glory in them as if they were hers,[22] but that she should rather thank God for such benefits and express her thankfulness by a discreet and wise use of such advantages. She has received the gift of good understanding, bodily health, and beauty, comes from the highest lineage, has married into the greatest family of the Kingdom, has beautiful children, a good name, and great riches. Her only suffering is the imprisonment of her husband, the Duke Jean de Berry, and this itself can be put to good advantage by the exercise of patience and fortitude.

IV

Christine de Pisan was the first woman to protest in writing against the slanderous attacks of the anti-feminist authors of the Middle Ages. She was the first to defend womanhood against the wholesale generalizations and prejudices of Jean de Meung, author

---

[21] *L'epistre, op. cit., ibid.,* 286.
[22] " Le beau corps fort sain et puissant." *Ibid., op. cit.,* 296.

of the *Roman de la Rose*. The antifeminists, led by Mahieu, a married cleric of the thirteenth century,[23] openly claimed that on the day of the Last Judgment God would give back to Adam the rib from which woman was created. Thus women would disappear and would not take part in the joy of Paradise.

> Adam par entier ne seroit;
> Se sa coste n'estoit remise
> En son lieu, ou elle fu prise,
> . . . .
> Femme sera destituée
> Ainsi saulvée ne sera
> Ne ja ne ressuscitera.[24]

In her two poems, *L'Epistre au Dieu d'Amours* (May 1399) and *Le Dit de la Rose* (Feb. 14, 1401),[25] Christine vigorously denounced the immoral literature and the disloyal attitude of Jean de Meung:

> Se bien veulx chastement vivre,
> De la Rose ne lis le livre

A champion of edifying readings, she bade parents put good stories into the hands of their children.[26] In her teaching, addressed to her son, Jean Castel, she begged him not to believe those detractors of womankind. Experience would show him that there are many good women in the world:

> Ne croy pas toutes les diffames
> Qu'aucuns livres dient des femmes,
> Car il est mainte femme bonne,
> L'experïence le te donne.[27]

Woman is the ever present companion of man. She nurses his child, she cares for him during his lifetime, she is man's companion from birth to death:

> A son naistre, au vivre et au mourir
> Lui sont femmes aidans et secourables.[28]

On the dignity and worth of women Christine borrows her arguments from the writings of great theologians. Profiting from such

---

[23] A. G. Van Hamel, *Les lamentations de Matheolus* (Paris, 1892, I–II, 1892–1905).

[24] *Ibid., op. cit.,* I, 200; vv. 1442–1445 and 1450–53.

[25] M. Roy, *op. cit.,* II, 29.

[26] *Les enseignemens moraux,* ed. M. Roy, *op. cit.,* III, 39, strophe 77.

[27] *Ibid.,* 33, strophe 38.

[28] *L'epistre, op. cit.,* vv. 176–177; Roy, *op. cit.,* II, 6–7.

tradition as that represented by Robert de Sorbonne, she thinks woman is a nobler creature than man. Adam was made from dust, Eve from bone. Man was created outside of Paradise, while the creation of woman was among the delights of a joyful place. If woman is so weak and easy to conquer, why did Jean de Meung and the other anti-feminists write such lenghty treatises on how to secure a woman's love? Men should cherish and love the sex from which they descend, because men are never happy without women, who are to them mother, sister, and friend: [29]

> Homs naturel sanz femmes ne s'esjoye:
> C'est sa mere, c'est sa suer, c'est s'amie.

In her attack on the opinions of Jean de Meung, who scoffed at both the married and the cloistered life, she found a faithful ally in the person of Jean Gerson, powerful chancellor of the University of Paris, " un tres vaillant docteur, et maistre en Theologie, souffisant, digne, louable, clerc solempnel, esleu entre les esleus." Reason and wit, strength and affection characterized this alliance against the Roman de la Rose.[30]

There is a striking resemblance between Christine and Gerson. Both started their careers around 1390. They had the same adversaries, the Burgundians, they had the same ideals. They wrote without exaggerated mysticism or fruitless discussion. They wanted a solid piety rooted in the respect of neighbor and love of God. After the death of Gerson, we hear nothing more from Christine de Pisan.

Besides Gerson, Christine found wholehearted support in such influential men as Jean le Meingre and Marechal of Boucicaut, who founded a gallant " order " to defend the honor of womanhood.[31]

Thanks to Christine de Pisan, the popularity of anti-feminist literature was losing its force. With her calm and dispassionate arguments she made the case of her sex her own problem. In attacking the Roman de la Rose, she kept the controversy on a high level, never losing her intellectual curiosity to find woman's place in society.

V

Mediaeval educators were not content to compose elementary treatises for training children; they looked ahead, they visualized the needs of grown-up men. Guibert de Tournai composed a treatise on how to teach boys, and as a theologian tackled the problems of rulers. Their faith in integrated education forced them to examine the prob-

[29] L'epistre, op. cit., vv. 732–3; ibid., II, 24.
[30] Pinet, op. cit., 69.
[31] A. Kemp-Welch, op. cit., 134.

lems of statesmanship and the qualities of a good prince.[32]
Christine de Pisan continued the mediaeval tradition of political
thinkers by outlining the most necessary qualities of a good government. John of Salisbury's *Policraticus* (1159), Gerald of Welsh's
De principis instructione, Guibert de Tournai's *De eruditione regum,*
Giles of Rome's *De regimine principum* constituted some of the phi-
losophico-political tradition for her model, Raoul de Presles' *Compendium morale rei publicae* (1361-64).

Christine's purpose in composing the *Chemin de long estude* was
simple. She wanted to attract the French people to noble morals by
displaying before them the features of an ideal ruler. In the dispute
of Richness, Nobility, Chivalry, and Wisdom, allegorical persons of
the poem, the decision is left to Reason. The conclusion of the dispute (which ends in the scholastic tradition of the "determinatio"),
is that one wise man assisted by a council of learned and wise men
should govern the whole world (thus she passed judgment on one-
world government):

It would also be necessary to lead this low world to peace, by putting
one man over it who would rule the whole earth.[33]

Her method of composition was simple. She applied the wisdom
of the ancient writers to the daily problems of political science. The
arguments and illustrative examples are old, but their arrangement
is new and entirely hers. As a moralist, she was deeply concerned
about the ethical dynamism of human behavior. Always inclined to
moralize, she used her source-material for ethico-didactic purposes.
She saw the disorders of her time, wars, suicides, betrayals, snares.
In her desire for peace she looked for remedies and explanations.
God permits such things in order to direct our thoughts to the eternal
destination of mankind. The cause of all miseries is the unrestrained
desire for power on the part of man and political ambitions on the
part of nations.

Christine de Pisan is more than a simple ethical compiler, because
with courageous mind, she solved certain problems of her time. In
the *Chemin de long estude* she showed how to heal the wounds of
ailing humanity by treating it with the medicine of virtue.[34] *Le
Livre des fais et bonnes meurs du sage roy Charles V* is an illustration

[32] A. De Poorter, "Un traité de pédagogie mediévale: le DE MODO
ADDISCENDI de Guibert de Tournai, notices et extraits," *Revue Neo-Scolastique
de Louvain,* 24 (1922), 216–228. Same author: Le Traité ERUDITIO REGUM
ET PRINCIPUM de Guibert de Tournai (Louvain, 1914).

[33] *Le chemin de long estude,* vv. 3037–40; Pinet, *op. cit.,* 300.

[34] Madeleine Rosier, *Christine de Pisan as a moralist* (Thesis, University of
Toronto, 1945; manuscript).

of the principles and virtues required by different authors on the Government of Rulers and Mirror of Princes.[35] Christine's aim is nothing less than to convince us that the virtues required by the *Nicomachean Ethics* of Aristotle were really practised by Charles V. Christine, sitting in her pulpit " in the shadows of ignorance, searching for clear understanding," labored hard for the good of her " doulce France ":

In order to draw the French heart to noble morals by good example.[36]

In the *Livre de la paix* (1412) written after the treaty of Auxerre, when hope was high for prosperity and peace, she exhorts those in power to use Liberality, Clemency, and Justice in order to restore peace in the troubled world.[37]

One of her best treatises, which is, so to speak, a complete course on feminine education, is the Book of the Three Virtues, *Le Livre des trois vertus*. Christine addresses herself to all women of all social classes, princesses and servants, Parisian ladies and villagers, laborers and poor helpless " little women," *petites femmes*.[38] She follows the rational educational thesis of the Fathers of the Church, that a woman should be womanly. This does not exclude her being the " strong woman of the Gospel," ready to face the troubles, temptations, and deceptions of the world. Christine's pedagogy is based on giving good example. A man of high position should serve as a mirror of perfection. Good example should be given by the lord to his subjects, by parents to their children, by the master to his pupil, by the rich to the poor, by the clever to the simple:

Doivent estre si comme mirouer et exemple de toutes bonnes meurs à leurs subgetz.[39]

Religious teaching should be the foundation of any further education. Christine agreed with Gerson, who in his *ABC des Pauvres Gens* suggested that the mother should teach the first elements of religion, the Our Father, Hail Mary, and Creed.[40]

[35] Abbé Lebeuf, " Vie de Charles V dit le Sage, roy de France," *Dissertations sur l'histoire ecclésiastique et civile de Paris* (Paris, 1743), III, 81–484.

[36] Wilhelm Berges, *Fürstenspiegel des hohen und späten Mittelalters* (Leipzig, 1938), 267.

[37] K. Sneyders de Vogel, " Une oeuvre inconnue de Christine de Pisan," *Mélanges de philologie romane et de littérature mediévale offerts à Ernest Hoepffner* (Paris, 1949), 369–370.

[38] Mathilde Laigle, *Le livre des trois vertus de Christine de Pisan* (Bibliothèque du XVe siecle, XVI, Paris, 1912), 56.

[39] Laigle, *op. cit.*, 114.

[40] B. N. Ms. Fr. 1843, fol. 16–19: Laigle, *op. cit.*, 124.

VI

The aim of feminine education in the view of Christine de Pisan is the acquisition of *moral wisdom*. She insists in every page of her writings on the necessity of instruction. As a champion of education, she thinks that knowing is a duty and a benefit for all. But Christine warns that knowledge alone is not sufficient. It must be developed alongside of and in harmony with virtue. Her true aim is to prepare girls to meet the joys and sorrows of life, to be ready to repel temptations and fit to endure life's many deceptions.[41]

Discussing the education of the young girl, she does not want the same type of learning for the two sexes. The girl's education should be less varied than that of her brother. The acquisition of moral science will enable the woman to become a helpful associate of her husband. Christine stresses the necessity of practical sciences useful for the administration of the lands, the revenues, and the " castles " of the young lady's noble husband, who because of duty in war or pleasure in travels is often absent from the home. The knowledge involved is not primarily of the speculative order. Latin is not recommended. Mathematics is of primary importance. The womanly arts of sewing, knitting, embroidery, and weaving are highly recommended for all types of women.[42] Out of this should come the strong woman spoken of in the Bible.

Christine harks back to Quintilian's idea of the educated man as one who can express himself with prompt readiness, possessing the gift of speech and all the excellences of character as well: in one word, someone who lives up to the principles of upright and honorable living.[43] In Christine de Pisan's conception, reason is one of the adornments of the educated man. She renews the warning of Clement of Alexandria, the Father of Christian paideia, that we must form man to live as the image of God, according to LOGOS—Reason personifying Christ.[44]

As far as the proper extent of a woman's knowledge is concerned, Christine's theory is that she should have an understanding of all things, for the person whose knowledge is limited is not really wise:

[41] Laigle, *op. cit.*, 5.
[42] Laigle, *op. cit.*, 189–90.
[43] " My aim, then, is the education of the perfect orator. The first essential for such an one is that he should be a good man, and consequently we demand of him not merely the possession of exceptional gifts of speech, but of all the excellence of character as well." Quintilian, *Inst. Orat.*, I, Preface: *The Institutio Oratoria of Quintilian with an English Translation* by H. E. Butler (London, New York, 1933), I, 9–11.
[44] J. Giordani, *The Social Message of the Early Church Fathers* (Washington, D. C., 1944), 186–87.

C'est qu'elle se sache entendre de touttes choses, car, dit le Philosophe, que celui n'est pas sage qui ne cognoist aucune part de chascune chose.[45]

According to the shrewd male's statement, woman is just a little simple thing, easy to conquer:

> On peut vaincre une chose simplete
> Une ignorant petite femmelette [46]

and therefore she must be wise: men may study to be learned, women should study to be wise. She repeats the teaching of the Fathers, that nature is the same in each individual and that each is capable of the same virtue. Woman does not have one human nature and man another. Respiration, sight, hearing, knowledge, hope, obedience, love are all alike in man and woman.[47] Christine de Pisan logically concludes from the *Stromata* of St. Clement of Alexandria: if woman has the same qualities, talent, and aptitude as man, she has the right to the same education too.

Christine disagreed with her mother's conservative views, that purely domestic education is sufficient for a girl. She followed her father's advanced ideas, that learning is not injurious to the physical and mental integrity of a young girl. The formation of the whole person in its natural and supernatural powers with regard to its intellectual, moral, and religious being as well as to its social, economic, and professional life is one of the main features of Christine's educational ideas. This formation is to be obtained with the help of wisdom acquired through speculative and practical knowledge.

The indispensable virtues for a girl are sobriety and chastity. The first restrains her from excessive pleasure, controls her behavior, and keeps her in the line of discipline and reason. Chastity adorns her with respect and fortitude. It gives to the virgin the magic power which could even subdue such a legendary and fairy animal as the unicorn. (According to the belief of the vernacular literature of the time, represented in so many beautiful tapestries, the unicorn could be captured by no one but a virgin. The freshness of virginity provided her with extraordinary strength.)

The emphasis in Christine's moral teaching is on the good reputation of women. *A good name is better than precious ointments* (Eccl. vii.2.). To earn this good fame a woman must avoid detrac-

---

[45] Laigle, *op. cit.*, 187; L. McDowell Richardson, *The forerunners of Feminism in French literature of the Renaissance*, Part I (The Johns Hopkins Studies in Romance Literatures and Languages, XII; Baltimore, 1920), 32.

[46] *L'epistre au Dieu d'Amours*, vv. 549–50; M. Roy, *op. cit.*, II, 18.

[47] Clement of Alexandria, *Stromata*, IV, 8. PG 8, 12, 71A. Translation: W. Wilson, *The Writings of Clement of Alexandria* (Edinburgh, 1871).

tors (*Malebouche*) and lead a noble life. The question of honor appears in its classical importance: honor which is like lilies, fragile and delicate:

This flower which we call lily is white, tender, sweet-scented, and pleasant, but at the least touch it is already hurt and crushed.[48]

Defending the honor of her sex, Christine admits that women are by nature timid and fearful:

> Femenin sexe par droiture
> Craint et tousdis est paoureux.[49]

But let us not forget—she continues—that man's recklessness has brought us into wars, duels, and riots. It is true that women are easily moved to tears; but what a miraculous influence this gentle dew has been! St. Monica's tears gave St. Augustine to the Church. The anti-feminists always reproach woman's loquacity as a vice. But is not speech a positive gift? The desire for learning is as great in a girl as in a boy. Christine is, she admits, only a weak woman but she can defend the honor of her own sex. A very small knife can make a big hole in a sack.

As a convincing argument Christine appeals to the good example of the great women who have brought glory and honor to their sex. The deeds of these illustrious women are told in *La Cité des dames.*

VII

The *City of ladies* houses the heroines of the ancient past and some of the famous women of Christine's own time.[50]   In this work, written around 1404–1405, she recalls the illustrious deeds of the great women of all times. One of the miniatures that illustrates the manuscript of the *City of ladies* represents Christine as helping to build this imaginary city, a symbolic expression of her devout passion for virtuous life and noble example. The *City of ladies* or " The Golden Book of Heroines," is another defense of women's virtue against the anti-feminists' slanderous attacks. God created woman; He gave her a soul; therefore she cannot be evil. It is not difference of sex but the fulfillment of duty and the adornment of virtue which must be taken into consideration. Christine freely uses Boccaccio's stories from *De claris mulieribus,* interwoven with her moral inter-

---

[48] " C'est la fleur que nous appelons lis, lequel est blanc, tendre et souef flairant; mais de moult petit hurt est froissié et taché," Laigle, *op. cit.*, 136.

[49] *Le chemin de long estude,* vv. 1736–1737.

[50] Unpublished.   The most beautiful miniatures are in B. N. Ms. Fr. 607; O. Cartellieri, *The Court of Burgundy* (London, New York, 1929), 102; Kemp-Welch, *op. cit.*, 138.

pretations, in order to show that women can possess those qualities which were regarded as foreign to their sex.[51]

In the minature the allegorical persons, *Reason, Righteousness,* and *Justice,* are helping Christine to build the city of illustrious women. *Reason* testifies that a long line of princesses have governed their kingdoms more successfully than have many kings. They excel in learning, like Cornificie, Sappho, Manthoa, and Medea:

la tres soultille poete et philosophe.[52]

After Reason has built the City, *Righteousness* (*Droiture*) helps to bring virtuous women to live there. The problem of married life comes up in a discussion between Christine and *Droiture.* Christine's compassion towards married women compels her to say that a married woman's life is frequently worse than if she were captured by the Saracens. She openly protests against the accusation that women can not keep any secret unrevealed. She defends most vehemently woman's aptitude for learning. On this point she quotes the famous story of Novella, the daughter of a Law teacher, called Johannes Andrea, in Bologna (around 1270). Novella was born in 1312. She was so keen and learned that whenever her father was sick, she took over his law courses. However, the University authorities were very careful in using her talent. Before she started to lecture, they hooked up a curtain in the classroom, to make sure that only her voice and learning, and not her beauty, would enchant the boys in the school.[53]

The third part of the *City of ladies* deals with those distinguished married women, virgins, and saints who are assigned by *Justice* to defend this City. Magdalen, Catherine, Margaret, Lucy, Martine, Justine, Barbara, Dorothy, Christine, Anastasy, Affra (who was "folle femme"), and others are helped by the apostles and other saints in their duty of defending this City, built by Reason, populated by Righteousness (*Droiture*), and defended by Justice.[54]

Christine placed her talents at the service of virtuous womanhood, but at the same time she had a pious desire to save those "foolish women" who were addicted to the pleasures of sin, the numerous courtesans of love, the "folles femmes." She had pity for

[51] M. Jeanroy, "Boccace et Christine de Pisan LE DE CLARIS MULIERIBUS," *Romania,* 48 (1922), 93–105; Rosier, *op. cit.,* 14.

[52] Jeanroy, *op. cit.,* 99; cf. ch. 27 "Cy commence a parler d'aucunes dames qui furent enluminées de grans sciences, premierement de la pucelle Cornificie"; Pinet, *op. cit.,* 369.

[53] *Cité des Dames,* Bk. II, ch. 36: "Contre ceulx qui dient que il n'est pas bon que femmes apprennent lettres"; Fr. C. Savigny, *Geschichte des Römischen Rechts,* VI (1850), 109.

[54] It was translated into English and printed in London in 1521: Pinet, *op. cit.,* xiii.

these unfortunate creatures, whose life would end in misery and ugli-
ness. They deserved to be taught how to amend their lives. It is
the duty of society to save them. Christine, faithful to her ethico-
didactic attitude, energetically exhorted them:

Raise yourselves up, get out of the filth. God is merciful and ready to
forgive you if you repent.[55]

Christine de Pisan composed several other ethico-didactic treatises
in prose; most of them are still unpublished. *Le livre du corps de
policie* is an educational treatise for the three different classes of
mediaeval society. The first part is a true Mirror of Princes, borrowed either from Pseudo-Thomas *De eruditione principum*, Giles of
Rome's or Vincent of Beauvais' *De educatione filiorum nobilium*.[56]
The second part is written for knights and nobility; the third for the
common people, clerks, burghers, and their wives.[57]

Le Livre de la prodhommie de l'Omme or *Livre de prudence* is an
adaptation of different translations of the *De quatuor virtutibus*
literature. Prudence, Fortitude, Temperance, and Justice will help
to avoid the failures and abuses of public life.[58]

Another ethico-didactic poem is *L'Epistre d'Othea a Hector* or
" The Epistle of Othea to Hector," a *Lytil Bibell of Knythhood*, a
collection of quotations illustrating different legendary stories of
antiquity. Each of the hundred epistles, written in verse, is commented and re-commented upon in prose.[59] Othea, this very wise
lady, " moult sage dame," goddess of Prudence, a combination of
Minerva and Pallas, writes her advice in the form of an epistle to
Hector. The epistles are provided with " glosses " by Christine de
Pisan that give a literary explication of the historical facts. The influence of the *Ovid Moralisé* is manifest in the whole book. Christine's epistle has been translated into English several times.[60] It
was illustrated by beautiful miniatures during the fifteenth century.
The most marvelous are those rearranged by Jean Mielot, Canon of
Lille, by order of Philippe le Bon. One of them represents a teaching
scene, *Io* with her disciples. The teacher is dressed like a fashionable

[55] Laigle, *op. cit.*, 360–62.
[56] *Le livre du corps de policie*, Paris, B. N. Ms. Fr. 1197; 1198; 1199; 12439.
Ist part ch. 4: Cy dist a quel gens on doit bailler dans leur commencement les
enfans des princes; Pseudo-Thomas, *De eruditione principum*, Bk. IV, ch. 9: De
his quae requirenda sunt in electione magistri disponentia ad hoc ut bene doceat,
St. Thomae Opera Omnia (New York, 1950, Musurgia), XVI, 431.
[57] Rosier, *op. cit.*, 26; Pinet, *op. cit.*, 357 and xv.
[58] Paris, B. N. Ms. Fr. 605; 2240; Pinet, *op. cit.*, xv, 354–57.
[59] Pinet, *op. cit.*, 273.
[60] H. N. MacCracken, "An unknown middle English translation of l'Epitre
d'Othea," *Modern Language Notes*, 24 (1909), 122–123.

lady of the fifteenth century writing at a desk. Four students are engaged in active studying, writing and reading.[61]

The tender voice of the loving mother in Christine de Pisan never spoke on such a high level as it did in the *Enseignemens moraux,* moral teachings composed for the instruction of her son, Jean de Castel. She provides him with the soundest advice of Christian pedagogy. Her secret ambition is to awake the gentle heart of her son to respect for womanhood:

Thou shall not deceive nor slander women but respect them.[62]

She aims to prepare John for the various states of his future career. If in school he should strive for prudence:

Search out the studies which help you acquire prudence, because she is the mother of virtues who drives away bad luck.[63]

She recognized that her son must know the world in order to live as a man. By study he would acquire some polish, and when he was among clerks or scholars he would not appear rude:

> Se tu veulz en science eslire
> Ton estat par les livres lire,
> Fays tant, et par suivre l'estude,
> Qu'entre les clers me soyes rude.[64]

When teaching in "chair," he should use discretion and gentleness and take into account human frailty:

> S'as disciples, ne les reprendre
> En trop grant rigueur, se mesprendre
> Les vois; pense que foible et vaine
> Est la fragilité humaine.[65]

He should avoid unnecessary disputes, be prudent and not too loquacious in court, prudent in choosing his wife. If he wants to know something about his fiancée, he should first look at the mother:

> Se tu veulz femme espouse prendre,
> Par la mere pues tu apprendre
> Ses meurs.[66]

She warns him against blind idolatry of himself, and reminds him of the eternal values of the soul which will last forever:

> Car biens mondains vont a defin
> Et l'ame durera sans fin.[67]

[61] J. Van den Gheyn, S.J., *Christine de Pisan, Epitre d'Othea, Déesse de la Prudence à Hector, Chef des Troyens, reproduction des 100 miniatures du manuscrits 9392 de Jean Mielot* (Brussels), London, n. d.

[62] *Les enseignemens, op. cit.,* str. 47; Roy, *op. cit.,* III, 34.

[63] *Ibid.,* str. 4, p. 28.

[64] *Ibid.,* str. 6, p. 28.

[65] *Ibid.,* str. 18, p. 30.

[66] *Ibid.,* str. 51, p. 35.

[67] *Ibid.,* str. 113, p. 44.

The love and fear of God is ever present in the whole of her educational system. *Dieu premier servy*, "First serve God," said Joan of Arc to her judges. The main advice of the *Enseignemens* sounds a similar note:

> Aimes Dieu de toute ta force,
> Crains ley et du servir t'efforce.[68]

The manuscript, ms. français 836 in the Bibliothèque Nationale in Paris, has a delightful miniature representing a lovely scene of maternal instruction. Christine de Pisan, seated, with the open book of the *Enseignemens* before her, speaks to her son, Jean de Castel, attired in the costume of a young page, listening to her with devotion.[69]

Christine's common sense and experience is reflected in her Moral Proverbs, gathered like rare flowers from various collections of wise sayings.[70] The time that is lost cannot be regained; therefore we should put the time we have to good use. Seldom does keeping silence hurt, but too much talking often causes damage. Polite speech often restrains great anger, and to speak at the proper time is the indication of a wise man.

Christine used freely the proverbial literature at her disposal. These wise sayings were rather the popular maxims of philosophers and great men than proverbs. She simply followed the tradition of Raymond Lull and others in formulating moral proverbs for educational purposes. Mediaeval educators thought that those maxims were very useful and fruitful for the instruction of the laity, and that anyone knowing those proverbs would be much better off than another not familiar with these nuggets of compressed wisdom: [71]

> Prudence aprent l'omme a vivre en raison,
> La ou elle est eureuse est la maison.[72]

The moral proverbs of Christine were greatly enjoyed by the public in the fifteenth century. Anthony, Earl of Rivers, translated them into English.[73]

---

[68] *Ibid.*, str. 2, p. 27.

[69] H. Martin, *Les joyaux de l'enluminure à la Bibliothèque Nationale* (Paris-Brussels, 1928), 110, 129, fig. LXXXIV, pl. 68 (Paris, B. N. Ms. Fr. 836).

[70] *Prouerbes moraux*, ed. M. Roy, *op. cit.*, III, 45–57.

[71] [These proverbs] "contain many helpful subtleties. Any layman knowing them would excel in intellect any other ignorant of them." Berges, *op. cit.*, 336; Ramon Lull's proverbs: A. Morel-Fatio, "Proverbes rimés de Raimond Lull," *Romania*, 11 (1882), 188.

[72] *Prouerbes moraux*, ed. M. Roy, *op. cit.*, III, 45, no. 2.

[73] *Moral proverbs* (Westminster, William Caxton, Feb. 20, 1478). A copy in the Huntington Library: EH1; Pierpont Morgan Library: DeR. 27, 1; Stillwell, *op. cit.*, 143, C. 427.

Christine de Pisan did not segregate herself from the scholastic world, from the leaders of public opinion in Paris in the beginning of the fifteenth century. Love of science and affection for those who were carrying the lighted candle of scholastic learning reigned in her heart. She composed a prayer for the students and masters of the University of Paris:

May Thou keep the clercs, masters, and students of the noble and honored University of Paris, Thy theologians and others, whatever Faculty they are from. Likewise preserve all the other universities of Christendom under Thy holy protection, give them strength to endure the labor of studies and understanding of sciences in order to make profitable use of them to teach the ignorant and the common people.[74]

In a very interesting passage of " The Book of Fayttes of Armes," *Le Livre des faits d'armes et de chevalerie,* translated into English in 1489 by William Caxton, she brings up a touching problem of the Hundred Years' War, the question of the privileges of scholars at the University of Paris in time of war.[75] She considers the case of an English student, licentiate of Cambridge in England, who would like to come to France to study. Do the " men of arms " have any right to take him prisoner? The law denies it, and protects those who are seeking to know and to acquire learning. An affectionate description of the scholars almost reminds us of the enthusiastic speech of the Great Clerk of England, " Le Grand Clerc d'Angleterre," of Rabelais.[76]

In a dialogue touched with emotion she pays homage to the scholars who put aside riches, delicate things, and all bodily comfort, who leave their friends and their country go into voluntary poverty, and are banished from all other goods. They have forsaken the world and all its pleasures for love of science. They deserve all privi-

---

[74] L. Delisle, " Notice sur les Sept Psaumes allegorisés de Christine de Pisan," *Notices et extraits des manuscrits de la Bibliothèque Nationale,* XXXV, 2e p. (Reprinted, Paris, 1896), 9: " Cy commence les. vii. psaumes en Francoys allegorises." To each verse of the seven psalms Christine added a meditation and a prayer: " Que tous les clercs, maistres et estudiants de la noble honoree universite de Paris, tes theologiens, ou de quelque faculte que ilz soient, et semblablement de tous les autres estudes de crestiante, ayes en ta sainte garde, donne leur force d'endurer le labour d'estude, bien comprendre les sciences, et prouffitablement en user, enseigner les ignorens et le peuple." (Bibl. du Comte d'Ashburnham, fond Barrois, no. 203, f. 59 verso).

[75] *The book of fayttes of armes and of chyualrye,* translated and printed by William Caxton from the French original by Christine de Pisan, edited by A. T. P. Byles (London, 1932; E. E. T. S., no. 189), 226–229; Pinet, *op. cit.,* 358–362.

[76] *Oeuvres de François Rabelais,* ed. Abel Lefranc (Paris, 1922), IV, 210. " De faict, ouyant le bruyt de ton scavoir tant inestimable, ay delaissé pays, parens et maison, et me suis icy transporté, rien ne estimant la longueur du chemin, l'attediation de la mer, la nouveaulté des contrées, peour seulement te veoir, etc."

leges and advantages. The soldier retorts: what if he turns out to be a spy and informer of the enemy, or would engage in "sabotage" and various secret evils? The answer is that in this case he is not a "true" scholar, therefore not entitled to the privileges. The good reliable scholar should enjoy the privileges, not only for himself but for his servants taken with him from England.

Christine tries to solve another question involved in this privilege: may the father of a sick English scholar in Paris visit him in time of war? The answer is affirmative. She goes even further. He should be allowed to come even if he is healthy, provided he brings some food and other necessaries:

The love of the father and of the mother for their son so privileged, that no right of arms may surmount it.[77]

The Middle Ages respected the rights of scholarship even in the midst of cruel wars and battles. In this respect the "liberal" modern age still has something to learn.

VIII

Christine de Pisan loved science and learning, and rightly called herself *fille d'estude*, the servant of Science. In her mind, art and learning must serve the aims of moral teaching. For Christine, the value of moral sense and learning are not in the same category as far as their effect is concerned. While the latter does not offer any security, the first leads to eternal happiness. Learning must refine and improve our character. Consequently science without virtue is harmful and dangerous. Christine had a deep devotion to glorious "sapience," divine wisdom. Her pedagogy consisted in leading others to worship and imitate this Wisdom, the love of the Holy Spirit, Father of the Poor.[78]

Christine did not compose any specific book of good behavior. In her writing she simply represented the attractive side of religious ethics, triumphing over the deceptive illusions of the world. The heritage of the Christian pedagogues is well used in her poems, ballads, and historical writings which are sprinkled with moral truth, a mixture of philosophical maxims and Biblical sayings.

Her voice is definite and strong in recommending labor and courage to her contemporaries: "labor and do not be discouraged."[79] But in the depths of her heart she desperately looks for the means to spiritualize distress and melancholy, the permanent temptations of a lonely woman. Christine de Pisan had something of St. Anthony

---

[77] P. Rebuffo, *Privilegia universitatum, collegiorum, scholasticorum* (Frankfurt Main), 1575, 208–209; Christine de Pisan, *Fayttes of Armes, op. cit.*, 228.
[78] Rosier, *op. cit.*, 102.   [79] P. G., VII, I, 12.

the hermit's grace and urbanity. Her speech was seasoned with particular wisdom, like that of the great hermit, and everyone in her entourage enjoyed her sound mind and serene philosophy.[80] Her masters were the great thinkers of classical antiquity and of Christianity: Plato, Aristotle, Galen, Ptolemy, Democritus, Virgil, Horace, Ovid, Tibullus, Catullus, Juvenal, Boethius, Apuleius, Vegetius, Frontinus, Lucan, Cicero, Suetonius, Seneca, St. Augustine. She preferred Ovid to Virgil, but not without repudiating his anti-feminist views. She read much of the *Consolation* of Boethius, but did not use the doctrinal part of his work.

Christine de Pisan's personal experience and wide learning enabled her to illustrate the moral virtues. Her love of science and moral earnestness opened to her the ways of experimental ethics. Energy of soul, deep feelings, a sincere approach to problems favored in her development of the woman-moralist. She really deserved, in her distinction as the first woman-moralist of France, Gerson's compliment: *femina ista virilis*. Faith and Christian principles guided the life work of Christine to build an intellectual storehouse of culture for refined women.[81] Her exterior truly reflected the inner beauty of her soul. In miniatures she appears a woman of elegance, arrayed in high headdress, like a *dame de prix*.

Some time after the battle of Agincourt, around 1418, she retired from public life to the Convent of Poissy, cherished home of her daughter. She broke her silence only once, to sing her " prayers " to the glorious maiden Joan of Arc in 1429:

> O blessed be He
> That lent the life!—how word my grateful prayer?
> No prayer of thine was spoken fruitlessly,
> O Maid of God! O Joan! O Virgin rare!
> . . . .
> Honour to womankind! It needs must be
> That God loves woman, since He fashioned Thee! [82]

With praise of God and of her brave Maid, Joan of Arc, on her lips, she disappears from the world of letters. The date of her death is not known. It may have occurred around 1430. She cleared the way for the coming Renaissance.

The Mediaeval Institute, University of Notre Dame.

---

[80] *St. Athanasius, The Life of St. Anthony.* Newly translated and annotated by R. T. Meyer (Westminster, Md., 1950; Ancient Christian Writers; the Works of the Fathers in translation, no. 10), ch. 73, p. 81.

[81] F. C. Johnson's review in *Modern Language Review*, 24 (1929), 492.

[82] A. Kemp-Welch, *op. cit.*, 146 (no source given). Cf. J. Quicherat, *Procès de condemnation et de réhabilitation de Jeanne d'Arc* (Paris, 1849), 10, str. 22, 34.

IX

CHRISTINE DE PIZAN: THE POETESS AS HISTORIAN

By Nadia Margolis

The origins of Christine's preoccupation with history and the human condition may be found in her lyric poetry in such moving examples as the following:

> What is there in great people of whom
>   one reads in histories,
> Who accomplish great and difficult deeds
> For praise, high honors, and victories?
> Are they not dead and visible before
>   our eyes?
> Do we not see that all things, whether
>   visible
> Or not, must come to an end? They must
>   decay!
> Let us not, then, have faith in impossible
>   things,
> Let us decide that we're destined to die.
>
> *Autres Balades,* V:9-16

Such a passage reminds us of Aristotle's precepts (*Poetics,* IX) stating that history tells what has been, while poetry expresses what might be and is therefore the more philosophical, more enduring form. Christine (1365-1430?) may also have been familiar with the observation of Quintilian (X, i, 31), that history closely resembles poetry, that it is a poem in prose written to narrate, not to prove. The French feminist poet would devote her entire literary career to developing a discursive style for conveying spiritual and intellectual insight in an agreeable, accessible manner, without losing argumentative persuasiveness. A discussion of Christine's development from poetess to historian should pursue two levels: the generic transformation of poetry into history and the change of narrative gender necessary for the author in the shift from a traditionally feminine to a masculine form of discourse.[1] The meaning of the terms "masculine" and "feminine" will become clearer as my analysis unfolds, beginning with the Roman concept of history as a masculine genre because of its relation to politics.

Christine began her literary career by writing lyric poetry a few years after the death of her husband in 1390. Although she continued to

[1] See Natalie Zemon Davis, "Gender and Genre: Women as Historical Writers, 1400-1820," *Beyond Their Sex: Learned Women of the European Past,* ed. Patricia Labalme (New York, 1980), 153-83.

compose *ballades, rondeaux,* and *virelais* until about 1410, she had begun as early as 1399 to compose prose works on moral and political subjects. Her awareness of the separate purposes of her lyrics and serious narrative may be inferred from the fact that they arose from different motives on her part. Christine's overall motivation was to live by her pen and support her three children, her mother, and a niece after the death not only of her husband but also of her father soon after. At the time of her bereavement she was only twenty-five. Although associated with the royal court through her father, an astrologer from Bologna, and her husband, a royal notary, Christine had great difficulty in claiming her inheritance because she was a woman. Plagued by creditors and the demands of supporting a family, she turned to study and writing, first for consolation and then as a means of earning a living. Fortunately, she had received an education "toute virile" from her father, and in her reading of history, mythology, and romance (often the distinction among these subjects remained blurred concerning their factual truth) she would identify herself with the great figures of the past—both men and women. Such was her romantic side; she also revealed a more intensely philosophical, even pragmatic approach to her reading in her allusions to works like Boethius's *Consolatio.* "Boethius the profitable" she called this book, which proved so useful to her as a source of solace from the cruelty and injustice of Fortune and as a model for instructing others in methods of coping with unhappiness.

The Boethian presence haunts Christine's persona throughout her literary production, for though he is not alluded to directly in every work, one finds traces of the famous pupil of Lady Philosophy in every one of Christine's references to her personal misfortunes. The figure of the condemned philosopher, a victim of Fortune aided by a call to contemplate higher things, obviously appealed to the helpless widow seeking to survive by her intellect. One of Christine's admirable qualities lay in her selection of heroically moral literary and philosophical sources with a nonetheless pragmatic eye. Her resulting conviction as both author and narrator-heroine was that one learns from "within the system" and by serving "the enemy" before liberating oneself from it. Thus we see Christine the heroine serving Fortune in the *Mutacion de Fortune* (1403) in order to vanquish the fickle goddess and Christine the writer borrowing imagery from Jean de Meun (c. 1240-1305) or Cecco d'Ascoli (1269-1327)—men with whom she disagreed ideologically but whose more developed literary style was essential to her needs. If her erudite pursuits had taught her anything, it was that men, and often evil men, ran the world as she knew it because they held the secrets of learning.[2] It was

---

[2] This becomes an increasingly apparent theme, from some of her early poetry, esp. the *Epistle to the God of Love,* through the *Dittié de Jeanne d'Arc,* essential not only to her historiographical viewpoint but also to her self-awareness as an author. This is not to say that Christine felt all men to be bad rulers but that she perceived them as an

this arsenal of knowledge that Christine attempted to penetrate in order to win her place in the Parisian intellectual milieu. Boethius and another favorite, the Dante of the *Inferno,* taught Christine the value of self-knowledge as well.[3] Once she gained control over her own limitations, Christine then took on the qualities of the Cumaean Sibyl, who led Aeneas to the underworld and who, in another thread of tradition, offered prophetic books to Tarquin the Proud. Virgil's Cumaean Sibyl also predicted the Golden Age in the Fourth *Ecloque,* and it is no coincidence that Dante chose the Roman epic poet to guide him through the Underworld; nor is it accidental that Amaltheia ("Almethee") led Christine on a prophetic, learned journey in the *Chemin de long estude* (1402-03). Sibyls and sibylline figures appeared in many of Christine's writings as wise women linking Troy to Rome and Rome to Italy and, most important politically as well as culturally, as the foreteller of the Golden Age of Rome as coming to France rather than remaining in Italy. Even in Christine's earliest didactic work, the *Epistre d'Othea* (1399-1400), the Sibyl predicts not only this triumph of *translatio studii* (with an eye toward *translatio imperii*) but also the growing role of women in shaping the New Order.[4]

---

integral part of the decaying order, with certain notable exceptions among her contemporaries, such as Charles V of France and Richard II of England. In Greek and Roman antiquity men earned their superiority by noble deeds; in modern times, Christine avers, deserving women should be given more responsibility because men have slackened in their official and professional duties. Shulamith Shahar, *The Fourth Estate: A History of Women in the Middle Ages* (London, 1983), treats Christine's idealization of women and her definition of the feminine (168-70).

[3] The classic study on Christine's real knowledge of Dante's Italian works is that of Arturo Farinelli, "Dante nell'opere di Christine de Pisan," in *Aus romanischen Sprachen und Literaturen: Festschrift Heinrich Morf* (Halle, 1905), 117-52.

[4] Christine's conclusion to her *Othea,* Chap. C:

> Cent auctorités t'ay escriptes,
> si ne soyent de toy despites;
> Car Augustus de femme aprist
> Qui d'estre aoure le reprist.

Quoted in P. G. C. Campbell, *L'Epitre d'Othéa: Etude sur les sources de Christine de Pisan* (Paris, 1924), 78. As Campbell points out, the basic material, the Cumaean Sibyl's revelation of the Virgin and Child before Augustus, is not original but most likely taken from Jean de Vignai's translation of the *Legenda Aurea.* The following translation renders the meaning better than the style:

> One hundred authoritative stories have I written,
> May you not disdain them;
> For Augustus learned from a woman
> Whom he should worship (in order to be worthy of
>   adoration himself).

Thus to the merging of Christian and pagan legends and to the conceptual balance of political power between Church and State, Christine adds the defense of women, a

Yet Boethius and the Sibyl, whatever their worth as examples of wisdom conquering adversity, are passive. They know, but they do nothing to communicate what they know, to the masses. Sibyls and sibylline figures must be sought out by divinely designated heroes for aid. Christine came to see her personal misfortune as a small part of a troubled time suffered by many: the Schism, the Black Death, the Hundred Years' War ravaged countries already weakened by civil strife and incompetent or unscrupulous rulers.

Christine's professed reasons for writing history in the early fifteenth century can be compared to the reasons for women's dominating novels in the eighteenth and early nineteenth centuries. Just as writing novels offered tremendous opportunities for self-examination and defense and even for attacking social oppression,[5] so did historiography provide a convenient and powerful framework upon which Christine could build a different story of humanity, as in her *Cité des Dames* (1405), a very literal example of her concept. Gabrielle Spiegel has demonstrated the conscious attempts of certain medieval chroniclers to explain and to legitimize the prevailing political situation.[6] We shall see how Christine carries this tendency a step further, both stylistically and ideologically.

Unlike the various poetic genres, whose rigid stylistic rules reflected—and eventually even dictated—an equally formalized ethical code itemizing each sentiment and significant potential, historical writing was less crystallized. Within the category of historiography there was little differentiation among chronicles, biographies, and systematic theological visions. Both history and poetry were dominated by men as perceivers and the perceived; but in history, especially the chronicles, the characterization was often so skeletal, its nuances so hackneyed, that the genre seemed to cry out for a vivid stylist with a keen sense of cause and effect. The discursive voice, because of the lack of personality and psychological insight, was often not so much masculine as it was asexual. Furthermore, despite its superficial depersonalization, the chronicle, composed to fur-

---

contribution which becomes even more meaningful in the light of *translatio studii* and *translatio imperii*, for it implies the triumph of women along with that of France as heir to the Golden Age.

[5] Madelyn Gutwirth, *Madame de Staël, Novelist: The Emergence of the Artist as a Woman* (Urbana, 1979), 14.

[6] See especially "Political Utility in Medieval Historiography: A Sketch," *History and Theory*, 14 (1975), 315-25, devoted to the chronicles of Saint-Denis. Prof. Spiegel also discusses the role of these chronicles in creating, as well as preserving, dynastic continuity between the Carolingian and Capetian lines in "The *Reditus Regni ad Stirpem Karoli Magni*: A New Look," *French Historical Studies,* 7 (1971), 145-75. More recently, in conjunction with Prof. Sandra Hindman, Prof. Spiegel has treated iconography and historiography in manuscripts of Guillaume de Nangis's *Chronique abrégée* in "The Fleur-de-lis Frontispieces. . .: Political Iconography in Late Fifteenth-Century France," *Viator,* 12 (1981). Prof. Spiegel effectively incorporates and develops the standard works of Bloch (1924), Brandt (1966), Hanning (1966), Guenée (1973), and others.

ther the interests of its patronage at least as much as other court literature, abandoned the objectivity often associated with the historian's professed mandate. Consequently, if a woman, particularly from outside the nobility, were to write history from her point of view, she could achieve her ideological goal without totally upsetting the genre of medieval histo-riography. She could not have done the same with a romance or an epic without overthrowing the male-oriented order. True, many romances concerned women, but only as objects and types. Allegories, such as the *Othea* and *Chemin,* she used to the same purpose, but they lacked the authority of a weighty chronicle or history. While the *songes* (such as those by Jean de Meun and Philippe de Mézières) could exert greater subliminal influence over a reading public, they lacked the immediate respect, the official presence, of a *chronique* or *livre des fais.*[7] In the *Mutacion* Christine appeared to experiment by fusing annals with allegory with enough success to further her prestige at the Burgundian court. In Christine's history, even when dealing with male subjects, the woman is more than the object, more than the subject—she is the perceiver and narrator.

As stated by way of introduction, Christine's interest in history is evident in her earliest poems. In the *Cent Ballades,* composed between 1395 and 1400, Christine begins by admonishing the reader that she "has neither the desire nor the space// to make poems of solace or joy" (ed. Roy, I:1:9-10) because of her grief over her husband's death. She also claims to write at the behest of her friends, that is, by responding to the will of *others* (a topos nonetheless sincere in this context, as is often the case with her use of commonplaces). In the second ballad of the same sequence she evokes the past: "In olden times, in the city of Rome," describing the classical world in medieval terms (*preux, sage, beau vas-selage*). The impact of the *ubi sunt* topos strategically culminates, after the midpoint of the ballad, in a structural evocation of decadence, as our attention is turned to "modern" times, when things are far less utopian, despite the similarity of exteriors to those of Rome. Static qualities based on past glory (*heritage, lignage*) conflict with *corage* (vv. 20, 21, 23) as

---

[7] There is no doubt that an occasional fine line exists between the role of Christine's allegories and that of her more chronicle-like *Charles V* in achieving her didactic purposes, particularly in analyzing the structures of the *Mutacion,* an experiment in combining not only historiographical genres but also other compilations of knowledge in search of causal continuity. On the development of medieval prose writing and its origins in allegory, chronicle, and romance, see Chap. 10 and other pertinent sections of *Précis de littérature française du Moyen Age,* ed. Daniel Poirion (Paris, 1983). Janet Ferrier points to the similarity between the language of certain major French chronicles and that of the common people as another source of the chronicle's credibility, in *French Prose Writers of the Fourteenth and Fifteenth Centuries* (Oxford, 1966), x, as does Stephen G. Nichols, Jr., "Discourse in Froissart's *Chroniques,*" *Speculum,* 39 (1964), 279-87, in greater detail.

well as with the noble traits listed above from the first two stanzas, as Christine effectively uses rhyme scheme and word play. All symptoms of decline seem to rhyme, appropriately enough, with *domage*. The exhortation at the end, in the *renvoi*, is stronger in its message to the Prince than the conventional final display of reverence and obeisance: it is the princes of France who must guide France to emulation of Roman virtue. This use of classical models in historical writing marks Christine as a humanist worthy of the greatest intellectuals of the time.[8]

Her interest in the past did not stem from passive nostalgia. In the later *Autres Balades,* the thirty-ninth poem begins with "There was once in the city of Athens" (ed. Roy, I:250:1) and forms part of the corpus of Christine's poetic and prose polemic against the *Roman de la Rose.* In this ballad chivalry is described entirely as a function of learning rather than of military prowess. We hear, instead of real swords, the clash between *sens* (reason) and *erreur* in the battle for truth. "One is often beaten down for speaking the truth" serves as the refrain to a poem containing examples not of Christian martyrs, as one might expect, but of classical philosophers, notably Aristotle and Socrates, tormented by *mensongeurs* (liars). The last third of the ballad typically associates past injustice with present iniquity: a direct equivalence is established between Jean de Meun and the liars and between the wise men of old and Christine. We also recall that Paris had been dubbed the "second Athens," and this provides another diachronic analogy. This ballad reveals the poetess's desire to transcend the Boethian and Sibylline sphere. She would try to extend her historical sense beyond uniting individual and exterior phenomena to depicting causal continuity between past and present on both personal and universal levels.

Time and space do not permit here a full discussion of Christine's role as instigator of France's first literary dispute, the Quarrel of the *Roman de la Rose* (1401-1404), in which she publicly matches wits with Jean de Montreuil (1354-1418), France's "first true humanist," with the help of none less than Jean Gerson (1363-1429), chancellor of the University of Paris.[9] It is important to remark, however, that Christine's concern did not only center on the misogynistic content of the Rose but also aimed at restating the need for authorial responsibility with regard to the public. Jean de Meun had in a sense disguised his subversive doctrine by presenting it in the discursive sheep's clothing of a *songe*—what could be considered the late medieval equivalent of the *Bildungsroman*—before what Christine saw as an unsuspecting public. If an author

---

[8] Certainly if one follows the definition of humanists and humanism given on various occasions by Paul Kristeller and more specifically in Christine's case by Gilbert Ouy, "Paris: L'un des principaux foyers de l'humanisme en Europe au début du XV⁰ siècle," *Bulletin de la Société de l'Histoire de Paris et de l'Ile-de-France* (1967-68), esp. 85-90.

[9] See the excellent study and edition by Eric Hicks, *Le Débat sur le "Roman de la Rose"* (Paris, 1977), which supersedes all other research on the question.

knows more than his reader, especially concerning a moral concept, such information should be conveyed so as not to corrupt the reader. A sense of moral responsibility is essential for a writer, for he or she must strive to improve society's attitudes, whether in lyric, epic, or epistle.

In her early poems Christine could manipulate her audience through stylistic games such as *jeux partis,* an amusing genre. She was at first content to "chanter par couverture" but gradually expressed her convictions more openly. Stylistic control, she discovered, could be employed for edification as well as for diversion without extending into outright polemics, as is exemplified in the *Epitre d'Othea* to Hector (1399-1400). In composing this work, Christine culled from a variety of sources one hundred historical moments, each presented as a text and followed by a gloss and an allegory—just in case the young reader (first, her son, Jean de Castel) were to miss the moral lesson of the story.[10] Rosemond Tuve has described the work as an exceptional example of an author stating very clearly how she wished to be read as she recounted the history of Greece, Rome, and Troy interpreted in terms of the Bible and the Church Fathers.[11]

Like many such works by Christine, the *Othea* enjoyed great popularity in the French and in the English courts, surviving in 43 manuscripts and having been offered to such illustrious patrons as Louis of Orleans, Charles VI, Philip the Bold, and John of Berry.[12] Though certainly not as widespread as the *Othea,* the manuscript tradition of that versified behemoth, the *Mutacion de Fortune* (1403), a 24,000-line journey through Christine's life in relationship to the history of the world, flourished sufficiently to provide ten extant manuscripts.[13]

The *Mutacion* is of even greater interest to us for several reasons. While providing an inventory of historical sources popular in the late fourteenth century, it sheds light on Christine's genre-gender shift very explicitly, as when she relates the story of her bereavement using the classical image of her being left alone to guide a ship through a terrible storm. In this portentous episode Christine incorporates Ovid's hauntingly tragic story of Ceyx and Alcyone (*Met.* XI, 411-750). Then, as if undaunted by any danger of destroying pathos by potential irony, she adds elements of Ovid's account of Tiresias and his sexual transformation and ensuing gift of prophecy (*Met.* III, 324-36). Christine's often un-

---

[10] Gianni Mombello, "Per una edizione critica dell'*Epistre Othea* di Christine de Pisan III," *Studi francesi,* 9 (1965), 1-12, lists other possible "Trojan princes" for whom the various MSS of the *Othea* were destined, aside from Christine's son, Jean Castel: Louis of Orleans, Charles VI, Philip the Bold, and John, Duke of Berry.

[11] Rosemond Tuve, *Allegorical Imagery: Some Medieval Books and Their Posterity* (Princeton, 1966), 230-35.

[12] Mombello, *Studi francesi,* 8 (1964), 402ff, and 9 (1965), 12, lists 43 MSS of the *Othea.*

[13] Intro. to *Le Livre de la Mutacion de Fortune,* ed. S. Solente (Paris, 1959), I, xcix.

derrated skill somehow fuses the two contexts into a convincing unity. Fortune, whom Christine had reproached for being so changeable (*muable*), deploys her mutability to the young widow's advantage as the ship is about to crash against the rocks:

> Transformed I felt all over.
> My arms and legs feeling stronger
> Than ever before, the great suffering
> And sorrow in which I had languished up to now
> Had subsided; I felt myself over
> All in astonishment.
> Fortune had not been cruel to me,
> She who transformed me,
> For she all of a sudden changed
> This great fear and doubt
> In which I used to wallow,
> And now I felt more confident.   (ll. 1336-47)

Then, as a superhero bursting from the final restraints of his ordinary condition, Christine bursts from her wedding ring, which will never again hold her down in the "stagnation of sorrow" (*la parece de plour*) over the loss of her beloved.

The meaning of her transformation from female to male operates on more than one level. When Christine changes sexually, the range of her activities also changes as she moves from passive to active. Like Tiresias, she can transcend the limits of normal experience, although in pursuit of knowledge greater than that required to appease the frivolous curiosity of Ovid's gods. She is seeking knowledge about herself and her world and how to remedy the evils of her time—undeniably a humanist perspective. As a writer, she wants to help her readers to do the same for themselves, in keeping with her notion of the author's moral responsibility toward the public. Christine assures us that she would rather remain a woman, "but Fortune has estranged me from this. . . . I shall remain a man . . . for the rest of my life" (*Mutacion*, vv. 1398-1407).[14] She feels singularly destined to gain greater insight, as symbolized by her new competence and independence at repairing, maintaining, and steering the ship of life, than that which is conventionally given to women *and* men.

Christine conveys the elements of divine designation, prophecy, and

---

[14] Diane Bornstein, in "Self-Consciousness and Self-Concepts in the Work of Christine de Pizan," *Ideals for Women in the Works of Christine de Pizan*, ed. D. Bornstein (Detroit, 1981), 11-28, also discusses this passage. It is particularly rewarding to study this episode in the light of such new feminist criticism as Sandra Gilbert, "Costumes of the Mind: Transvestism as Metaphor in Modern Literature," in *Writing and Sexual Difference*, ed. Elizabeth Abel (Chicago, 1982), 193-219, as well as that surveyed by Jonathan Culler in "Reading as a Woman," *On Deconstruction: Theory and Criticism after Structuralism* (Ithaca, 1982), 43-64.

gender consciousness by manipulating the legend of Tiresias in a subtle and innovative manner. Greek and Roman authors had tended to separate the sexual transformation, with its humorous connotations of his having been chosen for the gods' amusement because of his grave, portentous presence as blind soothsayer warning men against offending the Gods. Christine, however, unites both traditions, so that Ovid's victim of Olympian diversion assumes the serious stature of Sophocles's blind seer of Oedipus's tragic fate. Christine's Tiresias is able to foresee *because* of his sexual transformation, just as her real-life misfortunes transformed and enabled her to know more. Also like Tiresias, she received such revelations whether she wished to or not at that point, at the whim of a higher being, Fortune instead of Jupiter. Furthermore, if Dante saw his appointment to begin the journey of the *Divina Commedia* as oscillating somewhere between Aeneas and Paul (*Inferno,* I, 32), a pagan and a Christian founder, Christine chose Tiresias as the proper embodiment of her privileged, dualistic situation as she stands poised to begin her voyage through human history. She stays within the pagan realm, the shift being one of gender rather than of relationship to original sin. Her Tiresias, alternately experiencing gain and privation of sexual (and visual) potential, ignores the erotic in favor of the spiritual and social; and so he sees what others (i.e., mortal men) cannot, in a way finally deeper than the mere symbolic blindness, devoid of sexuality, with which previous authors had contented themselves. For Christine's mythopoesis such figures as Tiresias represent a development beyond the phase marked by her use of the Cumaean Sibyl. For while the Sibyl signified female superiority through desexualization, Homer's and Ovid's prophet points toward what Joan Kelly has labeled the "universalist outlook" characteristic of the early feminists.[15] The poetess's use of Tiresias furnishes a fine example of how she was often forced to search out and to amplify evidence from classical sources instead of borrowing from the more frequent and easily recognizable *exempla* so effectively incorporated by her male humanist colleagues.[16]

---

[15] "Early Feminist Theory and the *Querelle des Femmes,* 1400-1789," *Signs,* 8 (1982), 6-7.

[16] Kelly oversimplifies in her generally excellent overview of the inherent problems of the early Feminists, particularly Christine, when she states, "Unlike the male humanist, however, Christine could not draw on the classical learning to guide her toward her new intellectual position. She had to oppose what seemed and still seems to be the overwhelming authority of the learned on women's inferiority" (13). It is not that Christine could not use any classical examples but that she was obliged to find different ones. Charity Willard, *Christine de Pizan: Her Life and Works* (New York, 1984), esp. Chaps. 5, 6, contains much valuable information on her use of classical and medieval sources. For Christine's occasional ironic re-creations of figures from antiquity, see Christine Reno, "Christine de Pizan: Feminism and Irony," in J. Beck and G. Mombello (eds.), *Seconda Miscellanea di Studi e Ricerche sul quattrocentro francese* (Chambéry-Torino, 1981), 125-34.

Her metamorphosis can also be seen to represent her bursting forth from the more passive, decorative—and therefore more "feminine"— genres of courtly poetry. No more coy love-casuistry for her: there was too much to resolve in the real world. Because it did relate to the world outside the courts of love and other *loca amoena* so dear to static meditation, historiography could correspondingly be typed as a "masculine" genre. It was produced by men endowed with education in both arms and letters and often with the mobility to view events and people firsthand. Even those not composing these accounts from eyewitness experience at least had access to other works and conversation with colleagues on politics, war, finance, and books. These were distinctly masculine objects. The central focus of the authors, whether conscious or unconscious, was power and the interrelationships of power.

Christine herself had enjoyed what she herself even termed a "masculine education" because of her father's enlightened attitude. Although women were not as helpless as previously believed, especially those in the Italian university milieu, Christine nevertheless received better training and experience in the domains traditionally ruled by men. In years to come she would compose military and political treatises and translations, most of which became influential and widely read. She would also instruct women on how to use their already existing strengths to greater advantage. However, she would never really advocate feminine supremacy; she could be at times surprisingly conventional in her assessment of most women's lot in life, while praising the deeds of famous women in history as exceptional and not to be emulated by all.

It is significant that she chose as her heroes Boethius and then the more mobile Dante—both political minds and poets—instead of Lancelot and Tristan, the warrior love poets. Following the example of the courageous Florentine in his search for Beatrice with the help of Virgil, she must go on to see history as a privileged pupil of its guiding force, Fortune.

Then there remained the problem of writing it down for her public. How aware she was of her historiographical abilities is somewhat obscured by her persona of modesty and even incompetence. Using such diminutives as *femmelete, seulete,* she often poses the question, directly or indirectly, at the beginning of her polemical and historical works, "How can someone of such meager intellect [*faible engin*] accomplish the great task before me? I shall do my best" (e.g., *Mutacion,* vv. 1-20). It would be too easy to interpret this reticence and modesty on her part as a result of the fact that she was a woman and therefore unaccustomed to exercising her new-found strength. Rather, she has revitalized an old offertory topos and turned it into a polemical weapon.

Such calculated self-deprecation can be seen in the prefaces to works by her male colleagues as well, especially in the works of the translators claiming to be awed by the great writings of ancient authors in Latin, a more complex language than was their French. This self-effacement of moderns before the ancients produced a variety of results: it put the reader at ease and thus facilitated communication, and it served as a handy pretext for incorporating many neologisms into the then primitive language of translation, thereby enriching the intellectual range of Middle French.

Christine certainly enjoyed using the profusion of learned words from Latin and even Greek—the longer the better—as any index to her serious works will show.[17] The freshness and spontaneity of her style may be seen to come in part from a mixture of quadrisyllabic bombast and Italianate diminutive,[18] lending an aura of engaging, though cumbersome, dedication to her narrative. Her association with Jean Gerson and Jacques Legrand seems to have contributed to her sermonizing and visionary tendencies.[19] Another significant linguistic trait of Christine's discourse stems from her familiarity with the legal profession, no doubt through her husband and possibly through her father as well. Legal language, which was to reach its fullest development in the sixteenth century in France, gave her both power and precision of expression in her histories and political treatises, freeing her from poetic and romance convention. Gradually, she was acquiring her own arsenal of knowledge to express the impossible, thus following her dictum of the *Autre Balade* quoted at the beginning of this paper.

In advocating that history be written to move the public towards virtue, Christine echoes an old Roman ideal which she most likely read about in the early seventh-century *Etymologiae* (I, 40-44) of Isidore of Seville, who in turn had recorded the principles of such writers as Sempronius Asellio (second century B.C.). Both sources also distinguish between history and annals, the former being an account of events personally lived by the author and the latter recording events never known firsthand to the author. Isidore goes on to define *history* as telling what has happened, *arguments* (plots, as in a play) involving potentially possible events not having occurred, and *stories* or *fables* as differing from the above in that they concern things which have not happened, nor could

[17] See glossary to Solente's edition of *Mutacion,* vol. IV, and her study on Christine in *Histoire Littéraire de la France* (Paris, 1969), XL, 84. For information on learned vocabulary of the time, see glossary to Oresme, *Le Livre du Ciel et du Monde,* ed. Menut and Denomy (Milwaukee, 1968), and A. J. Denomy, "The Vocabulary of Jean de Meun's Translation of Boethius's *De Consolatione Philosophiae," Medieval Studies,* 15 (1953), 19-34.

[18] Lucy M. Gay, "On the Language of Christine de Pisan," *Modern Philology,* 6 (1908-1909), 16-28.

[19] For Jacques Legrand's influence on Christine's moralizing, see Evencio Beltran, "Christine de Pizan, Jacques Legrand et le *Communiloquium* de Jean de Galles," *Romania,* 104 (1983), 208-28. Beltran demonstrates textual borrowing from the Augustinian monk's translation, the *Sophilogium,* in Christine's *Chemin de long estude* and *Corps de policie* and stylistic similarities in the *Charles V.*

ever happen, because they are against nature. Christine interwove all of these to convey her message in a manner both engaging and credible. Whatever her self-consciousness as an historian, Christine's "feminine sense" seems to have pleased the men in power. As an example, Philip the Bold, Duke of Burgundy, was so impressed by the *Mutacion de Fortune* that he commissioned her to write a biography of his deceased brother, Charles V. *Les Fais et bonnes meurs du sage roy Charles V* (1404) is her most purely historical work, yet it reveals as much about its author as it does about its subject. An unstinting panegyric with a strong personal touch, her biography reflects the flowering of the new chivalric ideal. Charles V is portrayed as the perfect monarch and the perfect knight. Christine's idealization transcended the conventional necessity to please her patron, the Duke. Rooted more in admiration than in sycophancy, Christine's adulation was inspired by personal acquaintance, for Charles V had presided over the golden age of her youth as her father's protector as well as ruler in a time of peace for France. Christine's prosperity and that of France are entwined.

While some modern scholars are skeptical of Christine's success in reconciling the figures of perfect king and perfect knight within the unprepossessing, yet extraordinarily competent reality that was Charles,[20] others argue that she produced an image of rebirth and hope rather than one of decline. Instead of interpreting the increasing military impotence of the nobles as a mandate for disabusement, the poetess turned political theorist sees, and causes us to see, the King as part of a new wave of learned, rational rulers guiding France into an era of peace and prosperity, which replaced the domination by warlords and an effete landed aristocracy.[21] Pursuing this all-pervasive thesis, Christine also shows herself capable of exacting detail. Her biography provides us with the most true-to-life description of his physical appearance.[22]

In the *Charles V,* Christine elucidates her historical method:

I can answer that just as a builder or mason works with stone and other materials with which he builds and constructs a castle or house . . . (selecting his materials) according to the purposes and concepts which he intends, also the embroiderers, who do a variety of designs according to the subtlety of their imagination . . ., so I too bring together all of my materials, that is, other works, of which my compilation is composed; I need only know how to apply them correctly in the interests of my imagination. (Solente ed., 191)

So what is a woman doing writing about chivalry and knighthood? To

---

[20] Raymond Kilgour, *The Decline of Chivalry* (Cambridge, Mass., 1937), 137-40.

[21] George H. Bumgardner, "Tradition and Modernity from 1380 to 1405: Christine de Pisan" (Ph.D. Diss., Yale 1970), 98-99. Percy Schramm discusses Christine's omission of unfavorable characteristics in her portrait of Charles in *Der König von Frankreich* (Weimar, 1960), I, 246.

[22] Claire R. Sherman, *The Portraits of Charles V of France* (New York, 1969).

this typical question Christine answers with a paraphrase of Hugh of St. Victor: a wise person looks at the doctrine itself and not at the one who wrote it.

Is there a feminine style of writing history? There is certainly a special quality to Christine's style of history. When one compares her narratives to those of her early contemporary, Jean Froissart, one notices a striking difference in attitude and focus. For example, in examining both authors' accounts of the last moments of Charles V, it is clear that Froissart describes appearance and gesture in careful detail, while Christine devotes her attention to the abstract and symbolic. Froissart concentrates on the King's medical problems, giving a seemingly eyewitness account—in particular, of an evidently fatal fistula and accompanying maladies— with almost Balzacian relish. Like Christine, the author of the *Chronicles* was both poet and historian, though perhaps because of his willingness to rely on dramatic second-hand accounts as uncritically as on his own direct experience, his sensibility is more novelistic. Christine's voice alternates between the poetic and the erudite.[23] Froissart concerns himself with surface and sequence, while the poetess of imposed allegory is ever on the lookout for the hidden meaning of a real event, refusing what Paul Archambault has characterized as the "horizontal construct" in mid-fourteenth-century historical perception.[24] Her relation of the King's death describes the "beautiful end" of the monarch, using words meaning conscience, devotion, contrition. She does mention his physical sickness but with no detail whatsoever, preferring to enumerate its psychological manifestations, anguish, torment, peril of the soul—in any case, there is not a fistula to be found here. Although Christine's description abounds in erudite intangibles, her account is more moving, more emotional, even more uplifting. Froissart's somber impassivity leaves the reader more

---

[23] Suzanne Solente, the editor of *Le Livre des fais et bonnes meurs du sage roy Charles V par Christine de Pisan* (2 vols.; Paris, 1936), I, xxxiv, gives many sources for her biography, of which the main one on the King's final moments is the *Relation latine de la mort de Charles V*, in accordance with Henri Duchemin's conclusions (*Positions de Thèse à l'Ecole des Chartes*, 1891). Solente also agrees with Duchemin in attributing certain eyewitness details of the death scene to Christine's father, Thomas de Pizan, who, as court astrologer, functioned in such situations as a doctor to the King. Charity Willard notes that Christine was therefore more familiar with the court than Froissart (132). Further on in the same chapter in Christine's account (chap. LXXI), Charles is shown giving an oration on the crown and its responsibilities and burdens. Roland Delachenal, *Histoire de Charles V* (Paris, 1926), III, 92, n.1, labels this passage a *ressouvenir* of Valerius Maximus (*Facta et Dicta*, ed. Kempf, Bk. VII, ii, 5) as transmitted to Christine's time most likely by the *Somnium Viridarii* (1376) and its widely influential French adaptation the *Songe du Vergier* (c. 1378), both done for Charles V in his lifetime as didactic works.

[24] Paul Archambault, *Seven French Chroniclers: Witnesses to History* (Syracuse, N.Y., 1974), 15.

stoical, and perhaps prepared to deal with the demands of daily survival in a difficult epoch.

In these and other episodes of his *Chronicles* Froissart expresses the point of view of a member of the established order: he had always been "part of the system," whereas Christine, forced out of a life of sheltered ease and esteem into one of oppressive marginality, had to fight her way back into security and respectability. She thus shows a heightened understanding of the poor, of widows and of other unfortunates and did not confine her energies to praising the upper classes as did Froissart.[25] Somehow she did not offend her aristocratic patrons by her attention to the *menu peuple.* She also criticized dishonest lawyers and clerks, at whose hands she suffered in real life, and, with a keen satirical eye, corrupt members of the clergy and government.

Generally, her works after about 1407 became more impersonal, as though there were too much to accomplish to be at all lyrical. After prolific output of political treatises, religious commentaries, and even military manuals, Christine seems to have fallen silent for about ten years, starting from about 1418. Her inactivity coincided with the great mental and physical depression of the Dauphin, later Charles VII. She then composed what could be considered the culmination of her poetic and historiographical talents, the *Dittié de Jehanne d'Arc.* As the only possibly eyewitness, certainly contemporary, narrative in French of the heroine's exploits, the *Dittié* (literally, "tale," a late medieval narrative genre) portrays the maid of Orleans as the epitome of Christine's ideal of active virtue: what the poetess had hoped to do with her pen the military heroine was accomplishing with the sword. One could almost say that both Christine and the Dauphin were restored by Joan's presence as evoked in this almost hagiographic vision. The poem is full of patriotic verve coupled with personal emotion, so much so that one hopes, as does Liliane Dulac,[26] that Christine did not live to see Joan imprisoned by the English, the victim, ironically enough, of the treachery of the poet's onetime patron, Isabel of Bavaria.

In her love of learning and her sense of commitment toward her intellectual ideals, Christine ranks with such early humanists as Jean de

---

[25] See Brian Woledge, "Le Thème de la pauvreté dans la *Mutacion de Fortune* de Christine de Pisan," in *Mélanges... Guiette* (Paris, 1961), 97-107. On Froissart as *littérateur,* see Stephen G. Nichols, Jr. "Discourse in Froissart's *Chroniques,*" Daniel Poirion, *Le Moyen Age II—1300-1480* (Paris, 1971), and Archambault's chapter, "Froissart: History as Surface," in *Seven French Chroniclers.* The collection of essays, *Froissart, Historian,* ed. J. J. N. Palmer (Totowa, N.J., 1981), are concerned more with the chronicler's historical background, career, and manuscripts, with the possible exception of the essay by Philippe Contamine.

[26] Liliane Dulac, "Un Ecrit militant de Christine de Pisan: *Le Ditié de Jehanne d'Arc,*" in *Aspects of Female Existence: Proceedings from the St. Gertrud Symposium, Women in the Middle Ages, 1978,* ed. Birte Carlé *et al.* (Copenhagen, 1980), 115-33.

Montreuil and Jean Gerson. The eloquent fusion of literature and history provided her with a source of personal consolation and models for revelation to enhance the glory of her adopted country.[27] Her example refutes Paul Zumthor's observation that "the bookish culture of the fifteenth century French 'humanist' [quotation marks his] thus adds little to the learning of the old schoolbooks."[28] She used both fact and fable to construct her moralized histories designed to prove something new, and as a committed thinker she demonstrated that the road to dissidence can be paved with good inventions, though not exclusively feminist ones.[29]

University of Utah.

I am indebted to the helpful comments and suggestions made by Professors Natalie Zemon Davis and Sandra Hindman, and Donald Kelley, who read an earlier draft of this manuscript. Any remaining deficiencies are of course my own.

[27] Christine's conscious deployment of eloquence to promote the fame and glory in connection with history approaches Nancy Struever's characterization of the Florentine humanists' writing of history in *The Language of History in the Renaissance: Rhetoric and Historical Consciousness in Florentine Humanism* (Princeton, 1970), 62-63. The Italian humanistic aspect of Christine's historiography warrants further investigation, beyond the limits of this study, which has confined itself primarily to the French tradition. Christine may have been exposed to Italian humanist ideas through her father and perhaps more through the Parisian humanistic circle, some of whose members corresponded with Petrarch and Salutati.

[28] Paul Zumthor, *Le Masque et la lumière: La Poétique des grands rhétoriqueurs* (Paris, 1978), 100.

[29] Christine's concepts of feminism and femininity influenced her philosophical viewpoint despite their complex and even contradictory nature. Charity Willard, in "A Fifteenth-Century View of Woman's Role in Medieval Society," in *The Role of Woman in the Middle Ages*, ed. R. Morewedge (Albany, 1927), observes that Christine is quite traditional in her perception of women's place with regard to men, with a few exceptions. See also Constance Jordan, "Feminism and the Humanists . . . ," *Renaissance Quarterly*, 36 (1983), 181-201. Joan Kelly has provided the most persuasive interpretation of Christine as "the first . . . feminist thinker" (*op. cit.*, n.15, p. 5), Michèle Sarde refers to her as "la première de nos intellectuelles professionnelles," who understood that a woman's speaking out necessitated renouncing her femininity, in *Regard sur les Françaises* (Paris, 1983), 334. Historiography was for Christine a primary vehicle for speaking out, as I have demonstrated.

X

THE DOUBLE STANDARD *

By Keith Thomas

" Anything wrong about a man was but of little moment . . . but anything wrong about a woman, . . . O dear! "—Mrs. Wortle, in *Dr. Wortle's School* by Anthony Trollope (1881).

This paper is an attempt to explore the history of an idea which has been deeply rooted in England for many centuries and which by its effect upon law and institutions as well as upon opinion has done much to govern the relations of men and women with each other. Stated simply, it is the view that unchastity, in the sense of sexual relations before marriage or outside marriage, is for a man, if an offense, none the less a mild and pardonable one, but for a woman a matter of the utmost gravity. This view is popularly known as the double standard.

It is an idea which has made itself felt in most aspects of English life. In the field of opinion it gives rise to such maxims as " young men may sow their wild oats," " a reformed rake makes the best husband," " two maidenheads meeting together in wedlock, the first child must be a fool " or, in modern language, " it is best if the man is ' experienced '." Correspondingly, it teaches that a woman who has lost her honor has lost all and it leads to a great exaltation of female virginity for its own sake. " Chastity in women," said a politician in 1923, " is a star that has guided human nature since the world began, and that points far higher and teaches us of the other sex things which we could not otherwise know. We bow in humble reverence to that high star of chastity, and we celebrate it in song and poetry. But I do not think that any mere man would thank us for enshrining him in such a halo." [1] Both before and after marriage men were permitted liberties of which no woman could ever avail herself and keep her reputation. From Henry I to George IV most of the Kings of England kept mistresses and their examples were followed by many of their subjects. At the court of Charles II, where debauchery was almost a proof of loyalty, Francis North, Lord Guildford, was seriously advised to " keep a whore " because, we are told, " he was ill looked upon for want of doing so." [2] But on the other hand if a woman once fell from virtue her recovery might be impossible.

From this state of affairs sprang the extreme wenching attitude associated with periods like that of the Restoration. Society trained up its daughters to trap men into matrimony without yielding any of its benefits in advance, so the men hit back in the only way they

* I am much indebted to discussions with Mr. Alan Tyson, although I fear that he is unlikely to accept many of my conclusions.

[1] *Parliamentary Debates (Commons)*, 5th Ser., Vol. 160, col. 2374.

[2] R. North, *The Lives of . . . Francis North, Baron Guildford, . . . Sir Dudley North . . . and Dr. John North* (London, 1826), II, 164.

could.[3] The illicit nature of their attempts on female chastity constituted a large part of their attraction. " I'd no more play with a man that slighted his ill fortune," says Fainall in Congreve's *The Way of the World*, " than I'd make love to a woman who undervalued the loss of her reputation."[4] Or, as Jeremy Collier put it, " difficulty and danger heighten the success, and make the conquest more entertaining."[5] The role of seducer and rake was more attractive than that of husband. As Mr. Badman remarked, " Who would keep a cow of their own that can have a quart of milk for a penny?"[6] It has been argued that in eighteenth-century England there was a decline in marriage, or at least a rise in the proportion of bachelors.[7] It is perhaps significant that it was also in the eighteenth century that the demand for virginity in the brothels of England culminated in a mania of defloration which contemporary observers agreed was without parallel in Europe.[8]

When men took liberties, women had to be educated to tolerate them, and in the great mass of didactic literature for young ladies one of the main themes was that women should recognize that the double standard was in the nature of things, that model wives should turn a blind eye to their husband's liaisons. Here is the first Marquis of Halifax writing to his daughter at the end of the seventeenth century:

You are to consider you live in a time which hath rendered some kind of frailties so habitual, that they lay claim to large grains of allowance. The world in this is somewhat unequal, and our sex seemeth to play the tyrant in distinguishing partially for ourselves, by making that in the utmost degree criminal in the woman, which in a man passeth under a much gentler censure. The root and excuse of this injustice is the preservation of families from any mixture which may bring a blemish to them: and whilst the point of honour continues to be so plac'd, it seems unavoidable to give your sex the greater share of the penalty . . . . Remember, that next to the danger of committing the fault yourself, the greatest is that of seeing it in your husband. Do not seem to look or hear that way: If he is a man of sense, he will reclaim himself . . . if he is not so, he will be provok'd, but not reformed . . . . Such an undecent complaint makes a wife much more ridiculous than the injury that provoketh her to it.[9]

[3] On this see Mr. Christopher Hill's brilliant article, " Clarissa Harlowe and her Times," *Essays in Criticism*, IV (1955), esp. 324.   [4] Act I, scene 1.
[5] " Of Whoredom," in *Essays upon Several Moral Subjects*, III (3rd ed.) (London, 1720), 114–115.
[6] J. Bunyan, *Life and Death of Mr. Badman*, ed. J. Brown (Cambridge, 1905), 154.
[7] H. J. Habakkuk, " Marriage Settlements in the Eighteenth Century," *Trans. Roy. Hist. Soc.*, 4th Ser., Vol. 32 (1950), 24.
[8] I. Bloch, *Sexual Life in England Past and Present*, trans. W. H. Forstern (London, 1938), 176.
[9] *Miscellanies by the Right Noble Lord, The Late Marquess of Halifax* (London, 1700), 17-18.

But if society was to allow men comparative sexual freedom and at the same time keep single women virgin and married women chaste then a solution had to be found which would gratify the former without sacrificing the latter. The answer lay in prostitution and the widespread view that a class of fallen women was needed to keep the rest of the world pure. The classic statement of this belief is to be found in W. E. H. Lecky's *History of European Morals*, where he describes the prostitute:

a figure which is certainly the most mournful, and in some respects the most awful, upon which the eye of the moralist can dwell. That unhappy being whose very name is a shame to speak; who counterfeits with a cold heart the transports of affection, and submits herself as the passive instrument of lust, who is scorned and insulted as the vilest of her sex, and doomed, for the most part, to disease and abject wretchedness and an early death, appears in every age as the perpetual symbol of the degradation and the sinfulness of man. Herself the supreme type of vice, she is ultimately the most efficient guardian of virtue. But for her, the unchallenged purity of countless happy homes would be polluted, and not a few who, in the pride of their untempted chastity, think of her with an indignant shudder, would have known the agony of remorse and despair. On that one degraded and ignoble form are concentrated the passions that might have filled the world with shame. She remains, while creeds and civilisations rise and fall, the eternal priestess of humanity, blasted for the sins of the people.[10]

But the view of the prostitute as a necessary evil and a buttress for the morals of the rest of society goes back to a time long before Lecky. " Remove prostitutes from human affairs," wrote St. Augustine, " and you would pollute the world with lust." [11] Aquinas compared her to a cesspool in a palace, unpleasant but necessary.[12] And in the eighteenth century that engaging writer Bernard Mandeville, who argued that private vices were public benefits, produced *A Modest Defence of Publick Stews* (1724) in which he made a strong case for state-regulated brothels. The existence of male lust had to be recognized; even Socrates had confessed in his old age that when a girl touched his shoulder " he felt a strange tickling all over him for five days." [13] This lust had to be channelled off by way of the stews if female chastity (which he shrewdly analyzed as an artificial combination of honor and interest [14]) was to be preserved. " If courte-

[10] W. E. H. Lecky, *History of European Morals* (London, 1913), II, 282-283.
[11] *De Ordine*, ii, 4, quoted in E. Westermarck, *Christianity and Morals* (London, 1939), 363.
[12] Cited in G. R. Taylor, *Sex in History* (London, 1953), 21.
[13] Mandeville, *A Modest Defence*, iv.   [14] *Ibid.*, 42.

zans and strumpets were to be prosecuted with as much rigor as some silly people would have it, what locks or bars would be sufficient to preserve the honor of our wives and daughters? " [15]

Whether or not it existed for the sake of wives and daughters there can be no doubt that prostitution was widespread in England throughout the whole of medieval and modern times. It was regarded as universal and inevitable and it received a good deal of official sanction from the state. Regulations for the management of the stews at Southwark were issued by Henry II and these licensed brothels survived until the reign of Henry VIII. They came under the jurisdiction of the Bishop of Winchester and their inhabitants were popularly known as " Winchester geese." It is impossible to quote reliable figures, but it is clear that by Victorian times prostitution in London and the industrial cities was carried out on an enormous scale. In 1841 the Chief Commissioner of Police estimated that there were 3,325 brothels in the Metropolitan district of London alone [16] and this calculation takes no account of part-time prostitution produced by inadequate female wages. " I am afraid," said Gladstone in 1857, " as respects the gross evils of prostitution, that there is hardly any country in the world where they prevail to a greater extent than in our own." [17]

The most horrible aspect of this state of affairs lay in the different standards applied to the prostitutes themselves on the one hand and to the men who availed themselves of their services on the other. As late as 1871 a Royal Commission declared, " we may at once dispose of (any recommendation) founded on the principle of putting both parties to the sin of fornication on the same footing by the obvious but not less conclusive reply that there is no comparison to be made between prostitutes and the men who consort with them. With the one sex the offence is committed as a matter of gain; with the other it is an irregular indulgence of a natural impulse." [18] Such indulgence was made possible by the law. In 1881 a Select Committee reported: " In other countries female chastity is more or less protected by law up to the age of twenty-one. No such protection is given in England to girls above the age of thirteen." [19] Until 1875 the age of consent had been only twelve and when in 1885 it was finally raised to sixteen the vehement opposition which had previously greeted this proposal was only overcome by the publicity afforded to the sensational prosecution of the journalist W. T. Stead who had delib-

[15] *The Fable of the Bees*, ed. F. B. Kaye (Oxford, 1924), I, 95-96.
[16] G. R. Scott, *A History of Prostitution from Antiquity to the Present Day* (London, 1954), 98.   [17] *Parliamentary Debates*, 3rd Ser., Vol. 147, col. 853.
[18] *Report of the Royal Commission upon the Administration and Operation of the Contagious Diseases Acts* (London, 1871), I, 17.

erately purchased a young girl from her mother for five pounds, had her virginity certified by a midwife, took her to a brothel for a night and finally shipped her abroad—all to show just what could be done under the then existing state of the law. His subsequent articles in the *Pall Mall Gazette,* entitled *The Maiden Tribute of Modern Babylon,* caused an outcry and made reform inevitable. Yet Stead himself was sent to prison and, as he remarked of the House of Lords, "Stringent legislation against the fraud and force by which brothels are recruited could hardly be expected from legislators who were said to be familiar visitors at Berthe's in Milton Street, or Mrs. Jeffries's in Chelsea." [20]

In no way did these legislators demonstrate the direction of their sympathies in this matter more clearly then in the passing of the Contagious Diseases Acts. These were a series of measures issued in the 1860's. They were modeled on a scheme devised by Napoleon and they provided for a system of state regulated prostitution in the garrison towns of England. Under their provisions any woman could be arrested merely on the suspicion of a plain-clothes government spy and be compelled to sign a voluntary submission to be medically examined once a fortnight or else vindicate her character in the police court. After a notable campaign led by Mrs. Josephine Butler the Acts were repealed in 1886. They had led to much incidental hardship and cruelty, but their main relevance to our purpose here is that they represent the high-water mark of the tendency we have been describing. By their bland assumption that prostitution was a permanent and necessary evil and by their direct application of the double standard in that all regulation and medical examination applied to the women alone they yield an interesting commentary on a too often forgotten aspect of Victorian England.

The branch of English law, however, which best illustrates the effects of the double standard and the tenacity with which it survived is that relating to divorce. Here we see how, during those periods when divorce and remarriage have been allowed, adultery on the part of the married woman has almost invariably been recognized as valid grounds for such a divorce, but the wife, on the other hand, has very seldom been entitled to seek the dissolution of the marriage solely on the grounds of a similar offense on the part of her husband. A brief survey of the facts should serve to demonstrate this point.

In Anglo-Saxon times the conventions governing marriage and divorce are shrouded in a certain amount of obscurity, but it appears that under ancient Germanic law adultery was, strictly speaking, not a crime that a man was capable of committing against his wife at all.

[19] *The Truth about the Armstrong Case and the Salvation Army* (London, n.d.), 6. [20] *Ibid.,* 7.

If he were punished, it would be not for unfaithfulness to his wife, but for violating the rights of another husband. For similar misconduct on her part, however, the wife was sometimes put to death—which would have obviated the need for any divorce proceedings.[21] The code of King Ethelbert suggests that divorce was possible at the will of either spouse,[22] but in the penitentials of Theodore we see the clear operation of the double standard. In cases of adultery discretion was exercised in favor of the husband. Should the wife be unfaithful he had the right to repudiate her, but if he committed adultery she was unable to free herself from him save by his departure for a monastery.[23]

After the Norman Conquest all matrimonial cases were dealt with in the spiritual courts and came under the jurisdiction of the canon law. This did not recognize the existence of divorce at all, at least not in the sense of divorce with the right of remarriage (*divortium a vinculo matrimonii*); although, if the parties were sufficiently rich or influential, it was usually possible to find an impediment on the grounds of which the marriage might be annulled, so that it was deemed never to have taken place. The ecclesiastical courts, however, could grant a separation (*divortium a mensa et thoro*) by which the marriage was effectively brought to an end, although neither party would be allowed to remarry. Adultery by either partner was good grounds for a separation and here it might seem as if the double standard went into abeyance. But such an impression would be misleading, for in practice it usually only the husband who was in a position to take advantage of this. The wife was seldom able to claim a separation from her husband. The reasons for this were economic; she would probably be unable to support herself during such a separation, because, although separated, she was still subject to all the legal disabilities of a married woman. In other words, she was now in a state of virtual outlawry, for her husband retained all his rights over her property, including even the wages she might earn after her separation; she was incapable of conducting a legal action by herself, and she could not even claim access to her children. All she had was a small allowance in the shape of alimony and the payment of this was often difficult to enforce. As a result it was only those wives of higher social status with independent property rights secured to them by

[21] G. E. Howard, *A History of Matrimonial Institutions* (Chicago & London, 1904), II, 35–36. Cf. J. R. Reinhard, " Burning at the Stake in Medieval Law and Literature," *Speculum*, XVI (1941).

[22] F. L. Attenborough, ed., *The Laws of the Earliest English Kings* (Cambridge, 1922), 15.

[23] A. W. Haddan and W. Stubbs, *Councils and Ecclesiastical Documents* (Oxford, 1871), III, 199.

equity who were in a position to take advantage of their theoretical right to gain a separation from a husband on the ground of his adultery.

The jurisdiction of the spiritual courts survived the Reformation and the law remained unchanged until 1857. But from the end of the seventeenth century a new factor emerged: divorce by Act of Parliament. A marriage might be dissolved and the partners allowed to marry again as a result of a petition and bill presented to the House of Lords. This procedure made divorce with the right to remarriage legal in England for the first time since the Norman Conquest, but its effects were limited. The process was enormously expensive and few people were in a position to take advantage of it—to be precise, there were only a little over 200 such divorces granted in the whole period up to 1857. Of these only about half a dozen were granted at the suit of a woman. Whereas adultery by the wife was regarded as good grounds for granting the husband a divorce, she on the other hand had no hope of getting her bill through if she had no stronger claim than that of infidelity on the part of the husband. The doctrine was that the marriage should be dissolved only if circumstances had arisen which were deemed such as to make the continuance of the union impossible. Adultery by the wife *was* such a circumstance, but adultery by the husband was not. In *Mrs. Moffat's Case* (1832) it was stated that the husband had " committed an act of infidelity on the very night of his marriage, and occupied himself afterwards in constant experiments on the chastity of his female domestics, by one of whom a child was born to him." Her petition for divorce was rejected.[24] The opinion of parliament was that the wife should forgive the guilty husband but that the husband *could not* forgive the guilty wife. Another rejected petition was that of Mrs. Teush in 1805, whose husband had treated her with great brutality and was living openly with a mistress by whom he had had several children. Lord Eldon said that " he never recollected a more favorable representation given of any woman; but yet, on general grounds of public morality, he felt it his painful duty to give a negative to the original motion; " and the Bishop of St. Asaph was of the opinion " that however hard the rule might press upon a few individuals, it would, on the whole, be better if no bill of this kind were passed." [25] Only if her husband's adultery was incestuous adultery or was greatly aggravated by other circumstances was the wife entitled to expect a divorce.

Although England was the only Protestant country in Europe to maintain this distinction, it was not discarded in 1857, when matri-

---

[24] J. Macqueen, *A Practical Treatise on the Appellate Jurisdiction of the House of Lords and Privy Council* (London, 1842), 658.　　　　[25] *Ibid.*, 603–4.

monial jurisdiction was transferred from the realm of canon law to a
new civil divorce court. In permitting dissolutions of marriage the
new court was to follow the rules which had governed the earlier
divorces by Act of Parliament. The husband merely had to prove
one act of adultery committed by his wife, but his wife had to show
her husband guilty of adultery *plus* some other injury—bigamy,
cruelty, desertion, incest, rape, or unnatural offenses. "It had ever
been the feeling of that House," said that Lord Chancellor, intro-
ducing the bill in the Lords, "indeed, it was a feeling common to
mankind in general that, although the sin in both cases was the same,
the effect of adultery on the part of the husband was very different
from that of adultery on the part of the wife. It was possible for a
wife to pardon a husband who had committed adultery; but it was
hardly possible for a husband ever really to pardon the adultery of a
wife." [26] Despite a good deal of opposition, notably from Gladstone,
the double standard was preserved in the act of 1857 and it was only
in 1923 that the grounds for divorce were made the same for both
sexes.

Prostitution and divorce have provided us with two examples of
the way in which the law enforced the double standard, but there are
many others, for instance, the laws relating to the property of married
persons. Should either spouse die intestate, the surviving partner
was allowed to retain a proportion of the property of the deceased.
The wife had a third of the estate as her dower, the husband was permitted by what was called *courtesy* to remain in possession until his
death of all the land which the couple had held during the wife's lifetime in her right, provided a child had been born to them. The double
standard appears in the conditions under which dower or courtesy
might be forfeited. The wife lost her dower if she was proved to be
unfaithful, but a similar act of adultery did *not* deprive the husband
of his courtesy.[27] The same distinction applied also to unmarried
women, for under feudal law an heiress who was demonstrated to have
been unchaste was deprived of her inheritance—a penalty which was
not demanded of a man who had behaved in a similar manner.

As a final instance of the double standard at work in English law,
let us recall that until half-way through the nineteenth century the

[26] *Parliamentary Debates*, 3rd Ser., Vol. 145, col. 490. A stronger view was expressed by Sir John Nicholl in 1825: "Forgiveness on the part of wife, especially
with a large family, in the hopes of reclaiming her husband, is meritorious; while a
similar forgiveness on the part of the husband would be degrading and dishonour-
able." J. Haggard, *Reports of Cases argued and determined in the Ecclesiastical
Courts at Doctors' Commons, and in the High Court of Delegates* (London, 1829–
1832), I, 752.

[27] T. E., *The Lawes Resolutions of Womens Rights* (London, 1632), 146 has
some spirited remarks on this topic.

husband was entitled to use violence and physical restraint to secure the person and services of his wife (her *consortium*) whereas she was able to regain her renegade husband only by means of a court order for restitution of conjugal rights.

There is therefore abundant evidence for the extensive operation of the double standard in both English law and opinion in medieval and modern times.[28] But it is hardly necessary to add that this double standard did not meet with uncritical acceptance by all elements in the community. In particular, two main currents of opinion ran counter to it. The first was that of Christianity.

The idea of reciprocal fidelity was not unknown in pre-Christian times, but it is undeniable that it received a new emphasis from Christian teaching. Christ's own treatment of the woman taken in adultery was frequently cited as justification for not discriminating against the woman alone. The attitude of the medieval church was mixed and it is easy to detect a wide discrepancy between theory and practice; nevertheless, the idea that unchastity was as much a sin for the one sex as for the other steadily gained ground,[29] and with the Reformation the attack on the double standard grew stronger. The English Reformers of the sixteenth century were generally in favor of divorce and most of them would have allowed it to the wife for the husband's adultery. The *Reformatio Legum Ecclesiasticarum* drawn up under Edward VI would have permitted the innocent party of either sex to remarry.[30] Similarly, most of the later Puritan writers urged equality of the sexes in divorce and enjoined chastity as a duty for men and women alike. " Keep chaste till the coming of the Lord Jesus," wrote Daniel Rogers; " Know that this is an equal duty of both, . . . think not thy husband tied to this rule, O woman; nor thou thy wife tied, O husband, and the other free: the tie is equal." [31] Perkins declared that the husband's superiority gave him no immunity from the prohibition against adultery,[32] and William Gouge wrote, " I see not how that difference in the sin can stand with the tenour of God's Word." It might be that greater consequences followed from a lapse on the part of the wife, but at least " God's Word

[28] For a discussion of some of the consequences of the double standard as it operates in modern American society see I. L. Reiss, " The Double Standard in Premarital Sexual Intercourse. A Neglected Concept," *Social Forces*, Vol. 34, No. 3 (March 1956).

[29] *Dives and Pauper* (1493), 6th Commandment, cap. 5, actually says that the husband's adultery is the more serious offense, on the grounds that he is the woman's superior and the greater the sinner, the greater the sin.

[30] E. Cardwell, ed., *The Reformation of the Ecclesiastical Laws* (Oxford, 1850), 51.

[31] *Matrimonial Honour* (London, 1642), 181-2.

[32] *Workes* (Cambridge, 1609-1613), III, 53.

maketh no disparity between them."[33] By the time of the Restoration the attitude of most divines was that adultery was as great a sin in the husband as in the wife, but that account had to be taken of the more enduring consequences when it was committed by the latter.[34] Up to the nineteenth century this position was the standard one, and in the debate on the Divorce Bill in 1857 most members agreed that the sin was the same but that the effects were different. By itself, therefore, the Christian insistence upon the equality of the two sexes before God was not sufficient to bring about a radical change in social attitudes, since by their own admission its exponents did not claim to provide a yardstick by which the full consequences of unchastity might be measured.

The other main source of opposition to the double standard was the ever-growing current of what can only be described as middle-class respectability. From the seventeenth century, if not earlier, there becomes apparent a strong tendency to place a new and heightened emphasis upon the values of family life and to deplore any aristocratic or libertine conduct which would be likely to jeopardize domestic security. This attitude is intimately connected with Puritanism, though it stems from certain strong material values as well. It is associated with propriety and prudery and is exemplified in the attack on the Restoration stage. It is also essentially a middle-class morality, which the rich despise and the poor cannot afford. Sexual promiscuity was condemned because it was incompatible with the high emotional values expected from marriage, because it was wasteful, and because it took time and money which would have been better spent in the pursuit of a gainful occupation.

The representative exponents of this outlook were totally opposed to the double standard. "It is certain," wrote Richard Steele, "that chastity is . . . as much to be valued in men as in women."[35] He deplored the state of affairs by which the world "instead of avenging the cause of an abused woman, will proclaim her dishonour; while the person injured is shunned like a pestilence, he who did the wrong sees no difference in the reception he meets with, nor is he the less welcome to the rest of the sex who are still within the pale of honour and innocence . . . I know not how it is, but our sex has usurped a certain authority to exclude chastity out of the catalogue of masculine virtues, by which means females adventure all against those who have nothing to lose."[36] Jeremy Collier attacked the aristocratic seducer.

[33] Of Domesticall Duties, Eight Treatises, 3rd. ed. (London, 1634), 221.

[34] R. B. Schlatter, The Social Ideas of Religious Leaders, 1660–1688 (London, 1940), 28–9.

[35] Tatler, No. 58, also quoted by R. Blanchard, "Richard Steele and the Status of Women," Studies in Philology, XXVI, 3 (1929), 349.

[36] The Guardian, No. 45 (2 May, 1713).

"Why," he asked, "is not he that steals a woman's honour as un-creditable as a common surpriser of property [37] . . . . What think you of sending a wench to Bridewell, and doing nothing to the fellow that debauch'd her, tho' sometimes the first is single, and the other married? " [38]

Since the late seventeenth century there has always existed a large body of middle-class opinion which has regarded illicit sexual activity outside marriage as equally unrespectable in men and women alike. Yet its influence has been limited, in that its main attention has always been directed towards safeguarding the chastity of married women and of the daughters of respectable families. Towards the large body of lower class and of "fallen" women it has been less indulgent. Moreover, the emphasis on outward respectability has resulted in the absence of any serious deterrent against successfully conducted clandestine activity. Concealment has always been more difficult for women than for men; as for the Victorian father the volume of nineteenth-century prostitution tells its own tale.

Before we embark upon the question of why this double standard existed, there are two observations which should be made.

The first is that the double standard is in no way peculiar to England. The moral and legal codes of most advanced peoples reflect the same distinction. The Hindus, the Mohammedans, the Zoroastrians, the ancient Hebrews, all to a greater or lesser extent regarded chastity as primarily a female virtue, an essential quality for all women, but for men, if perhaps an ideal, yet scarcely an attainable one.[39] But it is not true that a high value has been set on female chastity by the whole human race at every stage in its development. As Locke remarks, "He that will carefully peruse the history of mankind, and look abroad into the several tribes of men, and with indifferency survey their actions, will be able to satisfy himself, that there is scarce that principle of morality to be named, or rule of virtue to be thought on . . . which is not, somewhere or other, slighted and condemned by the general fashion of whole societies of men, governed by practical opinions, and rules of living quite opposite to others." [40] Some societies have set great value on female chastity; some have not. And if it is admitted that it is comparatively rare for infidelity by married women to be condoned, then it has also to be recognized that active contempt for unmarried females who are still virgin is by no means infrequent. There is, therefore, no reason to believe that the origin of the double standard lies in the nature of things. It is

<hr>

[37] "Of Whoredom," *op. cit.*, 123.   [38] *Ibid.*, 129.
[39] E. Westermarck, *The Origin and Development of the Moral Ideas* (London, 1906–1908), II, 427–8.
[40] *An Essay Concerning Humane Understanding* (London, 1690), 19.

not to be found in every society and we may reasonably conclude that when it does appear, as in England, we may discuss it as a genuine product of historical circumstance.

The second observation is that the double standard is not to be found in all levels of English society with the same intensity. In particular, it has been much less marked in the lower classes. This is made clear by a volume of nineteenth-century comment the force of which cannot be gainsaid, even when all allowances for the deficiencies of the observers have been made. " There is no chastity among the absolute poor," wrote Place in 1822.[41] A country vicar reported to a Royal Commission, in 1843, " I remark also a particular deficiency of the women as to chastity; in many instances they seem hardly to comprehend or value it as a virtue." [42] The Poor Law Commissioners of 1834 were told that " it is scarcely possible in a civilised country, and where Christianity is professed, for there to be less delicacy on the point of chastity than among the class of females in farm service and the labouring community generally [43] . . . . The moral sanction is wholly ineffective amongst the labouring classes." [44] " Sexual intercourse was almost universal prior to marriage in the agricultural district," wrote Gaskell; " marriage was generally deferred till pregnancy fully declared itself." He went on to explain that this kind of intercourse " must not be confounded with that promiscuous and indecent concourse of the sexes which is so prevalent in towns, and which is ruinous alike to health and to morals. It existed only between parties where a tacit understanding had all the weight of an obligation—and this was, that marriage should be the result. This, in nineteen cases out of twenty, took place sooner or later.[45] But there is little doubt that what indignant observers like Gaskell mistook for the effects of the Industrial Revolution upon the morality of the cotton mills represented merely the standards which the laboring classes had always known and which overcrowded housing conditions now did everything to encourage.[46] Among the lowest classes of society the tradition of promiscuity was too strong to allow the emergence of so sophisticated a concept as that of the double standard.

[41] Quoted in M. C. Stopes, *Contraception*, 6th ed. (London, 1946), 280.

[42] *Reports of Special Assistant Poor Law Commissioners on the Employment of Women and Children in Agriculture* (London, 1843), 201.

[43] Parliamentary Papers, 1834, XXXVII (Appendix C to Report of Poor Law Commissioners), 407.

[44] *Ibid.*, 394.

[45] P. Gaskell, *The Manufacturing Population of England* (London, 1833), 28, 31.

[46] M. Hewitt, " The Effect of Married Women's Employment in the Cotton Textile Districts on the Organization and Structure of the Home in Lancashire, 1840–1880 " (London, Ph.D. thesis, unpub'd) 1953, 73.

With these reservations in mind we may now turn to consider some possible explanations as to the origin and cause of this double standard.

Of these explanations the first is the one which the present writer is least competent to discuss, for it is matter of psychology, but it is an important one which has to be considered at the very outset. In one of his essays Freud describes what he regards as a common characteristic of civilized men: their inability to fuse the two currents of love and sensuality into love for one person and the resulting tendency to find with women of a lower social order, whom they despise, that sexual satisfaction which they are unable to obtain from their relationship with their wives, for whom they feel only tenderness, affection, and esteem. Of such men he says that " where they love they do not desire and where they desire they cannot love." [47] This dissociation of sexual attraction from the other elements of love and the inability to focus both on a single object Freud attributes to the frustration of intense incestuous fixations in childhood. He admits that women to some extent are also subject to this dissociation, which in their case takes the form of frigidity and occasionally produces Lady Chatterley–like situations. But, on the whole, it seems fair to say that the conclusion which follows from Freudian psycho-analysis is, in the words of one of its best-known exponents, that " with women the directly sexual elements of love are more frequently aroused together with the elements of tenderness and esteem, than is the case with men." [48]

Now if this were true it would suggest that when people have regarded an act of marital infidelity on the part of the woman as having far greater significance than a similar act committed by the man they were doing no more than stating a psychological fact. Such an explanation would go a long way towards accounting for the existence of a double standard of morality. It lends much support to Mr. Gladstone's analysis in the debate on the 1857 divorce bill of the " mode in which temptation operates on parties guilty of adultery according as they are men or women. I believe that a very limited portion of the offences committed by women are due to the mere influence of sensual passion. On the other side, I believe that a very large proportion of the offences committed by men are due to that influence." [49] The findings of the Freudian school of psycho-analysis have to be considered by the historian of morals who endeavors to disentangle the permanent factors from the variable. Thus Dr. Ernest

[47] " On the Universal Tendency to Debasement in the Sphere of Love," (trans. A. Tyson), in *Works* (Standard Ed.), ed. J. Strachey *et al.*, XI (1957), 183.

[48] J. C. Flügel, *The Psycho-Analytic Study of the Family*, 3rd ed. (London, 1929), 112.

[49] *Parliamentary Debates*, 3rd Ser., Vol. 147, cols. 1273–1274.

Jones once declared that " prostitution is not altogether a mere *faute de mieux* replaceable, for instance, simply by making early marriage possible." [50] He added that " in a large number of typical cases potency is incompatible with marital fidelity, and can be attained only at the cost of adultery," [51] and that " there is reason to think that the state of affairs would not be so very dissimilar if the social restrictions on sexuality were greatly diminished." [52]

If all this is accepted, then our search for the origins of the double standard would be at an end, for it would have to be recognized that it was no more than an inevitable by-product of a permanent feature of human pyschology, namely the inability of the male to find complete satisfaction within marriage. But it is scarcely as simple as all that. There are good reasons to believe that the conclusions of Freudian psycho-analysis, represented as valid for the whole human race and reinforced by numerous indisputed case-histories as they are, do not necessarily hold outside the nineteenth-century, Western European middle-classes from whom they were derived. It is not just that Freud held many of what we would now regard as characteristically Victorian prejudices and in his attitude to women embodied many of the patriarchal assumptions of his time.[53] What is more serious is that he rarely seems to have considered the possibility that what he regarded as permanent attributes of human nature might have been more temporary affairs influenced or determined by economic and social factors which his investigations did not take into account.

It is true that the incestuous motif which he identified as the fundamental cause of dissociation and therefore of the double standard is less easy to explain away as merely the product of one society than are the various subordinate causes such as the view of the sexual act as something degrading. On the other hand the universal existence of this incestuous fixation would seem to be equally hard to establish. It is not clear exactly how propositions relating to the unconscious are to be proved or disproved, but it can at least be seen that Freud's account of dissociation can hardly be a complete statement of the facts, since there obviously do exist men who succeed in uniting the two streams of love, and since he leaves curiously uncertain the plight of the large majority of men—those of the lower strata of society for whom there exists no class of socially inferior women at whose expense they may gratify their sexual appetites.

[50] E. Jones, *Papers on Psycho-Analysis*, 3rd ed. (London, 1923), 569.
[51] *Ibid.*, 575.
[52] *Ibid.*, 576.
[53] Cf. C. Thompson, " Cultural Pressures in the Psychology of Women," *Psychiatry* (Aug. 1942) V, 3.

Those features of sexual morality which Freud explains by reference to incestuous fixations can, I think, be equally well accounted for in terms of the *mores* of a society that held that sexual desire unadorned was something no respectable lady could ever confess to having known, that produced prostitution by paying single women inadequate wages, and, by assuming that men should conduct the political and professional affairs of the world while women confined themselves to domestic affairs, created a situation in which the casual onlooker would have agreed with Byron that

> Man's love is of man's life a thing apart,
> 'Tis woman's whole existence.

In short, it may be argued that Freud was analyzing not the cause of the double standard, but the result.

A better-known solution to our inquiry was provided by a highly successful interpreter of English life, Dr. Johnson. He regarded female chastity as of the utmost importance because " upon that all the property in the world depends." [54] As for adultery, " confusion of progeny constitutes the essence of the crime; and therefore a woman who breaks her marriage vows is much more criminal than a man who does it. A man, to be sure, is criminal in the sight of God; but he does not do his wife a very material injury, if he does not insult her; if, for instance, from mere wantonness of appetite, he steals privately to her chambermaid. Sir, a wife ought not greatly to resent this. I would not receive home a daughter who had run away from her husband on that account.[55] . . . Wise married women don't trouble themselves about infidelity in their husbands . . . . The man imposes no bastards upon his wife." [56]

There is obviously a good deal of truth in this. A valid reason for discriminating against the adultery of a married woman is that it might well produce bastard children who then intrude into the husband's inheritance. But as an explanation for the double standard it is far from complete. If " confusion of the progeny constitutes the essence of the crime," then the woman should be blameless if there is no confusion or if there is no progeny. When Boswell quoted the example of the lady who " argues that she may indulge herself in gallantries with equal freedom as her husband does, provided she take care not to introduce a spurious issue into his family," Johnson retorted, " this lady of yours, Sir, I think is very fit for a brothel," [57] yet there was logically no reason why he should have disapproved of her argument. Even on Johnson's premises it is clear that the double standard derives from something more than fear of bastard children.

Yet, fundamentally, female chastity has been seen as a matter of

[54] G. B. Hill and L. F. Powell, eds. *Boswell's Life of Johnson* (Oxford, 1934– 1950), V, 209. Cf. *Ibid.*, II, 457.   [55] *Ibid.*, II, 55–6.   [56] *Ibid.*, III, 406.

property; not, however, the property of legitimate heirs, but the property of men in women. The language in which virginity is most often described should tell us this, for it is that of the commercial market. " The corrupting of a man's wife, enticing her to a strange bed," says *The Whole Duty of Man,* " is by all acknowledged to be the worst sort of theft, infinitely beyond that of goods." [58] A maid who loses her virginity is described by a sixteenth-century writer as " unthrifty " [59] and a hundred years later a poet tells us that "Wives lose their value, if once known before." [60] In other words, girls who have lost their " honor " have also lost their saleability in the marriage market.

The double standard, therefore, is the reflection of the view that men have property in women and that the value of this property is immeasurably diminished if the woman at any time has sexual relations with anyone other than her husband. It may be that this only pushes our investigation back one stage further, for the reasons for the high value set on pre-marital virginity, on retrospective fidelity, as it were, are hard to find and they certainly spring from something more than mere certainty of the legitimacy of the children. Nor do they derive entirely from the fear that a woman who has been unchaste before marriage is likely to be unchaste again, for there have always been men like Angel Clare in *Tess of the d'Urbervilles* who are totally unable to entertain the idea of marriage with a woman who has experienced sexual relationships with another man, no matter how extenuating the circumstances, or who in casual or venal intercourse would insist on a virgin for a partner.[61]

At all events this attitude is to be found in many different kinds of patriarchal society, even if it has varied in intensity according to the social level of the persons concerned and has been weakened by some economic circumstances and strengthened by others. Although reinforced by the growth of capitalism and the influence of the middle-classes it was not entirely derived from those phenomena in the way that some Marxist writers, for example, have suggested. " The heaven-blest merit of chastity," which is so exquisitely celebrated in *Comus,* one of them asserts, " is not unconnected with the Puritan-capitalist reaction against irresponsible consumption." [62] Despite its

---

[57] *Ibid.,* III, 25.   [58] London (1804), 152.

[59] L. Vives, *The Instruction of a Christen Woman,* trans. R. Hyrde (1541), f. 16ᵛ.

[60] G. Goodwin, ed., *The Poems of William Browne of Tavistock* (1894), II, 160.

[61] Flügel, *op. cit.,* 115–6. By way of example, we may cite the customers of the eighteenth-century brothels mentioned above.

[62] E. Rickword, " Milton: The Revolutionary Intellectual," in C. Hill, ed., *The English Revolution, 1640* (London, 1949), 108, note 1. Cf. C. Hill, " Clarissa Har-

comic overtones, there is an element of truth in this statement in that the middle-class outlook which emerged in the seventeenth and eighteenth centuries, although superficially opposed to the double standard, did much to intensify existing ideas on the subject of female chastity. But it is not a complete answer and the thinly-veiled implication—banish capitalism and banish the double standard—is, it has to be recognized, just not true. What, for example, could provide a better instance of this allegedly peculiarly *bourgeois* view than this law dating from the pre-capitalist times of King Ethelbert? " If one freeman lies with the wife of another freeman, he shall pay the husband his or her wergeld and procure a second wife with his own money, and bring her to the other man's home." [63] The adulterer was expected to buy the aggrieved husband a new wife because the first had been paid for in money. Modern anthropologists, however, agree that the insistence on pre-nuptial chastity is not a result of the system of wife-purchase, but goes back before it, and that the most that can be said is that such a form of marriage provided an additional reason for an existing prohibition. [64]

Yet much of English feudal law was based on the need to protect the property rights of the woman's father or husband. A female heir who was unchaste during the period of her custody was excluded from her inheritance because the advantage to the lord of her marriage might now be lost through her having lost her honor. [65] At a lower social level the same principle applied. The lord of the manor assumed the right to take a fine from girls who bore illegitimate children in exactly the same way as he took fines from those of his tenants who sought permission to give their daughters in marriage. [66] In each case he was losing the value of the woman's marriage, because that depended upon her chastity.

The laws relating to seduction illustrated the same principle. The abduction of heiresses only became a public crime as opposed to a private injury in the reign of Henry VII, and under Elizabeth I it was made a felony without benefit of clergy. [67] But everything depended upon the woman's being an heiress. [68] If she owned no land

---

lowe and her Times," *loc. cit.*, 331. " Insistence on absolute pre-marital chastity goes hand-in-hand with the bourgeois conception of absolute property, immune alike from the king's right to arbitrary taxaticn and the church's divine right to tithes."

[63] Attenborough, *op. cit.*, 9.

[64] M. Ginsberg, *Essays in Sociology and Social Philosophy*, II, *Reason and Unreason in Society* (London, 1956), 81.

[65] G. May, *Social Control of Sex Expression* (London, 1930), 6, note 1.

[66] D. M. Stenton, *The English Woman in History* (London, 1957), 83.

[67] 3 Hen. VII, c. 2. 39 Eliz., c. 9.

[68] W. S. Holdsworth, *A History of English Law* (London, 1925), VIII, 427-9.

or goods then her forcible abduction was a much less serious offense. In the late seventeenth century men were hanged for stealing heiresses, but the women had to be heiresses. In feudal society there was always somebody with a financial interest in every woman's marriage whether she was an heiress or not, but when this situation disappeared it was only the chastity of women with property which continued to be legally protected, because the loss in the case of landless women was nobody's but their own. On the other hand, the father was always at liberty to bring an action against his daughter's seducer on the grounds of the loss of her services which he had thus incurred.[69] Similarly the injured husband could bring against his wife's seducer an action for criminal conversation to recover damages for the loss of his wife's *consortium*. This action was based on the legal fiction that as the husband and wife were one person at law the wife was consequently incapable of consenting to adultery and the husband might therefore claim damages for trespass and assault. This action for criminal conversation was abolished in 1857 but survived in the form of the damages the husband might claim from the co-respondent, the adulterer being liable because he had infringed the husband's right of property in his wife.

Needless to say, none of this worked in reverse. The wife had no claim for damages against her husband's mistress; and on the only occasion in modern English history when adultery was made a criminal offense, and a capital one at that, in 1650, it was the adultery of the married woman and not of the married man which was made punishable.[70] The Puritans took such strong action against adultery, partly because of their respect for the Mosaic law and partly because of the great value they set on family life, but they still adhered to the double standard, based as it was on nothing more than men's property in women.

This deeply entrenched idea that woman's chastity was not her own to dispose of persisted for a long time and was reinforced by the system of arranged marriages which prevailed in the higher reaches of society for most of English history. As long as these unions were a means of social and economic advancement and as long as the bridegroom expected his partner to be a virgin, so long have the arrangements of society been specially designed to preserve female chastity. A woman could no more be unchaste than she could resist her parents' commands concerning her marriage. Rogers tells us how a Puritan preacher " once said to a coy virgin, ' thy virginity is not all thine to dispose of: in part it's thy parents ', father hath a stroke in it, mother another, and kindred a third: fight not against all, but be his whom they would have thee.' " [71] Once married, her chastity was transferred to another owner. "A woman hath no power of her own body, but her husband," wrote Vives; " thou dost the more wrong to give away that thing which is another body's without the owner's licence." [72]

The absolute property of the woman's chastity was vested not in the woman herself, but in her parents or her husband. And it might be sold by them. "For very need," writes one of the Pastons, " I was fain to sell a little daughter I have for much less than I should have done by possibility." [73] Even the husband might do a little marketing himself. In 1696 Thomas Heath was presented by the churchwardens of Thame for cohabiting unlawfully with the wife of George Fuller, " having bought her of her husband at 2¼d the pound." [74] In the eighteenth and nineteenth centuries foreigners were firmly of the opinion that Englishmen could sell their wives, provided they put a halter around their necks and led them into the open market; and in fact many actual transactions of this kind seem to have taken place.[75] One does not have to prove the widespread existence of wife-selling in order to be able to assert that until the mid-nineteenth century the ownership of most women was vested in men, but it provides an interesting if somewhat exaggerated illustration.

The double standard, therefore, was but an aspect of a whole code of social conduct for women which was in turn based entirely upon their place in society in relation to men. The value set on female chastity varied directly according to the extent to which it was considered that women's function was a purely sexual one. Until modern times women were, broadly speaking, thought of as incomplete in themselves and as existing primarily for the sake of men. Hence the contempt for unmarried women—" old maids " who had failed to achieve the main purpose of their existence. The virtue of women was relative to their function and their function was to cater to the needs of men. For this task the first qualification was chastity;

[71] D. Rogers, op. cit., 303.   [72] L. Vives, op. cit., f. 66ʳ.
[73] J. Gairdner, ed. The Paston Letters, 1422–1509 (London, 1900–1901), Introduction, clxxvi.
[74] S. A. Peyton, ed., The Churchwardens' Presentments in the Oxfordshire Peculiars of Dorchester, Thame and Banbury (Oxford Records Society, 1928), 184.
[75] Notes and Queries, 1st Ser., VII (1853), 602–3; 4th Ser., X (1872), 271, 311, 468–9; H. W. V. Temperley, " The Sale of Wives in England in 1823," The History Teachers' Miscellany (May 1925), III, 5.

hence, chastity was the essence of female virtue. In the sixteenth century Vives had written that "no man will look for any other thing of a woman, but her honesty: the which only, if it be lacked, is like as in a man, if he lack all that he should have. For in a woman the honesty is instead of all." [76] Three hundred years later the sentiment was repeated when Josephine Butler in the course of her travels was told that "A woman who has once lost chastity has lost every good quality. She has from that moment ' all the vices.' " [77]

It is not for us to comment here on the ironies of a code of morality which made virtue and honor a mere physical fact to which intention and circumstance were not relevant. As finally developed in the eighteenth century, this view of honor held out no hope to an injured girl save the unlikely *deus ex machina* of marriage, what Fordyce called "a sponge to wipe out in a single stroke the stain of guilt." [78]

From this prime insistence on woman's chastity emerged most of the other social restrictions upon her conduct. As Mrs. Knowles said to Dr. Johnson, " the mason's wife, if she is ever seen in liquor, is ruined; the mason may get himself drunk as often as he pleases, with little loss of character.[79] And not only sobriety was expected, but modesty, delicacy, bashfulness, silence and all the other " feminine " virtues. For centuries the ideal woman was a Griselda, passive and long-suffering, or a Lucrece who put death before dishonor.[80] And in courtship women existed to be pursued, not to do the pursuing. Ultimately such conduct was regarded as springing not merely from the usages of society, but from the fundamental attributes of female nature itself. The claim of men to the exclusive sexual possession of women resulted not only in two separate codes of conduct, but in a highly exaggerated view of the innate differences between the two sexes themselves.

[76] Vives, *op. cit.*, f. 17ᵛ.

[77] J. Butler, *Personal Reminiscences of a Great Crusade* (London, 1896), 149.

[78] Quoted on 171 of I. Watt, *The Rise of the Novel: Studies in Defoe, Richardson, and Fielding* (London, 1957).

In this connection it is noteworthy to see how Richardson advances from the repulsive marriage-covers-all morality of *Pamela* (the story of a maid-servant who holds off the advances of her lecherous employer until he has agreed to marry her) to the superior theme of *Clarissa*, who is raped after being drugged and can find escape only in death, yet whose chastity of intention remains unchallenged. See C. Hill, " Clarissa Harlowe," *loc. cit.*

[79] G. B. Hill and L. F. Powell, *op. cit.*, III, 287.

[80] For example, Isabella in *Measure for Measure* (III, i, 104–106). She cannot yield her chastity to save her brother but

Isabella: O, were it but my life,
                    I'd throw it down for your deliverance
                    As frankly as a pin!
Claudio: Thanks, dear Isabel.

The final step in the campaign to protect female chastity was the most remarkable of all, for it amounted to nothing less than the total desexualization of women. It is now well-known how the eighteenth century witnessed the triumph of the new feminine ideal afforded by Richardson's Pamela—delicate, insipid, fainting at the first sexual advance, and utterly devoid of feelings towards her admirer until the marriage knot was tied.[81] Slowly there emerged two quite different standards of what constitutes propriety for either sex. And the origin of these standards can be seen quite clearly in the male desire to build a protective fence round male property—female chastity.

The association of sexuality primarily with men and the male organ was not new and may well have some basis in fact, particularly in the case of younger people. Dr. Kinsey tells us that " the average adolescent girl gets along well enough with a fifth as much sexual activity as the adolescent boy." [82] Be this as it may, this distinction was fostered out of all proportion by the tendencies we have been describing. An article in *The Westminster Review* for 1850 remarked that, save in the case of fallen women, sexual desire in women was dormant " always till excited by undue familiarities; almost always till excited by actual intercourse. . . . Women whose position and education have protected them from exciting causes, constantly pass through life without ever being cognizant of the promptings of the senses. . . . Were it not for this kind decision of nature, which in England has been assisted by that correctness of feeling which pervades our education, the consequences would, we believe, be frightful." [83] Less stress on the effects of education was laid by the leading authority on sexual matters in later Victorian England, who declared that " happily for society " the supposition that women possess sexual feelings could be put aside as " a vile aspersion." [84]

Respectable Victorian wives therefore were educated to regard the act of procreation as a necessary and rather repulsive duty; and of course the process was circular. The sense of shame in the woman and the lack of consideration on the part of the man, who was, after all, encouraged to regard this particular part of matrimony as existing primarily for his benefit, led women to take an unduly fastidious attitude and helped to create the enduring legacy of frigidity in women, all traces of which have not yet departed.

As a final proof that the double standard was based on something

[81] See R. P. Utter and G. B. Needham, *Pamela's Daughters* (London, 1937) and I. Watt, *The Rise of the Novel.*

[82] A. C. Kinsey, W. B. Pomeroy, C. E. Martin, *Sexual Behaviour in the Human Male* (Philadelphia and London, 1948), 223.

[83] *The Westminster and Foreign Quarterly Review* (April–July 1850), 457.

[84] Acton, quoted by H. Ellis, "The Erotic Rights of Woman," *The British Society for the Study of Sex Psychology, Publication No. 5* (London, 1918), 9.

more than fear of the risk of illegitimate children, some of the arguments deployed by the opponents of birth-control may be cited. Although a modern feminist work speaks in passing of "the comparative unimportance of physical fidelity now that birth-control is possible," [85] it does not seem that contraception by eliminating some of the consequences has eliminated everything which went into making the double standard. At the famous trial of Mrs. Besant and Charles Bradlaugh for publishing Knowlton's *Fruits of Philosophy*, a manual on birth control, the prosecuting counsel described the work concerned as a "dirty, filthy book" which would enable the "unmarried female" to "gratify her passions." [86] In doing so he was clearly revealing that his demand for female chastity was not based upon the dread of illegitimate children at all. And yet it may be that all the details of the double standard are mere elaborations of the central fact that when a man and a woman have sexual relations the woman may conceive whereas the man will not. The whole social and ethical structure may well follow from this in practice without following logically. "When a general rule of this kind is once established," says Hume, "men are apt to extend it beyond those principles from which it first arose . . . and though all these maxims have a plain reference to generation, yet women past child-bearing have no more privilege in this respect than those who are in the flower of their youth and beauty . . . the general rule carries us beyond the original principle, and makes us extend the notions of modesty over the whole sex, from their earliest infancy to their extremest old age and infirmity." [87]

Hume's remarks notwithstanding, it seems that the English insistence on female chastity cannot be explained by reference to the fact of child birth and elaborations thereon, but that the solution is more likely to be found in the desire of men for absolute property in women, a desire which cannot be satisfied if the man has reason to believe that the woman has once been possessed by another man, no matter how momentarily and involuntarily and no matter how slight the consequences.

I am well aware that this conclusion leaves many questions unanswered, notably why this desire for property in women should vary in degree according to the social level of the men concerned. This problem, together with allied questions, must be left to future investigators. My main concern here is to pose the question, not to provide all the answers.

St. John's College, Oxford.

---

[85] I. Clephane, *Towards Sex Freedom* (London, 1935), 230.   [86] *Ibid.*, 108.
[87] *Theory of Politics*, ed. F. Watkins (London, 1951), 124–5.

XI

THE ENGLISHWOMAN'S SEXUAL CIVIL WAR: FEMINIST ATTITUDES TOWARDS MEN, WOMEN, AND MARRIAGE 1650-1740

By Jerome Nadelhaft

The contemptuous descriptions of women in seventeenth-century England are well-known. The wisdom of the Bible in relegating women to marital servitude was supposedly borne out by their predictable daily behavior. Women were mentally inferior, irrational, often given to hysteria and superstition. Their hot, moist humors made them overly passionate and emotional, sometimes more violent and rebellious. They were chatterers and scolds, flirts, and spendthrifts. Only marriage justified their existence, providing companionship for men, a cure or moral outlet for lust, and a renewal of the species. While there was some softening regarding women in laws relating to marriage and greater acceptance of the idea that women were to be help-meets, partners rather than simple drudges, women's subservience and overwhelming inferiority were as plainly written in 1700 as they had been one hundred years earlier.[1]

Not surprisingly, the stereotype originated with and was perpetuated by men, who monopolized institutions of power and education and the means of communication. Too often, however, their opinions have been accepted as their society's exclusive opinion, as though no other did or could exist. Certainly many women had so internalized the common beliefs that they felt no need to resist their own degradation. Others—most women—had neither the opportunity nor the education to sustain widespread protest. Nevertheless, between 1650 and 1740 there was a remarkable expression of another, sharply contrasting view. A few women, and some supporters whose anonymity hid their sex, went beyond easy descriptions and probed more deeply into women's feelings and the male rationale. Assuming that women were human, and even the equal of men, they developed a sweeping and powerful criticism of men's attitudes towards and treatment of women.

---

[1] Louis B. Wright, *Middle Class Culture in Elizabethan England* (Chapel Hill, 1935), ch. 13, "The Popular Controversy over Woman"; Robert H. Michel, "English Attitudes towards Women, 1640-1700," *Canadian Journal of History*, **13** (1978), 35-60; Margaret George, "From 'Goodwife' to 'Mistress': The Transformation of the Female in Bourgeois Culture," *Science & Society*, **37** (1973), 152-77.

Historians have not done the dissenters justice, and the failure is more than a disservice to individuals. Since women were not so totally repressed or made speechless that protest was impossible, the absence from historical studies of detailed summaries and analyses of contemporary criticisms implies that women lacked either the courage or ability to resist. Consider, for example, how the works of Margaret Cavendish and Mary Astell, the two outstanding, identifiable spokeswomen for a radical female viewpoint have been ignored, slighted, or misrepresented. Cavendish (1624-1674), Duchess of Newcastle, was born into a large, wealthy family and brought up freely, inclined to ignore certain social and womanly graces and to follow the intellectual pursuits that appealed to her. At eighteen she became maid of honor to the Queen. Two years later she married the fifty-two year old Duke of Newcastle, commander of the King's northern troops during the Civil War; he was "the onely Person I ever was in love with." Their marriage was childless. Cavendish began writing while in exile with her husband, and she published books with regularity during the 1650s and 60s.[2] Her works, however, are often slighted because of her personal eccentricities, prolixity, and somewhat apparent unwillingness to be consistent. She wrote on religious, philosophical, and scientific subjects without consulting any authorities, relying on her own observations and judgment. "She wrote and wrote," Ida O'Malley concluded in her scholarly study, Women in Subjection, "but wrote nothing well." Neither Lawrence Stone, in his exhaustive analysis of The Family, Sex and Marriage in England 1500-1800, nor Robert Michel, in his recent article, mentions Cavendish's writings at all. But if Cavendish failed to achieve fame through scholarly researches, she nonetheless set down in lively prose serious feelings about men, women, and seventeenth-century relationships which should not be overlooked.[3]

Mary Astell (1668-1731) has been more frequently discussed—and misused. Astell was from a much more modest background, born into a Newcastle merchant's family. Educated in her youth by a clergyman uncle, she moved to London in her early twenties and there continued, apparently on her own, a rigorous program of reading and

[2] Douglas Grant, Margaret the First: A Biography of Margaret Cavendish, Duchess of Newcastle (London, 1957); the quotation is taken from Myra Reynolds, The Learned Lady in England, 1650-1760 (Boston, 1920), 48.

[3] Ida B. O'Malley, Women in Subjection: A Study of the Lives of Englishwomen before 1832 (London, 1933), 102; Lawrence Stone, The Family, Sex and Marriage in England 1500-1800 (New York, 1977); Michel's "English Attitudes towards Women, 1640-1700," is mistitled, since it deals almost exclusively with the attitudes of males. Joan K. Kinnaird characterizes Cavendish as a "learned lady," a woman who "while often critical of males, is concerned only with her own pursuits." She is not a "true feminist," a woman who identifies "with her sex as a whole" and is committed "to the advancement of women." "Mary Astell and the Conservative Contribution to English Feminism," Journal of British Studies, 19 (1979), 58.

study which equipped her for some of the day's spirited controversies in print. In her first major work, *A Serious Proposal to the Ladies for the Advancement of their True and Greatest Interest* (1694, with a Second Part in 1697), Astell urged the creation of a female seminary for the improvement of women's minds. Although she never married, her book, *Some Reflections on Marriage*, which appeared in 1700, was a comprehensive description of marriage from a woman's perspective, its popularity demonstrated by further editions in 1706 and 1730. Some of her arguments were similar to those of Cavendish and to those of the anonymous author of *An Essay in Defense of the Female Sex*, which first appeared in 1696. Astell's work, however, is fuller, more subtle in its concern for motives and responses, and richer in psychological insight than previous works and than *Woman Not Inferior to Man*, an angry pamphlet of 1739 which the anonymous Sophia modelled on Poulain de la Barre's book: *De l'égalité des deux sexes* (Paris, 1673).[4] At great length and carefully, Astell described society not only as it was and as it could be, were oppressed people treated more kindly, but also society as it ought to be.

Historians have often noted Astell's work on education, but they have generally ignored the anti-male theme which runs throughout it; Stone concluded simply that Astell pushed the scheme with the argument "that it would be to the benefit of husbands." Many, while acknowledging the keenness of her observations on marriage, slight her contributions by repetitious quotation of only one section: "She then who Marries, ought to lay it down for an indisputable Maxim, that her Husband must govern absolutely and intirely [sic]. . . ." But the quotation is taken out of context. It could be balanced easily by Astell's other remarks; for example: women, wrote Astell, "are no where that I know of forbidden to claim their just Right[s]. . . ."[5]

----

[4] The best study of Astell is still Florence M. Smith, *Mary Astell* (New York, 1916). For a long time Astell was thought to be the author of *An Essay in Defense of the Female Sex*, but scholars no longer accept that view. See Smith, *Astell*, 173-7. *De l'égalité des deux sexes* was published in England as *The Woman as Good as the Man: Or, the Equality of Both Sexes* (London, 1677). For a brief analysis of this work, see Michael A. Seidel, "Poulain de la Barre's *The Woman as Good as the Man*," *Journal of the History of Ideas*, 35 (1974), 499-508.

[5] Stone, *The Family*, 345; Ada Wallas, *Before the Bluestockings; Essays on Six Englishwomen from 1660-1835* (London, 1929), 111-30; for examples of the use of the quotation, see Reynolds, *The Learned Lady*, 301-02, which cites Smith, Astell, and, more recently, Kinnaird, *op. cit.*, n.3 *supra*, 68. Scholars have not understood that the quotation, as will be evident later, describes what is, not what ought to be. They have also sometimes confused Astell's call for better, kinder treatment of wives with the ultimate change that she could envision for society. Kinnaird does recognize Astell's "anti-male bias," but she describes it as "a decided and, in most ways, unattractive feature of . . . [her] personality." *Ibid.*, 67. For the second Astell quotation, see *Reflections upon Marriage. The Third Edition. To which is Added a Preface, in Answer to some Objections* (London, 1706), [xxi]. In this and subsequent notes numbers in brackets refer to unnumbered pages.

Collectively, despite class limitations, shifting emphasis, and developments over time, Cavendish, Astell, the anonymous authors, and a few others disclose in their consistent arguments a female view of life. Leaving unchallenged no element of the male argument, these authors despaired over marriage and damned men, identifying them as dangerous enemies who have conspired, lied, and distorted history to maintain a sexist power. At the same time they praised women and demonstrated a sexual awareness which suggested a desire to go it alone. They were early feminists, anticipating arguments that would not become current for centuries. But the forces against them were great, so they were not optimistic.

The feminist reevaluation of women and their social position was a natural consequence of the Civil War when power, allegiance, liberty, and slavery became subjects of debate. The bonds of society were so tightly woven that no fundamental assumption could be questioned by itself; change or criticism enveloped institutions and relationships without check. Although the controversies first involved church and state, they soon of necessity took in monarchs and their subjects, and then all supposed superiors and inferiors, rich and poor, masters and servants, men and women, husbands and wives. All authority was joined. So, too, were arguments. In much the same way that nobles and gentlemen characterized the lower orders as a rude multitude, giddy headed, ignorant and cruel, so men described women. And the world turned upside down as much when women demanded new recognition and attacked marriage and men as when "the very dregs and scum" challenged clergy and king in the name of liberty.[6]

Women first became visibly active in Protestant sects, debating, voting, sometimes preaching; usually, even as wives, they were accepted as the spiritual equals of men. They sought political power, recognizing that participation in government was necessary to protect their religious equality. And power was due them, women sometimes argued, because of their Civil War activities: they had acted as spies, had built fortifications, and had raised money for the war effort.[7]

---

[6] For an analysis of upper class attitudes towards the mass of the English population, see Christopher Hill, "The Many-Headed Monster in Late Tudor and Early Stuart Political Thinking," in Charles H. Carter, ed., *From the Renaissance to the Counter-Reformation: Essays in Honor of Garrett Mattingly* (New York, 1965), 296-324. The quotation is from page 310.

[7] Keith Thomas, "Women and the Civil War Sects," *Past and Present*, No. 13 (April 1958), 42-62; Christopher Hill, *Milton and the English Revolution* (New York, 1977), 118; Patricia Higgins, "The Reactions of Women, with Special Reference to Women Petitioners," in Brian Manning, ed., *Politics, Religion and the English Civil War* (London, 1973), 212, 215-21.

While scholars have not yet determined whether the condition of women was actually worsening, there were clearly many changes isolating and restricting them. Even in the religious sphere, losses accompanied gains. Protestantism encouraged spiritual equality, but it also emphasized paternal authority through a patriarchal God. No longer could women pray to female saints or choose celibate lives in convents. Economically, also, many women lost ground. Not only had women worked the land with male peasants in the past, but they had been active in numerous trades. By the end of the seventeenth century, however, men had frozen women out of those occupations. Women from the upper and commercial classes, on the other hand, benefitted from better marriage settlements which granted them independent incomes, and the greater protection of their property by the Court of Chancery.[8]

Whether the feminist criticism of male ideas about women was based on the rising status of some or was a reaction to the declining fortunes of others is not yet known. But whatever the cause or causes, the early feminists unceasingly rejected the idea of their own inferiority. Because men and women had been created equal, women objected to the "Lampoons, Impertinent Ballads, and Malicious Pamphlets" and to the "Calumnies dayly cast" on them. Sarcastically, Mary Astell argued that if women were as bad as men said, they ought to be confined "with Chain and Block to the Chimney-Corner."[9] Women argued their equality both by pulling men down and by extolling themselves. Men, possessed of an overweening conceit, monopolizing self-granted titles, were not nearly as impressive as they made themselves out to be. What men saw as their strength women denounced. For the Puritan preacher William Whately, man's "more sterne, lesse delicate" face was evidence that man was made to govern. Women rejected the idea that hardness was a qualification for government. Men used their strength destructively, seeking opportunities to intimidate others and thereby weakening their own moral standing. As Margaret Cavendish wrote, men "make Enemies

[8] On patriarchalism see Stone, *The Family*, ch. 5, "The Reinforcement of Patriarchy," 150-218, and Michael Walzer, *The Revolution of the Saints: A Study in the Origins of Radical Politics* (Cambridge, Mass., 1965), 183-98; on economic changes, Sheila Rowbotham, *Hidden from History: 300 Years of Women's Oppression and the Fight Against It* (London, 1974), 2-3; Kathleen Casey, "The Cheshire Cat: Reconstructing the Experience of Medieval Women," in Berenice A. Carroll, ed., *Liberating Women's History: Theoretical and Critical Essays* (Urbana, Ill., 1976), 224-49; on legal changes, Stone, *The Family*, 244, 330-31; Michel, "English Attitudes towards Women," *op. cit.* (n. 3 above), 53-55.

[9] Anonymous, *The Ladies Vademecum, or The Excellency of the Female Sex, above that of the Male, Proved by divers Arguments taken from Scripture, History, and Reason* (Edinburgh, 1702), [ii]; Astell, *Reflections*, [xxv].

to fight with''; they assault ''Peaceable Neighbours'' who have done them ''no Injury.''[10] Sophia thought men a sex ''enslaved to the most brutal transports'' which, of course, put women in a dangerous position. Women nourish and propagate the human race; men murder and destroy their neighbors, argued the author of the *Ladies Vademecum or The Excellency of the Female Sex, above that of the Male.*[11]

Stern faces and good government did not go together. As far as women were concerned, hardness led only to oppression. One proved that not only from the way women were treated, but from the plight of the poor, whose meagre profits were drained away, according to one of the speakers in Cavendish's *Orations*, to be spent in idleness by courtiers. They ''tread upon the *Bellies, Backs,* [and] *Heads* of the Poor.'' Sophia found men excelled in a ''spirit of violence, shameless injustice, and lawless oppression.'' Hence, they filled public offices ''so miserably.''[12]

As usual Astell was pointed. Men had done all the great things in the world: ''They make Worlds and ruine them, form Systems of universal Nature and dispute eternally about them.'' They invented everything from ''Guns to the Mystery of good Eating,'' and even ''brought *Gaming* to an Art and Science.''[13] The author of *An Essay in Defense of the Female Sex* also found men incompetent, their vaunted brains and education notwithstanding. Men ''may know perfectly the Sense of the Learned Dead,'' but they were ignorant of their own country's affairs. ''Bigotted Idolaters of time past,'' they lacked the judgment that comes from independent thought. Sophia thought men labored with drudgery to bring forth ideas. Taken in by appearance, they ''blindly'' accepted everything around them, including their religion. Men were unimpressive, unimposing figures, making, Astell wrote, poor returns ''to all the cares and pains that is [*sic*] bestow'd on them.''[14]

Praising women was as necessary for the feminists as damning men. However, because women thought ''as humbly as their Masters

[10] Sophia, *Woman Not Inferior to Man: or, A short and modest Vindication of the Natural Right of the Fair-Sex to a perfect Equality of Power, Dignity, and Esteem, with the Men* (London, 1739), 26-27; Whately, *A Bride-bush, or a Wedding Sermon; Compendiously describing the duties of married persons* (London, 1617), 18; Cavendish, *Orations of Divers Sorts Accommodated to Divers Places* (2nd ed., London, 1668), 4.

[11] *Woman Not Inferior to Man,* p. 53; *Ladies Vademecum,* 5; see also, Anonymous, *An Essay in Defense of the Female Sex . . . In a Letter to a Lady* (2nd ed., London, 1696), 17-18.

[12] *Orations,* 218; see also 127-28; *Woman Not Inferior to Man,* 36, 28.

[13] *Reflections,* 56, 88.

[14] *An Essay in Defense of the Female Sex,* 27, 29; *Woman Not Inferior to Man,* 40, 5; Astell, *A Serious Proposal to the Ladies, for the Advancement of their True and greatest Interest* (London, 1694), 21.

can wish," such praise contradicted their education and their learned values. Even attempting to applaud female achievements exposed one to denunciation; self-congratulations violated the valued, supposedly feminine, trait of modesty. But the feminists recognized the need to strengthen themselves, to overcome the internalization of society's centuries-old propaganda. The only way for women to force men to be just to them was for women to be just to themselves. If we give in, "if we think meanly of ourselves," Sophia wrote, men will seize on that self-deprecation as justification for treating us "with the contempt we seem conscious of deserving."[15] To make certain that women knew they were not "so despicable as the *Men* wou'd have them believe," the authors introduced proper role models, providing what men deliberately denied them. "Histories are writ by them," Astell wrote. "They recount each others great Exploits, and have always done so." In another context, the author of the *Essay* bemoaned the lack of information about women's roles in ancient times. "If any Histories were anciently written by Women, Time, and the Malice of Men have effectually conspir'd to suppress 'em. . . ." Tacitus was Sophia's favorite historian, "but still he was a *Man*, and like the rest of *Men* prejudiced in favour of his sex."[16] Perhaps with Astell's idea in mind that the best of each sex "should be the Standard to the rest," writer after writer introduced famous, worthy women. Queens—Elizabeth and Anne; military leaders—Joan of Arc and Boadicea; strong Biblical women—Sarah, Deborah. There were so many that Astell found it "tedious to enumerate all the excellent Women."[17]

But the case for women could hardly rest on isolated figures scattered through the ages, although clearly it was important to argue that if women of the past had achieved, so could those of the present. To give themselves full credit, however, feminists had to face one major problem and a key to male stature and success: as Lady Mary Wortley Montagu wrote, prejudiced men would not give women "any Degree of that Fame which is so sharp a spur to their Greatest Actions."[18] Men defined what was worthy of praise and doled out all the rewards. They had made hardness a virtue and the study of dead

[15] Astell, *Reflections*, [xxv]; Sophia, *Woman's Superior Excellence over Man: or, A Reply to the Author of a late Treatise, entitled, Man Superior to Woman. . . .* (London, 1740), 87.

[16] Sophia, *Woman Not Inferior to Man*, 56; *Reflections*, 88; *An Essay in Defense of the Female Sex*, 23; *Woman's Superior Excellence over Man*, 52.

[17] *Reflections*, [xxii, xxvii]; see also, Anon., *Ladies Vademecum*, p. 9; Sophia, *Woman Not Inferior to Man*, 46-48, 55.

[18] Montagu, *The Nonsense of Common-Sense*, No. VI, 24 Jan. 1738, reprinted in Montagu, *Essays and Poems, and Simplicity, A Comedy*, ed. Robert Halsband and Isobel Grundy (Oxford, 1977), 134.

languages more important than knowledge of the present. The feminists pushed forward women's claims, not so much by anticipating what women might accomplish if given the opportunity, but mostly by concentrating on their visible achievements. Women, for example, excelled in arts practiced by both sexes: "*Embroidery* and other *Needle-Work,* working *Tapestry* and other very curious Arts." And, in particular, women's worth could be measured by their roles in the home and family—managing and raising children. For that private work, Sophia thought women deserved, but did not get, the highest esteem; they were contributing most to the public good.[19]

Almost by definition, however, men labelled what women did or seemed to excel in as either meaningless or so common as to be beneath special notice. Perhaps Sophia had that rejection in mind when she wrote that men thought "the office of nursing children" was "despicable, . . . low and degrading." As the author of the *Essay* noted, the "Erroneous Conceit" of Men leads them to conclude that "those things in which they are little concern'd, or consulted, are triffles below their care or notice, which indeed they are not by Nature so well able to manage." If women talked with each other about managing households, regulating families, governing children, men "condemn us for impertinence," impertinence being the "humour of busying ourselves about things trivial."[20] Women's work was little rewarded because women did it and because they did it as a matter of course, perpetually.

The feminists defended women and their work, not with the idea that such work was adequate but by arguing that if women did the meaningful work at home, they could work successfully elsewhere as well. One was proof of their abilities to do the other: "our being so much more capable than the male kind to execute that office well, no way proves us unqualify'd to execute any other."[21]

Anticipating yet another argument to be more fully developed by twentieth-century feminists, women recognized that they were victimized by language. In the same way that men controlled rewards, they also, these critics argued, determined the way words were used, especially the words of war. Cavendish noted the usual practice of making women cowards through words. Women who were not meek and submissive were unwomanly; men who were not warlike were unmanly, hence womanly. One should not stop fighting because women want you to, one of Cavendish's male orators said. Such "Effeminate Fears" ought not to be decisive. Soldiers who ran from battle had "*Effeminate Spirits,* though *Masculine Bodies.*"[22] Sophia

---

[19] Anon., *Ladies Vademecum,* 14, 15; *Woman Not Inferior to Man,* 13.
[20] Sophia, *Woman Not Inferior to Man,* 12; *An Essay in Defense of the Female Sex.* 85, 84.
[21] Sophia, *Woman Not Inferior to Man,* 15.
[22] *Orations,* 20, 35.

also noted the same, and for her inaccurate use of the words *"ef-feminate"* and *"manly."* They were arbitrary expressions "and but a fulsom compliment which the *Men* pass on themselves; they establish no truth." In fact, Sophia, agreeing that men and women had different natures, perceptively called attention to the guilt assigned through distorted language and suggested a reversal.

The real truth is, That humanity and integrity, the characteristics of our sex, make us abhor unjust slaughter, and prefer honourable peace to unjust war. And therefore to use these expressions with propriety, when a *Man* is possest of our virtues he shou'd be call'd *effeminate* by way of the highest praise of his good nature and justice; and a *Woman* who shou'd depart from our sex by espousing the injustice and cruelty of the *Men's* nature, should be called a *Man*: that is, one . . . whom no blood-shed can deter from the most . . . violence and rapin[e].[23]

The real point of the feminists' lengthy argument was simply that women were at least the equal of men in virtue, honor, and capabilities, although there were some statements in these works that show contrary feelings, perhaps a backsliding or unwillingness to go too far, as when Cavendish noted that women could not govern. Perhaps, too, praising women for suffering in silence and establishing a kind of moral credit by putting up with inferior men was unproductive because it blunted anger. But one also could argue that the praise at least gave women a sense of worth for surviving in a situation that might have seemed inevitable or unchangeable.[24] Mostly, however, the women writers stressed equality. "We were made equal by Nature," said Cavendish expressing a sentiment duly echoed by others. Men knew that "in the Infancy of the World [we] were their Equals and Partners in Dominion."[25]

Clearly the writers rejected what male clerical voices never tired of preaching: female inequality was natural and ordained by God. Astell found in the Bible evidence that women played key roles, but she had another, more subtle objection to the invocation of sacred texts. She argued, in effect, that men had too much at stake to be trusted as explicators of the Bible. Just as later feminists would reject the 'objective' scientific facts which proved female inferiority, noting that women were not allowed to become scientists and so remained incapable of checking the so-called evidence, Astell rejected the male's Biblical evidence: women were not taught to read the Bible for themselves, and they could not know what distortions had crept into translations or interpretations.[26]

---

[23] *Woman Not Inferior to Man*, 51.
[24] Cavendish, "Preface," *The World's Olio* (London, 1655); Astell, *Reflections*, 16; Montagu, *The Nonsense of Common-Sense*, 133–34.
[25] "Preface," *World's Olio; An Essay in Defense of the Female Sex*, 21.
[26] *Reflections*, [x, xxii, xxiii].

Other feminists continued the religious argument. Sophia acknowledged that women could not hold religious office, but she attributed the prohibition to the fact that women were naturally more religious and men had to be enticed into the church with the prospect of position. One could not see inferiority in the creation of women after men, for one could argue that what came second was more refined, just as man came after animals.[27] Biblical references to weak women referred only to physical strength, noted the author of the *Ladies Vademecum,* and physical strength, others emphasized, did not indicate bravery or worth. "An Ox is stronger than a Man, yet none will think the Ox is therefore *Preferable.* . . ." Were strength the determining factor, one needed only to find the strongest porter to uncover the wisest man.[28]

If women were not created inferior by nature or religious dictate, what then explained their subordination? There were two essential explanations, one dealing with the origins of female oppression, the other with its continuance. Acknowledging that in general women were physically weaker, the feminists argued that men simply used their strength to guarantee dominance. Cavendish wrote that men "usurped a Supremacy to themselves" and permanently enslaved women.[29] The "Usurpation of Men, and the Tyranny of Custom" were responsible for women's lowly position, said the Essayist. Sophia returned more often than any to the idea, referring to the "tyrannical usurpation of authority" men exert, the "unjust usurpation on their side."[30]

Nobody explained the process itself, but perhaps Cavendish had in mind a similarity with the way property had been greedily acquired. In one oration, a lawyer pleaded for a man who stole to maintain his old parents, young children, and sick wife. Theft should not have been necessary since nature had "made all things in common." There should have been no rich and no poor, but "Usurping Men," who were called "*Moral Philosophers,* or *Commonwealth-makers,*" devised governments and laws and "robbed most of Mankind, of their Natural Liberties and Inheritances."[31] The motives were clearer than the process. Men excluded women from power because all men needed to command and because they feared female competition. Men were aware of female ability and "began to grow Jealous" that women, who were originally their "Partners in Dominion," might become their superiors. Therefore, said the author of the *Essay,* they used force, "the Origine of Power, to compel us to a Subjection."

---

[27] *Woman Not Inferior to Man,* 11, 45-46.
[28] *Ladies Vademecum,* 12; Astell, *Reflections,* 87.
[29] "Preface," *World's Olio;* see also Astell, *Reflections,* 90, [xii].
[30] *An Essay in Defense of the Female Sex,* 3; *Woman Not Inferior to Man,* 2, 9.
[31] *Orations,* 91-2.

Sophia too found in men's fear of competition the basis of women's subjection. Because men feared women would outshine them, "the same sordid selfishness which urged them to engross all power and dignity to themselves, prompted them to shut up from us that knowledge which wou'd have made us their competitors."[32]

The institution of marriage was intimately connected with man's need to command. The feminist response to the nature and condition of marriage was acute and based not only on ideas of right and wrong and political analogies but also on an understanding of people, both men and women, and their psychological nature and needs. Astell was most explicit. As both king and priest, a man issued orders, prescribed duties, administered justice. Astell knew that women's oppression gave men a sense of control over their own lives. Nothing pleased a man as much as "intire subjection." A slaving, passively obedient wife was a healing balm for a husband who suffered wounds inflicted by other, daily conflicts. When a man was "contradicted and disappointed abroad," rejected, a subservient woman put him again in control.[33]

The feminists complained of the hard work, the drudgery and servitude of marriage. But more than that they complained about the psychological demands. Women, wives, were to stamp into their minds one idea, regardless of how bad their husbands were, how mean their condition: "*Mine husband is my superior, my better.*" Subservience alone was not enough; it had to be joyfully and cheerfully given. Like the later idealized singing and dancing black slaves, women were supposed to internalize male rules, serving without disagreement, without hint of displeasure or disapproval. No out of place gesture was allowed. Mildness of countenance, action, and carriage was required. William Gouge, a Puritan minister, declared unacceptable "a sullen looke, a powting lip, . . . a disdainfull turning of this side and that side of the body, and a fretfull flinging out" of a husband's presence. All those and "other like contemptuous gestures," he added in a masterly phrase, "make it very uncomfortable." So much was that obedience to be a part of a wife's natural behavior that Whately could define "impudencie" as "unwomanhood."[34]

Silence was one of the most valued aspects of obedience. One after another, writers urged that silence on women. "*Paul commands the*

[32] *An Essay in Defense of the Female Sex*, 21; *Woman Not Inferior to Man*, 28.

[33] *Reflections*, 55, 35. A subscriber to the *Spectator* was blunt: "Nothing is more gratifying to the mind of man than power or dominion; and this I think myself amply possessed of, as I am the father of a family." No. 500, 3 Oct. 1712.

[34] The first and last quotations in the paragraph are from Whately, *A Bride-Bush*, pp. 36, 38; William Gouge, *Of Domesticall Duties. Eight Treatises* (London, 1622), 278-79.

women to *learne in silence*. The word is, *in quietnesse*," Whately wrote. When a husband was around, he even argued, a wife should speak more quietly to children and servants, not in as "snappish" a manner. She should not then speak without necessity, even to correct faults. One character in a marriage manual by Robert Snawsel learned her role perfectly: "I resolved to pray continually, that God would set a watch before my lips, lest I should offend in my tongue. . . ."[35]

Part of the rationale for such behavior was phrased so as to make women beneficiaries. Silence was acceptance which made "injuries and crosses" easier to bear, William Fleetwood argued. One adapted; one lost one's rage; one broke "the force of . . . misfortunes by patience and submission." As Fleetwood put it: "Wild birds beat themselves almost to pieces in the same cage where tame ones sit and sing; and yet the prison is the same. . . ." Calm, quiet behavior was valuable too because it might reform husbands, sinners who could not be persuaded through argument.[36]

In the age-old manner in which individuals were made to assume the guilt for their own victimization, wives were told that their contrary behavior caused strife and enraged men. They were to bear the guilt for making men angry and the responsibilities for the consequences. "A soft answer stayeth wrath," Snawsel noted. To avoid inducing bad treatment women had to overlook their husbands' flaws, Gouge wrote, reflecting instead "their eies on their owne infirmities." Cavendish was succinct. One of her critical wives is denounced as a *"Scold"* who gave her husband more *"unkind Words"* than he gave *"blows."* Anyway, "her *Tongue* provokes his *Hand* to strike her."[37]

A well-instructed wife, however much she was part of a sympathetic, loving marriage, stood before her husband in "loving feare," aware she was being judged. Every action and gesture spoke of inferiority. Her behavior was ingratiating. Nothing should make a man doubt the correctness of his behavior. For him there should be no question of guilt or wrongdoing; a wife was voluntarily to become a non-person. "You shall not be mistress of yourself, nor have any desire satisfied, but what is approved of by your husband," Fleetwood declared.[38] In the writings of seventeenth-century marriage

---

[35] *A Bride-Bush*, 40, and also 38, 41; Robert Snawsel, *A Looking-Glasse for Maried Folkes* [London, 631], rpt. *The English Experience*, No. 763 (Amsterdam, 1975), 43.

[36] Fleetwood, *The Relative Duties of Parents and Children, Husbands and Wives, Masters and Servants, considered in Sixteen Practical Discourses* [1705], in *The Works of the Right Reverend William Fleetwood* (Oxford, 1854), 380, 381, 378; see also Sophia, *Woman Not Inferior to Man*, 22.

[37] *A Looking-Glasse*, 42; *Of Domesticall Duties*, 279, 276; *Orations*, 98.

[38] Whately, *A Bride-Bush*, 37; Fleetwood, *Relative Duties*, 320, and also 323; see Gouge, *Of Domesticall Duties* 274, for another statement on "fear" in marriage.

counsellors there is scarcely a hint that total subservience, the destruction of self, would cost a woman anything. One of the signs of women's inferiority, to be deduced from these writings, is that women do not have the same emotions as men. They have no need to achieve; they do not feel pain, rejection, or despair over being despised. One comes close to an understanding of women's real reactions only in the words of one Snawsel character, words which are of course rejected by the author's spokeswoman. One woman bemoaned her husband's practice of ignoring her feelings and complaints. Her husband laughed, played his fiddle, or slept to avoid her voice. "It grieves me indeed to the very guts, and I do so chafe sometimes that I can hardly hold my hands," she said.[39]

Feminists thought women enslaved, rejecting the male argument that lawful duty was not slavery, and they had no doubt about the nature of that condition. Women, Cavendish saw, "*live* like Batts, or Owls, *labour* like Beasts, and *dye* like Worms," which seemed to indicate that men were "made for *Liberty*, and *Women* for *slavery*."[40] Lady Montagu compared wives with other lowly people, servants who might be released from service if defrauded, wounded slaves who became free; but she found wives, no matter how ill used, condemned "to daily Racks . . . and to eternal Chains." Astell perceived that women were yoked because men thought them created to be slaves to their will, and she complained that Milton was not ready to "cry up Liberty to poor *Female Slaves*." In strong language she asked: "If all Men are born free, how is it that all Women are born Slaves?"[41] While the Essayist thought women might have been better off in England than elsewhere (except among the Dutch), she noted nonetheless that "Fetters of Gold are still fetters, and the softest Lining can never make 'em so easy, as Liberty."[42]

At best, wives had a hard lot, sufficiently oppressive so that Astell suggested that if women thought more about their lives "they seldom

[39] *A Looking-Glasse*, 38-39. Jeremy Taylor showed some understanding of women's feelings: "If the man cannot endure her talking," he asked, "how can she endure his striking?" But Taylor still affirmed the notion that women were to obey men voluntarily as a sign of love and reverence. "The Marriage Ring; or, The Mysteriousness and Duties of Marriage," sermons XVII and XVIII, *Twenty-Five Sermons preached at Golden Grove, being for the Winter Half-Year* (1653), in *The Whole Works of the Right Rev. Jeremy Taylor*, ed. Reginald Heber (15 vols., London, 1828), V, 268, 272-73.

[40] *Orations*, 195.

[41] Isobel Grundy, ed., "Ovid and Eighteenth-Century Divorce: An Unpublished Poem by Lady Mary Wortley Montagu," *Review of English Studies*, New Series, 23 (1972), 424; Astell, *Reflections*, 47, 27, [xiii].

[42] *An Essay in Defense of the Female Sex*, 22, 16, 25; see also *Woman Not Inferior to Man*, 3, 18.

wou'd Marry," for they had no reason to be fond of being wives, however much pleasure and happiness men got from being husbands. Far too many were "yok'd for Life" to despicable men, their miseries so great that "none can have a just Idea of [them], but those who have felt it."[43] Cavendish, whose marriage to a man thirty years her senior was happy, nevertheless thought a single life safest and most rewarding. Then, you were "Mistress of your self." Believing that the wedding day, "consecrated to *Love, Joy,* [and] *Pleasure,*" was the "only *happy Day*" of a girl's life since marriages soon turned nasty, she understandably concluded that "a Bad Husband is far worse than No Husband."[44] Even more significantly, she was so filled with despair over the "*Unsufferable Condition* of a Married Life" that she returned repeatedly to the drastic idea that death was preferable to marriage. "Why do you mourn, that *Death* must be your *Son-in-Law?*" a dying daughter asks her father. "He is a better Husband, than any you could chuse me, or I could chuse myself." The happiest women are those who never marry or those who die young.[45] Montagu made the same point, reversing the order of death. She answered writers who made fun of women for not adequately mourning their husbands' deaths with the succinct reply that men, and hence marriages, were not worth grieving over.[46]

Why, then, did women marry? Ignoring one aspect of the obvious, that there was no practical alternative, feminists focused on training, ignorance, and deceit. Girls learned that marriage was the end and purpose of their lives. They valued themselves for their attractiveness to men.[47] That intense indoctrination could not be countered even by education. Cavendish found that despite the "examples of the *Evils* that are in Marriage, Men and Women will take no warning." Marital grief could only be learned at first hand. How, Astell wondered, could you warn a friend of her danger, of the mistake she might be making? "She will hardly forgive the Affront. . . ." Somehow, even if problems made an impression on observers, each woman had enough confidence in her own ability to think she would control her life and husband better; she would avoid the common tribulations of the married woman. "We may be told of the Danger, and shown the Fall of others," but "we are all so well assur'd of our own Conduct, as to believe it will bring us safe off those Rocks on which others have been *Shipwrackt*."[48]

[43] *Reflections*, 34, 89, 92, 4.
[44] Cavendish, *Sociable Letters* (London, 1664), 4, 184; *Orations*, 193, 181.
[45] *Orations*, 211, 143, 179, 195.
[46] In defending women for not mourning, Montagu wrote in *The Spectator*, No. 573, 28 July 1714: "my first [husband] insulted me, my second was nothing to me, my third tormented me," and so on through number six. The essay is reprinted in Montagu, *Essays and Poems*, ed. Halsband and Grundy, 69-74.
[47] See, for example, Astell, *Reflections*, 53.
[48] Cavendish, *Orations*, 211-12; *Reflections*, 47, 67, 74, 80.

One after another, the women noted that men were deceitful: they crooned, humbled themselves, sighed, moaned, and almost expired before marriage testifying to their love and devotion, their enraptured enslavement. Girls swallowed poison because it came in golden cups.[49] After marriage, Sophia thought, a *"spaniel* [is] metamorphosed into a *tyger.''* Cavendish thought that ''Defects of the Mind, Soul, or Appetities'' may not be discovered until after marriage, when ''you find you are Unhappy by them.''[50]

Women felt marital victimization acutely, and they were shaken by the realization that man's ''love [of] power and superiority'' erased even traces of empathy.[51] ''Men in *Prosperity,* feel not the *Misery* of others in Adversity,'' Cavendish wrote. ''Are we not form'd with Passions like your own?'' Montagu asked, wondering how men expected women to ''sigh in Silence.'' Suffering without redress was more grievous than being murdered, Astell wrote. For a woman to obey ''an absolute Lord and Master,'' no matter how ignorant, was ''a misery none can have a just Idea of, but those who have felt it.'' No one, she thought, was capable of such self-abnegation, of catering to a man's sense of superiority, which was likely to be based on nothing more than his knowledge of how to tie a bow or how to ''keep himself clean.'' Nature was averse to it.[52]

Since women were men's equals, they refused to destroy themselves. In countless acts and statements they expressed their desires to be human, to be individuals, to achieve and be taken seriously. Astell, addressing herself to the ''Glory of her . . . Sex'' and to ''the great things that Women might perform,'' could not value marriage in which a wife was forced to ''lay aside her own Will and Desires'' so that a man could shape her to ''his will and liking.''[53] Cavendish, writing of her needs, was far more personal, perhaps more forthright and extreme. She spent her life writing ambitiously meaningful texts and appealing to a public and the universities for recognition. ''They are poore, dejected spirits that are not ambitious of Fame.''[54] Perhaps

---

[49] Astell, *A Serious Proposal to the Ladies, for the Advancement of their True and greatest Interest* (London, 1694), 36; *Reflections,* 66. Because it was difficult for a woman to pass from ''a State of Empire and Adoration to a State of Obedience and Subjection,'' the anonymous Philogamus advised men to impose their rule gradually and not put ''on the Husband too soon.'' *The Present State of Matrimony: or, the Real Causes of Conjugal Infidelity and Unhappy Marriages* (London, 1739), 4, 53, 54.

[50] *Woman Not Inferior to Man,* 17, 18; *Sociable Letters,* 425; see also *An Essay in Defense of the Female Sex,* 115.

[51] The quotation is from Fleetwood, *Relative Duties,* 378.

[52] *Orations,* 191; Grundy, ed., ''Ovid and Eighteenth-Century Divorce: An Unpublished Poem by Lady Mary Wortley Montagu,'' 425; *Reflections,* 4, 33, 63.

[53] *Reflections,* [27] 89, 35.

[54] Cavendish, *Poems and Fancies* (London, 1653), 162, and see also the ''Dedication.''

that desire was too strong for many to acknowledge, or for women whose ambition had been bred out of them even to have, but more could identify with Cavendish's rehearsal of a woman's loss or lack of identity. A wife might desire children to keep alive her husband's memory but not for her own sake, for when she marries, "first her Name is Lost," and then "her Family, for neither Name nor Estate goes to her Family. . . . Daughters are to be accounted but as Moveable Goods or Furniture that wear out. . . ."[55] Mary Collier, in her poem "The Women's Labour" (1739) complained of work so tedious and drawn out that women "have hardly ever *Time to dream.*" She might as accurately have worried that their dreams would have been owned or controlled by men. Cavendish described and rejected the morality of the ultimate act of non-existence. Not only was a wife, according to one of her characters, bound to risk her life "for her Husband's *Safety, Honour,* and *Pleasure,*" as well as for his "*Humour,*" leaving her parents, country, everything, travelling on "Dangerous Seas, or into Barren Desarts, or Perpetual Banishment, or Bloody Warrs," some of which she herself had suffered through, as had thousands of colonizing women, but "Loving Wives," another character testified, "ought, nay, do desire to live and dye with their Husbands."[56] Having no independent lives, they were to follow their men to the grave. Neither in life nor in death, however, did women exist, for their very names were "buried in the Grave of the Males."[57]

Marriage was the fate of most women, and it highlighted the terrible difference between what was and what ought to have been. Feminists described the contradictions and explained how the loss of women's natural equality was made permanent. Having once been denied their rights, women were kept in place largely by custom, of which marriage was a part, and ignorance. "Time and Custom by Degrees destroy'd/ That happy State our Sex at first enjoy'd," wrote Collier. Sophia was the most vehement: men in their simple-minded and blind way were taken in by appearances. There was no notion derived from custom "more absurd," none more "ancient or universal" held by learned and illiterate alike, than that of the inequality of the sexes.[58]

The feminists agreed that enforced ignorance ensured the continued enslavement and degradation of women, and they protested eloquently. The male philosophy, expressed by William Fleetwood,

---

[55] *Sociable Letters*, 183-84.

[56] Collier, *The Woman's Labour* (3rd ed., London, 1740), 11; *Orations*, 97, 85.

[57] Cavendish, *Sociable Letters*, 184.

[58] *The Woman's Labour*, 6; *Woman Not Inferior to Man*, 3, 6; also Astell, *Reflections*, [v, vii].

that no education could train women "for the performances of the great businesses" wasted human capacity by rendering useless the minds of half the world's population. Because of men's "groveling jealousy," Sophia wrote, the world has been robbed of an "immense fund of knowledge, and useful discoveries." For Astell, women's ignorance was virtually a sin, the improvement of one's mind being one reason for existing.[59] Collier's life as a slave in drudgery was sufficient reason that, as she wrote, "No Learning ever was bestow'd on me." Sophia was more detailed. Men stopped at nothing "to give our sex a degenerate way of thinking." Men even invented dolls and put them in girls' hands "to confine us to trifles."[60] But the upper-class and ambitious Cavendish was more angry and effective in prose than any other feminist. Because men used women "like Children, Fools, or Subjects, . . . we are become so stupid, that Beasts are but a Degree below us." Not exercising one's reason or understanding permanently damaged one's ability to think. "We are become like worms that onely live in the dull earth of ignorance. . . ." Worse, women were "kept like birds in cages to hop up and down," thus deprived of experiences which might have substituted for other forms of education.[61]

The frustration and irritation of the writers were great, for they recognized their entrapment. Because they were not educated they were ignorant and unqualified for important jobs, and because they were unqualified men were judged superior and trained for public office. The author of the *Essay* complained of men valuing themselves for being wiser. It was like a man boasting of "his Courage, for beating a Man when his Hands were bound." The author of the *Ladies Vademecum* made the same point: "Can the Husband-man Expect as good a Cropt upon the Ground which he has not Tilled or Sown, as of that which has been duly Cultivated, *Manured* and *Strawed* with *Seed*?" Astell also objected to praising men for becoming wise and learned after years of study while damning women because they "are not Born so." Had so little care been taken of men's education, men would "sink into stupidity and brutality."[62]

Women who, despite social pressures, persevered and tried to fulfill their intellectual potential were rejected, in stark contrast to men who sought education. Men were encouraged and rewarded for

---

[59] *Relative Duties*, 318; *Woman's Superior Excellence over Man*, 2; *A Serious Proposal*, 63.

[60] *The Woman's Labour*, 5; *Woman's Superior Excellence over Man*, 69, 27-28.

[61] "Preface," *World's Olio*; Cavendish, "To the Two Universities," *The Philosophical and Physical Opinions* (London, 1655); see also Astell, *A Serious Proposal*, 48, 81.

[62] Sophia, *Woman Not Inferior to Man*, 27; *An Essay in Defense of the Female Sex*, 20; *Ladies Vademecum*, 13; *Reflections*, [xxiv]; *A Serious Proposal*, 20.

their efforts with fame, "Title, Authority, Power, and Riches themselves." Women were "restrain'd, frowned upon, and beat, not for
but from the Muses." They were laughed at and ridiculed for attempting to learn. At best men were condescending, picking books for
women, making one, as Astell angrily commented, "walk with the
Crutches they are pleas'd to lend her." Women who rise from their
unnatural ignorance "are star'd upon as Monsters, Censur'd, Envy'd,
and every way Discourag'd, or at the best they have the Fate the
Proverb assigns them, Vertue is prais'd and starv'd."[63] Cavendish
thought women's counsels "despised and laught at." She fully expected scorn and derision for her works because men thought women
who wrote books did "incroach too much upon their Prerogatives."
Sophia found that "the vulgar of both sexes" had "disadvantageous
notions" of educated women. Men thought educated women became
"proud and vicious," she wrote, not adding that perhaps they meant
and feared that women might acquire the strength to resist. Sophia
excused any excess pride with the understanding that the hardships
put in the way of women who desired an education "will apologize for
the little vanity they may have shown."[64]

Ignorance hurt women throughout their lives, as Astell pointed
out. It mired women permanently in an inferior position and subjected
them to male criticism and abuse. Clearly, cause and effect reinforced
each other. Ignorance prevented women from fulfilling what for these
leaders was their natural role. It prevented them from resisting the
evils and temptations presented by men, a consequence men also
acknowledged. Because the world was "too full of Craft, Malice, and
Violence for absolute Simplicity," ignorant women, those who could
not "Dissemble," did not know how to survive. Women were constantly attacked for their follies, time wasting, card playing, gambling,
dancing, although Astell noted that women's unprofitableness was not
to be regretted for the man's sake but for woman's. In any event, it
was not to be avoided. Men denied women a choice. "Ignorance and
a narrow Education," Astell wrote, "lay the Foundation of Vice."[65]
Men encourage our vices, said the Essayist; they create our faults,
wrote Sophia. Women, thought Cavendish, simply were not taught
"to Temper their Passions, and Govern their Appetites." Indeed,
only their bodies were educated, parents taking "more care of their
Feet than their Head, . . . their Musick than their Virtue."[66] Their

[63] Reflections, [xxiv], 65.
[64] "To the Two Universities;" "To All Noble, and Worthy Ladies," Poems and
Fancies; Woman Not Inferior to Man, 38, 25, 26.
[65] The first quotation is from An Essay in Defense of the Female Sex, 111; the
second is from Astell, A Serious Proposal, 44, but see also 25, 31.
[66] An Essay in Defense of the Female Sex, 6; Woman Not Inferior to Man, 57-58;
Sociable Letters, 50.

bodies became courtiers and their minds clowns. Women were nursed in the vices they were blamed for, taught to be attractive for men and denounced for attracting them. If women subsequently turned their attention to plays and romances rather than to the useful, again they could not be faulted. "A rational mind *will* be employ'd," Astell wrote; "if you neglect to furnish it with good materials, 'tis like to take up with such as come to hand." If that was silly, it was inhuman to blame women. Sophia agreed. With education women would "despise those follies and trifles for which they are at present unjustly despised."[67]

Once women fell behind men, for whatever reason, they were doomed. Although Astell argued that one could not prove what was right from current conditions, men tended to think that what existed was natural and desirable. As Sophia said, because men see women in subjection, they necessarily "conclude that we ought to be so." So it would be "odd" for men to see women commanding armies or nations, acting as magistrates or university professors. But if men had not been so envious, if they had shared power, "they wou'd have been so accustom'd to see us filling public offices, as we are to see them disgrace them. . . ."[68]

Despite the impetus of the Civil War, these feminists made very little of political oppression, of their lack of political voice, although they obviously felt compelled to criticize their male rulers. If monarchy were a legitimate form of government or if any other system left any group powerless, the social contract required that rulers govern with the true interests of their unprotected subjects in mind. Usurping men failed. Sophia was most telling, complaining that if one woman was improved by male rule, millions were ruined. It could not be otherwise since to govern wisely rulers needed to know and understand their subjects. But men could never know women because they "force *Women* to live in constant masquerade."[69]

Political ideology, however, provided Astell with an additional argument. She found some support for her positions in one of the controversies of the day. Towards the end of the seventeenth century the debate over the origin of monarchy began again, centered on the exclusion controversy, Parliament's attempt to remove James, Duke of York, from the line of succession. The duke's supporters pushed forward the patriarchal philosophy, and Robert Filmer's major work, *Patriarcha*, written in the 1640s, was published for the first time in 1680. Monarchy, Filmer argued, was a natural form of government, directly related to and logically derived from the age of the patriarchs

---

[67] *A Serious Proposal*, 26, 84; *Woman Not Inferior to Man*, 57-58.
[68] *Reflections*, [vii], *Woman Not Inferior to Man*, 35-37.
[69] *Woman Not Inferior to Man*, 30, 33.

or from rule within the family by the father. Astell accepted the analogy between family and state and used it in her own cause. Filmer, John Locke, and others started with the family and moved, though in somewhat different directions, towards their conclusions about the necessary state. Astell worked in the opposite direction, using her political knowledge to attack the existing family dynamics. Focusing on the democratic ideal implicit in Locke's doctrine of consent, Astell argued that if tyranny was bad in the state, it was equally bad in a family. If it was acceptable in families, why not then in a state? "If Arbitrary Power is evil in it self, and an improper Method of Governing Rational and Free Agents, it ought not to be Practis'd any where," she wrote. People, Astell pointed out, were not made for their prince even if princes have dominion over subjects. Likewise, wives were not made for their husbands. Unfortunately, however, "Superiors indeed are too apt to forget the common Privileges of Mankind; that their Inferiors . . . are as capable as themselves of enjoying the supreme Good. . . ." In the state, apparently, monarchs who governed unwisely were more and more criticized and disobeyed. But men who would not accept the idea of "Passive-Obedience" in a political sense approved of it for women married to unjust rulers.[70]

[70] For background information, see Gordon J. Schochett, *Patriarchalsim in Political Thought* (New York, 1976); for Astell's remarks, *Reflections*, [xii], 12, 47, 45, 27. Kinnaird argues that Astell, "a staunch royalist," used the analogy between state and family ironically, "to expose . . . a double standard." It was, for Astell, legitimate that the family remain "a little monarchy, patriarchal and authoritarian." Astell continued to believe that "families need[ed] the rule of a male sovereign," a conclusion Kinnaird supports by quoting Astell's statement that there could be no "Society, great or little, from Empires down to Private Families, without a last Resort, to determine the Affairs of that Society by an irresistible Sentence." "Mary Astell and the Conservative Contribution to English Feminism," 55, 68-70, 72. But Astell was not just highlighting a double standard. Again and again she returned to the same idea. In addition to what has already been quoted in the text, see, for example: "For Covenants betwixt Husband and Wife, like Laws in an Arbitrary Government, are of *little* Force, the Will of the Sovereign is all in all." That statement is not meant to justify arbitrary rule in state or family. How should one interpret the following remark? "Far be it from her to stir up Sedition of any sort: none can abhor it more; and she heartily wishes, that our Masters would pay their Civil and Ecclesiastical Governors the same Submission, which they themselves exact from the Domestick Subjects." The comment is followed closely by one in which Astell attributes her ignorance of women's "Natural Inferiority" to her lack of "Learning, and of that Superior Genius which Men, as Men, lay claim to." *Reflections*, 37 for the first quotation, and [iv-v] for the next two. When Astell, in non-sexist language, argues that societies need "a last Resort," she is not describing the world as she thinks it could be. She is simply making the point that, in her world, contention was resolved through force, not reason. Men were stronger; hence they had to rule so as to avoid conflict. Again, she made her argument frequently. God, telling Eve that "Her Husband shou'd Rule over her," was only "foretelling what wou'd be," not "determining what ought to be." If custom allowed, women might rule in families without usurping power. *Reflections*, [xiii, xxi].

In this sexual civil war, men took no chances. They kept women ignorant, denied them role models by controlling written history, and prevented women from appreciating the full horrors of their situation. Except for allowing women to worship together, men discouraged women from associating with one another for anything more serious than the playing of meaningless games, for which they could then be denounced. Men recognized the value of proper peer pressure, as in Robert Snawsel's work in which women are set on the right path of honor and obedience by already socialized and molded models. They feared unsupervised female gatherings which could have dispelled ignorance and brought to light not only common problems but deep hostility. That was why William Whately demanded submissiveness in thought and speech even in a husband's absence.[71]

The feminist authors knew men had successfully divided women. They had fostered competition among women for men and so made them jealous of each other. Men had so trained them up that women "tamely give up their Liberty, and abjectly submit their Necks to a slavish Yoke."[72] Astell knew women would not rebel, no matter how sad their case and how eloquently she argued, because they were "for the most part Wise enough to Love their Chains." So the critics expected denunciation from their own sex. "I believe all of my own Sex will be against me," Cavendish wrote. She would be censured for neglecting housework, though, as she noted, she had none to do and was incompetent at it anyway.[73]

Recognizing a desperate need for unity, the authors urged sexual identity and encouraged consciousness arousing groups. Collier wrote about her life as a reflection of all women's lives. Anticipating trouble over one of her books, Cavendish sought to enlist female support, again urging a sexual self-consciousness, a redefinition of the struggle from a personal one to a sexual one. "Strengthen my Side, in defending my Book; for I know Womens Tongues are as sharp, as two-edged Swords, and wound as much, when they are anger'd. And in this Battell may your wit be strong, as to beat them out of the Field of Dispute."[74] A number of times Cavendish called for such group action. In one of her *Sociable Letters,* a few women met for gossip. As usual they talked of childbirth, children, nurses, servants, the trivialities men ridiculed. "At last they fell into a Discourse of Husbands, Complaining of Ill Husbands, and so from Husbands in General, to

---

[71] *A Looking-Glasse,* 41-42; *A Bride-Bush,* 41.

[72] For the competition see Cavendish, *Sociable Letters,* 331-32, 345; for the quotation, *An Essay in Defense of the Female Sex,* 21.

[73] *Reflections,* [xxv]; "Preface," *World's Olio;* "An Epistle to Mrs. Toppe," and "To the Reader," *Poems and Fancies.*

[74] *The Woman's Labour,* 5; "To All Noble, and Worthy Ladies." See n. 64 above.

their own Particular Husbands. . . . '' One of her male speakers in the book of *Orations* demanded the banning of all female societies because women "corrupt and spoil each other, striving to out-brave, out-beauty, and out-talk each other,'' and then more meaningfully noted that he was sure the very proposal would lead the female societies to damn him with *"Railing Tongues.''* Two female speakers provided effective, clearly radical, feminist answers. Women, said one, should "make frequent Assemblies, Associations, and Combinations amoungst our Sex, that we may unite in Prudent Counsels, to make our selves as *Free, Happy,* and *Famous*, as Men. . . .'' And another called for behaving like men, hunting, racing, and the like, and conversing "in Camps, Courts, and Cities; in Schools, Colledges, and Courts of Judicature; in Taverns, Brothels, and Gaming-Houses,'' which would make them known to men and to themselves, "for we are as ignorant of our selves, as Men are of us,'' ignorant of our *"Strength and Wit.''* Rather than let us assemble, men "would fain bury us in their Houses or Beds, as in a Grave.''[75] Indeed, for the Essayist, men did not want women to meet to talk of things trivial, presumably because it wasted time, but perhaps, although the author did not say it, because any meeting joined women's minds and heightened their awareness. Astell proposed a female seminary to remove women temporarily from men who "under pretence of loving and admiring . . . [them] really served their *own* base ends.''[76]

Women's need for self knowledge formed the basis of Astell's desire to establish a female seminary for learning. Because of the temptations to which ignorant women were prone, because of the natural tendency "to do what others do round about us,'' and because of "the hurry and noise of the World,'' it was difficult to find time or inspiration to "stand still and reflect on our own Minds.'' It took courage and prudence to quit old habits, hence one needed organized female support. Men would "resent'' her proposal, but that was unimportant.[77]

Astell's proposal was the only suggestion of any of these writers which offered women organized help in their efforts to change society. Mostly the authors simply urged on women the difficult task of girding themselves up to fight or to encourage women to improve despite obstacles. We should not respond to husbands' ill usage by punishing ourselves, said Astell. Falling prey to temptations and vices hurts us and justifies to men their continued oppression. We are good but we can be better, said the author of the *Ladies Vademecum*.[78] But the feminists were not optimistic. Certainly, in the immediate future, they

---

[75] *Sociable Letters*, 207; *Orations*, 236, 235, 239, 242, 240.
[76] *An Essay in Defense of the Female Sex*, 85-86; *A Serious Proposal*, 64-65.
[77] *A Serious Proposal*, pp. 46, 47, 121, 86.
[78] *Reflections*, 4-5; *Ladies Vademecum*, [ii].

expected little change. Sophia hoped only that women would not submit "tamely" to man's "misplaced arrogance." Astell was left with warning a woman not to marry unless she accepted the "indisputable Maxim that her Husband must govern absolutely and intirely." Otherwise she was not "fit to be a Wife."[79] But women would at least continue to complain and might possibly do more. "*An Ass tho' slow if provok'd will kick*," commented Astell. Her analysis again owed something to political controversies, and she framed her comments in broad terms: "I don't say that Tyranny *ought*, but we find in *Fact*, that it provokes the Oppress'd to throw off even a Lawful Yoke that sits too heavy. . . ."[80]

In the final analysis, women must depend on men, and that was disappointing. Women were surprised, tormented, and disturbed that even men who loved them treated them ill. The anonymous author of *The Hardships of the English Laws in Relation to Wives* (1735) included on the title page an excerpt from Psalm 55, taken somewhat out of context but astonishingly relevant:

For it was not an Enemy that reproached me, then I could have born it; neither was it he that hated me, that did magnifie himself against me, I then would have hid myself from him.
But it was thou, a Man, mine Equal, my Guide, and mine Acquaintance. We . . . [had taken] sweet Counsel together, and walked into the House of God in company.

Men benefitted too much from female oppression to end it or to encourage women to help themselves. One of Cavendish's speakers on behalf of women angrily noted: "Men, that are not only our *Tyrants*, but our *Devils*, keep us in the Hell of *Subjection*, from whence I cannot perceive any Redemption, or getting out." Complaints, murmurings, were useless. "Our *Words* to Men, are as empty *Sounds*; our *Sighs*, as Puffs of *Wind*; and our *Tears*, as *Fruitless Showers*; and our *Power* is so inconsiderable, that Men laugh at our *Weakness*." Astell agreed that there was no relief. A ruler "does not value the Provocations of a Rebellious Subject, but knows how to subdue him with ease. . . ." Men might dislike arbitrary power on a throne, but they welcomed it at home.[81]

Without power, women had little hope. Sophia in the end could suggest nothing more than setting a good example: "In a word, let us shew them, by what little we do without aid of education, the much

---

[79] *Woman Not Inferior to Man*, 17; *Reflections*, 56, 57. Again, it is important to emphasize that Astell is not defending absolute rule by husbands. She is describing here only what exists and warning women who marry that they had better like slavery. Necessity, not reason, compels women to obey. *Reflections*, 56-7, 26.
[80] *Reflections*, 59, 90-91.   [81] *Orations*, 240, 241; *Reflections*, 27, 36.

we might do if they did us justice; that we may force a blush from them, if possible. . . ."[82] That was a philosophy not far removed from the old advice of marital counsellors who urged quiet obedience on wives as ways of reforming refractory husbands.

Astell was in a similar bind. A man with a disagreeable temper would be impossible to reform. And even one with "some good Qualities" would not change. "Pride and Self-conceit" would prevent a man who was more humane than "most of his Neighbours, from growing better." To change would be an open and embarrassing admission of having been wrong, and "Penitence and Self-condemnation are what his Haughtiness cannot bear. . . ." Perhaps, too, such a man, responding to male peer pressure, would be embarrassed to behave better.[83] Astell, on another occasion, had pointed out that people curiously avoided acknowledging their good actions. Indeed, both sexes delighted in detracting from their neighbors' virtue. Rather than deal with his own feelings of guilt, "the reproaches of his own Mind," by "Humbling himself and making Peace with Heaven," a man who senses the wrongness of his behavior, "bids Defiance to it."[84] Accepting, charitable, subservient female posturing, then, would work no better than persuasion to end the civil war. Not only did men's self interest dictate continued oppression, so did an external pressure which each man internalized.

Astell's words, closing the preface to the second edition of *Some Reflections Upon Marriage,* are a glorious summary of the feminist argument: men tyrannical, women now accepting unnatural enslavement, men imposing ignorance, women playing at dress and games— in short, a division between the haves and the have nots, between unrestrained rulers and quiet subjects. Astell did not mention England's Civil War, but in some ways her words reflected the failure of that revolution to produce the radical shift in society that some people craved. She was writing about men and women, but there was a connection between the sexual battles and others in society:

As to those Women who find themselves born for Slavery, and are so sensible of their own Meanness as to conclude it impossible to attain to any thing excellent, . . . She's a Fool who wou'd attempt their Deliverance or Improvement. No, let them enjoy the great Honor and Felicity of their Tame, Submissive and Depending Temper! Let the Men applaud, and let them

---

[82] *Woman Not Inferior to Man,* 62.
[83] *Reflections,* 29, 30. William Heale's reason for pessimism was somewhat different: "And most of all men being evil themselves, love but few things that are good, and so perchance hate women." *An APOLOGIE for Women* [Oxford, 1609] *The English Experience,* No. 665 (Amsterdam, 1974), 2.
[84] *A Serious Proposal,* 49; *Reflections,* [xxv], 30.

Glory in, this wonderful Humility! . . . Let . . . [women] enjoy the Glory of treading in the Footsteps of their Predecessors, and of having the Prudence to avoid that audacious attempt of soaring beyond their Sphere! Let them Huswife or Play, Dress and be pretty entertaining Company! . . . Let them not by any means aspire at being Women of Understanding, because no Man can endure a Woman of Superior Sense, or wou'd treat a reasonable Woman civilly, but that he thinks he stands on higher ground. . . . Let them in short be what is call'd very Woman, . . . but let them not Judge of the Sex by their own Scantling.

Astell was not at all optimistic, but she had a vision. She looked forward to "those Halcyon . . . Millennium Days, in which the Wolf and the Lamb shall feed together, and a Tyrannous Domination which Nature never meant, shall no longer render useless if not hurtful, the Industry and Understandings of half Mankind!" The other feminists, outspoken and clear-sighted critics of the prevailing view of women, shared the gloom and the dream.

University of Maine

Research for the above article was partially funded by a grant from the Faculty Research Funds Committee of the University of Maine, Orono.

XII

MARY WOLLSTONECRAFT: EIGHTEENTH-CENTURY COMMONWEALTHWOMAN

BY G. J. BARKER-BENFIELD

The subject to which Mary Wollstonecraft devoted the largest amount of her prose was politics. *Vindication of the Rights of Woman* (1792) should be grouped with the preceding *A Vindication of the Rights of Men* (1790) and the succeeding *An Historical and Moral View of the French Revolution* (1794) as her contributions to the great Anglo-French revolutionary debate of the 1790s. Wollstonecraft tells us in the dedication of *Vindication of the Rights of Woman* that it was intended to influence the revisions to the French revolutionary constitution then being made. She and others in her radical, "Jacobin" circle in England were in close touch with French revolutionaries. And she, no less than her fellow urban radicals, drew upon "the antiquarian and Commonwealth tradition handed on by the Protestant Dissenters. . . ."[1] Contrary to the opinion of the most recent historian of "the eighteenth-century feminist mind" there was a relationship between eighteenth-century feminism and "other political ideas of the time. . . ."[2] Wollstonecraft's achievement was to extend the Commonwealth analysis of male corruption and program for male reform to women. The following essay discusses those elements of Commonwealth thought on which Wollstonecraft would draw and suggests, moreover, that one can see signs of its influence in her early work. The essay then argues that the key moment of Wollstonecraft's breakthrough as a political thinker was her answer to Edmund Burke's *Reflections on the Revolution in France* in her *A Vindication of the Rights of Men*; and finally it demonstrates that her second and more famous *Vindication* is a result of this breakthrough.

English radicals of the 1790s were the latest exemplars of an indigenous tradition of political and moral thought. Identifying themselves as "Real," "True," and "Honest" Whigs, they looked back to the "Commonwealthmen" of the English revolutions of the seventeenth century.[3]

This article was written under a summer research grant awarded by the State University of New York Research Foundation. The author wishes to thank Patricia West, Warren Roberts, and Carolyn Lougee for their generous assistance and encouragement.

[1] Albert Goodwin, *The Friends of Liberty: The English Democratic Movement in the Age of the French Revolution* (Cambridge, Mass., 1979), 99.

[2] Alice Browne, *The Eighteenth-Century Feminist Mind* (Brighton, U.K., 1987), 19.

[3] Caroline Robbins, *The Eighteenth-Century Commonwealthman: Studies in the Transmission, Development and Circumstance of English Liberal Thought from the Restoration of Charles II until the War with the Thirteen Colonies* (Cambridge, Mass., 1961); J. G. A. Pocock, "The Varieties of Whiggism from Exclusion to Reform: a History of Ideology

Among the leaders of this tradition were religious nonconformists, the Dissenters, who suffered legal and political disabilities imposed by the Test and Corporation Acts, part of the religious settlement following the "Glorious Revolution" of 1688. They saw themselves barred from the full expression of individual talents and understood that the removal of these disabilities required Parliamentary reform: annual Parliaments, the removal of placemen, the redistribution of seats; and extension of the franchise, eventually to universal manhood suffrage.[4] In the latter part of the eighteenth century English Dissent was headed by the Reverend Richard Price (1723-91) and his friend, the Reverend Joseph Priestley (1733-1804). They were at the heart of the last Commonwealth generation, and for a time they were close to the pinnacle of British political power as part of Lord Shelburne's brain trust. Moreover, Price contributed importantly to Pitt's economic reforms.[5] A third Dissenting Commonwealthman of whom we must take note was James Burgh (1714-75), Price's close friend and neighbor in Newington Green. His *Political Disquisitions* (1774, 1775), "the most elaborate and detailed indictment so far available of the corrupt nature of English parliamentary representation and its social and political consequences," was "the standard source book for reform propagandists in the 1780s," "the key book of this generation."[6] These Commonwealthmen linked the revolution of 1688 to the American Revolution, to which they were sympathetic. They were to look favorably on changes in France in 1789 and call for similar changes in Britain.[7]

---

and Discourse," *Virtue, Commerce, and History: Essays on Political Thought and History, Chiefly in the Eighteenth Century* (Cambridge, 1985), 215-310.

[4] H. T. Dickinson, *British Radicalism and the French Revolution 1789-1815* (New York, 1985), 1-8, provides a succinct summary of these reform proposals.

[5] Robbins, *Eighteenth-Century Commonwealthman*, 335-53; Carl Cone, *Torchbearer of Freedom: The Influence of Richard Price on Eighteenth Century Thought* (Lexington, Ky., 1952); Bernard Peach (ed.), *Richard Price and the Ethical Foundations of the American Revolution: Selections from his Pamphlets with Appendices* (Durham, N.C., 1979); D. O. Thomas, "Richard Price, 1723-91," *Transactions of the Honourable Society of Cymmrodorioun* (1971), 46-64; D. D. Raphael, "Introduction," Richard Price, *A Review of the Principal Questions in Morals* (Oxford, 1974); Joseph Priestley, "Memoirs of the Rev. Dr. Joseph Priestley to the Year 1795, Written by Himself," in Ira V. Brown (ed.), *Joseph Priestley: Selections from his Writings* (University Park, Penn., 1962) 4, 3-75; Joseph Priestley, *Priestley's Writings on Philosophy, Science, and Politics*, ed. John A. Passmore (New York, 1965); Derek Jarrett, *The Begetters of Revolution: England's Involvement with France, 1759-1789* (Totowa, N.J., 1973) is valuable for Price's and Priestley's relations with Shelburne.

[6] Carla H. Hay, *James Burgh, Spokesman for Reform in Hanoverian England* (Washington, 1979); Robbins, *Eighteenth-Century Commonwealthman*, 363-68; Goodwin, *Friends of Liberty*, 52; Black quoted by Hay, *Burgh*, 4; Bernard Bailyn, *The Ideological Origins of the American Revolution* (Cambridge, Mass., 1967), 41.

[7] Robbins, *Eighteeth-Century Commonwealthman*, 7 and ch. 9; John Brewer, *Party Ideology and Popular Politics at the Accession of George III* (Cambridge, 1976), ch. 10.

The Dissenting edge of this tradition emphasized that to be virtuous one must be free. Time and again Dissenters insisted that independence of mind was the individual's essential right: in Price's words, "to be obliged from our birth to look up to a creature no better than ourselves as the master of our fortunes and to receive his will as law—what can be more humiliating? What elevated ideas can enter a mind in such a situation?" One can see how the Dissenters' demand for freedom of religious conscience could be extended to the rights of men generally, but one can see, too, its appeal to women.[8] The Dissenters identified such independence with the exercise of reason: their party is often called that of "Rational Dissenters," in contrast to "enthusiasts" like the Methodists. They urged that the individual be freed from the control of his own and government's unnatural passions and prejudices. Like other Commonwealthmen, they were deeply critical of the luxury and dissipation of the "ins," the ruling class. Conversely, they presented "the middling people" as the repository of morality and civic virtue. It was a class which Edmund Burke and the traditional rulers whose power he justified would find "increasing reason to fear. . . ."[9]

The moralizing perspective of the Commonwealthmen was a response to conditions particular to the modern state. For example, in the late seventeenth century, the phrase, "standing army" was beginning to denote an army of professional officers and long-service soldiers . . . paid for by the state." The Commonwealthmen opposed "the poor swaggering idler(s) in a red coat" who made up this force. A "financial revolution" allowed the state "to maintain larger and more permanent armies and bureaucracies . . . increasing the resources at the disposal of political patronage. . . ."[10] As Professor Pocock has argued, in earlier times an Englishman's civic consciousness had been first rooted in "the bearing of arms" under circumstances where "the possession of untenured land in nondependent tenure" was its "material basis." James Harrington's notion of *populo armato* was "the foundation on which a republican

[8] Price quoted in William Stafford, *Socialism, Radicalism, and Nostalgia: Social Criticism in Britain, 1775-1830* (Cambridge, 1987), 88-89; Goodwin, *Friends of Liberty*, ch. 3.

[9] *Priestley's Writings*, 17; Priestley, *Memoirs*, 37; Wollstonecraft shows contempt for Methodists in, for example, her *Vindication of the Rights of Woman*, 225, n. 2. For the aggrandizement of the middle class, see James Burgh, *Political Disquisitions: An Enquiry with Public Errors, Defects, and Abuses* (3 vols.; New York, 1971 [1774, 1775]), II, 39; Priestley, *An Essay on the first Principles of Government*, in *Priestley's Writings*, 203-4; Priestley, *Memoirs*, 49-50; Price, *Additional Observations on the Nature and Value of Civil Liberty and the War with America* in Peach, *Price . . . Selections*, 146-47; Pocock, "Varieties of Whiggism," 281.

[10] J. G. A. Pocock, *The Machiavellian Moment: Florentine Political Thought and the Atlantic Republican Tradition* (Princeton, 1975), 411-12; Pocock, "Varieties of Whiggism," 246; Robbins, *Eighteenth-Century Commonwealthman*, 104; Pocock, *Machiavellian Moment*, 411, 425.

people erects the structure of its civic virtue." The eighteenth-century Commonwealthmen continued to adhere to these republican beliefs. One can see how this foundation for the Commonwealthmen's civic consciousness excluded women. As Professor Kerber points out, "republican" ideologues had not yet included women as political agents. Burgh held that God intended women "to be submissive to men . . . as loving wives, prudent mothers and mistresses of families, faithful friends, and good Christians. . . ." Price and Priestley thought of political rights strictly as a male prerogative. On the other hand Commonwealthmen *were* keenly interested in gender.[11] They inherited from seventeenth-century republicanism a powerful emphasis on "the release of personal virtue through civic participation," its trope, the parable of the talents: "God hath given no man a talent to be wrapped up in a napkin and not improved. . . ." The replacement of the citizen army by the state's mercenaries, the state's own "standing army," was seen as a degeneration of both civic virtue and manhood. This affected those exercising a corrupt political power, but also it contributed to an enervation of the whole of male society.[12] Burgh's vision is striking in this respect. Man's disposition had become "perverse," "degenerated into luxury," and the upper classes were refined into "adultery, gambling, cheating, blasphemy, rookery, and sodomy."[13] According to another expression of the same vision, England, far "from being the nursery of heroes, became the residence of musicians, pimps, panders, and catamites."[14] Burgh's conclusion about the tendency of such behavior illustrates the gender specific meaning of the *populo armato*: "A people enervated by luxury are but a nation of women and children."[15]

A vision of civil society's being corrupted by luxury and false refinements pervades Burgh's *Political Disquisitions*, both in his own language and in that of the Commonwealthmen he quotes. Burgh introduces the following quotation from Adam Ferguson's *History of Civilized Societies* as a description of "a people sliding into luxury and corruption."

The increasing regard with which men appear in the progress of commercial arts, to study their profit, or the delicacy with which they refine on their pleasures, even industry itself, or the habit of application to a tedious employment

---

[11] Pocock, *Machiavellian Moment*, 335, 390, 372, 389; Linda Kerber, *Women of the Republic: Intellect and Ideology in Revolutionary America* (Chapel Hill, N.C., 1980), 27-32; Dickinson, "The Rights of Man from John Locke to Tom Paine," Owen Dudley Edwards and George Shepperson, *Scotland, Europe, and the American Revolution* (Edinburgh, 1976), 38-49: 45; Burgh quoted in Hay, *Burgh*, 65. See, too, Ruth Bloch, "The Gendered Meanings of Virtue in Revolutionary America," *Signs*, 13 (1987), 98-121: 102-05.

[12] Pocock, *Machiavellian Moment*, 394, 313, 411-12.

[13] Burgh, *Political Disquisitions*, III, 59; III, 11.

[14] Bernard Bailyn, *Ideological Origins*, 136.

[15] Burgh, *Political Disquisitions*, III, 59.

in which no honors are won [a reference to the preceding more virile and chivalric age], may perhaps be considered an indication of a growing attention to interest, or of effeminacy contracted in the enjoyment of ease and conveniency. Every successive art by which the individual is taught to improve on his fortune, is in reality an addition to his private engagements, and a new avocation of his mind from the public . . . it is in the midst of ["higher"] engagements that they are most likely to acquire or to preserve their virtues. The habits of a vigorous mind are formed in contending with difficulties, not in engaging the repose of a pacific station; penetration and wisdom are the fruits of experience, not the lessons of retirement and leisure.[16]

As Pocock argues, such a change (or more precisely, such a belief), the "decisive abandonment of the classical (and at the same time Gothic) ideal of the citizen as an armed proprietor, and his replacement by a leisured, cultivated and acquisitive man who paid for others to defend and govern him" entailed "the emergence of new types of personality," that is of *male* personality. Here Ferguson characterizes such personality—refined, delicate, tediously employed, enjoying ease and convenience, above all, absorbed by the private—as "effeminate." The same political tradition also interpreted it as "hysterical and unstable" and Professor Pocock demonstrates further that the modern figure of degenerate manhood was associated with a female symbol of "Credit."[17]

The qualities Ferguson associates with "masculine" manhood, vigor of mind, penetration, and wisdom, were derived from "higher engagements." If "feeble and interested men" give up their "national and political efforts" and grow indifferent to "objects of a public nature" and "the exercise of freedom," Ferguson predicts "corruption to the national manners, as well as remissness to the national spirit." It is worth our while to read more of Ferguson's description of the kind of "effeminate" character to which absorption of private life led.

Men being relieved from the pressure of great occasions, bestow their attention on trifles; and having carried what they are pleased to call sensibility and delicacy on the subject of ease or molestation, as far as real weakness or folly can go, have recourse to affectation, in order to enhance the pretended demands, and accumulate the anxieties of a sickly fancy and enfeebled mind.

Such men degrade the "former ages" celebration of masculine "ardour, generosity and fortitude," explaining it away as mere necessity.

They congratulate themselves on having escaped the storm, which required the exercise of such arduous virtues; and with that vanity which accompanies the

---

[16] Burgh, *Political Disquisitions*, II, 85-86. See Robbins, *Eighteenth-Century Commonwealthman*, 199-203.
[17] Pocock, "Varieties of Whiggism," 235; Pocock, *Machiavellian Moment*, 410-42 and ch. 13, *passim*. See, too, Bloch, "Gendered Meanings," 106-7.

human race in the meanest condition, they boast of a scene of affectation of languor, or of folly as the standard of human felicity. . . .[18]

The Commonwealthman's particular sexualization of virtue and of corruption would provide a *point d'appui* for Wollstonecraft.

Wollstonecraft had already been introduced to the real Whig/Dissenting tradition when she moved to the Dissenting community at Newington Green in 1783. Price was its minister, and Burgh had kept a successful academy there with his wife until his death in 1775. His widow, Hannah Harding Burgh (1710-88), played a key role in Wollstonecraft's life, treating her as if she had been, in Wollstonecraft's words, "her own daughter."[19] In the end Wollstonecraft would break free of this complex relationship;[20] but Hannah Burgh's introduction of Wollstonecraft to her and her husband's circle of friends, her experience running a school with her husband, her willingness to lend Wollstonecraft money, and her practical and emotional support for Wollstonecraft and her sisters over the next few years were crucial. Most important, Hannah Burgh, it seems clear, introduced Wollstonecraft to her husband's ideas and his writings. According to another leading Dissenter and the Burghs's good friend, the Reverend Andrew Kippis, Hannah Burgh "zealously concurred with [James] in promoting all his laudable and useful undertakings."[21] We can imagine this zealous and childless widow, taking the twenty-four-year-old Wollstonecraft under her wing, identifying herself closely with her efforts to perpetuate education in her community, and pulling out copies of her dead husband's books to aid in those efforts, perhaps first his *Thoughts on Education* (1747).[22] (She may well have proudly shown her "daughter" Burgh's *magnum opus*, his *Political Disquisitions*, although Price or Joseph Johnson, her publisher, could have loaned it to Wollstonecraft.) It is possible that the title of Wollstonecraft's first book, *Thoughts on the Education of Daughters* (1787), was a tribute to the Burghs.

Devoting only five pages of the *Thoughts on Education* to female education, Burgh had intimated the need for a more extended work on the subject. The chief burden of those five pages was that women are as rational as men and as accountable in the world to come, that they should develop their minds rather than their shortlived charms, that they should resist the male flattery and rakery fostered by plays and novels, and that

---

[18] Burgh, *Political Disquisitions*, II, 86.

[19] Hay, *Burgh*, 20, 114, n. 47; Wollstonecraft to Eliza W. Bishop, Sept. 23, 1786 in Wardle (ed.), *Collected Letters of Mary Wollstonecraft* (Ithaca, N.Y., 1979), 113. These are the best source for Wollstonecraft's relationship with Hannah Burgh.

[20] Wollstonecraft to Everina Wollstonecraft, Feb. 10, 1787; March 4, 1787; and Nov. 7, 1787 (*Collected Letters*, 134, 142, and 164).

[21] Kippis quoted in Hay, *Burgh*, 19.

[22] Eleanor Flexner, *Mary Wollstonecraft: A Biography* (Baltimore, 1972). 48; Claire Tomalin, *The Life and Death of Mary Wollstonecraft* (New York, 1974), 40.

they should do so in the interest of a rational marital partnership. Burgh provided Wollstonecraft with the nub of her first book, *The Female Reader* (1789), as well as a theme that would culminate in *A Vindication of the Rights of Woman*. Burgh's views were part and parcel of a political vision in which education was crucial.[23] Wollstonecraft's other early work—all published by Joseph Johnson—can be linked to the same political views. One also finds in her *Original Stories From Real Life* (1788) views of economic relationships which have been informed by the views of the Commonwealthmen. Her story of the indebtedness of the stationer's wife and family embodies exactly that perspective on the "client economy [that] was an integral part of aristocratic and courtly politics," a politics buttressed by "a system of graft and corruption." Wollstonecraft's writing here may be seen as an expression of the "out-of-doors" politics described by John Brewer.[24] Her 1788 translation of Jacques Necker's *De l'importance des opinions religeuses* is another in-triguing link with politics.[25] Commissioned by Johnson, Wollstonecraft must have undertaken it at first for income, but she told her sister in Paris that the book pleased her and she wanted "to know the character of the man [Necker] in domestic life and public estimation and the opinion the French have of his literary abilities." We cannot ignore the personal links between Price and Necker and the fact that Wollstonecraft wrote to Necker and sent him some papers while working on the translation.[26] Necker was famous in England as the reformer of French governmental finances but famous, too, as a Protestant who had risen to power in a Catholic country. He was seen by British Dissenters as a symbol of "the movement for the civil emancipation of the French Protestants" and thereby of their own aspirations in their campaign against the religious and political establishment. Chapter XVI of *De l'importance* makes a strong case against "religious intolerance."[27] Above all, we should note the timing of Wollstonecraft's translation in the midst of three successive applications for the repeal in Parliament of the Test and Corporation Acts by Dissenters and their allies in March 1787, May 1789, and March 1790.

[23] Burgh, *Thoughts on Education: Tending chiefly to recommend to the Attention of the Public, some Particulars relating to that Subject; which are not generally considered with the Regard their Importance deserves* (Boston, Mass., 1749 [1747]), 53-58.

[24] Wollstonecraft, *Original Stories from Real Life: with Conversation, Calculated to Regulate the Affections, and Form the Mind to Truth and Goodness* (n.p., 1972 [1791]), 83; Brewer, "Commercialization and Politics," Neil McKendrick, John Brewer, and J. H. Plumb, *The Birth of a Consumer Society: The Commercialization of Eighteenth-Century England* (Bloomington, Ind., 1982), 195-262, 199.

[25] London, 1788.

[26] Wollstonecraft to Everina Wollstonecraft, March 22, 1788 (*Collected Letters* 173); Wardle, *Wollstonecraft*, 33; Cone, *Torchbearer*, 160; Peach, *Price . . . Selections*, 14, 177.

[27] Jarrett, *Begetters of Revolution*, ch. 7; Goodwin, *Friends of Liberty*, 91, 92, 81; Necker, *Religious Opinions*, ch. 16, "Reflexions on Intolerance," 204.

In a letter written in March 1788 to her sister, Everina, who was in Paris, and while working on the translation of Necker's *De l'importance*, Wollstonecraft requested her sister "*immediately*, without delay" (her emphasis) to deliver a letter to the French minister by way of a French contact, Mr. Laurent, together "with some papers" and reiterated her urgency a third time, "do not lose time." Professor Wardle suggests that Laurent was a business associate of Johnson.[28] Those mysterious papers cry out for research. In any case one can see the political value of Wollstonecraft's translation of Necker's book to the British Dissenters' Parliamentary campaign, then at its height. Not only was Necker seen by *them* as a symbol, he was also deeply respected by more conservative Whigs for his efforts at financial reform, which Burke attempted to emulate in 1780 and cited frequently in his *Reflections on the Revolution in France*, that is, even after his break with the Dissenters and their Whig allies.[29] Necker's views could serve to broaden the appeal of the upcoming assault in Parliament on the Dissenters' disabilities. Johnson's commissioning Wollstonecraft's translation was characteristic of his lifelong habit of publishing radical works of the greatest political immediacy to the Dissenting group to which he and Wollstonecraft belonged.

Johnson played an important part in the publication of the original work by Wollstonecraft which illustrates unequivocally and dramatically her participation in British politics, her *A Vindication of the Rights of Men*.[30] This was her response to Burke's *Reflections on the Revolution in France* of the same year, in turn provoked most immediately by Price's "A Discourse on the Love of Our Country" a sermon delivered November 4, 1789, the anniversary of England's 1688 revolution. It was an annual event, and its place, audience, and occasion epitomized the expression and values of this last generation of Commonwealthman: Price preached at the Dissenters' Meeting House at Old Jewry, before members of the London Revolution Society, preceding their formal proceedings and dinner at the London Tavern.[31] By November 1789 Price could feel buoyed by the near-success in May of the challenge in Parliament to the Test and Corporation Acts; Price's sermon linked that challenge expressly to the return that summer of Necker, (characterizing him as "a professed Dissenter") to power in France. Price could also celebrate the fall of the

---

[28] Wollstonecraft, *Collected Letters*, 174, n. 2. For unofficial contact between Shelburne (Price's patron and a Dissenters' supporter) and Necker in the spring of 1789, see Goodwin, *Friends of Liberty*, 104-6.

[29] Jarrett, *Begetters of Revolution*, 160; Burke, *Reflections on the Revolution in France and on the Proceedings in Certain Societies in London Relative to that Event*, ed. Conor Cruise O'Brien (New York, 1968 [1790]), 220-21, 232, 234-35, 238, 367.

[30] William Godwin, *Memoirs of Mary Wollstonecraft*, ed. W. Clark Durant (New York, 1969 [1798]), 52-53; I have used the edition of *Vindication of the Rights of Men* published in Boston, 1790 (Gainesville, Fla., 1960).

[31] Goodwin, *Friends of Liberty*, 106.

Bastille that July.[32] The failure in Parliament the following May to repeal the Test and Corporation Acts was largely because of the decisive intervention of Burke, who read Price's sermon to Parliament. Burke was then hard at work on his counter-revolutionary manifesto. This was a turning point in British politics, confirming "the inherent radicalism of Dissent and provid[ing] the new working-class reformers with the political leadership and intellectual stamina that enabled them in the years ahead to acquire political credibility and to develop . . . large-scale organization."[33]

Wollstonecraft, then, was a participant in this struggle, an ally of Price, the most celebrated Dissenter in England, who, because of his relationship with Shelburne and Pitt, was the symbol to Burke of the political principles that threatened his road back to office. The Dissenters' abandonment of the Rockinghamites in the 1784 election in favor of Pitt had sent Burke into the political wilderness.[34] In his *Reflections*, as in his *Thoughts on the Present Discontents* twenty years earlier, Burke was attempting no less than a redefinition of the Whig party. It was this that Wollstonecraft was taking on.[35]

Wollstonecraft's closeness to Price as she was writing this reply is indicated by her inclusion in a footnote of the correction Price made in the fourth edition of his *Discourse* to Burke's misrepresentations. Her identification with Price and his fellow "revolutionaries" is further suggested by her addressing precisely those reform issues, the repeal of the Test and Corporation Acts, the blatant inequity of "the penal law," the press gang, and the game laws, which were the subjects of toasts by the London Revolutionary Society at its 1788 meeting, and whose proceedings, published in 1789, she very probably had at hand. Wollstonecraft gives a post-Bastille definition of liberty: "the birthright of man . . . such a degree of liberty, civil and religious, as is compatible with the liberty of every other individual . . . in a social compact. . . ." Her representation of the effects of luxury, idleness, and the maldistribution of power and property shows the influence of Burgh as well as Price.[36]

[32] Price, "A Discourse on the Love of our Country . . ." (London, 1790), 31-32; Goodwin, *Friends of Liberty*, 88, 90, 92.

[33] Goodwin, *Friends of Liberty*, 96-97, 98.

[34] Priestley, "A Discourse on the Occasion of the Death of Dr. Price; delivered at Hackney, Sunday, May 1, 1791," *Gentleman's Magazine*, I, xi, no. 1 (1791), 557-59; Burke, *Reflections*, 25; Goodwin, *Friends of Liberty*, 76; Pocock, "Varieties of Whiggism," 279. Burke's hostility to Dissenters went back to the early 1770s, Frank O'Gorman, *Edmund Burke: His Political Philosophy* (Bloomington, Ind., 1973), 64.

[35] *The Writings and Speeches of Edmund Burke*, ed. Paul Langford (Oxford, 1981), II, 203-4; O'Gorman, *Burke*, 109.

[36] Wollstonecraft, *A Vindication of the Rights of Men*, 55n; the fourth edition of Price's "Discourse" was published one week earlier; James Boulton, *Language of Politics in the Age of Wilkes and Burke* (London, 1963), 266; Goodwin, *Friends of Liberty*, 85-86; Wollstonecraft, *A Vindication of the Rights of Men*, 7-8 and 22, 100. Stafford, *Socialism,*

Most striking in Wollstonecraft's *A Vindication of the Rights of Men* is its focus on Burke (in her correspondence she referred to it as her "answer to Burke"). Her title could well have been a reference to Burke's early satire on the intellectual tradition Wollstonecraft was now defending, entitled *A Vindication of Natural Society*; if so, she is calling his satire truth.[37] But there is no doubt of Wollstonecraft's sustained, two-pronged attack on Burke in her text. The first prong is composed of a series of references to his political career. That he was in 1790 "an old Member of Parliament"; a man not born to office but having had to win it for himself, now sunk into oblivion. It was from that position that he was represented by Wollstonecraft as envious of Price who, like Burke, had supplied his aristocratic patrons with economic expertise.[38] Wollstonecraft refers to Burke's plan of "oeconomical reform" and, it seems, to its being nipped in the bud by the Gordon Riots.[39] She suggests that his concern for the plight of Indians under corrupt British rule is now revealed to have been concern for the caste system, above all Brahmin domination. With similar irony she refers to Burke's defense of "disinterested conduct" in relation to his constituents, and she mentions his erstwhile sympathy for revolution in the American case. She tells Burke that she has "been reading . . . several of your insensible and profane speeches during the King's illness" that is, during the Regency Crisis the previous year, which Burke had seen as an opportunity to regain office under the Prince of Wales.[40] Here, too, the Dissenters had been on the opposite side to Burke and it was likely that one of them, Price perhaps, or Johnson, supplied Wollstonecraft with the published speeches on the controversy, for example, Stockdale's *The History of the Lords and Commons of Great Britain . . . with regard to the Regency* (1789). She refers to Burke's reputation for unbridled passion and even madness;[41] she alludes throughout to his putative Catholicism[42] (his mother was Catholic and he was intensely loyal to his Catholic kin) and, more slyly but with equal nastiness, to his Irishness.[43]

Radicalism, and Nostalgia, 77; Dickinson, "Rights of Man," 45; Dickinson, "The Eighteenth-Century Debate on the 'Glorious Revolution,'" *History*, 61 (1971), 28-45.

[37] Wollstonecraft to William Godwin, Oct. 26, 1796 (*Collected Letters*, 358); Burke, *A Vindication of National Society*, in *Works* (8 vols.; London, 1854), I, 1-49.

[38] Wollstonecraft, *A Vindication of the Rights of Men*, 42, 107, 110.

[39] *Ibid.*, 20, 89; Jarrett, *Begetters of Revolution*, 174-75.

[40] Wollstonecraft, *A Vindication of the Rights of Men*, 130, 85, 87-88, 61; Pocock, "Varieties of Whiggism," 279.

[41] Wollstonecraft, *A Vindication of the Rights of Men*, 4, 6; these are running themes. Compare O'Gorman, *Burke*, 127, n. 57, 140; Jarrett, *Begetters of Revolution*, 175; F. P. Lock, *Burke's Reflections on the Revolution in France* (London, 1985), 147-48.

[42] Wollstonecraft, *A Vindication of the Rights of Men*, 17, 18, 21, 23, 32, 40, 74, 81, 93, 120, 124-25.

[43] O'Brien's introduction to Burke, *Reflections*, 29-30; Wollstonecraft, *A Vindication of the Rights of Men*, 23.

The second prong was pointed at Burke's hitherto most famous work, most influential in literary and artistic culture, his *A Philosophical Enquiry into our Ideas of the Sublime and the Beautiful*, to which she referred throughout her *A Vindication of the Rights of Men*.[44] She saw that Burke's "categories" in his *Reflections* "were essentially his own aesthetic ones of the *Enquiry*," which she replaced with her own definitions of the sublime and the beautiful.[45] Her immersion in the *Enquiry* was linked to her extremely close intellectual and personal relationship with the painter, Henry Fuseli, who was deeply influenced by Burke's aesthetics and whose unhappy experience as a tutor to Lord Chewton Wollstonecraft mentioned obliquely in *A Vindication of the Rights of Men*.[46]

The climax of this, the most striking organizing principle of her answer to Burke's *Reflections*, is Wollstonecraft's quotation of and commentary on Burke's prescriptive depiction of women in his *Enquiry*: "little, smooth, delicate fair creatures, never designed that they should exercise their reason . . ." but taught they "should lisp, to totter in their walk and nick-name God's creatures."[47] The former phrases show Wollstonecraft's understanding of Burke's identification of "the beautiful" with women as a separate human and aesthetic category. Burke's sexual invidiousness here is, of course, the same as Rousseau's (particularly in *Emile*), a primary target of Wollstonecraft's second *Vindication*.[48]

By contrast, she identifies *herself* with the rights of man: "I reverence the rights of men. Sacred rights for which I acquire a more profound respect the more I look into my own mind. . . ." She writes of "our liberty," "our constitution," and "our faculties." She will fight Burke with the manly "weapons" of reason. He on the other hand, is infantile and effeminate, "the slave of impulse," at the mercy of his organs and passions. She compares him to a coquette, ever on the watch for conquest by way of exercising emotion, a creature that had never exercised reason.

[44] Boulton, "Editor's Introduction" to Burke, *A Philosophical Enquiry into the Origin of Our Ideas of the Sublime and the Beautiful* (Notre Dame, Ind., 1958), xv-cxxvii. Wollstonecraft refers on her first page to the fact that Burke's "literary abilities have raised him to notice in the state" and thereafter mentions or quotes the *Enquiry* throughout, 2, 5, 6, 10, 11, 13, 28, 42-43, 76-77, 78, 98, 111-14, 116, 117, 119, 120, 121, 122, 131, 136-37, 140-41, 150, 152-53.

[45] Ronald Paulson, *Representations of Revolution, 1789-1820* (New Haven, Conn., 1983), 81; Wollstonecraft, *A Vindication of the Rights of Men*, 2, 5-6, 136-37, 140, 141, 145.

[46] Godwin, *Memoirs*, 57-62; Boulton, *Language of Politics*, cxiv-cxvi; Wollstonecraft, *A Vindication of the Rights of Men*, 90.

[47] Wollstonecraft, *A Vindication of the Rights of Men*, 113, 112; see Paulson, *Representations of Revolution*, 79-87.

[48] Wollstonecraft, *Vindication of the Rights of Woman* (New York, 1975 [1792]), 173-91 and *passim*. In that book she does not refer to Burke by name although she does refer to his views of women, for example, "libertine notions of beauty," 83. See, too, 288.

He is, then, an illustration of the rich she describes on the next page who, because they "supinely exist without exercising mind or body, have ceased to be men." Wollstonecraft argues for a course of action which will "unfold the mind, and inspire a manly spirit of independence."[49] Her use of "manly" here and throughout this book is the same as the Commonwealthman's usage, manifest, say, in Burgh's *Political Disquisitions*; but is also represents Wollstonecraft's extension to women of the principles of true Whiggery and political radicalism.

This breakthrough was sponsored, as it were, by Wollstonecraft's Burgh-like characterizations of the English magnates Burke was defending. Her standards of healthy citizenship, the receipt of a good education, and the exertion of mind and body under the bracing condition of liberty in order to produce virtue, look back to the "manly" political, moral tradition epitomized by Price, Burgh, and Priestley. What she says in *A Vindication of the Rights of Men* in criticism of upper-class degeneracy is identical to the description in Burgh's *Political Disquisitions*, of "a people" (those men entrusted with power) "sliding into luxury and corruption." How, she asks, can "a man of rank and fortune" "discover that he is a man, when all his wants are instantly supplied, and invention is never sharpened by necessity? Will he labour, for everything valuable must be the fruit of laborious exertions, to attain knowledge and virtue . . . pampered by flattery . . . the senses meet allurements on every side. . . ." The significance for the manhood on which civic virtue depends, is clear.[50]

Prescription, the centerpiece of Burke's argument in his *Reflections*, Wollstonecraft writes, is "raised as an immortal boundary against innovation." The minds of the hereditarily rich "have been . . . warped by education. . . ."[51] Were politics to be opened to "talents," an old Commonwealth theme, "luxury and effeminacy would not introduce so much idiotism into the noble families which form one of the pillars of our state." The effect of such "restless idleness" is contagious, spreading "through the whole mass of society."[52] Already "the profligate of rank, [are] emasculated by hereditary effeminacy. . . ." The tendency can be reversed only in the way pointed to by Ferguson and heralded by Price in his 1789 peroration, welcoming the revolutions in America and France. "Such a glorious change," wrote Wollstonecraft in 1790, toward the rational values signified by the word "manly," can only be produced by greater liberty and by less inequality. Finally, and crucially, she states

[49] Wollstonecraft, *A Vindication of the Rights of Men*, 78, 16-17, 23, 24, 9, 56, 6, 4-5, 10-11, 28.

[50] *Ibid.*, 103-4.

[51] O'Gorman, *Burke*, 117-18; Brewer, "Rockingham, Burke and Whig Political Argument," *The Historical Journal*, 18 (1975), 188-201; 198-201; Wollstonecraft, *A Vindication of the Rights of Men*, 104.

[52] Wollstonecraft, *A Vindication of the Rights of Men*, 51-52. See, too, 96-97, 104-5.

in her first *Vindication* that the same effeminizing system, (isolating, pampering, and warping the childrearing of a group defined hereditarily) "has an equally pernicious effect on female morals."[53] *Vindication of the Rights of Woman* was essentially the exposition of this embryonic point.

Before showing that to have been the case it is necessary to note another, related aspect of Wollstonecraft's intellectual tradition. To the list of factors Wollstonecraft brought to her exposition of true Whiggery's moral vision for women in her *Vindication of the Rights of Woman* must be added her serious engagement (as reader, fiction writer, and reviewer of fiction) with the literature of sensibility. In fact she first approached Burke as a "literary" figure and took him on as an aesthetic theoretician whose sensibility could not be detached from his party politics. She criticizes him throughout for affecting sensibility rather than being genuinely a man of feeling. This criticism was a convention of her age. Her language in reviewing the sentimental novel, *Julia de Gramont* in the July 1789 issue of Johnson's *Analytical Review*, is identical in tone to the one she would use in condemning the sentimental and infantile coquette, Burke, in the following year. It is with heavy irony that she suggests the novel's artifice resembles a translation of "one of the *sublime* French romances" (her emphasis). She challenges its notion of "*inborn sensibility*," just as she will challenge "inbred" sensibility in *A Vindication of the Rights of Men*, only in the latter case she attributes it directly to one of the cult's chief theoretical sources, Burke's *Enquiry*, because she is writing a political pamphlet. In another review, she urged the replacement of "the *cant* of sensibility" (her emphasis) by the criterion of reason, just as she wishes "sentimental jargon" to be replaced in *A Vindication of the Rights of Men*. One can see in the reviews she was writing immediately before that book the further growth of the argument that would culminate in *Vindication of the Rights of Woman*. "Why do [female writers] poison the minds of their own sex, by strengthening a male prejudice that makes women systematically weak? We allude to the absurd fashion that prevails of making the heroine of a novel boast of a delicate constitution. . . ."[54] In the second *Vindication* Wollstonecraft will make her most thoroughgoing criticism of "the reveries of stupid novelists who,

---

[53] *Ibid.*, 97, 16-17, 47.
[54] Wollstonecraft, review of *Julia de Gramont, Analytical Review*, 1 (1788). 334; Wollstonecraft, *A Vindication of the Rights of Men*, 74 (and see 68); Wollstonecraft, review of *Edward and Harriet or the Happy Recovery: A Sentimental Novel, Analytical Review*, 1 (1788), 207; review of *A Simple Story* by Mrs. [Elizabeth] Inchbald, *Analytical Review*, 10 (1791), 102; for the still unsettled question of the attribution of Wollstonecraft's reviews, see Wardle, "Mary Wollstonecraft, *Analytical Reviewer*," *PMLA*, 62 (1947), 1000-9 and Derek Roper, "Mary Wollstonecraft's Reviews," *Notes and Queries* (Jan. 1958), 37-38.

knowing little of human nature, work up stale tales, and describe mer-
etricious scenes all retained in a sentimental jargon."[55]
One can see how Wollstonecraft's immersion in the literature of
sensibility (a subject on which she had been and continued to be
ambivalent[56]) prepared her for a broadening of the "effeminacy" theme
of Commonwealth thought. Other writers would also politicize the cult
of sensibility much more directly in the 1790s, as part of the Jacobin—
Anti-Jacobin debate. Jacobin novelists (of whom Wollstonecraft was one)
were also heirs and heiresses of the Commonwealth tradition. They were
accused by Anti-Jacobins of being led by Rousseau into over-cultivated
sensibility and into revolution: indeed, the former led to the latter. But
Jacobins, too, joined in criticizing the over-cultivation of sensibility in
girls and women.[57] In her second *Vindication* Wollstonecraft united that
Jacobin theme with its Commonwealth politics by way of the breakthrough she had made in the first *Vindication*, observing that half "the
sex [women] in its present infantine state, would pine for a Lovelace. . . ."[58]
Wollstonecraft begins *Vindication of the Rights of Woman* with the
same, typically Commonwealth account of the falsely refined, idle, and
unnatural rich, "weak artificial beings, raised above the common wants
and affections of their race," which she gave in her first *Vindication*.
They "spread corruption through the whole mass of society." The lower
classes become "obsequious slaves." Wealth, she reiterates, has "enervated" men to the extent that "something more soft than women is
sought for; till in Italy and Portugal, men attend the levees of equivocal
beings, to sigh for more than female languor." In Burgh's version they
turned to "sodomy." Wollstonecraft brings this traditional perspective
to the lives of middle-class women, in fact, to "the whole female sex,"
who are acculturated into "the same condition as the rich, for they are
born—I was speaking of a state of civilization with certain sexual privileges; and whilst they are gratuitously granted them, few will ever think
of works of supererogation." It is women who, under the influence of
an industrializing, consuming civilization, are now being required to

[55] Wollstonecraft, *Vindication of the Rights of Woman*, 305.
[56] G. J. Barker-Benfield, "Mary Wollstonecraft's Depression and Diagnosis: the Relation between Sensibility and Women's Susceptibility to Nervous Disorders," *Psycho-
history Review*, 13 (1985), 15-31.
[57] Barker-Benfield, "Approach and Avoidance: Women, the Cult of Sensibility and
the Man of Feeling, 1790-1800." Paper presented at the Annual Meeting of the American
Historical Association, Chicago, 1984; Marilyn Butler, *Jane Austen and the War of Ideas*
(Oxford, 1975); Gary Kelly, *The English Jacobin Novel* (Oxford, 1976). Jocelyn Harris
(*Samuel Richardson* [New York, 1986]) has demonstrated that Samuel Richardson was
a Commonwealthman in his political thought and that his novels are fraught with
Commonwealth values. This is widely true of the literature of sensibility.
[58] Wollstonecraft, *Vindication of the Rights of Woman*, 224.

perpetuate and spread "the seeds of false refinement, immorality, and vanity previously shed by the hereditarily great."[59]

Women, like rich, hereditarily defined men, are proscribed from work, from life, and corrupted by idleness and wealth. They are therefore susceptible "to enervating vices. . . ." It is those unnatural males' unnatural demand "for more than female languor" that also leads to the exaggerated effeminization of women.

To satisfy this genus of men, women are more systematically voluptuous, and though they may not carry their libertinism to the same height, yet their heartless intercourse with the sex, which they allow themselves, depraves both sexes, because the taste of men is vitiated; and women, of all classes, naturally square their behavior to gratify the taste by which they obtain pleasure and power.[60]

Men's turning themselves into sodomites and catamites in pandering to power had shown women the way. Wollstonecraft goes on to suggest that the female equivalent of such an abrogation of manhood is the loss of motherhood—of republican motherhood as it were.

Women becoming, consequently, weaker, in mind and body, than they ought to be, were one of the grand ends of their being taken into account, that of bearing and nursing children, have not sufficient strength to discharge the first duty of a mother; and sacrificing to lasciviousness the parental affection that enables instinct, either destroy the embryo in the womb, or cast it off when born.

In sum the Commonwealthmen's moral view of the ultimate degeneracy from the Harringtonian ideal of masculine civic consciousness is central to Wollstonecraft's explanation for the degeneracy of women.[61]

We have seen that in the Commonwealth view the release of civic virtue and patriotism required a turning away from private preoccupations to politics. Wollstonecraft applies this to women, by showing them to be imprisoned in privacy, in contrast to men who "have various employments which engage their attention, and give a character to the opening mind." You men, she writes, "*force* all women, by denying them civil and political rights to remain immured in their families . . ." (her emphasis).[62] In that famous 1789 sermon Price had warned that "we are

[59] *Ibid.*, 81, 141, 249; 147-48; 81.
[60] *Ibid.*, 144, 249.
[61] *Ibid.*, 249.
[62] *Ibid.*, 144, 131, 87. This is a persistent theme. The emphasis in the following example alludes to Burke's invidious view of women in his *Enquiry*, which she quoted in her previous book: "*littlenesses* would not degrade their character, if women were led to respect themselves, if political and moral subjects were opened to them . . ." (288). The passage goes on to "affirm" that such an opening would improve a woman's "domestic duties." Wollstonecraft wished to square an improvement of women's lot on the basis of commonwealthman's ideology—including its gender-shaped diagnosis of degeneracy— with the preservation of the commonwealthman's definition of "masculine virtues."

too apt to confine wisdom and virtue within the circle of our own acquaintance and party," including "our families."[63] Wollstonecraft has realized that if men have fallen off from civic virtue by their idleness, their preoccupation with "objects of sense," their refinement of feelings, and their abjuration of rights, in sum, by their effeminacy, how much more is that true of women, above all those novel-reading women, immersed in the cult of sensibility from womb to tomb? Thus, she writes, their "natural emotion" and "true dignity" are stifled, when such qualities "ought to sweeten the exercise of those severe duties, which educate a rational and mortal being for a nobler field of action." Women's effeminacy is the result of "prescription" just as privileged men's effeminacy is the result of the "principle of heredity. In her view women's feebleness "arises less from nature than from education."[64]

Wollstonecraft's solutions in this book are inspired by the Commonwealth tradition. "How can a being be virtuous if not free?" She can be virtuous only "if freedom strengthens her reason till she comprehends her duty." Her duty includes the rearing of children inculcated with notions of civic virtue and patriotism. The book's "patriotic" note draws from the earlier tradition and it continues into a widespread, ideological view of childrearing, that "republican motherhood" described by historians Mary Beth Norton, Linda Kerber, and Jane Rendall.[65]

But beyond motherhood, Wollstonecraft insists on women's economic "independence," "supporting themselves by their own industry." The cluster of values one can detect here and in her thoroughly Protestant emphasis on self-improvement for one's life-to-come focuses on the parable of the talents, which she quotes. If Pocock sees a link between the vision this parable embodies and the emergence of male civic consciousness, we can see how it would be linked to a new female consciousness. In sum, one finds throughout *Vindication of the Rights of Woman* a corollary of liberty for self-improvement that we saw in Ferguson's *History*, but now it is applied to women as well as men. "Happy is it when people have the cares of life to struggle with, for these struggles prevent their becoming a prey to enervating vices. . . ."[66]

Wollstonecraft asks her audience, if "the abstract rights of man will bear discussion and explanation, those of woman, by parity of reasoning will not shrink from the same test. . . ."[67] Explicitly recognizing the arbitrariness of characterizing "talents and virtues" as "masculine" and

---

[63] Price, "Discourse," 7. 8.

[64] Wollstonecraft, *Vindication of the Rights of Woman*, 81-82; 126 n. 2.

[65] *Ibid.*, 259, 86-87; Mary Beth Norton, *Liberty's Daughters: The Revolutionary Experience of American Women, 1750-1800* (Boston, 1980); Kerber, *Women of the Republic*; Jane Rendall, *The Origins of Modern Feminism: Women in Britain, France, and the United States* (Basingstoke, U.K., 1985), ch. 2.

[66] Wollstonecraft, *Vindication of the Rights of Woman*, 261, 262, 139, 144.

[67] *Ibid.*, 87.

"manly" in the context of a debate over the rights of man, Wollstonecraft, vindicating the same rights for woman, declares that men who call women "masculine" are inveighing,

against the imitation of manly virtues, or more properly, the attainment of those talents and virtues, the exercise of which ennobles the human character, and which raises females in the scale of animal being, when they are comprehensively termed mankind, all those who view them with a philosophic eye must, I should think, wish with me, that they may every day grow more masculine.[68]

That masculine standard is upheld in the Commonwealth tradition, as we have seen, by the middle class. "Abilities and virtues are absolutely necessary to raise men from the middle rank of life into notice, and the natural consequence is notorious—the middle rank contains the most virtue and abilities." Necessity stimulates improvement, including virtue: "Men have thus, in one station, at least, an opportunity of exerting themselves with dignity, and of rising by the exertions which really improve a rational creature. . . ." Women, she infers, should be exposed to such necessities too.[69] It is the application of this value that leads Wollstonecraft to introduce her *Vindication of the Rights of Woman* by addressing "my sex . . . in the middle class because they appear in the most natural state."[70]

We have seen that Commonwealthmen urged men to move out from the preoccupations of private life "to the higher engagements of public life," the "release of personal virtue through civic participation." It is in accordance with that principle that Wollstonecraft proposes women break out of their domestic "immuring," their preoccupation with sensual triflings, and the psychological and physical *sequelae*, including the "delicacy," "refinement," "leisure," "sensibility," "weakness," "folly," "sickly fancy," "enfeebled mind," and "affectation of languor," all of which Ferguson saw in feminized males. Such language permeates Wollstonecraft's second *Vindication*, assimilated therein to her criticism of women's acculturation into over-developed sensibility. This was in an England where, she writes, an obsession with "shopping," fashions, and emulation marked a new level of refined civilization among middle-class

---

[68] *Ibid.*, 80; see, too, 288. These passages may also be read as part of the lengthy eighteenth-century debate in England and its American colonies over the definition of manhood. Wollstonecraft's contrasting definition here includes "ardour in hunting, shooting and gambling" (80), which should be compared to Burgh's slighting those upper-class men who prefer "a cock-match, a horse-race, the preservation of the game, or the preservation of the court-places." Quoted in Hay, *Burgh*, 24. Directly relevant is Rhys Isaac, *The Transformation of Virginia, 1740-1790* (Chapel Hill, N.C., 1982).
[69] Wollstonecraft, *Vindication of the Rights of Woman*, 147-48. Compare Priestley, *Memoirs*, 49.
[70] Wollstonecraft, *Vindication of the Rights of Woman*, 81.

women, of easeful, materialist culture. It is precisely the view that is characteristic of eighteenth-century, Commonwealth jeremiads.[71] The alternative to this way of life, Wollstonecraft says, is for woman to be "an active citizen . . . discharge her civil duties," as well as those of a wife and mother. Thus free, she can exhibit virtue. To this end, women "ought to study politics, and thereby settle their benevolence on the broadest basis." Arguing the traditional case for women's education, that women have souls just as men do, Wollstonecraft also develops the Protestant notion of improvement in the typical language of Rational Dissent, "the perfectibility of human reason," the forming "of a being advancing gradually towards perfection . . ."; and she quotes Anna Laetitia Barbauld to make this point. This also illustrates that Puritan element in the origins of civic consciousness, picked out by Pocock, a "millennial expectation serv[ing] as a framework in which to present schemes of rational optimism and rational explanation. . . ." One finds this typical view in Burgh's *Thoughts on Education*.[72]

It is only by realizing that Wollstonecraft's intention in her most well-known and revolutionary book is to extend the political values of the eighteenth-century Commonwealthman to woman that one can appreciate the value of her consideration of a "standing army." Based upon the Burghian effeminacy argument, Wollstonecraft's analogy between such soldiers' idle lives and that of women is her own. Secondly, like her Commonwealthmen colleagues, Wollstonecraft distinguishes between, on the one hand, the dynastic wars of greedy, overweening princes and corrupt, imperialistic governments and, on the other, wars necessary for defense. But it is consistent with her understanding of those virtues arbitrarily termed "masculine" that in such a "justifiable war" where "virtue can show its face and ripen amidst the rigours which purify the air on the mountain's top . . . the true heroism of antiquity might again animate female bosoms." Such invocations of ancient virtue was a commonplace of Commonwealth thinking. One may interpret Wollstonecraft here to be reaching back to the civic consciousness men had claimed as a *populo armato*. Women, she suggests, should have "the power to take the field and march and counter march like soldiers or wrangle in the senate to keep their faculties from rusting."[73]

Wollstonecraft's account of the corruption of British politics ("multiplying dependents and contriving taxes which grind the poor to pamper the rich"), using a war as "a lucky turn-up of patronage for the minister, whose chief merit is keeping himself in place," must also be explained as her self-conscious adherence to this reform tradition. So too is the

---

[71] *Ibid.*, 260, 170.
[72] *Ibid.*, 259, 261, 141, 143; Pocock, *Machiavellian Moment*, 404; Burgh, *Thoughts on Education*, 11.
[73] Wollstonecraft, *Vindication of the Rights of Woman*, 97, 105-6; 258-60.

context within which she frames her "hint . . . that women ought to have representatives" in Parliament, "instead of being arbitrarily governed without having any direct share allowed them in the deliberations of government." She laments "that women of a superior cast have not a road open by which they can pursue more extensive plans of usefulness and independence."[74] The body of thought she drew from, itself radicalized under the impact of the defeat of the Parliamentary campaign on behalf of the political rights of Dissenters and the French Revolution, was the true Whig, Pricean assault on the unrepresentative distribution of Parliamentary seats and franchise. Wollstonecraft writes:

> But as the whole system of representation is now, in this country, only a convenient handle for despotism, they [women] need not complain, for they are as well represented as a numerous class of hard-working mechanics, who pay for the support of royalty when they can scarcely stop their children's mouths with bread.[75]

Wollstonecraft's unmistakable call for a standard of political virtue common to both sexes was lost in the 1790s. Propertyless men came to claim citizenship on the basis simply of their physiology: Sheffield petitioners to Parliament in 1793 argued "though they may not be free holders, they *are men*, and do not consider themselves fairly used in being excluded from the rights of citizens" (emphasis in original).[76] By then this had been part of Commonwealth thought for twenty years. It seems clear that women's writings of all kinds, private correspondence through novels, as well as the pamphlets I have mentioned, together with a host of other political activities, from the salons to the streets, can be considered part of the "alternative structure of politics" under the eighteenth-century condition that the great mass of people were unenfranchised. But at the crucial, tavern level of this alternative structure, the culture was powerfully, self-consciously male, responding *en masse* to the insistently dramatized sexual style of Wilkes, a "belligerent scourge," "a wit, a rake and a man of extraordinary boldness," a member of the Hell-Fire Club and author of *The Essay on Woman*.[77] In Wollstonecraft's

[74] *Ibid.*, 259-60, and see *A Vindication of the Rights of Men*, 43. Fox may have been referring to these passages in a 1797 Parliamentary speech. See Karl von den Steinen, "The Discovery of Women in Eighteenth-Century Political Life," Barbara Kanner, ed., *The Women of England, From Anglo-Saxon Times to the Present: Interpretive Bibliographical Essays* (Hamden, Conn., 1979), 229-58; 242.

[75] Wollstonecraft, *Vindication of the Rights of Woman*, 260.

[76] The Sheffield petitioners quoted in Cone, "English Reform Ideas During the French Revolution," *Social Science Quarterly*, 27 (1946-47), 368-84; 380; for their political circumstances, see E. P. Thompson, *The Making of the English Working Class*, (New York, 1963) 149-52.

[77] Brewer, "Commercialization of Politics"; Barker-Benfield, "Approach and Avoidance." For the appeal of Wilkes's sexual style, see Brewer, *Party Ideology and Popular Politics at the Accession of George III* (Cambridge, 1976), 171 and ch. 9. *passim*.

conception Wilkes, and, presumably, his followers, "were always men in company of women," when she would have it that both sexes be capable of laying aside sexuality, as it were, "excepting with a lover," in order to be "agreeable and rational companions."[78]

Price, Burgh, and other Dissenters wished to separate reform from Wilkes's or Fox's style of masculinity. Of course, however modified their alternative style, it did not encompass the single standard of behavior and psychology (let alone politics) which Wollstonecraft came to envisage, any more than the archetypal Rousseau did. Thus Price addressed his "brethren" reformers, when he took up this issue in his famous 1789 "Discourse":

brethren, while we shew our patriotic zeal, let us take care not to disgrace the cause of patriotism, by any licentious or immoral conduct—Oh! how earnestly do I wish that all who profess zeal in this cause, were as distinguished by the purity of their morals, as some of them were by their abilities. . . . Oh that I could see in men who oppose tyranny in the state, a disdain of low passions in themselves.[79]

Price's own personal style, unaffected, self-effacing, patient, paradoxically well-known for its "candour," "meekness," "benevolence," "kindness," "sincerity" and "simplicity"—Hester Chapone represented him as "Simplicius"—was in keeping with the kind of manhood advocated in the literature of sensibility as the "man of feeling," a rebuke to the hard rake epitomized by Lovelace as well as Wilkes.[80] One can see the connection between that last sentence of Price's, inferring the tyranny of low passions in men, and Wollstonecraft's extension of its value to men's relations with women. "Let not men, in the pride of power [over women], use the same arguments that tyrannic kings and venal ministers have used. . . ."[81]

That line of Wollstonecraft's recalls Abigail Adams's famous adjuration to her husband in 1776: "Remember all Men would be Tyrants if they could." John Adams and American revolutionaries generally were saturated in Commonwealth thought, and so too were their womenfolk. It is not surprising that one can detect the application of Commonwealth

---

[78] Wollstonecraft, *Vindication of the Rights of Woman*, 230 n. 99.

[79] Price, "Discourse," 35-36; for the general point see Hay, *Burgh*, 36.

[80] Priestley, "A Discourse on the Occasion of the Death of Dr. Price"; Hester Chapone, "On Affectation and Simplicity," *Miscellanies in Prose and Verse* (London, 1787), 20-23 (the relevant section is printed in Cone, *Torchbearer*, 57-58). See, too, Wollstonecraft's description in *Vindication of the Rights of Men*, 34-36, where she depicts Price as a saint, to be "reverenced," his "hands clasped, and eyes devoutly fixed, praying with all the simple energy of unaffected piety. . . ."

[81] Wollstonecraft, *Vindication of the Rights of Woman*, 132.

ideology to gender relations in the letters of such American women.[82] (Indeed the application of seventeenth-century natural rights theory to the relations of husbands and wives goes back at least to Mary Astell's *Some Reflections upon Marriage* of 1700, although she was a High Tory. She derived it from John Locke.[83]) And the greatest of female "Commonwealthmen," the transatlantic Catherine Sawbridge Macaulay, grasped the potential of that tradition for women in her last book, *Letters on Education*, published the same year as Wollstonecraft's *Vindication of the Rights of Men*. She did so with precisely the same argument that Wollstonecraft used, although it was far briefer than that of her younger contemporary and buried within a book devoted to other things.[84] In any case, on both sides of the Atlantic, "republican motherhood" came to be the counterpart of republican politics (as Burgh, typically, had believed it should be). Women, by definition and by prescription, remained locked in their particular sphere and identified with the home. The movement of middle-class women outward into civic life would be on that basis. Such a counterpart must be seen as one element in Wollstonecraft's thinking. Her broader attack on the belief that women were too weak physically and psychologically to sustain the world's full challenge was defeated for now but not forever.

State University of New York at Albany.

---

[82] Lyman Butterfield (ed.), *Adams Family Correspondence* (Cambridge, Mass., 1963), I, 370; Norton, *Liberty's Daughters*, 225-27, 242, 270; Nancy Woloch, *Women and the American Experience* (New York, 1986), 92, 94; Jay Fliegelman, *Prodigals and Pilgrims: The American Revolution against Patriarchal Authority* (New York, 1982), ch. 5.

[83] Mary Astell, *Some Reflections upon Marriage, occasion'd by the Duke and Dutchess of Mazarine's case; which is also considered With Additions* (New York, 1970 [1700]); Ruth Perry, *The Celebrated Mary Astell: An Early English Feminist* (Chicago, 1986), ch. 6.

[84] Macaulay, *Letters on Education: with Observations on Religious and Metaphysical Subjects* (New York, 1974 [1790]), 24-5, 49, 48, 61, 221. Intriguingly, John Wesley and James Otis also detected that Price's and the Commonwealthman argument (respectively) for political rights for men could be extended to women. Wesley, *Some Observations of Liberty Occasioned by a Late Tract*, "Appendix Three to Peace," *Price ... Selections*, 245-52; Otis quoted Kerber, *Women of the Republic*, 30-31.

XIII

The Eleventh Commandment: Sex and Spirit in Wollstonecraft and Malthus*

Mervyn Nicholson

Had Adeline read Malthus? I can't tell;
I wish she had: his book's the eleventh commandment,
Which says, "thou shalt not marry," unless *well*:
This he (as far as I can understand) meant:
'Tis not my purpose on his views to dwell,
Nor canvas what "so eminent a hand" meant;
But *certes* it conducts to lives ascetic,
Or turning marriage into arithmetic.

Byron, *Don Juan* 15: 297-304

Wollstonecraft and Malthus are virtual opposites: archetypal rebel, archetypal conservative. Malthus discharged his task of defending the status quo far more effectively than the more prestigious Burke. Burke gave conservatism its rhetoric, Malthus gave it its artillery. For Malthus produced scientific *proof* that altering social relations was not merely immoral, it assaulted the constitution of nature itself, thus retiring dubious arguments based on tradition to cosmetic operations. Malthus consciously assimilated his defense of the status quo to physics; and doing so, he pre-empted the language of freethinking intellectuals. "The eighteenth century took the model of Newtonian mechanism as its scientific paradigm; the Malthusian theory . . . was an attempt to apply this model to economics."[1] He saw the nucleus of his theory as an axiom, the equivalent in moral philosophy to Newton's in natural philosophy—and equally unanswerable. His argument was practical: based in statistics, it had an application

---

* This paper is dedicated to the memory of F. E. L. Priestley.

[1] Salim Rashid, "Malthus's *Essay on Population*: The Facts of 'Super-Growth' and the Rhetoric of Scientific Persuasion," *Journal of the History of Behavioral Sciences*, 23 (1987), 22-36.

in practical affairs, notably the notorious 1834 Poor Law.[2] No thinker has had more influence on society than Reverend Malthus, who proved, to speak plainly, that helping people was really hurting them, and hurting people was really helping them.

By contrast Wollstonecraft was a thoroughgoing rebel—a rebel not just intellectually, like her husband Godwin, but in her life too. She was in some ways a female Byron—passionate, charismatic, and bold in both life and writing; a lover of independence and travel; a supporter of revolution, democratic principles, and self-determination. She was publicly maligned—as Byron was—and for similar reasons. She died at 38, he at 36. Byron died a martyr—as did Wollstonecraft, a witness to the rights of women who died from childbirth, the death no man ever faces. Her son-in-law Shelley grasped this, for the martyrdom finales of *The Revolt of Islam* and *The Cenci*, with their sense of sexual as well as social martyrdom, imply a reference to her attempted suicide—and her actual death.[3]

Given such differences, it is striking that Wollstonecraft and Malthus should agree on two crucial points: sex and spirit. For both sex is dangerous morally—and socio-politically. Both, furthermore, view the aim of the Creator as the conversion of body to spirit: "The Holy purpose to which Malthus saw the principle of population directed . . . was nothing less than the transmutation of matter into mind/spirit."[4] Malthus responds to the idea of equality by focusing on sex and reconstituting spirit. Likewise Wollstonecraft's response to equality focuses on sex and reconstitutes spirit. In the history of ideas both display with unusual clarity the way thinkers deduce social principles from beliefs regarded as axioms embedded in the very constitution of nature itself. Hence their concerns are functions of a cosmology: a cosmology in crisis in the 1790s.

Keynes's sketch of Malthus is quite wrong in seeing him as a scientific enquirer in a logical positivist mode. Despite being a bureaucrat with very practical concerns—as "professor" he taught East India Company employees how to do their job (a fact Indians should ponder)—yet Malthus in no way abjured metaphysics. *Essay on Population* is metaphysical through and through; its "socio-political problem translates into a prob-

---

[2] For Malthus's consistency with laissez-faire see D. Bland, "Population and Liberalism 1770-1817," *JHI*, 34 (1973), 113-22; Rajani Kanth, *Political Economy and Laissez-Faire: Economics and Ideology in the Ricardian Era* (Totowa, 1986), 129-32, hereafter cited as "Kanth."

[3] Wollstonecraft's influence on Shelley intellectually—and as example—cannot be exaggerated; see Nathaniel Brown, *Sexuality and Feminism in Shelley* (Cambridge, 1979), 187-96. Malthus also affected Shelley—but negatively; see Roger Sales, *English Literature in History 1780-1830 Pastoral and Politics* (London, 1983). Godwin was the link connecting Malthus, Wollstonecraft, and Shelley.

[4] M. Harvey-Phillips, "Malthus' Theodicy: Intellectual Background of His Contribution to Political Economy," *History of Political Economy*, 16 (1984), 591-608. J. M. Pullen summarizes *Population*'s theology in *History of Political Economy*, 13 (1981), 39-54.

lem of theology."[5] Similarly Wollstonecraft's *Vindication of the Rights of Woman* is only partly on the "woman question."[6] Just as *Population* expands into an immense sociohistorical theory, so the *Vindication* is a wide-ranging study in the relations subsisting between God, nature, and society. The specific concerns of each, preserving oligarchy in one and female emancipation in the other, involve each in an immense revision of religious, historical, and social models.

The way society understands the divine is, inevitably, as a function of society itself—especially the *image* that society visualizes for God. This image is of more practical import than theological concepts, for religion is a social reality shared by educated and uneducated alike. The image of God as patriarch has had incalculable influence on Christianity; for many, this image is what Christianity is. Eighteenth-century attempts to reinvent God not only reconceptualized but revisualized Him. Before, in the *ancien régime* of the Authority-Subordinate hierarchy rooted in feudal relations, God is visualized as a bearded king on a throne in Heaven, a wise master in the mold of invincible aristocratic lord. "Subordination was indeed the very soul of order, and the Almighty as a god of order formed his earthly kingdom in a pattern of subordination."[7] But in mercantile and later manufacturing culture—in "the great transformation," as Polanyi put it—new ways to visualize God emerged in accord with the growing force of commercial market principles in society. Capitalist social relations implied a god more like an engineer—a god, in Newton's words, "very well skilled in mechanics"[8]—a practical artisan or merchant who must plan ahead for all contingencies ("Providence"): *not* like a "lord" of special privilege, an absolutist god who interferes in the mechanism of nature at whim. In short, according to Margaret Jacob, "The radical mind of the eighteenth century extracted from the Scientific Revolution a reverence for and understanding of nature that rendered the God of traditional Christianity superfluous."[9]

[5] Edmund Santurri, "Theodicy and Social Policy in Malthus' Thought," *JHI*, 43 (1982), 315-30.

[6] See Carol Kay, "Canon, Ideology, and Gender: Wollstonecraft's Critique of Adam Smith," *New Political Science*, 15 (Summer 1986), 63-76; cf. Elissa Guralnick: "the *Rights of Woman* is a radical political tract even before it is a radical feminist tract . . . the feminism [of] the *Rights of Woman* is merely a special instance of the political radicalism that animates the *Rights of Men*" ("Radical Politics in Wollstonecraft's *Vindication of the Rights of Woman*," *Studies in Burke and His Time*, 18 [1977], 155-66); it is also a *metaphysical* manifesto, unlike their writings on Scandinavia.

[7] Edmund S. Morgan, *The Puritan Family: Religion and Domestic Relations in Seventeenth-Century New England*, rev. ed. (New York, 1966).

[8] Quoted in Alexandre Koyré, *From the Closed World to the Infinite Universe* (Baltimore, 1957), 186.

[9] *The Radical Enlightenment: Pantheists, Freemasons and Republicans* (London 1981), 65; see chapter 1, "Science and the Philosophical Origins of the Radical Enlightenment," 29-64. "The experimental philosophy . . . was ultimately destructive of traditional theism . . . , a critical mentality that would screen all unverifiable affirmations about the supernatural from legitimate claims to rational belief" (Donald Meyer, *The Democratic Enlighten-

Commerce needs consistent systems of weights, measures, taxes—
equal, uniform, universal laws that apply everywhere to everyone, just as
gravity rules equally all physical bodies. "The commercial system has
long been undermining the distinction of ranks in society," laments Robert
Southey in 1807: "Mushrooms are every day starting up from the dunghill
of trade."[10] Thus the ancient belief in two levels of reality (upper/perfect
world vs. lower/sinful world) collapses. Newton showed that both the
aristocratic stars in the upper world above *and* the humble apple below
act by the same equalizing laws. In this he was showing what Galileo had
done when he revealed the sun to be made of the same mutable stuff as
changing, fallen earth: no special dispensation for the aristocrats of nature.
Commerce does not want a class of hereditary privilege: "idle people, who
produce nothing in return for their consumption," as Adam Smith puts
it in a passage Ricardo cites.[11] For the advanced thinker an absolute
monarch in heaven is no more desirable than an absolute monarch on
earth—not an *arbitrary* god exempted by special privilege from lawful or
predictable ways. A god who does miracles as *violations* of nature's law
can hardly be God. We need a working god, one who builds and maintains
the system of nature. Cleanthes crystallizes the updated god in Hume's
Dialogues Concerning Natural Religion—a god of the type expounded by
the deist Elihu in Blake's illustrations to *Job*. The necessity for a "reasonable" god in what Paine called the "age of reason" arises not merely for
intellectual reasons but for solid practical ones.

Out of this revisualization emerges a new model of the divine—first a
severe Roman-Republican deity with pure clean ethical lines and values
based on reason, on respect for the individual and property. A god of
freedom and equality must necessarily be impersonal—not preferring one
group above another: a detached god that embodies what Godwin calls
the "principle in the nature of human society by means of which everything seems to tend to its level, and to proceed in the most auspicious
way, *when least interfered with by the mode of regulation.*"[12] In the words
of the Anglican divine, Edmund Law (1745): "as we continually advance
in the study of God's *works*, we shall come to a proportionally better
understanding of his *word*." Burke articulates the assumption here in his
Thoughts on Scarcity: the "laws of commerce" are the "laws of nature"
and the "laws of nature" are the "laws of God."[13] The divine is mirrored

---

ment [New York, 1972], 44).

[10] Quoted in P. J. Corfield, "Class by Name and Number in Eighteenth-Century
Britain," *History*, 72 (1987), 38-61, 60-61.

[11] *Principles of Political Economy and Taxation*, ed. R. Hartwell (Harmondsworth,
1971), 238.

[12] William Godwin, *Political Justice*, ed. Isaac Kramnick (Harmondsworth, 1965),
765.

[13] *The Collected Works of Edmund Burke* (London, 1825), V, 151.

in the market place, which is mirrored in the array of material objects in space: God is deduced from nature, not nature from God.

This god is an impersonal stabilizer like the Invisible Hand that harmonizes the chaos of the market place; indeed he personifies the market and its automatic equilibrating action. The deity (embodying Necessity, space, or natural law) is a god that people of advanced ideas can accept—mostly merchants, artisans, and a dissenting middle class. Paine shows that Republican values and belief in nature as a mechanism conduce to an image of God as a sort of Cosmic Energy—a divinity utterly unlike the spiteful old man he lampoons in *The Age of Reason*, a god suited to "Gothic" feudalism or absolutist monarchy (the god Blake called the effluvium of priest and king). J. C. D. Clark shows how Paine rooted his arguments (from *Common Sense* to *The Age of Reason*) in religion, but a religion increasingly heterodox, establishment Christianity being identified with the existing social structure, especially aristocratic privilege.[14] Similarly, "Godwin's ideas on politics represent a secularized version of the English dissenting tradition in religion."[15]

The point of this re-vision of God for our authors is that the ancient split between fallen and unfallen nature, between a lower world of sin, mutability, and mortality on one hand, and an upper world of permanence and authority on the other, disappears. This split has dominated Christianity. Two levels of nature correspond to two kinds of people—nobles and commons. Social principles are woven into the fabric of the cosmos itself: in order to function, feudalism *had* to have a belief such as the split between upper (unfallen) nature and lower (fallen) nature, an order of grace and an order of sin.[16] The idea that all men are created equal, with liberty a natural right, expresses a need to equalize aristocrats and property-owners which in turn exerts an equalizing pressure on the two levels of reality. This impulse is not aimed at equality for all but at weakening the privilege of aristocracy over property in general: a "society which demanded formal equality but required substantive inequality of rights."[17] All men are created equal—but some are more equal than others. "The phrase 'the people' . . . was a synonym for the middle classes and those few among the laboring masses who could demonstrate loyalty

---

[14] *English Society 1688-1832: Ideology, Social Structure and Political Practice during the Ancien Regime* (Cambridge, 1985), 324-29.

[15] Richard Fenn, *The Spirit of Revolt* (Totowa, 1986), 165.

[16] This split always had political significance, even that of Being vs. Becoming in Plato; see Alban Winspear, *The Genesis of Plato's Thought*, 2nd ed. (New York, 1957). A subsidiary correspondence holds between males (= permanence/authority) and females (= mutability/subordination).

[17] C. B. Macpherson, *The Political Theory of Possessive Individualism* (London, 1962), 247. Locke *assumes* religion to be a means of bringing "the labouring class . . . to obedience by believing in divine rewards and punishments" (Macpherson, 226).

to 'middle-class' society, a loyalty indexed, initially, by property ownership" (Kanth, 139).

With the two levels of reality now discarded, this must necessarily be
the best possible world, not one blighted by human sin and God's wrath.
The doctrine of original sin also must be jettisoned, practically if not in
theory. Hume observes this shift in *Dialogues Concerning Natural Religion*: Philo notes that divines have lately changed their tune. The old vale
of tears has become the best of all possible worlds.

> They know how to change their style with the times. Formerly it was a most
> popular theological topic to maintain, that human life was vanity and misery,
> and to exaggerate all the ills and pains which are incident to men. But of late
> years, divines, we find, begin to retract this position, and maintain, though still
> with some hesitation, that there are more goods than evils, more pleasures than
> pains, even in this life. When religion stood entirely upon temper and education,
> it was thought proper to encourage melancholy; as indeed, *mankind never have
> recourse to superior powers so readily as in that disposition*. But as men have now
> learned to form principles, and to draw consequences, it is necessary to change
> the batteries, and to make use of such arguments as will endure, at least some
> scrutiny and examination.[18]

"Superior powers" implies aristocrats: those who extort obedience. The
change—proud optimism supplants humble submissiveness—marks a
shift in worldview. In creating one fitting its needs, society reconstitutes
parts of the earlier worldview.

What is striking about Malthus, writing in 1798, is just how far down
the road of revisualizing God—and thus of reinventing the relations between society and nature—he is. His language is that of the sophisticated
intellectuals who realize God is not, and so cannot be visualized as, a
feudal potentate in an upper-world kingdom. *Population* takes for granted
that God is a personification of natural law. Scripture, Malthus indicates,
is fine for academics. But to be serious about what God is like, we must
cast "our eyes to the book of nature, where *alone* we can read God *as
he is*" (my emphasis).[19] Whatever is, therefore, is right. An ingenuous
biographer says: "Malthus was drawn to this unorthodox conclusion by
the need to reconcile the cruel general law of population with his belief

---

[18] *Dialogues Concerning Natural Religion* (New York, 1949), 213, my emphasis; cf.
Marx on the French Revolution: its heroes "performed the task of their time in Roman
costume and with Roman phrases, the task of unchaining and setting up modern bourgeois
society. The first ones knocked the feudal basis to pieces and mowed off the feudal heads
which had grown on it ... a century earlier, Cromwell and the English people had
borrowed speech, passions and illusions from the Old Testament for their bourgeois
revolution. When the real aim had been achieved, when the bourgeois transformation of
English society had been accomplished, Locke supplanted Habakkuk" (*The Eighteenth
Brumaire of Louis Napoleon* [Moscow, 1935], 11.)

[19] Thomas Robert Malthus, *An Essay on Population*, ed. Philip Appleman (New York,
1977), 201 (this is from the 1803 edition).

in an omnipotent and loving God."[20] His fascination with the new god had, like everything in Malthus, a practical base: he "was obsessed with the heuristic power and efficacy of natural theology."[21] That is, natural theology is a validation device—a way of endowing authority. By identifying God's nature with nature, Malthus literally deifies his theorem: the population law not only has the unanswerable authority of number, it incarnates the deity. Blake satirizes this "deism" in his geometrizing deity Urizen: one begins to understand why Blake treats deism—historically a clear instance of "the liberating effect of rationalism"[22]—as essentially devil worship.

Within the orderly structure of nature, humans are driven by self-interest. Malthus euphemistically calls it self-love. He assimilates self-interest to Newtonian physics: "self-love," he declares, is "the moving principle of society" (Marx uses the same metaphor when he speaks of finding the "laws of motion" of capitalism). It "is to the established administration of property and to the apparently narrow principle of self-love that we are indebted for all the noblest exertions of human genius, all the finer and more delicate emotions of the soul, for everything, indeed, that distinguishes the civilized from the savage state" (Malthus, 98). Self-interest is not corrupt, as in Christianity—a manifestation of the original sin that infects the will. It is the very engine of civilization: *everything good*, says Malthus with bold hyperbole, stems from the operation of self-interest. To doubt the privilege of self-interest is literally to blaspheme. Malthus conceived *Population* as an assault weapon against Godwinian benevolence—a very thin shadow indeed compared to this all-creating self-interest.

Inevitably this view collides with the doctrine of original sin, which Malthus logically proceeds to redefine in a form he can use. "The original sin of man is the torpor and corruption of the chaotic matter in which he may be said to be born" (Malthus, 118). This is hardly intelligible: man is not born in chaotic matter but from the womb of woman. It is an absurd definition, for original sin is the corrupted will disseminated by birth from Adam. "Malthus constructed a theodicy without ever mentioning Jesus, perhaps because Christ saved men from sin, not laziness."[23] His views, R.

---

[20] Patricia James, *Population Malthus: His Life and Times* (London, 1979), 67; James portrays Malthus as a veritable saint of conscientious benevolence—genuflecting to Malthus being a scholarly subgenre, e.g., Santurri (n. 4 above); Ezra Talmor, *History of European Ideas*, 4 (1983), 121-22.

[21] A. M. C. Waterman, "Malthus as Theologian," J. Dupâquier (ed.), *Malthus Past and Present* (London, 1983), 195-201.

[22] Hilda L. Smith, *Reason's Disciples: Seventeenth-Century English Feminists* (Urbana, 1982), 53.

[23] D. L. LeMahieu, "Malthus and the Theology of Scarcity," *JHI*, 40 (1979), 467-74.

Remond says mildly, "ran counter to religious orthodoxy."[24] LeMahieu notes restrainedly that his "theological ruminations have not found a place in the anthologies of religious thought" (LeMahieu, 467). But his "ruminations" are not casual: Malthus is attaching his theory to the updated model of God that hitherto—in Paine or the Declaration of Independence—validated equality. He appropriates the language of Godwin and his type and turns it against them; he also neatly makes reason endorse attitudes otherwise indefensible. The theology provides theory, the law of population a necessary application.

Deleting the split between upper and lower worlds and viewing God as a deity who gave nature its present form marked a shift from the earlier cosmology in another way as well. In the earlier model this world is only partly a creation: it was *originally* made by God, but His perfect creation is damaged by sin. The result of human folly, its horrors are intelligible. Malthus's project is to *reconstitute* the ancient split between upper and lower, fallen and unfallen, worlds—but in new terms. Instead of an eternal upper world he installs "spirit"; instead of a lower world he gives us Newtonian inert "matter" that is by nature shapeless and lazy. Like other "conservative theorists," Malthus "repudiated the notion that all men were naturally equal."[25] The revised split articulated social relations better: property-owners—both commercial and aristocratic—vs. a new laboring class detached from traditional small-holding culture: laborers who need "checks," to borrow his power term. Malthus "work[s] with a simple view of society as divided into two classes: a small group controlling enough wealth to escape the general misery and the great mass of the laboring poor."[26] Thus his spirit/matter split corresponds to those with property and those without it. Original sin becomes propertylessness. His "theology of scarcity" (LeMahieu, 467) could hardly have less to do with Christianity. Malthus was asked to delete it and obligingly did so (not all, as often assumed; see Santurri). Having done its job of validating inequality, it became unnecessary. The Godwinian dragon turned out to be a harmless chameleon anyway. "The first national censuses, of 1801 and 1811 provided unassailable proof of a sharp upswing in population"—the *"Essay* was no longer seen as economic astrology but rather as a *conven-*

---

[24] R. Remond, "Malthus and Religion," J. Dupâquier (ed.), *Malthus Past and Present* (London, 1983), 157. Compare F. Rausky, "Malthusianism and the Secularization of Jewish Thought," *Malthus Past and Present*, 183-93. While Malthus's theology interests scholars, few note its obvious *tactical*—not theological—nature. A theology that proclaims scarcity as *primum mobile* is simply canonized political ideology.

[25] H. T. Dickinson, *Liberty and Property: Political Ideology in Eighteenth-Century Britain* (London, 1977), 302.

[26] Peter Bowler, "Malthus, Darwin, and the Concept of Struggle," *JHI*, 37 (1976), 631-50.

tional wisdom about the inevitability of famine unless population could be controlled."[27]

The shift in viewing spirit parallels "a great secular change in sexual attitudes and sexual behavior"[28]—a "great awakening of sexual concern."[29] "Generation, i.e. reproduction, was a central biological problem in the eighteenth century."[30] In a model where nature is a constructed object—not generated but engineered by a male God—sex is inherently problematic. Sex traditionally is part of fallen life and must be understood in that context. A consequence of sin, it displays the irrational impulse that human reason, damaged by the fall, is prey to. Sex is for reproduction not pleasure: "Augustine indicates that sex is a necessary evil, necessary, that is, for having children."[31] Reproduction, in turn, is part of the burden woman must bear because of Eve. Sex-as-reproduction is constituted as a subordination of women; indirectly of males as sinful beings. "Christianity portrayed women as the daughters of Eve and accordingly as lacking in rational control and sexually voracious. A woman's innate interest in sex was considered not so much a matter of her sensibly seeking pleasure as giving in to self-destructive urges."[32] Eve's disobedience is a revolt of appetite against reason, inferior against superior, a kind of insane attempt to reconstruct the cosmos. To visualize sin *per se* is to see it as sexuality; thus Milton personifies sin as a sexual female. Sexual desire is hard to control and an obvious link to the animals that Christianity declared inferior. Sex pushes the life cycle of bodily existence and is inseparable from the nauseating facts of body decay and death. The horror of sex in a worldview based on artificial creation, especially of the mechanical type crystallizing in the enlightenment, is epitomized by Yahoo sex and Gulliver's reaction to it.

Foucault attributed the shift to a new scientific approach to sex. The new science did not automatically encourage equality between the sexes. Thus the microscope, a major scientific invention, was used to prove the theory that women had no role in conception.[33] The idea that "the female

[27] Michael Bentley, *Politics without Democracy: Great Britain, 1815-1914: Perception and Preoccupation* (Oxford, 1984), 20; my emphasis.

[28] Alan MacFarlane, *Marriage and Love in England: Modes of Reproduction 1300-1840* (Oxford, 1986), 322.

[29] Michel Foucault, *The History of Sexuality*, tr. Robert Hurley (New York, 1973), 151. On the rise of "a science of sex" see G. Rousseau, "Nymphomania, Bienville and the Rise of Erotic Sensibility" and Roy Porter, "Mixed Feelings," both in P.-G. Boucé (ed.), *Sexuality in Eighteenth-Century Britain* (Manchester, 1982), 45-119, 159-75.

[30] L. J. Jordanova, "Natural Facts: A Historical Perspective on Science and Sexuality," Carol McCormain (ed.), *Nature, Culture, and Gender* (Cambridge, 1980), 42.

[31] Daniel Dombrowski, "St. Augustine and Abortion," *JHI*, 49 (1988), 151-56.

[32] Angus McLaren, *Reproductive Rituals: The Perception of Fertility in England from the Sixteenth to the Nineteenth Century* (London, 1984), 15.

[33] See Carolyn Merchant, *The Death of Nature: Women, Ecology, and the Scientific Revolution* (San Francisco, 1980), 153-63.

is no more than a material cause of the animal" was in some ways reinforced: "the female as an accidental necessity *of the species*, the norm of
which species is obviously male."[34] This view goes back to Aristotle; he
"associate[s] men with the rational part and women with the irrational
part of the soul."[35] Since women are constituted as less rational, hence
prone to superstition, "The ideology of progress which was so deeply
entrenched in Enlightenment thought meant that the growth of a humane,
rational, and civilized society could also be seen as a struggle between the
sexes, with men imposing their value systems on women in order to
facilitate social progress."[36] Hence the "scientific" approach to sexuality
was essentially an *objectifying* of women:

Despite the claims of some historians that it was only in the eighteenth century
that the pleasure principle emerged, we discovered that as a consequence of the
elaboration of more sophisticated models of reproduction in the later 1700s the
rights of women to sexual pleasure were not enhanced but eroded. Medical
scientists were, of course, not the only ones seeking in the eighteenth century to
redefine sex roles. [It was not] that doctors alone created the new ideal of female
sexual passivity (McLaren, 146).

In Ruth Perry's words, "By the eighteenth century, decent women were
no longer expected to enjoy their sexuality."[37] The new science encouraged
what Ellen Pollak calls "the myth of passive womanhood,"[38] in which
woman is not only a passive object of male appetite but a supply of
male appetite generally: a paradigm Wollstonecraft's *Vindication* attacks
continuously.

Historians observe "a bourgeois sexual mythos whose values differed
from those implicit within earlier sexual codes" (Pollak, 2), including
what John Gillis calls "the triumph of new conceptions of family and
sexual life among the upper classes."[39] "From the mid-eighteenth century

[34] Lynda Lange, "Woman is not a rational animal: On Aristotle's Biology of Reproduction," Sandra Harding and Merrill Histikka (eds.), *Discovering Reality: Feminist Perspectives on Epistemology, Metaphysics, Methodology and Philosophy of Science* (Boston, 1983)
1-15.
[35] Elizabeth Spelman, "Aristotle and Politicization of the Soul," in Sandra Harding
and Merrill Histikka, eds., 16-26.
[36] Jordanova, "Natural Facts," 42-69.
[37] Ruth Perry, *Women, Letters, and the Novel* (New York, 1980), 151; see 137-68.
[38] Ellen Pollak, *The Poetics of Sexual Myth: Gender and Ideology in the Verse of Swift
and Pope* (Chicago, 1985), 22. Mary Poovey's "Proper Lady" paradigm is similar. "Men
want women to be passionate, but, because they fear the consequences of this appetite,
they want to retain control over its expression." (*The Proper Lady and the Woman Writer:
Ideology as Style* [Chicago, 1984], 191-92.) See John O'Neal, "Eighteenth-Century Female
Protagonists and the Dialectics of Desire," *Eighteenth-Century Life*, 10:2 (1986), 87-97;
and John Price, "Patterns of Sexual Behaviour in Some Eighteenth-Century Novels" in
Boucé, ed. 159-75.
[39] John Gillis, *For Better, For Worse: British Marriages, 1600 to the Present* (New York,
1985), 135.

onward sexual politics became increasingly bitter as the propertied classes attempted to impose their standards on the rest of society."[40] Sex is to be a function of marriage, and marriage a function of the State, i.e. of established property relations, as expressed for instance by the 1753 Marriage Act, by Blackstone's *Commentaries* on the law (1758)—and by Malthus himself. "Thou shalt not marry—except well," in Byron's words. Hence Wollstonecraft's rejection of marriage had a *political* (not merely sexual-personal) meaning.

The new "sexual mythos" is not a "scientific" rationalizing, then, as Foucault argues. Rather, commercial relations based on individual choice come to supply the paradigm. In Stone's model ("affective individualism")[41] the individual is freed to love and marry his personal choice, whomever he likes. Free choice is the essence of what MacFarlane terms the "Malthusian marriage system": "Marriage was not automatic, it was a choice, the outcome of cost-benefit calculations for both men and women" (MacFarlane, 321; note the commerce metaphor). Randolph Trumbach contrasts "patriarchy" in the nobility with an innovative "domesticity": "a partial egalitarianism in familial relations."[42] But "domesticity" (paralleling Stone's "affective individualism") "increased patriarchal control over women and children since men believed they could not love what they did not own. But domesticity was based on the friendship of husband and wife, and friendship, as the feminist writers said, could exist only between equals" (Trumbach, 123).

Regarding sexuality in terms of ownership relations is the point: "A form of social relations which treated persons as objects."[43] Loving becomes a kind of owning, a commercial transaction based on "free" exchange. This sounds liberating: an open exchange chosen consciously by independent individuals. People are not bound by feudal ties of fealty/bondage but by free desire, just as one buys/sells according to free desire. But paradoxically female emancipation appears on the agenda of history just as most women are increasingly subordinated—subordinated for the same reason that weak competitors in commercial society lose even the

[40] John Gillis, "Married, but not Churched: Plebeian Sexual Relations and Marital Nonconformity in Eighteenth-Century Britain," *Eighteenth-Century Life*, 9:3 (1985), 31-42.

[41] See *The Family, Sex and Marriage in England 1500-1800* (New York, 1977), 221-69.

[42] Trumbach, *The Rise of the Egalitarian Family: Aristocratic Kinship and Domestic Relations in Eighteenth-Century England* (New York, 1978), 122. Surprising political implications flowed from these changes in "family relations" as Jay Fliegelman shows: "An older patriarchal family authority was giving way to a new parental ideal" including a more "equalitarian relationship with children" (*Prodigals and Pilgrims: The American Revolution against Patriarchal Authority 1750-1810* [New York, 1982], 11.)

[43] L. J. Jordanova, "Naturalizing the Family: Literature and the Bio-Medical Sciences in the Late Eighteenth-Century," *Languages of Nature: Critical Essays on Science and Literature*, ed. L. J. Jordanova (London, 1986), 112.

little they have when competing with large owners. In a "reasonable" cosmology—one in which reality consists of material objects in space—conviction necessarily grows that the aim of existence, as Hume's Philo implies, is happiness. Happiness is in essence personal self-gratification. Such gratification is inseparable from, indeed is a synonym for, the enjoying of property. "The pursuit of happiness" in practice is the pursuit of property. The dominance of commercial relations in society came to provide the paradigm of human relations generally, and specifically between the sexes, with women inevitably understood as object-commodities. "Women became commodities more than helpmates or independent economic actors."[44]

In this context sex pleasure is a mode of male gratification divorced from reproduction: "In the eighteenth century sexual continence became a predominantly female virtue" (Todd, 18). Such sexuality is fundamentally a *purchase*: one with property pays for what he buys. Sex is an exchange act, not a fertility act. It may include pleasure for both parties—as in a successful business deal—but not necessarily. Paralleling marriage with prostitution, Wollstonecraft attacked this paradigm: her "most striking innovation was to introduce Maria's sexuality into the discussion. . . . Wollstonecraft insisted that sexual relations should never be forced by duty"—duty meaning obligation contracted by marriage. "She emphasized motherhood over wifehood" (Smith, 192, 246): marriage is the means of reproduction and child-rearing, not the arena of contractual sex.

"Population" in Malthus's text is also a codeword for sex: the result (population) stands metonymically for its cause (sex). Thus his theory of population is also a rudimentary theory of sexuality. Jacques Solé opens his historical study of sex with Malthus: the exemplar of a "christianisme où la chastété devient la vertu sociale essentielle" and whose defense of the status quo was identical with the repression of sex—"la joie," as Solé says sarcastically, of "un célibat prolongé."[45] Malthus visualizes sex in revolutionary terms. "Population" is a force that by its very nature would shatter the world: a Blakean Orc whose yearning for self-gratification is so intense that nothing can stand against it, whatever barricades reason, religion, or authority can throw up in its path. "Marriage discipline was" not only "of great concern to the elite throughout the eighteenth century," but "From the 1790s, propertied classes listened with growing anxiety to the voices of those such as Tom Paine, who, himself illegally divorced before leaving England, praised the Native Americans for having 'no other ceremony than natural affection'" (Gillis, "Married," 33, 38). "The nexus of fears generated by the French Revolution . . . significantly shaped the

[44] Janet Todd, *Sensibility* (London, 1986), 17.
[45] Solé, *L'Amour en occident à l'époque moderne* (Brussels 1984), 23, 24.

contours of 'Victorian' sexuality."[46] Just as Blake's Orc unites sex appetite with revolutionary impulse and popular yearning for better life, so "population" consists of propertyless masses who own nothing but dangerous sexual—and illusory political—wishes. Only the severest counter forces, famine and epidemic, can check population's world-shattering power. Civilization thus *depends* on sexual repression (that is, the repression of the desire of those without property for better conditions). In this Malthus anticipates the oddly similar thinking of Freud, for whom the conflict between sex appetite and the repressive superego is the mechanism of civilization: in both, reason/control is to replace desire/appetite.[47] Law—property—must hold sway over those who own nothing but their reproductive apparatus.

"Given the natural tendency of population to increase faster than capital" in Malthus, "the only hope for real relief of poverty was a drastic reduction in the numbers of the poor" (Kanth, 52): *not*, as in Godwin, to alter property relations. The poor must curtail their proclivity for "reckless breeding," as J. Banks delicately puts it.[48] The laboring class can survive only by neutralizing itself as a sexual agent—metaphorically as an impulse to change reality. *Their* sex = insubordination: *our* sex = privilege of property. "Critical factors in promoting rapid demographic growth were the proletarianization of the mass of producers, peasants, and artisans and their integration into an extralocal commercial system." "Proletarianization was accompanied by a reduction in age of marriage" and "rising fertility."[49] Population increase resulted from social changes not caused by population at all: a byproduct of the same property relations Malthus was so anxious to deify as the inviolable construction of the cosmos. The Old Poor Law so detested by Malthus did not cause population increase—it did give modest support to the laboring class. Population was ascertained to be increasing only in Malthus's own time.[50] By the revolutionary 1790s famine and epidemic had weakened, hence the "de-

---

[46] Jeffrey Weeks, *Sex, Politics and Society: Regulation of Sexuality Since 1800* (London, 1981), 14.

[47] Freud assumes the same kind of cosmology as Malthus, one in which capitalist property relations and Newtonian physics are identified; see Richard Lichtman, *The Production of Desire* (New York, 1982), 211.

[48] J. Banks, *Victorian Values: Secularism and Size of Families* (London, 1981), 19.

[49] David Levine, *Essays on the Family and Historical Change* (New York, 1977), 146, 147. See also Nancy Birdsall, "Fertility and Economic Change in Eighteenth and Nineteenth Century Europe," *Population and Development Review*, 9 (1983), 111-23. By contrast "The choice for most wives during their teeming years, in pre-industrial England was an infant in the womb or at the breast. Since most women chose to have an infant at the breast, their fertility lagged well behind their fecundity" (Dorothy McLaren, "Marital Fertility and Lactation 1570-1720," Mary Prior [ed.], *Women in English Society 1500-1800* [London, 1985] 22-53).

[50] See James Huzel, "The Demographic Impact of the Old Poor Law: More Reflexions on Malthus," *Economic History Review*, 33 (1980), 367-81.

cline in mortality in the later eighteenth century."[51] "After about 1750 subsistence crises, no matter how severe . . . no longer produced major mortality crises in western and central Europe" due to "environmental and behavioral changes concomitant with economic growth and modernization," "improved nutritional and social conditions," and "effective quarantine measures instituted by the better organized governments of Europe."[52] "Human action . . . freed western Europe from plague in the later seventeenth century and early eighteenth century."[53]

Sex was as disturbing to Wollstonecraft as to Malthus. Wollstonecraft loved love: "Love is a want of my heart,"[54] but she saw that sexual love as currently practiced meant subjection for women. "A heavy emphasis in the *Vindication* lies in devaluing passionate love."[55] This devaluation informs the "Rights of Woman"—not because sex makes babies, the reason it worries Malthus—but because for men sex was co-extensive with the enjoyment of dominating. Since for women sex meant the role of masochistic arouser of male aggressiveness, sex gratification was identical with female enslavement. Woman's weakness was a precondition of men's sexual pleasure. Love became the exercise of male power, the cradle, so to speak, of tyranny: the training-medium, incitement, and occasion for male force, male greed. Female powerlessness was the inevitable concomitant of political tyranny—as Wollstonecraft never tires of pointing out. Sexual love was inherently *physically* dangerous to women. *Maria, or The Wrongs of Woman* "declares a woman's erotic rights": "the most important is her right not to submit to be disgusted by a brutal husband"; hence "much more of *Maria* is devoted to the indignities of the relations with men than to its ecstasies" (Blake, 104).

Thus for Wollstonecraft sex is dangerous not as anarchic desire, a willingness to rip up the fabric of society for momentary pleasure, as in Malthus. Existing sexual practice reproduces established power relations. The task of middle class women is self-neutralization in order to maximize gratification for their husbands, very much as in Veblen, where women are a mode of conspicuous consumption: a display of male ranking as power over objects. (Neutralizing sexuality, especially female sexuality, is central to Wollstonecraft's daughter's novel *Frankenstein*.) Both Woll-

---

[51] Andrew Appleby, "Famine, Mortality, and Epidemic Disease: A Comment," *Economic History Review*, 30 (1977), 508-12.

[52] J. D. Post, "Famine, Mortality, and Epidemic Disease in the Process of Modernization," *Economic History Review*, 29 (1976), 14-37.

[53] Paul Slack, "Disappearance of Plague," *Economic History Review*, 34 (1981), 469-76. In the 1800s hunger was common, starvation rare (D. J. Oddy, "Urban Famine," *Economic History Review*, 36:1 [Feb 1983], 68-86).

[54] Quoted in Ralph Wardle, *Mary Wollstonecraft* (Lawrence, 1951), 169. Her intense devotion to eros did not block her perception that love without equal rights/power was not love.

[55] Kathleen Blake, *Love and the Woman Question* (Brighton, 1983), 102, 104.

stonecraft and Malthus are negative about sex—but for opposite reasons. For one, sex is bad because it enforces the existing social structure—for the other, it is bad because it threatens that structure. The object of intense social anxiety, sex has become for both the enjoyment of power—but to Wollstonecraft such enjoyment is evil; to Malthus it is, for propertied men, the will of God. Whereas in Malthus sex as reproduction becomes, in effect, theft—stealing what one cannot buy—in Wollstonecraft it is a complex spiritual duty. Specific concerns for each—female emancipation in one, population in the other—require far-reaching changes in society. Malthus won, and subsequent social legislation, especially the 1834 Poor Law, reflect his program.

The overt argument of the *Vindication* is that women's relation to men is the same sort of relation as that between commons and aristocracy. Wollstonecraft argues exactly along the lines of Tom Paine, for whom the nobility were, in his phrase, the "no-ability"—a "fungus" on the parent branch of the society of workers.[56] Since all men are created equal, the hierarchic relation of king and commoner is obsolete, evil, socially corruptive in every way: the essence of tyranny for it infects all aspects of human life, including sexual and domestic life, as Wollstonecraft shows. She then takes this argument the next logical step: if commons and aristocrats are equal and a power-over relation based on coercion can no longer be legitimated—then neither can male tyranny and female peonization: a republic of equals with half the population essentially serfs, "like a creature of another species," as Jemima says in *Maria*.[57] As Astell complained a century before, "If all men are born free, how is it that all women are born slaves?"[58]

The Rights of Woman remains vital and contemporary. But in one area it is very un-modern: its obsession with God. The appeal to a Supreme Being *defines* Wollstonecraft's discourse. The preoccupation with God's attributes is no idiosyncrasy: as in Malthus, God makes the argument. Her God is not the male autocrat tradition venerates, an index of female enslavement.[59] "God himself cannot be a tyrant . . . he must be rational and virtuous, so that his character may serve as a foundation for human morality" (Guralnick, 163). "The Deity," her term for God, created in order to increase happiness. What makes one happy is virtue: virtue = happiness; and happiness = fulfilling God's will. But virtue in turn requires reason, for reason shows what virtue is and how to pursue it—hence the obsession of the *Vindication* with education. Wollstonecraft

[56] Thomas Paine, *Essential Works*, ed. S. Hook (New York, 1969), 183, 181.

[57] *Maria, or The Wrongs of Woman* (New York, 1975), 83. Even the rational Bentham—an early advocate of homosexual rights—resisted this reasoned view (Douglas Long, *Bentham on Liberty* [Toronto, 1977], 167; J. S. Mill was of course more receptive).

[58] See Ruth Perry, *Women*, 22.

[59] Feminists grasped this point early; see Naomi Goldberg, *Changing of the Gods: Feminism and the End of Patriarchal Religion* (Boston, 1979).

insists "that education rather than nature was responsible for perceived differences of intellect between the sexes."[60] Education is not merely acquiring facts, it is an expansion of consciousness that enables one to act authentically; it includes sublime emotion. This world is constituted as the locale of virtue-stimulating struggle, not of individual self-gratification. The aim is to achieve growth, not property.

Wollstonecraft goes further. Reason, virtue, and education prepare us for *immortality*, for changing body to spirit where there is no marrying or giving in marriage. The design of creation is not happiness *qua* enjoying property but happiness as self-transformation. But distinction of spirit by sex is nonsensical, Rousseau and others notwithstanding. Like reason, the soul is without sex. To say "men and women are ontologically similar"[61] is not quite accurate: they are ontologically identical. Hence sex is subordinate to life's real function, education—expanding consciousness to prepare for immortality, freedom from the body and its sexual itches and urges. Thus sex as vehicle for arbitrary power violates not only the personal integrity of women, like rape, but in fact denies God, immortality, and so the meaningfulness of existence and the very rationality now seen to constitute reality. Sex as currently practiced = personal gratification = power over others = a violation of equality before God: a metaphysical crime.

The purpose of sex is not personal gratification (= male owning power) but to bond husband and wife as matrix for child-rearing, for literally the creation of immortal spirits.[62] As *spirits* we are unsexed; in the afterlife we are not sexual beings generating more sexual beings. Since we are here to train for the next life our spirit-identity requires equalizing men and women in *this* life. Wollstonecraft's argument thus (1) requires God's existence, (2) makes spirit supreme over body, (3) subordinates this life to the next, hence (4) establishing the necessity of female emancipation, which begins with (5) education for women and (6) devaluing sexuality as a mode of self-gratification and marriage *qua* property-ownership. We need equality and emancipation in order to conform with the Deity's will.[63] Thus while pietistic "religion was the basis of women's education" in her time,[64] a heterodox religion was the basis of her emancipatory

---

[60] Sara Mendelson, *The Mental Web of Stuart Women* (Brighton, 1987), 191.

[61] Josephine Donovon, *Feminist Theory: Intellectual Traditions of American Feminism* (New York, 1987), 8.

[62] For actual child-rearing in the age (not Wollstonecraft's proposals), see Alice Miller, *For Your Own Good: Social Roots of Violence in Cruelty to Children*, tr. H. Hannum (New York, 1983), 3-91.

[63] On the links of Deism and female emancipation see Harrison 86-87, 120-21, and Donovon, *Feminist Theory* 1-30; also Smith (n. 20) and Katherine Rogers, *Feminism in Eighteenth-Century England* (Brighton, 1982).

[64] Lynne Agress, *The Feminine Irony: Women on Women in Early Nineteenth-Century English Literature* (Cranbury, 1978), 71.

program—just as natural theology validated Malthus's defense of existing property relations.

A Vindication's God is very anthropomorphic: He loves justice, freedom to develop as an individual, equality; He wants us to transform ourselves to better beings, to multiply happiness. In Wollstonecraft's book on Sweden, God is a mind-expanding spiritual energy manifest in sublime nature (she "experienced ecstatic religious feelings").[65] Her anthropomorphic God modulates into a God of personal spiritual transformation. Wollstonecraft understands the new up-to-date model of God that advanced, educated people of the same class as Malthus is appealing to could believe in. But she *skips* the phase of God conceived as Malthus does, personification of implacable physical laws. Wollstonecraft needs God because God needs the emancipation of women, just as God, in Malthus— the inexorable law of nature—needs poor people to be abandoned to poverty. If you believe in God, Wollstonecraft argues, then you must also believe in educating women and transformating society: she enlists spirit in her sexual argument. They both assume Paley's view: "a future state alone rectifies all disorders."[66]

Wollstonecraft's God is not as highly evolved (or devolved) on the road to personifying natural law as God emphatically is in Malthus. Her God is moving in a very different direction. God in Malthus is really a numeric formula, inscrutable exactly as natural data are inscrutable—one cannot imagine praying to it. "Man suffered; some starved, but overall there was an economy of evil as just and compensatory as the Law of supply and demand" (LeMahieu, 468). But Wollstonecraft's God demands struggle against tyranny and irrationality to reform society. Her son-in-law Shelley crystallizes her religious thinking in believing that the soul is immortal, that the deity is a personal power that enters one's life as moments of ecstatic or expanded consciousness, and that the aim of this power is the renovation of society. The spirit is not just an impersonal force but the will to know more and live better, an energy in one's personal

---

[65] Emily Sunstein, *A Different Face: The Life of Mary Wollstonecraft* (New York, 1975), 251.

[66] *The Works of William Paley* (London, 1825) I, 282. Significantly, Paley was a major popularizer of Malthus. His sermon "Reasons for Contentment addressed to the Laboring Part of the British Public" was published in 1792: the year of *Vindication* and Paine's *Rights of Man*, part 2. Paley's natural theology, instead of implying reform, coheres with the defense of the status quo (as the textbook use of *Natural Theology* [1802] at university in the nineteenth-century indicates) and even with Malthus's repressive theology. J. C. D. Clark analyzes Paley's political use of natural theology (80); see also Thomas Schofield, "Conservative Political Thought in Britain in Response to the French Revolution" (*Historical Journal*, 29 [1986], 601-22), 605-7. The nexus of religion, natural philosophy, and defending established social relations pivots on worldview, for it is worldview that connects and integrates disparate beliefs, disciplines, and practices.

life.[67] The next step logically from Malthus's deism is atheism; in Woll-stonecraft it is a Romantic god like the "presence" of Wordsworth's *Tintern Abbey* or "Eternity" in Shelley's *Adonais*.

By rigorous deduction from her image of God, Wollstonecraft reaches a concept of female emancipation hardly realized in nearly 200 years. But her sexual argument hinges on a spiritual one: immortality demands a certain kind of sexual life now. General approval met the *Vindication* in 1792;[68] but by the time of *Population* (1798), things had changed: "The shift in the treatment of feminist works between 1792 and 1798 indicates the continuing approbation of improved education for women and the solidifying opposition to works that seemed to threaten the established relations between the sexes": most disturbing of all "was the attack on the sexual character of women. . . . Men who were glad to agree that mind is of no sex were not pleased to acknowledge that manners [i.e., power] should be of no sex." (Janes, 302). Equalizing thought became anathema. The years 1792-98 mark the end of the optimistic phase of the mechanist equilibrating cosmology and the advent of a reactionary phase of the same worldview. Natural theology now justifies the existing social structure; Malthus's economics rationalized—so as to irritate Ricardo—the unproductive consumption built into that structure ("his unrelenting defence of the landlord class . . . still causes one to wince today").[69] Unlike Ricardo, Malthus defends hereditary landowners while showing their essential identity of interest with commercial capital against a common, propertyless, potentially revolutionary enemy.

An unbroken chain of deductions leads Wollstonecraft from her image of God to the emancipation of women. Similar deductive reasoning constitutes Malthus's thesis, again arguing from a certain kind of God. In Malthus population increase naturally exceeds increases in the food supply. Food is limited not by labor but by the soil fertility: nature (deified as the will of God) forbids emancipation/equality. The incompatibility of the power to reproduce, on one hand, and the power to produce, on the other, is conveyed as a difference between geometric and arithmetic rates of increase. Harelike, population will always outstrip the tortoise-like increase of food. The argument reduces to laws of arithmetic. "There is

---

[67] Wollstonecraft's religion—very differed from her husband's—arose from a history of female spirituality. Astell's feminism was religious. "Instead of being Eves, as in former times, symbols of sexuality and opacity through their crucial part in the myth of the fall, [women] grew into Protestant virgins, the consciences of society" (Todd 18). In the resulting "sexualization of religion," "Men become the evil sexual force in culture and women become suffering servants, guardians and emblems" (Rita Goldberg, *Sex and Enlightenment: Women in Richardson and Diderot* [New York, 1984], 205).

[68] R. M. Janes, "On the Reception of Wollstonecraft's *Vindication*," *JHI*, 39 (1978), 293-302; America reacted negatively; see Marcelle Thiébaux, "Wollstonecraft in Federalist America," Donald Reiman (ed.), *Evidence of Imagination* (New York, 1978), 190-205.

[69] Alexander Field, "Malthus's Methodological and Macroeconomic Thought," *History of European Ideas*, 4 (1983), 135-49.

so little ground for assuming a geometrical progression on the one hand, an arithmetical one on the other, that one may well ask whether this genial trick is not at bottom a mathematical expression of nature's superior creative power as against man's."[70] "The principles were stated in a manner which made them incapable of clear proof or refutation, once the initial assumptions were granted."[71] The numbers *subordinate* people: they signify power relations and are not a demographic tool but a validation device. They assimilate Malthus to his model Newton, whose numbers brooked no argument, who found a determining simplicity beneath all apparent complications. This Newtonian imperative explains why Malthus insists his "law" of population is not just demographic description— it determines *all* human phenomena: a fixed point in moral philosophy like Descartes's *cogito*. As the Newton of moral philosophy Malthus deduces everything from his Law, even civilization itself.

The chief reason why the Law of population is so sweeping in scope is that, while conclusively limiting human reproduction, it evacuates human desire for better conditions. The most the majority can ever hope for, Malthus explains, is the state of laborers in *pre*-revolution America. It is no accident that Malthus dates a maximum condition to a period before revolution. Revolutionary desire is precisely what Malthus's *Population* is designed to abort. In a very real sense the *Essay* is not about demography at all: its *raison d'être* is to rule out social changes of the type Godwin promoted, proving them a violation of the physical construction of nature and the will of the Deity incarnate in that construction: metaphysical crime. The role of desire is self-neutralization; in Wollstonecraft it is to transform society. For her, converting matter to spirit *subverts* established power relations; for Malthus, it deifies those relations.

But Malthus's attack is too effective: it generates serious religious, ethical, even metaphysical problems. What sort of God commands humans to be fruitful and multiply—yet arranges nature as a doublebind, implanting urges for sex while penalizing (with death, poverty, and degradation) those who involuntarily come into being because of this built-in "passion between the sexes"? Why did God not decrease sex appetite or provide a more enharmonic relation between production and reproduction? Malthus answers: this system converts matter to spirit. The harder things are, the better the system works: by this reasoning, the worse things are, the better—and the more God likes it. The God that emerges is hardly distinguishable from a monster that enjoys his creatures' suffering: the God Blake, Shelley, and Byron satirize. It is also the kind of God who presides in the horrifying religious structures of the Gothic fiction contem-

[70] Louis Dumont, *From Mandeville to Marx: Genesis and Triumph of Economic Ideology* (Chicago, 1977), 172-73.

[71] Frederick Rosen, "The Principle of Population as Political Theory: Godwin's 'Of Population' and the Malthusian Controversy," *JHI*, 31 (1970), 33-48.

porary with Malthus: imaginative illustration of the religious crisis Malthus himself implies.

To solve the problem he creates for himself, Malthus argues the purpose of creation to be the conversion of matter to spirit. This trendy notion that God wants humans to cease being material and become mind, is an ideological rabbit pulled out of a metaphysical hat. Its absurdity is plain when translated from theory to actual practice. Thus: restraining sex is the grand design of creation. Conversely, the having of children by rich people advances the conversion of matter to mind that God designs. The rich are more spiritually evolved than the poor. Property is index of spirit: the propertied may indulge *ad libitem*. "The profane and secular have become, in a word, sacred."[72] The reward for property—for spirit—is personal gratification, especially sex. Again, ideology is inscribed in the metaphysics of creation. Unlike modern Malthusians, Malthus hated contraception,[73] as the fifth edition makes clear (Banks, 19-20). Birth control is worse than the famine, plague, and war that population causes and that he imagines with intense rhetorical relish (see the apocalyptic fantasia on Famine [Malthus, 57]). Contraception would short-circuit the power relations in society (no doubt one reason why it was resisted so intensely), allowing people to have sex *and* democratized property relations.

Interestingly Byron made Malthus a significant target in *Don Juan*; he appears as one more figure in its huge cast. For Byron Malthus is, like all pious, self-righteous people in his work, a hypocrite: indeed, a byword for hypocrisy. "Malthus does the thing 'gainst which he writes" (12:160). *Preaching* frustration to check population, he *practices* sexual intercourse so avidly as to produce numerous offspring. This attack seems lame. After all, Malthus did *not* say Do Not Have Children, but Do Not Have Children You Can't Afford: " 'Thou shalt not marry,' unless *well*"—as Byron put it, "the eleventh commandment," recognizing Malthus's ideological importance. This harmless-sounding advice is in fact the heart of his satire. For Malthus imposes frustration on the majority, and extends license to the rich. His commonsense advice not to have children you can't afford is really a shocking, mercenary vulgarity—essentially prostitution, where sex, if you can pay, is always available. "Malthus preferred vice to babies" (James, 124). Property-ownership licenses sex gratification, and spirit identity.

The apparatus about God in Malthus is an elaborate blind, a red herring to distract attention from the injustice of existing conditions. Belief is still vital—but as what I called a *validation device*, a way to valorize an argument or social practice. Malthus needs God to rationalize

---

[72] Rita Goldberg, *Sex and Enlightenment: Women in Richardson and Diderot* (New York, 1984), 205.

[73] James, 388-98; see Charles Kegel, "William Cobbett and Malthusianism," *JHI*, 19 (1958), 348-62.

a ghastly system. In Wollstonecraft God is also a validation device, a means to sustain the argument: He is needed to make necessary the educating and freeing of women. Malthus's God is deconstructible—a God whose purpose is to paper over the suffering that so obviously fascinated Malthus. Two Gods emerge: his *justifies* existing power relations, hers *struggles against* such relations. Today his God is extinct. But hers anticipates liberation theology, a God whose "preferential option" is for the oppressed. The only God visible in *The Wrongs of Woman* is the power to endure, "the will to struggle" that typified Wollstonecraft,[74] to struggle on even in apparently hopeless conditions: a conviction that, one day, things *will* be better.

Cariboo University College.

---

[74] Moira Ferguson and Janet Todd, *Mary Wollstonecraft* (Boston, 1984), 116. *Maria or The Wrongs of Woman* shows Wollstonecraft's growing awareness that "the oppression of women is related in theory as well as in practice to the oppression of other groups" (Spelman, 18): the underside of Malthus's equations: spirit = property-ownership = divine authority (= males); whereas women = objects = inert matter = the torpor of original sin = sexual reproduction (owned by males) = object of repression = laboring class.

PART THREE

POLITICS AND ECONOMICS OF RANK

XIV

SOCIAL EQUALITARIANISM IN A TUDOR CRISIS

By W. Gordon Zeeveld

I

Intellectual historians have quite properly emphasized the general acceptance in the sixteenth century of the classical concept of a fixed social order as a basis for Tudor authoritarianism;[1] but it is equally true that this order was being inevitably and permanently destroyed even while Tudor theorists praised with one voice the traditional principle of "degree." The event had outrun theory. Yet if the historian of ideas is to account for the theories of social leveling of the Puritan Revolution, he must be prepared to find equalitarian notions in formulation at least in the sixteenth century.[2]

Troeltsch understood the importance of the problem of equality in the development of European society,[3] though his influence may be the reason for its being overlooked in sixteenth-century England. Since Troeltsch, it has been customary to associate the first burgeoning of the democratic spirit with socially radical movements of the Reformation such as the Peasants' War and the rising of the Anabaptists on the continent and the Lollard movement in England, in which the rebels were the spokesmen for democracy.

[1] See J. W. Allen, *A History of Political Thought in the Sixteenth Century* (London, 1928), Part II, ch. iii, and James E. Phillips's elaborate citations of the idea in *The State in Shakespeare's Greek and Roman Plays* (New York, 1940), 76–92. Its *locus classicus* is Ulysses' speech on degree (*Troilus and Cressida*, I. iii. 75–137).

J. H. Hanford has traced the idea to Plato in "A Platonic Passage in 'Troilus and Cressida,'" *Studies in Philology*, XIII (April, 1916), 105, but it is, of course, a far more general inheritance. Aristotle found the principle of degree in a law of nature (*Politics*, II, 2; VII, 8, 9); Aquinas in the order of the universe as originally established by God (*On the Governance of Rulers*, ch. xiii).

[2] G. P. Gooch (*English Democratic Ideas in the Seventeenth Century*, ed. Laski, Cambridge, 1927) passes over the sixteenth century with a brief mention of More and Ponet. So far as I know, the only discussion of the subject is by Professor Helen C. White in an important recent book, *Social Criticism in Popular Religious Literature of the Sixteenth Century* (New York, 1944), with which this paper will be found to be in substantial agreement. Professor White does not emphasize the Pilgrimage of Grace, however, when the idea was forced into the open for the first time in the Tudor period.

[3] *The Social Teaching of the Christian Churches* (London, 1931), 902.

229

But in the most important social revolt of the Tudor period, the Pilgrimage of Grace of 1536, the fact is clear, as this paper will show, that paradoxically, principles of social equality were voiced, not by the "outs" but by the "ins," not by the Pilgrims but by Henry VIII's own apologists in tracts issued from the king's press. Such an inconsistency, superficially an act of expediency in a crisis, is significant not merely as a revelation of democratic modes of thought not far below the surface of a nominally authoritarian regime, but as the earliest official application in England of an equalitarian formula in a purely secular context. There was nothing new in the principle in and of itself. As an ecclesiastical conception, equalitarianism was as old as the church. But it is characteristic of a point of view eager to clothe a policy of expediency in the language of tradition that they made it serve their own purposes. Confronted by the hard and dangerous fact of the Pilgrimage of Grace, they sought the refuge of the old patterns in order to legitimize novelty in practice, and thus evolved, almost, it would seem, against their will, a theory whose general application and ultimate implications they would certainly have rejected.[4]

It would be strange, in fact, if the loosening of class distinctions, which has often been observed as characteristic of the Tudor period, did not find expression in theory. The ground was being prepared, not merely by the increasing independence of the yeoman class,[5] but by the policy of the government itself. The absorption by the crown of powers of administration over courts of law, the great shift of landed wealth from the church into the hands of a new class of royal servants, the depressing of the traditional aristocracy in favor of a newly created and prospering middle class— all are too familiar aspects of social change to be stressed here,[6] but all tended to cut across the established social barriers and to assist the rise of the lower classes. What does need emphasis is the fact that most of these changes were accelerated by commoners

    [4] On this characteristic of reformist thought, see White, *op. cit.*, 1–2, 132 ff.

    [5] R. H. Tawney, *The Agrarian Problem in the Sixteenth Century* (London, 1912), 325, and the cases cited by I. S. Leadam, *Select Cases in the Court of Requests* (Selden Society, 1898), lv.

    [6] W. S. Holdsworth, *A History of English Law* (London, 1937), IV, 402–7; Rachel R. Reid, *The King's Council in the North* (London, 1921), 48, 90–7; Edward P. Cheyney, *Social Changes in England in the Sixteenth Century* (University of Pennsylvania, 1895), 105–6; S. B. Liljegren, *The Fall of the Monasteries and the Social Changes in England* (Lund, 1924).

whom Henry VIII had elevated to the highest offices in the kingdom. Wolsey, Cranmer, and Cromwell were obscure men until the
king chose to disregard class distinctions and employ their services.
Social equalitarianism may thus be regarded as sanctioned, however unintentionally, by the crown itself.

There is every reason to believe that this break with tradition
was recognized by Henry's low-born officers. A. F. Pollard doubts
Leadam's thesis that Wolsey created the policy of relying on the
people against the aristocracy,[7] but the truth remains that through
Wolsey's efforts, particularly in establishing the Court of Requests
for the arguing of poor men's causes,[8] the position of the common
man in court was greatly strengthened. And contemporary testimony reveals Wolsey's similar disregard of social position in his
diocese of York as advocate of the commons,[9] and in his household
as a patron of letters. Learning, Richard Pace wrote in 1517, was
now better than ignorance and noble blood.[10]

This democratic policy of advancement, begun by Wolsey, was
continued by Archbishop Cranmer. On the occasion of the secu-

[7] A. F. Pollard, *Wolsey* (London, 1929), 78–9.

[8] Pollard, *op. cit.*, 79 and the references there cited, 81–7; Reid, *op. cit.*, 97.

[9] Richard Morison, Cromwell's secretary, testified in *A Remedy for Sedition*
(Berthelet, 1536), sig. E ii^r–iii: "Who was lesse beloued in the northe, than my lorde
Cardynall, god haue his sowle, before he was amonges them? Who better beloued,
after he had ben there a whyle? we hate oft times, whom we haue good cause to loue.
It is a wonder, to see how they were turned, howe of vtter ennemyes, they becam his
dere frendes. He gaue byshops a right good ensample, how they might wyn mens
hartis. There was fewe holy dayes, but he wolde ride. v. or. vi. myle from his howse,
nowe to this paryishe churche, nowe to that, and ther cause one or other of his doc-
tours, to make a sermone vnto the people. He sat amonges them, and sayd masse
before al the paryshe. . . . He broughte his dinner with hym, and bad dyuers of the
parish to it. He enquired, whether there was any debate or grudge betwene any of
them, yf there were, after dinner he sente for the parties to the church, and made
them at one."

Note also a Northern criticism of Wolsey's appointment of Thomas Donyngton
as his steward that "he never had staff in his hand." *Letters and Papers, Foreign
and Domestic, of the Reign of Henry VIII* [referred to henceforth as "*L&P*"], IV
(3), no. 6447.

[10] *L&P*, II, no. 3765, cited by Pollard, *op. cit.*, 79; John Strype, *Ecclesiastical
Memorials* (London, 1816), I, 199–200.

Wolsey made provision in his college at Oxford for twenty rich young commoners, to be maintained at their own expense. Poor commoners were supported as
"petty canons" with tutors to look after their funds. C. E. Mallet, *A History of
the University of Oxford* (London, 1924), II, 38, note 2. Richard Morison was one
of these. *L&P*, XIII (2), no. 817, p. 325.

larization of the cathedral church of Canterbury, he was able to override those who argued that only the sons of gentlemen should be put to school there, on the grounds that

pore mennys children arr many tymes enduyd with more synguler giftes of nature, which are also the giftes of God, as with eloquence, memorie, apte pronunciacion, sobrietie, with suche like, and also commonly more gyven to applie thair studie, than ys the gentilmannys sonne delicatelie educated.

To exclude the plowman's son and the poor man's son from the benefits of learning is as much as to say that

almightie God sholde not be at libertie to bestowe his greate giftes of grace apon any person, nor no where els but as we and other men shall appoynte them to be enployed according to our fansey, and not according to his most godlie will and pleasure : who gyveth his giftes both of lernyng and other perfections in all sciences, unto all kinde and states of people indifferentelie.

It was satisfying for one who, having been scorned as an hostler, was now establishing a place of learning, to hew a new line for the founders of the King's School:

I take it that none of us all here being gentilmen borne (as I thincke)[11] but hadd our begynnyng that wey from a lowe and base parentage; and thorough the benefite of lernyng and other civile knowlege for the moste parte all gentil ascende to thair estate.[12]

What Cranmer thus expressed as theory, Thomas Cromwell was putting into practice. Indigent university students like Richard Besiley of Oxford and William Byrlyngham of Cambridge recognized in Cromwell a benefactor "especially of poor men, whom you are always glad to help."[13] Furthermore, Wolsey's occasional disregard of rank in appointing bright young scholars to offices of political usefulness in the state had now become known policy. In 1535, Richard Morison, once a petty canon in Wolsey's college at Oxford, now a poor student at Padua, closed one of his frequent appeals to Cromwell's generosity with the acid remark that the cardinal, had he been living, would never have suffered him to remain in such mean circumstances.[14] Morison hoped for, and at-

[11] None of the commissioners was high-born, according to W. F. Hook, *Lives of the Archbishops of Canterbury* (London, 1868), VII, 24.

[12] Ralph Morice, servant of Cranmer, in *Narratives of the Days of the Reformation*, ed. J. G. Nichols, Camden Society, no. 77 (1859), 273–5.

[13] *L&P*, VIII, nos. 68, 828; IV (2), no. 5069. For Besiley's later career, see C. H. Garrett, *The Marian Exiles* (Cambridge, 1938), 85.

[14] *L&P*, IX, no. 198.

tained, even greater success than his fellow student, Thomas
Starkey, who a year earlier had also found in humanistic studies
a by-pass to political preferment.[15] Such circumstances account
for Roger Ascham's nostalgic complaint to Cranmer four years
after Cromwell's fall that new students at Cambridge

were for the most part only the sons of rich men, and such as never intended
to pursue their studies to that degree as to arrive at any eminent proficiency
and perfection in learning, but only the better to qualify themselves for some
places in the state, by a slighter and more superficial knowledge.[16]

The breakdown of the traditional social stratifications implicit in
Tudor policy was presently to be illustrated in Ascham's own
career. In 1550, he realized his ambition to travel abroad as secretary to an ambassador; his superior was Sir Richard Morison,
newly knighted and appointed to the Emperor's court, he who
fifteen years earlier had been relieved from penury by Cromwell
to employ his learning in defense of the policy which had made his
rise possible.

II

That this democratization of social classes, deliberately fostered
by those who had themselves risen from low to high degree, was
being felt as a serious menace to the stability of the social structure,
may be inferred from the demands of the Pilgrims voiced during
the Pilgrimage of Grace, when for the first time the policy of the
government was publicly challenged. The outcry in the North
against Cromwell and the king's other low-born officers arose from
commonalty as well as nobility, a circumstance not unnaturally
perplexing to the king's low-born officers.[17] As a class, the Northern commons were far more conservative than the commoners in
the South, but the seeds of class discontent were there. That condition of society which Thomas More had ascribed in 1516 to a conspiracy of rich men had even further deteriorated in 1536. Poverty
stalked the North, induced by a series of bad harvests and high
prices.[18] The Poor Law, passed in the year of the Pilgrimage,
represented official recognition of a social emergency. But the
inertia of the lords of the North, to whom the commons tradition-

[15] W. Gordon Zeeveld, "Thomas Starkey and the Cromwellian Polity," *Journal
of Modern History*, XV, 179.
[16] *Works*, ed. Giles, I, 69, translated in Strype's *Cranmer* (Oxford, 1812), 242.
[17] And to modern scholars as well. See Tawney, *op. cit.*, 333-7.
[18] W. J. Ashley, *English Economic History and Theory* (London, 1925), 355.

ally looked to present their case to London, caused resentment, and resentment undoubtedly sharpened the perennial and radical cleavages between the estates.[19] For the most part, it remained inarticulate. One would hardly expect it to appear in such public declarations as the Pilgrims' manifesto to the king, which was dominated by aristocratic sentiment and hence conservative in tone, the commons apparently deferring to the nobles in its formulation. But ominously, ubiquitously, "Master Poverty" sprang up throughout the North as "conductor, protector, and maintainer of the whole commonalty,"[20] and in less ambiguous language Robert Aske accused the temporal lords of not properly providing for the poverty of the realm, so that of necessity, the North country should

either patyssh with the Skotes,[20a] or for of very pouertie, enforced to make comocions or rebellions; and that the lordes knew the same to be trew and had not down ther dewtie, for that they had not declared the said pouertie of the said contrey to the kinges highnes, and the dangers that otherwise to his grace wold insew, alleging the holl blame to them the nobilite therin, with other lyke reasons.[21]

Government apologists did not overlook Master Poverty in assessing the dangers of the Pilgrimage.

Yet it was not as radicals but as conservatives that the Pilgrims seemed most threatening. A challenge to the existing order as clearly radical as Robert Aske's could be met and was met, as will

[19] Not resentment on the part of the commons at the success of individuals among their own number, as in M. H. and R. Dodds, *The Pilgrimage of Grace and the Exeter Conspiracy* (Cambridge, 1915), I, 177. Likewise open to question is Kenneth Pickthorn's belief in *Early Tudor Government: Henry VIII* (Cambridge, 1934), 306, that the Pilgrimage "showed from the outset, what remained true and decisive to the end, the common people's intimate and ineradicable persuasion that they must have at any cost the leadership of their betters." As will presently be shown, the latter view had appeared by 1549; but in 1536, the evidence makes it clear that although the rank and file suspected their noble leaders from the first,— and that their suspicion was well-founded was borne out by events—they felt incapable and unwilling to proceed without the help of their social superiors. See Tawney, *op. cit.*, 322; *L&P,* XII (1), no. 70 (x).

[20] *L&P,* XI, no. 892 (1) and (2); XII (1), nos. 411, 467, 687 (1) and (2), 786 (18), 849 (27), 914.

[20a] Froude is doubtless correct in reading this phrase "perish with the skaith." *History of England from the Fall of Wolsey to the Death of Elizabeth* (New York, 1871), III, 133.

[21] Mary Bateson, "Robert Aske's Narrative of the Pilgrimage of Grace," *EHR,* V (1890), 336.

SOCIAL EQUALITARIANISM IN TUDOR CRISIS 235

presently be shown, with an easy conscience and with the gloves off; but when in the name of tradition Pilgrims of all ranks proposed to remove radicalism in the existing order, they became both united and embarrassing to the government. For however far apart they might drift on the issue of poverty, in restoring and conserving traditions which they felt were endangered by current governmental policy, noble and villein had discovered a genuinely common objective. No small part of their strength derived from the conviction that ecclesiastical traditions were being destroyed by radical reformers who had won the ear of the king. It is indicative of the Pilgrims' conservative temper on ecclesiastical issues that they viewed the revolutionary Anabaptist uprisings in Germany with abhorrence, determined that neither Reformation nor reformers should gain a foothold in England. At home, all ranks recognized the monastic suppressions as a blow at the very foundations of the social structure as they had known it,[22] and Thomas Cromwell as the chief perpetrator of these reforms.[23]

This community of interest against Cromwell the suppressor of monasteries, could not be expected to obtain against Cromwell the social climber, where the interests of the aristocracy were primarily at stake. The fact that the northern nobles made common cause with the lower classes was in itself a tacit acknowledgment of the jeopardy to their caste in the rise of Cromwell. Already their

[22] "Wherfor the said statut of subpression was greatly to the decay of the comynwelth of that contrei, & al those partes of al degreys greatly groged ayenst the same." Ibid., 562.

[23] "Cromwell is in such errour and hatred with the peple in thos partes [second version: "in all partes"] that in maner they wold eat him. . . . And ther especiall great groge is ayenst the Lord Cromwell, being reputed the distrewer of the comynwelth, as well emonges most parte of the lordes, as all other the worshipfull and comyns." Ibid., 340, 342–3.

Cromwell's reputation in the North should be balanced against a southern view: "He perswaded the king by maintteininge of equum jus, and by holdinge-downe the over-emminent power of soche greate ones as in time paste, like bell-wethers, had led the sheppeshe flockes of England against their prince, to knett fast to him the love of his commons and specially of his cittie of London." According to this report, Cromwell sold much monastic property "to many men four reasonable prises, exchainging many of them with the nobilitie and other for their auncient possession to their greate gaine with whome he exchainged, preferring many sufficient persons to the kinges servis who were sone raised to nobilitie and to worshipe and good calling, and all indewed with maintenaunce out of the revenewes of abbyes." Three chapters of letters relating to the suppression of monasteries, ed. Thomas Wright, Camden Society, no. 26 (1843), 114–5.

dignities had been superseded by the parvenu Wolsey, and were passing further into eclipse by the appointment of Wolsey's and later of the king's servants.[24]   And now Cromwell, an upstart like his master, had catapulted into office and was misguiding the king.[25] To the feudal lords of the North, the presence of men of such humble and ignoble origins as Cranmer and Cromwell in the king's council was an open challenge to the traditional principle of degree exactly in the quarter where it should have been most scrupulously observed.[26]   The records in the *Letters and Papers of Henry VIII* leave little doubt that the Pilgrimage of Grace was precipitated in part by the increasing apprehensions of the older nobility that their accustomed world was falling about their ears, and that the traditional social ranks were being dangerously invaded.

It is even conceivable that the plea of Northern aristocrats for ousting Cromwell and Cranmer and substituting noble blood in the king's council might not have prevailed with the commons had not all classes been united by a deep-rooted respect for social degree. On this ground, the Pilgrims unanimously took their stand as spokesmen and guardians of the commonwealth.   Under an oath to be true to king, church, and commonwealth, they would expel "all villain blood from the King's grace and his privy council for the common wealth, and restoring of Christ's church."[27]   The king's council must be composed of virtuous men "as would regard the commonwealth above their princis lo[ve]," and the king in turn must be counselled by nobles, baronage, and commons for the said

[24] Holdsworth, *op. cit.*, IV, 39; Reid, *op. cit.*, 92, 102–114. For the possible enlistment of Skelton's pen on the side of the aggrieved Howards, see William Nelson, *John Skelton, Laureate* (New York, 1939), 210–11.

[25] Darcy, on trial for his part in the Pilgrimage, accused Cromwell directly: "Cromwell, it is thou that art the very original and chief causer of the apprehension of us that be noblemen, and dost daily earnestly travail to bring us to our end and to strike off our heads, and I trust that or thou die, though thou wouldst procure all the noblemen's heads within the realm to be stricken off, yet shall there one head remain that shall strike off thy head." Dodds, *op. cit.*, II, 186–7, quoting *L&P*, XII (1), no. 976.

[26] "The nobility despised him [Cromwell], and thought it lessened the greatness of their titles, to see the son of a blacksmith raised so many degrees above them." Gilbert Burnet, *The History of the Reformation*, ed. Pocock (Oxford, 1865), I, 441. See also *The Correspondence of Edward, Third Earl of Derby*, ed. Toller, Chetham Society (1890), 50, 52.

[27] *L&P*, XI, no. 622, p. 249; no. 705 (i, ii, iv); no. 892 (ii), p. 356; no. 902 (ii), p. 358.

commonwealth. They warned Henry's commander, Norfolk, "and such noble folke as are of ancient blood with baronage of the sowth and commonalty also" to recall how Suffolk dealt with Lincolnshire men in 1525, "for their part is not unlike to be in after this." Not that they insisted on a fixed social order at the expense of their responsibility as human beings. There is a striking family likeness in the candid independence of Shakespeare's common soldier, Williams, and in the Pilgrims' blunt reminder to the king that "when he has killed a man he [cannot] make a man alive again.'"[28] Henry's position was vexing. Were the "subverters of the good laws of the realm'"[29] the rebels or Henry's agents? In 1536, the charge against the new men was serious enough and the government's case vulnerable enough to make justification necessary, and the process of justification forced government apology into a premature but unmistakable expression of equalitarian social theory.

For the government apologists found themselves in the uncomfortable and ironic dilemma of justifying a government whose chief officer was regarded by the Pilgrims as a flagrant violator of the traditional order. Under these circumstances, it was tactically safe to ignore the nobles who had joined the Pilgrimage and to confront the rest of the Pilgrims with their audacious disruption of political unity; it was undoubtedly good politics to compare their act of rebellion with that of the Münster Anabaptists, the infiltration of whose beliefs they had specifically decried in their petition to the king. But how could the attack on Cromwell and his officers be answered in terms of conventional social theory? This was the embarrassing question that government apologists were called upon to answer; the manner in which it was answered betrays their grave anxiety over an alarmingly widespread social discontent during the very years sometimes referred to as the "Henrician tyranny."

III

Henry's personal response, as a matter of fact, was truculent and inflexible. At first, he answered force with force; only when he felt that the rebellion was definitely under control did he reply to the Pilgrims' criticism of the new social order. Then, in contemptuous and minatory language, he categorically denied the right of

[28] *L&P,* XI, no. 1244; *Henry V,* IV. i.
[29] The eighth demand of the Pilgrims at Doncaster: *L&P,* XI, no. 1246.

"common and inferior subjects," of "rude and ignorant common people," to question his appointments to the council:

How presumptuous then are ye the rude commons of one shire, and that one of the most beastly of the whole realm, and of least experience to find fault with your prince for the electing of his councillors and prelates; and to take upon you, contrary to God's and man's law to rule your prince.[30]

This was mere bluster. But later, in answering the Pilgrims' petition at Doncaster, he denied that the principle of degree had been violated, inasmuch as now there were more noblemen in his council than at the beginning of his reign. Of his first councillors, only two, Surrey and Shrewsbury, were "worthie calling noble"; Marney and Darcy were "scant well borne gentilmen, and yet of no grete landes, till they were promoted by Us."[31] The fact that he named nine temporal lords in his present council was cold comfort to the northern nobility. They were only too painfully aware that he had discreetly omitted mentioning Cromwell, Cranmer, Audeley, and Rich, the objects of their protests. As a matter of fact, he had consistently flouted the principle of degree by appointing no one to the Council in the North above the rank of knight.[32] Consequently, when the Duke of Norfolk dared to suggest that only noblemen were fitted to keep order in the West Marches after the Pilgrimage of Grace, the Privy Council sent the curt rebuff:

If it shal please his Majesty to appoynt the meanest man . . . to rule & govern in that place; is not his Graces aucthoritie sufficient to cause al men to serve his Grace under him without respect of the very estate of the personage?

Significantly, Cromwell and Cranmer were among the signers of that statement. To it, the king added his own comment: "For surely we woll not be bounde of a necessitie to be serued there with lordes. But we wolbe serued with such men what degre soeuer they be of as we shall appointe to the same."[33]

Insofar as Henry undertook to defend his position at all, he addressed himself to the Pilgrims of high rather than low degree. But as he must have known, the feudal nobility as a class were no longer a serious threat. While there is ample evidence that they

[30] *Answer to the Petitions of the traitors and rebels in Lincolnshire, State Papers* . . . *Henry VIII* (London, 1830–52), I, 463.

[31] *Ibid.*, 507–8.

[32] Reid, *op. cit.*, 103.

[33] *L&P*, XII (1), nos. 636, 1118.

felt their danger, they were timid and inclined to acceptance and collaboration.[34] One finds Norfolk, for example, currying the favor of his hypothetical enemy Cromwell and sharing the spoils incident to the dissolution of the monasteries; Shrewsbury, a member of the council at the king's accession, profiting from transactions involving the alienation of ecclesiastical property; and the Marquis of Exeter accepting a grant of priory lands and property in November, 1536, while the North was still seething.[35] In the end, they capitulated to the spirit as well as the fact of the new order. Thomas, Lord Darcy, admitted to Thomas Treheyron, Somerset herald of arms, that he was sorry he had spoken foolishly of Cromwell at Doncaster, "for to say truth every man had a begynnyng and he that the kyng will have honored wee must all honor and god forbyde that any subject shuld goo about to rule the kyng in his owne realme."[36]

The real social problem behind the Pilgrimage of Grace, the new independence of the commons, Henry chose to ignore. Having sown the dragon's teeth, he preferred to leave the rationalization of his policy to his official apologists. They approached it in precisely the manner in which they approached the political problem, as traditionalists rather than as innovators, but as the supporters of a tradition as venerable as the principle which their practice apparently violated. And they arrived at a theoretic justification of current social policy quite as novel if not quite as unassailable.[37] Since they were responsible only and directly to Henry, they could, of course, take the position that the king on his mere prerogative might advance whom he pleased, regardless of his birth or his riches. We must obey the rulers constituted by the king, said one apologist in an unpublished treatise written to support the government policy in 1536,[38]

[34] Geoffrey Baskerville, *English Monks and the Suppression of the Monasteries* (London, 1937), 161–3.

[35] S. B. Liljegren, *The Fall of the Monasteries* (Lund, 1924), 33, 110.

[36] Dodds, *op. cit.*, I, 305; *L&P*, XI, no. 1086, p. 437.

[37] For their solution to the political issues, see *The Journal of Modern History*, XV, 177–191.

[38] Public Record Office, S. P. 6/4, fols. 173–210 (*L&P*, XI, no. 1420, p. 567). Fol. 210 is headed "This boke intreateth of obedience to Princes." It is undated, but a reference to the Ten Articles as "set forthe" (fol. 197) places it after July 11, 1536; and internal evidence clearly identifies it as a contribution to the campaign against the Pilgrims.

not hauyng respecte to ther richesse, to ther nobilite, to ther honour to ther
birthe but as his cõmyssioners because god cõmmandeth us so to do. A kyng
in his Realme maye promote whom he liketh whom he thynketh meete to be
his deputie or Connsailor, be he neū so pore and so beyng promoted we ought
to haue hym in as high honour in as high reverence in as high reputacon, as
though he beside wer borne to enherit by the Lawes of the Realme the greatest Dukedome of the same, not for hymselfe, but because god cõmmandeth us
so to do; as one that is advanced by the kyng that is goddes mynyster.[39]

This was no more than Henry's argument for unrestricted appoin-
tive power, supported by the usual Biblical citations,[40] and the writer
was conscious that so stated and without qualification, it meant the
overthrow of degree—and hence of the traditional social system—
without offering anything in its place. He therefore sought to
temper its naked and arbitrary character by grounding it in principles just as traditional. The crux of the matter is in the
phrase ''not for himself.'' Granted full honour and reverence
and reputation to the king's commoner-appointee because God
commanded it, could not that same honour and reverence and reputation be granted also for himself? And if this were granted, did
it not abrogate the whole artificial set of distinctions represented in
the principle of degree? The only logical answer must admit a
theory of equality, and the apologist stated it boldly. The concept
of degree, he argued, was a violation of the natural order of society.
Originally all men had been created equal; ever since, virtue, not
birth, had been the measure of true nobility:

At the begynnyng of the wordle [sic] ther was no difference of persones
but afterward dyuers for ther holynes and gode qualitees wer ordeyned and
constituted by god to be Rulers, dyuers also afterward which wer but of
base byrthe and cam not of that stocke lyneally that were first ordeyned by
god to be rulers beyng but poore men for ther vertue wisedome and qualitees
and by the favour of noble Emperours and kynges wer constituted and put
in high auctorite.[41]

The Pilgrims themselves had demanded virtue as the qualification
of the king's officers; government spokesmen merely substituted a

[39] Fols. 192–3.
[40] *Romans*, 13: 1–7; *Titus*, 3: 1–2; *1 Peter*, 2: 13–15, 18; 5: 5.
[41] PRO, S. P. 6/4, fol. 193.   Cf. William Marshall's gloss on "universal multitude" in his translation of Marsilius of Padua's *Defensor Pacis* (1534), sig. f4ʳ–f5:
"He meaneth suche offyces as yᵉ prynce or kynge wyll haue instytuted by acte of
parlyament els all other officers & degres it lyeth ĩ yᵉ kynges absolute power to
appoĩte at all tymes."

principle of equality for a principle of degree as a basis for social relations. But by that simple substitution, they had acclimatized the radicalism of John Ball's

> When Adam delved, and Eve span,
> Who was then a Gentleman?

and at the same time forged a link between the social thinking of the middle ages and the seventeenth century.

What is at once apparent is the eclecticism of the official position. The formula proposed was derivable from both classic and Christian thought and traditional enough to appeal to all sorts and conditions of men. Aristotle placed political virtue above either birth or wealth (*Politics,* III. 9) and maintained that those superior in virtue and in power of performing the best actions should be obeyed (*Politics,* VII. 3), but the construction of Aristotle's state did not allow for a free access to political office of all social ranks (*Politics,* III. 12) nor for social equality except in a very limited sense (*Politics,* II. 7; III. 9, 13). In Cicero, however, a natural and historical principle of equality, the Stoic *omnes homines natura aequales sunt,* was explicit.[42] It is a provision of nature, he said, that only those superior in virtue and in spirit should rule the weaker, and that the weaker should be willing to obey the stronger. Indeed, only ignorance of virtue leads men to think of the rich, prosperous, or well-born as the best men; for riches, names, and power, when they lack wisdom and the knowledge of how to live and to rule over others, are full of dishonour and insolent pride (*Republic,* I. xxxiv. 51). Cicero observed this principle in use among the early Romans, who, rustic though they were, saw even then that kingly virtue and wisdom, not royal ancestry, were the qualities to be sought (*Republic,* II. xii. 24).

Christian ideology, likewise, offered a limited authority for a theory of social equality. It admitted an original equality among men, but inequality after the Fall. It accepted a spiritual equality among all men, but limited it to the spiritual realm. The first ecclesiastical government as established by Christ ignored degrees, though the present status of the church hardly conformed to that pattern.

[42] For the significance of this development in political thought, see R. W. and A. J. Carlyle, *A History of Mediaeval Political Theory in the West* (Edinburgh, 1903), I, 8. McIlwain, *The Growth of Political Thought in the West* (New York, 1932) 115, calls it "the profoundest contribution of the Stoics to political thought."

But while there was ready at hand both classical and Christian support for advancing a doctrine of equality to meet a current situation, and while the apologists were anxious to align the government position with traditional thought on the subject, they were alive to the danger of its literal adoption as a social program, and their use of it was consequently defensive, not doctrinaire. For pressed to its logical conclusions, equalitarianism led either to the fanciful land of Utopia or to the real and bloody insurrections of Münster. Tradition in the form of man's law must prevent the anarchic excesses of equalitarianism implicit both in the law of Christ and the Stoic law of nature. According to Thomas Starkey, a plowman is ideally as dear to God as is the most royal king or prince in his high majesty, a cobbler as is the greatest philosopher, a merchant abroad in the world as is the monk in his cloister. In spite of the diversity among men, "before God . . . there is no regarde of person nor degree."[43] On the other hand, there are men of arrogant blindness who

if hit were not for feare of mannes lawe, wolde brynge to ruyne all order and policye, they wolde haue all thynges whyche nature hathe broughte forth to the common comforte of manne, to be in common, iudgynge this inequalitie in possession of thynges, where as somme have to lyttell, and some ouer moche, to be playne ageynste Nature, and manyfeste iniurye. They wolde in all thinges serue their owne fantasye, they wolde in harte be subiecte to no ceremonie, lawe, nor mannes tradition: for that they saye agreethe not to the libertie of a Chrystian manne, who is free frome all bondage of lawe, and subiecte to no ceremonye, the whiche they say be only snares and stayes vnto weke myndes, nothynge agreing vnto theyr dignitie.[44]

Indeed, an ideal of equality based solely on classical virtue and Christian humility was far from compatible with the practical exigencies of the present crisis. Cuthbert Tunstal, the king's appointee to the office of President of the Council in 1530, could cite Christ's warning to the apostles that the first among them would be servant of all (*St. Mark* 10:43): "Here we doo see, that Chryste wolde haue the mekest and moste humble to be chiefe in his flocke, by humilitie and by seruyce done to other."[45] But obviously, ambition rather than humility, active ability rather than passive virtue,

[43] *An exhortation to the people instructynge theym to unitie and obedience* (Berthelet, 1536), sig. D.

[44] *Ibid.,* sig. [F iii*v*]. A comma after *iniurye* has been changed to a period to clarify the thought.

[45] *A sermon . . . made upon Palme sondaye* (Berthelet, 1539), sig. C iii.

were the more immediate motives of the royal servants. And viewed externally for its uses as propaganda, with how good grace could they recount illustrations of the advancement of poor men "for ther vertue wisedome and qualitees" when the complaint of the Pilgrims against Henry's low-born officers lay precisely in their lack of virtue?

Redefinition of the concept of nobility in terms of practical politics was necessary, and Richard Morison, writing at a critical moment during the insurrection, recognized the need. For a man who was familiar with the works of Machiavelli,[46] the transposition of values was easy. In Morison's addresses to the Pilgrims, Aristotelian virtue has been replaced by Machiavellian *virtù*, Christian humility by ambition, theoretical by practical motives as a basis for social equality. "Who can justly blame him," he asked arrogantly in defending Henry's advancement of commoners, "for making them great, that indeed have all those things which at the beginning of nobility only made them noble?"[47]

They only ought to be officers, that are known to be discreet, politic, wise, and of such stomach that if need be, they can set little the hatred and malice of them that seldom love such as are in greatest authority.[48]

"Wherever virtue is, there is nobility," Dante had said, speaking in the Aristotelian tradition.[49] Nobility is what we make of ourselves since we are all by nature equal, Machiavelli makes the demagogue, Ciompi, say to stir the commons to revolt:

Nor must you let yourselves be cowed by that nobility of blood of which they make boast to us; for all men, having had the same beginning, are of equally ancient birth, and nature has made them all in the same fashion. Were we

[46] For Morison's knowledge of Machiavelli, see *PMLA*, LV (1940), 416–8. The influence was natural in view of the identity of their political objectives. Of Machiavelli's purpose, Allan H. Gilbert writes: "The great question for republic or prince is: how can turmoil and confusion be permanently avoided? Nothing else mattered in comparison, either present morality or hope of life hereafter. To this theory of the settled state all was subordinated." *Machiavelli's Prince and Its Forerunners* (Durham, 1938), 235.

[47] *A Lamentation in whiche is shewed what Ruyne and destruction cometh of seditious rebellyon* (Berthelet, 1536), sig. A iv.

[48] *A Remedy for Sedition* (Berthelet, 1536), sig. A iv.

[49] *Convivio*, IV, xvi. The statement is made in an extended passage showing true nobility as determined by moral and intellectual virtues. I am indebted to Professor Theodore Spencer for directing my attention to Dante's discussion of the subject.

all stripped naked you would find us alike; dress us in their clothes and they in ours, without doubt we should seem noble and they mean, forasmuch as it is only poverty and riches that make us inequal.[50]

Morison, familiar with both, paraphrased and integrated them with a prudential twist of his own. Henry, he claimed, had set up a new definition of nobility:

> True nobility is never but where virtue is . . . this only to be the way of promotion, and here nobility to consist. In all other things, it little availeth whose son a man be. . . . What shall we need to endeavor ourselves unto, when whatsoever we do, we must be tryed by our birth and not by our qualities?[51]

It is stated with even greater clarity in his translation of Vives's *Introduction to Wisdom* (Berthelet, 1540):

> What other thynge is nobylite nowe, but a chaunce, to be borne of this or that gentyll bloud, and an opinion grafte vppon the foolishness of rude and vnlerned people, whiche oftentymes is gotten by robberie and lyke wyaes.
>
> True and perfect nobilite, springeth of vertue, wherfore it is gret madnesse for any man, to crake of his parentes, beinge naught him selfe, dishonourynge theyr noble actes, with his lewed doinges.[52]
>
> Trewely we be all made of lyke elementes, and haue all oone god, father to vs all, yet to contempne the byrthe or stocke of any man, is vnder a color to reproue god, whiche is the autoure of euery mans natiuitie.[53]

Will the commons have no one rule but noblemen born? Morison's shrewd answer was an admission that the caste of the old nobility had gone forever: "Let them have that they require, whom toucheth this so sore as themself, and all their posterity? What doo they

[50] *Florentine History* (Everyman edition), 109.

[51] *A Remedy for Sedition*, sig. A iv[v]–B ii.

[52] Cf. Dante's view in *Convivio* that nobility is a broader term than virtue, including other kinds of excellence (IV, xix). No one, because he is able to say, "I am of such and such a stock," is entitled to believe that he is possessed of nobility, if the seed of blessedness placed by God in the soul is not in him (IV, xx).

For a similar expression of opinion in fifteenth-century Florence, see Hans Baron, "The Historical Background of the Florentine Renaissance," *History*, n. s., XXII (1938), 318.

[53] Sig. B vii[v]–B viii (*Introducción á la Sabiduría*, Madrid, 1918, pp. 23–4. Morison's preface, addressed to Cromwell's son, Gregory, makes it clear that in such a passage he had Cromwell in mind: "Folowe your leader, goo on with your guyde, you shall fynde all the steppes and grices, wherby not only my lord clymed to nobilitie, but all other, that in ded are or were atte any tyme noble." Sig. A v[v].

leave unto theirs, when they also take away the possibility of better fortune?"[54]

Such passages reveal the motive of ambition which prompted the apologists to advance a theory of social equalitarianism. These men were the obscure but talented authors of Henry's new order, trained in the classics, philosophy, scriptures, and the civil law, eager to use their learning in a society in which the old barriers had been broken down and new opportunities opened to them through the benevolence of their prince.[55] They thought within the framework of the present regime. With the more radical forms of equalitarianism, the communism of either More or the sects, they would have nothing to do. It was far from their intention to lend theoretic support to a classless society. They thought of equality, not in terms of property but of opportunity. Social rank existed, but limited only by a man's ambition, a point of view anticipating the "career open to talents" of a later era. As beneficiaries of the new order, they wanted to legalize their own rise; and they were anxious to maintain the privilege. There is no better proof of the new social outlook among the lower classes than their scorn of the caste system which the Pilgrims were willing to tolerate. In fact, one is quite prepared to see the same writers from their new position of security revert to the conventional theory of degree, but with personal inferences. If the commons accept Henry, said Morison flatly, they must accept his officers. "Lordes must be lordes, comunes must be comunes, euery man acceptynge his degree, euery man contente to haue that, that he laufully maye come by."[56]

The same note of expediency is apparent when they faced the problem of poverty in the North. As in the political realm, order —but the present order—must be maintained. Morison's sense of the social instability underlying the Pilgrimage of Grace becomes

[54] *A Remedy for Sedition*, sig. A iv^v–B ii.

[55] Starkey offered his services to the state as follows: "In dyuerse kyndys of studys I haue occupyd my selfe, euer hauyng in mynd thys end & purpos at the last here in thys commynalty where I am brought forth & borne to employ them to some vse; and though in them I haue not most profyted, yet dylygence & wyl hathe not lakkyd therto: but what so euer hyt ys that I haue by the gudenes of god attaynyd vn-to I schal most gladly . . . apply hyt to the seruyce of our prynce, and therby rekun my selfe to attayne a grete parte of my felycyte." *England in the Reign of King Henry the Eighth* (Early English Text Society, Extra Series, No. XXXII, 1878), p. x.

[56] *A Remedy for Sedition*, sig. B iii, B iv. See also Morison's *Invective against Treason* (Berthelet, 1539), sig. a ii^v.

apparent by comparison with Henry Parker's *Dives and Pauper,* which Berthelet, the king's printer, was reprinting at the same time as Morison's *A Remedy for Sedition* was rushed through his press. It is a defense of holy poverty in the mediaeval manner, the conclusion of which is the Augustinian doctrine that rich man and poor man are necessary to each other. Otherwise, says the poor man:

> Who shulde tyll your londe, holde your plough, repe your corne, and kepe your beastes? who should shape your clothes or sewe them? what myllar wolde than grynde your corne? what baker bake your breade? what brewer brewe your ale? what coke dyght your mete? what smith or carpenter amēde your house and other thinges necessarie? ye shulde go showles and clothles, and go to your bedde meateles, all muste ye than do alone.[57]

Significantly, the issue of disturbance of degree is not raised. Morison's argument, following similar lines but loaded with poignant sarcasm for "Captain Poverty," reveals the tensions now racking the social structure:

> We thinke it is very euyll, that soo many of us be poore, we thynke it were a good worlde, if we were al ryche. I pray you for a season, let it be as we desire, let us imagine, we be al ryche, doth it not streight folow, I as good as he, why gothe he before, I behynde? I as ryche as he, what nedeth me to labour? The mayde as prowde as her dame, who mylketh the cowe? The fermour hauing no more cause to toyle than he that loketh for the rentes, who shall tyl the grounde? His meny ye say. How so? why they more than he, if they be ryche to? What were more to be wayled, than suche welthe, that shuld bring either euery man, or the mooste parte of men, to extreme confusyon.[58]

Like Starkey, Morison perceived that the ultimate cause of poverty was idleness;[59] hence he took the position natural enough for a commoner raised from poverty because of his learning and basking for the first time in the king's favor, that while everyone must labor in his calling, the solution to the problem of poverty was in education both in the crafts and the professions. By this means, poverty would be banished and equality of opportunity would indulge the ambitions of the lower classes to rise.[60]

[57] Sig. A iii^r–A iiii.

[58] *A Remedy for Sedition,* sig. A iii–A iii^r.

[59] "Men wylle steale, thoughe they be hanged, excepte they may lyue without stelyng." *Ibid.,* sig. E iii^r.

See Starkey's *Dialogue between Pole and Lupset* (Early English Text Society, New Series, XII, 74–80.

[60] "Shall they, that be not ryche, by and by say, they wyll no more be ruled by their prince, by his coūsaylours, by his lawes? God sende vs more grace, for lesse

IV

The rapid development of social thinking during the reign of Henry VIII may best be measured by comparing the position taken by the government *vis-à-vis* the rebels of Devonshire and Norfolk in 1549. In 1536, government spokesmen were accusing the commoners of advocating social equality so that all commoners could be gentlemen; in 1549, the commoners were charged with advocating social equality so that gentlemen would be destroyed altogether. A new note of leveling had become articulate.[61] To the demand of the Devonshire rebels ''that no Gentleman shal have any mo servants then one, to wait upon him, except he may dispend one hundred mark land, and for every hundred mark we think it reasonable he should have a man,'' Archbishop Cranmer responded in terms that show his awareness of the new danger:

It was not for good mind, that you bare to the Gentlemen, that you devised this Article; but it appeareth plainly, that you devised it to diminish their strength, and to take away their friends, that you might command Gentlemen at your pleasures.[62]

Social equalitarianism seemed now to have become proletarian:

For was it ever seen in any country since the world began, that Commons did appoint the Nobles, and Gentlemen, the number of their Servants? Standeth it with any reason to turn upside down the good order of the whole world, that is every where, and ever hath been? That is to say, the Commoners to be governed by the Nobles, and the Servants by their Masters. Wil you now have the subjects to govern their King, the Vilains to rule the Gentlemen, and the Servants their Masters? If men would suffer this, God wil not; but wil take vengeance on al them, that wil break his order.[63]

Writing against the Norfolk rebels in the same year, Morison's friend, John Cheke, like Cranmer, was conscious of the leveling motive now implicit in social equalitarianism. Cheke paraphrased Starkey and Morison in warning the rebels that if everyone were

wytte we can not haue. There is a way to ryches moche better, than in sekynge goodes to lese al goodnes. Moche nygher, than in sekynge riches, to defye al regarde of honestie. There be handy craftes, there be honest occupations, whereby pouertie may be dryuen away.'' *A Remedy for Sedition*, sig. C iiiᵛ. So Starkey's *Dialogue,* 152 ff.

[61] Potentially recurrent, as Professor White points out, in every social rebellion. *Op. cit.*, pp. 118–120.

[62] John Strype, *Memorials of the Most Reverend Father in God Thomas Cranmer* (Oxford, 1812), II, 835–6.

[63] *Ibid.*, II, 837.

rich, the commonwealth would be destroyed by idleness. But equality had come to mean quite the reverse of what it meant in Morison's day. In 1536, Morison, observing the attack on the rigid system of degree, thought of equality as the opportunity to rise; in 1549, Cheke, observing the threat of leveling of all ranks, thought of equality as the stultification of it:

if there should be such equalitie, then ye take awaie all hope from yours to come to anie better estate than you now leaue them. And as manie meane mens children doo come honestlie vp, and are great succour to all their stocke: so should none be hereafter holpen by you, but bicause ye seeke equalitie, whereby all can not be rich.

Morison invoked a theory of equality to break down the social barricades to the lower classes; Cheke foresaw the barricades levelled and the lower classes a victim of their own theory. You pretend a commonwealth, he mocked, but

if riches offend you, because yee wish the like, then thinke that to be no common-wealth, but envie to the common-wealth. Enuie it is to appaire an other mans estate, without the amendment of your owne. And to haue no gentlemen, bicause ye be none your selues, is to bring downe an estate, and to mend none.

Then Cheke addressed himself directly to the issue of social equality, in the most elaborate analysis of the motives behind the idea in the Tudor period:

But what meane yee by this equalitie in the common-wealth? If one be wiser than an other, will ye banish him, because yee intend an equalitie of all things? If one be stronger than an other, will yee slaie him, bicause ye seeke an equalitie of all things? If one be well fauourder than an other, will yee punish him, because yee looke for an equalitie of all things? If one haue better vtterance than an other, will ye pull out his toong to saue your equalitie? And if one be richer than an other, will ye spoile him to mainteine an equalitie? If one be elder than an other, will ye kill him for this equalities sake? How iniurious are ye to God himselfe, who intendeth to bestow his gifts as he himselfe listeth: and ye seeke by wicked insurrections to make him giue them commonlie alike to all men as your vaine fansie liketh? Whie would ye haue an equalitie in riches & in other gifts of God? There is no meane sought. Either by ambition ye seeke lordlinesse much vnfit for you; or by couetousnesse ye be vnsatiable, a thing likelie inough in ye; or else by follie ye be not content with your estate, a fansie to be plucked out of you.[64]

[64] *The Hurt of Sedition*, reprinted in Holinshed's *Chronicles* (London, 1808), III, 989–990.

The royal apologists couldn't have it both ways, and subsequent history was to prove that the break in the elaborate mediaeval social structure would not be repaired by a mere reiteration of the principle of degree. But granted that the points of view were incompatible, the remarkable fact is that under a Tudor monarch a theory of social equality was voiced at all. Evaluated as propaganda, it reflects a new and increasing independence in the commons. It takes on meaning to the degree that propaganda accurately measures the minds of its intended audience. Regardless of the motive for its promulgation, it constituted by implication an unmistakably democratic challenge in the sixteenth century to the authoritarian tradition.[65] It was inevitable that the same challenge should have been raised wherever in sixteenth-century Europe inquiring minds perceived that the incompatibility of the "callings" and Christ's injunction that the first shall be last and the last first, implicit in the Protestant ethic, was a socially disruptive force. Henry's propagandists were astute enough to put the simple question: If the principle of equalitarianism were divested of its ecclesiastical connotation, what then?[66] In such questionings, the Puritan Revolution germinated.

The University of Maryland.

[65] Thomas Elyot approached the idea in *The Governour*, ed. Croft, I, 6: "They which excel other in this influence of understanding, and do employ it to the detaining of other within the bounds of reason, and show hoe to provide for their necessary living; such ought to be set in a more high place than the residue." But Elyot does not face the crucial question of nobility vs. men of noble birth.

[66] A. S. P. Woodhouse, *Puritanism and Liberty* (London, 1938), pp. 68–9, 81.

XV

THE PURITAN ETHIC AND THE DIGNITY OF LABOR: HIERARCHY VS. EQUALITY

By Charles Constantin

During the first two centuries of American life, that cluster of ideas and attitudes usually designated as the "Puritan Ethic" underwent certain changes. Though the precepts of the Puritan ethic remained intact, the intellectual and social contexts did not. At the beginning of the colonial period, the religious impulse was paramount since the leading colonial intellectuals were mostly ministers. By the end of the Revolution, attitudes were no longer dictated primarily by religion because intellectual leadership was firmly in the hands of statesmen who thought about politics. Edmund S. Morgan informs us that "the Puritan Ethic as it existed among the Revolutionary generation had in fact lost for most men the endorsement of an omnipresent angry God. The element of divinity had not entirely departed, but it was a good deal diluted."[1] More specifically, the different emphasis was reflected in changes in the concept of the "calling," core of the Puritan ethic. Such a transformation involved a movement from a "spiritual" doctrine of work toward a "secular" doctrine, the upshot being an uneasy, even an unholy relationship between one's piety and his daily occupation or trade in the world.[2]

What follows is an inquiry into the subject from a new perspective, with its focus on developments in the idea of a "calling" in seventeenth- and eighteenth-century New England. The idea itself contained important equalitarian implications which paradoxically sprang from a hierarchical conception of society. Yet a curious continuity underlay Puritan attitudes toward a "calling" during those two centuries. Attitudes in sermons and treatises gave servile labor an intrinsic dignity even at the

[1] Edmund S. Morgan, "The Puritan Ethic and the American Revolution," *William and Mary Quarterly*, 3rd ser. 24 (Jan., 1967), 3-8. See also Morgan, "The American Revolution Considered as an Intellectual Movement," in *Paths of American Thought*, Arthur M. Schlesinger, Jr. and Morton White, eds. (Boston, 1963), 11-33. I use the term "Puritan Ethic" to denote both religious and secular attitudes towards *work*, rather than to describe attitudes that evolved into the "spirit of capitalism." In this respect, unlike Morgan's first article, above, my essay attempts to distinguish between earlier *religious* attitudes toward work and later *secular* attitudes.

[2] See Robert Michaelson, "Changes in the Conception of the Calling or Vocation," *New England Quarterly*, 26 (1953), 315. one of the few articles that points out the levelling implications of a "spiritual" doctrine of work.

expense of higher levels or "stations" of work. In certain cases the evolution of "calling" from a spiritual to a secular orientation was not as clear-cut as scholars like Max Weber have usually indicated. Evidence of such continuity, understood in the context of an objective social and intellectual order hierarchical in structure, sheds new light on Weber's assumptions about economic activity and religious motivation. Did the Puritan doctrine of the calling provide an ideological framework for the emergence of a capitalistic ethos? Was it primarily a spiritual principle that evoked as a sign of salvation[3] an equalitarian glorification of labor releasing men from the compulsion to seek worldly success?

To Luther and Calvin, the idea of a "calling" meant that ethical behavior was subordinate to spiritual piety. As an expression of one's "particular" calling, everyday work had to be conceived in terms of a "general" or spiritual calling by God to eternal life in the next world. The worth of any calling must be measured not by success in a *hierarchy* of occupations, but by a profound coherence between mundane activity and the saving "temper" of one's own heart. Both Luther and Calvin contended that the deepest gratitude for the gift of salvation in Jesus was working in one's calling. A person's body was not his but God's, and all labor involved the presentation of one's body as a "living sacrifice, holy, acceptable unto God." In this light, Luther and Calvin concluded: "The works of monks and priests, be they never as holy and arduous, differ no whit in the sight of God from the works of the rustic toiling in the field or the woman going about her household tasks. . . ."[4]

The significance of this comment has sometimes been overlooked by historians, but it can hardly be overestimated. As Robert Michaelson has pointed out, "The common endeavors of the ordinary worker received new status and new meaning in Christian thought. The doing of ordinary work was hallowed by the touch of God's grace; the humblest sinner was given ample incentive to glorify God by grateful response to the divine grace in daily living." A classic expression of this "spiritual" interpretation of the calling was given by John Cotton in his 1641 sermon, *The Way of Life*. Echoing Luther's declaration that "truly good works . . . become good only when they flow from faith," Cotton declared that diligence and success in an individual's calling *"is but dead works"* if he lacks piety. Suggesting that even servile labor was a kind of sacrament, he insisted that preoccupation with social status was often the product of a "carnall" rather than a "faithful" heart. A man of rank and breeding was not wonted to hired servile work, but the same faith that made him desirous to be in a calling, made him stoop to any work his calling led him to;

---

[3] See Perry Miller, *The New England Mind: From Colony to Province* (Boston, 1953). Miller's theme of leading New England ministers unselfconsciously accommodating their piety to growing secular pressures is ably challenged by Robert Middlekauf, *The Mathers* (New York, 1971), esp. Ch. I.

[4] Quoted in Michaelson, *loc. cit.*, 316-18.

there is no work too hard or too homely for him, for faith is conscious, that it hath done most base drudgery for Satan. No lust or pride, or what else insolent, but our base hearts could be content to serve the Devil and nature in it, and therefore what drudgery can be too homely for me to do for God? . . . . So faith is ready to embrace any homely service his calling leads him to, which a carnall heart would blush to be seen in. . . .

While diligence in "homely employment" might make men grow rich and New England prosper, the true "Christian would no sooner have his sinne pardoned than his estate to be settled in some good calling, though not as a mercenary slave, but he would offer it up to God as a free-will Offering, he would have his condition settled in God's purpose, . . . though it be but a day labourer. . . ."[5] In effect, an important goal of manual labor was to *free* the individual rather than enslave him; herein lay the clue to a different meaning for Cotton's famous dictum: "Diligence in worldly businesse, and yet deadnesse to the world; such a mystery is none can read, but they that know it." Such a standard exalted the common and refused to say that any calling was to be valued above others.[6]

Both Cotton and his grandson, Cotton Mather, insisted that common callings were inseparable from Christ's redemptive role. This divine function began with "the revolutionary obedience of the Son" in living a lowly life and dying a criminal's death on the Cross. As Cotton observed in the *Way of life:*

Let the same mind be in you that was in Christ Jesus, he made himself of no reputation. He stood not upon it, that he was borne of God, and equal to the most high, but he made himself a servant, and of no reputation, and so to serve God, and save men; and when his father called him to it, he stooped to a very low employment, rose up from Supper, and girded himself with a Towell, and washed his Disciples' feet.

Indeed, a "right apprehension" of Christ's redemption enabled the regenerated individual in society to be released from the powers of mere men by functioning in his daily work. Cotton contended the laborer stood "directly before God, free to pursue the special duties of [his] lawfull calling without lesser earthly control or domination. Such freedom is his inheritance, it is the hallmark of his new life."[7] Like his predecessor, Mather also was concerned with subordinating all worldly occupations to his vision of a universal piety for mankind. His approach to the doctrine of the calling was predicated upon the inseparability of daily "work" from eternal predestined "vocation." Only in this way

---

[5] John Cotton, *The Way of Life* (London, 1641), 437, 449, 455-57.

[6] Michaelson, 320.

[7] Cotton, *The Way of Life,* 458. See also David Little, *Religion, Order, and Law* (New York, 1969), 52-54. Little makes an important distinction between "differentiation" and "subordination" in discussing the meaning of freedom in a spiritual doctrine of work.

could a genuine union of Christians be achieved, thereby preventing the kind of social fragmentation and alienation that resulted from the private pursuit of economic gain. In the *"business* of our *personal callings,"* he asked, "hast thou no dispositions to raise thy soul, unto some thoughts, *what may be done for GOD and CHRIST* . . . ? My friend, thou art one that makes but a *little figure* in the world, and *a brother of low degree,* behold a vast encouragement! A *little* man may do a great deal of *hurt.* And then, why may not a *little* man, do a great deal of *good!* It is possible the *wisdom of a poor man,* may start a proposal, that may *save a city,* serve a nation! A *single hair* applied unto a *flyer,* that has other whells depending on it, may pull up an *oak,* or pull down a *house."* The intensity of Mather's piety suggested that the ultimate value of work superseded the distinctions between rich and poor, or masters and servants.[8]

Not all Puritans, whether in America or England during the seventeenth century, emphasized the dignity of the common callings when compared with other forms of work. William Perkins suggested that the idea of the calling itself produced permanent conditions of inequality in society. Husbandmen, laborers, and the like did not deserve and should not aspire to expect the same degree of deference shown to a magistrate or a merchant. But even Perkins viewed all "particular" callings, whatever their status might be, as an expression of the "general" calling and of the almost infinite qualities of diversity in Christ's Work of Redemption for mankind. The basic reason for upholding the doctrine of the calling was the subordination of all work to the common good, just as "In mans bodie there be sundrie parts and members, and every one hath his severall use and office, which it perfecteth not for it selfe, but for the good of the whole bodie. . . ."[9]

On the eve of the English Civil War, some of Perkins' fellow divines drew more radical implications from this Puritan conception of work. John Dod and Robert Cleaver noted that since God "doth prefer the poor, despised, industrious, laborious, and giveth His voice for their precedency, why should we give titles to ruffians and roisters . . . that have nothing in them of grace and goodness, . . . of art or skillfulness?" Emphasis on the dignity of labor meant that "Every man, of every degree, as well rich as poor, as well mighty as mean, as well noble as base, must know that he is born for some employment to the good of his brethren, if he will acknowledge himself to be a member, and not an ulcer, in the body of mankind."[10] This equalitarian strain in Puritan thought was

[8] Cotton Mather, *Bonifacius: Essays for the Doing of Good,* ed. David Levin (Boston, 1967), 23-25; Middlekauf, 260.

[9] William Perkins, "A Treatise of the Vocations or Callings of Men," *Works,* I (Cambridge, 1608), 187; see also Michaelson, 323.

[10] Quoted in Christopher Hill, *Society and Puritanism in Pre-Revolutionary England* (New York, 1967), 140.

reinforced by traditional biblical sources. Though St. Paul's conception of a Christian community was conservative and hierarchical, the ideal itself stressed the inherent equal worth of each individual within that social structure. Individual values were measured by the proper performance of worldly work as well as by the spiritual state of sinner-believers. As a marginal note in the later Genevan Bible pointed out, Abraham's "great riches gotten in Egypt, hindered him not to follow his vocation." Real inequality arose, not when individuals worked industriously and diligently in their callings, but rather when they failed to do so at any level in the hierarchy of occupations.[11]

Puritans like Mather, Dod, and Cleaver were saying that even though there might always be gradations in talent and various distinctions between rich and poor in society, the nature of any kind of labor however low or mean was of equal value in the eyes of God. What gave all work, and especially common work, dignity was the kind of discipline which, as John Milton had written in 1641, included "not only the removal of disorder, but if any visible shape can be given to divine things, the very visible shape and image of virtue."[12] The employment of everyone in a useful calling gave a certain "structure" to society, but such employment did not prevent highly competitive, iron-willed men from being constantly at one another's throats. Attempting to define satisfactorily the difference between praiseworthy industry and the *"Cursed Hunger of Riches,"* for example, a New England Election Sermon in 1717 declared that men would lack "Some Motives and Encouragements to Vertue and Restraint from Vice, that they now have," if not distributed into "various Ranks and Degrees." The thrust of Puritan discipline—and of Puritan virtue—was to liberate men as much as possible from their natural state of sin by placing "over against the carnal aristocracy which ruled the world, . . . an aristocracy of the spirit, chosen by God and destined to inherit heaven and earth." This process involved a heightened awareness of paradox concerning hierarchy and equality that many Puritans continued to maintain in their faith even when confronted with situations in which the command to worship God conflicted with a social structure that placed a premium on getting ahead in this world. John Robinson's early seventeenth-century admonition to his Plymouth followers that "man is borne to sore labour, in body, in minde, as the spark to fly upward" provided no little comfort to sinner-believers who knew that the "upward goal was not of this world, and that in "Heaven . . . onely" was there "rest without labour." When considered in conjunction with a view of Christian redemption working throughout history to "free" men of all possible "Ranks and Degrees"

---

[11] *Ibid.,* 144; see also Ernst Troeltsch, *The Social Teaching of the Christian Churches,* I (New York, 1960), 76-77.   [12] Quoted in Hill, 225.

from their sinful bondage, such a statement pointed to an egalitarian notion of work while at the same time reflecting a hierarchical conception of society.[13]

This dual perception of the world and of work had its religious antecedents for the Puritans in the doctrine of the calling. What is interesting, however, is that in the eighteenth century another tradition, more secular in orientation and long known in literature as the "Great Chain of Being," gave expression to these tensions between hierarchy and equality in almost exactly the same way as the doctrine of the calling had done. While seventeenth-century Puritans had thought about vertical order and the equal dignity of each "station" within that order in almost complete ignorance of the "Chain," spiritual descendants like Jonathan Edwards in the following century were not unaware of the governing assumptions behind such an intellectual construct. Appealing to the Gospels of St. Paul as earlier Puritans had done, Edwards and other major Calvinist evangelicals reaffirmed both their religious piety and a spiritual doctrine of work by also evoking the fundamental premises of the Great Chain. From the Great Awakening revivals to the end of the Revolutionary era, their efforts produced a sense of continuity with the original Protestant idea of the calling that resisted the growing secularization of the Puritan ethic in eighteenth-century America. Stressing the equal dignity of all socially productive worldly activities, they operated within a hierarchical framework based on the general conception of the Great Chain of Being. It may be instructive, therefore, to review the main outlines of the Chain as the educated public of that period defined and saw them, before we discuss its implications for religious attitudes toward work as expressed by Edwards and his followers.[14]

In a century that has been described as an "Age of Sentiment" as well as an "Age of Reason," it is hardly surprising that a Neoplatonic scheme of ideas based on hierarchy, continuity, and plenitude should have been so popular. As Arthur O. Lovejoy has observed, in its broadest sense the Chain of Being affirmed what many Enlightened people in Europe and America believed most fundamentally, that man was endowed with a moral sense and that the universe was comprehensible by reason and becoming more so. Such an affirmation, implying arguments for "design" in the cosmos, had been given tentative expression by Locke in his *Essay Concerning Human Understanding:*

And when we consider the infinite power and wisdom of the Maker, we have reason to think, that it is suitable to the magnificent harmony of the universe,

---

[13] *Ibid.,* 249; see also John Robinson, "Diligent Labor and the Use of God's Creatures" in *Tensions in Puritanism,* ed. R. Reintiz (New York, 1970), 12, 66.

[14] Arthur O. Lovejoy, *The Great Chain of Being* (New York, 1960), 43-45, 183. Lovejoy in his analysis of the Platonic origins of the idea of the Chain, cites Edwards' views on the "disinterested" character of the entire design of creation.

and the great design and infinite goodness of the architect, that the species of creatures shall also, by gentley [sic] degrees, ascend upwards from us toward his infinite perfection, as we see they gradually descend from us downwards.[15]

Postulating the notion of an orderly and coherent universe whose harmony had been originally illuminated by a divine and benevolent Architect, Locke went on to stress the fullness or "plenitude" of the creation, with everything in it arranged in an infinite number of links according to the minutest degree of differentiation, from the lowest to the highest possible form of "Being." Implicit in Locke's formulation was an emphasis, which other writers made more explicit, on the constant activity of creation itself. The rationality of the cosmos in terms of a "ful and infinitesimally graduated Scale of Being" meant that each link or "species of creatures" existed not only for their "utility" to any other, but also, as Lovejoy put it in paraphrasing Leibniz, for "the maximization of diversity that [Nature] seeks."[16] Hierarchy was important primarily in the sense of defining and evaluating man's place in the cosmic scheme of things. Though not denying the almost limitless potentiality of human worth, many proponents of the Great Chain used the concept in part to protest against the equally boundless forms of human vanity. Man's position in the Scale of Being was seen as approximating that of a "middle rung." Locke had even suggested that "there are far more species of creatures above us, than there are beneath; we being in degrees of perfection much more remote from the infinite Being of God, than we are from the lowest state of being, and that which approaches nearest to nothing."[17] The thrust of these pronouncements was toward a cosmic and increasingly non-utilitarian view of man and the world in which he lived and worked. "Not for the actors, but for the action" were life's many mechanisms contrived and functioning, observed the early eighteenth-century deist Lord Bolingbroke, whose mildly agnostic attitudes concerning the specific purposes of creation did not prevent him from declaring, as many nineteenth-century Romantics would, that the completeness of the total cosmic scheme was the true *raison d'être* of the universe.[18]

This appeal to nature in terms of Newton's mechanical universe and, conversely, as an evolving organism underscored not only the complex

[15] Quoted in Lovejoy, 184.
[16] *Ibid.*, 256-57, 268-69. My discussion of the tensions between hierarchy and equality in the Chain of Being idea is heavily indebted to Lovejoy's seminal study.
[17] *Ibid.*, 185.
[18] *Ibid.*, 189. I am referring here to what Henry F. May has called "Moderate Enlightenment" thinkers who stressed optimism and harmony in the universe, rather than to skeptics like Voltaire who denounced the fundamental principles of the Great Chain. See Henry F. May, *The Enlightenment in America* (New York, 1976), Ch. XIV.

range of Enlightenment patterns of thought but also the variety of ways in which the Chain of Being reflected many levels of mental construction, whether in politics, religion, philosophy, or social theory. Traditionally, the implications of the concept had been conservative. The following Federalist partisan chant denouncing the levelling excesses of the French Revolution, for example, was a familiar refrain to many Americans steeped in the heritage of the Puritan Ethic:

> Next, every man throughout the nation
> Must be contented with his station,
> Nor to think to cut a figure greater
> Than was designed for him by nature.[19]

But the idea of the Chain of Being as a way of ordering nature's differences was not necessarily limited to a static world view. Leibniz had suggested an alternative, an almost aesthetic approach in his late seventeenth-century vision of a "pluralistic universe," which perceived each individual substance or link in the Scale of Being as not simply a preordained "fragment" of the universe but "the universe itself" seen from a particular, lively, and even mystical viewpoint. During the eighteenth century this vision began to be affected by what Lovejoy has referred to as "evolutionistic theories" or the "temporalizing" of the Chain of Being (especially by Leibniz) which stressed degrees of differentiation and not only degrees of "subordination" between each link or species in the Great Chain. For certain *philosophes,* nature came to be seen as no longer "always equally perfect" but "always increasing in perfection, with the Scale of Beings constituting a whole infinitely graduated, with no real lines of separation; . . . only individuals, and no kingdoms of classes or genera or species."[20] The individual's status before his Creator and before his fellowmen might no longer depend primarily upon his particular "calling" or "estate" in this world but instead upon his general "existence" or "humanity." Rousseau's entreaty that man "Remain in the place which Nature has assigned to thee in the chain of beings," for example, was designed not to confine but to broaden and deepen the range of human experiences. "Man is strong," Rousseau contended, "when he contents himself with being what he is; he is weak when he desires to raise himself above *humanity.*"[21]

Rousseau's pre-existential concern with defining daily living in general terms like "humanity" rather than in the particular terms of one's place in a hierarchical social structure, represented a secularized restatement of what many Puritan theologians had been saying for nearly two

[19] Quoted in Winthrop Jordan, *White Over Black* (Chapel Hill, 1968), 185.

[20] Lovejoy, 274-75. For certain aesthetic tendencies in Leibniz's thought, see Ernst Cassirer, *The Philosophy of the Enlightenment* (Boston, 1955), 32-33.

[21] Quoted in Lovejoy, 201-02. My emphasis.

centuries about the inseparability of everyday "work" from eternal "vocation." During the Great Awakening revivals in New England, Jonathan Edwards suggested that an important reason for these religious upheavals stemmed from guilt-feelings aroused in men who had failed to subordinate their business pursuits to larger religious and moral goals.[22] Subjecting his own community at Northampton to intensive scrutiny, he declared that all "works," whether they took the form of good deeds or meant simply earning a livelihood, must be conceived as a kind of communal conversion experience that would bring every personal calling into harmony with transforming grace. If the social conflicts that stemmed from individual acquisitiveness were to be healed and "God's people in this land [abound] in . . . deeds of love," the "fruits" of these various vocations must be made to cohere with their holy "antecedents" in Christ. Even more than Cotton had done before him, Edwards made the pursuit of one's calling inseparable from the Work of Redemption in history. Playing upon any sense of guilt produced by the drive to wealth and power, he preached to ambitious men the meaning and necessity of conversion as a "new birth":

Not only are our best duties defiled, in being attended with the exercises of sin and corruption, that precede them and follow them, and are intermingled with holy acts; but even the holy acts themselves, and the gracious exercises of the godly, though the act most simply considered is good, yet take the acts in their measure and dimensions, and the manner in which they are exerted, and they are corrupt acts; that is, they are defectively corrupt, or sinfully defective. . . .[23]

The purpose of working hard and performing good acts, he told them, was not to gain "eternal blessings in reward for them, for it is in consequence of our justification, that our good deeds become rewardable with spiritual and eternal rewards. The acceptableness, and the rewardableness of our virtue, is not antecedent to justification, but follows it, and is built entirely upon it; . . . Hence, though it be true that the saints are rewarded for their good works, yet it is for Christ's sake only, and not for the excellency of their works considered, or beheld separately from Christ."[24] Denouncing the principle of "utility" as the basis for a

[22] Richard Bushman, "Jonathan Edwards as a Great Man: Identity, Conversion, and Leadership in the Great Awakening," *Soundings,* 52 (1969), 40-41.

[23] Jonathan Edwards, "Justification by Faith Alone," 1738, in *Jonathan Edwards: Representative Selections* (New York, 1962), Clarence H. Faust and Thomas H. Johnson, eds., 109. Edwards' evangelical counterpart in the middle colonies, Gilbert Tennent, preached similar sermons that questioned the value of all economic activity when it was identified with the profit motive. See J. E. Crowley, *This Sheba, Self* (Baltimore, 1974), 66-67.

[24] Edwards, "Justification by Faith Alone," 111; "God Glorified in Man's Dependence," 92-93.

Godly-ordered society, he insisted that genuine callings, from the lowliest "labourer" to the highest "Governor," must be viewed not as a way of reconciling egotistical impulses with the good of the whole but rather as a way of totally subjecting the human will to God. The true sign of holiness in communities as well as in individuals was not fanatical self-control but humble self-surrender.[25]

Even after the fervor of the Awakening had subsided in New England, Edwards continued to preach that "the nature of things will not admit of a man's having an interest given him in the merits or benefits of a Saviour, on the account of any thing as a righteousness, or virtue, or excellency in him."[26] Rather than justifying such anti-utilitarian reasoning by appealing to a chaotic universe, where "all men . . . allied themselves with [God's] sovereignty or rebelled against it," he declared that "an entire new method" had been designed for uncovering "all parts of the grand scheme, in their historical order." Though this design was only partially realized in his unfinished *History of the Work of Redemption* the "method" itself was predicated upon an interesting juxtaposition of concepts which combined a traditional Augustinian approach to history with a major assumption behind the Chain of Being theory. The purpose of creation, and the purpose of his *History,* Edwards readily conceded, was to demonstrate how " the WORK OF REDEMPTION is a work that GOD carries on from the fall of man to the end of the world," so that every doctrine will appear "beautiful and entertaining; . . . in the highest light, in the most striking manner, shewing the admirable contexture and harmony of the whole." But in the philosophical conception of his plan, he evoked a Neoplatonic ideal that was a central premise of the Great Chain theory: the notion that "Change" throughout the creation as well as "Redemption" working throughout Christian history could be explained by a principle of "identity" rather than by one involving a strictly "chronological or causal development."[27]

Presupposing the existence of a divine, unitary "Being" whose very "otherness" inspired in lesser beings an oddly exuberant king of "this-worldliness," the notion of "identity" suggested that the "connexion" of a thing with "some antecedent cause, ground or reason of its existence"

---

[25] See Richard Bushman, *From Puritan to Yankee: Character and the Social Order in Connecticut, 1690-1765* (Boston, 1967), 275 ff.

[26] Quoted in Perry Miller, *Jonathan Edwards* (New York, 1949), 79.

[27] Edwards, "Letter to the Trustees of the College of New Jersey at Princeton," in *Selections,* 411-12. For a very general and illuminating discussion of these seemingly opposing ways of interpreting experiences, especially as they relate to a "traditional" vs. a "modern" world-view, see Sidney E. Mead, "Church, State, Calvinism and Conscience," in *Perspectives in American History* (Charles Warren Center for Studies in American History, Harvard), III, 1969, 443-59. See also Erich Auerbach, *Mimesis; the Representation of Reality in Western Literature* (Princeton, 1953).

was comprehensible only in a cohering sense, or as Edward put it, "in the whole continuance of the thing created." What gave each "being" or "link" in a hierarchical universe equal or "sufficient reason" for existing was the fact that there was an absolute "moral necessity" rooted in the "natures of things" themselves, which constituted an immutable order of right and wrong in the universe and ultimately represented the "reason and ground of their being what they are." With respect to the origins and activities of creation, Edwards saw no inconsistency between this "nature of things" and the fluctuating operations of "divine Providence" because both concepts were seen as mutually "reflecting" or "cohering" entities, rather than "antecedent" or "consequent" to each other. In the light of Edwards' principle of "identity," God had neither been compelled nor had he acted arbitrarily in creating a world and assigning its offspring to specific stations in life. Instead, he had acted upon "good and sufficient reason" in the form of a "direct call to man to accept both freely and humbly his individuality and the position it occupies in the plan of the whole." In this way, as proponents of the Chain of Being theory increasingly emphasized during the eighteenth century, man would "add something of his own" to a hierarchical cosmos in which God himself, from the standpoint of both spiritual intentions and worldly commitment, appeared to be almost "insatiably creative."[28]

For Edwards, it was this sense of *collaboration* between man and God in fulfilling the "universal Design" in history which gave shape and meaning to that inherited set of values clustered around the Puritan ethic and the idea of "calling." Max Weber later expressed vividly the social implications of this ideal when he wrote that "the God of Calvinism demanded of his believers not single works but a life of good works combined into a unified system." Edwards had outlined the philosophical significance of such a "system" in *Two Dissertations* ("Concerning the End for which God Created the World" and "The Nature of True Virtue") completed in 1755. Describing this interaction in the aesthetic terms of "Man's high calling . . . to enrich the sum of things," the *Dissertations* consistently invoked both the notion of "identity" underlying the Chain of Being and its functioning principles of "variety" and "plenitude." There could be "no solid objection against God's aiming at an infinitely perfect union of the creature with himself," Edwards contended, even though "the particular time will never come when it can be said, the union is now infinitely perfect. [For] God [also] aims at satisfying justice in the eternal damnation of sinners; which will be satisfied by their damnation, considered no otherwise than with regard to its eternal damnation."[29] There has been speculation that Edwards him-

[28] Edwards, "Dissertation Concerning the End for which God Created the World," *Selections,* 348; Lovejoy 296.
[29] Edwards, "Dissertation . . .," 348.

self intended the *Dissertations* to be published as one major treatise in conjunction with his last completed work, *The Doctrine of Original Sin,* which developed more fully the premise of the "identity" of mankind with Adam's fall and God's redemptive promise.[30] Taken together, a dominant emphasis in all three works was on the "plenitude" and "variety" of the creation itself and of man's role in it as he related both to his Creator and to his fellow men. Edwards constantly cautioned that God had never been obliged to produce a world that would represent a mere addition to his already "infinite excellency," or "imply . . . any dependence of the Creator on the creature;" nonetheless, he insisted, a "natural world" had in fact been created in which the "creature's good" was seen both as "an emanation of God's fulness, [and as] the subject of the fulness communicated." This process of "emanation" was reflected primarily in the universal drama of salvation, but the sense of aesthetic collaboration between man and God also extended to mundane activities. Whether these connections involved the temporary exercise of a particular calling or the eternal fulfillment of a divine one—whether indeed they were "enjoined by God, by history or by philosophy," as Edmund Morgan has asserted about the ideas and attitudes surrounding the Puritan Ethic— they were "explicable," from Edwards' viewpoint only "in mutual relationship, as they reflect one another."[31]

While Edwards drew upon major assumptions and principles of the Great Chain in discussing the purpose of creation and the place of the Puritan ethic in both the "work of redemption" and the ultimate "nature of things," his terminology was a product of many sources. His description of the divine "coherence" of the creation and its creatures, for example, made use of the language of religious typology by appealing directly to Newton's "law of gravity":

The whole material universe if preserved by gravity or attraction, or the mutual tendency of all bodies to each other. One part of the universe is hereby made beneficial to another; the beauty, harmony and order, regular progress, life, and motion, and in short all the well-being of the whole frame depends on it. This is a type of love or charity in the spiritual world.[32]

Passages like this one evoked the rational universe of the Enlightenment and attempted to spiritualize it by employing an ancient Biblical device. At the same time, however, Edwards' harmonious picture of a symmetrically progressive creation also corresponded with the "cosmical order" of the Chain of Being philosophy, which was "conceived not as a process

---

[30] Jonathan Edwards, *Original Sin,* ed. Clyde Holbrook (Yale, 1970), intro. by Holbrook, 22.

[31] Edwards, "Dissertation . . .," 344-46. Morgan, "The Puritan Ethic and the American Revolution," 7-8.

[32] Quoted in Ursula Brumm, *American Thought and Religious Typology* (New Brunswick, 1970), 99.

of infinite static diversity," but as one of "increasing diversification." Enhancing this "cosmical order" was a certain "cosmical piety" radiating from a hierarchical theory of the universe that involved a peculiar and absolute "delight in the world which can arise, not from any belief in its adaptation to man's need or hopes, but from its infinite richness and diversity as a spectacle, the prodigious sweep of the complex and often tragic drama which it exhibits."[33]

It would be no exaggeration to say that it was this kind of pietistic "spectacle" which Edwards had in mind when he attempted to explain the meaning of virtuous callings for mankind. "When we are called to a secular business, . . . if we improve our lives to any other purpose, than as a journey toward heaven, all is lost," Edwards declared in *The Christian Pilgrim,* adding somewhat caustically in a similar sermon that the utilitarian consequences of earthly success in a calling "are things which God in his providence throws out to those whom he looks on as dogs; but Christ's peace is the bread of his children."[34] This challenge to the belief, increasingly assumed by practitioners of the Puritan ethic in the eighteenth century, that one's own betterment in a productive calling contributed automatically to the greatest happiness of the greatest number in the best of all possible worlds, was given a more precise formulation in the writings of two leading followers of Edwards who became important theologians in their own right, Joseph Bellamy (1719-90) and Samuel Hopkins (1721-1803). Like Edwards, both Calvinist divines conceived of all callings in terms of their subordination to the doctrines that they preached. Two of the most striking of these doctrines involved the integration of worldly activity with the Work of Redemption. In explaining this process, Bellamy and Hopkins found justification for restating the original spiritual version of the Puritan ethic and much of this reaffirmation evoked the basic premises of the Chain of Being.[35]

The first doctrine proclaimed the idea of a "General Atonement" in which Christ's suffering, death, and resurrection was considered to be not a limited process but for all men at every level of "being," including the damned as well as the saved. "The Redeemer has made an atonement

---

[33] Quoted in Lovejoy, 294-96; 187-89. Though the language here is Lovejoy's, the phraseology almost duplicates that of Edwards in certain passages from the "End for which God Created the World," "The Nature of True Virtue," and the "History of the Work of Redemption." See, respectively, 345-47, 352-55 in *Selections.*

[34] Edwards, "The Christian Pilgrim," 130; "The Peace Which Christ Gives," 137, in *Selections.*

[35] On the whole, Edwards' followers have not received a favorable treatment from historians. See Joseph Haroutunian, *Piety versus Moralism* (New York, 1935). Alan Heimert's *Religion and the American Mind* (Boston, 1967), while critical of Hopkins, does give a sympathetic and perceptive analysis of Bellamy's religious vision for society.

sufficient to expiate for the sins of the whole world, and, in this sense, had tasted death for every man," wrote Hopkins, the complex and often cranky theoretician of what became known as the "New Divinity" movement in eighteenth-century New England. Though only a relative few had actually been saved throughout history, he declared that Christ's atonement nonetheless had been and would continue to be "sufficient" for the salvation of all to the end of time, whether they were sinners or saints, ministers or laymen, rich or poor, laborers or merchants. Seeing the General Atonement as a logical projection of the principles of "identity," "variety," and "plenitude" underscoring Edwards' own view of the nature of redemption, Hopkins tied this redemptive process to secular callings as well as to one's spiritual election. As he observed in his theological *summa,* the *System of Doctrine,* "All the created universe, containing every creature and thing, visible and invisible, greater and less, are here said to be created for Christ—considered as God, Man, and Mediator—the redeemer of man." Hopkins saw the climax of such a creation in a this-worldly millennium, when the Puritan ethic would finally be divested of its profit motive, thereby subsuming man's rapacious competitive instincts under more ennobling "sentiments." The selfish and the greedy, he contended, "will be . . . diminished, by their destroying themselves and one another" over the use and control of "Property." The structure of society would then flow naturally and inevitably from the very nature of "rebirth," because grace would conform the mind and nature to the moral image of God, reborn men being made "partakers of his holiness, . . . which summarily consists in benevolence."[36]

Hopkins' notion of "holiness" as "benevolence" pointed to a second fundamental doctrine of the New Divinity, a belief that men could find their unity only in "disinterested benevolence" of which God himself, who was identified as "Being in General," was the crowning culmination. This altruistic conception of virtue proposed that genuine morality in one's calling and conduct was a spontaneous demonstration of the "taste and expression of the heart," not of the understanding. As Alan Heimert has perceptively observed of the social significance of such a notion, virtue was defined "not as a variety of deportments that differed from class to class and calling to calling but as a 'temper' essentially the same for all men, regardless of station."[37] Restructuring the basis of virtuous callings

---

[36] *The Works of Samuel Hopkins, D. D.,* with a Memoir of His Life and Character, ed. Edwards A. Park (Boston, 1854), I, 173-365; see also Bushman, *From Puritan to Yankee,* (Boston, 1967), 276.

[37] Hopkins, Works, I, 369-71; *The Works of Joseph Bellamy* (Boston, 1850), I, 68. See also Heimert, *Religion and the American Mind,* 55-56; Ernest O. Tuveson, "The Creed of the Confidence-Man," *ELH,* **33,** No. 2 (June 1966), 247-70.

by stipulating that every form of selfishness, including a "natural esteem" of self, was sinful, both Bellamy and Hopkins viewed the pious exercise of individual occupations in cosmic, almost sublime terms. Bellamy appealed to the origins of creation itself in order to reiterate that the connection between faith and experience should not be "regarded as primarily a . . . causal development but as a oneness with the divine plan, of which all of the occurrences are parts and reflections." Though "long before the foundation of the world [God] had his choice [of] all possible . . . systems that equally lay open to the divine view," his creative activity with respect to this world was performed in total coherence with "a perfectly good taste, . . . infinite wisdom and perfect rectitude being the judges." This "taste," inherent in the creation and yet beyond it, subsequently enabled every kind of "being" to have an equal claim to "existence" in the "divine plan," even though one's "earthly connection" might, in the very "nature of things," be unequal. What mattered about the individual's "connection" or "calling" in this world and in the next was that it existed primarily "for the sake of completeness . . . , the realization of which was the chief object of God in creating the world." What was socially and spiritually redeemable about man was the fact that even the lowliest of individuals on the scale of human worth could experience, through the proper cultivation of disinterested benevolence in the practice of earthly callings, a sense of equal "completeness" with the highest of individuals.[38]

In *True Religion Delineated,* his impressionistic synthesis of Edwardsean theology, Bellamy patterned such an integrated experience after the hierarchical symmetry of the Great Chain of Being. "There are valuable things in mankind," he declared:

Some have one thing, and some another; some have gifts, and some have grace; some have five talents, and some two, and some one; some are worthy of greater esteem, and some less, considered merely as they are in themselves; and then some are by God set in higher station, and some in a lower, sustaining various characters and standing in various relations; as magistrates and subjects, ministers and people, parents and children, masters and servants, etc. And there is a certain esteem and respect due to every one in his station. Now, with a disinterested impartiality, and with a perfect candor, and a hearty good will, ought we to view the various excellencies of our neighbors, and consider their various stations, characters, and relations; and, in our hearts give everyone his due honor and his proper place, being perfectly content, for our parts, to be and to act in our own sphere, where God has placed us; and, by our fellow mortals, to be considered as being just what we are; and, indeed, this, for substance, is the duty of everyone in the whole system of intelligent creatures.

---

[38] Bellamy, *Works,* I, 120; Auerbach, *Mimesis,* 490.

We could not be satisfied, Bellamy contended, with cultivating a purely "impartial" appreciation of the "place that God has allotted to us in the system, and to be and act in our own proper sphere, and willing to be considered by others as being just what we are." It was further required "that we be perfectly *benevolent* towards all beings, that is, that we consider their happiness as to body and soul, as to time and eternity, as being what it really is, and are, according to the measure of our natural capacities, thoroughly sensible of its value and worth, and are disposed to be affected and act accordingly; that is, to be tender of it, value and promote it, as being what it is; to long, and labor, and pray for it, and to rejoice in their prosperity, and be grieved for their adversity; and all from a cordial love and genuine good will."[39] Considered in this light, Bellamy's emphasis on pursuing one's calling according to one's "station" in society was hardly intended to preserve an inequality of condition in a close hierarchial system. Bellamy as well as Hopkins appealed to the "temporalized" kind of hierarchy contained in the Chain of Being theory as a means of checking the growing secularization of the Puritan ethic. Human drives, whether they be socially, economically, or religiously motivated, must cohere always with "True Holiness," which Hopkins defined as a "disinterested," rather mystical, but esthetically knowledgable "consent" of individual being to "Universal Being." A genuine sense of "identity" among human beings meant "that by which intelligent beings are united together in the highest, most perfect and beautiful union. It consists in the harmony of affection and union of heart by which the intelligent system becomes *ONE,* so far as holiness prevails." Applying the principles of "variety" and "plenitude" to such a structure, Hopkins concluded that "holiness" in individual callings "fixes every being, by his own inclination and choice, in his proper place, so as in the best manner to promote the good of the whole."[40]

Describing man and society in terms of the precepts of the Chain of Being was not an isolated phenomenon among ministers in eighteenth-century America. For rationalist theologians like Charles Chauncy (1705-87) and Jonathan Mayhew, (1720-86), the concept not only provided "pleasure and assurance" but was "the foundation of all social wisdom." But unlike Edwards and many other Calvinist evangelicals. Chauncy and Mayhew stressed "hierarchy" and "subordination" rather than "identity," "variety," and "plenitude" as the essential elements of the Great Chain. "'Tis unalterably right and just there should be rule and superiority in some and subjection and inferiority in others," Chauncy announced in the aftermath of the Great Awakening. Just as there were infinite distinctions regarding beasts, men. angels, and God, there were also numerous sub-links within the society of mankind itself

---

[39] Bellamy, 121-22, 583-85.
[40] Hopkins, *Works,* III, 11-13; Lovejoy, 316.

founded upon what appeared to be permanently descending gradations from "superior" to "inferior" beings. Edwards and his followers drew nearly opposite conclusions from the Chain of Being than these conservative implications. Their notion of "hierarchy was one of holiness and increasingly visible likeness to God." "'Tis certainly beautiful," Edwards wrote of the Chain, "that it should be so—that in the various ranks of beings those that are nearest to the first being should most evidently and variously partake of his influence." Both in the exercise of virtue and in the performance of work, the focus was always on "the 'pleasing' equality of all nature, . . . in which the sweet concord of equals might be discerned."[41]

It has already been suggested that such an aesthetic equalization of hierarchy while evoking a Chain of Being framework represented a contradiction in terms and a symptom of an inherent inconsistency between that "traditonal" framework and a so-called "modern" representation of reality like the Puritan ethic. That this "figural" apprehension of particular occurrences in the universe basically resembled a "pre-modern" worldview has been pointed out by numerous scholars. To the same degree that the Great Chain envisioned a "world-historical context" in which each part of that context was interdependent with every other part and in which the whole was "regarded as being of all times, or above all time," the notion of "work" itself was perceived as having a constant value in the ultimate scheme of things. But interpreting daily events primarily in terms of a timeless, "invisible world" rather than in terms of a "chronological or causal connection" did not necessarily mean a negation of the latter conception. The "invisible" drama of redemption, as we have seen, was portrayed by prominent theologians in the seventeenth and eighteenth centuries as a "work" progressively revealing itself in many different forms throughout "history." In a similar manner, the principles of "identity," "variety," and "plenitude" behind the idea of the Great Chain were gradually conceived by eighteenth-century interpreters as the basis for a belief that "progress" throughout the hierarchy of beings "will never come to an end." From this standpoint, the secular as well as the religious value of laboring in the world lay not in the fact that it was instrumental to the individual's advancement in society, but rather because it brought the individual into equal coherence with the wholeness or "completeness' of creation. When applied to human relationships, this redemptive emphasis meant that every graduation or "station" in the society of mankind shared equal diginity with every other. But more important, the later tendency by theorists of the Chain to "temporalize" or "romanticize" it while paradoxically retaining its hierarchical structure involved tensions that were at work in much the

41 Quoted in Heimert, *Religion and the American Mind* (Boston, 1967), 262, 307.

same manner within the Puritan ethic. Broadly speaking, these tensions might be described as a *secular-utilitarian* as opposed to a *religious-aesthetic* conception of the values which productive diligence in the performance of one's calling ought to promote. Increasingly, Americans affirmed the secular-utilitarian version of the Puritan ethic because it encouraged upward mobility and tended to associate both "liberty" and "property" with "virtue." However, the reaffirmation of the spiritual basis of work by theologians like Edwards, Bellamy, and Hopkins indicates that a subtle continuity persisted in attitudes toward the Puritan ethic. Their particular notion of work and morality derived the support, not just from the original pietistic motivation behind the doctrine of the calling but from that anti-utilitarian and aesthetic perception of the universe expressed in eighteenth-century views of the Chain of Being. Advocating a renewal of the notion of "work" as "vocation," these theologians insisted that the Puritan ethic derived its validity and power less from the actual "ethic" than from an internalized sense of piety which was very much like the cosmic reverence toward all life that the Great Chain theory evoked.[42]

To write off these criticisms as the work of a small clique of tradition-fixated, otherworldly Calvinist divine who had "lost confidence in the calling's ability to integrate social and spiritual life" contributes little to our own understanding of alternative ideas and possibilities which have at every moment affected the final outcome in history.[43] Recently scholars have begun to question, for example, the "ease with which most past Americans affirmed the Protestant work ethic" in its "modern" secularized form. Revolutionary statesmen like Franklin, John Adams, and Alexander Hamilton constantly worried about the presence of "alien" virtues among "good workmen from the several countries of Europe." Herbert Gutman has observed that these tendencies persisted well into the present century: "Even in the land of Benjamin Franklin, Andrew Carnegie, and Henry Ford, non-industrial cultures and work habits regularly thrived and were nourished by new workers alien to the 'Protestant' work ethic."[44] It would be presumptuous to ascribe the source of these different attitudes directly to *religious-aesthetic* tendencies in the Chain of Being and in the spiritual idea of calling. But this so-called "alien" deference to "nonindustrial" and even "pre-modern" values points to nearly identical concerns with the nature and the purpose of work in daily life. Though Gutman has indicated that these qualities were seemingly antithetical to the "Protestant"—or "Puritan"—work ethic, the above evidence suggests that similar alternative approaches to labor continued to exist within the Puritan ethic itself and that they were

---

[42] Auerbach, 136; Mead, 448.   [43] Crowley, 71.

[44] Herbert Gutman, "Work, Culture, and Society in Industrializing America, 1815-1919," *American Historical Review*, 78 (June, 1973), 531-32.

reinforced philosophically by the paradoxical emphasis in the Great Chain on the " 'pleasing equality" of every level of activity in society. Rapid economic growth in the new nation was not always paralleled by immediate changes in social attitudes toward "work," and one reason for this cultural lag both during and after the colonial period was the persistence of what have been called "traditional artisan work habits" among diverse working-class populations. Accepting loose "Old World" distinctions concerning occupational hierarchies while stressing the individual dignity of each of these occupations, these groups rejected the kind of mass regimented labor that would make, in Hamilton's prophetic words, "the spirit of manufacturing . . . become the spirit of the nation." What has been overlooked, however, in explaining this resistance among not only artisans and laborers but also certain evangelical ministers was an important theoretical basis for it. The very concept that encouraged work habits which, whether intentional or not, led to dynamic economic expansion, continued to evoke in its original form values which undermined the utilitarian rationale behind that expansion. This does not mean that exponents of the Puritan ethic usually preached the efficacy of viewing economic success as a sign of salvation. Whether they imparted to it a secular or a religious orientation, Puritans had always minimized the importance of earthly accomplishments at the same time that they sanctified work. But in the literature on the calling, the nature of the tasks that were sanctified was subject to different interpretations.

Beginning with Luther and Calvin in the sixteenth century, a consistent theme runs through the writings of theologians like John Cotton, Cotton Mather, Jonathan Edwards, Joseph Bellamy, and Samuel Hopkins which placed special emphasis on the dignity of labor. Ordinary work was singled out in order to demonstrate the subordinate quality of all worldly activity to a creation whose true value lay in the image of spiritual piety which God had breathed into its creatures. To sustain this piety not only required the spiritualization of work, but also involved an aesthetic conviction, as important Calvinist divines saw it by the eighteenth century in America, that the individual in his calling was made for the sake of his creation and not the other way around. No one calling, therefore, was more or less higher than another. It is not without irony that, in order to rationalize this belief in the levelling of all occupations before God, these theologians appealed to a world-view that was hierarchical and "traditional" rather than to one that was egalitarian and "modern."[45]

North Carolina State University.

[45] *Ibid.*, 560, 580-81.

XVI

"CLASS VERSUS RANK": THE TRANSFORMATION OF EIGHTEENTH-CENTURY ENGLISH SOCIAL TERMS AND THEORIES OF PRODUCTION

BY STEVEN WALLECH[1]

Asa Briggs's article, "The Language of 'Class' in Early Nineteenth Century England," stated that the term "class" did not come into general use until "the large scale economic changes of the late eighteenth and early nineteenth centuries."[2] Instead of "class," words like "rank," "order," "station," "degree," "estate," and "post" made up the social vocabulary. Briggs's article focused on the relationship between the word "class" and the events of social strife during that period to account for this shift in social language. What Briggs left out of his discussion, however, was an explanation of the conceptual framework that made the word "class" more effective in the description of that social strife he identified.

The use of "class" in nineteenth-century Great Britain depended on changes in the perception of social division that occurred in the eighteenth century. Concepts of status in the eighteenth century associated specific occupations and types of property with particular "ranks," "social character," and "distinction." The relationship between words like "rank," "station," and "order" and the social identity they defined depended on a sense of stability found in the organization of eighteenth-century British society. In reality, however, new ideas explaining the nature of the social structure undermined this stability and placed too much conceptual strain on the language. These conventional words, which functioned interchangeably, gave way to the term "class." The area where this conceptual strain occurred with the greatest regularity was in the new discipline called political economy. There the idea of production undermined older notions of where one stood in society.

Eighteenth-century concepts of status based on the language of "rank" associated a person's social position with a calculus of property, privilege, dress, education, honor, obligation, residence, occupation, friendship,

[1] The author wishes to thank Professors J. G. A. Pocock, Paul Fideler, Fred White, Sara Varhus, Bill and Miram Haskett, Ben Kennedy, Gerry DeMaio, LeAnne Thurmond, Dennis Kline, Don Wester, Anton Donoso, Richard Reitsma, and Fred Conrad for commenting on a draft of this essay during a summer seminar offered by the N.E.H. at The Johns Hopkins University. Their help and critical evaluation made the final form of this project possible.

[2] Asa Briggs, "The Language of 'Class' in Early Nineteenth Century England," *Essays in Labour History,* ed. Asa Briggs and John Saville (London 1960), 43.

beauty, strength, and wisdom.[3] These features of status derived from an individual's personal merit and estate. This approach to social division reflected the habits of British authors to weigh and to measure all the qualities of distinction that placed one person above another in eighteenth-century society. Each "rank" isolated by such an approach could be located on social maps that cast society in complex hierarchies of "subordination." Political arithmeticians like Sir William Petty, Gregory King, and Charles Davenant urged that the true picture of the nation required the "weight, number, and measure" of all the things and people identified in the social fabric.[4]

The precision of such an approach endowed the language of "rank" with a wealth of meaning. In contrast the word "class" imparted an essentially hollow signification during this era. "Class" was hollow in the sense that it identified only a "species," "sort," or "type" of person or thing. For example, an eighteenth-century English-speaking author might say that fops were a "class" of people found among the distinguished "ranks" of society. "Class" was most frequently used to generate categories within a taxonomy, while the real wealth of social meaning belonged to "rank." "Rank" communicated the specific details of status that were tangible and visible to the eighteenth-century observer.[5]

The history of the emergence of "class" saw the erosion of that

---

[3] Adam Smith, *An Inquiry into the Nature and Cause of the Wealth of Nations*, ed. Edwin Cannan, intro. Max Lerner (New York, 1965), 670-672; Roland Mousnier, *Social Hierarchies 1440 to the Present*, trans. Peter Evans, ed. Margaret Clarke (New York, 1973), 25; and Frank Parkin, *Class, Inequality, and Political Order: Social Stratification in Capitalist and Communist Societies* (New York, 1971), 24, 28-29.

[4] Sir William Petty, *A Treatise of Taxes and Contributions* [1662], in Charles Henry Hull (ed.), *The Economic Writings of Sir William Petty* (Cambridge, 1899), 63. Petty emphasizes the need to focus on "weight, number, and measure" in order to understand the wealth and power of a nation; Sir William Petty, *Political Arithmetic or a Discourse Concerning the Extent and Value of Land, People, Buildings; Husbandry, Manufacture, Commerce, Fishery, Artisans, Seamen, Soldiers; of Militia, Harbours, Situations, Shipping, and power at Sea, &c.: As the Same Relates to Every County in General, but more Particularly to the Territories of His Majesty of Great Britain, and his neighbours of Holland, Zealand, and France* [1677], *An English Garner, Later Stuart Tracts* (New York, 1909); note that the title alone reveals how Petty divides a nation into a calculus of parts and wealth; see also Gregory King, *Natural and Political Observations Upon the State and Condition of England* (Lancaster, 1696), 31; and Charles Davenant, LL.D., *An Essay Upon the Probable Method of Making A People Gainers in the Balance of Trade* [1699], *The Political and Commercial Works of that Celebrated Writer Charles Davenant*, II, ed. Sir Charles Whitworth, M.P. (London, 1771), 184-85.

[5] See definitions of "rank," "order," "station," and "class" in Samuel Johnson, *A Dictionary of the English Language* (London, 1755); Thomas Dyche and William Pardon, *A New English Dictionary* [1774] (New York, 1972); Thomas Sheridan, *A General Dictionary of the English Language* (Dublin, 1784); Nathan Bailey, *Dictionarium Britannicum* [1730] (New York, 1969); C. Cole, *An English Dictionary* (London, 1724); and Edward Phillips, *The New World of Words or, Universal English Dictionary* (London, 1720).

calculus identified by "rank" and the substitution of a "species" of roles involved in production. The concepts developed by the authors of political economy imparted new meaning to a system of social division that became rooted in the word "class." As the concept of production developed, roles identified in the economy took precedence over and were substituted for "rank," "estate," and "personal merit." French theorists like Richard Cantillon, François Quesnay, and Anne Robert Jacques Turgot joined British theorists like Joseph Harris, Adam Smith, and David Ricardo to play a part in the transformation of the concepts and language of status. When they completed their work, the new theory of status was locked in place and identified by the word "class." This new conceptual foundation isolated and captured the sense of social division found in nineteenth-century Great Britain.

The use of the term "class" in the history of political economy, however, did not follow as even a development as the other social concepts found within that field. At first "class" appeared consistently among the French authors who launched the inquiry; their "class" identified "species" of people in production. Then "class" came to challenge specific "ranks" and "orders," when political economy was imported into Great Britain, but here eighteenth-century authors wavered between social languages. Eventually, in David Ricardo's writings, "class" overcame this inconsistency to become the sole term for identifying social division.

While the word "class" challenged the language of "rank," the divisions identified by production modified "class" behavior by such terms as "productive," "unproductive," "useful," "higher," "lower," "middle," "labouring," "capitalist," and "landlord."[6] These modifying terms described the value and conduct of each "class" isolated by the productive process and contributed a new understanding for what was believed to be the real interests behind social behavior. The identification of these interests and the ways they appeared to conflict combined to present a conceptualization of social conduct and strife that Asa Briggs's article developed. Readers of these theories of production received a new conceptual framework to which they could attach ideas they thought accounted for behavior in society. The evolution of that framework and its association with "class" are the subject of this essay.

I. The Irish-born French banker Richard Cantillon wrote his *Essai sur la nature du commerce* sometime between 1730 and 1734. Although this work remained unpublished until 1755, Cantillon launched the inquiry into the theory of production. Cantillon's *Essai* argued that the real determination of value (i.e., that quality that made wealth and property desirable) rested on what land alone could produce. Production centered attention on the creation of new wealth and shifted attention

---

[6] These modifying terms match closely the words associated with "class" in Raymond Williams, *Keywords: A Vocabulary of Culture and Society* (New York, 1976), 15-16.

away from older notions that wealth existed only in trade, treasure, or landed estates.[7] In terms of the concepts of status, this shift suggested the possibility that roles in production might be more important than social positions identified by property. Combined in Cantillon's theory was an explicit link between production and the generation of new wealth and an implicit link between the roles played in production and the status they created.

The significance of Cantillon's approach lay in his concern with "intrinsic value." Cantillon defined intrinsic value as the productivity of the soil measured against the amount of labor necessary to get the land to yield crops. The soil alone was the productive agent, but different organizational uses of labor could effect higher yields. Furthermore, Cantillon's use of intrinsic value replaced John Locke's popular notion that such value depended on the consent of rational individuals to accept gold and silver in exchange for goods.[8] Such a shift in definitions replaced the idea of centering an account of wealth on the monetary value of an estate with consideration of the ways labor divided itself and worked the soil. A shift of this nature also suggested that estates were of secondary importance when describing the material reality of a nation; rather, the productivity of the soil took precedence. Finally, if estates were of secondary importance to material reality, then implicitly they lost importance in terms of the "weight, number, and measure" of status.

The value of all goods, agricultural or industrial, always took expression in terms of land and labor. The value of any enterprise depended on how much produce from the land a nation was willing to commit to sustain that form of work. If a particular industry was of special value to a community, then each year that community committed a large share of its produce to that particular enterprise. According to Cantillon, ". . . it is seen that the value of day's work has a relation to the produce of the soil, and that the intrinsic value of any thing may be measured by the quantity of land used in its production, and the quantity of labour which enters into it, in other words by the quantity of land which is allotted to [feed] those who have worked upon it. . . ."[9]

Spending the produce of land and labor occurred among those in

---

[7] This assertion undermined the approach taken by the mercantilists that wealth resided in trade and treasure. See Mark Blaug, *Economic Theory in Retrospect* (3rd ed.; London, 1978), 18-19 and 21; Joseph A. Schumpeter, *History of Economic Analysis* (New York, 1974), 338-47; and Daniel R. Pusfeld, *The Age of the Economist* (Glenview, Illinois, 1966), 9-11.

[8] Richard Cantillon, *Essai sur la nature du commerce en general*, ed., trans. Henry Hull (London, 1931), 3; John Locke, *Some Considerations of the Consequences of the Lowering of Interest and Raising the Value of Money* [1691], *The Work of John Locke*, V (London, 1963), 22; and John Locke, *Two Treatises of Government*, ed. Peter Laslett (New York, 1963), sections 32 and 33.

[9] Cantillon, *Essai*, 41.

society who had sufficient income to dispose of wealth as they pleased. Such individuals shaped society according to their "fancies" and "tastes."[10] The owners of this wealth Cantillon called "proprietors of land." These few individuals formed a distinct body in society, but Cantillon did not put them into a "class." He saw their independence from concern—i.e., the mundane process of making a living—as liberating them from any "species" of activity (such as labor). Hence, they must have been, for Cantillon, merely a collection of like individuals giving free reign to their tastes as they spent the new wealth produced by land and labor.

The fancies of these "proprietors of land" animated the labor of others. Those people who worked for the proprietor fell into two large categories Cantillon called "classes": the "entrepreneur" and the "hired people." The "entrepreneur" (i.e., undertaker or go-between) typically located himself near the "proprietor of land" and arranged various services to satisfy the landlord's desires. As the "entrepreneur" made the necessary connections between the laborer and the consumer (i.e., landlord), all forms of luxury appeared.[11] With luxury came the establishment of towns and cities, and the nation grew into a fully developed civilization.[12]

The "class" of "hired people" comprised a network of occupations each with a specific minimum income. This minimum income represented a subsistence level that had to be paid for in order for this expression of labor to exist. The lowest level of labor, the slave, required a specific income corresponding to ". . . double the produce of the land needed for their maintenance."[13] All other occupations required an additional payment above the income of slaves. Artisans and craftsmen, for example, required an extra payment to support them during their training; overseers and tenant farmers required additional income to pay either for their authority (in the case of overseers) or for the terms of their leases.[14] In all cases, however, these occupations fit within the general "class" of "hired people."

The network of occupations found within Cantillon's "class" system named all the basic roles he identified within an advanced society. The "class" system itself drew the necessary lines of connection between

[10] *Ibid.,* 3 and 7. Here Cantillon defined "maintenance" as the goods and food that sustained the various forms of labor. Cantillon said that wealth had to first support agriculture and then could be used to meet the tastes and fancies of landlords.

[11] As *entrepreneur* satisfied the desires of the landlord, so "aggregate demand" functioned to shape a nation. Richard V. Eagly called Cantillon's theory of "fancies" as the first expression of a "quasi-real aggregate demand." See Richard V. Eagly, *The Structure of Classical Economic Theory* (New York, 1973), 19.

[12] Cantillon, *Essai,* 43. Cantillon groups with *entrepreneurs* people he also calls merchants.

[13] *Ibid.,* 7, and 33-35, for a discussion of the subsistence wage and why it took specific forms.

[14] *Ibid.,* 35.

occupations and the process of production. This "class" system constituted the framework of the nation; except for the "proprietors of land"
everyone else fell within a "species" of labor identified by "class": ". . . all
inhabitants of a state, it may be laid down that except the prince and
the proprietor of land, are . . . dependent; that they can be divided into
two classes [*en deux classes*] undertakers and hired people. . . . Finally
all the inhabitants of the state derive their living and advantage from the
property of the landowners and are dependent."[15]

Cantillon's use of "class" here conformed with the eighteenth-century
definition of that term. An English-speaking reader would observe that
Cantillon had identified two great "species" or "sorts" of people that cut
across the "ranks" and "orders" of society. The minimum wage system
of Cantillon's occupational structure specified such specific and stable
incomes that they conformed to the status concepts of that century. Only
Cantillon's "entrepreneurs" lived on an unfixed revenue. Cantillon referred to these occupations as the "other orders" (*les autre ordres*) of
society.[16] What is significant here, however, is that Cantillon subordinated
these "other orders" to the network of connection (i.e., production and
consumption) based on his "class" system.[17] This network made his
"class" system the independent variable that determined the existence of
the "other orders." Hence, Cantillon had created a simple economic
hierarchy whose activity determined the distribution of people within the
social structure.[18]

Cantillon's *Essai* proceeded with an explanation of economic growth
and development, but his contribution to the emergence of "class" ended
with his two-"class" system. A reader of his *Essai,* François Quesnay
picked up Cantillon's theory of production and incorporated it into a
program of economics. Quesnay used Cantillon's system to found the
first school of economic theory; this school, variously called the *secte,*
the *économistes,* and *physiocratie,* comprised a collection of French intellectuals who used "class" to create an economic policy they believed
would solve France's problems. The members of the *secte* sought to

[15] *Ibid.,* 17.

[16] *Ibid.,* 43.

[17] See Cantillon cited in Ronald Meek, *Studies in the Labor Theory of Value* (London,
1956), 29.

[18] Mousnier, *Social Hierarchies,* 16-17. Mousnier describes five hierarchies used to
determine status. The third is the economic. Since no such scale existed before Cantillon,
he may be the author of the modern version of this third division of society.

Complementing Mousnier's account of social division, Frank Parkin distinguishes
between concepts of "status" and "class" by assigning to class the inequality associated
with the rewards of one's occupation. According to Parkin, "class" division is the result
of the distribution of material wealth, while "status" like "rank" is the result of *honor.*
"Class" is more an economic division, while "status" follows the personal distinctions
identified by such words as "rank, degree, order, character, and station." Frank Parkin,
Class, Inequality, and Political Order, 13, 18, and 28-29.

explain the nature of human relations based on what they called "a natural order, essential and general which formed the fundamental and constitutive laws of all societies."[19] The physiocrats analyzed what they believed was a universal economic structure divided into "classes," whose roles in production indicated the best program for the nation to follow.[20]

Quesnay's system appeared in his articles "Farmers" and "Grains" (1756) and his *Tableau Economique* (1758-59). Within these three brief works Quesnay developed an "analytical model for the description of the economic structure, performance, and strength of an imaginary state."[21] This ideal agricultural kingdom comprised only three bodies of people: "proprietors of land," a "productive class," and a "sterile class." "Class" identified for Quesnay the species of economic activity a person engaged in and outlined the structure of supply and demand that became the core theory of exchange in the *secte*'s writings.[22]

The third edition of the *Tableau* (1760) added a list of lengthy explanations that Quesnay used to outline the best economic policy for production. Rather than rely on the "fancies" of landlords, Quesnay turned to the power to shape society that Cantillon's intrinsic value offered. Quesnay wanted to use that power to create an ideal society with the greatest productive capacity the combination of its soil and labor had to offer. To achieve this goal, Quesnay self-consciously avoided the "ranks" of his own society and created a realm without a feudal past. Quesnay believed that feudalism, with its "ranks," customs, and seignorial rights, placed obstacles in the way of exchange. Consequently, he sought a term like "class" because that word was theory-free and simply assigned roles within society. "Class" allowed the system of supply and demand to create wealth; such a system followed the principle of *laissez-faire, laissez-passer* and ignored all inhibiting (i.e., feudal) features.[23]

In the explanations accompanying the third edition of the *Tableau,* Quesnay argued that prosperity depended on the behavior of the people as they were divided into "classes." Growth and prosperity always required a basic investment of 50% or more in "la classe des dépenses

[19] Pierre Samuel Dupont de Nemours, *De Origine et des progrès d'une science nouvelle* [1767] (Paris, 1911), 7.
[20] Elizabeth Fox-Genovese, *The Origins of Physiocracy: Economic Revolutions and Social Order in Eighteenth Century France* (Ithaca, 1976), 43-49 and 137; Ronald I. Meek, *The Economics of Physiocracy: Essays and Translations* (Cambridge, Mass., 1963), 27; and Steven L. Kaplan, *Bread, Politics, and Political Economy in the Reign of Louis XV* (The Hague, 1976), I, 113-16.
[21] Fox-Genovese, *The Origins of Physiocracy,* 262.
[22] Meek, *The Economics of Physiocracy,* 28.
[23] This is one of Elizabeth Fox-Genovese's arguments in her first chapter. She reinforces this view by stating that Quesnay derived many of his conclusions from English land tenure practices. For the phrase *laissez-faire, laissez-passer* see François Quesnay, *Tableau Economique,* ed. Marguerite Kuezynski and Ronald L. Meek (London, 1972), xxxv-1.

productive" (i.e., labor that worked the soil).[24] Only in this manner could the next year's yield equal or exceed the existing supply. To reinforce this argument, Quesnay cautioned against investing too much in "la classe des dépenses stériles" (i.e., labor involved in industry).[25] These same proposals appeared earlier in his articles "Farmers" and "Grains" where he systematically attacked the wasteful use of the land found in the French system of agriculture.[26] Like Cantillon, Quesnay did not place landlords within a "class"; this group of individuals existed above the economic process and spent the "aggregate demand" found in their rents in intelligent ways to foster economic health.[27]

Quesnay's *Tableau* and two articles revealed his desire to modernize French agriculture. The power to improve society found within his system inspired a throng of followers, each of whom contributed to Quesnay's original theory in some individual way. For example, Victor de Riquetti, Marquis de Mirabeau, helped Quesnay flesh out his tenets and organized a coherent philosophy around the *Tableau*.[28] Also Le Mercier de la Rivière explored in detail the relationship between what he called the physical and natural laws of production and the political society they shaped.[29] Finally, Pierre Samuel Dupont de Nemours provided the energy and enthusiasm needed to make Quesnay's theories public.

Complementing Quesnay and his followers was the work of Anne Robert Jacques Turgot. Somewhat more independent than other members of the *secte,* Turgot created his own "class" system. In his work *Réflexions sur la formation et la distribution des richesses* (written in 1766 and published in 1770) Turgot placed all members of society within a specific "class" and proposed a hypothetical history of how society changed through time. Here Turgot's objectives included broadening the view of how each "class" interacted in a developing society to see how membership within these "classes" functioned to improve production.

Turgot stated that in the beginning of each society people first cleared and settled the land. Settlement invariably led to inequality, for no matter how a community started, those with talent and good fortune ended up

---

[24] *Ibid.,* i-ij.

[25] *Ibid.,* i-ij and 6-12.

[26] *Ibid.,* iv, and Denis Diderot, Jean le Rond d'Alembert, and others, *Encyclopédie, Selections,* ed. Nelly S. Hoyt and Thomas Cassirer (New York, 1965), 88-89, 95, and 105-06.

[27] Quesnay, *Tableau Economique,* xxxv-1.

[28] See Victor de Riquetti, Marquis de Mirabeau, *Philosophie Rural ou Economique General et Politique De L'Agriculture* (Amsterdam, 1972), 14-15, to see how Quesnay's *Tableau* fit within Mirabeau's philosophy.

[29] See Le Mercier de la Rivière, *L'Ordre naturel et essential des société politique* (London, 1767); part I explores the physical and natural laws of production, and part II explains the consequences to political society.

in control of the land.[30] These individuals who controlled land acted upon the rest of the population to distribute people into two "classes." These "classes" Turgot called "une classe productrice et une classe stipendée."[31] Like Quesnay's "class" system, Turgot's two "classes" found themselves engaged in a circulation of goods and services based on supply and demand. Turgot, however, did not stop with these two "classes"; rather, his society included a third.

As the rich emerged through talent and good fortune and as the market tied all economic activity into a common web of exchange, so a third "class" eventually appeared. This "class" Turgot called "une classe disponible" i.e., the available class (available for public service) because it had enough wealth to guarantee leisure time.[32] Unlike Cantillon and Quesnay who had named only two "classes," Turgot placed everyone within a specific economic role. Turgot converted "the proprietors of land" into this third "class" and locked them into his conceptual framework of exchange and mutual dependence. Of society Turgot wrote:

Here then we have society divided into three classes; the class of husbandmen for which we may keep the name productive class; the class of artisans and others who receive stipends from the produce of the land; and the class or proprietors, the only one which, not being bound by the need of subsistence to a particular labour, can be employed for the general need of society [i.e., as public servants] . . . the name which for this reason suits it best is that of the available class.[33]

Once Turgot had established the three basic "classes," he proposed a hypothetical account of how society evolved into its "modern" form (i.e., modern for Turgot). Starting with slavery, then developing into serfdom, and emerging into tenant-farming, each phase represented the way labor exchanged its service for use of the land.[34] In the final phase, the landowner left the farm, moved to the city, and spent his wealth on newly created arts and crafts. Together all three—the landowner, the tenant-farmer, and the artisan—represented the variety of occupations and statuses that filled Turgot's "class" system. The way these occupations and statuses changed through time reflected the shifting nature of the social structure within this economic system. The "modern" form of society was by no means the final form; Turgot, like Quesnay, proposed

---

[30] Anne Robert Jacques Turgot, *Reflections on the Formation and Distribution of Riches* [1770] (New York, 1963), 13. This is the "pure" text—free from Dupont de Nemour's attempts to edit Turgot to fit within Quesnay's *secte*.

[31] Eugene Daire (ed.), *Oeuvre de Turgot* (Paris, 1844), 12. Turgot called the second class a stipend class because it received its payment in the form of a stipend from the soil.

[32] Turgot, *Reflections,* 5; also see Daire, *Oeuvre,* 14.

[33] *Ibid.,* 15.

[34] *Ibid.,* 18-22.

the possibility of improving society through judicious investments in agriculture. The future of society could take any form depending on how well one understood production.[35]

Turgot's intention in this "history" of agriculture was to establish a view of contemporary society that could be useful in correcting the problems of production. What Turgot communicated was a highly malleable perception of the social structure. The proper understanding of the typology of "classes" he created projected an image of society that could be used to change the existing social system. Consequently, whatever forms estates or statuses took within society depended on understanding his conception of the economic "class" structure. Social status was in effect subordinate to one's understanding of production.

Cantillon, Quesnay, and Turgot exemplified the French theorists who established the initial link between "class" and production. Cantillon started the process by identifying the "classes" of activity essential to production and by relocating the foundation of status and occupation within his system of generating new wealth. Quesnay continued this process by consolidating the relationships of supply and demand in an integrated "class" system that tied together the whole fabric of society. Finally, Turgot projected this network into a complete "class" structure including everyone within society. Turgot also identified the changeable character of social distinction within each "class." Together these three French authors created the means to explore status in terms of production.

II. In 1757 the theory of production crossed the English channel to appear in a book entitled *An Essay upon Money and Coins* written by Joseph Harris. This author, along with Adam Smith and David Ricardo, represented how production became a British theory. At first Harris and Smith contributed substantially to this theory while channeling the language of status back into that of "rank." Smith more than Harris was responsible for redirecting production into the language of "rank," while both Smith and Harris represented a serious effort to integrate production with what was actually seen in society. Since both were accustomed to the language of "rank," direct empirical evidence would be couched in such terms. Both men, however, contributed to the language of "class," directly and indirectly, while both dealt with the issue of production. When they had completed their work, they had prepared the way for Ricardo to convert the whole structure of production into a "class" dominated system.

Joseph Harris wrote his work within two years of the publication of Cantillon's *Essai*. In the introductory section of his treatise, Harris expressed ideas remarkably similar to Cantillon's—so similar, in fact, that

[35] *Ibid.*, 22-23.

they were probably derived from Cantillon's *Essai.*[36] Harris's book introduced Cantillon's theory of intrinsic value into English thought. Harris varied from Cantillon only by adding skill to the combination of land and labor needed to produce goods. Hence all commodities received their value "in proportion to the land, labour, and skill that are requisite to produce them."[37]

Having established intrinsic value, Harris then moved to a theory of relative value; here he anticipated Smith in several basic features of social perception. Harris showed that the price paid labor had to conform to both the laborer's needs and the circumstances of the market. Using Cantillon's minimum wage for slaves, Harris identified what Smith would later call the "natural price" of labor (i.e., that wage that must be paid to support specific occupations): "It may be reasonably allowed that a labouring man ought to earn at least, *twice as much as will maintain himself* in ordinary food and cloathing; that he maybe enabled to breed up children, pay rent for a small dwelling, find himself in necessary utensils, etc. So much at least the labourer must be allowed, that the commodity may be perpetuated. . . ."[38] Feeding the laborer and sustaining his family maintained his occupation within the community. A laborer, however, could only sell his goods according to the demand that existed for them. Demand represented the conditions of the market; what Smith would later call "market price" (i.e., what people were willing pay for goods).[39]

The price set by the laborer had to conform to the circumstances of demand. If workers asked too much, then either one of two conditions occurred: ". . . their goods [would] remain on their hands . . . [,or] there [would] be others ready to step into their places. . . ."[40] Consequently all workers had either to conform to demand or cease their labor. Should

[36] Harris plays a relatively minor role in the overall history of political economy when contrasted with figures like Quesnay, Smith, and Ricardo, but is important to the concept of "class" in that he retained so much of Cantillon's language while writing in English. Furthermore, he anticipated Smith in certain key concepts such as "natural price and market price." Harris therefore is important in the history of the language of "class" in that he converted Cantillon's *classe* to the English term "class," while expanding the economic foundation of that social concept. See Edmund Whittaker, *Schools and Streams of Economic Thought* (Chicago, 1960), 112; Ronald L. Meek, *Studies in the Labour Theory of Value* (London, 1956), 29-30; and Lewis Henry Haney, *History of Economic Thought* (New York, 1917), 159 and 161.

[37] Joseph Harris, *An Essay Upon Money and Coins* (London, G. Hawkins, 1757), 5.

[38] *Ibid.,* 9-10. The underlined section in this quotation is Cantillon's base price for slave labor; the rest is remarkably similar to Smith's definition of natural price. See Adam Smith, *Lectures on Jurisprudence,* ed. R. L. Meek, D. D. Raphael, and P. G. Stein (Oxford, 1978), 495-96.

[39] For a discussion of Adam Smith's sociology see David A. Reisman, *Adam Smith's Sociological Economics* (New York, 1976), 124.

[40] Harris, *An Essay Upon Money and Coins,* 9-10.

demand be very high for a specific commodity and offer the opportuity for a specific occupation to rise in status, then laborers in other forms of employment would leave their former jobs and compete for these wages. Consequently more men would "enter into that business, and their outvying [would] undersell one another, till at length the great profit of it [was] brought down to *par* with the rest.[41] In Harris's opinion, the dynamics of the market would invariably sustain labor at a subsistence level.[42] This dynamic shaped society— getting rid of some occupations and expanding others—while placing the great body of workers essentially in the same status. All these people Harris placed in the "lower class"; this "class" needed to be handled both with benevolence and discretion.[43] Since they really could not expect to rise in status above the conditions they enjoyed near the subsistence level, Harris recommended not teaching their young to read or write. He believed that this was "a kind of intrusion upon *the class* above them; . . . and [it] . . . inspire[d] them [i.e., workers] with notions subversive of society."[44]

Harris's use of "class" in his analysis of the market conditions of labor provided several conceptual features important to both the language of "class" and the theory of production. Instead of following the French example of only identifying broad "species" of occupations, Harris used "class" as a status term. "Class" comprised people at the bottom of society; "class" was modified by the adjective "lower." To this identity Harris added the adjective "useful"; the "lower class" was also called the "useful class."[45] Consequently, this social category entailed an eco-nomic identity; production distributed people within a social hierarchy according to income received from the economy, while this distribution comprised "classes" that were beneficial to the community.

Because Harris had converted "class" into a concept that now de-scribed status, when he looked above the "lower class," his social vision was blurred by the language of "rank." Just above the "lower class," Harris identified "another class [comprised of] . . . dealers of all sorts, from the meanest shop-keeper to the merchant."[46] Above this "class," however, Harris became lost in "all [the] ranks" that comprised society— especially those of the "higher stations."[47] The phrase "higher station" would not be converted into "higher class" until 1795, when it would join the "middle class" in Thomas Gisborne's title, *Enquiry into the Duties*

---

[41] *Ibid.*, 9.

[42] *Ibid.*, 10.

[43] *Ibid.*, 11, 12, 13, and 84 are all pages on which Harris uses the phrase "lower class" consistently when talking about this body of people.

[44] *Ibid.*, 11-12.

[45] *Ibid.*, 12.

[46] *Ibid.*, 18.

[47] *Ibid.*, 11 and 85.

of Men in the Higher and Middle Classes of Society in Great Britain. For Harris, however, such a combination did not occur even though "class" appeared more frequently than "rank" or "station" within his text. A reader of Harris, Adam Smith, took several of the ideas suggested by the *Essay upon Money and Coins,* combined them with concepts of production articulated by French theorists, and worked them into a distinctive economic system bearing his own stamp.[48] Smith converted the theory of production from a concept discussed by a few men into a general social science that reached many readers. Smith's *Inquiry into the Origins and Nature of the Wealth of Nations* (1776) created a complete system of economics set in a pattern of stable and recognizable empirical terms common to eighteenth-century English. Smith diverted the theory of production back into the language of "rank," but at the same time he made all forms of status dependent on the circumstances of production. Thus Smith created a thorough-going sociological theory that could later easily be returned to the language of "class."

Rather than confound his theory of production with the standard of land and labor, Smith focused on labor alone. Labor represented for Smith the one central feature to measure value; labor was the sole agent that created new wealth, new property, and ultimately society itself. The ways in which human energy expressed itself in an organized fashion identified both the material conditions of society and the foundations of the social structure. Labor in all its various forms created each year the annual supply, while at the same time shaping the occupational framework of the nation.[49]

As the source of new wealth and the foundation of society, labor took on two important roles in the community's history. In one sense labor remained a continuous feature of society—an everpresent, essential ingredient of social and economic existence. In another sense, however, labor was always changing; at any given moment the current division of labor could undergo reorganization and transform the shape of society.

---

[48] Harris was only one of many authors read by Adam Smith. Given the major issues associated with political economy in the 1760s and '70s, such as the grain trade and mercantile regulations, when Smith read Harris the latter author probably was only a minor voice compared to Cantillon, Quesnay, and Turgot. If one reads Steven Kaplan's *Bread, Politics, and Political Economy in the Reign of Louis XV,* or Istran Hont and Michael Ignatieff's "Needs and Justice in the *Wealth of Nations:* An Introductory Essay," *Wealth and Virtue: The Shaping of Political Economy in the Scottish Enlightenment,* ed. I. Hont and M. Ignatieff (Cambridge, 1983), one sees that such issues as mentioned above would have sharply influenced Smith. Still Harris had clearly stated the concepts of "natural price and market price" before Smith, and Harris along with Cantillon and Quesnay are cited in Smith's *Wealth of Nations*—see 26-27 for Harris, and 68, 637, and 643 for Cantillon and Quesnay.

[49] Smith, *Wealth of Nations,* lvii.

Labor thus functioned as an essential economic constant and existed in specific, changeable patterns.[50] The organization of labor in both these forms Smith called the "division of labor." The division of labor separated individuals into complex networks of occupations. Each occupation became the "principle or sole trade ... of a particular class of citizen."[51] The phrase "labouring classes" combined the historical pattern of occupations with the everpresent and essential features identified by Smith's concept of labor. In the historical sense, these "classes" were "that great multiplication of production of all the different arts ..., which extend[ed] itself [from the top of society] to the lowest ranks of the people."[52] Here "class" merely identified a "species" of status in the old sense of "rank," "station," and "order." Yet, these "classes" also functioned as a united and essential force holding society together; hence, the "labouring classes" took on new meaning as the singular force of production.[53] This was a whole new identity for "class," for such a definition became the criterion for the modern concept of "class": "Social classes [taken collectively] as a category of social strata that exist in a market economy where the production of material goods ... is judged the most important [of] social functions...."[54]

Smith's two meanings found in the phrase "the labouring classes" became the focal point for his sociological theory. As is well known, Smith defined labor as the source of "real value:" "Equal quantities of labour, at all times and places, may be said to be of equal value to the labourer.... Labour alone, therefore, never varying in its own value, is alone the ultimate and real standard by which the value of all commodities can be estimated and compared."[55] Real value replaced Cantillon's intrinsic value and functioned as the key feature that tied one form of labor in the marketplace to the rest. What was truly available for exchange was not so much the goods for sale but various forms of labor that produced those goods. Every sale represented one pattern of labor exchanging for and supporting another pattern; the exchange itself became a reciprocal relationship of support.[56]

---

[50] See Paul J. McNulty, "Adam Smith's Concept of Labor," *Journal of the History of Ideas,* 34 (1973), 345-47.

[51] Smith, *Wealth of Nations,* 10.

[52] *Ibid.,* 11.

[53] The division of labor is seen as a single economic force in various examples of productive capacity at different times in human history. Smith compares the wealth of a civilized nation to that of an African king in one of these examples.

[54] See Mousnier, *Social Hierarchies,* 35-40 for the criteria defining class, and Parkin, *Class, Inequality, and Political Order,* 18: "The backbone of the class structure, and indeed the entire reward system ... is the occupational order ...," and 20: "At least so far as modern ... societies are concerned, the role of the market in allocating rewards via the occupational order seems crucial to the entire stratification system...."

[55] Smith, *Wealth of Nations,* 33.

[56] See Smith, *Lectures on Jurisprudence,* 495-96, and *Wealth of Nations,* 55-56; R. H.

Having established the concept of real value and the mechanism of mutual support found in exchange, Smith could account for every moment in the evolution of a nation's social and economic structure. Each "class" of labor formed a unit in production; adding or subtracting units of labor occurred as conditions of production changed. Each labouring "class" became in a sense a building block within the whole edifice of society. If an item sold very well, certain blocks of labor expanded; if an item did not sell, certain blocks of labor disappeared. How stable each block was depended on the basic minimum price one had to pay to sustain labor itself. That price was essentially the price of food, which functioned for Smith as a second standard to measure the real value of goods: "Equal quantities of corn [i.e., the subsistence of the laborer] . . . will at distant times be more nearly of the same value, or enable the possessor to purchase or command more nearly the same quantity of the labour of other people." [57]

Since equal quantities of corn remained basically the same in value over long periods of time and since the possessor of such quantities controlled equal value in terms of labor, the stability of the price of corn imputed stability to the price of labor. Stability in the price of labor meant that most laborers lived on incomes near the subsistence level and converted their work into a low and stable wage. The cost of labor in purchasing goods therefore was stable in general; consequently, the cost of goods became equally stable. Stability in terms of the value of goods, in turn, assigned stability to property in general; such stability allowed Smith to use the old language of "rank."

This view of stability was reinforced by Smith's explanation of economic growth. Economic growth for Smith occurred through adding units of "stock or capital" to the productive process. Added units of stock meant increased demand for production and therefore labor. Smith did not see that capital-intense investments like machinery might reduce the demand for labor. Therefore, an added unit of stock always meant, for Smith, an added unit of labor. Such a view reminded Smith's readers of his image of labor as being so many building blocks one could add or subtract from the social structure. [58]

This image of building blocks received further support when Smith revealed how the drudgery of work held labor consistently in low status. The amount of work required by the poverty of the "labouring classes"

Campbell and A. S. Skinner, *Adam Smith* (New York, 1982), 119-20; and M. L. Myer, "Adam Smith's Concept of Equilibrium," *Journal of the History of Ideas*, 36 (1975), 566-68.

[57] Smith, *Wealth of Nations*, 35.

[58] *Ibid.*, 17 and 260 for the relation of stock and the market to labor; Adolph Lowe, "The Classical Theory of Economic Growth," *Social Research*, 21 (1954), 132-41, for an explanation of economic growth. Smith's view of economic growth is one area that Ricardo will attack to create his image of the social structure.

reduced their members to a "drowsy stupidity, which in every civilized society seem[ed] to benumb the understanding of almost all the inferior ranks of people."[59] Even when economic growth was at its peak and the opportunity to improve one's "condition in life" presented itself, the laborer was so crushed by the simple tasks of his daily occupation that he could not see what to do. Smith recommended benevolently that society ought to intervene and educate the poor. Even then, however, the likelihood of many members of the "labouring classes" escaping their status seemed improbable. Caught, therefore, at the bottom in a general state of poverty, the "labouring classes" could not avoid the numbing habits that perpetuated their condition, fixed their income at the price of corn, and assigned the stability of that price to all goods for sale.

While stability appeared in Smith's account of the price of corn, economic growth, and the mental state of the poor, the terms "rank," "station," and "order," which riddled his text, were themselves undermined by his theory of production. The meaning of these terms could survive only so long as they directly identified status. Smith's theory of production, however, created a pattern of "labouring classes" that took precedence over all status terms. Granted these "labouring classes" were themselves very stable; now, however, they were subject to the conditions of production and had displaced the language of "rank" in its primacy of communicating the structural sense of society. All one had to do now was to undermine Smith's conditions of stability, and the rigid qualities of the vocabulary of "rank" would collapse.[60]

When Smith established production as the foundation of the social structure, he also created five descriptive categories into which people fell: "landlords or proprietors of land," "labourers," "owners of capital or stock," "productive labourers," and "unproductive labourers."[61] These five descriptive categories figured prominently in the future use of "class." Behavior described by Smith with such terms as "labourer" or "landlord" imparted values to these groups that future authors could identify with.[62] When Smith added that "some of the most respectable orders in society . . . [were] unproductive labourers," he raised (unintentionally) the question as to whether or not their services were worth the respect they

[59] Smith, *Wealth of Nations,* 734.

[60] *Ibid.,* 248, where Smith concludes Book I of the *Wealth* with three great "orders" that form the natural foundation of all societies. These three great "orders" become the structure that Ricardo will convert into a "class" system once he reevaluates Smith's theory.

[61] "Landlord" and "proprietor of land" are used interchangeably, while "capital" substitutes for "stock" in Smith's text. "Landlord," "labourers," and "owners of stock" derive from Smith's history of natural price and each is sustained by its own income—rent, wages, and profits.

[62] This is the source that could shape opinion and lead to "class" consciousness.

received.[63] In a changing society, especially one like Great Britain's, where the distribution of wealth was undergoing redefinition, "productive labourers" were particularly sensitive to their role within the whole process of creating wealth. The low status of "unproductive labourers," because they were also the poverty-ridden "labouring classes" or the upwardly mobile "owners of capital," raised many questions. Since Smith had placed the "Sovereign, . . . with all his officers both of justice and war," among the "unproductive labourers," and since they enforced the law and resisted changes demanded by the "labouring classes" and "owners of stock," Smith's five descriptive categories figured prominently in the literature of protest and social strife circulated in the nineteenth century.[64] This was the literature that led to the "language of class" identified by Asa Briggs.

Judging from the elements offered in his vision of social organization, Smith communicated a mixed set of old and new status concepts. The degree of stability his system identified suggested a tendency to return to the older language of "rank." The fact, however, that he converted the entire structure of status into a system dependent on economic circumstances laid the foundation for the modern language of "class." Changing the language of status now only required changing the circumstances of the market, for Smith had subordinated the language of "rank" to the concept of production.

David Ricardo completed the transformation of social language and established the conceptual framework that made "class" adaptable to the nineteenth century. In his book *On the Principles of Political Economy* (1817) Ricardo challenged the assumption of stability suggested by Smith's analysis. At the same time Ricardo substituted the word "class" for the language of "rank" and swept aside all the features of the old language.

Ricardo launched his revision of Smith in two key areas: the price of corn and the impact of machinery. Smith's observations that equal quantities of corn allowed its possessor to command equal quantities of labor, while the price of corn remained the same over long periods of time, had imputed a sense of stability to labor. Ricardo denied that stability by showing how population and the history of rent caused the price of corn to vary sharply over short periods of time. Furthermore, Smith's theory of economic growth, which did not see capital intense investments like machinery as sharply influencing the role played by labor in production, also fell victim to Ricardo's analysis. These two changes undermined the stability of Smith's system; Ricardo transformed the price of corn and machinery into elastic variables. With these changes

---

[63] Smith, *Wealth of Nations*, 315.
[64] *Ibid.*, 315.

the mixture of old and new status terms found in Smith's *Wealth of Nations* collapsed in favor of the language of "class."

Ricardo's account of status, like Smith's, depended on the concepts of real value and the reciprocal relations of exchange. For Ricardo, however, the value of a commodity depended on the relative quantities of labor necessary for its production. The degree to which the amount of labor expressed itself collectively in the production of an item, given in the form of the current wage paid for that labor, measured the value of that commodity when compared to the amount and cost of labor in some other item for sale. Unlike Smith, who saw labor as comprised of precise and stable units, one being exchanged for another, Ricardo saw labor as a commodity that fluctuated in price like all other goods for sale. If the *price* of labor for a commodity changed sharply, then the cost of production equally varied; if the *amount* of labor needed in production for that same item changed, then again so did the cost of production.

In terms of the *price* of labor, the principal cost one had to pay was that cost identified originally by Cantillon—i.e., the cost of maintaining workers in their occupations. The basic item that indicated what that cost might be was Smith's second standard of value—the cost of corn or ". . . the subsistence of the labourer. . . ."[65] Unlike Smith, however, Ricardo regarded the price of corn as a flexible standard. Fluctuations in the price of corn always meant fluctuations in the price of labor; those who paid the wages of workers (i.e., capitalists) always had to provide sufficient income so that "labourers" could purchase food. This rule was Ricardo's famous "iron law of wages." As the cost of food changed, the iron law of wages dictated a variation in the cost of labor and thus always influenced two forms of income: one, the wages of the "labourer," which became a cost that affected two, the profit margins of "capitalists."[66]

The regulating feature behind Ricardo's iron law of wages—the price of corn—depended on the cost necessary for producing that item. The cost of producing corn, in turn, followed the history of population as represented in the history of rent (i.e., the income of landlords). In order to understand the relative value of corn and its impact on the price of labor, then, one has to understand Ricardo's theory of rent.

The rules governing rent took shape for Ricardo after he had read Thomas Robert Malthus's *Essay on Population* (first and second editions, 1798 and 1803). The first edition established to Ricardo's satisfaction that population would always grow at a rate that exceeded food production; the pressure of population therefore would always place high

---

[65] *Ibid.,* 35.

[66] See David Levy, "Ricardo and the Iron Law: A Correction of the Record," *History of Political Economy,* 7 (1976), 235-51; also see David Ricardo, *On the Principles of Political Economy,* Volume I, *The Works and Correspondence of David Ricardo* (Edited by Piero Sraffa in collaboration with M. H. Dobbs; Cambridge: 1951), 93.

demand on food and food cultivation.[67] The second edition established the principle of "diminishing returns"—i.e., that as population grew, the most fertile sections of land became fully occupied and forced farmers to cultivate less fertile fields at higher costs of investment.[68] Higher costs of investment meant that the relative cost of labor involved in producing corn, relative to the cost of labor for other items, varied so that the value of corn increased. At the same time the differences in cost necessary to cultivate the less fertile fields, relative to the returns on the same investment on the better land, measured the value and demand for the more productive soil. According to Ricardo, then, this newly identified superior fertility of certain fields became the source of their rent, while the increased value of corn indicated the degree to which the cost of labor would have to rise.[69]

The appearance of rent served as an accurate measure of the cost of corn. With the steady growth of population, there was a steady rise in rent and the relative value of corn. As the value of corn went up, there followed a steady rise in the cost of labor and the cost of production; this gradual but steady rise would become a permanent feature of the marketplace and created what Ricardo called "the natural tendency of profits to fall."[70] Consequently, as rents went up and satisfied the interests of "landlords," profits fell, and this conflicted with the interests of "capitalists."[71]

Happily for "capitalists," the tendency for profits to fall could be reversed temporarily with the introduction of machinery. Machinery reversed the influence of population on the cost of production wherever machines appeared. Machinery comprised labor-saving devices that allowed investors to reduce the *amount* and therefore the cost of hiring workers in the production of specific items. Whenever machines were introduced, there the cost of labor fell, and the "tendency, this gravitation as it were of profits, [was] happily checked. . . ."[72]

The impact of machinery, however, was complex. On the one hand lower costs of production meant higher profits for "capitalists," who saved the expense of hiring laborers. At the same time lower costs of production meant those goods produced by machinery were now cheaper, and therefore the purchasing power of everyone with an income increased.

[67] Thomas Robert Malthus, *The First Essay on Population* (Ann Arbor, 1960), 22-23.

[68] See Malthus cited in George J. Stigler, *Essays in the History of Economics* (Chicago, 1964), 166.

[69] Ricardo, *Principles of Political Economy*, 70; also Ronald P. Bird, "A Reinterpretation of Ricardian Rent Theory," *The American Economist*, 19 (1975), 69 for a short and clear statement of Ricardo's theory of rent.

[70] Ricardo, *Principles of Political Economy*, 104.

[71] *Ibid.*, 49, for Ricardo's use of the terms "capitalists" and "landlord" in his statement on relative status.

[72] *Ibid.*, 120.

This improved the circumstances of life for "landlords," since they had a steady and generally rising income—thanks to continuous population pressure. Lower costs of production, however, meant a decrease in the demand for labor, and therefore a certain number of workers became unemployed. Machines consequently forced workers to intensify competition among themselves to acquire fewer jobs in general, and hence the whole body of "labourers" suffered. After reading John Barton's *Observation on the Labouring Classes of Society* (1817), Ricardo stated in the third edition of his *Principles* (1821) that machinery was "very injurious to the interests of the class of labourers" and generated immediate conflict between "capitalists" and workers.[73]

Ricardo's treatment of real value, the cost of producing food, and the introduction of machinery—and their consequences: the appearance of a conflict of interests between "landlords," "capitalists," and "labourers"—created the foundation for his use of "class." The rising costs of food and the introduction of machinery caused real value to vary sharply and often in opposite directions. At the same time these variations caused the distribution of wealth to change dramatically, and therefore the status of individuals also varied. These changes were accompanied by conflicts of interest, which established degrees of hostility within society as certain groups of people rose in the social scale and others fell. The net result was that status had become extremely elastic, and conflicting attitudes were fixed to those shifts that occurred in one's standing within the community.

All these qualities combined to upset the "regular, established, settled, and proper" features of Smith's system of status.[74] Status was too elastic to be established or settled on any firm footing; at any moment a new innovation could upset the regular or proper features found in the fixed

---

[73] *Ibid.,* 338; also John Barton, *Observation on the Labouring Classes of Society* [1817] (Baltimore, 1934), 17, and Samuel Hollander, "The Development of Ricardo's Position on Machinery," *The History of Political Economy,* 3 (1971), 105. John Barton figures prominently in Ricardo's understanding of machinery. Barton observed that machinery affected labor in three significant ways: first, capitalists gained increased control over production through their ownership of machines; second, machines were expensive and therefore reduced the funds a capitalist had to pay wages; and third, machines cut back on the cost of labor itself and therefore the weekly use of capital for the regular payment of wages. Ricardo read Barton's book and saw that all three features of machinery identified by Barton would work to the interest of the capitalist and against those of the laborer. After some correspondence with Barton, Ricardo revised his understanding of machinery in the third edition of the *Principles.*

[74] See "order" in Samuel Johnson, *Dictionary of the English Language;* Thomas Dyche and William Pardon, *A New English Dictionary;* Thomas Sheridan, *A General Dictionary;* Nathan Bailey, *Dictionarium Britannicum;* C. Cole, *An English Dictionary;* and Edward Phillips, *The New World of Words.* The definition of "order" is important because the features of that term were precisely the qualities that Ricardo undermined in his revision of Smith's theory. Also Ricardo substituted the word "class" for Smith's use of "order."

qualities of "rank," "station," and "order." Hence, Ricardo returned to the term selected by the French theorists—i.e., "class"; that word was both free from old notions of status and flexible in meaning. Of social division Ricardo stated that:

The produce of the earth—all that is derived from its surface by the united application of labour, machinery, and capital, is divided among *three classes* . . . the proprietors of land, the owners of stock or capital, and the labourers. . . .
But in different stages of society, the proportion of the earth which will be allotted to each of these *three classes,* under the name of rent, profit, and wages, will be essentially different; depending mainly on the actual fertility of the soil, on the accumulation of capital and population, and on the skill, ingenuity, and instruments employed.[75]

This variation in allotted wealth led Ricardo to reformulate completely the nature of status itself. The way one judged the status of a "class" was not how much wealth that "class" had in terms of a specific quantity; rather, status depended on a "class's" relative position within society. A "class" was superior or inferior only in terms of where it stood relative to other "classes." Status, consequently, arose from a comparative evaluation of the whole community rather than a simple judgment of what a "class" owned:

It is not by the absolute quantity of produce obtained by either class, that we can correctly judge the rate of profit, rent, and wages [i.e., estates and status], but by the quantity of labour required to obtain that produce. By improvement in machinery and agriculture, the whole produce may be doubled; but if wages, rents, and profits be also doubled, these three will bear the same proportion [i.e., status] to one another as before, and neither could be said to have relatively varied. But, if wages . . . instead of being doubled, were only to increase by one-half; if rent, instead of being doubled, were only to increase by three-quarters, and the remainder went to profits, . . . I . . . say, that rents and wages have fallen while profits had risen; for . . . we should find that a less value had fallen to the class of labourers and landlords, and a greater to the class of capitalists.[76]

Ricardo's perception of status utterly eliminated a tabulation of property and its consequent pattern of "ranks," "stations," and "orders." Not only had the conditions of real value, the cost of producing food, and the introduction of machinery forced status into an elastic condition identified by "class," but now the very nature of status itself required a comparative and relative evaluation. Hence, Ricardo identified the word "class" with his revision of production, which upset the stable elements developed by Smith, while Ricardo included in this term Smith's use of the entire vocabulary of "rank." Ricardo had therefore compressed within his use of the word "class" the two features of Smith's phrase "the

---

[75] Ricardo, *The Principles of Political Economy,* 5.
[76] *Ibid.,* 49.

labouring classes"—i.e., the historical pattern of occupations found within society and the everpresent and essential force that held society together. Ricardo's redefinition of status changed the word "class" so that it now functioned on two levels: first, identifying "species," "sorts," or "types" of social strata that functioned as everpresent and necessary divisions of society that emerged with the evolution of production, and second, as specific statuses whose "real and tangible" interests (i.e., real and tangible to Ricardo) fluctuated with the conditions of the market.

Ricardo's perception of these real and tangible interests led him to formulate proposals for political conduct based on his understanding of "class." In the case of the Poor Laws, for example, money spent to support a population living on charity was money not spent on production. Such money took potential investments away from purchasing "productive labour" and machinery while maintaining an "unproductive" population. Such a policy injured the "capitalists" and "labouring classes" while it rewarded the "landlord class." The sheer number of people supported by charity increased the population and caused demand for food and land to go up. Therefore, rents increased rewarding "landlords," while profits declined, and wages, though large in the actual amount of money, were merely a subsistence income. Consequently, as Ricardo saw it, one's socioeconomic identity quickly determined one's political reaction to the Poor Laws.[77]

A second issue explored through "class" interests revealed another significant political concern of Ricardo's day. The Corn Laws, a tariff on imported grain, was a major issue that dominated political debate during the first half of the nineteenth century. Ricardo's perception of "class" interest animated a good portion of that debate. As early as 1815, in an essay that anticipated his *Principles,* Ricardo argued that such a tariff artificially increased the price of food while draining off money that could be invested in improving production. The artificial increase in the price of food injured every consumer, while money flowed into the hands of those who owned land. Even the farmer suffered, for artificial increases in the price of food stimulated competition to acquire land and therefore raised rents. Increases in rents rewarded the "landlord class," but led Ricardo to conclude "that the interest of the landlord [was] always opposed to the interest of every other class in the community. His situation [was] never so prosperous, as when food [was] scarce and dear: whereas, all other persons . . . greatly benefitted by procuring food cheap."[78]

Ricardo's perception of "class" conflict, i.e., the "landlord" against

---

[77] *Ibid.,* 106-08.

[78] Ricardo, *An Essay on the Influence of the Low Price of Corn on the Profits of Stock; Shewing the Inexpediency of Restrictions on Importation,* ed. Piero Sraffa, in *The Works and Correspondence of David Ricardo,* IV, 12.

the rest of society, or the "labourer" opposing the "capitalist's" desire to use machinery, undermined the eighteenth-century tendency to see society as a "commonweal." Commonweal—a body politic or community where benevolence and mutual support of wealth and property were central—appeared to some degree in the earlier works of both Harris and Smith.[79] For Harris, benevolence appeared as a concern for the "lower class," whose poverty placed them in a precarious condition in society; for Smith, benevolence surfaced in the form of education which he felt society owed the "labouring classes," whose drudgery and poverty reduced them to "drowsy stupidity." Ricardo abandoned completely such benevolence; for him the conditions of the market and the interests of "classes" directed them into opposition. A "commonweal" collapsed in the presence of such "class" hostility. "Class" attitudes shaped by production revealed for Ricardo the "real" mechanism to explain behavior in society. "Classes," however, had to remember that each was a necessary and natural component that appeared as the community evolved.

Ricardo's use of "class" launched that word on a new career. In Ricardo's perception of status, "class" completely swallowed the language of "rank," while "class" identified a conceptual framework that revealed the true and hostile interests that animated society. So clearly had Ricardo drawn the lines of conflict between "classes" that to defeat his theory of society and production required adopting his language. The language of "class" outlined in Asa Brigg's article shows how such a debate unfolded. Along with Brigg's observations, one should add that "class" now dominated the language of economic theory. When that theory spilled over into popular reviews such as the *Edinburgh Review,* the *Quarterly Review,* the *Westminster Review,* and *Blackwood's Magazine,* "class" invaded popular language. The numerous dailies and weeklies that were growing popular during the nineteenth century also picked up this term. "Rank" retained some vitality among those who sought to hold on to the older notion of status that "class" challenged, but the power of economics as a field of inquiry and the strife generated by the Industrial Revolution gradually undermined this attempt. The concept of "class" had by 1821 captured the imagination of Great Britain's thinking population, while the term and the concept combined to absorb what people believed to be the way society divided itself.[80]

Marymount Palos Verdes College.

---

[79] For "Commonweal" see dictionaries cited above, n. 74.

[80] Ricardo's perception of "class" conflict made this term useful in the political debates of the early nineteenth century. Not only did his perception appear in the major Reviews but this term also appeared in many of the newspapers. The three social divisions of "upper," "middle," and "lower" conveniently matched Ricardo's "landlords," "capitalists," and "laborers" and captured the imagination of most social commentators of that period. See R. S. Neale, *Class and Ideology in the Nineteenth Century* (London, 1972), 4-5 and 15.

XVII

THE CONCEPT OF CLASS IN FRENCH CULTURE PRIOR TO THE REVOLUTION

BY DALLAS L. CLOUATRE[1]

Introduction.—In modern French thought, as in European thought in general, it is now commonplace to apply the term *classe* to describe a way of ordering society and to describe particular social formations; hence we talk of "class stratification" and of *particular* "classes" in society. The present essay explores the emergence of this modern pattern of thought. In the first section the linguistic inheritance from antiquity and the Middle Ages provides the background necessary for an examination of sixteenth-century innovations in which *classe* came to be applied to socio-economic issues, at first apparently as aspects of the sphere of activity of the Third Estate and yielding the concept of "class stratification." The second section details the mid-eighteenth century application of this categorical term for the first time to the socio-political world, the usage which is basic to the notion of particular "classes" as being active political units with discrete economic interests and their own social, political, and cultural organizations.[2] The conclusion draws important distinctions between pre- and post-Revolutionary employments of *classe* as a political term.[3]

Class, Society and Economy—Although *classe* comes from the Latin word *classis*, the development is not direct from either the ancient or the medieval forms. In medieval usage *classis* seems to have meant (1) group, company, throng, with the related meaning of a "class" in the scholastic sense, i.e., a group of students; (2) fleet; (3) the peal of bells, especially as a funeral knell; also a steeple or "clapper;" the peal of guns;

[1] The author wishes to thank Professors Lynn Hunt, Martin Malia, Arthur Quinn, and Gerard Caspary of the University of California at Berkeley for commenting upon drafts of this essay. Special thanks are due Max Grober for help with the Latin sources cited and also Gabriel Motzkin, now of Hebrew University, Jerusalem, for help in defining and applying the distinction between essentialism and nominalism.

[2] For the philosophical work available on the English "class" one should consult the *Oxford English Dictionary* (1971) and the somewhat different interpretations given by Raymond Williams in *The Long Revolution*, Pelican edition (Harmondsworth, England, 1965), note to 343, and in *Keywords* (Oxford, 1976), under "Class." The only similar work on the French case consists of the brief and unanalytical remarks in William H. Sewell, Jr., *Work and Revolution in France* (Cambridge and New York, 1980), 81, 282-83.

[3] Peter Clavert, *The Concept of Class* (London and New York, 1982) provides an interesting analysis of the concept, but one which can be consulted with confidence only for the post-1789 developments.

(4) a trumpet or horn; (5) a summons.[4] The related term *classicus* was in many cases used interchangeably, although it also could mean (1) belonging to the highest class [i.e., group], preeminent, 'classical'; (2) naval or military; naval or military force; (3) a trumpet call or trumpet; (4) the right to sound the summons; (5) the sound of all the bells.[5]

This range of clearly affiliated meanings is comparable to that actually found in Classical Latin with the exceptions that Classical Latin does not use this family of terms to refer to the peal of bells or sound of guns or to the height of a steeple, on the one hand, but does elaborate references to military bodies, especially marines or sailors, or via the sea, naval forces and naval warfare, on the other hand. The other major exception— *the* exception for our purposes—is that in Classical Latin *classis* referred to one or other of the five groups into which Servius Tullius is said to have divided the Roman people according to wealth for military purposes. Significantly, always absent in both Classical and medieval usage is the sense of "class" as a general term for "category."[6] Likewise, the term is never used with the connotations of a verb, as in the sense of "to put into groups."

It is not entirely clear at what point *classis* passed into the vernacular. Modern French etymologies universally declare that *classe* was borrowed from Latin in the fourteenth century. *Larousse* follows *Littré* in pointing to Bersuire, 1355, as having used the word in reference to the divisions

---

[4] This conflates the range of meanings available from both British and French sources taken from Albert Blaise, *Dictionnaire latin-français des auteurs du Moyen-age* (Turnholti: Typographi Brepols, 1975); R.E. Latham, under direction of the British Academy, *Dictionary of Medieval Latin from British Sources* (London and Oxford, Fascicule II, 1981). The latter has only progressed as far as "C" at this writing.

[5] *Ibid.*, including obviously variant spellings and grammatical forms.

[6] For the range of Classical Latin meanings, see the *Oxford Latin Dictionary* (Oxford: Clarendon Press, 1969). It is sometimes proposed that in Classical Latin *classis* also referred to "a class, a division in general," but this seems a doubtful modernism for a term better left defined as "band or group" because the references are always explicitly to particulars, hence extensions occur by analogy rather than from a general term for category. Thus, although Charles Short and Charlton T. Lewis, *A Latin Dictionary* (Oxford, 1980, impression of 1879 edition) give "pueros in classes distribuerant" as an example of the word's use as a division in general, this interpretation is unnecessary. Likewise, Lewis and Short cite Suetonius, *The Twelve Caesars*, "Tiberius," 46, translated along these lines by Robert Graves (New York: Penguin Books, 1979, revised edition), 136-137, as "Tiberius then arranged them [these friends] in three categories according to their rank. . . . ," but *classis* could just as readily be rendered "groups" in this instance, and thus maintain a better symmetry with its other classical usages. Cf. A. Ernout and A. Meillet, *Dictionnaire étymologique de la langue latine*, fourth ed. (Paris, 1959); they consider the original meaning of *classis* to be "summons" and cast doubt upon attempts to derive the term from the Latin *calare* or from some imagined Greek root. A Momigliano, in Hammond and Scullard, *The Oxford Classical Dictionary*, second ed. (Oxford: Clarendon Press, 1970), argues that *classis* "was at first the whole Roman army; later it was a division of the army in the reform attributed to Servius Tullius." This etymology leads us even further from attempts to derive *classis* from *calare*.

of the Roman populace in antiquity and in reference to divisions in his own period according to birth and vocation. *Littré* gives the actual citation as "Servius ordena tout le pueple [*sic*] romain en cinq grandes distinctions, lesquelles il appela classes."[7] This, however, appears to be an example of the use of a latinism at a period during which Latin terms were in common currency, the use being not so much a "borrowing" as the employment of a simple analogy. Moreover, this particular employment must have been rare, for studies of the vernacular through the Middle Ages do not cite *classe* with this usage. Instead, one finds the word *clas* (or *claz, clac, chlas*), which was associated with noises and with a fleet. The related term *classique* referred either to the horn of war or to the one who sounded it (both *clas* and *classique* thus showing themselves as vernacular adaptations of *classis* in the perhaps most common of its medieval usages).[8] The orthography of *clas* and these meanings are important in that as *classe* began to acquire its modern meanings, *clas* was dropped in its original form and its place was taken by the modern *glas* (for knell or tolling), just as *classique* also was transformed. In brief, by the mid-sixteenth century *clas* had become restricted in its references to noise or a resounding sound.[9] Through the seventeenth century this form underwent a marked retreat. In the *Dictionnaire de Trévoux* of 1734 it appears as a sort of curiosity meaning the sound of church bells to mark deaths and burials. The compilers were careful to note that the word was not used at all in Paris at that time, although it was still popular in some provinces. *Classique*, by way of contrast, by the early sixteenth century already could refer to "classic French poets" but not to its earlier meanings.[10]

As for the term *classe* itself, its adoption into the vernacular appears to have been a development from one of the standard meanings in medieval Latin, but with important changes. *Classis* in the medieval period had as one of its chief meanings "group, company, throng," a set of meanings also found in Classical Latin and from which the usage "a class of students" was probably derived. In the oldest surviving major compendium of the French language, Robert Estienne's *Dictionnaire françois—latin* (1549), *classe* is defined directly as *bande* (the French

[7] *Le grand Larousse de la langue française* (Paris, 1977); Emile Littré, *Dictionnaire de la langue française* (Paris, 1960).

[8] Frédéric Godefroy, *Dictionnaire de l'ancienne langue française et de tous ses dialectes du IXe au XVe siècle* (Paris: F. Vieweg, 1881-1902); Edmund Huguet, *Dictionnaire de la langue française du seizième siècle* (Paris, 1929-1965, including supplements). Gilles Ménage, *Dictionnaire étymologique de la langue françoise* (1694) derives *clas* from *classicum*.

[9] Huguet, *ibid.*; also Randle Cotgrave, *A Dictionarie of the French and English Tongues* (London, 1611), entry "Clas" defined "m. as Glas; a knell, or woeful noise."

[10] Huguet; Oscal Bloch and W. von Wartburg, *Dictionnaire étymologique de la langue française*, second ed. (Paris, 1950) lists the borrowing of *classique* as 1548. Bloch and Wartburg also consider all the meanings of *classe* other than "a class of citizens" as being developments indigenous to French.

term) or *classis*, and the examples in both include the division of students: (1) To be the first and most knowledgeable of the class [*classe*] or of the group [*bande*]—*ducere classem.* (2) To divide the students into classes [*classes*] or by groups [*bandes*]—*distribuere pueros in classes.* To Estienne *bande* was clearly the more important of the two words, for its entry is easily ten or more times longer than that of *classe.* Significantly, a number of entries under *bande* are in fact defined by the Latin *classis*, although Estienne is unwilling to use these same examples to define or elaborate on the French term *classe*, something which indicates that *classe* not only had been adopted into the vernacular relatively recently and hence was a far less common word, but also that it was seen as having connotations which somehow set it off from the range of meanings in the Latin term. The definitions and examples of the usage of *bande* are quite revealing in this regard. Under *Bande de gens de guerre*, Estienne gives a number of obvious substitutions for Latin:

—Les cinq bandes des hommes d'armes Romains . . .;

—Qui estoyent de la première bande, *Classic*;

—Une armée sur la mer partie en deux bandes, *Bipartitò classis distributa*;

—Distribuer en cinq bandes, *In quinque classes distribuere.*

One way of interpreting this material is to see *bande*, which is probably Italian in origin and had long been used in the French vernacular,[11] as being in the process of absorbing the military meanings of "troop" or "group" or "company" which had been associated with the late medieval Latin *classis*, leaving *classe* free to become a general term for "category" in a sense not true of either *bande* or *classis*. Indeed, Estienne's examples of the use of *classe*, although apparently referring to classes of students, already indicate this type of change in that the association of *classe* and *bande* in this context means that *classe* (a) does not have the military connotations found in the Latin or in the vernacular *bande*; (b) does not possess the meanings other than "group" found in the Latin; and (c) is not limited only to an application to divisions of students because *bande* does not have this type of limiting association. A real distinction between *classe* and *bande*, however, and one easily overlooked in the twentieth century when we have become accustomed to the abstract use of *classe* whereas *bande* retains particular associations, which is one reason why Estienne gives so many instances of its uses. This way of thinking also would seem to characterize the Latin *classis* in its extension to various groups, in one case students, for its extension is by analogy rather than as an attribute to some general meaning. *Classe*, in contrast, groups particulars without being itself associated as a particular. By the mid-sixteenth century the only major continuation of the older restrictions upon the use of *classe* as a general term for a type of category seems here to be the application to groups of people as opposed to things, and

[11] *Larousse.* (See note 7 above.)

even this restriction appears uncertain. Under *Distribuer* Estienne gives the somewhat unusual Latin "causas describere [*sic*] in classes, atque in singulos inspectores quod & conscribere dicitur" as the meaning of the French phrase "faire les distributions des procez," which Cotgrave in 1611 translated as "the sorting of causes unto their several days of hearing, and Courts to be heard in," but Cotgrave's rendering sidesteps the meaning of *in classes*, which seems to involve some sort of categorization. Estienne's example, significantly, is not drawn from a classical or even a medieval author, but from his own teacher, Guillaume Budé, who died in 1540!

The evidence that *classe* had in fact become somewhat of a general term for "category" by the mid-sixteenth century is fairly widespread. Claude de Sailens in *A Treasurie of the French Tongue* (London, 1580) defines *classe* as "a form in the use in schools," "form" here being itself a word applied to school-classes only from about 1560 in England as an extension of the usage "a grade, degree or rank."[12] As in the case of *bande*, this equation is misleading, in this instance because "form" starts from the perspective of the general rather than the particular. As a "grade, degree or rank," it must distinguish the parts of some preëxistent whole, hence Thomas Cooper in the *Thesaurus linguae romanae & britannicae* (London, 1573) gives as a root meaning of *classis* "an order of forms or seats, where men sit according to their degrees," and retains this connotation under *Ducere classem*, which he translates as "to be chief of the band or form." By way of contrast, Estienne translates *Ducere classem* with *bande* and *classe*, although *forme* is the French equivalent of "form," thus emphasizing particulars via an *abstracted* general category rather than a *substantive* general category with its variations and elements. By the end of the century it seems to have become commonplace for authors of multi-language dictionaries to indicate some type of special meaning for the French, although the shadings of the term continued to elude translation. For example, Henri Hornkens in the *Recueil de dictionaires françoys, espaignolz et latins* (Bruxelles, 1599) defines *classe* in Spanish as *orden, vanda, renglera* and in Latin as *classis, ordo*. (*Vanda* was the Spanish form of the Italian *banda* and disappeared in the early seventeenth century.) The equation of the French term with these three Spanish terms is repeated in César Oudin's *Tesoro de las dos lenguas francesa y española* (Paris, 1607), although in this case the Spanish list includes its own *classe*, even though in the Spanish-French section of the dictionary the two terms are simply equated, indicating that the French term adequately translated the Spanish word, but not vice versa.[13]

---

[12] *OED.* (See note 6 above.)

[13] John Florio in *A Worlde of Words* (London, 1598) does not give "class" as an English word, but does give to the Italian *classe* the definition "a degree or form in schools, a company; also a navy or fleet at sea." In Italian the schoolroom and the naval uses of *classe* predominate into the eighteenth century; unlike the French, the Italians

The culmination of the development of French dictionaries before the appearance of those of Richelet and Furetière at the end of the century was Randle Cotgrave's *Dictionarie of the French and English Tongues* (London, 1611), which radically revised and extended Jean Nicot's *Thresor de la langue françoise tant ancienne que moderne* (Paris, 1606), which largely repeats the French parts of Robert Estienne's earlier dictionary. Cotgrave confirms much of the new status of *classe* and informs the reader that the word is still used chiefly in a school-room setting. His definition runs as follows: "A rank, order, or distribution of people according to their several degrees; in schools (wherein this word is mostly used) a form or lecture restrained unto a certain company of scholars, or auditors. . . ."[14] All the points made above clearly apply to this definition, and the implicit etymological issue is whether *classe* is taking on the meaning of "rank" and "order" or whether the reverse is occurring. By the middle of the century the evidence leaves no doubt that the process is the latter and not the former. After Nicot's work, dictionaries, for example, no longer list *bande* as a synonym, thus leaving *classe* free from prior particular and limiting associations.

There are several reasons for so diligent an examination of *classe* as a term expressing a particular type of logical relation among elements within an abstract framework. The most important of these reasons is given by the compilers of the *Oxford English Dictionary* in their observation that although *classis* had a clear connection with Roman social divisions, in fact the application of "class" to English society seems to have derived from its more general meaning as a "number of individuals (persons or things) possessing common attributes."[15] Since the *OED* sug-

---

do not use the word to describe logical relations until that late date, at which time its references to a fleet disappear. Cf. Lorenzo Franciosini, *Vocabolario italiano e spagnolo* (Venice, 1636 and 1735 editions); Antoine Oudin, *Dictionaire italien et françois* (Paris, 1681); *Vocabolario degli Accademici della Crusca* (Venice, 1697 and 1721 editions); F. Altieri, *Dizionario italiano ed inglese* (London, 1726), and also the numerous editions of Joseph Baretti's English-Italian dictionary which superseded Altieri's work and which list *classe* in Italian as used to refer to a navy or fleet only in poetical references. Finally, I have examined Salvatore Battaglia's *Grande dizionario della lengua italiana* (still in progress, vol. III published in 1964), which varies somewhat from my etymological argument, but whose pre-eighteenth century examples can readily be reinterpreted along the lines I outline.

As for the German case, until sometime in the eighteenth century *class* referred to classes in school, but *Ordnung* remained the translation for *classe* in the sense of order, rank, etc. Cf. Nathanael Duez, *Dictionnaire françois-allemand-latin* (Amsterdam, 1664); R.P. François Pomai, *Le Grand dictionnaire royal: françois-latin-allemand* (Frankfurt, 1709); *Nouveau dictionnaire du voyageur: françois-allemand-latin* (Geneva, 1732).

[14] Thomas Blount's *Glossographia* (London, 1656) appears to have taken much of its definition of the English term directly from Cotgrave's earlier definition of the French.

[15] By the end of the seventeenth century there is a tendency even to reinterpret the Classical Latin meanings of *classis*. Along with the emphasis upon its naval meanings and the order and distribution of citizens according to property and honor, which are the recommended meanings in a number of late sixteenth- and early seventeenth-century handbooks, such as Alexander Scot, *Apparatus latinae locutionis, in usum studiosae*

gests that in the seventeenth century "class" was borrowed from the
French *classe*, the etymology of the French word takes on added significance. Much of the material already discussed buttresses the contention
that the English usage was in fact a borrowing, and to this one might
add that when Jean Bodin's *Les six livres de la République* was translated
into English in 1606 as *The Six Bookes of a Commonweale*, neither *classis*
(from the Latin version) nor *classe* were rendered as anything other than
estate, degree, rank, etc., terms implying a hierarchical ordering absent
in Bodin's actual passages.[16]

Bodin's use of *classe* parallels Budé's use in the Latin cited above
and provides an early case of the application of the term to French society
qua French society rather than as an analogue of antiquity. In Bodin's
République (first ed., 1576) *classe* is used neither simply in reference to
the Roman model nor to its analogy in contemporary society, but is used
to discuss abstract models of societies such as are found in the works of
Plato and Aristotle. Regarding Plato's *Republic*, Bodin notes that there
were three classes (as distinct from estates) of citizens which were quite
unequal in property.[17] In another place he abstracts from the Roman
instance in order to write of the "great estates of the people" being
divided into six classes.[18] These instances repeat the same way of using
classe as a term allowing abstract theorizing which Bodin had pursued
in *Methodus ad facilem historiarum cognitionem* (Paris, 1572),[19] i.e., *classe*
is used to denote a collection of individuals with common attributes, in
these cases persons and groups. (This 'nominalist' use is discussed below
under *Classe and Politics* and in footnote 52.)

Conspicuously absent, however, is any immediate identification of
classe with such terms as *ordre* and *rang* in their contemporary political

---

iuventutis (Lyon, 1608), one begins to find *classis* treated as "any division of men appointed
to any employment," as in Robert Ainsworth's *Dictionary of the Latin Tongue* (London,
1736). There actually seems to be a difference in national traditions in this regard, for
English Latin dictionaries to the present day are more inclined to stress its substantive
aspects of the term, whereas the French are more commonly inclined to stress its derivation
from a verb form. Hence Antoine Furetière in the *Dictionnaire universel* (Paris, 1691)
insists that the word comes somehow from *kalo, congrego* and *convoco*, and that "classe
n'est autre chose qu'une multitude assemblé à part." There is more the sense in some of
the major early French works that somehow one is getting at the idea behind the usage
to uncover elementary logical forms. Cf. the *Encyclopédie*.

[16] I am working from the 1583 edition, but according to Douglas McRae this is largely
the same as the 1576 version. See Jean Bodin, *The Six Bookes of a Commonweale*, a
reprint of the 1606 Richard Knolles translation from the French and Latin texts, edited
and introduced by Kenneth Douglas McRae (Cambridge, Mass.: Harvard University
Press, 1962), pp. A79-A80. The translation on pp. 53, 193 and variously in Bk. III, ch.
viii, should be compared with the citations below in notes 17, 18 and 19.

[17] Jean Bodin, *Les six livres de la République* (1583), Bk. II, Chap. i, 265.

[18] *Ibid.*, 267-268.

[19] See Jean Bodin, *Methodus ad facilem historiarum cognitionem* (Geneva, 1610),
Chapter VI, pp. 142, 167 and 173.

roles. Both the novelty and the implications of Bodin's way of analyzing social and political issues become clear only through a juxtaposition of Bodin's language with the much older traditional vocabulary. The key words here, all of which by the early seventeenth century have been employed in defining *classe*, are *ordre, rang* and *degré*, to which should be added *état* for reasons which should shortly become clear. *Degré* is perhaps the least interesting of the four, and is defined fairly simply in Jean Nicot's *Thresor* as *marche*, or the Latin *gradus*. The sense of its connotation or nuance of ranking, a step in a row, etc., is unproblematic. *Rang* comes from the Frankish *hring* meaning ring or circle of judicial or military assembly, hence the "ordre, rang des personnes assistant à une assemblée."[20] Nicot, following Estienne, offers as Latin equivalents *ordo, series,* and *striga,* and his list of examples of usage stresses the word's affinities with operations of ranging, ranking, setting within a group of some sort of order, etc.

État and *ordre* have more elaborate definitions and affinities, no doubt in part because they are also legal concepts. *État* comes from the Latin *status,* which means "set, appointed, settled, fixed, certain, ordinary, never failing,"[21] and also attitude, situation, stability, form of government, etc.,[22] definitions which are basically extensions of the notion of settledness. At least as early as 1213 the word applied to the juridical status of persons,[23] and this sense of the word is greatly elaborated by lexicographers such as Nicot, who notes that *estat (état)* signifies the rank (*rang*) and the political order among men of a realm, a country, and so forth, and thus, according to Nicot, one refers to the three "estates" or sometimes simply to the "estates."

It is *ordre,* however, which among these terms possesses the richest and the most significant past and contemporary usage. For the jurist Charles Loyseau in the first decade of the seventeenth century, orders and estates were deeply interconnected, for

Some are devoted particularly to the service of God; others to the preservation of the State by arms; still others to the task of feeding it by peaceful labors. These are our three orders or estates general of France, the Clergy, the Nobility, and the Third Estate.[24]

In linking *état* to *ordre,* Loyseau also linked it to that word's overt cosmological overtones. *Ordre* is taken from a Latin root and early had been given a central place in explaining the Church's vision of the world. Loyseau, consciously or not, drew upon this tradition in much of his *Traité des Ordres et simples dignités,* and he actually attached to his

---

[20] *Larousse* (see note 7 above) citing *Chanson de Roland,* 1080 A.D.
[21] Ainsworth, confusing the nominative form with the past participle.
[22] *Larousse.* (see note 7 above).
[23] *Ibid.*
[24] Opening paragraphs of Loyseau's *Traité* (1610) as quoted by Georges Duby, *The Three Orders: Feudal Society Imagined,* trans. Arthur Goldhammer (Chicago, 1980 and first published as *Les trois ordres ou l'imaginaire du féodalisme,* 1978), 1.

"Prologue" a Latin text taken from the Decretum of Gratian (1130 A.D.), in this instance quoting Pope Gregory the Great (595 A.D.):

Providence has established various degrees [*gradus*] and distinct orders [*ordines*] so that, if the lesser [*minores*] show deference [*reverentia*] to the greater [*potiores*], and if the greater bestow love [*dilectio*] on the lesser, then true concord [*concordia*] and conjunction [*contextio:* the word evokes a fabric or weave in a very concrete way] will arise out of diversity. Indeed, the community [*universitas*] could not subsist at all if the total order [*magnus ordo*] of disparity [*differentia*] did not preserve it. That creation cannot be governed in equality is taught to us by the example of the heavenly hosts; there are angels and there are archangels, which clearly are not equals, differing from one another in power [*potestas*] and order [*ordo*].

[Inserts are those of G. Duby, the translator from the Latin.][25]

The contrast between *classe* and these terms is in many ways quite stark, for all the above have connotations of hierarchy, order, place, and of bringing to human institutions aspects of an objective and enduring way of things, hence that institutions are not the products of human caprice or invention. Moreover, all these terms share with the example of "form" examined earlier two attributes, to wit, they are drawn from the language of universals and they are "qualitative" terms expressing the "essences" or essential qualities of which experience can give only particular cases. In other words, they are "metaphysical" in the Aristotelian sense of expressing the reality behind the flux of experience. *Ordre* in particular has overtones linking it to doctrines of intelligible essences (which today positivists generally associate with magic) and certainly to doctrines of transcendence. *Ordre* and *état* also clearly had special roles within the French monarchy's legal framework, just as both *degré* and *rang* were related to these roles. Finally, since the ultimate justifications for the social relations and the established laws of the *Ancien Régime* were themselves metaphysical, all of these terms, insofar as they apply to law, politics, and society, from yet another angle implied the tacit acceptance of some notion of religious transcendence. The seemingly objective and permanent character of social and institutional arrangements was often associated explicitly with a divine ordering of the cosmos, either via analogies (e.g., the king is to the people as God is to His creation) or by ontological extension such as is found in the neo-platonic conception of the "great chain of being." Indeed, Loyseau employs both types of argument.

The peculiarity of *classe* in Bodin's usage, a usage which with time becomes more or less standard, lies not just in its sharp contrast to this older vocabulary, but also in the sphere of socio-political activity to which it was applied. This peculiarity stands out if, for example, one considers Loyseau's paraphrase of the Decretum of Gratian as he applied its principles to his own society.

---

[25] *Ibid.*, as translated from the Latin by Duby, 3-4.

There must be order in all things. . . . The world itself is so-named for that reason in Latin. . . . The inanimate creatures are all placed in it in accordance with their higher or lower degree of perfection. Their times and seasons are certain, their properties regulated, their effects assured. As for the animate creation, the heavenly intelligences have their hierarchical orders, which are changeless; and, with regard to men, who are designated by God to rule over the other animate creatures of this world, though their order may be changeable and subject to vicissitude, owing to the particular capacity and freedom that God has given them to choose between good and evil, it is the case that they cannot survive without order, for we should not be able to live together in a state of equality, *but of necessity some must command and others must obey. Those who command have many orders and ranks.* . . . Thus, through these order is established . . . so that, in the end, by means of order, a number numberless achieves oneness.[26] [emphasis added]

In this passage Loyseau's use of "order" differs significantly from that of the document he is paraphrasing; in the Decretum the emphasis is upon the great order [*magnus ordo*] which links the disparate elements of the community, the higher and the lower all falling within the same continuum, whereas Loyseau's usage draws a sharp dichotomy between those who rule and those who obey, just as he emphasizes less the qualities of the various elements of society as a whole than the multitude of orders and ranks of those who command.[27] Moreover, this important jurist was joined in these distinctions by authors whose stations and purposes were quite different, indicating that these distinctions either were or were becoming commonplace. For instance, Antoyne de Montchrétien in the *Traicté de l'OEconomie politique* (1615) remarks that in general all of society seems to be composed of government and commerce, the first being absolutely necessary, but the latter only secondarily so.[28] The first two orders performed the duties of government, whereas the "third order" included the merchants and those who performed all the other roles in society. Finally, although he observes traditional language in his descriptions of the elements of government, his characterizations of groups within the Third Estate could easily pass in part for modern descriptions of classes, for the "third order" in his view is composed of three sorts of people who share in each case the same quality and type of life, i.e., the same values and mores, the same humors and types of actions and conditions.[29]

To return to the earlier point, Bodin uses the term *classe* in the portions of his works in which he refers to social elements without

[26] Charles Loyseau, *Traité des Ordres et simples dignités*, as cited in Roland E. Mousnier, *The Institutions of France under the Absolute Monarchy, 1598-1789*, trans. Brian Pearce (Chicago, 1979), 5-6. This is from the Preamble.

[27] Mousnier, 3.

[28] Antoyne de Montchrétien, *Traicté de l'OEconomie politique* (1615), edition introduced by Th. Funck-Brentano (Paris, 1889), 137.

[29] *Ibid.*, 12. Montchrétien should also be compared with Bodin in important respects, for his doctrine of harmonies depends upon the claim of worldly perfection. This early utilitarian could follow Aristotle in describing the State as having persons of "haute, de moyenne et de basse qualité" when speaking of France rather than of only a city-state

indicating either inherent nature (something implicit in the early modern conception of corporate groups) or necessary political relationships such as are expressed by *ordre, état,* and *rang.* To put this another way, Bodin does not use *classe* with reference to the political aspects of society (which by definition involve corporate bodies and "qualities") but only to those aspects of society which in fact characterize either "those who obey" or all groups that merely constitute society as some great whole. Political society, to the contrary, consists of corporate groups with inherited rights and privileges, distinctions which Bodin notes, especially in the relevant sections of the *Methodus,* are made at all times and in all societies.

The major hurdle to be overcome (before *classe* could be accepted as a common term by other than highly educated authors inclined toward neo-platonic abstractions of either the Ramist or later the Cartesian variety) was the substitution of an inductive analysis of particulars to replace the earlier approaches dependent upon a metaphysics of substance and quality.[30] For this substitution the middle years of the seventeenth century were the turning point as philosophies of mechanism and attacks upon Aristotle grew apace. *Classe* remained a relatively uncommon word until the last third of the century, but there is evidence of its increasing application as a social term. When the Cardinal de Retz in 1648 wrote

---

in part because he also thought that government could be made to follow the universel harmony of the world (238-39). This notion of earthly harmony separates Montchrétien from earlier "realists" such as Machiavelli, for they saw a large state such as France as being too diverse and extended to be compared to the antique models for city-states, and they also did not view the natural world as subject to complete rationality, but to elements of chance. On a vulgar level, Montchrétien presaged the doctrine of a totally filled mechanistic universe elaborated in the next several decades by Descartes and his followers. In such a model of the world all the old fears of merchant greed and love of gain could be seen as working through hidden ways for the public good (137-141). It should be added that only when the claim that private activities led necessarily to public welfare had been largely accepted could modern capitalism emerge. See the remarks in notes 30 and 36 below.

[30] Alexander Koyré deals at length with the "platonization" of the material world in classical physics, in *From the Closed World to the Infinite Universe* (Baltimore, 1957), and more briefly in his *Galileo Studies,* trans. John Mepham (Atlantic Highlands, N.J., 1978), 1-38, 154-236, which show that the anti-Aristotelian scientists, from Galileo to Descartes, expressed their preference for mathematics and for treating the material world on the same level with the celestial bodies. In the sphere of economics it would seem similarly appropriate to point out that such Renaissance neo-platonists as Copernicus and Bodin are generally credited with having invented the quantity theory of money, and that such continued mathematicization was essential to all pre-nineteenth century economics. Likewise, in political theory Bodin's notion of sovereignty relied heavily upon the mental abstraction from the everyday world of contending hierarchies, jurisdictions, and privileges to an ideal world of mathematical completeness. On economic theories, see Henry William Spiegel, *The Growth of Economic Thought* (Englewood Cliffs, N.J., 1971), 86-92, as well as the general argument of Guy Routh in *The Origin of Economic Ideas* (London, 1975). For Bodin's views upon sovereignty, see *Les six livres de la République,* Bk. I, ch. viii. On the related nominalist logic, see note 52 below.

of "ce maudit esprit de classe," he meant what today would be termed *esprit de corps*, yet given the associations then growing up around *classe* there was certainly lacking the sense of general "relatedness" which earlier would have enveloped the groups involved in this sort of sentiment.[31] *Classe*, furthermore, never really carries very well the connotations of hierarchy which belonged to the older vocabulary to which it was increasingly equated by the end of the century and for which it was even substituted. The tension involved comes out somewhat in two instances drawn from La Bruyère's *Les caractères* (1688-1696), for a remark about a group or class of lawyers ("il est de la classe de ces avocats. . . .") seems unproblematic, but we are less certain when it is combined with the older terminology ("Se dit aussi de l'ordre, du rang dans lequel l'estime publique met les individus d'après leur mérite et leur capacité. Ils ne peuvent tous au plus qu'être les premiers d'une seconde classe.")[32]

Nevertheless, after the mid-century there can be no doubt that *classe* was increasingly employed to describe elements of what we would now term social stratification. In this it was at first largely limited to the Third Estate, as in Maréchal de Fabert's proposals of 1660 to create tax classes. Such limitations, however, quickly passed. Furetière in his *Roman bourgeois* (1666) refers to the differentiation of society by income as involving "classes" and notes the attendant possibilities for social climbing.[33] In 1673 the official legal designation of the ranks (of *qualité*) by the collectors of the *taille* is as *classes*, and the use of this non-hierarchical term in a legal context indicates in an important sense the subtle triumph of a new sensibility.[34] Two decades later in the *capitation* (poll-tax) of 1695 the entirety of the French nation was divided into twenty-two tax classes according to wealth or assumed income (and although this tax may have marked the success of the Crown in the realm of bureaucratic rationalization, it also undermined the traditional political/legal forms upon which Absolutism depended for legitimacy).[35] The ramifications of

---

[31] Cardinal de Retz, *Oeuvres*, ed. by Alphonse Feillet (Paris, 1872), II, 83. Also see Louis-Adolphe Regnier, *Lexique de la langue du Cardinal de Retz* (1896), vol. X of the *Oeuvres*.

[32] Jean de La Bruyère, *Les Caractères ou les moeurs de ce siècle* (Paris, 1962), under "De quelques usages," no. 49, p. 429 for reference to lawyers. The second passage is quoted in *Dictionnaire national ou dictionnaire universel de la langue française*, 15th ed. (Paris, 1874), without exact citation.

[33] Jules Bourelly, *Le Maréchal de Fabert* (Paris, 1885), 250-53; Antoine Furetière, *Roman bourgeois* (Paris, 1958), 921.

[34] Letter from M. de Saint-Contest, intendant at Limoges, to the Controller-General, August 2, 1687, referring to the regulation of 1673 which had created *classes* or *échelles*. See A. de Boislisle, *Correspondance des controleurs-généraux des finances avec les intendants des provinces, 1683-1715*, 3 vols. (Paris, 1874-1897), I, p. 114, no. 444.

[35] *Ibid.*, I, App., 565-74 for text of *Déclaration du Roi portant établissement de la capitation*, as well as Vauban's reasons for the tax, p. 561. On a more general level, the late seventeenth-century's version of *raison d'État* (not to be confused with that of the Cardinal de Richelieu) self-consciously applied neo-platonic principles of the new sciences.

the new language, especially in its official use, had already begun to appear earlier in the types of distinctions which it encouraged, as when in 1684 the tax-collector at Moulins wrote to Colbert that the capitation then in effect inconvenienced both the *gentilshommes* and the *classes non-privilégiées*.[36] By 1718 Philibert Le Roux, in the compilation *Dictionaire comique, satyrique, critique, burlesque, libre & proverbial* could write regarding *classe* that it was a word greatly in fashion and that it was used in place of *ordre, rang*, etc.

The "fashionableness" of *classe* by the end of the reign of Louis XIV was hardly without consequences or implications. For instance, different rights and material conditions are the implicit concomitants of the particular social role (again with its implied "qualities") of the "rank" of *gentilshomme*. To distinguish this rank from that of the non-privileged classes reduces this complex intermingling of role, quality, and *état* to a simple question of political/legal entitlements based upon comparisons along some common measure. One indication of how far this altered perspective had permeated French culture by the end of the century can be found in the fact that all the major dictionaries created at the end of the century define *classe* much as does Richelet's work of 1680, that is, as the grade or rank *attributed* to persons or things according to their importance or qualitites,[37] in contrast to the earlier definitions of *classe as* an order or rank, or, as Cotgrave puts it, "a rank, order, or distribution of people according to their several degrees." Two points are important in this contrast. First, by the end of the century the word had been accepted as a general term for categorical groupings in terms of qualities abstracted from particulars. Second, the earlier definitions had been to a certain extent circular, that is to say, to determine a rank or order in terms of "degrees" is to move within descriptions continuing to emphasize the complex relatedness mentioned above in which "order" included the arrangement of elements by "degrees" as a ranking of their "qualities"; in the case of persons, this involved their condition, titles, and so forth.

Administrators under Louis XIV had a tendency to apply principles of mechanics to the workings of government in a quite explicit fashion. For instance, in 1698 Jean Pothier de la Hestroye described the recently deceased Colbert as one of France's greatest ministers, and then went on to proclaim that in the State all must work—the poor by hand and the rich by spending so as to provide work for others. His analysis compared "state and society to a cosmos devoid of hierarchy and personality; an inanimate system of corpuscular and mechanical forces . . . money, dissolving traditional values and social structures, was said to enable the state to shape human beings into more easily combinable parts of a total pattern." See Lionel Rothkrug, *Opposition to Louis XIV* (Princeton, 1965), 104-06. The spirit of mechanism, so closely connected with the idealization of the State, was very much a part of administrative drives to inventory national wealth; cf. Rothkrug, 108, and Spiegel, 86-92.

[36] De Boislisle, I, 16, no. 56.

[37] *Larousse*; cf. same point in Antoine Furetière, *Dictionnaire universel* (Paris, 1691), under *Classe*.

(See Estienne or Nicot for examples of all of these. Cotgrave's dictionary, when compared with these two, already in 1611 reflected enormous changes in standard usage.) Distinctions drawn from "merit, value, nature, [personal] qualities, etc." effectively cut this link to the older vocabulary with its interconnecting hierarchies.

In the first decade of the eighteenth century Boisguilbert took a large step toward making this position explicit in his meditations upon the problems of taxation and commerce in France, for example in his observation that "privilege" served to mask the "solidarity of [economic] interests" common to all the members of a state, from the highest to the lowest.[38] The great crime in his eyes was that human institutions had corrupted the created order and divided people into two classes [classes], those who did not work and yet enjoyed every pleasure, and those who worked from dawn to dark from painful necessity and yet often possessed hardly anything at all.[39] In this judgment Boisguilbert does not so much attack disparaties of wealth as he does the political/legal distinctions upon which the *Ancien Régime* rested, portraying the essential roles and activities of various groups as fundamentally involving their interaction in the sphere of economics.[40]

Boisguilbert, a member of the judicial nobility and a landowner, argued his case indefatigably through his books and especially his letters to French ministers of finance. Although he followed the same mechanistic physical models as Colbert, he considered agriculture to be the basis of the French economy and furthermore sought higher general prices for farm goods, greater export of foodstuffs to aid farmers, greater

[38] Pierre de Boisguilbert, "Mémoire sur l'assiette de la taille et de la capitation," in *Pierre de Boisguilbert ou la naissance de l'économie politique*, collected by L'Institut National d'Etudes Démographiques (Paris: Institut d'Etudes Démographiques, 1966), II, 695-96. This is from Chap. IV "Sur la capitation." Boisguilbert was not exactly alone in these sentiments. Abbé Girard in *Synonymes françois* (Paris, 1718) explains under "De-condition, De-qualité" and "Condition, État" that nobility is an employment rather than a personal condition, as well as speaking of the "diverse orders which form the economy of the Republic." Likewise, Girard distinguishes between *l'état* as linked to one's manner of life, occupation, and so forth, and *la condition* as having overtones of one's rank in society.

[39] *Ibid.*, Boisguilbert, 979, from "Dissertation de la nature des richesses. . . . ," Chap. III.

[40] In the light of the argument made above concerning the distinction between ruler/ruled and public/private functions, it is surely significant that the distinction between *état* and *nation*, which appeared in the 1690s, implies that the government and its functions and enterprises can be separated clearly from the situation in society at large. Once this distinction is made, one need not conclude with Loyseau and Montchrétien that government is necessary, but in fact may conclude that government is an interference in an otherwise self-regulating sphere, as is the position of libertarians. For the etymologies of *état* and *nation*, see Ferdinant Brunot, *Histoire de la langue française des origines à 1900* (Paris, 1930), VI, part I, 137.

price stability, and increase in the wealth *of the poorest elements* of French society as the key to general prosperity (he favored a type of multiplier theory in which he claimed that consumption, especially by those groups unable to hoard, led to a rapid circulation of money). His attacks upon "privileges" as impediments to the proper working of the economic system did not mean, nevertheless, that he sought the elimination of the society of estates in all of its manifestations. It should be borne in mind that the major distinction between the social order of estates and that of classes is the barrier of political/legal entitlements, entitlements only partially removed in the transition to modern social forms.[41] Following somewhat the models of "political arithmetic" employed by William Petty in England and by Vauban in France (models clearly related to the physical sciences of the day), Boisguilbert sought to employ a notion of "equilibrium" in order to understand the French economy, and, not incidentally, to solve the intense financial problems besetting the Crown at the end of the reign of Louis XIV.[42]

The heirs to Boisguilbert's economic arguments were the Physiocrats, both in continuing a line of thought fairly widely current in the late seventeenth century and in an even more aggressive employment of "political arithmetic," "equilibrium theories," and the model of the physical sciences.[43] Significantly, it was also the Physiocrats who gave the greatest impetus to *classe* as a way of describing various social groups as components of an economic system. Beginning in the 1750s a string of new words appeared from their pens, for example: *la classe stérile* (Quesnay, 1758), *la classe laborieuse*, and *la classe productrice* (Turgot, 1766),[44] and similarly *classer* as part of the argument that in order to understand human interests, it is necessary to classify the various forms of work (DuPont de Nemours, 1772).[45] Since many of the Physiocrats were nobles either of old stock (e.g., Turgot) or of new standing (e.g., Quesnay, the physician to Louis XV) and served as government officials generally bent on economic reform in the fiscal interests of the Crown, at least for a time they possessed excellent positions from which to popularize their theories. Turgot, as Controller-General in 1774, sent hundreds of copies

[41] Roberto M. Unger, *Knowledge and Politics* (New York, 1975), 164-67.

[42] For a good brief discussion of Boisguilbert's work, see Spiegel, 172-75, *op. cit.* (note 30 above).

[43] Spiegel, 183-99; Jean Molinier, "L'Analyse globale de Boisguilbert, ou l'ébauche du Tableau économique," in *Boisguilbert*, I, esp. 97; Routh, 29-79; and for physiocratic language, Brunot, 28-31.

[44] Turgot uses *classe productrice, classe stipendiée, classe disponible, classe industrieuse*, and refers to the *classe de laboureurs, capitalistes*, etc. at least as early as 1766. See Gustave Schelle, ed., *Oeuvres de Turgot* (Paris, 1914), II, "Les réflexions sur la formation et la distribution des richesses," Chapters xv, xcvi, xcviii, and literally throughout. See also Brunot, 191-95.

[45] DuPont de Nemours, *Abrégé des principes de l'économie politique*, 1772 (Paris, II, 376, as cited in Brunot, 31.

of Abbé Morellet's physiocratic tracts to *intendants* throughout France.[46] In any case, by the middle of the eighteenth century *classe* as a term for social groups was no longer uncommon and furthermore it was applied freely as a description of social elements, especially in their economic relations, without any connotations of hierarchy. Moreover, this was not a result of the machinations of any one school of thought, but seems to have been part of a general acceptance of nontraditional ways of viewing society, as evidenced by both the remarkable lack of emphasis given to terms such as *ordre* in many works composed from roughly the 1730s onward and by the variety of contexts in which *classe* was used as a social term by mid-century. For instance, although M. de Réal (de Curban), Grand Sénéchal de Forcalquier, is chiefly concerned with legal and diplomatic issues in *La science du gouvernement* (1761), he offers such offhand observations as "the plowman and the men of the countryside form the first class of those cooperating [with regard] to the wealth of the state,"[47] and the reader is not at all surprised when the same author later recommends that titles of ancient nobility and the advantages of station should be cherished "as property."[48] Likewise, in Du Chesne's *Code de la police ou analyse des réglemens de police* (1767) under "Laboureurs" is the advice that the "profession of the peasant is the basis of society; if it is relegated to the last classes [*les dernières classes*] by a vulgar frivolity and ingratitude, all those whose judgments are regulated by reason and feelings honor these men. . . ."[49] In the same vein is the chapter "Du Commerce," which speaks glowingly of commercial activities and of the "different classes of citizens" involved in them.[50]

Thus, by the middle of the eighteenth century an influential segment of French society tacitly regarded the polity as being composed of classes. By this was meant simply that if one considered society as a whole in its economic aspects, one could discern particular economic roles which could in their turn be related to specific social elements. This outlook reflected, first of all, the application to society of a nominalist logic of categories, an application which can be traced to the first third of the

---

[46] Steven L. Kaplan, *Bread, Politics and Political Economy in the Reign of Louis XV*, vol. LXXXVI in the *International Archives of the History of Ideas* (The Hague, Martinus Nijhoff, 1976), 67-68; also, Georges Weulersse, *La Physiocratie sous le ministères de Turgot et de Necker, 1774-1781* (Paris, 1950), 246.

[47] M. de Réal de Curban, *La science du gouvernement* (Amsterdam, 1764), VI, 105. This should be compared with Montesquieu's transparent application of *classe* to his contemporary societies in defending the aristocracy in France in *Esprit des Lois*, Bk. III, ch. ii. Montesquieu realized that the nobility had ceased to perform legitimate roles in the eyes of many in France and he hoped to show that it could regain such a position. Franz Neumann in the introduction to Thomas Nugent's translation of *The Spirit of the Laws* (New York, 1949), xii, shows that although the work was first published only in 1748, Bks. I-VIII had been written by 1720.   [48] De Réal, VI, 366.

[49] Du Chesne, *Code de la police ou analyse des Réglemens de police* (Paris, 1767), I, 133.   [50] *Ibid.*, 329.

sixteenth century. Its elaboration with regard to economics entailed the adaptation to this end of the mechanistic models of physics developed in the following century. Implicit was the rejection of the medieval essentialist ontology and the logic derived from it. The extension to society of this rejection of essentialism necessarily involved the weakening of the normative forms and language dependent upon essentialism for meaning. Hence, as Roberto Unger has put it, the development of the concept of *classe* involved "the rejection of the idea of a fixed social hierarchy, in which each social group has settled duties to obey or entitlements to govern."[51] Finally, the separation of function from status implicit in the concept of social stratification left problematic the relation between the interests of groups and the interests of society at large. The need to establish a framework for relating public and private interests once these had been accepted as distinct was the basis for new developments in the concept of class after the mid-eighteenth century.

Class and Politics.—Functionally *classe* is actually closely related to a term such as *espèce* or the Latin *species*. Like *classe*, *espèce* indicates a category of beings or things with some sort of common character which allows distinctions within the field of a larger whole. Unlike *classe*, it also indicates characterization by essential qualities. We can translate *espèce* as "a sort, a type, a variety," etc., and in related usages as "an appearance, an image, a representation," but not generally as a *classe*, the two terms being used together unambiguously only in a special sense in biology.[52] (Similarly, in early modern French dictionaries *classe* itself is almost never used as a synonym for another word, something which again indicates the term's singularity in usage.) Of the two terms *espèce* is older in the vernacular by centuries, having been employed as a categorical term since the mid-thirteenth century. Moreover, unlike *classe*, its meanings in the Latin root, whether in antiquity or in the medieval period, are not markedly different from those in French.[53]

Just as the central meaning of *species* is "form"—one should associate this with Plato's doctrine of "Forms" or "Ideas"—the central meaning

---

[51] Unger, 165. (See note 41 above.)

[52] Cf. *Larousse, Godefroy, Huguet* as well as the meanings given in the dictionaries of Richelet, Furetière, and the *Encyclopédie*. Samuel Johnson's *A Dictionary of the English Language* (London, 1755) makes the pertinent distinction about "class" when it defines the term as "a set of beings or things; a number ranged in distribution under some common denomination." This "under some common denomination" is precisely the point of contrast with *espèce*, and the discussion below merely draws this out. Additionally, it should be noted that *classe* is a categorical term dependent upon a type of logic related to modern forms of induction, and this logic itself can only be traced to the late thirteenth or the early fourteenth century with the creation of the philosophical concept of the "transcendental," regarding which see Gabriel Motzkin, "The Problem of Transcendence in the Secular Age from Kant to Heidegger," unpublished Ph. D. dissertation, University of California, Berkeley, December 1982, Chapter 1.

[53] Cf. *Larousse*, A. Blaise and R. E. Latham, cited above.

of the vernacular stresses the "intelligibility" of an object to the mind, especially by way of "participation" of the particular in some universal form, the "reality" of the particular being perceived only through this participation. By way of contrast, *classe* as a term for "category" connotes a relation of particulars to the whole through membership, i.e., a "class" is a collection of entities falling under stipulated conditions of membership, their relations being merely "formal." Significantly, "classes" are the same only if they have the same members—the emphasis is upon the particulars and upon the (mentally) abstracted formal characteristics which they share, but which may be otherwise insignificant or accidental, just as in a "class of students" the only similarity between the students mandated is that they be members of that group. *Espèce*, however, indicates something qualitatively and internally "essential" to the nature of those things of which it is predicated. To place these distinctions within the traditional language of the *Ancien Régime* one should consider that the term *ordre* indicates the "qualities" and the *état* (or "state" and general disposition, condition, place, etc.) of its members in a very complex web of relations from which any given individual may stray without ceasing, except in very limited circumstances, to be a part of his "order." With *classe* the opposite is true, for either an individual's characteristics or activities are sufficient for the particular purposes of the classification or he is not a member. Thus a class also is *sui generis*—classes are the same only if so defined as to contain numerically, that is, in each separate particular, the same elements or members; otherwise the relations are between classes, not between members. Classes in the *capitation* of 1695 were such that a noble's *état* did not link him to other nobles, but he could be lumped together with a wealthy peasant if their presumed incomes were the same, the common thread being that of wealth.

The significant point about *classe* as a concept in the sense discussed here is that it replaced only part of the function of the traditional vocabulary of words such as *ordre, état, rang,* etc. The older terms in their medieval usages were socio-politico-economic in meaning. More or less at the same time-period that *classe* was entering the vernacular these terms underwent a partial truncation towards usages more limited to socio-political roles. One sees this clearly in the works of Bodin, Loyseau, and Montchrétien cited above, and it is certainly related to the use of *classe* in reference to the economic activities of French society. The point of overlap between *classe* and the traditional vocabulary is in the reference to society, specifically to the relations of various groups as parts of society. The type of description given via *classe* until the mid-eighteenth century does not so much replace the older terms as sap them of meaning; in the period starting at the mid-seventeenth century and running up to the French Revolution the connotations of the older terms became more and more confused.

Classe could not, however, replace these terms until the mid-eighteenth century precisely because of those characteristics specific to it which were necessary for its use as a "nominalist" categorical term (including its logical implications). As an anti-essentialist concept it could express the static picture of a quantitative division of society into various economic elements, but it was limited to expressing abstracted relations imposed for the purpose of ordering and necessarily left undefined— indeed left implicitly "empty"—the natures of the elements so related. *Precisely because it was not an essentialist concept it could express the capacity for function, but not for activity as intrinsic to the elements involved.* In its socio-economic or nominalist sense, after all, the ranging is by "membership" in functional units rather than in terms of the innate propensities and possibilities of elements *qua* exemplars and variations of elemental substances. Moreover, this limitation was as true of its use in the hands of the Physiocrats as it had been of its use by Bodin.

The domain in which *classe* had been adopted and in which its antiessentialist functions were for the first time dismissed was biology, the same area in which mechanistic models from the physical sciences first came under sustained attack. The term was first used taxonomically for living things in 1733,[54] and by the time of the publication of the *Encyclopédie* in the 1760s its use in biological taxonomies as a division between kingdom and genus (just as the term species ranked in this schema below genus) had become its leading scientific meaning. In point of fact, all of these biological classifications depended upon some notion of "form" or essential quality for which the taxonomy merely detailed the degrees of variation. It is not important for our purposes whether the biologist believed himself to have found a real essence in the ontological sense or merely to be employing a convenient logic. Buffon, widely read after the publication of two volumes of his natural history in 1749, believed, for example, that species are real, and his works would have done much to popularize *classe* in its new usage.[55] In either case important elements of the old Aristotelian distinctions between form and accident are employed via taxonomies which endeavor to identify the most general categories of life and then the multitude of their variations.

Significantly, in philosophy one of the chief reasons for the Aristotelian distinctions between form and accident had been the need to allow for "generation" or the appearance of variety and of change in nature and human experience, a great difficulty in Platonic thought. Time obviously is an important consideration here and the difficulty involved is the need to construct a concept which connotes a "change" as well as a "state." This problem, in fact, haunts physics as well as biology, but the application of mechanistic categories to the human world created an especially acute need for some type of resolution to the conundrums created. The traditional doctrines had allowed "generation" or variety

---

[54] Larousse, see note 7 above.
[55] Norman Hampson, *The Enlightenment* (New York, 1968), 221-22.

via the multitude of corporations, degrees, privileges, local associations, and so forth within the orders and had radically demoted the importance of change over time. The new categories, with their dependence upon antecedent causation, knew no change other than over time. The only apparent answer was to reintroduce an essentialist logic in biology, to relate parts to the whole through innate qualities, which explains the employment of *espèce* in biology with all its ancient ramifications. With regard to *classe* this move involved a grafting of essentialism onto nominalist stock, something which at the same time allowed a flexibility not previously possible. In essentialism logical "inversion" is acceptable to the extent that essence is prior to existence so that one can say, and as it became a Romantic commonplace, *either* that the part is contained within the whole *or* that the whole is contained within the part. This logic had not previously been possible with *classe*.

Such a notion of the embodiment of the whole within the part is in fact the key to the employment of the traditional vocabulary in the socio-political sphere. Moderns are more familiar with the issues involved under the heading of "representation," hence it may be helpful here to consider an example of the characteristic medieval attitude toward the role of corporate bodies as political entities. In 1489 the Parlement of Paris remonstrated against the claims of the King's Council under Charles VIII and proclaimed itself "un *corps mystique* meslé de gens ecclésiastiques et lais . . . representans la personne du roy," because this highest court of the kingdom was the "sovereign Justice of the Realm of France, and the true throne, authority, magnificence, and majesty of the king himself."[56]

The claim expressed by the Parlement is quite simply that it is the person of the king in the same sense that the king, in his official capacity, embodies the kingdom. Moreover, despite the common description of the three orders by modern historians as being a sort of functional division of labor, this notion of "representation" was the hallmark of corporate bodies in general: a nobleman, for example, performed a certain role because he literally, not figuratively, participated in a particular sphere of potentiality through his essence as a noble. This is the reason for the tremendously complex web of interrelated meanings which characterized *ordre, état*, etc., in their medieval and early modern usages. Likewise, for this reason the socio-political connotations of the traditional vocabulary were more resistant to dissolution than were the socio-economic ties. The economic sphere could be described by referring to activities or functions laid out in a static tableau and then divided into parts, but the political sphere ultimately requires that some individuals or groups

---

[56] "The Remonstrance of 1489" found in Edouard Maugis, *Histoire du Parlement de Paris* (Paris, 1913), I, 374ff, as given in Ernst H. Kantorowicz, *The King's Two Bodies: A Study in Medieval Political Theology* (Princeton, 1957), 220-221. Kantorowicz examines the issue of representation at great length and with equal profundity.

act *for* others, thus avoiding the necessity of "representation" and its complications. (The latter was the standard practice of antiquity whenever this type of issue arose, neither direct democracy nor its variations being strictly comparable to their later European counterparts—as Rousseau noted in his *Social Contract*, Bk. III, ch. v.)

Again, it must be stressed that prior to the second third of the eighteenth century *classe* could not be fully substituted for the older vocabulary precisely because it was used in opposition to the type of logic necessary for the older language's political functions. This point is readily apparent in the not uncommon instances in which *classe* is used in a political context but without political overtones. For instance, under "Egalité" in the *Dictionnaire philosophique* (1764) Voltaire judges that society consists of a multitude of classes, the chief conflict being between the rich and the poor (the rich always winning, of course). This usage is tantamount to saying that society consists of groups—one of the oldest meanings of the word *classe*.

Voltaire earlier in the 1750s had observed that previously philosophical questions were beginning to take on economic overtones;[57] it was also in that decade that Rousseau made his name discoursing upon inequality, and Linguet declared that society was born from violence and property, from usurpation.[58] The frequent and often applauded declaration of such sentiments gives us some idea of the extent to which the traditional vocabulary and the doctrines for which it was essential had lost their power to compel conviction. Those least convinced by the old claims of legitimacy often were those at the top of the social hierarchy. For example, competing with Rousseau in 1754 for the prize at Dijon on the topic of the evils of inequality was René–Louis de Voyer de Paulmy, Marquis d'Argenson, Conseiller au Parlement (1715), Conseiller d'Etat, *intendant* for Hainaut and Cambrésis (1720), and minister for foreign affairs (1744).[59] D'Argenson was clearly a noble of some importance, yet in his essay he remarks quite openly that inequality is the foundation of tyranny and the destroyer of mores and liberty. Indeed, he writes, it is the source of that ambition found in all estates which causes children to leave the class of their fathers (*elle fait sortir les enfants de la classe où étaient leurs pères*) and to be indignant at the profession to which they are born. The Marquis d'Argenson placed these observations within the context of Roman history, but the application to contemporary society was transparent, not only in his references to inequality, but also in his observations upon the manner in which inequality

---

[57] Kaplan, 118.

[58] René Roux, "La Révolution française et l'idée de lutte des classes," *Révue d'Histoire économique et sociale*, XXXIX, 3 (1951), 254.

[59] Roger Tisserand, ed., *Les concurrents de J.-J. Rousseau à l'Académie de Dijon pour le Prix de 1754* (Paris, 1936), 16.

and the desire for it led the bourgeoisie to buy nobility without the necessary merit, just as it led to intrigues among the nobility, to the corruption of great nobles, and to the failure of princes to fulfill their proper functions.[60]

D'Argenson's essay won praise from, among others, both the Président de Brosses and Diderot.[61] If anything, his later work was more radical. In his *Considérations sur le gouvernement ancien et présent de la France*, which was privately circulated before his death in 1757 and published in 1765,[62] he challenged tradition directly by asserting that "everything is reduced to knowing if an order separated from the rest of the citizens, much closer to the Throne than to the People . . . if a grandeur by birth, independent of the graces of the Prince, is more submissive to Royal authority than [are] Subjects equal among themselves." The nature of these "Subjects equal among themselves" is also given—they work for themselves and are treated only according to their reputations and their personal merit.[63]

The complaint that the nobility, especially the nobility of the sword, offered little of importance to society was not new with d'Argenson. Already in 1732 Boullainvilliers was responding to obviously well-entrenched attacks upon the nobility, especially the nobility of the sword, as having no real role, or as he put it, "three general causes of the decadence of the old nobility."[64] By the 1750s this theme of noble superfluity had become a staple of public debate, only by then applying to *privilèges* in a more general sense. The wording *"privilèges particuliers"* seems to have been applied especially to ascriptive privileges, and privileges as such were often characterized as meaning interests (which is chiefly an economic word here) separate from and opposed to those of the nation, the people, the prince, or commonly of all three. Much of the time the vehicles for these criticisms of historical prerogatives were, appropriately enough, themselves "histories," such as Mably's transparent *Observations sur l'histoire de France* (1765), which is sprinkled with remarks about how such and such ceremony had removed the would-be noble from the common class of citizens (*la classe commune de Citoyens*) and raised him to a "superior" order having personal nobility and privileges (*privilèges particuliers*), such as occupying a distinguished place in the general Assemblies and alone having the public charge and the right to form the council in which was to be found the [political] nation.[65]

---

[60] *Ibid.*, 127-28, in what is listed as "Discours V."

[61] *Ibid.*, 15, editor's Introduction.

[62] René-Louis de Voyer de Paulmy, Marquis d'Argenson, *Considérations sur le gouvernement ancien et présent de la France* (Amsterdam, 1765), "Avis du Libraire," 3.

[63] *Ibid.*, 190-91, 212, 305.

[64] Henri, Comte de Boullainvilliers, *Essais sur la Noblesse de France* (Amsterdam, 1732), 230-300.

[65] Abbé de Mably, *Observations sur l'histoire de France* (Geneva, 1765), 44.

Mirabeau does something very similar in *L'Ami des hommes ou Traité de la population*, which was in its fifth edition in 1760.[66] Sometimes this theme appears in indirect ways, such as in the "explanation" given for how the word *travail* had come to be associated with degraded aspects of society (*Nouveaux synonymes françois*, by Abbé Roubaud, 1786).[67]

The reinterpretation of the political world which was behind the attack upon "feudalism" (*féodalité*) and privilege clearly was related to the type of transformation in thought and values already outlined in the discussion of the substitution of *classe* for words such as *ordre* and *état*. The slow process of the withering away of the meanings of the older terms did not lead to the incorporation of their meanings and functions into *classe* until the 1760s, at which point the incorporation primarily took the form of what might be characterized "negative representation." That is, the prior claims of the nobility to "represent" by virtue of their *ordre* or *état* (through which they actually *were* the political nation, to paraphrase Mably) were simply reversed so that now they were characterizable as an impediment to the common good—by virtue of their *ordre*. The reasoning here has already been discussed, to wit: if all groups have "private" interests by virtue of their economic functions, to what extent can any group (however defined) claim to represent in its own interests the general interest?

In the mid-eighteenth century this issue was dealt with at length in precisely these terms. Such was the basis of Rousseau's *Social Contract*, and the discussion was titled appropriately in 1765 in one of the most widely read publications of the eighteenth century—the *Encyclopédie*, in this case in d'Holbach's article "Représentans." D'Holbach leaves no room to doubt that representation involves representing groups with interests and that this representing can be done only by those who come from the groups involved. As he puts this, "the leaders of political society are interested in maintaining among the different classes of citizens [i.e., groups characterized by economic functions and interests] a just equilibrium [Boisguilbert's economic term now applied to political society] . . . each class should be represented by men who know its state and needs; these needs can of course be known only by those who feel them. . . ." Likewise, the state whose constitution permits one order [or class] of citizens to speak for others—as in the systematic anarchy of the nobles under feudalism—creates an *aristocratie* which sacrifices the needs of the nation and of the sovereign to its own ends.[68] D'Holbach repeats this

---

[66] Victor Riqueti, Marquis de Mirabeau, *L'Ami des hommes, ou traité de la population* (Hamburg, 1760), esp. Chap. VIII, "Travail & Argent."

[67] Abbé Roubaud, *Nouveaux synonymes françois* (Paris, 1786), 432-33, under "Travail, Labeur."

[68] "Représentans," in the *Encyclopédie* (1765), towards the end of the article. In the 1780 printing of the edition published "à Berne et à Lausanne," this is in vol. XXVIII, 367-68.

point in various places: "no order [which he equates simply with 'class'] of citizens should always exercise the right to represent the nation"; likewise, " 'representatives' suppose constituents from whom their power emanates; to whom they are as a consequence subordinated, and of whom they are merely organs." In other words, groups which are merely "classes" with their own (private economic) interests, i.e., the nobility, through their privileges are an *aristocratie* which is inherently pernicious to the needs of the society as a whole.

Epilogue and Conclusion

When any function is made the prerogative of a separate order among the citizens, has nobody remarked how a salary has to be paid not only to the man who actually does the work, but to all those of the same caste who do not, and also to the entire families of both workers and the non-workers? Has nobody observed that as soon as the government becomes the property of a separate class [*classe*], it starts to grow out of all proportion. . . ? (M. Blondel trans. from Ch. 1 of *Qu'est-ce que le tiers état?*)

The meaning of d'Holbach's argument for the *Ancien Régime* was ominous (his position was expanded and sharpened by Sieyès in 1789 in *Qu'est-ce que le tiers état?*), for if the privileges of nobility were merely "property," as De Réal had claimed in 1761 and the *avocats* of Nuit (Burgundy) affirmed as a principle of law in 1788,[69] then the privileged corporate groups, which as "classes" were merely groups with private (economic) interests, had simply usurped public functions for private gain. This way of relating political, social, and economic issues is familiar to us and almost "modern"—but not quite. References to the conflict between the classes, to *la classe aristocratique du bourgeois*, etc., which began to appear in 1790, did not refer to classes as specific socio-economic formations in the modern sense. They referred most commonly to the revolving door of "negative representation" as applied to whatever group was in power, there being little sense of "classes" as fixed socio-economic formations other than in terms of rich and poor, the dividing line often being, as it long had been in French law, between those who did not do manual labor and those who did. Moreover, denunciations of *la classe aristocratique du bourgeois* reflected the true legal nature of the *bourgeoisie* until 1789—a *bourgeois de Paris*, for instance, was as privileged as a noble of considerable standing.[70] The Revolution ushered in the use of a

---

[69] J. Egrét, *La Pré-révolution française, 1787-1789* (Paris, 1962), 532.

[70] On the meaning of social titles, see Joseph di Corcia, "*Bourg, Bourgeois, Bourgeois de Paris* from the Eleventh to the Eighteenth Century," *Journal of Modern History*, **50** (June 1978), 207-33. Much of the confusion over the meaning of the language of the Revolution stems from the fact that the denunciations remained largely political by virtue of various groups' perceived roles vis-à-vis the Revolution, but were social in the sense that the same type of "negative representation" which had been applied to the nobility could be applied to any other group in power. See, e.g., Marat's views in *L'Ami du peuple*, 6 September, 1790 and 13 April, 1791 in *French Revolution Documents*, vol. I, ed. by

variety of categorical terms for expressing either approval and inclusion or rejection and denunciation, i.e., nation, people, proletariat, etc.; yet as important as these terms were for allowing the expression of new senses of the polity, they are also extraordinarily amorphous. It is almost surprising how slow the French were to adopt more specific references to socio-economic groups, preferring generalities such as *toutes les classes, les classes privilégiées, la dernière classe, les classes populaires, la classe mitoyenne, tous les propriétaires,* etc. until 1830.[71]

There is certainly nothing in the concept of "class" itself, either in its early modern or its modern versions, which would determine that there be a specific number of classes with particular characteristics. One may contend as much on other analytical grounds, but that is another issue. Indeed, the debates within the disciplines of history and the social sciences regarding class analysis and other forms of social analysis move almost entirely within the framework of questions regarding the "boundaries" of given social groups, on the one hand, and questions regarding the nature of the "interests" of social groups, on the other hand. Significantly, the analytic focus is nearly always upon the nature of the particular groups which compose societies and almost never calls into question the assumption that societies are necessarily "stratified," indicating clearly that the concept of social stratification is logically prior to any particular analysis of the elements of stratification.

The history of the emergence of the concept of "class" in the early modern period, more than anything else, is the history of the development of this concept of social stratification. The tendency to analyze society in the abstract in terms of functional component parts possessing formal or nominal rather than inherent or essential relations appears to have

---

J.M. Roberts (Oxford, 1966), 268-69, 280. Additional material from Marat and also from Brissot can be found in *French Revolution Documents,* vol. II, ed. by John Hardman (New York, 1973), 21, 50. This material should be compared with that found in Shirley M. Gruner, "Le concept de classe dans la Révolution française: une mise à jour," *Histoire sociale,* XI, 18 (Nov. 1976), 416-21, in René Roux, cited above, note 58; and in Jeremy D. Popkin, *The Right-wing Press in France, 1792-1800* (Chapel Hill, 1980), 104-21.

[71] Antoine Fantin-Desodoards, *Histoire philosophique de la Révolution de France* (Paris, 1807), 27, 33, and discussion 1-27; J.A. Dulaure, *Esquisses historiques des principaux évènemens de la Révolution française* (Paris, 1823), 39, 52, 76, 267, 302; "Opinion de M. Le Duc de Fitz-James, sur le Projet de Loi relatif aux Journaux," delivered in the Chambre des Pairs (December 1817) and published (Paris, 1818), 14, 28. For references to property, see Popkin's material mentioned in note 70 above; *La Quotidienne,* **184,** 2 (July 1820), 2; *Bulletin général et universel des annonces et des nouvelles scientifiques,* vol. II (Paris, 1823), article 362. For economic doctrines see J.C.L. Simonde [Sismondi], *De la richesse commerciale ou principes d'économie politique* (Geneva, 1803), 90ff, where Sismondi speaks of three productive or economic classes and three administrative classes, i.e., the old distinction between government and society which had appeared during the sixteenth century; also J. Dutens, *Analyse raisonnée des principes fondamentaux de l'économie politique* (Paris, 1804), 57ff for a tripartite class structure. For popular usages after 1830 see Sewell, esp. 194-218.

been a sixteenth-century development, very likely one pioneered in France. The etymology of *classe* provides a window upon this new way of thinking as it took shape and spread within French culture. As we have seen, the word was applied first to non-political aspects of the polity, hence to social elements in their most general senses as components of society as a whole and to economic activities, then to social elements as related to particular economic activities. At the same time, traditional social terms tended to be increasingly truncated to their political/legal meanings, necessarily leaving the Third Estate and its activities most fully described by the new language as well as isolating intellectually the public functions of the first two Estates from their private or economic activities. By the last third of the seventeenth century this process had advanced to the point that *classe* could replace traditional hierarchical terminology in all but a narrow range of political and legal usages.

By the eighteenth century educated Frenchmen had no difficulty conceptualizing their society as being "class-stratified." Conversely, the traditional language which still provided an alternative to this picture of the polity had lost so much force that it no longer could bear the full weight of its political meanings. At some point during the mid-century these socio-political meanings were re-associated with the socio-economic aspects of society which had begun to diverge from them at least as early as the sixteenth century. The result of the grafting of essentialist socio-political meanings onto the nominalist socio-economic meanings of *classe* was a new concept which was frankly limited as to how much political legitimacy it could convey, for the economic interests of socio-economic groups are by definition potentially in conflict. *Classe* thus by the mid-eighteenth century offered a type of analysis, and especially a type of polemic, which challenged the inherited notion that the polity contained specific "public" social elements which constituted the "political" nation by virtue of ascriptive qualities and duties. Unlike the older language of orders, estates, degrees, and so forth, *classe* was part of a new language and a new way of thought which specifically isolated public functions from private (economic) interests and activities in a way which allowed the two to be cogently contrasted and opposed to one another. The elaboration of the language of social stratification to include fixed socio-economic formations does not seem to have occurred until the early nineteenth century for a variety of reasons. The chief of these is that *classe* in its combined socio-economic/socio-political usages is by its nature a polemical concept, one useful for expressing what has been called here "negative representation." The actual elimination of the public orders of French society would have been one condition for more positive notions to have become attached to "classes" as special types of enduring social groups.

Berkeley, California.

PART FOUR

HUMAN NATURE AND COMPASSION

XVIII

THE MIME OF GOD: VIVES ON THE NATURE OF MAN

By Marcia L. Colish

Until recently, Juan Luis Vives' philosophy of man has been of peripheral interest to scholars. Working primarily from his psychological and educational writings and his social and political thought, most commentators have drawn Vives into focus either by viewing him as a precursor of subsequent contributors to these disciplines [1] or by using him to support a religious or nationalistic bias.[2] With the printing of an English translation of his *Fabula de homine*, however, a fresh approach to Vives has been made which starts from his ideas on the nature of man. Yet, although placed among the selections published by the editors of *The Renaissance Philosophy of Man*, the *Fabula* has been included only as a "sort of appen-

[1] See especially W. C. Atkinson, "Luis Vives and Poor Relief," *The Dublin Review*, CXCVII (July–Sept. 1935), 93–4, 102; H. Barnard, "Giovanni Ludovico Vives: His Pedagogy and Influence on Education," *American Journal of Education*, XXVII (April 1877), 342; A. Bonilla y San Martín, *Luis Vives y la filosofía del renacimiento* (Madrid, 1929), II, 341–2, 347–9; G. Desdevises du Dezert, "Luis Vives, d'après un ouvrage récent," *Revue hispanique*, XII (1905), 406, 407, 410; E. D'Ors, *Estilos del pensar* (Colección temas actuales, III, Madrid, 1945), 102; P. Graf, *Luis Vives como apologeta: Contribución a la historia de la apologética*, trans. J. M. Millas Vallicrosa (Madrid, 1943), 16–7; R. Günther, *Inwieweit hat Ludwig Vives die Ideen Bacos von Verulam vorbereitet?* (Borna-Leipzig, 1912), 16–7; J. M. Hofer, *Die Stellung des Desiderius Erasmus und des Johann Ludwig Vives zur Pädagogik des Quintilian* (Erlangen, 1910), 101; G. Hoppe, *Die Psychologie des Juan Luis Vives* (Berlin, 1901), 119; A. Lange, "Luis Vives," *La España moderna: Revista de España*, VI (April 1894), 185–6; M. Menéndez Pelayo, *La ciencia española* (Edición nacional de las obras completas de Menéndez Pelayo, LVIII, Santander, 1953), I, 306; *idem, Estudios y discursos de crítica histórica y literaria* (Edición nacional de las obras completas de Menéndez Pelayo, VII, Santander, 1941), II, 7–8. The works of Foster Watson are a prime example of this sort of predilection, particularly the introduction to his translation of Vives' *De tradendis disciplinis* (Cambridge, 1913), lxvi–ii, xcv, cl; and his articles "The Father of Modern Psychology," *The Psychological Review*, XXII (Sept. 1915), 334; "J. L. Vives and St. Augustine's 'Civitas Dei,'" *The Church Quarterly Review*, LXXVI (April–July 1913), 145–6; and "Juan Luis Vives: A Scholar of the Renascence, 1492–1540," *Essays by Divers Hands, being the Transactions of the Royal Society of Literature of the United Kingdom*, ed. Sir Henry Newbolt. N.S., I (London, 1921), 92, 97–101.

[2] Religious interests are reflected by W. A. Daly, *The Educational Psychology of Juan Luis Vives* (Washington, D. C., 1924), 64–5; Georg Siske, *Willens- und Charakterbildung bei Johann Ludwig Vives (1492–1540)* (Breslau, 1911), 51–2; Graf, *op. cit.*, 31; Bonilla y San Martín, *Luis Vives*, II, 339–40, 344–5; Menéndez Pelayo, *Ciencia*, I, 311. Menéndez Pelayo links his religious concerns with a florid Spanish nationalism in *Estudios y discursos*, II, 7–8, and is joined here by his compatriot Juan Estelrich in the preface to his edition *Vivès: Exposition organisée à la Bibliothèque nationale* (Paris, 1941), xvi–xvii. Nationalism is also a concern of Desdevises du Dezert, "Luis Vives," *loc. cit.*, 396, although with an anti-Spanish viewpoint.

321

dix . . ." [3] to the volume. The editors, finding "the basic idea of this elegant little work . . . closely related to Pico's *Oration*," [4] the views of which are indeed "repeated by Vives," [5] and the translator of the *Fabula*, who readily agrees that its story "is directly based on Pico's conception of the dignity of man . . . ," [6] thus place Vives in this constellation of greater lights merely because the *Fabula*, "written by a friend of Erasmus, . . . may well illustrate the interdependence of the cultural movements of the Renaissance" [7] as well as "the influence which the thought of the Italian Humanists and Platonists exercised in the rest of Europe. . . ." [8] No one as yet has seen fit to comment on the merits of the *Fabula* as a piece of humanistic philosophy in itself or to place the work in the context of Vives' writings as a whole. Until this is done, however, it remains impossible to discern both the precise extent of Vives' debt to Pico della Mirandola and the position he occupies in the thought of the Renaissance.

The *Fabula de homine* (1518) is one of Vives' earliest works, written when Vives (1492–1540) was twenty-six, and had recently come to Flanders after completing his formal education at the University of Paris. Employed at the time as tutor to William de Croy, Cardinal and Archbishop-elect of Toledo, and Antoine de Berges, the young Belgian nobleman to whom the opuscule is dedicated, the youthful Valencian had already composed a series of brief devotional works [9] and several commentaries on classical authors. [10]

[3] *The Renaissance Philosophy of Man*, ed. Ernst Cassirer, Paul O. Kristeller, and John H. Randall, Jr. (Chicago, 1958), 16.   [4] *Ibid*.

[5] *Ibid.*, 19. This opinion is reiterated by Kristeller, "Ficino and Pomponazzi on the Place of Man in the Universe," *Studies in Renaissance Thought and Letters* (Rome, 1956), 285: the *Fabula* is "based entirely on Pico's conception" of the dignity of man.

[6] Nancy Lenkeith, *Renaissance Philosophy of Man*, 385.

[7] *Ibid.*, 386. It should be noted that Miss Lenkeith here de-emphasizes the usual interpretation of Vives as a mediator of Erasmianism to Spain by depicting him as a cultural intermediary between Italy and the Low Countries. Cf. Marcel Bataillon, *Érasme et l'Éspagne: Recherches sur l'histoire spirituelle du XVIe siècle* (Paris, 1937), vi, 656, 658; Adolfo Bonilla y San Martín, *Erasmo en España: Episodio de la historia del renacimiento* (Paris, 1907), 8.

[8] Kristeller and Randall, *op. cit.*, 16.

[9] *Christi Iesu triumphus, Virginis Dei parentis ovatio* (1514?); *Clypei Christi descriptio* (1517?); *De tempore quo natus est Christi* (1518?); *Genethliacon Iesuchristi, Meditationes in septem psalmos poenitentiales* (1518). On the chronology of Vives' writings see A. J. Namèche, "Mémoire sur la vie et les écrits de Jean-Louis Vivès," *Mémoires couronnés par l'Académie royale des sciences et belleslettres de Bruxelles*, XV (Brussels, 1841), 13–126.

[10] *Poeticon astronomicon de Higino* (1517); *Anima senis, In Georgica Vergilii, De initiis, sectis et laudibus philosophiae* (1518).

Before his death in 1540, he was to produce forty-seven additional treatises on apologetic, social, political, psychological, philosophical, philological, and pedagogical subjects, as well as numerous letters. Although stating in 1518 his intention to develop the theme of human life in another, more extensive work, "if, some day, I should have the free time," [11] Vives deals with the nature of man *per se* in the *Fabula* alone. His intention was unrealized; the *Fabula* remains the point from which any discussion of his philosophy of man must begin.

The *Fabula* is conceived in theatrical terms. Jupiter, in compliance with Juno's wish to provide an entertainment for the gods on the occasion of her birthday feast, creates the vast amphitheatre of the world, containing celestial stalls occupied by the divine spectators according to their rank and the stage of the earth, where the action is to take place. Scenarist and director of the drama as well as creator of the amphitheatre, Jupiter "instituted everything and instructed all that they might understand. So that nothing might be done differently from what he pleased, he prescribed to the troupe of actors the entire order and sequence of the plays, from which not even by the breadth of a finger, as they say, should they depart." [12] So that his production may proceed as planned, Jupiter stands as it were in the wings, giving the starting signal and the cue for each of the players in turn.

The last to perform is the protagonist, man. The wisest in the audience and those sitting close to Jupiter do not hesitate to grant him critical recognition. The pleasure Jupiter takes in "the human archmime" [13] is enough to make his paternity patent; a closer look confirms the judgment. Recognizable as "the image of Jupiter," man, although "concealed under a mask," often seems on the verge of bursting through it, revealing himself "in many things . . . clearly divine," and participating in the immortality, wisdom, prudence, memory, and many other attributes of his celestial progenitor. [14]

As man's performance gets under way, the extent to which he partakes of the powers of the greatest of gods is made manifest. "Jupiter's own mime" [15] at once proceeds to "transform himself so as to appear under the mask of the plant," simple and devoid of sensation. [16] Withdrawing, he soon reappears in a thousand animal shapes, representing various moral traits. [17] Then, after a brief intermission, "the curtain was raised and he returned a man, prudent, just, sociable, human, kindly, and companionable. He frequented cities with other men; he ruled and was ruled in turn. With others

[11] Juan Luis Vives, dedication to *Fabula de homine. Opera omnia* . . . , ed. Gregorio Majansio (Valentiae, 1782–1790), IV,3.
[12] *Ibid.*   [13] *Ibid.*, 4.   [14, 15, 16] *Ibid.*   [17] *Ibid.*, 4–5.

he attended to matters of public interest and welfare, and, in a word, was in no way either uncivil or unsocial." [18] Having changed his masks with his own hands up to this point, man, much to the surprise of the gods, now indulges in a passive metamorphosis, being "remade into one of their own species, transcending the nature of man and relying entirely on a most wise mind." [19] Hailing him as Protean, the gods beg Juno to let him unmask and join them, "to make of him a spectator rather than an actor," [20] but before she can ask her husband's permission, man reappears in the rôle of Jupiter, mimicking his father with such accuracy that some of his fellow players, deceived into swearing "that this was not man but Jupiter himself, . . . underwent harsh punishment for such an error." [21]

The gods, however, are wiser than men. Although at first discomfited by man's performance, they at once realize that what they have witnessed has been but an imitation of the divine, albeit apt and skillful, rather than the divine itself. [22] Renewing their request, they obtain the compliance of Jupiter, who "granted the gods what he himself, long before, had decided to transfer to man," recalling him from the stage and seating him among the gods in triumph. [23]

With man in their midst, the gods avail themselves of the opportunity to scrutinize him closely. Stripped of the mask of his body, which had made him the desultory creature they had seen on the stage, "the whole man, laid bare, revealed to the immortal gods his nature akin to theirs. . . ." [24] Examining man's stage costumes themselves, and noting that his body is so ingeniously contrived as to be no less handsome and harmoniously disposed than it is useful and appropriate, "they praised Jupiter's wisdom and skill and adored him. . . ." [25] Man, received as a brother by the gods, [26] who deem it "unworthy of him to . . . practice the disreputable theatrical art," [27] is further perceived to possess wisdom, prudence, knowledge, memory, speech, and reason. By means of these faculties he brings forth institutions, arts and sciences, language, and writing, through which he transmits many doctrines, including religion. [28] Religion, linked with memory, enables man almost to approximate that power to know the future enjoyed by the divine.[29]

So delighted are the gods with their human guest that many of them pass the afternoon contemplating him and questioning him about his various activities, which he lucidly explains. Then, crowned and clad in purple, refreshed with nectar and ambrosia, he observes the festivities from the best seats in the house. As the *Fabula* draws to a close, man is seen reclining in honor at an Olympian repast. He replaces his bodily mask; "since it had suited the needs of man so

---

[18] *Ibid.*, 5.   [19, 20, 21] *Ibid.*   [22] *Ibid.*, 5–6.
[23] *Ibid.*, 6.   [24, 25] *Ibid.*   [26] *Ibid.*, 7.   [27, 28, 29] *Ibid.*

well it was judged worthy of the most sumptuous feast and of the table of the gods. Thus it was given the power of perception and enjoyed the eternal bliss of the banquet." [30]

There are many similarities between the conception of man which emerges from the *Fabula* and that voiced by Pico della Mirandola in his *Oratio de hominis dignitate*. Equally striking are the differences in terms of which Pico and Vives envisage the scope of man's powers, the nature of his end, and the means by which he is to reach it.

The formal structure of the *Fabula* is the first point at which it may be compared with the *Oratio*. Both works begin almost immediately with the framing of man as a changeable creature. It is only partially true to state that "Vives' version, in its mythological setting, is less precise than Pico's. . . ." [31] As a piece of deliberate mythography, the *Fabula*, with its cosmological scope, unity of theme, and full-blown pantheon, is at once more detailed and more compact than the *Oratio*. Unlike Pico, Vives makes no excursions from the text to comment on the opinions of a host of philosophers of varying degrees of relevance. In addition, his use of a narrative rather than a rhetorical style makes the *Fabula* a work with more economy and integrity than the rambling *Oratio*. The motif of the stage, left inchoate in the *Oratio*,[32] becomes the organizing principle of the *Fabula*.[33] In lieu of Pico's nondescript God, neither pagan nor Christian, Vives selects a coherent cast of classical deities with which man's nature may be compared. Although by no means a mystagogue of Pico's proportions, Vives indicates in this choice of a pagan setting that he wishes to cloak the sublime in the mythological rather than overtly to demonstrate the possible compatibility of Ciceronianism and Christianity.[34] Since the *Fabula* was directed to the *cognoscentes*, Vives could confidently express the profound parabolically.

In detailing the extent of man's powers, however, Pico is far more explicit than Vives. The God of the *Oratio* leaves nothing in question in His creation speech to Adam:

Neither a fixed abode nor a form that is thine alone nor any function peculiar to thyself have we given thee, Adam, to the end that according to thy longing and according to thy desire thou mayest have and possess what abode, what form, and what functions thou thyself shalt desire. . . . Thou,

---

[30] *Ibid.*, 8.

[31] Lenkeith, *op. cit.*, 385.

[32] Giovanni Pico della Mirandola, *Oratio de hominis dignitate*, trans. E. L. Forbes in *Renaissance Philosophy of Man*, 223, 238.

[33] It is surprising that Miss Lenkeith, so anxious to show Vives' dependence on Pico, does not note the latter's use of this motif although she does mention its classical sources. *Op. cit.*, 385.

[34] The filiation of this taste is given masterful treatment by Edgar Wind, *Pagan Mysteries in the Renaissance* (New Haven, 1958), 14–20, 24–30.

constrained by no limits, in accordance with thine own free will, . . . shalt
ordain for thyself the limits of thy nature. . . . We have made thee neither
of heaven nor of earth, neither mortal nor immortal, so that with freedom
of choice and with honor, as though the maker and molder of thyself, thou
mayest fashion thyself in whatever shape thou shalt prefer.[35]

For Pico man's freedom is hence unlimited. God posits no criterion
in whose light the exercise of man's creative volition is to be judged.
That human freedom is at all qualified by a moral imperative results
from the self-initiated action of man's will. Cognizant of his own
nature, he decides that some of his potentialities are better than
others, and that these must be developed toward the good in preference to the rest lest his freedom be rendered "something harmful
instead of salutary." [36] The good is the eternal; this must therefore
be his end.

Accordingly, Pico's man directs himself toward God, Who, having
left man to unravel his own destiny after the creation, now appears
only as an object of erotic contemplation. In spanning the gap that
separates him from God man is led by philosophy, a guide whose
powers enable him to carry out the three Delphic precepts. He can
comply with the injunction "Nothing in excess" with the aid of moral
philosophy, by which the grievous discord raging between the flesh
and the spirit is subdued, the animal passions are bridled, and internal
harmony is brought to his soul.[37] Man achieves knowledge of self
through natural philosophy, which, in addition to allaying "the strife
and differences of opinion which vex, distract, and wound the spirit
from all sides," [38] "urges and encourages us to the investigation of all
nature, of which the nature of man is . . . the connecting link. . . .
For he who knows himself in himself knows all things. . . ." [39]
Rational progress, "in a rhythmical measure," [40] is accomplished by
means of Platonic dialectic, appeasing "the tumults of reason made
confused and anxious by inconsistencies of statement and sophisms
of syllogisms." [41] Theology now ushers us to the final stage of supra-
rational mystic frenzy, at which point, "uttering the theological greet-
ing, . . . 'Thou art,' " [42] "roused by ineffable love as by a sting, . . .
rapt from ourselves, full of divine power we shall no longer be ourselves but shall become He Himself Who made us." [43]

Thus by his own efforts man transforms himself into God.
Endowed at first with an indeterminacy so unqualified as to be in
practice no different from divine omnipotence, man also shares with
his Maker the attributes of creativity and universality. In freedom
he devises his own end; the definition of the good and the desire for
it emanate from his own judgment and will. Perceiving the poten-

---

[35] Pico, *Oratio*, 224–5.   [36] *Ibid.*, 227.   [37] *Ibid.*, 230–1, 234, 235.   [38] *Ibid.*, 231.
[39] *Ibid.*, 235.   [40] *Ibid.*, 234.   [41] *Ibid.*, 231.   [42] *Ibid.*, 235.   [43] *Ibid.*, 234.

tialities of his unique Protean nature,[44] he decides that mutability is but a means, that the realm of process can be transcended, and that, since it does not exist for its own sake, it ought to be transcended. The achievement of this goal depends on man's successful completion of a personally instituted programme. The man who reaches the top of the ladder of the Lord is neither absorbed into the Godhead nor granted communion with God as a creature, albeit worthy. At the point of culmination, man actually *is* God. By his own powers he has created himself. God may contribute the raw matter of human self-deification, but man provides the guiding lines and conceives the end toward which he propels himself without outside aid.

Compared with this fully autonomous creature, Vives' archmime seems feeble indeed. The contrast may be placed in still clearer relief if the ideas on man found in Vives' other writings be brought to bear on the issue. Although testifying to human nature only in passing, these writings at no point contradict the views enunciated in the *Fabula*. The random references they provide are, in addition, more than merely consonant with Vives' central concept of man. His other works function as the *Fabula*'s embodiment, embellishment, and exegesis.

The limitations under which Vives' man labors are, like his potentialities, divinely imposed and regulated. Even as the creation takes place the outgoing gesture of a self-sufficient deity rather than the anthropomorphic manifestation of a supreme Architect [45] who subsequently packs up his tools and departs, so the play begins, proceeds at all points, and culminates in accordance with Jupiter's express directions. Man is given a script of the scenario; he may extemporize only within the limits of the stock situations and stock characters he is called upon to represent. Capable of donning the mask of the vegetable, the animal, and the human being by himself, he must be acted upon by an outside power before he can assume a celestial costume. He shares only some of the talents of the divine; his possession of "a most wise mind" enables him to be made godlike and his filial resemblance makes it possible for him to masquerade as Jupiter. At best, however, he is only the mime of Jupiter.

Vives makes it quite clear that man cannot *become* Jupiter, either actively or passively.[46] That those who are foolish enough to think so are subject to severe punishment is enough to correct Miss Len-

[44] *Ibid.*, 225.

[45] *Ibid.*, 224.

[46] Thus he does not have "an unlimited power of self-transformation," as Miss Lenkeith claims; also her opinion that "he transforms himself into the god Jupiter" is mistaken. *Op. cit.*, 386.

keith's interpretation of this point. She finds a reminiscence of the dogma of the Incarnation in the "co-essentiality of Jupiter and his son."[47] This proposed co-essentiality, as well as being non-existent in the text of the *Fabula*, is also less suggestive of Vives' man than of Pico's. Vives doubtless would have considered the idea blasphemous.

The mimicry of Jupiter is hence more of a warning than a mandate. Man's apotheosis for Vives consists in his recall from the stage and his permanent installation on Olympus as the honored guest and brother of the gods. This involves not self-transmutation in the crucible of frenzy but Jupiter's explicit invitation. No gate crashers are tolerated at the banquet of the gods. The welcome which renders the stage obsolete comes man's way less because of the virtuosity of his performance than because Jupiter has previously decided to extend it out of his gratuitous benificence.[48]

Escape from the domain of process is thus the goal for both Vives and Pico. Differing as to the extent to which man personally effects this redemption, they yet agree that his mutability is the pathway to the realm of eternal repose. Describing man as Protean, their allusion to the classical myth shares the same transformation of meaning. Vergil's Proteus is subject to endless indiscriminate metamorphoses simply because change is of his nature; the Proteus of Pico and Vives is a Proteus who climbs Jacob's ladder.

Process, although it cannot be conceived as an end in itself, still exerts a powerful attractive force upon both thinkers. This is particularly true of Pico. Unending peace seems wan and monotonous compared with the brilliant intensity of the colors he uses to delineate the luxuriant diversity of man's inner faculties and the exhilarating dynamism of man's creative powers. His is a philosophy of agency rather than a philosophy of Being. The vision of the Empyrean he finds infinitely less fascinating than the multiform paths by which man reaches it.

Vives, too, is struck by the range of man's activities, despite the fact that he dilates on the delights of beatitude somewhat more fully than Pico does. Both of them are deeply impressed by the interrelationship of human nature and human action. Pico treats the idea that one is what he does in explicit fashion:

For if you see one abandoned to his appetites crawling on the ground, it is a plant and not a man you see; if you see one blinded by the vain illusions of imagery, . . . and, softened by their gnawing allurement, delivered over to his senses, it is a beast and not a man you see. If you see a philosopher

[47] *Ibid.*, 385. [48] Miss Lenkeith, *ibid.*, 386, holds that this grant is a reward for man's activity.

determining all things by means of right reason . . . he is a heavenly being and not of this earth. If you see a pure contemplator, one unaware of the body and confined to the inner reaches of the mind, he is neither an earthly nor a heavenly being; he is a more reverend divinity vested with human flesh.[49]

Vives deals with this question more generally through the use of the image of the stage; in the first instance, the nature of man is approached in terms of the part he plays. His intrinsic self, however, fascinating as it may be, is not necessarily coextensive with his actions. Like Pico,[50] Vives deems the essence of man a marvel. On seeing man unmasked and stripped of his accidents, the gods of the *Fabula* are moved to silent wonder.[51] Yet it is the contemplation of his accomplishments and the inquiry into his manifold operations which evoke their insatiable curiosity.

This distinction drawn by Vives between man's essence and his activity springs from his conception of man's intellectual limitations. The essences of things may be objects of wonder; they are not, however, legitimate objects of knowledge. Although Vives as well as Pico is concerned with self-knowledge and repeatedly enjoins his readers to seek it,[52] he does not think that a grasp of the essence of the soul falls within its scope.[53] The intrinsic nature of the soul remains hidden from man.[54] "It is not a matter which should be too important for us to know what the soul is, but rather . . . what it is like and what its operations are," [55] he states. God has not granted us the faculties of intelligence, will, and memory so that we may know *what* they are; "what they may be is known to Him Who is their Author. . . ." [56] When Vives does at length analyze the nature of the soul, he proceeds not by definition but by description, in terms of its functions and its aptitudes.[57]

There are several reasons why the inquiry into essential qualities is forbidden to man. One is entirely practical. So immense, so unlimited is the nature of things that it is impossible for man fully to comprehend it. All efforts to do so will be unfruitful; man will only

---

[49] Pico, *Oratio*, 226.   [50] "It is a matter past faith and a wondrous one . . . that man is rightly called and judged a great miracle and a wonderful creature indeed." *Ibid.*, 223.   [51] Vives, *Fabula. Opera omnia*, IV,6.
[52] *Introductio ad sapientiam. Opera omnia*, I,2,48; *Excitationes animi in Deum. Opera omnia*, I,56; dedication to *De anima et vita. Opera omnia*, III,298; *De tradendis disciplinis*, V,iii. *Opera omnia*, VI,402.
[53] *De anima et vita*, I,xii. *Opera omnia*, III,332.   [54] *Ibid.*, II,xii. *Opera omnia*, III,388.
[55] *Ibid.*, I,xii. *Opera omnia*, III,332.   [56] *Ibid.*, II, introd. *Opera omnia*, III,342.
[57] *Ibid.*, II,xii. *Opera omnia*, III,388: " . . . the human soul is the spirit by which the body to which it is joined lives; it is capable of knowing and loving God, and of uniting with Him by Him for eternal beatitude."

dissipate the energies and abilities which might better be applied to endeavors more hopeful of results.[58] Idle curiosity may be dangerous to man as well as wasteful,[59] since the things that are hidden are the province of God, and of God alone.[60] Any attempt to penetrate them is rebelliously to presume the prerogatives of the Deity, to invite punishment at His hands, and this, to Vives, is distasteful as well as sinful. Pico, on the other hand, reveals in the *Oratio* a certain restlessness and, indeed, a trace of *libido sciendi*. The worship of God is not enough for him; it is an agency through which "we may like heavenly eagles boldly endure the most brilliant splendor of the meridian sun." [61] Vives is more cautious and more reverent. Majesty, in his opinion, should inspire not the perverted obsession to know all but the humble joy of adoration.[62] Moreover, to fix one's gaze on the eye of Apollo is to be met with a blinding stare. "He who searches into divine Majesty will be devastated by its glory," [63] he affirms. Human omniscience, in addition, would rob the universe of its rich, mysterious life, its drama, its arcane meaningfulness. It would make God an unwelcome stranger in His own dwelling place. To Vives such a world would have seemed sterile, hollow, and colorless, as disagreeable as it would have been inconceivable.

Man, then, can operate solely within certain specifically regulated areas of inquiry and endeavor. His freedom is qualified not only by the nature of its object but also by the composition of his will. The will tends toward the good; [64] it "can desire nothing except that which is seen under some aspect of the good and can reject only that which is seen under some aspect of evil. . . ." [65] Hence, "the will is free to the extent that it chooses between an act and its omission," [66] and to that extent alone. When faced with a good object, it may choose to react either positively or passively; it cannot react negatively. Similarly, when faced with an evil object, it may react either negatively or passively, but cannot react positively.[67] In deciding whether an object is good or evil, the will is counseled by the reason and the judgment. Despite the fact that it is not bound to accept their advice, it works out in practice "that the will craves or avoids

---

[58] *De veritate fidei Christianiae*, I,ii;iii. *Opera omnia*, VIII,10,14; *De tradendis disciplinis*, I,vi. *Opera omnia*, VI,268.

[59] *De tradendis disciplinis*, IV,i. *Opera omnia*, VI,348.

[60] *Excitationes animi in Deum. Opera omnia*, I,54,55; *Introductio ad sapientiam. Opera omnia*, I,11; *De tradendis disciplinis*, I,iv. *Opera omnia*, VI,259.

[61] Pico, *Oratio*, 236–7.   [62] Vives, *Introductio ad sapientiam. Opera omnia*, I,23.

[63] *Ibid. Opera omnia*, I,11. See also *Excitationes animi in Deum. Opera omnia*, I,54.

[64] *De anima et vita*, II,xi; III,ii. *Opera omnia*, III,382,428.

[65] *Ibid.*, II,xi. *Opera omnia*, III,383.   [66] *Ibid.*   [67] *Ibid.*

nothing which has not been made manifest previously by the reason."[68] What freedom can be salvaged from the inroads of these constitutional restraints is, however, seen by Vives as adequate for man's purposes. God has granted us liberty sufficient for us "to form ourselves as we wish with the aid of His favor and grace."[69] These aids and limitations mark the resources and boundaries of the territory wherein human creativity may function.

Although man's creative activity seems radically circumscribed here when compared with the scope it enjoys in the *Oratio*, the land it rules is for Vives both wide and fecund. Its dominion—what is generally described as man's natural life—may be subsumed in the *Fabula* under the masks of the vegetable, the animal, and the human being. The vegetable is not an object of undue concern for Vives. He quickly passes on to the animal, which symbolizes for him the reign of the passions and which acts as the setting of a psychomachia. Like Pico, he describes a state of civil war between the mind and the body, almost comparable to the schism existing in the soul of the sinner,[70] a breach which can be healed with the aid of moral philosophy.[71] The passions are not to be excised, even for therapeutic purposes, for this would place man "outside the human condition, to be sure, in a kind of mental eclipse or in a perpetual spasm of the spirit. . . ."[72] Rather, the passions are to be domesticated, reoriented, instructed in virtue. When ethics has completed its task of moral integration, the passions may be made to bear the classic fruits of prudence, justice, fortitude, and temperance, and man may begin to restore himself to his original humanity.[73]

Above all, Vives is fascinated by the mask of the human being. This is the rôle in which man's talents may be exhibited *par excellence*. To play it with all its innuendoes requires the fullest use of his freedom and the consummation of each of his natural faculties. The prudence and justice revealed in the man of the *Fabula* having been gained by the exercise of morality, it remains for him to develop his humanity, to become cordial, kindly, and wise, to be "in no way either uncivil or unsocial." Man reaches this goal by the twin paths of education and action. Education includes every ramification of the *studia humanitatis*. Vives defines the various disciplines so comprised as those "by means of which we separate ourselves from the

[68] *Ibid. Opera omnia*, III,382. [69] *Ibid. Opera omnia*, III,385.
[70] *Meditationes in septem psalmos poenitentiales. Opera omnia*, I,176.
[71] *De tradendis disciplinis*, V,iii. *Opera omnia*, VI,402; *Introductio ad sapientiam. Opera omnia*, I,17.
[72] *De veritate fidei Christianiae*, V,v. *Opera omnia*, VIII,436.
[73] *De initiis, sectis et laudibus philosophiae. Opera omnia*, III,23.

way of life and customs of animals and are restored to humanity. . . . ." [74] "The branches of learning are called humanistic; since they make us human." [75] This cultivation of the mind has a harvest richer than mere erudition; the more closely one approximates the ideal of *humanitas*, the more generous, courteous, affable, and well spoken will he be. [76] Thus the subject matter of education has both an inward and an outward dimension. Philosophy, for example, which enables man "to live well and happily," [77] to escape the humiliating allegiance exacted by Fortune, [78] to achieve inner composure, also imposes "truly human customs" in cities and households as well as in each man's heart. [79] "Without its principles and without its precepts, neither private nor public matters could exist; nor would it be possible to gather men together in groups." [80] Man can scarcely enter into harmonious relationships with others unless he is at one with himself; [81] conversely, true knowledge conduces to true action.

Learning must thus be put into practice in everyday life for the good of society as well as for the personal benefit of the savant. "This then is the fruit of all studies. . . . Having ourselves acquired the arts of scholarship, we should seek to apply them to the arts of life, and employ them for the public good. . . . Every study is unlimited in itself, but at some point we ought to begin to turn it to the convenience and advantage of other people." [82] There is one humanistic discipline in particular which is by nature supremely suited to this purpose: the study of history. Vives is explicit on the uses of the past:

The true usefulness, indeed also the necessity of history, is discerned in

[74] *De disciplinis. Opera omnia*, VI,5. See also *De tradendis disciplinis*, V,iii. *Opera omnia*, VI,401–2.

[75] *De vita et moribus eruditi*, II. *Opera omnia*, VI,429.

[76] *Introductio ad sapientiam. Opera omnia*, I,35.

[77] *De initiis, sectis et laudibus philosophiae. Opera omnia*, III,2.

[78] *Ibid. Opera omnia*, III,22.   [79] *Ibid. Opera omnia*, III,23.   [80] *Ibid.*

[81] *Excitationes animi in Deum. Opera omnia*, I,59.

[82] *De vita et moribus eruditi*, I. *Opera omnia*, VI,423–4. See also *De tradendis disciplinis*, I,iv. *Opera omnia*, VI,259–60. At times statements of this type lead Watson, in the introduction to his translation of *De tradendis disciplinis*, to depict Vives as a forerunner of modern utilitarian social theory. However, since human society is not an end in itself for Vives, neither can the social utility toward which he directs education be seen as an end in itself. Cf. Otto Burger, *Erasmus von Rotterdam und der Spanier Vives* (Munich, 1914), 20–1; Paul Jlg, *Die Selbsttätigkeit als Bildungsprinzip bei Johann Ludwig Vives (1492–1540)* (Langensalza, 1931), 18; Günther, *op. cit.*, 23; Hofer, *op. cit.*, 104–5. The humanistic ideal of *utilitas* has been understood most clearly in this connection by Florence A. Gragg, "Two Schoolmasters of the Renaissance," *The Classical Journal*, XIV (Jan. 1919), 211.

daily life. . . . What shall I say of its great importance for the conduct of public affairs and the regulation of the labors of the populace? . . . Yet there are those who persuade themselves that a knowledge of the past is useless, since the ways of life have changed everywhere. . . . It is undeniable that everything has changed, and changes daily, for, to be sure, these changes spring from our will and industry. But such alterations do not take place in those things encompassed by Nature. . . . It is more important by far to know this fact than to know how men of old dressed or constructed buildings. For what greater prudence is there than to know how and what the human passions are; how they are roused, how quelled? To know also what influence they bring to bear on the commonwealth, their motivating forces, how they can be contained, healed, put aside, or, on the other hand, inflamed and fomented, whether in others or ourselves? What can be more expedient either for the ruler of a city or for any of his subjects to know? And what can be more delightful, what more conducive to the most fruitful kind of prudence? For, in truth, is it not more auspicious to be warned by the evils others have suffered than to learn from one's own misfortunes? Thus it is that history acts as an example of what we should follow, and what we should avoid.[83]

History is thus useful to instruct as well as to delight, since it reveals the unchanging character of human nature, knowledge of which is indispensable to the conduct of public affairs. This places a great responsibility on the historian's shoulders, for "the first law of history is that it be true, insofar as the historian can achieve this." [84] The historian may neither add nor subtract; he must represent the facts in the same perspective in which they really appear.[85] The image produced by history, "the mirror of past things," [86] must be undistorted so that it can function didactically for the greatest benefit of society.

In social intercourse and civic and political life man's human rôle finds its most complete realization. These areas of existence are necessary for the attainment of *humanitas;* "we men are, in truth, born for society, and cannot live fully without it." [87] Acting in collec-

---

[83] *De tradendis disciplinis,* V,i. *Opera omnia,* VI,389–90. History is not only the most useful discipline, it is also the most delightful: "I know not how else history may be seen to surpass all other studies, since it is the only one which either gives birth to, or nourishes, develops, or cultivates all the arts. It does this not through bitter and troublesome precepts and exercises, but by delectation of the mind, so that you drink in at the same time the most noble and fruitful knowledge and a real recreation and refreshment of the mind." *Ibid. Opera omnia,* VI,391.

[84] *De ratione dicendi,* III,iii. *Opera omnia,* II,206.

[85] *Ibid.* Vives does not discuss either the extent to which objective history is possible or the point at which subjectivism is liable to misrepresent the facts.

[86] *Ibid. Opera omnia,* II,205.

[87] *De tradendis disciplinis,* I,v. *Opera omnia,* VI,262.

tive bodies implies mutual dependence among men and imposes upon them a joint responsibility for those unable to care for themselves.[88] Public life, law and order, productive work as well as the life of study and contemplation, "all those things which make men better," can flourish only in peace; hence Vives condemns war.[89] His pacifism also has Biblical roots: God is the Father of all men; they should therefore live together as brothers.[90] For Vives, men are equal in the eyes of God, but nowhere else. He is well aware that knowledge and power may be perverted and made instruments of evil by those who do not have the capacity or the inclination to use them properly. "One need not place a sword in the hands of a madman,"[91] he states. Men have been granted varying degrees of intelligence and judgment, qualities which he finds conspicuous for their absence in the ranks of the common people. The multitude he calls "a many-headed monster";[92] its opinions are notoriously erroneous and should be avoided by the seeker of wisdom even as they are by the ruler.[93] Clearly no democrat,[94] Vives believes that man can best perfect his social and political nature by fulfilling the duties of his own particular station conscientiously and cheerfully.

The very order and fitness which permeate the full blossoming of man's humanity bear witness to the wisdom which rules and attends it. This wisdom is prudence, born of man's judgment and experience. It is "the skill of accommodating all things of which we make use in life to their appropriate places, times, persons, and functions."[95] All the activities that fall within the scope of man's natural life should properly take place in accordance with it. There

[88] *De subventione pauperum*, I,xi; II,i. *Opera omnia*, IV,461,465. Vives' project for poor relief is an extension of Christian charity; he is not a socialist, Christian or otherwise. Watson misconstrues this point in his introduction to *De tradendis disciplinis*, lxvi–lxvii. He is corrected by Enrico Rivari, "Un grande umanista spagnuolo del secolo XVI contro il communismo," *Nuova antologia* (Dec. 1, 1937), 359–60, whose rabid partisanship, however, tends to prejudge the issue.

[89] Letter to Henry VIII of England, *De pace inter Caesarum et Franciscum Gallorum regem, deque optimo regni statu.* Bruges, Oct. 8, 1525. *Opera omnia*, V,180.

[90] *Introductio ad sapientiam. Opera omnia*, I,32.

[91] *De subventione pauperum*, I,xi. *Opera omnia*, IV,462.

[92] *Sattelitum animi. Opera omnia*, IV,55.

[93] *Ibid.; Introductio ad sapientiam. Opera omnia*, I,2.

[94] It would seem difficult to misconstrue this point; cf., however, Watson, "Juan Luis Vives," *Essays by Divers Hands*, 92, 97–8; Atkinson, "Luis Vives and Poor Relief., *loc. cit.*, 102; Joaquín Xirau, *El pensamiento vivo de Juan Luis Vives* (Buenos Aires, 1944), 35–6.

[95] *De tradendis disciplinis*, V,i. *Opera omnia*, VI,386.

is, however, another form of wisdom, whose sway extends over man's supernatural life. This is piety, which "stands alone and has a special claim to the name of Wisdom. . . . " It exists "to teach us who God is, and how we ought to act towards Him"; [96] it comprehends the celestial light that makes it possible for man to view the immutable.[97] The "most wise mind" upon which the protagonist of the *Fabula* relies entirely when he is made a god, "transcending the nature of man," is a mind illuminated by piety. The cultivation of this wisdom extends throughout the whole of life.[98] Compared with it the wisdom of the world is pure ignorance and folly.[99] Its beginning is the fear of God, its end is the vision of God; the pathway it follows is the love of God.

On the road that leads to beatitude man is by no means alone. He is guided by the mediatrix of religion,[100] theology, which for Vives, as for Pico, is the queen of the sciences. Religion has been granted to man by God; "it not only teaches us how to come to Him, but also leads us by the hand," [101] since man's natural powers are inadequate to secure that end:

This then is religion, which we receive from God Himself, a ray from His Light, strength from His Omnipotence. This alone leads us back to the source whence we came, and towards which we bend our way. Nor is there any other perfection of man, for when this is accomplished, every end for which he was formed is obtained. . . . Wherefore, since that is the perfection of man's nature, and the consummation of all its parts; and since piety is the only way of perfecting man, and accomplishing the end for which he was formed, therefore piety is of all things the one thing necessary.[102]

Man's aspiration to consummate his form is thus preceded, aided, and resolved by the grace of God. Vives describes man's love for God in terms of Platonic Eros: "Love is the desire to delight in the good, to unite with it, so that the lover, by contact with the beloved, that is, the good, may himself become good." [103] But the good must

[96] *Ibid.* See also *Meditatio in psalmum XXXVII. De passione Christi. Opera omnia*, VII,94.   [97] *De anima et vita*, II,ix. *Opera omnia*, III,379.
[98] *Introductio ad sapientiam. Opera omnia*, I,16.
[99] *Ibid. Opera omnia*, I,23; *Praelectio in sapientem. Opera omnia*, IV,29; *De tradendis disciplinis*, I,ii. *Opera omnia*, VI,248–9. Eugene F. Rice, Jr., *The Renaissance Idea of Wisdom* (Cambridge, Mass., 1958), 156ff., 177, distinguishes between the two forms of wisdom in Vives' thought, but incorrectly assimilates piety to prudence.
[100] *De initiis, sectis et laudibus philosophiae. Opera omnia*, III,13.
[101] *De tradendis disciplinis*, I,ii. *Opera omnia*, VI,248   [102] *Ibid.*
[103] *De anima et vita*, III,iv. *Opera omnia*, III,443. See also *ibid.*, ii. *Opera omnia*, III,428; *De veritate fidei Christianiae*, I,vi. *Opera omnia*, VIII,48.

be recognized as such before it can be desired by the will, that faculty of man which naturally tends toward it. Knowledge of the good must hence precede erotic desire; "before being loved, a thing must be known."[104] Man can identify the good only by virtue of the fact that the good introduces and manifests itself to him. The will has but to set out on the pathway of the good for the good "to approach it in order to embrace it, whence arises the desire for union."[105] Faith, man's response to this revelation, "will show what things ought to be loved. . . ."[106] God's abundant love for man cannot be confined to this one activity. After showing the will its proper object, it then "joyfully raises it as if on wings toward its good. . . ."[107] Thus man returns to God in the same way he came forth from Him, the way of gratuitous grace. Playing every part assigned to him, signifying his heavenly longings by his own ability and volition, he can be robed in celestial garb and crowned with physical resurrection only through God's loving indulgence, in accordance with the divine plan.

Although Vives sees piety, supernature, and the divine as discrete from prudence, nature, and humanity, he by no means holds that the one is irrelevant or unrelated to the other. The links between the two realms are forged by Vives' epistemology, which, like much of his theology, is fundamentally a Christianized Aristotelianism. Accordingly, he agrees that the knowledge of nature appropriate to man can be known inductively. The senses are the gateway of knowledge.[108] They cannot be deceived since they simply reflect the natural data they receive without judging them; and such data will not deceive the soul if the sense organ is healthy, if the natural object is close enough and stable enough to be perceived, if the medium through which it is perceived is clear, and if the spirit is attentive.[109] Accurate data may thus be referred to the mind so that accurate general ideas may be formed about nature.[110] This interest in precision does not stem from a purely scientific frame of mind;

---

[104] De anima et vita, III,iv. Opera omnia, III,448. See also De veritate fidei Christianiae, I,vi. Opera omnia, VIII,47; De tradendis disciplinis, I,iii;iv. Opera omnia, VI,252,256.

[105] De anima et vita, III,ii. Opera omnia, III,428. See also De tradendis disciplinis, I,iv. Opera omnia, VI,255.

[106] De tradendis disciplinis, I,iv. Opera omnia, VI,256.

[107] De anima et vita, III,iv. Opera omnia, III,440.

[108] Ibid., II,iv;viii;ix. Opera omnia, III,354–5,373,378; De tradendis disciplinis, I,ii; IV,i. Opera omnia, VI,250,348.

[109] De anima et vita, I,ix. Opera omnia, III,325–6.

[110] De veritate fidei Christianiae, I,iii. Opera omnia, VIII,20; De tradendis disciplinis, I,ii;v; IV,ii. Opera omnia, VI,251,264–5,352; De anima et vita, II,iv. Opera omnia, III,354.

for Vives, knowledge of nature is a means rather than an end.[111] Man must know nature because the works of creation proclaim the Creator.[112] If his conception of the cosmos be distorted, man would misconstrue the nature of God.

Vives sees the *analogia entis* less as a necessary ontological link between God and the world than as an expression of the harmony and benevolence with which God disposes His creation and draws it back to Himself. Even as man's spirit and body function in a comparable fashion,[113] so the operations of his soul reflect the activities of God.[114] All his potentialities are proportionate to their actualities; all his faculties correspond generically with their objects.[115] Man has been granted a full range of innate aptitudes which are conducive to his natural and supernatural ends.[116] Thus there exists a certain conformity between humanity and divinity, between prudence and piety, between the truths of reason and the truths of faith.[117] Emanating from the same source, they cannot contradict each other although they are different in kind.[118] Man is not abandoned to a mangled universe where the noumenal eludes him.[119] The unapproachable light in which Vives' God dwells is also "that sunny radiance which Christ brought into the darkness of the world." [120]

Christian humanism is indeed the term which describes Vives' philosophical interests most completely and most suitably. The points at which his conception of man diverge most radically from those

[111] Cf. Watson, "The Father of Modern Psychology," *loc. cit.*, 334, who thinks that Vives' empiricism entitles him to be named a predecessor of Descartes and Bacon.

[112] *De prima philosophia seu de intimo opificio naturae*, I. *Opera omnia*, III,186; *De veritate fidei Christianiae*, I,i. *Opera omnia*, VIII,6; *De anima et vita*, I,xi. *Opera omnia*, III,328–9; *De tradendis disciplinis*, I,iv; IV,ii. *Opera omnia*, VI,257,351.

[113] *De anima et vita*, I,x; II,ii;ix. *Opera omnia*, III,326–7,346,378.

[114] *De prima philosophia*, II. *Opera omnia*, III,227.

[115] *De anima et vita*, I,x;xii; II,i;x;xix. *Opera omnia*, III,326–7,335,344,381,407.

[116] *Ibid.*, II,iv;viii. *Opera omnia*, III,372,374; *De tradendis disciplinis*, I,ii. *Opera omnia*, VI,250; *De prima philosophia*, II. *Opera omnia*, III,227.

[117] Preface to *De veritate fidei Christianiae*. *Opera omnia*, VIII,2; *Meditationes in septem psalmos poenitentiales*. *Opera omnia*, I,166–7.

[118] *De veritate fidei Christianiae*, I,iii. *Opera omnia*, VIII,13–14; *De tradendis disciplinis*, I,iv. *Opera omnia*, VI,257. Desdevises du Dezert, "Luis Vives," *loc. cit.*, 407, does not acknowledge any distinction between the light of reason and the light of faith in Vives' thought; he has been corrected by Graf, *op. cit.*, 22–24, 30–31.

[119] None the less, there are commentators who insist on linking Vives and Kant. See in particular Bonilla y San Martín, *Luis Vives*, II, 341–2; Desdevises du Dezert, "Luis Vives," *loc. cit.*, 407, 410.

[120] *De tradendis disciplinis*, IV,ii. *Opera omnia*, VI,351.

of Pico are precisely those points at which his insights are informed by Scripture, the Church Fathers, and ecclesiastical tradition. Vives' final literary effort, barely completed before his death in 1540, is a work of Christian apology, conceived along conservative theological lines. The *De veritate fidei Christianiae* is rhetorical Thomism, but it is Thomism with a difference. While at no point diverging from Catholic doctrine, Christian apologetics witnesses in this tract a shift in emphasis at once striking and characteristic of the period. St. Thomas begins with the nature of God; Vives begins with the nature of man.[121] God, to be sure, is the keystone of Vives' apology, but this is so because He functions, in the first instance, as the perfection and eternal end of man. Thus ethics rather than metaphysics commands Vives' prime attention, a point of view early crystallized in the *Fabula*. This is the philosophical orientation of all his later works, the motivating concern of the systematic treatise on human nature which he did not live to write. Many of his contemporaries share the mental inclinations of Vives; by no means do they all seek to compass their ethical quest in so fully, so devoutly, so explicitly orthodox a fashion.

Vives' polygraphical talents, his erudition both wide and deep, his confident stylistic elegance evince beyond question his participation in the humanistic tastes and predilections of his times. His conception of human dignity should not, however, be seen as nothing more—or less—than that of a third generation Florentine Platonist. He is fully capable of employing the vocabulary of Pico della Mirandola, but he uses it to express a different order of ideas, with fundamentally different ultimate concerns. Faced with the rich resources of Renaissance humanism, he develops a view of man more heavily weighted toward the Christian than the classical. That Vives alone adopts this particular arrangement of ideas on human nature as a guide amid the free-flowing and often turbulent emotional and intellectual currents of the time renders it no less important as an indication of the kind of effort which the time evoked and made possible. Set against the kaleidoscopic scene of Renaissance thought, Juan Luis Vives' philosophy of man forms a coherent, if evanescent, synthesis.

Yale University.

---

[121] A clear and competent comparison between the *De veritate fidei Christianiae* and the *Summa contra gentiles* is provided by Graf, *op. cit.*, *passim*, and particularly 31ff.

XIX

"PROPERTY" AND "PEOPLE": POLITICAL USAGES OF
LOCKE AND SOME CONTEMPORARIES

By JUDITH RICHARDS, LOTTE MULLIGAN,
AND JOHN K. GRAHAM

Discussions of Locke's political use of the term *property* and of
the consequences of his usage are numerous, but they have not usually taken into account his own understanding of the possible il-
locutionary force of his words or his knowledge of how contemporaries were using the same terms. The purpose of this paper is
twofold. In the first instance, we propose to apply a prescription of
recent writers on the methodology of the history of ideas and to
attempt to recover something of the linguistic context[1] in which
Locke began writing his *Two Treatises of Government*. Accordingly,
Locke's use of *property* is compared with other contemporary usage
to identify clearly any peculiarities of his language and consequent
peculiarities in his political thought. Locke began his *Two Treatises*
as a contribution to contemporary political discussions,[2] and it is
treated here as part of those particular debates. What emerges from
this comparison is the conclusion that Locke, by his self-conscious
and particular use of *property*, arrived at a political definition of *the
people* radically different from that of most of his political associates.
Where they were rigorously and explicitly exclusive in their qualifications for full membership of the political nation, Locke was consistently inclusive.

The second and related concern is to reconsider possible explanations for the indifferent response to *Two Treatises* in the years after
their publication. John Dunn has argued that *Two Treatises* was taken

---

[1] "Linguistic context" is particularly the term used by Quentin Skinner in his
more recent writings to describe part of his recommended procedures. Recent
noteworthy contributors to discussions of the proper methodology for the history of
ideas must include J. G. A. Pocock, *Politics, Language and Time* (London, 1962);
John Dunn, esp. "The Identity of the History of Ideas," *Philosophy, Politics and
Society*, Series III, eds. P. Laslett and W. Runciman (1967); Quentin Skinner,
"Meaning and Understanding in the History of Ideas," *History and Theory*, 8 (1969),
and "Some Problems in the Analysis of Political Thought and Action," *Political
Theory*, 2 (1974).

[2] The argument which follows accepts that Laslett's textual scholarship has indeed established that the *Second Treatise* was substantially written 1679-83, and
probably 1679-80; *John Locke: Two treatises of Government*, ed. Peter Laslett (New
York, 1965).

by contemporaries, as Locke had intended it should be taken, as "merely the dignifying of the legal order of the polity"[3] and it contained principles recognized by its readers to be "of the most indubitable and parochial political orthodoxy."[4] The relative silence with which *Two Treatises* was received was because it simply confirmed principles established in 1688. But Martyn Thompson has more recently suggested that the relative lack of Whiggish interest in Locke's political writings was, essentially, because of a common preference for other defenses of their position. By 1705, it was still Algernon Sidney who was seen by leading Whig writers as the man who best understood "the constitution of the English Government."[5] Pufendorf and Tyrrell were also highly regarded by Whigs and more frequently cited in periodicals and political discussions than Locke. Among reasons proposed by Thompson for this relative lack of contemporary enthusiasm for *Two Treatises* was that it "appeared to sanction radical changes in the Ancient Constitution."[6] There is no suggestion that Locke's work was ever ignored; a quick glance at its publishing history would make nonsense of that. But Locke's political treatise did not give rise to any detailed critical replies before 1703. There was no systematic refutation of it published until 1705, and even then Charles Leslie's *Rehearsal* and the anonymous *Essay Upon Government* concentrated on the first treatise.

The Tory silence in the face of *Two Treatises* is not surprising. Having co-operated so extensively with the 1688 Revolution, the prime Tory concern in the following years seems to have been with explaining how those events were compatible with their own fixed political principles and why allegiance was due to William and Mary. There were few noteworthy exceptions,[7] but these critics were even more unlikely to see as a first object for attack the less popular versions of Whiggish arguments. The present paper suggests that the *Two Treatises*, although more radical than the preferred Whig case, echoed too much of the language and principles of other Whigs easily to be repudiated by them. To the extent that Locke's authorship was suspected, *Two Treatises* were believed to be by a prominent author well connected to important Whigs. Moreover, since the work was not published until the conservative revolution of 1688 had been

---

[3] John Dunn, "The Politics of John Locke in England and America in the Eighteenth Century" in *John Locke: Problems and Perspectives*, ed. J. W. Yolton (Cambridge, 1969), 54.   [4] *Ibid.*, 57.

[5] Martyn P. Thompson, "The Reception of Locke's *Two Treatises of Government* 1690-1705," *Political Studies*, 24, 2 (1976), 189.   [6] *Ibid.*, 190.

[7] Robert Nelson was one of the few devout Tories of principle prepared even to accept exclusion from Church attendance by his friend Archbishop Tillotson because he could not pray for the new monarchs, William and Mary. Tillotson to Nelson, 17 September 1692, Nelson Correspondence, Hoare's Bank, London.

safely accomplished, any implicit challenge to the established order of things could then be more easily disregarded.

The works with which Locke's writing will be compared were all begun during the Exclusion Crisis period.[8] The general level of discussion of the constitutional principles raised by the three attempts to introduce Exclusion Bills against the succession of Catholic James between 1679 and 1681 was not intellectually impressive. Most of it played on the popular potency of the anti-Catholic fervor, on *ad hominem* polemic, or on explicitly self-interested appeals to particular social groups. The rumour, for instance, that he might repossess former monastic lands was so effective that James was explicitly forced to promise to make no such attack on property-owners.[9] In general, the material was ephemeral and too closely connected to the details of the particular situation to have lasting significance; for theoretical defenses of their respective positions both sides also resorted to republishing works from the debates of the Civil Wars period. The best-known example of this was the Court-sponsored publication of Filmer's works in 1679 and 1680, but such authors as Prynne were also reissued.

Nevertheless, the polemics of the Crisis produced some more enduring discussions of political fundamentals. While Locke's *Two Treatises of Government* is now taken as the classic constitutional statement of the period, contemporaries saw Tyrrell's *Patriarcha non Monarcha*[10] and Sidney's *Discourses Concerning Government*[11] as more effective defenses of the Whig position. Both, like Locke, were concerned in the first instance to refute Filmer, and they all moved to more general issues. Another work of immediate impact was Henry Neville's *Plato Redivivus*.[12] Its quasi-republican views of the proper distribution of political authority created much more of an immediate stir amongst the politically articulate than did *Two Treatises*. *Plato*

---

[8] For works covering the history of this period, one might nominate for a general history, David Ogg's *England in the Reign of Charles II* (Oxford, 1934, 1967); as a study of a faction, J. R. Jones, *The First Whigs. The Politics of the Exclusion Crisis 1678-1683* (London, 1961); and as a biography of a participant, K. H. D. Haley, *The First Earl of Shaftesbury* (Oxford, 1968).

[9] See esp. O. W. Furley, "The Whig Exclusionists: Pamphlet literature in the Exclusion Campaign, 1679-1681," *Cambridge Historical Journal*, **13**, 1 (1957), 24.

[10] James Tyrrell, *Patriarcha non Monarcha. The Patriarch Unmonarched: Being Observations on a Late Treatise and diverse other Miscellanies, Published under the Name of Sir Robert Filmer* . . . (London, 1681).

[11] Algernon Sidney, *Discourses Concerning Government* (London, 1698). The edition referred to throughout is the third edition, 1741, reissued by Gregg International Publishers, 1968.

[12] Henry Neville, *Plato Redivivus: Or, A Dialogue Concerning Government*, rpt. in *Two English Republican Tracts*, ed. Caroline Robbins (Cambridge, 1969).

Redivivus brought forth three published attacks in its year of publication (1681) and continued to draw comment in subsequent years.[13]

These four works show a common concern to reach an audience
of politically aware Englishmen made uneasy by the Court's activities
and by a mistrust of suspected monarchical aspirations to enlarge
royal power. The traditions to which these writers appealed vary
considerably, but they also had much shared experience. There had
been considerable overlapping and interlocking of the political lives
of Sidney and Neville, and of them both with the first Earl of
Shaftesbury—Locke's political mentor—since the 1650's. Sidney's
relationship, however, with Shaftesbury had been almost always bad,
and the most likely opportunities for personal encounters between
Locke and Sidney did not occur until after Shaftesbury's death.
Locke's friendship since youth with Tyrrell has been well-
documented, and Tyrrell was an old friend of Henry Neville. There
was also a long-standing friendship between Neville and the remarkable John Wildman, onetime Leveller, prosperous lawyer, compulsive
conspirator, and client in the 1670s to Shaftesbury. Wildman was a
friend of Sidney throughout the 1670s, and Sidney and Neville had
been associates as erstwhile Commonwealthmen.[14]

Men who shared common political experiences and who appealed
to similar audiences may be assumed to have, at least in part, a shared
understanding of the political rhetoric of their day. This paper
suggests that these writers in particular were aware of the difficulties
arising from the words they used and that, initially at least, problems
arising from seventeenth-century word usage may be the result of
misunderstanding by the modern reader rather than of confusion on
the part of the author. In other words, the reader must be prepared to
take the writer's choice of words seriously.

This observation ought to sound pedantic and even redundant.
Unhappily, experience suggests that it is neither. There is little dispute that a concept central to Locke's political theory was *property*.
It remains to be settled what Locke meant this term to denote and
what he might have expected his readers to take it to mean. The
difficulties of Locke's use of the term *property* are usually noted,[15]

---

[13] Robbins, 17 and note.

[14] *The Dictionary of National Biography;* Robbins, *op. cit;* Maurice Cranston,
John Locke: A Biography (London, 1957); Laslett's Introduction to Locke's *Two
Treatises;* Robbins' Introduction to *Plato Redivivus;* and Maurice Ashley, John
Wildman, *Plotter and Postmaster* (London, 1947) all provide evidence of the com-
plex interrelationships.

[15] This is not always so. Robert Albritton, "The Politics of Locke's Philosophy,"
Political Studies, **XXIV**, 3 (Sept. 1976) begins his discussion of this issue, "Locke's
concept of property is crucial to understanding his thought," but nowhere is there a
suggestion that Locke ever implied that property was more than what is created "by
mixing the body's labour with external objects" (265).

but often only to be dismissed. A classic example of this process is provided by C.B. Macpherson:

It is true that Locke somewhat confused matters by sometimes defining that property . . . in unusually wide terms. "Man . . . hath by Nature a Power . . . to preserve his Property, that is his Life, Liberty and Estate". Men's "lives, Liberties and Estates . . . I call by the general Name, *Property*". "By *Property* I must be understood here, as in other places, to mean that *Property* which Men have in their Persons as well as Goods."

But he does not always use the term property in such a wide sense. In his crucial argument on the limitation of the power of governments he is clearly using property in the more general sense of land and goods, as he is throughout the chapter 'Of Property'. The implications of this ambiguity need not detain us here.[16]

But the reader concerned to understand the text fully must pause to examine "the implications of this ambiguity," particularly in the case of *property*, a word of considerable elasticity in the seventeenth-century. In fact, each writer under consideration felt the need to define *property* in the process of expounding his own argument.

The novelty of Locke's emphasis on *property* as a central political issue has been overstressed.[17] Furley may have been the first modern commentator to argue that an appeal to property was a fairly common feature of Exclusion writing and agitation, but contemporary commentators were well aware of the political potency of that word. John Dryden described the force of *property* among the disparate "Malcontents"

Who thought the power of Monarchy too much:
Mistaken Men, and Patriots in their Hearts;
Not Wicked, but seduced by Impious Arts.
By these the Springs of Property were bent,
And Wound so high, they Crack'd the Government.[18]

When uses of *property* in seventeenth-century discussions are examined, the modern reader is struck by the care *each* writer took to define this powerful word.

James Tyrrell saw the need to protect property as a fundamental reason for the rise of political society. His definition of property was clearly narrower than that of Locke, but the place of *property* in Tyrrell's argument was similar. Not only did Tyrrell see the accumulation of property as a dominant factor in men's decisions to establish political society, but he also appealed to *property* in order to define

[16] C. B. Macpherson, *The Political Theory of Possessive Individualism* (Oxford, 1962), 198.
[17] For example, Laslett, *Two Treatises*, 114.
[18] John Dryden, "Absalom and Achitophel," I, lines 496-500.

the attributes necessary to the possession of a political voice. He explained even the arguably self-evident exclusion of children from full membership in the political society because "Children in their Fathers Families being under the notion of Servants and without any Property in Goods or Land, had no reason to have Votes in the Institution of the Government."[19] Civil Society, then, in Tyrrell's view, was not established by God as an inescapable condition but as an institution available for the convenience of man and protection of his *property*—in land and goods—in accordance with reason, and where, as in "several parts of America" there was little need for possessions and consequently "no Disputes about them," there was no need of government.[20]

In *Plato Redivivus*, Neville also argued that it was with property that political society had begun. In the beginning everything was held in common, "which made a state of perpetual war"; in order to avoid it,

every man consented to be debarred of that universal right to all things; and confine himself to a quiet and secure enjoyment of such a part, as should be allotted to him. Thence came in ownership, or property: to maintain which, it was necessary to consent to laws, and a government; to put them in execution.[21]

He defined *property* as almost co-extensive with political power. "Dominion is founded in property"; it followed that a monarch "if he had no companions in the sovereign power, had no sharers likewise in the *dominion or possessions of the land. For that is all we mean by property, in all this discourse* . . . ."[22] Neville did not feel free to assume that his audience would automatically understand *property* in a "usual" sense; as a longstanding Harringtonian, he used *property* in the particularly narrow meaning of land-ownership. If Locke's definition of property was "unusually wide," Neville's was "unusually narrow." Yet both, like Tyrrell, were clear that *property* described the basis of political society and power. For each writer the proper understanding of *property*, as he used the term, was essential to the proper understanding of his perception of political society. Nor is it self-evident that Locke's *property* as "Life, Liberty and Estate" was so unusually wide. Hobbes had written:

Of things held in propriety, those that are dearest to a man are his own life, and limbs; and in the next degree, (in most men), those that concern conjugall affection; and after them riches and means of living.[23]

[19] Tyrrell, *op. cit.*, 83-84.   [20] *Ibid.*, 120-21.
[21] Neville, *op. cit.*, 85.   [22] *Ibid.*, 89-90. Emphasis added.
[23] *Hobbes's Leviathan*, ed. C. B. Macpherson (Harmondsworth, 1968), 382-83.

And Laslett has pointed to a usage even closer to Locke's in both sense and time; Richard Baxter wrote in *The Second Part of the Nonconformist's Plea for Peace* (1680):

Every man is born with a propriety in his *own members*, and nature giveth him a propriety in *his Children*, and his food and other just acquisitions of his industry . . . . And men's *lives* and *Liberties* are the chief parts of their propriety.[24]

Filmer had also seen a close connection between property owner-ship and political rights. He argued not only from *Genesis*, but also from the Ancient Constitution that all property-rights and all liberties derived initially from the King, and appealed in *The Freeholder's Grand Inquest* to no less an authority than Coke that "the first Kings of this realm had all the lands of England in demesne."[25] Summariz-ing his position, Filmer made the inexorably subordinate and depen-dent nature of subjects since Creation and throughout the world quite explicit.

The first government in the world was monarchical, in the father of all flesh . . . .
Adam was the Father, King and Lord over his family: a son, a subject and a servant or a slave, were one and the same thing at first; the Father had power to dispose, or sell his children or servants . . . . As for the names of subject, slave, and tyrant, they are not to be found in scripture. . . .[26]

Filmer worked from a religious imperative for all men to recognize their perpetual subjection to authority instituted by God. The counter-argument, that man was born naturally free and had made a considered, rational decision to establish civil society the better to protect his interests, was restated by Tyrrell and Neville. Sidney, on the other hand, preferred to describe the basic interest for which men entered society as the fundamental

principle of liberty in which God created us, and which includes the chief advantages of the life we enjoy, as well as the greatest helps towards the felicity, that is the end of our hopes in the other.[27]

The concept of property was appealed to very little by Sidney since in property-owning he saw another attribute of liberty, but even then he made explicit what *property* encompassed for him.

[24] Quoted in Laslett (ed.), *Two Treatises of Government*, 329 n.
[25] Robert Filmer, *The Freeholder's Grand Inquest* in *Patriarcha and Other Politi-cal Works of Sir Robert Filmer*, ed. Peter Laslett (Oxford, 1949), 182. See also 141.
[26] *Ibid.*, 187-88.   [27] Sidney, *op. cit.*, 5.

Property is . . . an appendage of liberty; and it is . . . impossible for a man to have a right to lands or goods, if he has no liberty, and enjoys his life only at the pleasure of another.[28]

Property was, for the Whiggish Exclusion writers, a word of such political significance, and yet of such multivalence, that it required particular definition to clarify the meaning or meanings they gave to it. The primary purpose of Filmer, writing some forty years earlier in the context of such issues as Ship Money and forced loans, had been to assert the unlimited obligations of subjects to their Kings. The contrary argument, for limited obligation, had not only to establish the thoroughly unsatisfactory nature of Filmer's use of his sources— in itself a task undertaken at length by Tyrrell, Sidney, *and* Locke— but also to establish an alternative view of the origins and purpose of civil society. The concept of the natural rights of all, and the property rights of some, had been one way of arguing that political power came from the people.[29] These writers turned again to the argument that property-ownership predated civil society as a means of describing the stake that men had in society. The definition of such pre-societal *property* was an essential prerequisite for understanding the composition of political society. It is in the context of this awareness of contemporary usages of *property* that the reader should turn again to Locke and to the implications of his significantly different use of that term.

After some preliminary definitions and distinctions Locke's *Second Treatise* turned to the origin of private property. On natural rights and private property he drew particularly from Pufendorf,[30] but with significant modifications. Although the primary purpose of Chapter V, "Of Property," was to explain Locke's view of how material goods could be appropriated by individuals out of their original common condition rather than bestowed by a monarch, it becomes evident that Locke—like the Levellers, Baxter, and Hobbes amongst others— held that even when "the Earth and all inferior Creatures be common

---

[28] *Ibid.*, 317-18. Elsewhere, Sidney made it clear when he sometimes used property in the even narrower sense. He complained of some writers, that not content to make kings "the fountains of honour, they proceed to make them also the fountains of property; and, for proof of this, alledge, that all lands, tho' held of mean lords, do by their tenures at last result from the king, as the head from whom they are enjoyed" (392).

[29] The Putney Debates provide an earlier formulation of this same argument.

[30] For a recent discussion of this, see Karl Olivecrona, "Appropriation in the State of Nature: Locke on the Origin of Property," *Journal of the History of Ideas,* 35, 2 (April-June 1974). Olivecrona's assertion, however, that Locke was not concerned to refute Filmer in Chapter V seems at best inconclusive. To demonstrate the "natural liberty" of men in society, Locke certainly *had* to demonstrate their "natural right" to private property quite independently of any grants from the king.

to all Men, yet every Man has a *Property* in his own Person."[31] From this basis Locke proceeded to explain the legitimate origins of private, and of unequal, possessions.[32] In Chapter VII, where Locke discussed the fundamental principles of society, he significantly and explicitly widened *property* to include those qualities which he believed gave man a stake in political society. Slaves were carefully distinguished from all other men by the loss of those attributes; this argument was also part of Locke's answer to Filmer's insistence that originally all men but the king had been as slaves. Locke said that slaves were those men who had, by their actions,

forfeited their Lives, and with it their Liberties, and lost their Estates; and . . . cannot in that state be considered as any part of Civil Society; the chief end whereof is the preservation of Property.[33]

All other men apparently had an interest in political society. Locke removed any possible doubt that he meant *property* to convey a wider constellation of attributes than material goods and possessions:

Man being born, as has been proved, with a Title to perfect Freedom, and an uncontrouled enjoyment of all the Rights and Privileges of the Law of Nature, equally with any other Man, or Number of Men in the world, hath by Nature a Power . . . to preserve his Property, that is, his Life, Liberty and Estate against the Injuries and Attempts of other Men.[34]

Far from it being the case, as Macpherson suggests, that Locke "somewhat confused matters" by sometimes defining *property* in "unusually wide terms," Locke was being consistent in maintaining his argument that each man, having property in his own person, possessed property more satisfactorily protected within rather than outside political society. It has commonly been noted that Locke explained each man's entry into civil society by the process whereby

---

[31] Locke, *Two Treatises*, II, 27.

[32] It is less clear that Locke was concerned to *justify* unequal possessions as Macpherson argues. There is a problem in how a modern reader can identify the tone of Locke's comment: "This is certain, that in the beginning, before the desire of having more than Men needed, had altered the intrinsick value of things, which depends only on their usefulness to the Life of Man; or [Men] had *agreed, that a little piece of yellow metal*, which would keep without wasting or decay, should be worth a great piece of Flesh, or a whole heap of Corn" (II, 37). John Dunn quotes from a passage which must increase the reader's doubt that Locke intended to justify the acquisition of unequal possessions and the function of gold in promoting this: "When private possessions and labour, which now the curse of the earth had made necessary, by degrees made a distinction of conditions, it gave room for covetousness, pride and ambition which by fashion and example spread the corruption which has so prevailed over mankind." Dunn, *Political Thought*, 115, n.4.

[33] Locke, *Two Treatises*, II, 85.   [34] *Ibid.*, II, 87.

he seeks out, and is willing to joyn in Society with others who are already united, or have a mind to unite for the mutual *Preservation* of their Lives, Liberties and Estates, which I call by the general Name, Property.[35]

We contend that in subsequent discussions of the nature, forms, and extent of political and civil society, it was Locke's purpose to sustain this explicitly wider definition; although his signification of *property* was not invariably consistent, he interspersed reminders of this wider meaning throughout the rest of the *Second Treatise*.[36] In Section 171, Locke reiterated that the function of political authority was "to preserve the Members of that Society in their Lives, Liberties and Possessions." In Section 173, he again asserted his definition of *property*:

Nature gives the first of these, viz. *Paternal Power to Parents* for the Benefit of their Children, during their Minority, to supply their want of Ability, and understanding how to manage their Property. (By *Property* I must be understood here, as in other places, to mean that Property which Men have in their Persons as well as Goods.)

That interpolation reads very like someone struggling to keep *his* meaning of a key word to the forefront of his audience's awareness. Like the other writers glanced at, Locke knew *property* was a multivalent word and was determined to make his definition understood. The wider reading was unequivocally thrust before the reader again in the final chapter, "Of the Dissolution of Government":

. . . whenever the *Legislators endeavour to take away, and destroy the Property of People* . . . they put themselves into a state of War with the People . . . Whensoever therefore the *Legislative* shall transgress this fundamental Rule of Society; and either by Ambition, Fear, Folly or Corruption, endeavour to grasp themselves, *or put into the hands of any other an Absolute Power* over the Lives, Liberties and Estates of the People; By this breach of Trust they *forfeit the Power,* the People had put into their hands. . . .[37]

It is beyond dispute that Locke, in this passage, equated the destruction of property with the assertion of absolute power over the "Lives, Liberties and Estate of the People."

---

[35] *Ibid.,* II, 123.

[36] There are, however, also examples of apparent inconsistency on Locke's own part, as in Section 131 where he describes the reason men enter society as "an intention in every one the better to preserve himself his Liberty and Property." But Laslett suggests that this section, and even the whole of the chapter, may be "an insertion of 1689," in which case it strengthens the argument offered here that Locke intended by Property the definition of "Lives, Liberties and Estates" in the section Laslett calls "a short restatement of his whole petition" (395, n. 123).

[37] *Two Treatises,* II, 222.

Locke certainly used *property* in the sense of material possessions in the chapter "Of Property." There he had addressed himself to the problem revived by Filmer concerning the source of private property, for Filmer's assertions that all property titles derived, with divine sanction, from patriarchal and monarchical authority, needed meticulous refutation. Locke approached the problem with much more care then was shown by Sidney's pragmatically assertive appeal to reason and justice. Responding perhaps, to Filmer's use of Coke in *The Freeholder's Grand Inquest* on the source of land titles, Sidney wrote:

if it be said that records testify all grants to have been originally from the king; I answer, that 'tho it were confessed (which I absolutely deny, and affirm that our rights and liberties are innate, inherent, and enjoyed time out of mind, before we had kings), it could be nothing to the question, which is, concerning reason and justice; and, if they are wanting, the defect can never be supplied by any matter of fact, tho' never so clearly proved.[38]

But even when responding to the specific issue of property ownership, Locke implicitly appealed to a wider sense of *property* than material possessions alone. When he moved on to detail his own views of the origins and purpose of political society, his wider definition was made explicit.

His incorporation of all men but slaves at the institution of society is not in dispute. The argument here is that, by his constant definition of *property* so that *all* were included in the joint communal purposes of society—the protection of property—Locke was unobtrusively suggesting that all had a claim to an active political voice. It will be shown that the more usual practice was either to exclude many from full political membership by a definition of *property* which emphasized economic independence as a necessary precondition for membership or to plead pragmatic reasons for limiting the numbers of those who could be politically active. Locke's distinctiveness lay in his consistent position that all men had a positive political interest through their non-material possessions, their self-propriety, and their natural rights. In *A Letter Concerning Toleration* (1689), Locke reiterated this fundamental political principle:

The commonwealth seems to me to be a society of men constituted only for the procuring, the preserving and the advancing of their own civil interests.
Civil interests I call life, liberty, health, and indolency of body; and the possession of outward things, such as money, lands, houses, furniture, and the like.[39]

Given his contemporaries' stress on "the possession of outward things" as a primary factor in the institution of political society,

---

[38] Sidney, *op. cit.*, 393.
[39] *The Works of John Locke*, (ed.) W. Otridge (London, 1812), VI, 10.

Locke's listing of them as a merely secondary consideration is particularly striking. It adds force to the suggestion that Locke's thought did repeatedly turn to a theoretically universal membership of, and participation in, political society.

If one ventures beyond a discussion of some uses of *property* in Locke's time and compares other current political terms, Locke's sympathy for a radically wider membership of political society becomes even clearer. Historians have argued that Locke was not intending to describe a political membership as inclusive as his words suggest. He must be read, they have explained, with a proper awareness of the basic assumptions of the age, especially the assumption that the laboring classes were in, and subject to the laws of, civil society, but were properly excluded from any political voice. Macpherson described his understanding of the status of *that* assumption:

These were not only Locke's assumption, they were also his readers'. . . . He could safely take them for granted, for they were well-established in the prevailing view. Ever since there had been wage-labourers in England their political incapacity had been assumed as a matter of course.[40]

Dunn has also, at times, argued for positions he ascribed to Locke from the shared assumptions of his age.[41] But the remarkable thing is that if one turns to Locke's contemporaries, they can be shown to have taken a good deal of care to spell out not only their assumptions about who were *the people* but also the reasons for which they adopted their particular positions. Even such a pre-eminently theological writer as Baxter felt the need to describe why the majority of men should be excluded from an active political voice. He pointed out that "the major part are ignorant men" and "enemies of piety. . . . The rabble hate both magistrates and ministers that would bring them up to piety, and restrain them from a licentious sensual life." He appealed to prudence:

---

[40] Macpherson, *op. cit.,* 226.

[41] Dunn, *Political Thought,* 122, n. 6. Dunn here remarks on Locke's "facile conventionalism" and arrives at this description by remarking that Locke had "not even" rejected the political implications of his naturalistic treatment of relations between men and women, and that for him "Convention is simply *assumed* to carry prescriptive weight." But one consequence of Dunn's procedure is that he arrives at a Locke whose writing was "patently inconsistent and absurd" (92). Given that other writers did *not* rely on "facile conventionalism" to sustain their much more conventional arguments, it may well be that both Macpherson and Dunn are wrong to obtrude their expectations into Locke's words. They both hinge their understanding of him on what he does *not* say to arrive at an interpretation of what they think he *should* have said. This is indeed to elevate unspoken assumptions into a central place in unravelling meaning. We suggest that Locke's works are a better guide to his meaning than his silences or his failure to express the attitudes expected of him by modern commentators.

Let us have the common reason to conceive that as a man that hath studied physic, divinity, or any art, or science, or doctrine, is likelier to be skilled in it than he that was never brought up to it: so it is about the government of Commonwealths also.[42]

Sidney had declared the primary purpose of political society to be the protection of liberty and had written "that the liberty which we contend for is granted by God to every man in his own person, in such a manner as may be useful to him and his posterity."[43] But at several points Sidney made clear how inappropriate it would be to draw any politically democratic implications from such an apparently inclusive fundamental principle. Only *some* men could help determine how that liberty was to be protected. The status of freeman was a *sine qua non*.[44] As part of a general argument about the distinctions between paternal and political authority, Sidney made clear that though all men might belong to a family, only some, and never servants, could be full members of political society. He was adamant about the qualitative distinctions:

the difference between "civis" and "servus" is irreconcilable; and no man whilst he is a servant, can be a member of a commonwealth; for he that is not in his own power, cannot have a part in the government of others.[45]

But Sidney did not always settle for such a simple description of who comprised the political nation. The old Commonwealthman shared a good deal of Neville's enthusiasm for the "divine Machavel," and echoed Machiavelli's requirement that *the people* should possess sufficient *virtù* to take a proper part in public affairs.[46] Although he often turned his mind to defining who was fitted for a voice in society, he never produced an entirely consistent answer. To explain the wide disparities in the electoral qualifications of his contemporary England, Sidney took refuge in what was "reasonable," even though the consequences differed widely. His account of the historical processes leading to the existing franchise situation served his polemical case that political power derived from the people, however variously *the people* were defined in practice.[47] But he did repeatedly spell out his fundamental assumption that only independent men and non-servants could ever be considered for a political voice.

James Tyrrell was also explicit about the distinctions to be drawn between the masses and *the people*, and, unlike Sidney, he faced at

---

[42] Quoted in Richard Schlatter, *Richard Baxter and Puritan Politics* (New Brunswick, 1957), 26-27.

[43] Sidney, *op. cit.*, 78.   [44] *Ibid.*, 68.   [45] *Ibid.*, 79.

[46] In one digression Sidney argued that in Roman history it had been proper first that the people had been excluded from political decisiontaking (the oppressions of the Tarquins having left them corrupt) and then that they should have been given a political voice, after the period necessary for political re-education. *Ibid.*, 134.

[47] *Ibid.*, 423.

least some of the problems such a distinction raised. Tyrrell made the qualifications for membership of the political nation clear when he accepted the challenge proffered many years earlier by Filmer, to

name any commonwealth out of History, where the Multitude, or so much as the greatest part of it ever consented, either by Voice or Proxies, to the election of a Prince; I will name his two Commonwealths: The first was Rome, where all the People or Freemen consented to the election of Romulus, being formerly proposed . . . And the second shall be that of Venice, where all the Masters of Families, or Freemen at their own dispose, had a Vote in the choice of the first Duke and Senate.[48]

Tyrrell also acknowledged that such a definition of the political nation, the membership of which was far from co-extensive with that of the population at large, posed some problems in describing the binding nature of political obligation on all. Women, children, and servants had had no direct part in the establishment of political society, but they still owed to it a high "obligation in Conscience and Gratitude" since they "might be supposed as represented by their Husbands, Fathers, and Masters: And since they enjoy all the common benefits of the Commonwealth, and are likewise capable of enjoying all those privileges and advantages which are proper and peculiar to Free Subjects, whenever they come to be at their own disposal, and that they owe their breeding up and preservation to its protection."[49]

There was not, then, such an easy consensus as to who should be excluded from the vote, and on what grounds, that writers on political matters felt able to pass silently over the issue. Some writers can be seen making a rather uncomfortable transition from theoretically inclusive principles to pragmatically exclusive procedures. There is a striking example emanating from the household of which Locke was frequently a member. The draft scheme for electoral reform, commonly attributed to Shaftesbury himself, makes a telling point of comparison with Locke on the subject of political participation. The document spelled out what was implicit in a writer like Sidney, that in principle every individual had a stake in political society, but then, like Sidney, explicitly retreated from that position. Practicality was the reason, particularly since

every pater-familias or housekeeper, is a natural prince, and is invested with absolute power over his family, and has, by necessary consequence, the votes of all his family, man, woman, and child, included in his.[50]

---

[48] Tyrrell, op. cit., 84-85.   [49] Ibid., 77-78.

[50] "Some Observations concerning the Regulating of Elections," Somers Tracts, vol. 8, 401. K. D. H. Haley, op. cit., 740, however, offers some cogent reasons for doubting this customary attribution.

Nor did this paper stop at the *pater-familias* in tightening the boundaries of the political nation. The "natural right" of "every individual person" was diminished further, for reasons which made no pretence of appealing to natural rights or laws of nature but to prudence, since most electors being of a "mean and abject fortune" were "under the temptation of being corrupted and seduced by the inveiglements of a little money, or a pot of ale, whilst those whose circumstances are most enlarged have their thoughts so likewise."[51]

The range of opinion about who should be represented is widened if one turns from political writings during the final quarter of the seventeenth century to a consideration of political practice. Lawrence Stone has argued that, after the Restoration, all avenues of social mobility in England were sharply restricted and that "rule by a narrow elite was strengthened at all levels of government."[52] But J. H. Plumb, on the contrary, has suggested a steady expansion of the franchise for most of the seventeenth century, only briefly interrupted by the Cavalier Parliament after 1661[53] and culminating in the Exclusion Parliaments. He cites as an instance the case of Aldborough, transformed as a result of a disputed return in 1679 from being a tight burgage borough with thirteen voters into an open borough with all male inhabitants enfranchised. In over fifty appeals to the new parliament that year, the decisions were consistently in favor of a wider franchise even where that ran counter to previous local custom.[54] Keith Thomas has also pointed to examples of the franchise being progressively widened even under the Cavalier Parliament, and certainly later.[55] The difficulties in drawing the lines between those who were agreed to be entitled to a political voice and those who were not are indicated in the reports of disputed elections, and distinctions between dependent and independent men become much more blurred. Thomas's examples demonstrate that in practice

---

[51] *Ibid.,* 400.

[52] Lawrence Stone, "Social Mobility in England, 1500-1700," *Past and Present,* 33 (1966), 47.

[53] J. H. Plumb, "The Growth of the Electorate in England from 1600 to 1715," *Past and Present,* **45** (1969), 90-116.

[54] J. H. Plumb, *The Growth of Political Stability in England 1675-1725* (Harmondsworth, 1969), 52.

[55] In 1662 it was testified that at St. Albans the almsmen "had had voices time out of mind," and their right to vote was upheld by the House of Commons. The same thing happened at Sandwich in 1690 when the parliamentary committee resolved "that the freemen of the port of Sandwich, inhabiting within the said borough (although they receive alms) have a right to vote in electing barons to serve in Parliament." In 1711 a witness declared that in Grantham freemen in receipt of weekly relief had voted in parliamentary elections for the past forty or fifty years. Keith Thomas, "The Levellers and the Franchise," in G. E. Aylmer (ed.), *The Interregnum* (London, 1972) 65.

voting rights could move far beyond the line of independence to regular almstakers. Part of the discussion of a disputed return from Aylesbury in 1695 suggests something of the difficulties in drawing the lines, even where they *were* agreed to exist:

John Hawkes said, that Edward Edwards liv'd with his Father *William Cooper:* but Spencer said that *Edwards* was a Housekeeper, and that he watched and warded. That John Colsom was no Housekeeper; but *Spencer* said he was, and that his Mother had yielded up the House to him: and that *Charles Noy* was no Housekeeper; but own'd he receiv'd the Till of the Market, and that he was Constable the last year.[56]

Locke was out of joint with his associates to the extent that he was reluctant to subscribe to any such easy transgression of the "natural right" of "every individual person" as the paper ascribed to Shaftesbury had suggested. But such a reluctance need not have seemed a complete break with customary thought to anyone familiar with electoral proceedings.[57] Bohun's reports show the distinctions and the qualifications to vote to have been variable and not always subject to judgments based on legal facts. Custom and hearsay were both important elements in the submissions, and surviving evidence suggests the decisions were often made on grounds quite other than those of dependence or independence. Moreover, John Dunn's reconstruction of the intellectual development of Locke has stressed, and very properly, "the axiomatic centrality of the purposes of God"[58] in the political work of Locke. That Locke saw politics as only a part of a much larger scheme of things imbued with a higher moral purpose was also suggested by his comment to Lady Peterborough in 1697: "True Politicks I looke on as a Part of Moral Philosophie."[59] Near contemporaries had noted, and were made uneasy by, the extent to which Locke's arguments rested on "an appeal to natural law, natural rights, and the dissolution of government."[60] The general preference, Thompson has shown, was rather for an appeal to the constitutional rights of the English, a concept much more amenable to restricting

---

[56] W. Bohun, *A Collection of Debates, Reports . . . Touching the Right of Electing Members to Serve in Parliament* (London, 1702), 12.

[57] The extent of Locke's involvement with active electoral campaigning is hard to document. His apparent destruction of papers relating to political activities was thorough. Only one letter from Shaftesbury requesting Locke to intervene in an election issue has survived (Shaftesbury to Locke, 19 February 1681), E. S. de Beer (ed.), *The Correspondence of John Locke* (Oxford, 1976), II, 378, but other correspondence certainly retains indications of Locke's interest in all aspects of politics.

[58] John Dunn, *Political Thought,* 12. See also, Dunn, 263.

[59] Quoted by de Beer, *loc. cit.,* 40.

[60] Thompson, *loc. cit.,* 188. He cites particularly William Atwood as expressing this concern in *The Fundamental Constitutional of the English Government* (1690).

change to what those in power chose to define as the Ancient Constitution. Locke departed from the usage of his contemporaries in that he did not apply qualifying restrictions when he based human rights on natural law. There was very little in Locke's *Second Treatise* to reassure those who sought to maintain essentially the customary distribution of authority. This was not so much because of what Locke did say, for in his language of natural right, natural liberty, and the right to withdraw consent he was not more inclusive than, say, Sidney. But Locke did not then adopt the qualifications of Sidney or Shaftesbury. By comparison with his contemporaries, what is remarkable about Locke is his consistency in adhering to the implications of defining *property* for the protection of which men enter civil society with laws to preserve their lives, liberties, and estates.

Indeed, Locke took some care to insist that his reference was to *every* man. Unlike Sidney, Tyrrell, and Neville, Locke did not take the ownership of land to be itself a sufficient qualification for political membership. On the contrary, where he discussed the nature of tacit consent, he stated quite clearly that land ownership did not distinguish an individual in political society at all:

Every Man being . . . *naturally free,* and nothing being able to put him into subjection to any Earthly Power, but only his own Consent; it is to be considered, what shall be understood to be *sufficient Declaration* of *a Mans Consent, to make him subject* to the Laws of any Government . . . And to this I say, that every Man, that hath any Possession or Enjoyment, of any part of the Dominions of any Government, doth thereby give his *tacit Consent,* and is as far forth obliged to Obedience to the Laws of that Government, during such Enjoyment, as any one under it; whether this his Possession be of land, to him and his Heirs for ever, or a Lodging only for a Week; or whether it be barely travelling freely on the Highway; and in Effect, it reaches as far as the very being of any one within the Territories of that Government.[61]

Owning land was, in itself, irrelevant to the degree of consent and by implication to the degree of involvement in political society, a view echoed in *A Letter on Toleration.*[62] On the subject of the franchise, Locke was reserved when compared with his Whiggish contemporaries who often chose that point to enunciate their limitations on political participation. He was vague as to how the representatives should be chosen, apart from his remarks that electorates should be more evenly drawn.[63]

---

[61] Locke, *Two Treatises,* II, 119. Moreover, in the *First Treatise* he quite specifically denied that land ownership *per se* conferred authority of one man over another. I, 126.

[62] See footnote 44 *supra.*   [63] *Ibid.,* II, 157.

But Locke was even less like his fellow polemicists in his defense of resistance to government and, above all, in his account of who may undertake such an enterprise. Tyrrell, more conservative than Sidney or Locke (perhaps because he was the only one to publish his work in Charles II's reign), brought out a formidable barrage of reasonable and natural sanctions against overthrowing existing forms of govern- ment. He admitted that disparity of property may make subjects dis- contented, but this gave them no rights of resistance

since no man can disturb the general Peace of humane society for his own pri- vate advantage, or security, without transgressing the natural laws of God, by bringing all things insofar as in him lies out of the settled course they are now in, into a state of Anarchy and confusion.[64]

Sidney had gone further in that he had headed a section of his *Discourses* "The general revolt of a nation cannot be called a rebel- lion," but the issue of resistance by the people was couched in non- specific terms and did not make a case for resistance by parts of "the people."[65] Locke discussed the whole question in much more detail. Unlike Tyrrell, he did not deny expression of private discontent; he offered a much more pragmatic observation that the "examples of particular Injustice, or Oppression of here or there an unfortunate Man" would probably not rouse *the people* to rebellion. This was entirely consistent with his general defense of the right of people to overthrow any part of the government which threatened the "Guards and Fences to the Properties of all the members of the Society."[66] He then confronted the obvious objection:

To this perhaps it will be said, that the people being ignorant and always discontented, to lay the Foundation of Government in the unsteady Opinion, and uncertain Humour of the people, is to expose it to certain ruine; And *no Government will be able long to subsist,* if the People may set up a new Legislative, whenever they take offence to the old one. To this, I Answer: Quite the contrary. People are not so easily got out of their old Forms, as some are apt to suggest.[67]

Particularly when compared with the utterly unambiguous statements made about the people by the other writers, this was a remarkable turn to Locke's argument. Other authors of the time forestalled such a challenge by redefining *the people* to mean *some of the people,* and preferably only the most substantial men of the community. Yet Locke did not adopt the customary solution of depriving most men of their generally agreed "natural rights" on "reasonable" or custom-

[64] Tyrrell, *op. cit.,* 147. Revised pagination, misprinted as 107.
[65] Sidney, *op. cit.,* section 36.
[66] Locke, *Two Treatises,* II, 222.   [67] *Ibid.,* 223.

ary or pragmatic grounds. Rather, he argued for the stability of a society grounded on the profound political apathy of most people, despite their wide-ranging rights. His argument for resting government on the "unsteady Opinion and Uncertain Humour of the People" was defended by an assertion of their comprehensive lethargy, capable of being shaken only by "a long train of Abuses, Prevarications, and Artifices."[68] In another work Locke indicated what abuses might have been calculated to stir *the people* to violent resistance, but "unless when some common and great distress, uniting them, in one universal ferment, makes them forget respect . . . this rarely happens but in the maladministration of neglected or mis-managed government."[69] He noted that under such conditions of bad government and extreme oppression resistance not only occurs but is justified. Furthermore, Locke echoed Machiavelli's belief that a well-educated people was likely to be politically more responsible than the nobility when he wrote privately that under better government "the well instructed minds of the people" would not "suffer them to be the instruments of Aspiring and turbulent men," such as "designing or discontended Grandees."[70]

Locke, then, did not turn away from the implications of his fundamental principles in the name of prudence; he began by including all men in political society, the foundation of which had been to protect property in all its forms. His insistence on the consistency of his definition, his repeated inclusion of "every man" and "each individual" in his argument, his failure to pronounce the customary limitations on who, politically speaking, were included among *the people,* his avoidance of the usual discussions on the franchise, and his acceptance that his theory of political society rested the security of government, finally, on those who were "ignorant and always discontented," all point to one conclusion. Locke may not have been prepared to go so far as to argue in detail for the inclusion of all people in political society with full political rights, but he did not argue against this position which was the logical outcome of his postulates. Following Hooker, he had begun with a formula which conferred a fundamental natural equality on all men from which he derived the humane qualities most highly prized: "The great Maxims of Justice and Charity."[71] Locke, however, had no intention of claiming from such natural equality any revolutionary formulae of social egalitarianism:

---

[68] *Ibid.,* 225.
[69] Locke, "Some Considerations of the Consequences of the Lowering of Interest" (1691), *Works,* V, 71.
[70] Quoted in Dunn, *op. cit.,* 235, n. 6.
[71] Locke, *Two Treatises,* II, 5.

Though I have said . . . *That all men by Nature are equal*, I cannot be supposed to understand all sorts of *Equality*: Age or Virtue may give Men a just Precedency: *Excellency* of *Parts and Merit* may place others above the Common Level: Birth may subject some, and *Alliance* or *Benefits* others, to pay an Observance to those to whom Nature, Gratitude or other Respects may have it due; and yet all this consists with the *Equality*, which all Men are in, in respect of Jurisdiction or Dominion one over another, which was the *Equality* I there spoke of . . . being that *equal Right* that every Man hath, *to his Natural Freedom*, without being subjected to the Will or Authority of any other Man.[72]

Apart from children who lacked this *"full state of Equality,"* though as they acquired *"Age and Reason"* they grew into it,[73] the only other possible grounds for exclusion from political society which Locke conceded were the irreparable loss of all rights, including the right of life (a condition which applied only to slaves), and the absence of *"Reason,"* which he specifically confined to the condition of *Lunaticks* and *Ideots,"* children as previously described, and *"Madmen."*[74] But Locke was quite explicit that the condition of being a servant did not impair that fundamental equality; servitude was in no way to be confused with slavery, as

a Freeman makes himself a Servant to another, by selling him for a certain time, the Service he undertakes to do, in exchange for Wages he is to receive: And though this commonly puts him into the Family of his Master, and under the ordinary Discipline thereof; yet it gives the Master but a Temporary Power over him, and no greater, than what is contained in the *Contract* between 'em. But there is another sort of Servants, which by a peculiar Name we call Slaves. . . . These Men . . . being in the *State of Slavery*, not capable of any Property, cannot in that state be considered as any part of Civil Society.[75]

There is no hint in this passage of the class differential in rationality which Macpherson ascribes as a basic assumption to Locke and other quasi-capitalists. On the contrary, a servant was a freeman who temporarily entered into a clearly defined and limited contractual relationship, one of a wide range of possible subordinate relationships in Locke's society which could *not* of itself dispossess him of all property nor of his fundamental equality.

Two further points remain to be made about Locke on the issue of class differentials in rationality and in rights. Whatever his contemporaries may or may not have believed, Locke was clear that there were no inherent distinctions in the power of reason. On the contrary, arguing that "more might be brought to be rational creatures and

---

[72] *Ibid.*, II, 54.   [73] *Ibid.*, II, 55.
[74] *Ibid.*, II, 60.   [75] *Ibid.*, II, 85.

Christians," he pointed out that "the peasantry lately in France (a rank of people under much heavier pressure of want and poverty than the day-labourer in England) of the reformed religion, understood it much better, and could say more for it, than those of higher condition among us." He could see no reason "that the meaner sort of people must give themselves up to brutish stupidity."[76] His vision of society was one which, ideally, encouraged all to develop their rationality and Christian understanding. It was also one in which children of whatever rank should be taught to respect the fundamental equality of all and eschew all temptations to be seduced by superficial hierarchies into any oppression of whatever kind.[77] It was precisely because of the power structure inherent in the family grouping that Locke had insisted that political society differed so much from "a *Family*, or any other Society of Men."[78]

For many of Locke's contemporaries, especially Tyrrell and Sidney, it was self-evident that political society was constructed on and after the model of the family. The natural head of the family group made the decisions on behalf of all his subordinates, thereby committing them to civil society. But Locke painstakingly broke entirely free from the familial model. He showed the qualitative difference of the "proper *power of the Magistrate*, of which the Father has not so much as the shadow."[79] Tyrrell and Sidney could have gone so far; it is clear they could have followed Locke no further. For Locke added that when any son had reached a "state of maturity," or had reason requisite to know the law under which he was to live, "that so he might keep his Actions within the Bounds of it. . . . Which is supposed by that Law, at the Age of one and twenty years, and some cases sooner," then, "after that, the Father and Son are equally *free* . . . equally Subjects of the Law together, without any Dominion left in the Father over the Life, Liberty, or Estate of his Son, whether they be only in the State and under the Law of Nature, or under the positive laws of an Establish'd Government."[80] The capacity reasonably to know the law was the only prerequisite for membership of political society; the freedom to use that reason in accordance with that law for the preservation of life, liberty, and estate was the political stake each man had in society. All men were in political society, and all men were of it, except slaves and anyone who "through defects which may happen out of the ordinary course of Nature" could not come "to such a degree of Reason, wherein he might be supposed capable of knowing the Law, and so living within the Rules of it."[81]

It has been shown that Locke and some contemporary writers were consistently self-conscious users of the word *property*. Where a

---

[76] Locke, *Works*, III, 207.   [77] *Ibid.*, IX, 115.   [78] Locke, *Two Treatises*, II, 86.
[79] *Ibid.*, II, 65.   [80] *Ibid.*, II, 59.   [81] *Ibid.*, II, 60.

word is demonstrably and constantly subject to redefinition the particular definitions of a given writer should be treated with scrupulous
care, not merely noted and passed over. To understand an author,
one must indeed begin by seeking to recover what he believed himself
to be saying and what he believed his audience might have understood him to be saying.[82] It is only by a careful comparison of Locke's
arguments with those of his immediate contemporaries, and an examination of the prevailing conventions which he failed to observe, that
the full implications of his argument are illuminated.

Like others, John Dunn has argued that Locke's commitment to
the principles of natural law, reason, and the natural equality of all
men was tempered by his silent acceptance of the traditional social
assumptions of his hierarchic and privileged community.[83] One
methodological observation emerges clearly from this study: it is a
very dubious procedure indeed to explain silence on particular issues
by appealing to unspoken assumptions so deeply lodged in a community that they need no articulation. Yet two widely differing interpreters of Locke —Macpherson and Dunn—have resorted at significant
points to this means of sustaining their particular interpretations.[84] Of
all the assumptions shared by a community, one might reasonably
expect the exclusion of *children* from full membership of political
society to be least in need of enunciation. Yet each of the
seventeenth-century writers under consideration took time to explain
precisely why children are not full members. Such spelling out of the
apparently self-evident qualifications for political membership leads
one to look carefully at what was and what was not explicitly considered to be a criterion for a political voice. Here the significance of a
silence may properly be appealed to, for where Locke does *not* qualify his inclusion of *all the people* in political membership and the right
to rebel, his very omission acquires meaning in the context of his
contemporaries' political discussions. Indeed this silence on who
might legitimately rebel may help explain what Thompson describes
as the curiously quiet reception of *Two Treatises*.[85] It is not surprising
that his more careful colleagues preferred the prudent incoherence of
Sidney's declaration that the recognition of an agreed "natural right
to vote" was simply impracticable.

The efforts of Opposition politicians to widen the political electorate throughout the period of the Exclusion Parliaments had led, as
early as 1679, to the complaint from a Tory that "the common un-

---

[82] Quentin Skinner made the point succinctly in his insistence on the need to
recover "the conventions surrounding the performance of complex linguistic acts."
Skinner, "Some Problems," 284.
[83] Dunn, *op. cit.*, 236.   [84] *Ibid.*, 235 ff and Macpherson, *op. cit.*, 226
[85] Thomson, *loc. cit.*, 190-91.

thinking people have a voice equal to a man of best estate."[86] There is evidence that Locke played an active part in these campaigns, but the post-1688 Whigs in general preferred a more unequivocal assertion of existing property rights. Above all, it was surely more reassuring not only to stay with Sidney's appeals to the Ancient Constitution but also to follow his explicit distinction between free men who were "of" political society and servants who were merely "in" it. Far from being the Marxists' "ideological hangman of the new [capitalist] regime"[87] or Dunn's spokesman for "principles of the most indubitable and parochial political orthodoxy,"[88] the Locke who is thrown into sharper relief by the recovery of his immediate linguistic context is very much his own man. Locke was a radical theorist, driven to his radical stance largely by his commitment to the view that politics was indeed but a branch of moral philosophy.

La Trobe University, Melbourne.

[86] Haley, *op. cit.*, 426.   [87] Dunn, *op. cit.*, 211.   [88] See *supra*, footnote 5.

XX

CHARITY VERSUS JUSTICE IN
LOCKE'S THEORY OF PROPERTY

By John C. Winfrey

Certain moral dilemmas are inextricably bound up with the arguments of social theorists. While the dilemmas may be framed in diverse terms and may or may not be explicitly treated, they nevertheless are inherent in the arguments. In some theories the attempt is made to identify these moral questions and isolate them from political and economic arguments. They then may be resolved and cast in the form of principles in some purely abstract model. However, certain moral dilemmas are the *bases* for the conflicting claims in the ever-changing polemics among competing political and economic groups. As such, it is necessary that they be treated explicitly at every stage of the argument.

The particular dilemma I propose to examine is one of those several fundamental moral questions which may be framed in any one of a number of ways. Charles Monson has illustrated how several of John Locke's interpreters have come to contrasting conclusions regarding one or more of Locke's positions by utilizing ''nothing but'' interpretations. Such interpretations necessarily leave out any treatment Locke gives to opposing moral claims.[1] Monson has identified ''consent, freedom, and equality'' as the distinct and competing claims around which Locke's political philosophy is formulated. When Locke's arguments

originating from different basic concepts are laid side by side, incompatibilities become evident. Locke's theory requires both obedience to the state and the right to revolt: consent versus freedom. He sanctions unlimited appropriation, yet an obligation to help preserve others: freedom versus equality. He relies upon majority rule, yet affirms the inalienability of an individual's consent: equality versus consent. It is no wonder, then, that some writers have concluded that Locke is ''a blundering incompetent'' or ''a man whose problem exceeds his powers.''[2]

The particular competing claims I wish to investigate are those which Locke terms ''charity'' and ''justice'' and which I refer to as ''need'' and ''desert,'' since by ''charity'' Locke means the responsibility that Christians have to provide sustenance for those in need and by ''justice'' he means the honoring of the claim that property owners have established through their industry (so that it has become

---

[1] Charles H. Monson, Jr., ''Locke and His Interpreters,'' *Political Studies*, **6** (1958), 120-35; reprinted in *Life, Liberty and Property*, ed. Gordon J. Schochet (Belmont, Cal., 1971), 33-48.   [2] Monson in Schochet, 46-47.

their "just deserts"). A more egalitarian interpretation might pose the dilemma as a trade-off between the present claim of each individual to a "fair start" (or an "equal opportunity") and the opposing claim of each person to keep all or at least a portion of the wealth which he and his forefathers have earned in a fair process over time. However, for the purposes of our investigation the terms "need" and "desert" are the most appropriate for structuring the dilemma.

Forms for Resolving Moral Dilemmas. I will not attempt to specify precisely how moral questions and principles should be treated in political and economic theories. It may be that useful, though limited, theories can be formulated in such a way that the moral principles and choices are assumed to be already settled and are somehow separated from the theory itself. Be that as it may, John Locke's purpose was to justify the Glorious Revolution and the Whigs' position of political and economic power, and he felt obliged to do so by appealing to his readers on both moral and scientific bases. His argument was designed not simply for the Whigs but to gain support for their position among moderates of all parties. Moreover, he addressed the moral questions at each methodological stage of his argument from the derivation of principles in his abstract models (the state of nature and the state of war) to their application in the context of current institutional arrangements.

There are various forms that the "solution" to conflicting moral claims may take. For example, in one of the many Utilitarian schemes in which the overriding goal is to maximize total happiness, the conflicting claims of individuals may be seen as resolved when each individual's total, average, or marginal utility of income is equal to that of all others. The notion of "balance" is certainly a most appealing method of resolving conflicting claims if it can be argued that such claims can somehow be measured by some common denominator. In some theories particular claims are seen to have priority over others and thus must be satisfied first. Locke believed the claim that all men are equal by nature to have such priority.[3] More recently, John Rawls has placed his own two principles in serial order so that no departure from the institutions promoting equal liberty (first principle) can be justified, or compensated for, by greater social and economic advantages even though the latter fulfill his second principle that they be (a) reasonably expected to be to everyone's advantage, and (b) attached to positions and offices open to all.[4]

The satisfying of a claim may involve either (1) devoting to it all available resources necessary for its maximization or (2) devoting to it only those resources necessary for its maintenance at a designated

---

[3] *Two Treatises on Government*, ed. Peter Laslett (Cambridge, 1960), *Second Treatise*, §§ 4 and 5.

[4] Rawls, *A Theory of Justice* (Cambridge, Mass., 1971), 60, 61.

level. This method of solution is often termed "satisficing."[5] For example, suppose the management of a large corporation sees both profits and sales as its joint goals. The management sees profits as necessary to appease the stockholders and believes that a certain level will keep them happy. However, each executive knows that his or her salary, status, and prestige are actually more dependent on the company's increase in sales and the attendant increases in the number of persons employed, the number of plants built, and other indications of additional management responsibilities. It follows that management will "satisfice" by bringing profits to the required level but will then go on to maximize sales. It is this treatment that theorists generally use in dealing with competing claims of the type we are considering. And this is the approach used by Locke for resolving the claims of need and desert in his theory of property.

Locke's Three States of Nature. Locke uses his state of nature model in three distinct ways, and these uses, which seem at first to be inconsistent, add great leverage to his argument. It is important for us to follow these uses if we are to see how in developing his theory of property he simultaneously resolves the need-versus-desert dilemma. Locke uses the state of nature as (1) an historically accurate depiction of man's condition immediately after Adam's fall, (2) an accurate depiction of existing conditions in the Americas and other primitive areas, and (3) a timeless, abstract model depicting the condition of every man in every society prior to the time he gives his consent to becoming a member of that society.

Locke begins his argument by utilizing the state of nature in its abstract and ahistorical form:

To understand political power right, and derive it from its original, we must consider what state all men *are naturally in*, and that is a state of perfect freedom to order their actions and dispose of their possessions and persons as they think fit, within the bounds of the law of nature, without asking leave or depending upon the will of any other man.[6]

Later Locke states that all men are naturally in a state of perfect freedom "and remain so till by their own consents they make themselves members of some politic society."[7]

In this light it would have been preposterous for Locke to claim that the current state of men in England was:

---

[5] Herbert Simon introduced this concept as part of his analysis of the behavior of business firms. See Herbert A. Simon, *Models of Man* (New York, 1957), Chap. 14, and "Theories of Decision Making in Economics," *American Economic Review,* **49** (June 1959). This approach has been elaborated by a number of investigators to include Cyert and March. See R. M. Cyert and J. G. March, *A Behavioral Theory of the Firm* (Englewood Cliffs, N.J., 1963).

[6] *Second Treatise,* §4, emphasis added.   [7] *Ibid.,* §15.

A state also of equality, wherein all the power and jurisdiction is reciprocal, no one having more than another; there being nothing more evident than that creatures of the same species and rank, promiscuously *born to all the same advantages* of nature and the use of the same faculties, should also be equal one amongst another without subordination or subjection[8];

Modern Christian thought treats the story of Adam's fall and the state of nature into which he was placed as an allegory. As such it can be seen as an abstract model depicting man's condition vis-à-vis God. Many, if not most, of Locke's contemporaries saw the creation story of Adam's fall and mankind's subsequent position in nature as historically accurate. Yet, on the other hand, the Biblical stories were also recognized to be vehicles for stating religious truths from which moral truths could be derived. Locke argued that the Indians in the Americas of his own day found themselves in situations similar to the original state of nature. But since the situation was different in Locke's England, application of the model's principles required a transition, be it across time, distance, or simply from the "abstract" to the "concrete."

In his arguments which employ the idea of the state of nature, Locke is not always clear as to which of these perspectives and transitions he is using. Consequently, the methodological difficulties which occur in proceeding from one of these perspectives to Locke's "real world" of England are often glossed over and are thus the source of considerable criticism. But while the ambiguous use of the idea of "state of nature" is a source of weakness, we shall see that it is also a source of strength.

In his opening argument on property Locke begins with a basically historical approach; he claims, however, that history, reason, and revelation all support the conclusion that man has the right to subsistence:

Whether we consider natural reason, which tells us that men, being once born, have a right to their preservation, and consequently to meat and drink and such other things as nature affords for their subsistence; or revelation, which gives us an account of those grants God made of the world to Adam, and to Noah and his sons; it is very clear that God, as King David says (Psal. cxv. 16), "has given the earth to the children of men," *given it to mankind in common.* But this being supposed, it seems to some a very great difficulty how any one should ever come to have a property in anything. I will not content myself to answer that if it be difficult to make out property upon a supposition that God gave the world to Adam and his posterity in common, it is impossible that any man but one universal monarch should have any property upon a supposition that God gave the world to Adam and his heirs in succession, exclusive of all the rest of his posterity. But I shall endeavour to show how men might *come to have a property* in several parts of that

[8] *Ibid.*, §4, emphasis added.

which God gave to mankind in common, and that without any express compact of all the commoners.[9]

Locke's argument reveals a strategic position relative to the particular polemics of his day. His most fundamental task is to justify the Whig position in the Glorious Revolution, especially the political and economic power of the landed gentry and the merchants. Consequently, his argument is directed against the divine right claim of the Stuart kings and the attendant rights and privileges imparted to the aristocracy. The Biblical argument that the earth was given to all mankind in common is advanced as one of Locke's several answers to Filmer who in his *Patriarcha* had purported to trace the Stuart claim directly from Adam by means of heredity.[10]

At the same time Locke utilized the principles of his predecessors concerning natural rights and the social contract which legitimized government by "express compact of all the commoners." Hobbes had already demonstrated that the consent argument could be used to justify a monarchical government with the power to dispense property rights arbitrarily. What Locke required in order to justify the claims of the Whigs to their property (and its political and economic leverage) was a theory making property a natural right established *prior* to the consent which legitimized government. Grotius' assumption that property was a natural right, derived from natural law, had been absorbed into the English tradition of accepting the common law and the Magna Charta as reflecting the laws of reason and nature.[11]

Within the Biblical-historical context, however, Locke depends primarily on an appeal to the common sense of his readers. In making the point that acquisition of property must precede general consent he states: "If such consent as that were necessary, man had starved, not withstanding the plenty God had given him." [12] Similarly, Locke links man's basic subsistence needs with the acquisition of goods by ap-

<hr>

[9] *Ibid.*, §25, emphasis added.

[10] It is somewhat ludicrous that Locke relies heavily, although not completely, on a Biblical-historical approach since his laborious criticism of Filmer is disdainful of that approach. In addition to raising questions about Filmer's arguments on the nature of Adam's sovereignty and its succession, Locke observes that even if that inheritance "had been determined, yet the knowledge of which is the eldest line of Adam's posterity being so long since utterly lost, that in the races of mankind and families of the world there remains not to one above another the least pretence to be the eldest house, and to have the right of inheritance." (*Second Treatise*, §1.) As we shall see, Locke's theory does rely heavily on an historical process of "just" transactions and to that extent is subject to a similar objection.

[11] John Seldon had accepted this basic premise even while attempting to refute Grotius's argument for freedom of the seas. See John Seldon's *Mare Clausum* (London, 1635) for a refutation of Grotius's *Mare Liberum* (1609). Other writers such as Cumberland, Parker, and Towerson reinforced the natural law approach to private property: Richard Cumberland, *De Legibus Naturae* (London, 1672); Samuel Parker,

pealing to the reasonableness of the proposition that "there must *of necessity* be a means to appropriate them some way or other before they can be of any use or at all beneficial to any particular man."[13]

The means of appropriation required in the state of nature is, of course, labor. And here again Locke's argument reflects the actual claims generated in the evolving economic relationships of his day. To justify economic power and its consequent political power on the basis of labor would have been irrelevant in the ancient and medieval setting where claims to land and station were a result primarily of military power bolstered by the institutions of the church and the aristocracy. Serfs and peasants were considered a part of the manor and their labor merely an extension of their station. The notion of a worker's labor being an activity detached from his station and thus somehow independently creating value became more appropriate as more sophisticated market relationships developed. The entrepreneurial roles of the landed gentry, in employing labor and land to produce and sell products on the market, and of the merchants, in creating value through their marketing prowess, were clearly not related to the stations which had made up the traditional institutional framework.

Locke argues that one's natural right to property exclusively "in his own person" extends to the products of his own labor:

> Though the earth and all inferior creatures be common to all men, yet every man has a property in his own person; this nobody has any right to but himself. The labour of his body and the work of his hands, we may say, are properly his. Whatsoever then he removes out of the state that nature hath provided and left it in, he hath mixed his labour with, and joined to it something that is his own, and thereby makes it his property. It being by him removed from the common state nature hath placed it in, it hath by this labour something annexed to it that excludes the common right of other men. For this labour being the unquestionable property of the labourer none but he can have a right to what that is once joined to, at least where there is enough and as good left in common for others.[14]

The idea that in nature man has property in himself had been central to the debates within Lilburne's Leveller party, especially with respect to the question of whether their radical egalitarianism required universal suffrage and radical redistribution of wealth. Richard Overton argued in 1647 that

> every individual in nature is given an individual propriety by nature, not to be invaded or usurped by any . . . ; for every one as he is himself hath a self propriety—else could not be himself—and on this no second may presume

---

A Demonstration of the Divine Authority of the Laws of Nature (London, 1681); and Gabriel Towerson, *Explication of the Decalogue* (London, 1676).

[12] *Second Treatise*, §28.   [13] *Ibid.*, §26, emphasis added.

[14] *Ibid.*, §27.

without consent; and by natural birth all men are equal, and alike born to like propriety and freedom. . . .[15]

But for Overton and others taking up this argument, the logical end of stressing the "equality" of men in their natural state was that it should carry over to an equal distribution of wealth in current society but certainly not to unlimited accumulation of property. The Levellers continually had to deny the claims that the Leveller position led necessarily to the abolition of private property. Moreover, the Levellers themselves were not able to forge a theory which satisfactorily resolved the conflicting goals of universal suffrage, greater equality of wealth, and the honoring of private property rights. In the constitutional debates at Putney in 1647, Henry Ireton argued for the conservative side against the natural right approach:

Now I wish we may consider of what right you will challenge that all the people should have a right to elections. Is it by the right of nature? If you will hold forth that as your ground, then I think you must deny all property too, and this is my reason. For thus: by that same right of nature (whatever it be) that you pretend, by which you can say, one man hath an equal right with another to choosing of him that shall govern him—by the same right of nature, he hath the same right in any goods he sees—meat, drink, clothes— to take and use them for his sustenance. He hath a freedom to the land, the ground, to exercise it, to till it; he hath the freedom to anything that any one doth account himself to have any propriety in.[16]

Thus, Ireton concluded that property rights were to be a product of a government.[17]

A related problem is how much property natural law allows an individual to claim as his own. Locke's resolution of this difficulty is to make labor the key to *excluding* property from "the common right of other men."

A Digression on Strong and Weak Claims. In light of the different types of claims contained in the various theories it seems appropriate to classify claims as "strong" or "weak." Claims, or claim rights, are most often defined in terms of one individual as he relates to another. My claim right against another individual means that he has a correlative duty to allow (or perhaps even to aid) me to perform the activity in question. This leaves open the question of whether my claim right is "strong" in the sense that it extends to *all of the relevant parties*. If I have a "strong" claim to free speech, it imposes obligations on all

[15] Richard Overton, *An Appeal from the Commons to the Free People* (London, 1647), reprinted in A.S.P. Woodhouse, *Puritanism and Liberty* (London, 1938), 327.

[16] Putney Debates in A.S.P. Woodhouse, *Puritanism and Liberty* (London, 1938), 59.

[17] "The Law of God doth not give me property, nor the Law of Nature, but property is of human constitution" (Ireton in Woodhouse, 69).

those who might interfere with my exercise of that claim. Correspondingly, a "weak" claim does not cover all the relevant parties. The extreme case, a privilege or liberty right, refers to the situation where I am free to do something only to the extent that I have no contrary duty to others not to do it. It may be the case that others have neither an obligation to help nor even an obligation not to interfere. It follows then that in a situation where all parties have only privileges or liberty rights with respect to a given object or activity, they have no corresponding duties or obligations to the others.

The idea that in the state of nature man has the freedom to all he can acquire was common to men of such diverse persuasions as those of Grotius, Hobbes, and Ireton. As quoted above, Ireton dismissed the natural right approach since it implies that everyone has "the freedom to anything that any doth account to have any propriety in." In Hobbes's state of nature every man has a liberty right to everything. Claims overlap in the sense that no one has a duty to honor the claims of others and everyone desires possession of the limited supply of goods.[18] And while Grotius purported to start with an abstract model featuring natural equality of rights and to derive property rights from that natural state, he in fact changed his argument in midstream and based property rights on mutual assent. Moreover, Grotius acknowledged that the processes of conquest and domination through which property had been appropriated are clearly unjust.[19]

The property theory of Pufendorf is similar to that of Grotius in many respects except that it is premised on a state of nature in which property is collectively owned by the community whose claim is "weak."[20] The claim of the original community is "negative" in the sense that nothing belongs to anyone. "Positive" community, on the other hand, refers to the state of nature envisioned by Grotius in which the community has a strong claim to property and everything is owned "jointly." As noted, in Hobbes's state of nature no man has a strong individual claim to property, yet "every man has a right to everything" and the wants of all overlap and conflict.

Locke's state of nature is similar to that of Pufendorf in that while the property there is "that which God gave to mankind *in common*,"[21] the claims of the community and each individual to that property are "weak." Consequently, Locke's labor theory of property allows the individual to create a strong claim that "excludes the common right of other men."[22] To bolster his case that the right

[18] "Naturally every man has a right to every thing" *Leviathan* [1651], ed. Michael Oakeshott (London, 1962), 103.

[19] Hugo Grotius, *De Jure Belli ac Pacis*, 1646 edition, trans. F. W. Kelsey *et al.* (Oxford, 1925); see esp. 89-90.

[20] Samuel Pufendorf, *De Jure Naturae et Gentium* (Lund, 1672), Book IV, Chap. 4, "On the Origin of Dominion."

[21] *Second Treatise*, §25, emphasis added.   [22] *Ibid.*, §27.

established by labor is stronger than the common right, Locke argues that the marginal value of the other factors of production is zero. Obviously, labor is not the only factor contributing to the utility of berries, venison, and other "products" of nature. But as long as there is an unlimited supply, the market value of such "free goods" as berries, deer, or land is zero, and Locke is correct in attributing all the value of the picked berries, dressed deer, or cultivated land to labor. However, in a crucial transition, Locke extends this argument to include the economic values created in the more advanced countries where the other factors of production are scarce:

I think it will be but a very modest computation to say that, of the products of the earth useful to the life of man, nine-tenths are the effects of labour; nay, if we will rightly estimate things as they come to our use and cast up the several expenses about them, what in them is purely owing to nature, and what to labour, we shall find that in most of them ninety-nine hundredths are wholly to be put on the account of labour.[23]

In a crucial part of his account of the transition from the state of nature to a more complex economic system such as in England, Locke develops the argument that capital or land imparts value because of the labor "embodied" in it. Locke uses the concept to explain the differences in value created by a given acre of land in America and one in England:

It is labour, then, which puts the greatest part of the value upon land, without which it would scarcely be worth anything; it is to that we owe the greatest part of all its useful products; for all that the straw, bran, bread of that acre of wheat is more worth than the product of an acre of as good land which lies waste is all the effect of labour. For it is not barely the ploughman's pains, the reaper's and thresher's toil, and the baker's sweat is to be counted into the bread we eat; the labour of those who broke the oxen, who digged and wrought the iron and stones, who felled and framed the timber employed about the plough, mill, oven, or any other utensils, which are a vast number requisite to this corn, from its being seed to be sown to its being made bread, must all be charged on the account of labour, and received as an effect of that; nature and the earth furnished only the almost worthless materials as in themselves.[24]

It is interesting to note the shift Locke makes in his justification of property. In his initial argument Locke states that God ordained that man labor and thus, by implication, created "God-given" property rights, but with the transition to a more complex society, Locke, in a rather startling shift, justifies the use of money and the claims to property (now "scarce") by what we may term the "consenting adults argument." If all the transactions leading to the more complex society could be considered *voluntary*, as Locke assumes, all would

---

[23] *Ibid.*, §40.   [24] *Ibid.*, §43.

involve only trades making both sides better off (or one side better off and the other no worse off). While the latter argument has much to recommend it on moral grounds, Locke does not develop it as such. Nor does he demonstrate how the process of "fair" transactions necessarily leads to a "fair" result. Moreover, it is disquieting to read Locke's argument as depicting an historical progression from man's condition in the post-Eden state of nature to Locke's England, since it can hardly be argued that property distribution at that time had resulted from a long series of transactions exhibiting voluntary consent.[25]

Nevertheless, it is the "time frame" or "sequentiality" of Locke's argument that is the essence of his justification of property; i.e., he attempts to show how the historical process from the original God-given distribution of wealth has been just. The justness of the accumulation process derives from two major premises: first, Locke used the labor theory of value to justify initial accumulation; and secondly, he assumes that subsequent transactions are voluntary. One condition that holds for both processes is that no one is to be made worse off.[26] As long as these conditions are met, greater accumulations of more durable goods and eventually money are justified. Here again, voluntary consent guarantees the fairness of the process:

And *if he also bartered away plums that would have rotted in a week for nuts that would last good for his eating a whole year, he did no injury*; he wasted not the common stock, destroyed no part of the portion of the goods that belonged to others, so long as nothing perished uselessly in his hands. Again, if he would give his nuts for a piece of metal, pleased with its colour, or exchange his sheep for shells, or wool for a sparkling pebble or a diamond, and keep those by him all his life, he invaded not the right of others; *he might heap as much of these durable things as he pleased*; the exceeding of the bounds of his just property not lying in the *largeness of his possession,* but the perishing of anything uselessly in it.

[25] If we view Locke's use of the state of nature here as simply an abstract model (rather than as historically accurate), there are still problems of consistency. Grotius had deigned not to employ the labor theory since he determined that more than labor would be required to set land apart. As he saw it, the transition to more complex society naturally went through a stage in which land suitable for cultivation was held in common and worked without the presumption of private ownership. Thus, it was clear that one's acquiescence to another person's working of the land did not confer ownership. According to Grotius, a more formal agreement was required. *De Jure Belli ac Pacis*, 206.

[26] Locke also includes the traditional sanction that one should not accumulate more than he can use if that accumulation will result in spoilage. In a state of nature where there are unlimited supplies this sanction is superfluous since there is always "enough and as good left in common for others." See §§27, 33, 36, and 50 of the *Second Treatise* for examples of Locke's use of the "no worse off" proviso, and §§31, 46, and 50 for the "no spoilage" proviso.

And thus came in the use of money—some lasting thing that men might keep without spoiling, and that *by mutual consent* men would take in exchange for the truly useful but perishable supports of life.[27]

Correspondingly, the governmental institutions protecting these property rights are likewise justified by an historical process of voluntary consent. To reiterate, it is hard to argue the injustice of a series of trades all made under voluntary consent. Presumably, a man would enter into trade only if he believed it made him better off (or certainly no worse off).[28] The process, especially when augmented by the use of money, inevitably leads to "a disproportionate and unequal possession of the earth," but this is just since it is agreed upon "by a tacit and voluntary consent" and "without injury to anyone."[29] Finally, we must remember that the original "just" situation that had been preserved was not merely some brutish, Hobbesian state but one where fair opportunities had been given by God.

One rather fundamental weakness of Locke's historical approach is that it does not take into account the actual prehistorical and historical events that had determined property holdings by Locke's time. If, with apologies to the Fundamentalist sects, we accept the theory of evolution, the specification of a unique "original" state and its sanctity becomes blurred. Moreover, while voluntary consent might have occasionally played a part in the transfer of property, certainly the "justice preserving" character of the process had been lost many times over by the unfair use of military, political, economic, and religious coercion.

And yet, when considered in the political context in which Locke was writing, the argument serves quite well as justification for the political and economic claims of the Whigs vis-à-vis the royalists. Both the landed gentry and the merchants had acquired their property primarily by the means which Locke acclaims as "just" (i.e., through labor and voluntary trades), and his argument gives little support to the property claims and the claims to additional privileges and power made by the monarch and the aristocracy.

The Transition from America to Locke's England. Locke's identification of America with the original state of nature served several purposes. As noted, it offered a familiar current example of the state

---

[27] *Second Treatise*, §§46 and 47, emphasis added.

[28] Robert Nozick has elaborated on this theme in his "entitlement theory" of property rights. He relies on an analogy to rules of inference which holds that "any conclusion deduced via repeated application of such rules from only true premises is itself true, so the means of transition from one situation to another specified by the principle of justice in transfer are justice-preserving, and any situation actually arising from repeated transitions in accordance with the principle from a just situation is itself just." Nozick, *Anarchy, State, and Utopia* (New York, 1974), 151.

[29] *Second Treatise*, §50.

of nature which could be used in essentially the same way as the original state of nature[30]; that is, principles could be derived which could then be applied to the situation in England. In addition, Locke had a second, and for our purposes more important, use for the "America" approach. It served the function of updating and perhaps bypassing the "historical process" argument. "America" offered an indication that God's original provision of economic opportunity and challenge was *still a valid norm*. Even if the process by which property had been transferred over time had not always followed "justice preserving" procedures, there currently existed opportunity at a level equal to or better than the one God originally ordained.

Consequently, Locke can employ the "no worse off" comparison once again in making the transition from America to England. Locke claims that the value added by labor to the wealth of England had increased not only the wealth of any given individual but also the "common stock"[31] so much that "a king of a large and fruitful territory there [in America] feeds, lodges, and is clad worse than a day-labourer in England."[32]

We can now see the leverage Locke gains by simultaneously referring to the state of nature model in three different ways.[33] The three perspectives are mutually reinforcing. Principles derived from the abstract model are given additional legitimacy by the model's relationship with the post-Eden state of nature ordained by God. Their efficacy for England is demonstrated not only by a "justice preserving" historical process but also by comparison with the current state in America, which at the same time allows the inference that God's original intent with regard to economic opportunity still holds.

Locke's Resolution of the Need-Versus-Desert Dilemma. While Locke does not explicitly set out to resolve the need-versus-desert dilemma, the comparisons and analogies he uses in his arguments necessitate that he do so. Locke's main focus is on the "deserts" of the landed gentry and merchants—their wealth and consequently their exercise of political and economic power. Since his argument

---

[30] In §49 of the *Second Treatise*, Locke uses the phrase "Thus in the beginning all the world was America. . . ."   [31] *Second Treatise*, §37.

[32] *Second Treatise,* §41. Although Locke does not explicitly use the term "economic opportunities" when comparing America and England, it is clear from his argument that this is what he means. The comparison he makes between the "king" in America and the "day-labourer" in England is made in terms of material well-being: how the king "feeds, lodges, and is clad." But the assumption here, as with Adam in the original state of nature, is that each starts with some given level of economic opportunity and must work to attain a higher level of well-being.

[33] As outlined above the three are: (1) the original, God-given, state of nature; (2) the existing situation in America; and (3) the "state of nature" as a timeless abstract model.

was primarily directed against the claims of the royalists, he paid less attention to the logical ends of his egalitarian arguments, i.e., to whether the needs and desires of those who made up the great majority, the peasants, represented significant claims against those of the property owners. Nevertheless, the format of his property rights argument requires that he address and resolve this dilemma. Our examination of Locke's development of his theory of property has already given us some clues as to how Locke resolves the dilemma. One clue is his repeated use of the "no-worse-off" proviso. Couched in terms of the "strong" and "weak" analogy, we see that the "no-worse-off" proviso serves to negate any claims of others which might arise in the process of one individual creating for himself a strong, exclusive claim to property. The process creates a just claim, or right, · on an individual's behalf. Moreover, others cannot argue that such a process simultaneously creates any claim by which they are "owed" something.

To summarize, the base or "satisficing" level of wealth and economic opportunity is that level originally ordained by God and then available in America. The day laborers of England were not only as well off but actually better off than that level (as noted in the comparison of England to the king in America). To this Locke adds the moral injunction that God gave the world "to the use of the *industrious* and *rational*—and labour was to be his title to it—not the fancy or covetousness of the *quarrelsome* and *contentious*" . . . and the latter "ought not to meddle with what was already improved by another's labour."[34]

But Locke recognizes that although this "satisficing" level of economic opportunity is ordinarily available to all, there may be isolated cases when calamity may befall even the most industrious. In such cases the claims of "need" must be given priority:

> But we know God hath not left one man so to the mercy of another that he may starve him if he please. God, the Lord and Father of all, has given no one of His children such a property in his peculiar position of the things of this world, but that He has given his brother a *right to the surplusage* of his goods, so that it cannot justly be denied him when his *pressing wants* call for it; and therefore, no man could ever have a just power over the life of another by *right of property* in land or possessions, since it would *always be a sin* in any man of estate *to let his brother perish* for want of affording him relief out of his plenty.[35]

Locke sees the dilemma we pose as the conflicting claims of justice (or the "just deserts" of labor) and charity:

> As *justice* gives every man a title to the product of his honest industry and the fair acquisitions of his ancestors descended to him, so *charity gives*

---

[34] *Second Treatise*, §34, emphasis added.
[35] *First Treatise*, §42, emphasis added.

every man a title to so much out of another's plenty as will keep him from extreme want *where he has no means to subsist otherwise*.[36]

This sentence combines several threads of our treatment of Locke's theory. First, we see that charity places a limit on the right of individuals to accumulate. Secondly, the claim that one person has on another's property is limited to a certain level: the subsistence level. After this level is "satisficed" the second person is free to accumulate indefinitely as long as the process is fair. Thirdly, this charity is owed only to those few who are industrious but by some calamity find they have "no means to subsist otherwise." Finally, we once again observe that Locke's property theory is based on a fair historical process which gives rise to a man's claim to property by means of "*honest* industry and the *fair* acquisitions of his ancestors descended to him."

It is appropriate to ask what might result if Locke's positive, or "strong," claim to property were missing. Suppose that somewhere in the historical process a given property was not created and/or transferred fairly. Then it would seem that the property "owner" would have little or no claim to his property vis-à-vis any other person. This leaves an area not covered by Locke since the only competing claim the other person has is limited to that needed for subsistence. Yet, if the present property owner has no real claim to his property, some other method must be found to assign ownership if property is to remain in private hands. One might speculate that the property for which no just claim can be made should be divided equally. The appraisal of how much property fits this description would itself depend on judgments as to the "fairness" of the historical process by which it was produced and transferred. Although many aspects of Locke's political theory are egalitarian, he does not address the possibility of redistributing property according to some egalitarian rule. Presumably he thinks that the "fair acquisition" process sufficiently covers the distribution in England.

Concluding Remarks. It has not been the task of this brief inquiry to render a thorough assessment of Locke's contributions to social theory or of his impact on the events of his and subsequent periods. The "given" dictum from which we have proceeded is that fundamental moral problems and choices are necessarily inherent—either explicitly or implicitly— in economic and political theories and that it is important to see the role their resolution plays at various stages in the argument. The specific moral choice examined in this inquiry has been the "need-versus-desert" (or in Locke's terms, "charity-versus-justice") dilemma in Locke's theory of property. This has required that certain aspects of his methodology be examined from

---

[36] *First Treatis*, §42, emphasis added.

perspectives appropriate to our inquiry. In particular, we have examined Locke's treatment and resolution of the dilemma within the context of his state of nature model and especially in the transitions required when he uses it alternatively as an abstract model, as a depiction of man's original post-Eden condition, and as a description of contemporaneous conditions in America. We noted that the sequence the argument follows in establishing property rights is important, especially with respect to their priority to government or "any express compact of all the commoners." The classification of claims into "strong" or "weak" allows further insight into how Locke resolved the conflicting claims.

At the same time Locke's argument should be seen in the context of the political and economic developments of his time (especially the position of the Whigs whose claims he wished to bolster) and in the context of competing political theories which to some extent dictated the course his argument took. Locke's audience was important not only in terms of their understanding of the developing political and economic environment but of how they related their own moral principles to their own positions.

Locke's resolution of the need-versus-desert dilemma appears less consistent today than it appeared to Locke's audience. In Locke's time "need" and "charity" were more readily associated with the provision of a rather low subsistence level. No confusion arose when Locke argued that man's equality demanded that this level of need be "satisficed" first regardless of what other claims others might have to wealth. We may argue that man's equality requires periodic redistribution of wealth so as to more nearly equalize economic opportunity. Locke argued that the appropriate "satisficing" level of opportunity was that ordained by God in the original state of nature and then available in America. Since the "day labourer" in England then had better prospects, Locke's theory did not threaten his audience with an obligation to radically redistribute wealth as some arguments, such as those of the Levellers, had seemed to advocate. Indeed, except for those rare occasions when one encountered a victim upon whom some misfortune had befallen, the labor theory of economic value justified unlimited accumulation of property as long as a fair process was followed.

By speaking of Locke "resolving" the "need-versus-desert" dilemma I do not mean to imply either that his methodology is faultless or that the particular moral choice he makes is generally acceptable. As our analysis has proceeded, several methodological weaknesses have become apparent. For example, the various uses of the state of nature model, while they add considerable leverage, seem to be of questionable compatibility and historical accuracy. Similarly, the processes by which property claims are generated and transferred by a "fair process" also appear to be dubious. Yet, in spite of these and other methodological difficulties, my analysis allows one to see that in some respects Locke is more consistent than he is generally supposed to be, at least with regard to this particular moral issue. We began by observing with Monson that "nothing but" interpretations are prone to focus on a governing principle that will require the interpreter to discount certain passages or to state simply that Locke is inconsistent. Thus, C. B. Macpherson suggests: "Locke could not have been conscious that the individuality he championed was at the same time a denial of individuality."[37] Even more strongly, Virginia McDonald states: "Whatever interpretation of Locke's moral and political theory we advance, we face incoherencies and inconsistencies. If we start as I do, from the universal initial premises, we inevitably face their incompatibility with his acceptance of the patent social and political inequalities of his own age."[38] Leo Strauss, arguing that Locke is fundamentally Hobbesian, concludes that Locke allows for "unlimited appropriation without concern for the needs of others."[39] Charles Monson, in his review of interpretations by Willmoore Kendall and Charles E. Vaughan, comments that "Kendall sees Locke as asserting obligations and denying rights; Charles E. Vaughan finds the positions reversed."[40] To the extent that the approach I have used is correct, it demonstrates that what seem to be inconsistencies may instead be the appropriate recognition of conflicting moral claims which must be taken into account simultaneously and resolved.

Had Locke written his theories of property and government in a later period, he would very likely have focused on the polemics among other groups; certainly the claims of the lower classes, the peasants, and urban workers would have been addressed. At a later period the nature of the interdependencies and complementarities among the factors of production (capital, technology, natural resources, and labor) would have been more evident. Moreover, the moral arguments that individuals and groups use to justify their claims vis-à-vis other individuals, other groups, and society as a whole would also have changed. Consequently, it is interesting to speculate how the theory of property developed by Locke would have faced those claims, and what would have been his resolution of the moral questions inherent in them.

Washington and Lee University.

[37] *The Political Theory of Possessive Individualism: Hobbes to Locke*, 3rd ed. (Oxford, 1965), 261.

[38] "A Guide to the Interpretation of Locke the Political Theorist," *Canadian Journal of Political Science,* **6** (1973), 609.

[39] *Natural Right and History* (Chicago, 1953), 240.

[40] Monson, *op. cit.*, 41; Kendall, *John Locke and the Doctrine of Majority Rule* (Urbana, Illinois, 1941); Vaughan, *Studies in the History of Political Philosophy* (Manchester, 1925).

XXI

IRRESISTIBLE COMPASSION: AN ASPECT OF EIGHTEENTH-CENTURY SYMPATHY AND HUMANITARIANISM

By Norman S. Fiering

In a well-known letter written late in life, Thomas Jefferson reiterated some of the essential elements in his ethical philosophy. At one point he asserted, "Nature hath implanted in our breasts a love of others, a sense of duty to them, a moral instinct, in short, which prompts us irresistibly to feel and to succor their distresses. . . ."[1] At least four distinct "natural" ethico-psychological qualities are reflected in these few words, though Jefferson unwittingly conflated them all into a single innate "moral instinct" and worried little about the separate historical life of the parts. Of the variety of interesting and typical eighteenth-century assumptions in the passage, it is the last one that is the subject of this paper: the belief that men irresistibly have compassion for the sufferings of others and are equally irresistibly moved to alleviate that suffering. My purpose is to trace back to its modern origins the assumptions about compassion that not only Thomas Jefferson but numerous other figures in the eighteenth century treated as self-evident fact.

The belief in what we shall call "irresistible compassion" expresses great confidence in the human personality, a confidence that goes considerably beyond trust in the free exercise of reason as a moral guide or political safeguard. Here we are presented with an automatic mechanism for social good, not simply an intellectual option. To a twentieth-century mind, doubts about the reality and the reliability of this mechanism arise quickly; history and analysis both undercut it. We know more about the perversions of "nature." But in the eighteenth century, among some groups, as Jefferson is a witness, the trust in certain qualities of human emotion was unbounded, as impressive certainly as the more often noted trust in rational faculties.

Irresistible compassion has another name commonly used in the eighteenth-century, "sympathy"; it was also called "humanity." When the ideal was truly practiced, or when the alleged mechanism really worked, we have one of the essentials of humanitarianism. Modern humanitarianism may be defined as the widespread inclination to protest against obvious and pointless physical suffering.[2]

[1]Jefferson to Thomas Law, June 13, 1814, in Andrew Lipscomb and Albert Bergh, *The Writings of Thomas Jefferson* (Washington, D.C., 1903), XIV, 141.

[2]The suffering must be obvious because usually even humane souls would rather avoid than have to confront the physical pain of others. It must be pointless because most humane men and women do not object to self-incurred purposeful suffering—let

The doctrine of irresistible compassion as found in the eighteenth century was probably not more than a hundred years old.[3] It grew up with and was one of the motivating forces behind humanitarianism, and it contributed to the spread of humanitarianism by establishing an image or an idea of human nature that made humanitarian feelings insistently "natural." If human beings were by nature irresistibly moved to relieve suffering, then those who were coldly indifferent to suffering were, by definition, something less than human.[4]

The seventeenth century inherited from the ancient world many of the ingredients of the doctrine of irresistible compassion. The most famous expression of the idea from classical times appears in the fifteenth satire of Juvenal. I quote from the translation best known in the eighteenth century, viz., John Dryden's edition of the *Satires* (1693):

> Compassion proper to mankind appears;
> Which Nature witness'd, when she lent us tears:
> Of tender sentiments we only give
> These proofs: to weep is our prerogative;
> To show, by pitying looks and melting eyes,
> How with a suffering friend we sympathize!
> Nay, tears will e'en from a wrong'd orphan slide,
> When his false guardian at the bar is tried:
>   *   *   *
> By impulse of nature (though to us unknown
> The party be) we make the loss our own;
> And tears steal from our eyes, when in the street
> With some betrothed virgin's hearse we meet;
>   *   *   *

us say, for example, to the rigors of certain kinds of athletic training or to a moderate ascetic regimen—nor do they protest against suffering imposed from outside when the goal is humane, as, for example, in some medical treatments. Finally, most kinds of *mental* suffering, because of the subtlety and intangibility of the event, far less readily stir up humanitarian concern. Maria Ossowska, *Social Determinants of Moral Ideas* (Philadelphia, 1970), 8, points out that we ignore suffering that is the result of the personal search for excellence.

[3] I agree with Geoffroy Atkinson, *The Sentimental Revolution: French Writers 1690–1740* (Seattle, 1965), v, that "what is important in the history of ideas is always their expression and frequency of expression by different authors, for the date of onset of ideas is impossible to find."

[4] Of all the great themes of eighteenth-century social thought, humanitarianism has received the least study in intellectual history. The new international edition of the *Encyclopedia of the Social Sciences* (1968) has no entry under the subject, though the 1932 edition, vol. VII, had an interesting and promising short essay by Crane Brinton. A. R. Humphrey's, " 'The Friend of Mankind,' 1700–1760—An Aspect of Eighteenth-Century Sensibility," *Review of English Studies,* 24 (July 1948), 203–18, expertly relates humanitarianism to sentimentalism. An archaic treatment but worth reading is Maurice Parmalee, "The Rise of Modern Humanitarianism," *American Journal of Sociology,* 21 (Nov. 1915), 345–59. Many standard studies of the enlightenment take up the subject, but there is need for extended treatment.

Who can all sense of others ills escape
Is but a brute, at best, in human shape.[5]

In twentieth-century translations these words read somewhat differently, suggesting that Juvenal had been distorted in this version to conform to the already existing predispositions of Dryden's time.

Next to the influence of Juvenal's words, probably most deeply received into eighteenth-century consciousness were various passages in Cicero. In the *De Officiis,* for example, Cicero is arguing against the rule of expediency in international relations:

The appearance of profit [may be the occasion in public affairs] of making false steps. . . . Thus our fathers, for instance, did ill in destroying and rasing of Corinth; the Athenians yet worse in making an order, that the people of Aegina should all have their thumbs cut off, because they were powerful at sea. This, no question, was thought a profitable decree . . . ; but nothing can be truly profitable that is cruel; for the nature of man, which we ought to follow as the guide of our actions, of all things in the world is most opposite to cruelty.[6]

One other inheritance from the ancient world should be mentioned here since it is frequently found in eighteenth-century moral philosophy: the idea of *storgè,* a Greek word meaning "natural affections," which St. Paul uses in *Romans* 1:31, and which appears also in *Timothy* 3:3.[7] Thus, to cite one example of many possible, the Scottish moralist George Turnbull in 1740 called attention to the social passions given us by nature that counter-balance the powerful natural feelings directed toward the preservation and care of our own bodies:

Our moral desires and affections are strengthened . . . by uneasy strong sensations to maintain a just balance [against bodily appetites]; so is plainly the Στοργὴ or natural affection to children, so is compassion or pity to the dis-

[5]The translation of this satire was by Nahum Tate (1652–1715).

[6]Thomas Cockman's translation from 1699, reprinted in the Everyman Library edition (London, 1909), 132. Humane remarks occur, too, in Euripides, Seneca, Plutarch, and some others. But the prevailing tone in the ancient world, it seems, was along the lines of Plato's warning in the tenth book of the *Republic* against indulgence in pity and compassion. Cf. David Hume's opinion: "Epictetus has scarcely ever mentioned the sentiment of humanity and compassion but in order to put his disciples on their guard against it." *An Inquiry Concerning the Principles of Morals,* ed. Charles Hendel (Indianapolis, 1957), 136. Of course, this refers to the Stoic view. Grace H. Macurdy, *The Quality of Mercy: The Gentler Virtues in Greek Literature* (New Haven, 1940), makes a case for the widespread existence of humanitarian feeling in Greek literature from Homer to Socrates, but her point is often forced. John Ferguson, *Moral Values in the Ancient World* (New York, 1958), gives many examples of the expression of pity among the ancients, but he notes that it always existed in defiance of other greater values. The Greek "philanthropia" and the Latin "clementia" were tinged with the quality of condescension, according to Ferguson, if not for which they could have become words of "immense moral power." Ferguson is writing out of a definite Christian commitment.

[7]It is also used in works by Plutarch, Antoninus, and Athanasius.

tressed, and many other moral passions, that thus the public and social ones might not be too weak and feeble. . . .[8]

Storgè differed from irresistible compassion, as it will be studied here, in that it was primarily applied to the natural affections between parents and children rather than to compassionate relations between all humans.[9]

The humanitarian principles asserted in the eighteenth century had much in common with those in classical literature. But the modern period added (often implicitly) all of the weight of Christian providential design to the authority of Cicero's "nature." The mere phrase "the author of nature," so frequently adverted to in the eighteenth century, said enough. In addition to a kind of secular sanctification of compassion in the eighteenth century, there was also a vast increase in the number of express advocates of the principle. The idea of irresistible compassion became a psychological dogma, and more than ever a touchstone not only of true civility but of human status itself. Finally, the discussion of irresistible compassion was at the very center of the general discussion in the eighteenth century of the nature of sympathy and in that way contributed mightily to the ramifications of the idea of sympathy in both philosophy and literature.

In the seventeenth century from both religious and secular sources human nature was widely disparaged. Puritan examples of this tendency are easy to find, of course, and in secular thought there were many other figures besides Hobbes who took a similar line.[10] The dominant theory was pessimistic: men were almost always guided in their behavior by self-interest or self-love. In Hobbes's definition even pity was egoistic: the "imagination or fiction of future calamity to ourselves," albeit provoked by the calamity of another man. Pity, that is, is a species of personal fear. Few human virtues seemed to be immune from the shrewd analyses of the cynics in France or England.

Not surprisingly, it was among the Cambridge Platonists, who as a school objected to both the Calvinistic and the Hobbesian depreciation of human nature, that the modern emphasis on the significance of compassion has its beginnings. In Henry More's *Enchiridion Ethicum* (1666, Latin ed.; 1690, English ed.), the phenomenon of natural com-

---

[8]*The Principles of Moral Philosophy. An Enquiry into the Wise and Good Government of the Moral World* (London, 1740), 73.

[9]In Classical literature the negative concept of *"astorge"* was more commonly in use, with reference to the man who was little more than a brute insofar as he lacked sympathetic feeling.

[10]The fullest discussion is in F. B. Kaye's introduction to his edition of Bernard Mandeville, *The Fable of the Bees,* 2 vols. (Oxford, 1924), lxxvii–cxiii. Equally informative is A. O. Lovejoy, *Reflections on Human Nature* (Baltimore, 1961). For valuable discussion of optimistic, pessimistic, and neutral views: J. A. Passmore, "The Malleability of Man in Eighteenth-Century Thought," in Earl R. Wasserman, ed., *Aspects of the Eighteenth Century* (Baltimore, 1965).

passion was introduced with new force and meaning. More asserted, in opposition to the prevailing neo-Stoic opinion, that the passions in general were good in themselves, and "singularly needful to the perfecting of human life. . . ." "These Natural and Radical Affections" were peculiarly important, More argued, because it is obvious they do not come from our own effort; they are not "the result of freethinking or speculation," nor can they be acquired. They are "in us antecedent to all notion and cogitation whatever," and hence " 'tis manifest they are from Nature and from God." Therefore, More deduced, "whatever they dictate as Good and Just, is really Good and Just," and even further, "we are bound to embrace and prosecute the same."

Our passions and affections reveal to us the authentic version of the Law of Nature that "bears sway in the animal Region," and they are, therefore, "a sort of confused Muttering, or Whisper of . . . Divine Law," though the same message is, of course, "more clear and audible" to the intellect.[11] More's trust in the passions was an extension of the similar but narrower Augustinian trust in the nonrational influence of divine grace upon the soul. The sanctified will in the seventeenth-century Augustinian conception was synonymous with a heart imbued with love, and essentially a passively experienced effect upon the self rather than a matter of effort or deliberation. In short, will itself was a form of passion (psychologically "suffered" instead of "acted"), rather than a function of intellect. More seems to have transferred to natural passions the authority of the sanctified heart.[12]

However, the main driving force behind the avidity with which More and eighteenth-century moralists studied human nature was the belief that all of nature is a form of divine revelation, and human nature particularly. Thus, More said, in order to learn how the passions are "rightly to be moderated and used," it is necessary simply to observe "the end unto which Nature, or rather God, who is the Parent of Nature, has destined each of them. . . ."[13] As we noted earlier, this device put the full weight of the Judaeo-Christian God behind the results of psychological investigation, an authority it is doubtful that Cicero could muster in his own time, even though he, too, believed, according to one eighteenth-century commentator, that "the natural end for which man is made, can only be inferred from the consideration of his

[11]Henry More, *Enchiridion Ethicum: The English Translation of 1690* (New York, 1930), 41, 78, 54, 78–79. On the neo-Stoic disparagement of the ethical value of the passions: Anthony Levi, *French Moralists: The Theory of the Passions, 1585–1649* (Oxford, 1964); Peter Gay, *The Enlightenment: An Interpretation, The Rise of Modern Paganism* (New York, 1966), 295–304, and the bibliography, 522–23; Rae Blanchard, "Introduction" to Richard Steele, *The Christian Hero* (Oxford, 1932), and Rudolph Kirk, "Introduction" to Joseph Hall, *Heaven Upon Earth and Characters of Vertues and Vices* (New Brunswick, N.J., 1948).

[12]For discussion of this point, see my "Will and Intellect in the New England Mind," *William and Mary Quarterly*, 3rd Ser., **24** (Oct. 1972), 515–58.

[13]More, *Enchiridion*, 54.

natural faculties and dispositions as they make one whole."[14] More then proceeded to give a number of examples of how the passions themselves declare their purposes and ends. Two of his examples are directly related to our theme.

Even unpleasant passions have their special purposes, More noted. Thus, we see, he said, in some of the manifestations of grief, those "efficacious sorts of Eloquence she has bestowed on so many of the Creatures when they are oppressed, for the drawing of Compassion towards them," such as a "lamenting tone of the Voice, the dejection of the Eyes and Countenance, Groaning, Howling, Sighs, and Tears, and the like." These involuntary expressions have the "Power to incline the Mind to Compassion, whether it be to quicken or Help, or to retard the Mischiefs we intended." Similar to this example is another based on the passion of "commiseration." "The use hereof," More said, "is in succoring the distressed, and defending him that has right. For to take away the Life of an innocent Man, is so monstrous a Crime, as tears the very Bowels of Nature, and forces sighs from the Breasts of all Men." In other words, the emotional effects of grief on the sufferer bring about a psychologically determined compassionate response in the observer, and both the grief and the reciprocal compassion serve as natural revelations of God's moral expectations of us. Likewise, the emotion of commiseration reinforces justice and plainly exists in us for that purpose.[15]

In the great *Treatise of the Laws of Nature* published by the Latitudinarian bishop, Richard Cumberland, in Latin in 1672, one finds some of the assumptions in More's work stated with greater explicitness. Cumberland also sets forth clearly the basic methodological axiom behind most eighteenth-century reasoning about ethical questions: human nature itself, he said, "suggests certain Rules of life . . . ," and from the study of it we can learn "for what kind of Action Man is fitted by his Inward Frame."[16] Cumberland was nowhere near as favorably disposed towards the usefulness and verity of the passions as More. He is often spoken of as the founder of utilitarian ethics because of the preeminent place he gave to universal benevolence as the basic moral commandment, but the source of the benevolence, according to Cumberland, is intellectual, not passional or sentimental. Even so, included in the evidence that he ingeniously amassed to demonstrate the natural, empirical, and necessary foundation of the law of benevolence, was the observation that men have "both an expectation of Compassion" from other men, which presumably would not exist if they were not entitled to it, "and a sympathy . . . by which they rejoice with those that rejoice, and weep with those that weep."[17]

[14]Turnbull, *Principles,* 9, referring to Cicero's *De Finibus.*

[15]More, *Enchiridion,* 59, 70.

[16]Richard Cumberland, *A Treatise of the Laws of Nature,* trans. John Maxwell (London, 1727), 99.

[17]*Ibid.,* 96; for similar material in Cudworth: Passmore, "Malleability," 24.

Other Latitudinarian Anglican preachers contemporary with Cumberland struck the same note. For example, Isaac Barrow, who was also a famous mathematician, delivered sermons that were a model for many other ministers in Britain and America. When Barrow turned to attack Hobbesian egoism he called attention to natural benevolence and compassion: "the constitution and frame of our nature disposeth to [natural affection]," he said; we cannot but feel this "when our bowels are touched with a sensible pain at the view of any calamitous object; when our fancies are disturbed at the report of any disaster befalling a man; when the sight of a tragedy wringeth compassion and tears from us. . . ."[18]

The most astute and original psychologist of the passions in the seventeenth century, the French Augustinian monk Nicolas Malebranche, whose main work, *The Search After Truth,* appeared in 1674 (and in English in 1694 in two separate translations), contributed his great authority to the argument and deepened it considerably. It is "chiefly by the Passions," Malebranche said, speaking directly against the neo-Stoics, "that the soul expands herself abroad, and finds she is actually related to all surrounding Beings. . . ." God has so "artfully united us with all things about us, and especially with those Beings of the same *Species* as our selves, that their Evils naturally afflict us, their Joy rejoyces us; their Rise, their Fall, or Diminution, seem to augment or diminish respectively our own Being. . . ." "The strongest *Natural Union* which God has established between us and his Works, is that which cements and binds us to our Fellow-Brethren, Men. God has commanded us to love them as our second-Selves," and He "supports and strengthens" this love

continually with a Natural Love which he impresses on us: and for that purpose has given us some invisible Bonds which bind and oblige us necessarily to love them. . . . All this secret Chain-work is a Miracle, which can never be sufficiently admir'd, nor can ever be understood. Upon the Sense of some sudden surprising Evil, which a Man finds, as it were, too strong for him to overcome by his own Strength, he raises, suppose, a Loud Cry. This cry forc'd out frequently without thinking on it, by the disposition of the *Machine,* strikes infallibly into the Ears of those who are near enough to afford the Assistance that is wanted: It pierces them, and makes them understand it, let them be of what nation or Quality soever; for 'tis a Cry of all Nations and all Conditions, as indeed it ought to be. It makes a Commotion in the Brain, and instantly changes the whole Disposition of Body in those that are struck with it; and makes them run to give succour, without so much as knowing it. . . .[19]

By the turn of the century, ideas like those of More, Cumberland,

---

[18]*Theological Works* (Oxford, 1830), II, 78–79.

[19]*Father Malebranche his Treatise concerning the Search After Truth . . . ,* trans. T. Taylor, 2 vols. (2nd ed., London, 1700), I, 165–66. Malebranche's status in English-speaking countries was enhanced by the fervid admiration of his disciple, John Norris of Bemerton. Atkinson, *Sentimental Revolution,* fails to mention Malebranche.

and Malebranche found immensely influential expression in the famous *Characteristics* of the third Earl of Shaftesbury and in the journalism and other work of Addison and Steele and their associates. Shaftesbury is virtually identified with the view that "in the passions and affections of particular creatures there is a constant relation to the interest" of all. This is demonstrated, he said, in the many examples of men's "natural affection, parental kindness, zeal for posterity, concern for the propagation and nurture of the young, love of fellowship and company, compassion, mutual succour, and the rest of this kind." He developed a whole "economy of the passions," which had to do with their proper balancing in the general social interest. Selfish as well as social passions are included in, and even necessary to, this economy when they are properly integrated into the whole divine system. Indeed, all human emotions are important to virtue and well-being—except for one class: those passions that have *neither* the public nor private interest as their end. These so-called "unnatural passions" were rejected as perversions or abnormalities of nature. Examples of unnatural passions or feelings, Shaftesbury wrote, are those in which there is an

unnatural and inhuman delight in beholding torments, and in viewing distress, calamity, blood, massacre and destruction, with a peculiar joy and pleasure. . . . To delight in the torture and pain of other creatures indifferently, natives or foreigners, of our own or of another species, kindred or no kindred, known or unknown; to feed as it were on death, and be entertained with dying agonies; this has nothing in it accountable in the way of self-interest or private good . . . , but is wholly and absolutely unnatural, as it is horrid and miserable.[20]

Animal victims were included in Shaftesbury's condemnation of unnatural passions, whereas Cumberland's benevolence had extended only to "rational creatures."[21] The cluster of English words cognate to "human" that refer essentially to compassion as a trait, such as "humane," "humanitarian," "humanity," have their firmest philosophical origins in the work of Shaftesbury. No one before him had argued so eloquently for the identification of fellow-feeling with the essence of true human nature.[22]

The genteel moral journalism of the early eighteenth century, exemplified by the *Spectator,* contains a number of references to the ethical significance of compassion. Ten years before Francis Hutcheson

[20]Anthony, Earl of Shaftesbury, *Characteristics of Men, Manners, Opinions, Times,* ed. John M. Robertson, 2 vols. in one (Indianapolis, 1964), I, 280, 289, 331; II, 287.

[21]Shaftesbury explicitly rejected Descartes's theory of animal insensibility. But others in the seventeenth century, including Henry More, had done so before. For a brilliant survey of the development of "humanity" towards nonhumans: John Passmore, "The Treatment of Animals," *JHI,* 36 (1975), 195–218.

[22]This is not to deny predecessors: Ficino's letter to Thomas Minerbetti, in Paul O. Kristeller, *The Philosophy of Ficino* (New York, 1943), 113.

set out to refute Bernard Mandeville's renewal of cynicism and psychological pessimism,[23] irresistible compassion was already being cited as proof of the real existence of unadulterated altruism. Thus, in *Spectator,* no. 588 (1714), a dissenting minister, Henry Grove, who went on later to become a moderately distinguished lecturer on moral philosophy, presented an argument for the irreducibility of kind and benevolent propensities in humankind:

[The] Contriver of human nature hath wisely furnished it with two principles of action, self-love and benevolence; designed one of them to render men wakeful to his own personal interest, the other to dispose him for giving his utmost assistance to all engaged in the same pursuit.

Man is led to "pursue the general happiness" through his reason, according to Grove, for he sees that this is the way "to procure and establish" his own happiness. Yet

if besides this consideration, there were not a natural instinct, prompting men to desire the welfare and satisfaction of others, self-love, in defiance of the admonitions of reason, would quickly run all things into a state of war and confusion.

But we are happily saved from this Hobbesian nightmare by "inclinations which anticipate our reason, and like a bias draw the mind strongly towards" social ends. As part of the evidence for this thesis, Grove adduced the following observation: "The pity which arises on sight of persons in distress, and the satisfaction of mind which is the consequence of having removed them into a happier state, are instead of a thousand arguments to prove such a thing as disinterested benevolence."[24]

Bishop George Berkeley, the famous philosopher, was a dedicated opponent of Shaftesbury, but his contributions in early life to Steele's *Guardian* of 1713, paralleled the Shaftesburian disposition: "Nothing is made in vain," Berkeley wrote, "much less the instincts and appetites of animals." This is a maxim that holds "throughout the whole system of created beings. . . ." And using a gravity image with antecedents from long before the time of Newton, Berkeley wrote:

As the attractive power in bodies is the most universal principle which produceth innumerable effects, and is the key to explain the various

[23]Bernard Gert, "Hobbes and Psychological Egoism," *JHI,* **28** (Oct. 1967), 503–20, has argued convincingly that for most purposes the term psychological "pessimism" is preferable to the term psychological "egoism." True egoism, Gert observes, defined as the view that "men *never* act in order to benefit others, or because they believe a course of action to be morally right," is almost never explicitly defended by anybody. The term "pessimism" is appropriate for the view that "most actions of most men are motivated by self-interest. . . ."

[24]Donald F. Bond, ed., *The Spectator,* 4 vols. (Oxford, 1965); also numbers 213, 243, 302, 397, 488, 601. This is the earliest use of the term "disinterested benevolence" that I have seen. It has a long career thereafter in American religious thought.

phenomena of nature; so the corresponding social appetite in human souls is the great spring and source of moral actions. This it is that inclines each individual to an intercourse with his species, and models everyone to that behaviour which best suits with common well-being. Hence that sympathy in our nature whereby we feel the pains and joys of our fellow-creatures. . . . Hence arises that diffusive sense of humanity so unaccountable to the selfish man who is untouched with it, and is, indeed, a sort of monster or anomalous production. . . ."[25]

It is easy to find similar statements to Berkeley's from the pens of others at the time, not only in *The Spectator* and *The Guardian* but in Richard Steele's *The Christian Hero* (1701).

Writing in 1722 for his brother's newspaper, when he was still a youth in Boston, Benjamin Franklin casually referred to that "natural compassion to . . . Fellow-Creatures" that brings "Tears at the Sight of an Object of Charity, who by a bear [sic] Relation of his Circumstances" seems "to demand the Assistance of those about him."[26] Franklin may have gotten this idea from one of the English periodicals. But the doctrine of irresistible compassion, even before this time, was hardly unknown to the New England clergy. Solomon Stoddard, a clerical leader from the Connecticut River valley town of Northampton, in a discussion of the proposition, axiomatic for him, that "natural men are under the government of self-love," had to take cognizance of the fact that men are

sometimes over-ruled by a spirit of compassion. Men that are devoted to themselves, are so over-born sometimes with a Spirit of Compassion, that they forget their own Interest. . . . There is no man so void of compassion, but upon some occasions [it] will prevail upon him. The seeing or hearing of the miseries of others, will extort acts of compassion, and they will be under a necessity to deny themselves, and relieve them. Men have not the command of their own compassions, their compassion doth prevail sometimes whether they will or no, and they are forced to neglect their own interest to relieve others in their distress: and this compassion is not only to friends, but to strangers, persons that they have no acquaintance with; . . . yea, to brute Creatures also.[27]

It is notable, however, that Stoddard, the Puritan, does not use this phenomenon of irresistible compassion as the foundation for a new philosophical anthropology; nor does he give compassionate impulses an authority comparable to the acting of divine grace in the soul.

By mid-eighteenth century, the opinion that a person who is unmoved by the pains and joys of others is a kind of monster, an unnatural creation, and that God has given men and women inborn feel-

[25]*Guardian,* No. 49 (May 7, 1713), and No. 126 (Aug. 5, 1713), printed in A. A. Luce and T. E. Jessop, eds., *The Works of George Berkeley* (London, 1955), VII, 194, 227.

[26]*The Papers of Benjamin Franklin,* ed. L. W. Labaree and W. J. Bell, Jr. (New Haven, 1959), I, 37.

[27]Stoddard, *Three Sermons Lately Preach'd at Boston* (Boston, 1717), 37.

ings of compassion, sympathy, and benevolence as a way of directly guiding mankind to virtue, this opinion became a virtual philosophical and psychological dogma. Part of the reason for this popular success was the authoritative confirmation given to these ideas by the two moralists whose writings were probably more widely approved of in Britain and America in the second quarter of the century than those of any other philosophers: William Wollaston and Francis Hutcheson.

Wollaston's *The Religion of Nature Delineated* first appeared in 1722 and was printed in eight other editions before 1759. It quickly won an esteemed place in the genre of writing on "natural religion." Wollaston was distinctly not a sentimentalist, and humanitarian arguments usually are not associated with him.[28] But all of the dogmas that I have already recounted are as clear in Wollaston as in Hutcheson a few years later.

There is something in *human* nature resulting from our very make and constitution . . . which renders us obnoxious to the pains of others, causes us to sympathize with them, and almost comprehends us in their case. It is grievous to see or hear (and almost to hear of) any man, or even any animal whatever, in *torment*. This *compassion* appears eminently in them, who upon other accounts are justly reckoned amongst the *best of men:* in some degree it appears in *almost* all . . . It is therefore according to *nature* to be affected with the sufferings of other people: and the contrary is *inhuman* and *unnatural*.

The difference between Wollaston and Hutcheson for our purposes may be summed up by noting that in *The Religion of Nature Delineated* this reliance on natural compassion was carefully qualified, whereas for Hutcheson it becomes the very cornerstone of his system. "The reports of sense may be taken for true, when there is no reason against it," Wollaston wrote, and "the same may be said . . . of every *affection, passion, inclination in general. . . . Sympathy* ought not to be overruled, if there be not a *good* reason for it. On the contrary, it ought to be taken as a *suggestion* of nature, which should always be regarded, when it is not superseded by something superior; that is, by *reason*."[29] Wollaston's position on this matter, then, is something like Henry More's.

Wollaston also introduced into his book what was possibly the most interesting discussion of pleasure and pain in English thought between

---

[28]Atkinson, *Sentimental Revolution,* 157, e.g., is puzzled by the praise from the translator in the preface to a French edition of the *Religion of Nature:* "Wollaston proceeds from one logical step to the next in his treatment of virtues and vices among men," according to Atkinson, "without much evidence of passion or emotion. . . . One can only conclude that his translator was reading emotions into its pages, or else that he may have been counting upon the emotional nature of prospective readers. As for the 'natural outpourings of a heart . . . ,' those qualities are precisely what is most absent in this theoretical work."

[29]Wollaston, *The Religion of Nature Delineated* (London, 1726), 139–40, 165; French trans. *Ébauche de la Religion naturelle . . .* (The Hague, 1726).

Hobbes and Bentham. This in itself is significant, for perhaps underlying even the widespread justification of natural compassion was some sort of profound change in the phenomenology of pain and pleasure. This possibility has recently been suggested by Professor Sheldon Wolin, who refers to the "exposed nerve ends of modern man," and his "heightened . . . sensitivity to pain." [30] Wollaston's extraordinary discussion in 1722 would support this opinion. On the basis of the necessary subjectivity of all experience of pleasure and pain, Wollaston called upon "princes, lawgivers, judges, juries, and even masters," to put aside what might be called rationalistic legal considerations and to mete out punishment *not* on the basis of what "a stout, resolute, obstinate, hardened criminal may bear," but on the basis of what "the weaker sort . . . can bear." [31] In effect, Wollaston advocated an expanded role for compassion in all penal matters.

The Scottish philosopher, Francis Hutcheson, as it is now well known, reduced reason to an ancillary role in ethics a half-generation before David Hume issued his famous dictum that reason "is and only ought to be the slave of the passions." [32] This fact, in addition to Hutcheson's remarkably pervasive role in British and American moral thought for fifty years or more, makes the publication of his first book, the *Inquiry into the Original of our Ideas of Beauty and Virtue,* a significant event in the history of humanitarianism. [33]

Hutcheson's *Inquiry* was in many ways the culmination of the trend in the preceding seventy-five years. He was greatly indebted to More,

[30] Wolin, *Politics and Vision* (Boston, 1960), 326. Nietzsche suggested that in earlier days "pain did not hurt as much as it does today. . . . For my part, I am convinced that, compared with one night's pain endured by a hysterical bluestocking, all the suffering of all the animals that have been used to date for scientific experiments is as nothing." *The Birth of Tragedy and the Genealogy of Morals,* trans. F. Golffing (New York, 1956), 200.

[31] Wollaston, *Religion,* 34. Wollaston was used as a text at Yale College under Thomas Clap's administration, which began in 1740 and ran for more than twenty years. But as early as 1726, James Logan, the learned Philadelphia Quaker, considered it "a piece for which one may justly . . . congratulate the age." Frederick B. Tolles, *James Logan and the Culture of Provincial America* (Boston, 1957), 198. And ca. 1727 or 1728, Jonathan Edwards entered in his "Catalogue" of reading: "Wollaston's Religion of Nature which I have been told Mr. Williams of Lebanon [Conn.] says is the best piece on the subject that he has ever read." I have deliberately excluded Edwards from treatment in this paper, since I am preparing a separate discussion of his relation to humanitarianism.

[32] *A Treatise of Human Nature* [1739–40] ed. L. A. Selby-Bigge (Oxford, 1928), 415.

[33] William Frankena, who has extensively studied eighteenth-century British ethics, has estimated that if the moral thinkers of that century were asked who was the most original and important among them Hutcheson would take the laurels; and this is probably true of America also, despite the fact that in the eyes of posterity figures like Bishop Joseph Butler and David Hume are far greater moralists; Frankena, "Hutcheson's Moral Sense Theory," *JHI,* **16** (June 1955), 356–75; also Adam Smith's famous tribute to Hutcheson, his teacher, in *The Theory of Moral Sentiments,* Part VII, Sec. ii. Hutcheson's *Inquiry* was well-known in America in the second quarter of

Cumberland, Malebranche, and Shaftesbury among the moderns. The class of passions that Shaftesbury and others had despised, abominated, and designated as unnatural was treated by Hutcheson as not only unnatural but as somewhat improbable. "Human nature," the Scottish philosopher wrote, "seems scarce capable of malicious disinterested hatred, or a sedate delight in the misery of others, when we imagine them no way pernicious to us, or opposite to our interests. . . ." Moreover, the psychological determinism that had been implicit in this benevolist trend from the beginning is overt in Hutcheson. God has determined "the very frame of our nature" to feelingful benevolence, and this fact is considered a great testimony to the divine element in human affairs. There is a "determination of our nature to study the good of others; or some instinct, antecedent to all reason from interest, which influences us to the love of others. . . ."

Hutcheson has also an economy and a teleology of the passions. Part of it is the close circle of emotions nature has established, whereby benefits to others evoke gratitude in the recipients, which is unfailingly pleasing to the benefactors, which in turn further stimulates benevolence. But beyond that, there is "a universal determination to benevolence in mankind, even toward the most distant parts of the species." Compassion is just one of a number of human traits that "strongly proves benevolence to be natural to us." And Hutcheson reiterated the by then commonplace example of how "Every mortal is made uneasy by any grievous misery he sees another involv'd in. . . ." Sounding much like Malebranche, whose work he knew well, Hutcheson wrote: "How wonderfully the constitution of human nature is adapted to move compassion. Our misery and distress immediately appears in our countenance . . . and propagates some pain to all spectators. . . . We mechanically send forth shrieks and groans . . . : Thus all who are present are rouz'd to our assistance." Hutcheson was not blind to the selfishness and depravity to be found everywhere. The point was that because of the intrinsic goodness of human nature, vice was a quite surmountable obstacle. The vicious passions do not necessarily disappear, but they are balanced out by divinely established benevolent affections.

Aristotle had persistently stressed the importance of "choice" in moral action. By choice he meant not just that an act was free or voluntary but that it was the result of conscious deliberation and right reason. The benevolists like Hutcheson turned this upside down and held, in effect, that deliberation was vicious if the suffering of another

---

the century; and the work of a thorough and unquestioning disciple, the *Elements of Moral Philosophy* by David Fordyce of Aberdeen, became the primary text in ethics at Harvard in the last half of the century. Fordyce's book first appeared in *The Preceptor,* ed. Robert Dodsley, 2 vols. (London, 1748), and in a separate edition in 1754. One or another of Hutcheson's works were used at the College of Philadelphia, Columbia (i.e., King's College), and Brown in the course of the century.

human being was before our senses. Rather than deliberation, the measure of the good person was to be found in the instantaneity of response, the unthinking, unreasoned animal (or spiritual) act of the virtuous soul. "Notwithstanding the mighty reason we boast of above other animals," Hutcheson wrote, "its processes are too slow, too full of doubt and hesitation to serve us in every exigency, either for our own preservation..., or to direct our actions for the good of the whole...."[34]

Wylie Sypher, Sr., has called Hutcheson "the first writer in any language fully to apply to the moral problem of slavery the 'romantic' ethics of pity instead of the 'classical' ethics of reason." According to Sypher, in Hutcheson the strong " 'sense of pity' swallows up all reasoning about 'just' and 'unjust' wars," or about natural inferiority.[35] In the lectures that Hutcheson was delivering at the University of Glasgow in the 1730s (but which were not published until 1755, nine years after his death), the essential principle that marks the "revolution in ethics" Sypher wished to emphasize, comes across clearly: "Must not all the sentiments of compassion and humanity, as well as reflection upon the general interest of mankind, dissuade from such usage of captives [i.e., enslavement], *even tho' it could be vindicated by some plea of external right*?"[36]

The main innovation in ethics and psychology that allowed unqualified humanitarianism to flower was the discrediting of rational justifications for inhumanity by opposing to them the *divine authority* of natural and instinctive compassionate feeling. A benevolent God gave man authoritative benevolent feelings, according to this reasoning. But it is important to note what is often overlooked in this matter, that in this case the discovery of the benevolent feelings seems to have preceded and forced the change in the understanding of God's will. Eventually, flogging, torture, chattel slavery, mistreatment of children, the sick, and the insane, and of animals, and "cruel and unusual punish-

[34]*An Inquiry into the Original of our Ideas of Beauty and Virtue* ... (London, 1723), 132, 182, 137-40, 176-77, 143, 195, 215-17, 245.

[35]"Hutcheson and the 'Classical' Theory of Slavery," *Journal of Negro History,* 24 (July 1939), 263-80. David Brion Davis, *The Problem of Slavery in Western Culture* (Ithaca, 1966), 378, has pointed out that Sypher exaggerated Hutcheson's originality in antislavery arguments.

[36]Quoted by Sypher from Hutcheson, *A System of Moral Philosophy* ... (Glasgow, 1755), II, 202-03; my italics. It should be kept in mind that antislavery sentiments and humanitarianism are not identical. But the success of the antislavery movement, when it used the presentation of the horrors of slavery to win converts, owed a great deal to humanitarianism. If humanitarianism is defined as active protest against obvious suffering, ostensibly benign slavery might not attract the opposition of the humanitarian. On the complex and paradoxical relationship of humanitarianism to the antislavery cause, see the excellent discussion in Winthrop Jordan, *White Over Black, American Attitudes Toward the Negro 1550-1812* (Chapel Hill, 1968), 365-72.

ments," would all come under powerful condemnation in the name of plain feeling.[37]

Both Hutcheson and his contemporary, Bishop Joseph Butler, were intent on proving that not all benevolent behavior was reducible to self-love, as Hobbes, Mandeville, and others had claimed. In this debate with the cynics (or the egoists or pessimists), the nature of spontaneous compassion was a prominent issue. Butler conceded implicitly that pity sprang from the imaginary substitution of the spectator in the place of the sufferer, but he denied that one could then correctly conclude that "it is *not another* you are at all concerned about, but *your self* only." (The imaginary substitution, we can see, is required for an accurate comprehension of the event, but it does not alter its nature.) Butler observed that in fact there were often "three distinct perceptions or inward feelings upon sight of persons in distress: [1] real sorrow and concern for the misery of our fellow-creatures; [2] some degree of satisfaction from a consciousness of our freedom from that misery; [3] and as the mind passes on from one thing to another, it is not unnatural from such an occasion to reflect upon our own liableness to the same or other calamities."

Hobbes, however, was "absurdly mistaken," according to Butler, in taking for the whole of pity what are concomitant elements only. Hobbes's interpretation, Butler noted, would make fear and compassion the "same idea, and a fearful and a compassionate man the same character, which every one immediately sees are totally different." Butler asserted categorically that "accidental obstacles removed, [men] naturally compassionate all in some degree whom they see in distress, so far as they have any real perception or sense of that distress."[38]

It would be hard to find anything in Thomas Jefferson's moral thought at the end of the eighteenth century that was not already present in some measure in Hutcheson and Butler fifty or more years earlier. The great Scottish moral psychologists of the second half of the century, David Hume and Adam Smith, contributed some finer discriminations, more extended analyses, and magisterial authority, but in the area of theory of the moral passions fewer new ideas than is sometimes supposed. Hume's tremendous powers of analysis came to a dead stop on the subject of compassion. After reviewing the familier facts— "that the very aspect of happiness, joy, prosperity gives pleasure; that

---

[37]Amendment VIII to the American Constitution, which prohibits "cruel and unusual punishments," is one of the least studied of all the parts of the Constitution. Beccaria's *On Crimes and Punishments* (1764) readily comes to mind as an influence in this case. But it should be recognized that humane sentiments, if not all of the cogency of Beccaria's reasoning, were already present in America and Britain by 1750.

[38]*The Works of Joseph Butler,* ed. W. E. Gladstone, 2 vols. (Oxford, 1896), II, Sermon V.

of pain, suffering, sorrow communicates uneasiness. . . . Tears and cries and groans, never fail to infuse compassion and uneasiness . . ."—the great philosopher remarked in a footnote:

It is needless to push our researches so far as to ask, Why we have humanity or a fellow-feeling with others? It is sufficient that this is experienced to be a principle in human nature. We must stop somewhere in our examination of causes; and there are, in every science, some general principles beyond which we cannot hope to find any principle more general. No man is absolutely indifferent to the happiness and misery of others. The first has a natural tendency to give pleasure, the second pain. This everyone may find in himself. It is not probable that these principles can be resolved into principles more simple and universal. . . .[39]

Like Hutcheson, Hume believed that "absolute, unprovoked, disinterested malice has never, perhaps, place in any human breast."[40]

The story of the idea of compassion in the eighteenth century is, of course, incomplete without some reference to Adam Smith, who gave the subject more extended treatment than any one else before and probably since. It is striking evidence of the central position the doctrine of irresistible compassion held in this period that Smith's *Theory of Moral Sentiments* (1759) in its very opening words refers to it: "How selfish soever man may be supposed, there are evidently some principles in his nature, which interest him in the fortune of others. . . . Of this kind is pity or compassion, the emotion which we feel for the misery of others, when we either see it, or are made to conceive it in a very lively manner. That we often derive sorrow from the sorrow of others, is a matter of fact too obvious to require any instances to prove it."[41]

Smith paid much more attention than any of his predecessors to the nature of the imaginative projection that makes possible not only pity but all forms of sympathetic response. "As we have no immediate experience of what other men feel, we can form no idea of the manner in which they are affected, but by conceiving what we ourselves should feel in the like situation." Our physical senses alone can never inform us directly of the suffering of "our brother . . . upon the rack"; but

---

[39] *An Inquiry Concerning the Principles of Morals,* ed Charles W. Hendel (Indianapolis, 1957), 47–48. Hume quotes another ancient source in this context, Horace's *Ars Poetica,* 101–02: "Ut ridentibus arrident, ita flentibus adflent/Humani vultus." "As the human face smiles at those who smile so does it weep at those who weep."

[40] Hume, *Inquiry,* 42. Glenn R. Morrow in "The Significance of the Doctrine of Sympathy in Hume and Adam Smith," *Philosophical Review,* 32 (1923), 60–78, demonstrates that Hume and certainly Adam Smith went further than their predecessors in grasping the social (i.e., the non-individualistic) nature of sympathy, defining sympathy as "the communication of feelings and sentiments from man to man" rather than as simply pity or compassion, and making sympathy in this broad sense the very basis of moral approbation.

[41] *The Theory of Moral Sentiments,* 2 vols. (10th ed., London, 1804), I, 1–2.

through the use of imagination we can form a conception of his sensations. Yet even imagination cannot "help us to this any other way, than by representing to us what would be our own, if we were in his case." Thus, our imagination discovers our own sensations, not the sufferer's.

By the imagination we place ourselves in his situation, we conceive ourselves enduring all the same torments, we enter as it were into his body, and become in some measure the same person with him, and thence form some idea of his sensations. . . . His agonies, when they are thus brought home to ourselves, when we have thus adopted and made them our own, begin at last to affect us, and we then tremble and shudder at the thought of what he feels.

But for all this, Smith remained quite convinced that sympathy "cannot, in any sense, be regarded as a selfish principle." Compassion or commiseration does "arise from an imaginary change of situations with the person principally concerned," but "this imaginary change is not supposed to happen to me in my own person and character, but in that of the person with whom I sympathize."

When I condole with you for the loss of your only son, in order to enter into your grief I do not consider what I, a person of such a character and profession, should suffer, if I had a son, and if that son was unfortunately to die: but I consider what I should suffer if I was really you, and I not only change circumstances with you, but I change persons and characters. My grief, therefore, is entirely upon your account, and not in the least upon my own.

As another example of the independence of compassion from self-interest, Smith cited the case of the man sympathizing with a woman in child-bed. "It is impossible that he should conceive himself as suffering her pains in his own proper person and character."[42]

Smith's book is full of subtle perceptions about the functioning of compassion, and of sympathy in general. He truly brought to fulfillment a hundred years of interest and investigation. One further instance of his extraordinary analysis of compassion deserves extended quotation:

The emotions of the spectator will . . . be very apt to fall short of the violence of what is felt by the sufferer. Mankind, though naturally sympathetic, never conceive, for what has befallen another, that degree of passion which naturally animates the person principally concerned. That imaginary change of situation, upon which their sympathy is founded, is but momentary. The thought of their own safety, the thought that they themselves are not really the sufferers, continually intrudes itself upon them; and though it does not hinder them from conceiving a passion somewhat analogous to what is felt by the sufferer, hinders them from conceiving anything that approaches to the same degree of violence.

[42]*Ibid.,* I, 2–3; II, 283–84.

Meanwhile, the miserable sufferer is aware of the spectators' detachment, and yet "passionately desires a more complete sympathy."

He longs for that relief which nothing can afford him but the entire concord of the affections of the spectators with his own. To see the emotions of their hearts, in every respect, beat time to his own, in the violent and disagreeable passions, constitutes his sole consolation.

Ironically, however, the sufferer can only hope to obtain this degree of commiseration "by lowering his passion to that pitch in which the spectators are capable of going along with him."

He must flatten . . . the sharpness of its natural tone, in order to reduce it to harmony and concord with the emotions of those who are about him. What they feel will indeed always be, in some respects, different from what he feels. . . . Though they will never be unisons, they may be concords, and this is all that is wanted or required.[43]

The doctrine of irresistible compassion has played a large part in the establishment of Western humanitarianism insofar as it was presented in the eighteenth century as both a normative and a descriptive concept. Men *are* natively humane; if not they *ought to be,* and those who are not so are something less than human. Humanitarianism in this sense is a historical stage in the education of the emotions. The "man of feeling" was a new social type as well as a literary type. For what the intellectuals of the eighteenth century attributed to "nature," we can confidently assign to "culture." It is hard to believe, furthermore, that the effects of this great "sentimental revo'ation," which has so much softened or suppressed many varieties of p; n-inducing human conduct, will ever be reversed.[44] However, as has of :n been noted, one of the things that happened to the man of feeling in t 'e romantic period is that the enjoyment of the emotion of pity, the sympathetic identification with the sufferer, became an end in itseli and the compul-

---

[43]*Ibid.,* I, 31–32. Bishop Edward Reynolds had noticed that the mind of a sufferer "doth receive (as it were) some lightness and comfort, when it finds itself *generative* unto others, and produces *sympathy* in them." The torment of hell will be all the greater, Reynolds commented, because grief there "shall not be any whit *transient,* to work commiseration in any *Spectator,* but altogether *immanent* and *reflexive* upon its self." *A Treatise of the Passions and Faculties of the Soul of Man* (London, 1678), in Edward Reynolds, *The Works* (London, 1679), 631.

[44]Cf. Dr. Samuel Johnson's comment on the novelist Samuel Richardson, that he had "taught the passions to move at the command of virtue." The complex of doctrines supporting the man of feeling "was something new in the world," according to Ronald Crane; "Suggestions toward a Genealogy of the 'Man of Feeling,' " *Journal of English Literary History,* I (1934), 207. "Neither in antiquity, nor in the Middle Ages, nor in the sixteenth century, nor in the England of the Puritans and Cavaliers had the 'man of feeling' ever been a popular type."

sion to relieve the suffering proportionately less urgent. This is the same as saying that compassion became more literary and less a matter of practical morals. The cultivation of humane literature, ironically, may be a refuge from and a substitute for feelingful responses to painful human situations in the real world.[45]

If the teaching of compassion sometimes resulted in people feeling more and doing less, it has also been noticed that the reverse can happen, too. Bishop Butler in his *Analogy* made one of the shrewdest observations about the practical distortions of fellow-feeling. The repeated exercise of compassionate responses, Butler noted, has the paradoxical effect of strengthening the *habit* of providing relief and succour while at the same time weakening the emotional impetus behind compassion. This is the result of the general psychological rule that repetition strengthens active habits but weakens passive impressions.[46] Repeated subjection to excitements or stimulants from outside will gradually weaken the effect these stimulants have; on the other hand, repeated action tends to form indelible habits.

Perception of distress in others is a natural excitement, passively to pity, and actively to relieve it; but let a man set himself to attend to, inquire out, and relieve distressed persons, and he cannot but grow less and less sensibly affected with the various miseries of life, with which he must become acquainted; when yet, at the time, benevolence, considered not as a passion, but as a practical principle of action will strengthen: and whilst he passively compassionates the distressed less, he will acquire a greater aptitude actively to assist and befriend them.[47]

Social reform or benevolence, in other words, always tends to become bureaucratic. Fervent reform ends up as mere form.

Even worse than the misplaced compassion of the littérateur or than the benevolence without heart of the professional social worker is the outright perversion of the doctrine of natural compassion. It has been fairly well established that the philosophical defense of cruelty and diabolism, beginning especially with the Marquis de Sade, which has followed like an ominous shadow behind humanitarianism, was an ironic by-product of the age of sensibility.[48] Philosophical sadism—as

[45]For discussion see George Steiner, *Language and Silence* (New York, 1967), 5, 61. Late in the nineteenth century William James lamented the "habit of excessive novel-reading and theater-going," which he felt would produce "monsters" of indifference to real life situations. "The weeping of a Russian lady over the fictitious personages in the play, while her coachman is freezing to death in his seat outside, is the sort of thing that everywhere happens on a less glaring scale." *Habit* (New York, 1890), 63.

[46]*Works of Joseph Butler,* ed. Gladstone, I. 111.   [47]*Ibid.,* I, 112.

[48]Nietzsche was perhaps the first to expose this relationship between Sadism and sentimental humanitarianism. De Sade is discussed in the context of eighteenth-century moral thought in Lester Crocker, *An Age of Crisis: Man and World in Eighteenth Century French Thought* (Baltimore, 1959), and as an influence on the nineteenth

opposed to simple Caligula-like corruption from unlimited power—becomes a real possibility when the "Nature" that the eighteenth-century moralists vaunted ceases to be a secular metaphor for the Creation and becomes an antigod in its own right. This fact should indicate to us the importance of Christian underpinnings in sentimental humanitarianism. The belief in the eighteenth century that natural compassion was a divinely ordained and sanctioned human expression saved the whole theory of the moral authority of the passions from unlimited distortion by the libertines.

Both politics and theology were profoundly affected by humanitarian forces in the eighteenth century, and therefore indirectly by the dogma of irresistible compassion. Philosophers in particular, more than historians, have stressed the revolutionary implications of the increase in the scope and intensity of sympathy.[49] In Hannah Arendt's *On Revolution* the connection between compassion and revolutionary politics, which first began in the eighteenth century, is stated explicitly. The "passion of compassion," Arendt believes, above all other forces has "haunted and driven" the best men in all the modern revolutions, with the exception of the American.

History tells us that it is by no means a matter of course for the spectacle of misery to move men to pity; even during the long centuries when the Christian religion of mercy determined moral standards of Western Civilization, compassion operated outside the political realm and frequently outside the established hierarchy of the Church.

But in the eighteenth century, Arendt observes, "this age-old indifference was about to disappear, and . . . in the words of Rousseau, an 'innate repugnance at seeing a fellow creature suffer' had become common in certain strata of European society and precisely among those who made the French Revolution."[50]

---

century in Mario Praz, *The Romantic Agony* (Cleveland, 1967; first publ., 1933); also Michel Foucault, *Folie et Déraison. Histoire de la folie à l'âge classique* (Paris, 1961), 437: "Le sadisme n'est pas un nom enfin donné à une pratique aussi vieille que l'Éros; c'est un fait culturel massif qui est apparu précisément à la fin du XVIIIᵉ siècle, et qui constitue une des plus grandes conversions de l'imagination occidentale."

[49]Thus, for example, Nietzsche's *Genealogy of Morals;* Alfred North Whitehead, *Adventures of Ideas* (New York, 1933); Bertrand Russell, *Human Society in Ethics in Politics* (New York, 1955), 155–56: "Sympathy has produced the many humanitarian advances of the last hundred years. . . . Perhaps the best hope for the future of mankind is that ways will be found of increasing the scope and intensity of sympathy."

[50]*On Revolution* (New York, 1963, 1965), 66. Arendt's analysis of the social and political implications of modern pity and compassion—she carefully distinguishes the two—is superb. It follows up an insight of Bernard Mandeville's that Arendt was probably unaware of: pity resembles virtue, Mandeville noted, "but as it is an impulse of nature, that consults neither the public interest nor our own reason, it may produce evil as well as good." See Lester Crocker's discussion of Rousseau in *An Age of Crisis, op. cit.*, 362, where may be found the above quotation from Mandeville.

Theology in the eighteenth century was faced with the difficult problem of reconciling the new psychological dogma of irresistible compassion with traditional Christian teaching on reprobation, hell, and eternal punishment. What had been earlier simply a perennial theological tension between God's mercy and His justice, became, as a result of humanitarian pressure, open conflict or contradiction. If God had in fact given man involuntary compassionate responses, then God must be at least as compassionate as man. Moreover, truly divine teaching could hardly include eternal punishment, since eternal punishment was wholly incompatible with the divine lesson taught to every man by his own instinct for pity and sympathy. As William Ellery Channing said early in the nineteenth century in opposition to the old orthodox teaching on reprobation, "We ask our opponents to leave us a God . . . in whom our moral sentiments may delight."[51] That is to say, a God that humanitarian feeling may approve of.

Channing's point of view has many antecedents, of course.[52] And the basis of opposition to the doctrines of hell and reprobation is quite varied.[53] But historians have more often mentioned the so-called "rational" objections to eternal punishment than the affective.[54] The doctrine of hell offended both reason and "humanity," good sense and compassion, and perhaps it was the latter that was more effective in changing minds than the former; but the most convincing argument in the eighteenth century was a mixture of feeling and logic: God gave men

[51]*Unitarian Christianity, and other essays,* ed. I. Bartlett (Indianapolis, 1957), 25.

[52]A weakness in the excellent article by Howard R. Murphy, "The Ethical Revolt Against Christian Orthodoxy in Early Victorian England," *American Historical Review,* **60** (July 1955), 800–17, is that the author seems to date the revolt against Original Sin, Reprobation, Eternal Punishment, etc., from the nineteenth century, whereas already in Britain before the mid-eighteenth century all of the humanitarian arguments Murphy cites had been fully expressed.

[53]Murphy, "Ethical Revolt," for example, singles out "meliorism," "the idea that the world was susceptible to systematic improvement through a sustained application of human effort and intelligence," as the force that "gradually took hold in men's minds and fired (or seduced) their imaginations." The root of humanitarian repugnance to doctrines like infant damnation and eternal punishment, according to this view, was the sense of incongruity between the Christian teaching and the meliorist bias of the time.

[54]Paul C. Davies, "The Debate on Eternal Punishment in Late Seventeenth- and Eighteenth-Century English Literature," *Eighteenth-Century Studies,* **4** (Spring 1971), 257–76, refers to the "reasonable" desire, on the part of opponents to orthodoxy, to avoid "extremism, absurdity, and irrationality." When it comes to the affections and passions, Davies primarily notes the manner in which their existence in the human breast tended to sustain teaching about hell: since men are motivated principally by hope and fear, or the desire for pleasure and the fear of pain, the threat of hell is necessary for social control. Davies observes in the romantic period the "insistence upon the human values of sympathy, compassion, and forgiveness," but scarcely mentions the growth of these values in the pre-romantic eighteenth century and their vital bearing on the debate over eternal punishment.

and women compassion, and He would not contradict in His own performance His moral expectations of His creatures.

The belief that God or even a pious man would feel the least bit of pity for the suffering of sinners in hell had to overcome a tremendous weight of tradition. The predominant view, which goes back to Tertullian at least, was that God and the angels together would derive not uneasiness but an augmentation of bliss from the contemplation of the punishment of the damned. D. P. Walker in *The Decline of Hell: Seventeenth Century Discussion of Eternal Torment*[55] remarks about Peter Sterry (d. 1672) and Jeremiah White (d. 1707), both of whom preached universal salvation based on God's preeminent attribute of love, that these men are "almost unique in the theology of that age," insofar as they expressed a "compassion for the suffering of sinners" and projected it unto God. In the eighteenth century, under the influence of figures like Bishop John Tillotson (d. 1694) and others, it became commonplace to reconstruct God's image into that of the benevolent ruler.[56] George Turnbull in 1740 spoke representatively for many when he maintained:

Nothing can be more absurd than the doctrine which has sometimes been advanced; that goodness in God is not the same as goodness in men, but something of quite another kind and which we understand not. . . . The true notion . . . of the divine benevolence must be learned by considering what it is in man. And by augmenting the idea of a good man to boundless perfection, we arrive at the nearest conception that is possible for us to frame of the goodness of an all-perfect mind.[57]

Since compassion by this time had become so conspicuous a factor in human nature, extension to the godhead of this quality of mercy would inevitably lead to the abolition of eternal torment.

The encounter in the eighteenth century between irresistible compassion and orthodox theology is a more complex matter than there is space to go into here. I will conclude, however, with an example of the conflict that shows clearly the tensions within theology. In America, at Harvard College, at almost the same moment that Turnbull was writing, the Hollis Professor of Divinity Edward Wigglesworth was also

[55](Chicago, 1964), 111.

[56]This point has been made many times; e.g., Norman Sykes, "Theology of Divine Benevolence," *Historical Magazine of the Protestant Episcopal Church*, **16** (1947), 278–91.

[57]Turnbull, *Principles*, preface. For the same idea in a later period: Tom Paine, *Age of Reason*, Part I: "The moral duty of man consists in imitating the moral goodness and beneficence of God. . . . The goodness of God to all men . . . is an example calling upon all men to practice the same toward each other; and consequently, . . . everything of persecution and revenge between man and man, and everything of cruelty to animals, is a violation of moral duty."

addressing the problem of reconciling God's sovereignty with human compassion. Wigglesworth had turned to the subject, he said, after reading some pamphlets from England that defended "Universal Redemption" on the basis of a "dangerous Deduction" from the consideration of divine mercy.

Wigglesworth's tack was to distinguish sharply the divine attribute from its human counterpart. Not surprisingly, however, he found the psychological doctrine of irresistible compassion altogether compelling, and elaborated on it in his address, never realizing that once he admitted its validity he would be trapped. "When we speak of the Mercy of Men," Wigglesworth said, "we intend by it a compassionate painful sense of the Miseries we see others groaning under . . . , which excites us to endeavour to prevent those Miseries . . . and to deliver them from, or to relieve and comfort them under those miseries." The Scriptures, in order to give us "a more lively affecting Sense of the Greatness of the Mercy of God," represent the divine virtue in the same way, "as attended with all that inward Commotion and uneasy Sensation, which we experience in ourselves upon the Appearance of an Object of Pity." But it is a serious mistake, Wigglesworth insisted, to use this analogy as the basis for attributing the "Imperfections of human Passions to the Divine Nature." Humankind, he explained, "whose Wisdom reaches but a little way," has been given by God a "Readiness to shew Mercy to all that are in Misery," for if left "to our own Liberty in this Matter," "many Mischiefs both of a private and publick Nature" would result. In the case of the passion of compassion, in other words, man could not be trusted with freedom and was given an indiscriminate or at least controlling amount. "We . . . whose Disposition to Acts of Kindness and Mercy is many times too feeble, and whose angry Passions are not seldom too strong, are not left to our own Discretion to shew Mercy, or to refuse it, when, and where we please."

On all of these counts, however, God is quite different. He experiences no "inward Disturbance or Uneasiness at the Misery of Creatures," for it would be inconsistent with His absolute perfections, and "an Interruption of his perfect Happiness." Moreover, God is "absolutely free and unconfined in his Acts of Grace and Mercy." He is not subject to the involuntariness or the passivity of any passion.[58] With these words Wigglesworth appears to be simply reiterating the old truths rather than confronting the disturbing challenges to them. In the end, all that Wigglesworth can offer, it seems, is the weak protestation

---

[58]The paradox of God's passions, especially the nature of His love in comparison to human love, was widely discussed in the patristic period. A Harvard College commencement *quaestio* in 1723, answered in the negative by the M. A. candidate Thomas Smith, reads: "An dentur in Deo affectus Vere & proprie dicti?" (Are there affections in God, truly and properly speaking?)

that God "hath the Government of the World upon him," and "Mercy and Justice are both alike dear and essential to him."[59]

Wigglesworth's evasiveness, the unsatisfying incompleteness of his response, only serves to point up the revolutions in theological and moral thought that irresistible compassion was working in his day. But he can hardly be blamed for his helpless predicament. When a human feeling is elevated to a moral absolute, there can be no answer to it.

Institute of Early American History and Culture, Williamsburg, Va.

[59]Edward Wigglesworth, *The Sovereignty of God in the Exercises of his Mercy. . . . consider'd in Two Public Lectures at Harvard College in Cambridge* (Boston, 1741), 6–12.